ENGLISH RECUSANT LITERATURE
1558–1640

Selected and Edited by
D. M. ROGERS

Volume 303

THOMAS HARDING
A Reiondre to M. Iewels Replie
1566

THOMAS HARDING

A Reiondre to M. Iewels Replie

1566

The Scolar Press
1976

ISBN 0 85967 310 3

Published and printed in Great Britain by
The Scolar Press Limited, 59-61 East Parade,
Ilkley, Yorkshire and
39 Great Russell Street,
London WC1

NOTE

Reproduced (original size) from a copy in the library of Ampleforth Abbey, by permission of the Abbot and Community.

References: Allison and Rogers 377; STC 12760.

A REIOINDRE TO M. JEWELS REPLIE.

❧ By perusing wherof the discrete and diligent Reader may easily see, the Answer to parte of his insolent Chalenge iustified, and his Obiections against the Masse, whereat the Priest sometime receiueth the holy Mysteries without present companie to receiue with him, for that cause by Luthers Schoole called Priuate Masse, clearely confuted.

By Thomas Harding Doctor of Diuinitie.

Prouerb. 25.

Nubes, & ventus, & pluuiæ non sequentes, vir gloriosus, & promissa non complens.

Like as is a cloude, and winde, and no raine folowing: so is a man, that craketh much, and performeth not his promises.

ANTVERPIAE.
Ex officina Ioannis Fouleri.
Anno. M. D. LXVI.

Regiæ Maiestatis Priuilegio permissum est Thomæ Hardingo Doctori Theologo librum ab se conscriptum hoc titulo, A Reioindre to M. Iewels Replie, &c. cuicunque velit ex typographis iuratis qui in Burgundica Ditione habitant, typis excudendum committere, atque eius seu cuiuscunque alterius opera ad exemplaria distrahenda uti. Datum Bruxellis .20. Maij. Anno. 1566.

Subsig.
Pratz.

TO THE READER.

Sith that I am not suffred Christian Reader, by vse of tongue to speake freely and openly in defence of the mater which concerneth thy soule health, by M. Iewels late Replie impugned: let it be lawful for the Truth, by secrete way of written treatises, to come vnto thy eares. That thou maist the better iudge of the whole, consider wisely the oddes of both our present states. He hath al the helpes, that in respecte of the worlde to the furtherance of such purpose can be desired, libertie to speake, vse of the pulpite, fauour of the time, benefite of the lawes, the sway of the worlde, the inclination of many hartes, besides al these, his owne peculiar pleasant eloquence. I on the other side, lacke al these. My voice is not heard, the pulpite is denyed, the time is contrary, the lawes threaten, the worlde frowneth, hartes repine, suche kinde of eloquence serueth not, nor is at al affected.

What is there then whereof in this enterprise I comforte my selfe? Soothly in the right of the cause, not doubting, but through Goddes power, naked Truthe shal in the ende ouercomme armed falshed. But our Aduersaries say, the Truth is of their side, and not of oures. Thereof to make credite, they reporte them vnto M. Jewels Replie. But what if as his Chalenge was vaine, so now his Replie also be founde vntrue, yea nothing els in manner, but a continual corruption of the Doctours, and a heape of lyes? That remaineth to be proued. I affirme, M. Jewel denieth. By whom shal we be iudged?

Here I must tel thee Reader by way of necessary digression, that forasmuch as Sathan hath now put in his foote, and plaid his parte, onlesse thou take good heede, and pray that thy harte may be staid with grace: thou arte in great danger to be deceiued, to be carried away into errours and heresies, and finally to lose the rewarde which is laid vp for the obedient children of the Church of Christe, and to haue thy portion with the rebellious synagogue of Antichriste.

What is then the parte that Sathan hath plaid? Marke, and consider. It is the breach of order. He seeth, that so long as due order is kepte in the Church, his deuises for heresies to be spred abroad, can not preuaile. Wherefore with al endeuour he hath euer gone about to transferre the iudgement concerning Doctrine of Religion, which is the key of order, from the lawful and ordinarie iudges, vnto others, to whose vocation no such auctoritie belongeth. And this hath he now brought to passe through his Ministers in diuerse Countries of Christendom. Albeit they agree not among them selues. For some appoint Princes to be iudges, some the common people, some euery Priuate man, so he be a member of the Churche.

Brentius in prolegomenis Cōtrà Petrū à Soto.

If thou wilt not be deceiued, be not thine owne iudge, heare ẏ

Ca-

Catholike Church. Stand to the iugement of thẽ, whom the holy ghost hath ordeined bishops (as S. Paul saith) to gouern ẏ church of god, which he hath purchased with his bloud. Heare them, to whõ Christ said, It is not you that speak, but the spirit of your father that speketh in you: He that heareth you, heareth me, he that despiseth you, despiseth me: To whom finally he said, I am with you al daies vnto the ende of the worlde. That thou shouldest be assured where to finde right iudgement touching causes of faith, Christ spake not thus to Princes, nor to the priuate people, nor to euery priuate man, but to the Apostles onely. Now whereas the Apostles liued but the time of common lyfe, and remaine not vpon the earth vntil the end of the worlde: it is most certaine, that he would these wordes to be vnderstanded of their lawful successours: which he shewed also most clearly when he said: I wil besech my Father, and he shal geue you an other comforter, to remaine with you for euer, the spirit of truth. Wherefore if thou seeke for sure iugement, whereby in controuersies and doubtes in religion thou maist with saftie of thy conscience be resolued, heare the Spirite of Christ speaking in the ordinarie gouernours of his Church.

Act. 20. Mat. 10. Mat. 28. Ioan. 14.

Neither let thy misliking of their life, if any do amisse, engender in thee discredite of their iudgement touching doctrine. Hereof our heauenly Master (as S. Augustine saith) hath geuen a forewarning, to thintent he might put the people in securitie of their euil gouernours, that for their sakes the chair of holsome Doctrine should not be forsaken, in which euil men be forced to say good thinges. For neither be the thinges which they speake theirs, but Gods, who in the chaire of vnitie hath placed the doctrine of veritie.

August. ad Donatist. Epist. 166.

To conclude, touching al pointes of Religion, by what

Consistorie can we be iudged, if we go from the Catholique Churche of God, where by his owne woorde we are assured of his wil? For of the Churche thus saith God by the Prophete Esay: Thou shalt be called by a newe name, which our Lords owne mouth shal name. Thou shalt be called no more the forsaken, and thy Lande shal no more be called the desolate (lande) but thou shalt be called, Voluntas mea in ea, My wil in her.

Esai. 62.

Of Her therefore let vs in al our doubtes and controuersies demaunde Gods wil and pleasure. There let vs seeke for it, there we shal finde it. But what neede we to seeke for it? Let vs onely beholde the custome of the Church.

Consider therefore how the case standeth. M. Iewel denieth the real presence of our Lordes body in the blessed Sacrament, he taketh away the singular and external Sacrifice of the Churche, he condemneth the Priest for saying Masse not hauing a companie to receiue the Communion in the same place with him, he abolisheth the external Priesthod of the newe Testament, the receiuing of the Communion vnder one kinde, the Latine Seruice of the Latine Churche, the Supremacie of S. Peters Successour, the being of Christes body in many places at one time, the Eleuation the Adoration, the Reseruation of the same, the pluralitie of Masses in one Church in one daie, secrete pronouncing of the Canon of the Masse, the Canon it selfe, the diuiding of the blessed Sacrament, the vse of Images, Prayer for the dead: al these, and many moe great points of Christian religion, and what so euer els almost is vsed and allowed in the Catholique Churche, be it of Doctrine, or of Religious obseruation, hee denieth, despiseth, and vtterly condemneth. Yet remember Reader, that

what

what M. Jewel denieth the Church affirmeth: what M. Jewel despiseth, the Church esteemeth: what M. Jewel condemneth, the Church Commaundeth. But what reasons, what Argumentes, what allegations, what shews of disprouses so euer he bring against these things, we ought to make smal accompt therof, forasmuch as we see them approued, and allowed by the continual custome of the Church.

In this case any stedfast Christian man, be he neuer so vnlearned, may thus say vnto him selfe. If M. Jewel kepe him selfe in the vnitie of the Churche, I holde with him: If he teach contrary doctrine, if he make him selfe wiser then the whole Churche, if he tel me that is Idolatrie, and superstition, which (as I vnderstand and see) the Church hath vniuersally vsed as a Seruice donne vnto God: there I leaue him, there I forsake him. For if the wil and pleasure of God be alwaies in his Churche, as by purporte of that newe name geuen vnto her by Gods owne mouth, Esay doth vs to vnderstande: if Christe remaine al daies vnto the worldes ende with the Successours of his Apostles, for the safe gouernement of his Church as the Scripture saith: if the heauenly Father at his Sonnes prayer haue geuen vnto the Churche the holy Ghoste, the spirit of Truth, to remaine with her for euer: if al this be true, as by Gods woorde we know it to be most true: let M. Jewel make hye Chalenges, and great Replies, let him sette his mouth against heauen, let him vtter the whole store of his Rhetorike, let him seme to speak like an Angel, yea if he were an Angel from heauen: I would beleue the Church, him I would not beleue: yea being the enemy of ẏ Church, & condemning so many things approued, vsed, taught & cōmaunded by the Churche,

Mat. 28. Ioan. 14. Esai. 59. Psal. 72. Galat. 1.

I

I would blesse my selfe from him, as from the disciple of Antichrist, as from the Minister of Satan, as from Gods open and professed ennemie.

Who so euer is at this point with M. Iewel, he shal not be deceiued by M. Iewel. Els if he seeke to be resolued in these, & other maters of faith & religiõ, which our Aduersaries would faine cal into cõtrouersie, by other meanes, as by his owne wit, by conference of their treatises, who haue written on both sides, by the opinion of priuate men whom he esteemeth and loueth, and by course of the times that he liueth in: onlesse he be learned, it is more then likely, that he shal wauer too and fro, be carried from one opiniõ to an other, & haue a mutable faith, or rather no faith at al, but onely a wandering phantasie. Therefore the surest way is, in al these doubtes to stand to the determination of the Churche. As for the more parte of the thinges by M. Iewels Chalenge condemned, let no man pretende ignorance of her determination: the custome of the Church sheweth to euery mans eye, be he neuer so simple, the same to be approued.

If then these maters wherevpon he hath made his Chalenge, be brought to that Consistorie, and to that seate of iudgement, wherevnto al controuersies ought to be referred, I meane
1.Tim.3. the Catholique Churche, the piller and sure staie of truth, in which the holy Ghoste the spirit of truth is resident: if our Aduersaries would condescend herevnto, we should soone be at acorde. But thereto they wil neuer yelde. For so be they sure, sentence should go against them, as it hath euer heretofore. And because they knowe so much, as al Heretiques haue
Tit.3. euer knowen: therefore S. Paule saith of euery such a one, He is condemned by his owne iudgement.

For

For this cause the face and the name of the Church, hath euer bene terrible vnto al Heretikes.

As concerning the Doctours of the Churche, like as the Jewes cannot be ouercomme by the Scriptures of the newe Testament, for that they do not admit them into their Canon of authentical Scriptures, nor acknowledge them, or any parte of them: so Heretikes of olde time and these false Gospellers of our time for the more parte, refuse the writinges of the holy Fathers, though to promote their owne purpose, sometimes they allege them. The Jewes kicke against Christe, these kicke and spurne against the Churche. The Jewes killed Christe, these do what in their power lieth, to destroy the spouse of Christe.

*B*Ut to returne from whence I haue digressed, by whom shall we be iudged? The iudgement of the Church is refused, specially for almost these M. yeres past. For these felowes would vs to beleue, that after six hundred yeres Christe waxed weary of his spouse the Church, as some men be of their olde wiues, and was diuorced from her. Which opinion is so vaine, so foolish, so wicked, so besides all reason and sense of Scripture, as nothing more, and is of late very sufficiently confuted by him, that wrote þe Fortresse of the faith first planted among vs Englishmē.

The case standing thus, what is now to be donne? Christ saith, Who heareth not the Church, let him be vnto thee, as a Heathen and a Publican. Therefore in dede I ought not to encounter, but quite to geue ouer M. Juwel, & to leaue him vnto þ iudgement of God, as the Church leaueth al such as he is, and acknowlegeth them for none of hers. And this were to be donne touching his person. Yet to thintent the canker of his false doctrine may in some persons be staid from creping further, and that by shewing the weakenesse of his parte, and the falshed of his dealing, the truth be laid forth to the comfort of the Catho- Mat. 18.

likes, & to the confusion of the Gospellers: I haue written against the Replie of his first Article, geuing thee thereby as it were a taste, what were to be looked for, if I would, and thought it expedient, in like sorte to examine and confute the whole,

Now sith it is so gentle Reader, that order is broken, and thou contrary to al good order must nedes be made iudge hereof thy selfe: consider (I require thee) what is thy dutie. Remember, thou be not parcial towardes either of our persons. Let al affection be laid aside. Let right conscience be the rule both of loue and hatred. Let neither hope, nor feare, haue place in thy harte to winne or lose by either of our fortunes. Let neither his preferment be enuied, nor my depriuation pitied. Yea if thou can so conceiue, let our bookes represent vnto thee, not Jewel, and Harding, but two men, John and Thomas departed this worlde, to no man lyuing knowen to haue lyued.

And when thou hast lefte of al affection touching our persons, then studie how to discharge thy mynde of al blinde parcialitie towardes both our doctrines. Put from thy harte the liking of their Gospel (for so they wil nedes cal it) because it is newe, because it is easy, because it semeth pleasant, and geueth more libertie vnto thy lustes. On the other side, let not lothsomnesse of the Catholike religion, which they cal Papistry crepe vpon thee, because it is olde, because it is austere and hard, because it requireth paineful workes, because it bindeth vs to a strait discipline and order of life, and bridleth the lustes of our flesh. Thus abandon al thy humaine likinges, and carnal phantasies, and with a single eye, and simple harte beholde and imbrace, what is good and true, onely for loue of good, and for the Truthes sake.

Being thus disposed, commend thy selfe vnto God with prayer, beseching him to lighten thy vnderstanding, and by his

holy

holy spirite to lead thee vnto the Truth. This donne, with an humble harte read both our Treatises, and iudge. Yet this much I say in case of necessitie, not to al in general, but to certaine, such, as by other meanes wil not, be induced to consider of the Truth. For otherwise I acknowledge, that both the Replie, and al other heretical bookes, by order of the Churche without special licence be vnlawful to be read, and are vtterly forbidden to be read or kepte, vnder paine of excommunication.

Whereas thou takest vpon thee Reader, to be iudge and vmpeer betwen M. Iewel and me: remember the parte of a Iudge is, to iudge (as the Lawiers speake) secundum allegata & probata, that is to say, accordingly as thinges be alleged and proued. But beware, euery thing is not proued, for which authorities be alleged: neither is al made good, which by probable argumentes semeth to be concluded.

Allegations must be true, plaine, and simple, neither weakened by taking away, nor strengthened by putting to of wordes, nor wrested frō the sense they beare in ẏ writer. Els they bewray the feblenesse of ẏ cause, for prouse whereof they be alleged, and also the great vntruth of him, that for furtherāce of his purpose abuseth thē. Verely if allegations made prouse of any doctrine, how soeuer they were brought: thē had M. Iewel largely proued the more parte of his negatiue Articles. For as euery man may see, with heapes of them his Replie is stuffed. But if he haue broken the condition which both right, and cōmon order bindeth vs vnto, I meane, if he haue corrupted his witnesses, if he haue brought in false witnesses, if he haue most vntruly reported his Doctours, and shamelesly falsifyed their sayinges: then oughtest thou Reader to geue sentence againste him, then is his honestie steyned, thē is his credite defaced, thē is his Chalenge quite dasshed. And for prouse that very oftentimes he hath so done, I referre thee vnto this present Reioindre.

Here shalt thou finde no small number of places by him falsified, and that in the first Article. Neither is his custome of falsifying and corrupting the Doctours of one only sorte. Sometime he corrupteth a place by clipping parte away, sometime by putting in of his owne, sometime he altereth the whole by hewing and mangling, sometime by false translating, sometime by laying together partes, that by the authour be laid a sundre: very oftetimes he taketh a peece of a sentẽce, that semeth to make for him, & leaueth out that whereby the doubte is discussed, and the whole mater answered. And as by false sleightes he corrupteth wordes, so much worse he corrupteth the sense, by racking and wresting it to proufe of a cleane contrary meaning.

Neither vseth he the only sleight of falsifying the Doctours sayinges (which of al other is a thing very vnworthy the profession of a reforming Preacher) but also sundry other sleightes. Of some parte of them I thinke good here to put thee in mynd, that being of the same forewarned, thou maist the better iudge of his whole Replie.

At the first he purposed to make his boke huge and great, that so he might gete vnto him opinion of learning, fray me from answering, or weary me in answering. But as we see, the greatest vessels holde not alwayes the best liquour, nor the largest romes stuffe of moste price: so neither many times conteine the greatest bookes the best learning. For some colour of vpright dealing, he hath caused my whole Answere to be printed within ye volume of his Replie, quartering and sorting it by his Diuisions so, as he might take moste aduantage. Thereby he maketh resemblance, as though he had left nothing vnanswered. But verely that geueth out a more shew, then it performeth truth. For in deede hauing laid forth certaine parcels together, of the whole he taketh some peece, and culleth out my sayinges, or rather

certaine

certaine wordes, & vnto them frameth his Replie. And doing this, he would be sure of ech heape to take vp no more, then he thought he was hable to beare away. And yet how farre he is ouercharged, and how he faileth vnder the weight that is laid vpon him, by this Reioindre it shal appeare.

He bindeth vs to conditions, wherunto he standeth not him selfe. Al that we bring, must be fetched from within the first six hundred yeres after Christe. Al our proufes must be taken out of the Scriptures, examples of the primitiue Church, Councels, or Doctours only of that age. If we allege ought that is vnder ye age of syxe hundred and three score yeres, be it but a yere or two: it is voide, and of no auctoritie, because it is without the compasse of time by him selfe allowed. As though Christ had withdrawen the holy Ghost the spirite of truth from his Church, which he prayde to his Father, that it might remaine with her for euer, suddeinly and iump at the ende of the six hundredth yere. Esai. 59. John. 14.
For this cause, and vpon this grounde, he refuseth the prouse of Masse celebrated without a companie of receiuers together by Iohannes Eleemosynarius that holy Patriarke of Alexandria, alleged out of his life written by Leontius. But he geueth him selfe licence to bring and allege against vs, and for maintenance of his owne strange doctrines, whatsoeuer it be, examples, stories, customes, Canons, Decrees, Gloses, Scholemen, Canonistes, Summistes, al Doctours, al writers of al ages, olde and young, so they seme to serue his turne, he refuseth none. Articulo primo In ye. 32. diuision. pag. 75.

I wil not trouble thee here Reader with a long rolle of their names, whome M. Iewel commonly allegeth against vs as he pretendeth in other partes of his Replie, making the vnlearned weene, they are famous and auncient Doctours, as one Iohn Belet, William Ockam, one Iohannes de torto collo, as much to say, Iohn with the wrye necke, and such other obscure and vnknowen writers: yet I will not let to put thee to knowlege, of what Doctours he hath stored him self for fournishing forth this first Article. which al be farre without the compasse of his first six hundred yeres, and most of them lyued within these three hundred yeres, and some within memorie of our age. They ar these, Anselmus, Rupertus, Innocentius tertius, Durandus, Alexander de Hales, Hugo, S. Thomas of Aquine, Bonauentura, Scotus, Gabriel Biel, Vincentius in Speculo, Gratian, Hugo Cardinalis, Nicolaus de Lyra, Nicolaus de Cusa, the glose vpon the Canō lawe, Hermannus Contractus, Summa Angelica, Micrologus, Bessarion, Eckius, Pighius, Doctor Smyth. These were wel learned men, I denie not, and for vertue, and knowledge to be honoured ech one in his degree: yet be they without M. Iewels compasse, yet be they for the more parte late writers, and young in comparison of the first six hundred yeres. Wherefore reason would he should beare ẏ more with vs, alleging sometimes vpon iust occasion, not Scholemen or glosers of the basest estimation, but men by confession of the whole worlde of excellent learning, though of later age then the first six hūdred yeres. As for exāple, Bessarion is alleged as a witnesse of the custome of the Greke Church for pronouncing the wordes of Consecration: M. Iewel voideth his authoritie in regard of his age, with this scorneful note in the margent, *Bessarion a yonge Doctour.*

In ẏ xvi. Article.

Replie. pag. 546.

And as he vseth a more libertie in the allowance of Doctours him selfe, then he graunteth vnto vs: so he demeaneth him selfe touching Councels. The Councel of Antissiodorum is light made of, because it was holden thirteen yeres after the first six hundred yeres. But he geueth him selfe leaue to bring in for him Councels, that were longe after, namely the Councels of Matiscona, of Cabilō, of Acon, of Lateran, of Constance, of Florence, the late Councel of Trente it selfe, and many other, in euery one

Article. xiii. pag. 487.

of

of which Councels his doctrine is condemned.

Verely he fareth with me much like, as if in a cōbate no other weapon agreed vpon to be vsed of vs both, but a sword onely, and that on foote: contrary to lawe of armes in that behalfe, he entred fight, and set vpon me on horse backe, with sword, speare, and shylde, with fiue or six dagges like a swart Rutter, with his Page at hand to helpe at nede. So in this strife to atteine ye victorie, as it semeth, not to trye out ye truth, he furnisheth him selfe with al manner of helpes, as it were with weapons, with ye Examples, Councels, & Doctours of al ages: as though it were so agreed vpō, admitteth me only to ye aide of the first six C. yeres for defence of our cause. which neuerthelesse is ynough, & would god according vnto his promise, therby he wold be tried.

As he maketh light of what soeuer is brought for proufe of any point out of them that liued after the first six hundred yeres, so he condēneth & denieth very many that be within ye compasse, namely S. Clemēt, S. Dionysius Areopagita, S. Martialis, S. Hippolytus, S. Iames Masse, S. Chrysostomes Masse, Leōtius. which al either I haue here fully proued, or thoroughly disproued ye objections made in their disproufe. As for ye storie of Abdias, or rather of Iulius Africanus, he hath fowly & impudētly belied. Against Amphilochius he vttereth more spite, & scorne, then learning or reason, albe it if such Visions like not faithles hartes, to godly beleuers for defence of the truth in my booke there is ynough besides.

His other shiftes be in maner infinite. He denieth sūdry Doctours, yet to the same he runneth for helpe. The Decrees & Decretal Epistles he condemneth altogether, the same he vseth very cōmonly, & to sundry purposes. How weakely he disproueth thē, here shalt thou finde. The auncient Fathers, where their only names for credite sometime I recite without rehersal of their words, as the custome of writers is, he calleth *Mummers.* Yet such *Mummers* he bringeth in him selfe very often,

He

He maketh his aduantage of the obiections, that he set forth by Innocentius tertius, Scotus, Bonauentura, and other Scholemen against the Truth, as though they were the censure and receiued doctrine of the Church. He allegeth the Schismatike Greekes touching the point of Consecration, as though their errour were of good authoritie. He allegeth them against the Masse, that openly impugne the Masse, as Gerardus Lorichius, and Georgius Cassander: as though the sclaunderous wordes of the ennemies of the Churche, were to be heard against the Church. He might as wel haue alleged Zuinglius, Oecolampadius, Caluine, Peter Martyr, Cranmare, and Hooper, against the real presence.

He falsifieth and peruerteth my wordes almost euerywhere, and when he hath made me to say, that he would faine I sayd, and say not in dede: then he taketh on, & triumpheth, as though he had me at greate aduantage. He forgeth peeuish and light argumentes of his owne head, such as a childe would not make, and laugheth at them him selfe, pretending them to be made by me. This is very common in him, specially in certaine the first Articles, where he thought by lyke to winne great praise by the arte of scoffing.

When he commeth to dispute and reason in earnest, the greatest grace he hath, standeth in denying one truth by the affirmation of an other truth: As for example, In sundry places of his first Article he maketh much adoo to proue, that the Communion in olde time was receiued of many, which no man denieth: and thereof concludeth the denial of the Masse without companie receiuing with the Priest, whereas both may wel be graunted.

Because the vertue of Christes Sacrifice vpon the Crosse endureth for euer, and is thereof by some called the euerlasting

Sacrifice: thereof he concludeth, the Sacrifice of the body and bloud of Christe in the Masse not to be the daily Sacrifice of the Churche. So otherwhere because Christe is eaten by faith and in spirite, thereof he inferreth, that Christe is not eaten in the blessed Sacrament by seruice of our mouth. Because Christe is corporally in heauen, thereof he concludeth that his body is not vnder the forme of breade. By as good manner of argument he might denie Christe to be God, because he is man.

Oftentimes he dissembleth the mater presently treated, and taketh occasion of a worde to enter into an other mater impertinent, as in ye.2. Diuision, where I say ye I leaue ye terme Priuate Masse to Luthers schole (vnderstanding no Masse as it signifieth the Sacrifice to be priuate) where it was first deuised, and so termed by Sathan him selfe: he sheweth nothing where it was euer so named before Luther, but saith much in excuse of Luther for his conference with the Deuil.

Likewise in the.5. Diuision, where I say, he pretendeth enmitie against priuate Masse in worde, but in dede against the Sacrifice commonly called the Masse: there he answereth not the point, but talketh much against that it is so commonly called. So he cauilleth at wordes, & leaueth the special mater. Sometimes he maketh him selfe mery, and taketh his pleasure at a worde reasonably vsed, with his owne imagination drawing it to an absurditie. As where in ye.34. Diuision I vse the terme of winding vp the mater, he scoffeth at the worde of *vvinding vp*, and there he calleth it *M. Hardinges Clevve*, and ceasseth not to sporte vpon a Clewe, as though either our tongue admitted no metaphorical speaches, or I had spoken of any Clewe at al.

Neither in that place only, but thorough his whole booke he entermedleth his scoffes and mockes, as it were his very purpose, with such sawce to make it pleasant, & to geue his readers,

 specially

specially those yͭ be delited wͭ that kinde of mery diuinitie, an appetite not only to taste of such cates, but also to feede of thē their fill. Such grace of writing I neither vse, nor couet, neither haue I it, nor if I had, should I thinke it meete to vse. The Truth of God would not be set forth wͭ scoffes. Whose desire to vnderstand yͤ truth is colde, the same is to be stirred vp rather wͭ graue and ernest exhortations, then with skornes, and mockes.

But when he is pressed with a manifest place, it is worthy to be considered, what shiftes he deuiseth. In yͤ .32. Diuisiō a testimonie for Masse celebrated by S. John Patriarke of Alexandria without a cōpanie of receiuers, is alleged out of Leontius, who wrote his life. To auoide this euident testimonie, it is a worlde to see, what sleightes he vseth. First he would deface the authoritie of Leontius, thē he pretēdeth, yͭ this Masse was said without yͤ cōpasse of his yeres, & by falsifying Vincētius in Speculo maketh yͤ Masse of yͤ age of Mahomet: as though ther had neuer Masse ben said before Mahomet beganne to raigne. After this he allegeth Decrees of Popes, & Cōcels, yͭ Masse might not be said in Chapels or priuate Oratories. If this wil not serue, he runneth to yͤ particulars not mētioned, as bread, wine, Cōsecration, Eleuatiō Aulter, Vestimētes, etc. Then he would it to be doubted who said yͤ Masse, yͤ Bishop, yͤ seruaunt, or the noble man, for of those three only yͤ Storie maketh mētion. Frō yͭ he goeth to finde fault with my trāslation. And then he steppeth asyde to yͤ Greke, where the worde Missa is not to be found. Now by him yͤ Interpreter was no good latine man. If al this wil not saue yͤ mater, thē must not Missa be yͭ which we cal yͤ Masse. Besides al this he maketh it a strāge case, yͭ I should seeke the Masse at Alexādria. And though it be founde there, yet is it not proued by S. Hierome, or S. Augustine, or by some other Catholike Doctour. If none of these shiftes would serue the turne, last of al he flyeth away as it were

out

out of the feelde, and pretendeth he meant in his Chalenge Masse said in open Church, in the face and sight of the People. This I lay before thy eyes here Reader, as I do hereafter in my Reioindre, to thinkẽ by this one example thou maist conceiue, with what a shifter I haue to do. Yet read the place, and I trust thou shalt iudge, that I ridde my handes of him wel ynough, such defence of Truth, the Truth it selfe ministreth.

But what shal I stand any longer in admonishing thee Christian Reader of M. Iewels shiftes, and false sleightes? Read this treatise, and of such ware thou shalt finde some stoare laid abroad for thee to beholde. He that of late gaue thee warning to BEWARE OF M. IEWEL, hath detected some, M. D. HESKINS, and M. DOCTOR SANDER, many moe. As for the late Treatise intitled A RETVRNE OF VNTRVTHES VPON M. IEWELS REPLIE, it turneth no smal heape of such stuffe vpon him. The number of Untruthes vttered of M. Iewels parte noted and confuted by M. Doctor Sander, by the author of the Returne, and by me, amounteth to a thousand and odde. And yet of his six and twenty Articles, onely fiue haue passed our examination. What number of Untruthes is like to rise of his whole booke, by this it may easily be conceiued. Whereas neither feare, nor shame could withholde him from vttering such a huge number of Untruthes in printed bookes, which he knewe wel should come to the vewe and examination of the Catholiques being loth to see Gods people deceiued with false Doctrine: what is it likely he wil sticke to vtter in pulpites, where he is sure no man shal control him!

M. Rastel.
D. Heskins.
D. Sander.
M. Stapleton.

If thou haue pleasure in Untruthes, the Replie may serue thy appetite. If it like thee better to vnderstãd ỹ Truth, & see vntruthes detected and confuted; the diligent reading of our bookes shal satisfie thy desire.

The thinges worthy to be most wondered at in M. Iewel, be these. His impudencie in lying, his falshed in corrupting the Doctours, his continual scoffing, his common running from the present mater into common places that be impertinent, his immoderate bragging, his common thrusting away of one truth by an other truth, his deepe dissembling where he is pressed with truth, his often ieasting and railing at the Pope and Cardinals, his vile, spiteful and blasphemous talke against our holy Mysteries. These in his Replie he vseth with so great excesse, as no man euer more.

Many haue thought, and so reported, this Replie to be such a peece of worke, as neither could, nor would be euer answered. But wilt thou knowe myne opiniō Reader, and what I thinke of it? Verely I iudge of it in much like sorte as Annibal did of Antiochus Armie. King Antiochus mynding to warre vpon the Romains, had caused a great Armie to moustre before him in sight of Captaine Annibal, who fled vnto him after he had ben ouerthrowen by the Romains. Whē al had shewed them selues, as them semed best, the foote men braue in their colours, ẏ horsemen sumptuous in their gilted harnesse, the Captaines al clad in golde and pearle passing rich: the king reioising hereat, how like you this Sir Annibal, quod he. Here is ynough, quod Anibal, for the Romains, if they be not insatiable. Antiochus looked for an other answere, thinking so wel an appointed Armie of so skilful a Captaine should haue ben praised. But Annibal, who had wel tried the Romains power, knewe al should be but a praye for them.

Right so when I consider this glorious Replie, I see there is Grammer, Sophistrie, Logique, & Rhetorique: there is Diui-

nitie

nitie and humanitie: there is lawe both Ciuile & Canon: there is Greke and Latine great store: there be stories and fables: there be Doctours of al sortes olde and newe, the Canonistes and Schoolemen, the Glosers & Summistes: there is gay eloquence, & Ministerly talke: there is much ioly sporte, and some sad hypocrisie with many a crying out, Blissed be God, O Maister Harding, Alas M. Harding, &c. there be strange Phrases, there be affected termes, there be pinching nippes, irksom cuttes, scorneful scoffes, & spiteful mockes: to be shorte what is there not to greue a godly man, to discredite the person of the Aduersarie, to cast a colour of truth vpon the cause, but specially to delite and please the baser sorte, as Prentises and light persons, the Ministers and their wiues, and al other the like riffe raffe of the people.

But in effecte al is nothing, because there is no force of truth. It monstreth gaye in the eyes of the deceiued frende, in the encounter with the learned Aduersarie it maketh weake resistance. It liketh them, that would al he saith were true: it liketh not them, that can examine what is true. Verely it geueth to the Aduersarie great aduantage, I meane abūdance of mater to confute, more then he would desire.

As it was said of the three hundred valiant men of Sparta, who fought against so many thousandes of Xerxes hoste in the straites of Thermopylæ, Vincēdo victi sunt, as much to say, with ouercomming they were ouercomme: So if the Catholikes take in hande to rensacke this Replie thorowout, the number of the Vntruthes and false partes wil rise so infinite, that (I wil not say they are like to be ouercomme, but) perhaps with abundāce of mater, being loth to let fowle pointes passe without control, they may be encombred. Certaine it is, rather shal they find distresse what to leaue, then what to touch, what to dissemble, then what to refel, what to winke at, then what to conuince. If euery their finger were a hande, and euery tooth a tongue, ther were stuffe ynough ministred vnto them to confute by writing, and to deface by preaching. Calling to thy consideration the great number of Untruthes which I and others haue deprehended in it, and that within the Compasse of fiue Articles: thou maist sone iudge, of what stuffe this Motley was made. A number of pretensed Untruthes he hath odiously scored vp as noted in my Answere vnto his Chalenge, but how truly, I reporte me vnto the Treatise intitled A Returne of vntruthes vpõ M. Iewels Replie, & to ỷ perhaps shal folow hereafter. Had he not begõne this dãce of scoring vp Untruthes himselfe, we should not thus haue folowed the rownde. For in dede I neuer knew any such a foolish daunce piped vp before. But it is often sene, He ỷ speaketh, what him listeth, sometime heareth, what him lotheth.

To confute any parte of the Replie, it is easy. by due examination to stay at euery Untruth, it is paineful. He doth not so much wring vs with fastnesse of close argumentes, as he encombreth vs with heape of loose sayinges. He presseth not with weighte, but troubleth with number. His blowes come thicke, but his weapõs lacke edge. Some in olde time likened Logique to the hand closed together, Rhetorique to the hand stretched abrode. Thereof it may be cõceiued, how much we feare this Rhetoriciã. Wel may he swepe duste frõ of our coates with flap of hand: he cã not hurte our boanes ẇ stroke of fiste. The onset of such an ennemie cãnot fray vs, the chasing of him may put vs to some labour.

Touching the state and issue of the mater in this parte of my Reioindre specially treated, sith it is of priuate Masse, remember Christian Reader for thy better instruction, what is to be vnderstanded by the name of priuate Masse. First it conteineth the signification of the Sacrifice, nexte of the Priestes single or sole receiuing. If the Sacrifice be sufficiently proued, and no reason can be shewed, why the Priest may not receiue alone in case of others negli-

Priuate Masse, what therby is meant.

negligence (where as of others it may be proued that within M. Jewels compasse of yeres they receiued alone) what wanteth to the ful prouse of Priuate Masse? Yet beware thou be not deceiued. whereas that which is signified by these two wordes, Priuate Masse, is quiddam compositum, as I may vse ẏ Schoole terme, I meane a thing consisting of Masse, in asmuchas it signifieth ẏ Sacrifice, & of receiuing, ŵ this cōdition that it be single or sole, & without companie (for els receiuing alone or otherwise on the Priestes behalfe, is an essential parte of Masse, for that the Sacrifice must of necessitie be receiued): M. Jewel ẏ rather to deceiue, & to confounde the whole mater, speaketh confusely of it in respect of both. By denying priuate Masse, he denyeth both. He then that wil proue it, must proue both aparte. Now marke M. Jewels Sophistrie. whē I bring prouse for ẏ Sacrifice, he wrāgleth vpon ẏ Priestes sole receiuing. when I proue the Priestes sole receiuing by examples of antiquitie, which reporte ẏ diuerse of the deuoute people receiued the blessed Sacrament alone, then he starteth vnto the Masse, and scoffingly demaundeth, whether the people, lay men, and women sayd Masse.

For which purpose, to speake exactly, & that wranglers thwartinges be stopped, ẏ Catholikes thinke good to say, there is no priuate Masse at al in respect of ẏ Masse it selfe. For as it implieth specially ẏ Sacrifice, it is cōmon & publike, and cā not be priuate. And whereas it cōsisteth of Consecratiō, Oblation, & receiuing, it ought not to be named of the only Receiuing. That which M. Jewel ŵ so much adoo hath impugned, may be called Priuate or sole Receiuing, priuate Masse reasonably it can not be called.

I acknowledge notwithstanding, that the Masse hath of learned men ben some times named Priuate, but in a far other sense, to witte, in consideration it is not solemne, or celebrated with publike solēnitie. But that it be called and accompted Priuate for that the Priest receiueth the blessed Sacrament alone, as it is taught by Luthers Schoole, it is not graunted. It was a terme by Sathans crafte deuised to begile simple soules.

Whereas by the importunitie of M. Iewels Replie I am driuen in this treatise many times to name Priuate Masse, remember gentle Reader, that where I seme to acknowledge it, the same is in respect of the Priestes sole receiuing, by which the Masse is not made of lesse vertue or worthinesse. Where I seme to reproue the terme, therein I haue respect to the Sacrifice, which is not, ne can not be priuate.

The issue is this, Seing the Sacrifice is cleare, and a thing confessed both by testimonie of al ẏ Fathers, and by practise of the Church, how so euer M. Iewel without grounde or learning striue against the manifest truth: and likewise seing it can not be denied, but that the blessed Sacrament was of olde time, and may now be receiued of one alone: what reason haue these men to shewe, why the Priest should be debarred from celebrating Masse, and from receiuing alone, when a companie is not disposed to receiue with him? To consecrate the body and bloude of Christe wherein the Sacrifice consisteth, and therfore also to offer it vp vnto God, by Christes owne Institutiō he is commaū-
Luc.22. ded, who said, Do ye this in my remembrance. But that he
1.Cor.11. should not so doo, onlesse there were a cōpanie presently ready to receiue with him: ẏ neither Christe cōmaunded, nor the Apostles preached, nor any of their Successours, or auncient Father euer wrote. This prohibition if they be not hable to shewe, let them ceasse barking against the holy Ghoste, by whose grace ẏ Church is gouerned, & hath oftentimes celebrated Masse through al the worlde these many hundred yeres the Priest receiuing alone, and for ẏ same was neuer cōtrolled vntil these late yeres, & ẏ by certaine, whose order of life hath declared them to be quite voide of the spirite of God, & to be lead altogether by ẏ spirite of Sathan.

The

The most they haue to say against vs is, that for the same we haue not many testimonies, nor examples of Antiquitie. For the Sacrifice which is donne in the Masse, we haue Scriptures, examples, testimonies of the auncienst and best learned Fathers in great aboundance. That the holy mysteries were alwaies receiued by the priest, that sacrificed, there is no doubt, for that is of the necessitie of the Sacrifice. But whether the priest had alwaies a companie to receiue with him, or sometimes receiued alone: that is a circumstance of a facte, the proufe whereof by manifest testimonies can not with reason be demaunded. If we proue the thing, it is contentious to put vs to the proufe of the circumstance. Yet some testimonies for it we haue, and though not many, no maruel, for such circumstances of factes, as it is knowen, be seldom expressed in writing: and certaine it is, that many thinges haue ben donne, which by witnesse of writers we can not auouch.

When Christe was at a feast in the house of Simon the Leper, Matth. 26.
whether he dranke wine without water, or water and no wine,
or wine tempered with water, neither I, nor M. Jewel, nor any Ioan. 12.
man lyuing can proue. What then? Shal we therfore conclude, that he dranke nothing at al? It doth not remaine in any recorde, that Christe, or his Apostles before his Ascension did euer eate flesh, but at the celebration of the Paschal Lambe: Shal we therfore pronounce and say, ỷ before that time they neuer eate flesh? Right so if we could not bring testimonies, that within the first six hundred yeres any Priest at Masse receiued the Sacrament without a number receiuing it with him, yet were not that a sufficient argument wherby to proue, there was al that time no such Masse at al. It were reason, that first these men agreed with vs touching the thing it selfe, so the disputation concerning the Circumstance, should procede more orderly. But M. Jew-

of purpose seeketh to confounde order, perceiuing he shal be best hable to set forth some colourable defence of his vaine Chalēge, if thinges be treated confusely.

To cōclude concerning this first Article, whereas the doctrine of the Sacrifice is certaine, and the priestes receiuing of it essential; but whether it be with companie of other receiuers, or without companie, ceremonial, which neither diminisheth, nor increaseth the vertue or worthinesse of the Sacrifice: I aduise thee good Reader, thou condemne not the Church for vse of the Accident, least so thou lose the fruit of the Substance.

That the people would dispose them selues worthily to receiue the blessed Sacrament with the Priest at euery time he saith Masse, it were to be wished: But that there be no Masse, but when a companie receiueth together with the priest, it is not of commaundement by Gods worde. Neither that the people should oftentimes receiue, is it of any commandement expressed in scripture, but of deuotiō, and (in the beginning) of order taken by the Church. And therfore the Fathers vse not wordes of commaundement vnto the people, touching often receiuing, but of exhortatiō. which they would haue donne otherwise, if to receiue oftentimes it had ben commaunded in Scripture. But as for the priest, he is expressely commaunded to consecrate the body and bloud of Christe, and therfore to sacrifice, & consequently to receiue it. The worde of Christe is this. *Do ye* Luc. 22. 1. Cor. 11. *this in my remembrance*, which the holy Ghoste hath taught the Church alwaies so to vnderstande. Sith then the one is of commaundement, the other of the peoples deuotion only, which in this case slaked, when persecution ceased: let it be wisely considered, whether that, which is necessary by Christes commaundement, may be abrogated for lacke of that sometime, which is not of his commaundement. If it may not, specially the common practise of the whole Church being to the contrary: thē is Masse

where

whereat the Priest receiueth alone, which they cal Priuate Masse, sufficiently auouched.

This being proued, it forceth litle, whether we bring forth testimonies of yͤ first six hundred yeres for it, or no. Testimonies proue not a thing, onely they report it to haue ben. And yet in my Answer to his Chalenge, I haue alleged mo testimonies of Antiquitie, then w reason or learning he hath hitherto auoided. If he haue a Commission for his owne parte to proue nothing, but onely to denie, and wrangle against our proufes: so may he a long while keepe vs occupied. For more may one froward wrangler, be he neuer so ignorant, denie, and demaunde proufes for more in one houre, then many wel learned men shal wel be hable to auouch and proue in many yeres. It remaineth he be demaunded to shewe an authentical prohibition, whereby it may clearely appeare, that the Priest is forbid to consecrate & offer the Sacrifice, onlesse he haue a number to receiue it with him forth with in yͤ same place. If for this he be hable to shewe vs neither Scripture, nor example of the primitiue Church, nor Councel, nor Doctour within the first six hundred yeres, nor at any time els from the Apostles age to this present day, as we are sure he is not: I trust good Reader thou arte not so farre wedded to fantasie, as to denie what M. Iewel denieth, rather thē to beleue, what yͤ whole Church hath with worde affirmeth, and by daily practise to al obedient beleuers commēdeth. Wher- Esai.59.
as the Scripture assureth vs that the Church is alwaies as- Mat.28.
sisted and lead into al truth by the holy Ghoste, and of M. Iew. Iohn.14.
it geueth vs no such assurance: euery faithful mannes iudgmēt herein is sone resolued, vnto whether parte most safely he may incline,

TO M. IEWEL.

Although M. Iewel, when you proclaimed your Chalenge at yͤ beginning, you promised to yelde & subscribe, if any mã a liue were hable to bring any one sentence out of any olde Doctour, Councel, Scripture, or example of the primitiue Church for proufe of any one of al your Articles: yet verely I am persuaded, no wise man beleued, what so euer, or how much so euer were brought, that you would stand vnto your promise. For if your mynde had ben to submit your selfe vnto the contrary iudgment, in consideration of any such sentence by any man to be alleged: You would neuer haue presumed so farre. And by yelding to any point now, were it neuer so assuredly proued, you should seme to confesse the ignorance and errour, in which you remained then: which humble confession agreeth not with the insolent sprite of such craking Chalengers. So then the largenesse of your promise, to others maketh shewe of your confidence, and to your selfe the regarde of it increaseth stubbornnesse. wherefore at yͤ first, when I addressed me to answer your Chalenge, I doubted not but sone after I should heare of some Replie. As I thought, so it came to passe. The sprite that stirred you to beginne arrogantly, driueth you to procede desperatly. And now that you haue weat your foote, you seme not to care how deepe you wade.

Our lorde yet (if it be his pleasure) once open your eyes, and geue you grace to see the danger of the poole you wade in. Beware by time M. Iewel, you fal not into the horrible gulfe, that Salomon speaketh of. *Impius cum in profundum malorum venerit, contemnit.* Prouer. 18. When yͤ wicked man commeth into yͤ bottom of euils, he becommeth carelesse setting al at nought. I once you fal into this bottom, what hope is there of your recouerie? For whereas none returneth from euil, but he ẏ repenteth him of euil: how can he repent, ẏ hath cast away al care? yea how can he steppe backe from euil, & be made good, ẏ saith (whose miserable state Esay lamenteth) euil is good, and good is euil? How can he see the right way, that maketh darkenes light, and light darkenes? How can he delite in swete thinges, that taketh sowre for swete, and swete for sowre? You say perhaps, But who be such? The prophete there discrieth them saying: woe be vnto you that are wise in your owne sight, and thinke your selues to haue vnderstanding in your owne conceite.

Esai. 5.

Returne not this scripture vpon me, as your manner is. Although through infirmitie otherwise oftentimes I offend, & the same to make exchange of euil for good, of light for darkenes, of swete for sowre, swaruing from the squire of Gods lawe, by which I ought to measure the actiōs of my life: yet verely touching maters of faith and religion, through Gods grace I am cleare frō gilt of such peruerse iugement. For now hauing learned to submit al my knowledge & vnderstanding vnto ẏ iudgement of the Catholike Church, what portion of witte or knowledge so euer is geuen vnto me, I am not wise in mine owne sight, neither thinke I not my selfe to haue vnderstanding in mine owne conceit. I resigne ouer al, & leaue it vnto ẏ discussion & trial of that Schole, whereof ẏ spirite of truth is ẏ euerlasting Schoolemaster.

Now because you wil not submitte your selfe vnto the Church, but cōtrarywise condemne the Church because you wil iudge, and not be iudged, because you control and refuse the learning of ẏ whole Church of Christe for nine hundred yeres past, & preferre your owne before al others of ẏ long time, and iudge of what so euer was said or written by any man before ẏ time, according to your priuate vnderstanding, & not according to the censure of the Churche: how can you not seme to be one of thē of whō Esaye meant? wherefore if my voice come to you frō to farre of, or be otherwise not lowde ynough: yet let ẏ wordes of Esaye, or rather ẏ wordes of God vttered by ẏ penne of Esaye, sownde in your eares: Woe be vnto you that are wise in your owne sight, and thinke your selues to haue vnderstanding in your owne conceite.

This mater is wel to be weighed, the case you stand in, is deeply to be considered. This much you can not denie. You haue for your parte broken the vnitie, that is so much commended vnto vs in ẏ scriptures, & al holy Fathers. The Catho- Cypriā.
like Church (saith S. Cyprian) can be one, it can not be cut and lib.2.ep.
diuided asunder. The Catholike Church alone is the body of 12.
Christe, saith S. Augustine, whereof he is the head, the Sauiour Aug.epi.
of his body. Without this body the holy Ghoste geueth life to 50.
none. Therefore in an other place he saith, Who so euer is sepa- Epist. 152.
rate from the Catholike Church, how laudably so euer he thinke himselfe to liue, for this onely wickednes that he is diuided from the vnitie of Christe, he shal not haue life, but the wrath of God remaineth vpon him. Tel vs thē what is your answer, & wherunto you wil stādе. If you remaine not a mēber of ẏ Catholike Church, thē can you haue no life. For as life redoundeth not vnto ẏ member ẏ is cut of from ẏ natural body, so neither geueth the holy ghoste life but only vnto such as be mēbers of Christes mystical body. That you are not a member of that body, which we esteme to be the catholike Church, your contrary doctrine, your bitter spite & hatred against it, manifestly declareth. For ẏ members of one body agree & loue together, they fal not out ne fight not one wᵗ an other. what resteth thē for you to answer, but ẏ the Church, whose faith we professe, is not ẏ catholike church?

If thus you be resolued, what nede we beate so long about so many your negatiue Articles? It were a shorter & a plainer way

 to

to conuert al our disputation vnto this issue, that we serched out, where the catholike Church is, and which it is, where it begãne, and by what succession it hath continued. Verely we acknowledge none other since Christes incarnation, but that which hath continued from the Apostles time by most certaine successions of Bishops vnto this day, and hath spred ouer the whole worlde. Because ye can not shew vs good euidence of such antiquitie, of such order of succession, of so long continuance, of so large spredding ouer the worlde in any of your Congregations, whether they folow the doctrine of Luther, or of Zwinglius, or of Brentius, or of Caluine, or of any other sith Luther beganne: you most beare with vs, if we can iudge neuer a one of them to be Christes Church. Yet if ye wil nedes dispute with vs about the Church, and wil claime that title for your brotherhed of Geneua, which of al other you fauer most: remember how farre ye are already confuted by S. Augustine writing against the Donatistes, who in much like sorte as ye do now, contented the Church was quite extincte in al other places of the worlde saue Africa, and was to be founde onely among them who tooke parte with Donatus.

But as it is certaine, you wil faile in proufe of your Church of the Caluinistes, so I doubte not, but the worlde ere it be long shal see, how weake are the other partes of your doctrine. A man would thinke who hath heard or read your Chalenge, that either you were wel fournished with substantial learning to defende what you tooke vpon you, or ẏ you were a man of passing impudẽcie, or of extreme madnesse. Your Chalẽge was answered you haue replied. What you could do, in this Replie you haue donne. What helpe might be had among ẏ whole syde, you haue not wanted. Schoolemasters, Greke Readers, Lawyers, Canonistes, Ciuiliās, Summistes Glose serchers, Diuines of al your sortes, & al others ÿ could do ought, haue put to their hãds. The whole forces of your side into your booke are brought together. God be thanked for it. Al shal turne to the ioyful victorie of truth, & to the glorie of God, & to your owne confusion at length.

Many thought, ye were inuincible: By this it is wel perceiued, ye are easy ynough to be conquered. Men supposed some great thing to be in you. Now al is sene, what ye haue. And when it shalbe made manifest that ye haue nothing in substance, but onely certaine shewes of thinges: your craking and boasting shal ende in your contempte and shame.

The euent of your vanitie putteth me in remembrance of one Megabysus a great Captain vnder the king of Persie. This Megabysus came on a time vnto the shop of Apelles that most famous painter at Athens. Beholding the Tables, and geuing his verdite of those excellent workes, he praised, and dispraised, liked, and founde faulte, as his fantasie blundered, not as skil directed. Apelles that while standing behind a cloth, and hearing what he said, stepte forth, and spake thus vnto him. Hitherto Megabyse thy purple, golde, and pretious stoanes, and the traine that waiteth on thee, made vs beleue, thou were a man of great worthinesse: now these boyes here that grinde my colours, hearing thee to speake so foolishly, set nought by thee, and laugh thee to scorne. Verely though I be not like to Apelles, yet is your case M. Iewel not much vnlike to Megabyses. Heretofore your Rochet, and your square Cappe (for I trowe you be not yet come to be one of the Roundcappe Ministers) your Bishoprike of Sarisburie, your sightly state and condition, your Rhetorical perswasions in the Pulpite with a holy holding vp of the handes, and casting vp of the eyes to heauen, and with

Megabysus.

 your

your lamentable crying out of your Oos, which you vse very commonly, weening therby to perswade the simple, your stoute asseuerations, your fauour of the common people and others, that clap you on the shoulder, your vaine pulpit buzzing, your Gloria patri at Powles Crosse: al this hath made many a one beleue, that M. Iewel was a great Clerke, a piller of the Gospel, a peerlesse felowe. But now that you haue said al that you, and your whole syde had to saye, now that you haue discouered that lay hidde before, now that your best stoare is laid abroade, now that you haue made the worlde witnesse of the proufes ye haue for your doctrine: they that haue but meane skil behold a further weakenesse to be on your side, then before they had conceiued. Better it had ben for you, ye had mainteined your opinion and estimation among your owne deceiued brotherhed with silence, and with your accustomed craking, without shewing forth any proufes.

Your case standing as it doth, the Catholikes contemne you, the mere Lutherans laugh at you, so do al others of any what so euer sect late sprong vp, and your owne dere brethren the Caluinistes be ashamed of you, as who confesse you gaue to large a scope to your Aduersarie, in plaine English nolesse to say, then that you had made your Chalenge so large, that it could not possibly be defended with any good colour of truthe. How litle truth you haue for your syde, and how many Untruthes you haue vttered in your Replie, partly by this Reioindre, and more largely by ye labours of other learned mē it is, & shalbe declared.

As concerning your Answere to my preface, it is like the rest of your booke, al together voide of truth and plaine dealing. To confute euery parte of it, would require an other booke. Your vntruthes euery where rise so in number, that it is more painful for multitude, then hard for pith of reason or stregth of your part.

to refel your sayinges. Here to touch some parte, You pretend, I misliked ẏ you should so precisely & so openly discouer the wants & weaknesse of our side. No M. Iewel, this is as sone denied, as you affirme it. I could not mislike a thing in you that you neuer did. Your vaine Chalenge I misliked, that you haue precisely and openly discouered our wantes & weakenesse: therein you speake as vntruly, as in your Chalenge you crake vainly.

You take light occasiō to twite me with the insufficiencie of my Answer, geuing forth a surmise, as though I complained of the largenesse of your Offer. How sufficient my Answer is, by the discussion of your Replie it shal appeare. If the Untruthes wherewith you charge me, be clearely iustified, and a farre greater number of Untruthes returned vpon you: my Answer shal seme sufficient, your Chalenge folish, your Replie fuller of gay shewe to the ignorant, then of substantial proufes to the learned. Of your large Offer as at the first I cōplained not, so now thereof I reioyse. For the larger it is, the more shal the arrogancie of your minde, the falshed of your Gospel, and the weakenesse of your parte be discouered.

The steining of your modestie, you haue not scoured away. In dede the men, whom I called wise, what so euer you make of thē, would haue conceiued better of you, if with such a sawcy bragge you had not made them witnesse of your folie. Where you say, of so many Doctours, I am not hable to shewe you one, these be your wordes of course, wherof contentious mainteiners of lyes must not be spareful. If I shew in dede, then am I able to shew. What I haue shewed, I report me vnto my Answere, and also to this Reioindre for defense of some parte of the same.

That ye looked fiercely, & shoke your sword terribly, I said it not, as you report me. By ẏ exāple of cowards, in way of cōparisō, I told you what you did, to shew your couragious hardines.

From thence to digresse to the odious vpbraiding of crueltie, charging vs with the terrour of our sworde, with hewing, cutting and sleaing, and with filling our handes with the bloud of our Brethren, it was a mater more spiteful, then to the present place pertinent, altogether violētly racked to stirre hatred against vs, of it selfe not aptly folowing. Neither were they our Brethren, vpon whom the Princes lawes were iustly executed, they were renegates, and Apostates, rebelles against God and man, and forsakers of al true Christian brotherhed.

Naming vs your Aduersaries, you say ye cal vs by a ciuile and a courteous name. How so euer the name ye geue vs liketh you, the dedes ye do vs, please not good men, neither can they seme to vs very ciuile or courteous. You seme to haue in minde reuenge. Els what meant you so sone againe to charge vs with sworde and fire, and to tel vs, we were embrewed with your bloude? wil you beare vs a bloudy harte M. Iewel, as you beare Gods truth a peruerse harte? Your Chalenge (you say) was not of Ambition, neither your reporte of our vnablenesse was of malice. But you were forced thereto by our importunitie, and with great griefe of minde. As for Malice, what measure you haue of it, I leaue to God, who seeth the secretes of al hartes. If you beare vs any, God amend you. If your Chalenge proceded not of Ambition, whereof proceded it then? God, that sercheth the inward affectes and thoughtes of men, discerneth from whēce it proceded. Soothly we may iudge, that it proceded not of humilitie. If your harte tel you therein you were ambitious, remember the plague of Core, Dathan, and
Num 16. Abyron: if, that you were proude, forgete not the fal of Lucifer.
Esay.14. Say for your selfe what you wil, to God your meaning is open, to men your doing appeareth vaine.

That you were forced therto by our importunitie, as you say, who

who cā beleue you? For who of vs al troubled you? who prouoked you? who did so much as pul you by the sleeue? Had ye not before shut vs vp in prisons? Had ye not bannished men out of your way? was there not greate silence of our parte ouer al England? was there any man that opēly did so much as hisse against you? By what importunitie of vs were you then driuen to blowe vp your trumpet, and make that Proclamation? Speake credibly M. Iewel, or els the worlde wil take you for such as you are. But you tel vs, you were forced with your great grief of minde. Yea forsooth it was a great griefe to your minde to see vs al depriued, and put to silence, your selfe to be exalted to the Bishoprike of Sarisburie, and set at libertie to crake what you listed. You shal hardly make the worlde beleue you wept, onlesse it were for ioy.

You finde want of Modestie in me for shewing forth your boasting. For my part, I pray God I be neuer more found faulty for want of Modestie. For excuse of your proude vaunting Goliathlike, you pretend to haue auouched the manifest & knowen Truth. Of your manifest and knowen truth you speake much, and proue litle. It is a thing very vaine, so often to speake it, and neuer to proue it.

If the truth you meane, were manifest and knowen, why could not Luther see it, by whose spectacles you haue espied many pointes of your Gospel, as otherwhere you affirme? He acknowlegeth pardy the true & real presēce of Christes body in ẏ blessed Sacrament, which is a greate point, wherein ye varie from him, and also from the Churche. Him herein follow al those that professe the Confession of Auspurg, as you knowe, which are the greater parte of Germanie, and Denmarke. So that if you wil be tried by the firste Founder of your owne Gospel, you may not say, the truth of you, that be Caluinistes,

In Apologia Ecclesiæ Anglicanæ.

Matthæus Iudex in lib. περὶ τοῦ ῥήσου, &c. is manifest and knowen. Yea he abhorred you the Sacramentaries, and your Communion, and not that onely, but also abhorred to receiue any letter that came from your sect.

Because (you say) I haue not Dauids sling in my hand, nor 1. Reg. 18 his stones in my skrippe, I am not likly to worke great maisteries, neither may I looke that the Ladies of Israel with their Lutes and Timbrelles wil receiue me in triumph. To this I answer. The working of great maisteries I leaue to God, by whose power Dauid maistred Goliath. Your Chalenge is so vaine, and in respect of learning so weake, that to ouerthrow it, it were no great maisterie. Yet neither may you thinke, we compared you with Goliath for strength, but only for craking and vpbraiding the whole armie of the Catholique Church. Goliaths wordes were terrible to them of Israel, because they saw his strength was great. The bragge of your wordes feareth vs not, because in dede we knowe your weakenesse.

By Dauids sling, and his skrippe with stoanes, what you meane, I know not: certainly to the foure weapons, by which you offered this fight to be tried, Scriptures, Auncient Examples, Doctours, and Councels, as it were with foure stoanes taken out of the skrippe of holy Churche, and slong at your forhed, you are ouerthrowen. Speake yet you may, who can let you, but with force rise vp against vs, you can not. Wel may we conquer you with Gods truth, but driue you to hold your noyse we can not. To stay the tongues of Heretiques, it belongeth to him onely, who rebuked Sathan the Father of Heretiques, Marc. 1. Luc. 4. saying: Obmutesce, & exi de homine, Hold thy peace and come out of the man.

For that I, and certaine learned men by sundry treatises, haue wrought to the confusion of your Goliathship, we loke not for the praise of Ladies. The looking after such reward we leaue to you, to you, whom the hope therof intiseth to sustein this wicked trauaile. But forasmuch as the soules of godly men reioise at our labours, and for the same praise God in vs, sith wel they may be called Ladies of Israel, for keping their faith vpright and vnsteined, preuailing with God, as Israel did, in these great temptations and assaults of Schisme and Heresie: there is no doubt, but that they receiue vs with their Spiritual Lutes and Timbrelles, in ghostly triumph. So they haue ioy, and God be praised: it is al the reward that here we looke for.

Your vaine and Ministerlike talke against the Pope, here I am content to dissemble. Now that you haue imagined him to be Goliath, how ye haue knoct him in ẏ forhead, as you crake, let it be iudged by that is of late returned vpon you, by him that wrote a RETVRNE OF VNTRVTHES vpon your Replie, specially where the great and manifest vntruthes of your Replie vpon the fourth Article, be to your vtter discredite and shame diligently noted.

But to what purpose is it, to stand long in ripping vp your Answer to my Preface? You start from place to place, and seriously prouing nothing, you fil your paper with much mater impertinent, neither in my Preface touched, & already for the more parte confuted, euery where shewing forth your spite against the Church of Christ, and the Catholike Religion. You are much beholden to certaine Canonistes, and to the Glose vpon the Canon law. For out from thence you store your self with much gay stuffe against ẏ Pope. But how false & forged stuffe it is, wrested from the writers meaning, it selfe also being of smal auethoritie: euery man that conferreth the places, may easily espie.

You make much a doo about your Negatiue, and beare the worlde in hande, you may lawfully and reasonably stand vpon ẏ Negatiue, in denying so many points of our faith and religion, because S. Gregorie vsed a negatiue propositiō writing to Iohn the Bishoppe of Constantinople, who ambitiously vsurped the title of vniuersal Bishop. What though S. Gregorie said by way of a negatiue: No Bishop of Rome euer tooke vnto him this name of singularitie? Againe what though S. Augustine (for him also you allege) hauing reckened vp al the Bishops of Rome before his time, said by a negatiue: In this order of succession there is found no Bishop, that was a Donatist? What though I would say, as I might truly say, Of ȳ whole number of them that haue ben Bishops of Sarisburie before this time: among them al there can none be found, that was a Caluinist? Likewise ȳ of al the Bishops that euer were in England, none was maried before Cranmare? Because these thinges be said by a Negatiue in defence of truth, shal it therfore be lauful for you to vtter your heresies and slaunderous doctrine by a Negatiue to impugne the truth? As for example, shal it therfore be lauful for you to say, that for the space of six hundred yeares after Christe, the people were neuer taught to beleue, that Christes body is really present in the Sacramente? That no Priest had aucthoritie to offer vp Christe vnto God the Father? That the body of Christe can not be in moe places then one at one time? To reherse the rest it is needelesse.

Gregor. lib. 4. epist 32.

August. epist. 165.

Vpon this Negatiue it liketh you wel to dally, and *because it offendeth vs so much of your side* (for so you say) of your liberalitie *you vvil turne it of our side*. Then you pretend to turne it so as it might like vs best, and as we would haue you say. And when you haue made al your turninges, you doo as much for vs, as if ye gaue vs a Snake for an Adder. This your Negatiue say you, we can not reproue: Our Affirmatiue can not be proued. Your doctrine is manifest and knowen Truth: we deceiue the people with errours: and the Churche hath erred these nyne

hundred

hundred yeres: And we haue haue nothing to say for vs. Thus you say & say againe. And whereas you proue nothing, but your selfe a great lyer: yet you thinke good to face out ẏ mater with bolde and impudent affirmations. What proufes we haue, and how iustly we confute your obiections and Replies, let our Treatises be examined.

You reporte my wordes vntruly, as your common manner is, making your reader beleue, as though I said, al your Articles were of light importance. No sir, I neither said it, nor thought it. Some of them are of right great importance, ẏ more hainous is your wickednesse: And ẏ lightest of them is of weight ynough to drawe you downe to the rueful state of damned soules, if for maintenance of your priuate opinion touching the same, ye feare not to breake the vnitie of the Church. Yet as though I had said, what you falsely reporte me to say, you procede, and scoffingly demaunde, whether ye may thinke that our Religion increaseth and vadeth, waxeth and waneth, as doth the Moone. If such gall be vttered, when no occasion is geuen, what venime may we looke for to be spitte forth, if by ouersight some peece of occasion be ministred vnto spite?

Concerning the rest of your Answer, wherein you treate certaine common places, and vtter much spite against the Pope, falsly bearing the worlde in hande, that he chalengeth vnto him the title of Uniuersal Bishop, and that he suffereth him selfe openly to be proclaimed by the name of God: wherein also you lay forth your common stuffe against the Canon of the Masse, against Transubstantiation, against Inuocation of Saintes, against Aulters, &c. (prayer for the dead ye condemne, though wisely without shewing cause why, for none ye haue to shewe) to refell euery one of these, it would require a longer treatise, *Why answer ye not the books made in*

 then

Defence of Purgatory, where prayer for the dead is auouched and proued.

then the nature of an Epistle, or Preface wil permitte, I thinke good therfore to let passe and contemne many thinges, that may apperteine to others as wel as to me, and which you would haue said to any other man, that had by writing controlled your temeritie. And to come to answer that, which concerneth my person specially.

You haue piked out, or set some a worke to pike out for you, and haue laid together al the termes and wordes vsed in my booke, which a good man may iustly bestow in rebuke of vice vpon euil mē, with which neuerthelesse the euil men be grieued. Those wordes be these, Thersites, Goliath, Heathens, Publicans, Sacramētaries, Lucians, Scoffers, Rash, Presumptous, Ignorant, Peeuish, and certaine other like. At the same you kicke and spurne, as if they had ben meant of your owne person, or of your owne brethren of Geneua only, and not of any Heretikes enemies of Gods truth in general. Why M. Iewel is your owne galde backe so sore, that if I reach forth my hande to touch an others, that is in like case, you can not stay your selfe from wincing? And that it may appeare how farre I haue offended herein, let the mater be wel considered, I pray you.

Thersites. Thersites is accompted of Homer the fondest of al the Greciās that came to Troye, because he boasted much him selfe, and twited other men of dastardnesse. By your arrogant Chalenge made to al the learned men aliue (for those wordes be blowen forth by the trumpet of your proclamation) do you not shew your selfe a vaine bragger, and to esteme al other men for vnlearned? May we not liken such a gentilman to Thersites?

Goliath. 1. Reg. 17. Goliath offered to fight but man for man with any one of Israel, you prouoke al men aliue to campe with you. And shal we not compare you with Goliath? Verely such a one

passeth

passeth Thersites, he passeth Goliath.

Christ saith in the Gospel, If one wil not heare the Church, let him be vnto thee, as a heathen and a publican. M. Iewel doth not only not heare the Church, but he resisteth the Church, he impugneth the Church, he fighteth with al his power against the Church. And may we not be so bolde as to say, we make no more accompt of him, then of an Heathen or a Publican? Heathen and Publican. Math. 18.

They that denie the body of Christe to be really present in the Sacrament, by the common reporte of the worlde, by Luther him selfe, and by them of Luthers schoole, be named Sacramentaries: and must M. Iewel alone be borne with al, and no man be so hardy, as to cal him a Sacramentarie, who most blasphemously both in his writinges and also preachinges inueigheth against the truth of the Real presence? Sacramentaries.

There was neuer any Dickescorner, that iested more pleasantly at any toye in an Enterlude, then M. Iewel scoffeth blasphemously at the most holy and dreadful Mysteries. And may no man be so hardy as to name him a Lucian, or a Scoffer? Lucian.

What madde man euer ouershotte him selfe so farre, as to make such a hasty Chalenge, specially in maters of Religion by so long practise of the Church determined? who euer presumed so to make defiance as it were to al learned men, yea to al men aliue? who euer defended a mater so stoutely auouched, with lesse learning? who euer in so weighty pointes made Argumentes of lesse pith, so light, and so childish? And yet this ioly felow standeth so high in his owne conceit, that whiles he laieth about him, stingeth, and stryketh at al men, spareth not the reuerence of his Mother, no not the Maiestie of the holy Ghoste, and Christe our Lord: he Rash, presumptuous, &c.

may not be touched, so much as it were with a venue of these most deserued termes, Rash, Presumptuous, Ignorant, Peuish. It were ouer long to prosecute the rest, for vse and application whereof, it is easy to render a due and iust reason.

Vetus Comœdia. You would haue men thinke, this were Vetus Comœdia. No M. Jewel, it is Zelus Dei, it is not Vetus Comœdia. The imitation of Vetus Comœdia hath euer ben taken for a badge of men of your profession. It is not like the olde heathnish libertie of railing, it is the zeale of God, and feruour of spirite, such as we finde to haue ben in the Prophetes, in the Apostles, in Christe him selfe. Ye mocke and scoffe not only at our persons, as the naughty boyes of Bethel did at Elizæus, but at our auncient *4. Reg. 2.* Religion, and at the Church of Christe. Yet we curse you not in the name of our Lorde, as he did those euil nourtered children, that ye might be torn of beares. Yet were it better for you to be torn and deuoured of beares, then thus to teare and deuoure so many Christian soules, as ye doo. With your wicked doctrine you haue so brought the people from God, as now for a great number, they may seme not to halt on both sides, but to be falle *4. Reg. 1.* downe right. Yet do we not cal for fire to descend from heauen *3. Reg. 18.* and burne you vp, neither do we stirre the people to take you, and destroye you, as Elias bad the people to destroye the false Prophetes.

Certaine false preachers for their great impudencie, and for that they barked at the light of the Gospel, as dogges do at the *Philip 3.* Moone by night, S. Paule called dogges, and bad the Philippians to beware of them. Your preaching is as impudent, *August. De vtilitate creden-* and dangerous as theirs was, ye neuer stinte barking at the Church (beare with the terme Sainct Augustine vseth it against such as ye are) and at the holy Catholike Religion,

naming

naming it Papistrie, Ignorance, Superstition, and Idolatrie: Yet we spare your worships, and put you in minde of your outrage with more courteous language. *di ad Ho noratum.*

Ieremie calleth them of Iewrie Staliens, for that they neyed ech one at an others wife. Ezechiel calleth the false Prophetes of Israel, Foxes, so Christe him selfe named Herode, a foxe. Your companions vnchast life, and lecherous neying at their strumpettes couered with the false cloke of Mariage, what godly hart doth not abhorre? Your spiteful guyles, and wyles, with which ye entrappe men, whom true deuotion, and vertuous liuing declareth to be Catholike, who feeleth not, and smarteth? Yet haue we not chastened your lewdnesse, and false dealing with such reuiling wordes. *Ierem. 5. Ezech. 13. Luc. 13.*

As for my selfe, how so euer it please you to charge me with Vetus Comœdia, verely I seme to men of right good discretion, rather to offende in lenitie and softenes: and many do wish I had tempered the Inche wherewith I wrote my Answer, with sharper ingredience then I haue. Albeit I sought not to please the homours of men, but rather to serue ẏ wil of God, & as I might, to defend ẏ truth, and discharge my conscience. wherein touching the order of my stile, I though good, to doo rather what became the cause, then what belonged to your deserte.

But with what face could you M. Iewel reproue me for the vse of wordes, that might offend? Is it not reason, who blameth an other, that in the thing he blameth, he be not founde faulty him selfe? A man would thinke to finde you softe and sweete, ẏ thus haue rebuked me for being rough and sowre. But whosoeuer wil come neare you & feele you, & pluck of your fruites, & taste of thē: shal soone perceiue what a pricking vrchin you are, & what Crabbes you beare. Verely of al ẏ writers ẏ I haue read, I neuer founde any, ẏ vseth ẏ lothsō mãner of scoffing & mocking, so much as you do. when reason faileth, a scoffe is at hande.

when an argument presseth, a mocke serueth for answer. When the mater goeth plaine on the contrarie side, then Dickescorner bestirreth him, and with iesting pulleth away the minde of the reader to an other light thought: that so al might be laughed out, and the chiefe point let passe.

εἴρων σκοτεινός

In olde time Philosophers had names geuen them of some special propertie and disposition of minde. Socrates was named the* dissembler, Plato the Diuine, Heraclitus, yͤ* Darke, Carneades the Subtile, Chrysippus, the Sharpe, Theophrastus, the Sweete, Diogenes the Doggish. Certainely had you ben aliue at those dayes, you had ben named, Iewel the Scoffer. Yet for your learning I weene you had not ben annumbred among Philosophers. Because I knewe of olde that scoffing witte of yours, in answering to your Chalenge, I tempered my stile so, both as the mater required, and as I might seme to geue you no occasion in replyng to runne out from the purpose, and to folow your peculiar scoffing vaine. And how so euer you haue laid forth in one heape, the wordes which you seme to charge me with, to be sene al atonce: Yet whosoeuer readeth my booke, and marketh it wel: shal see, that I applie not the most parte of them vnto your person, nor vnto your felowes particularly, but vnto Heretikes in general. with which order of writig no good man ought to be grieued. This not withstanding, how litle you haue withdrawen your selfe from your euil disposition, & frō your olde wonte of scorning & scoffing, your Replie hath at ful declared. In dede whosoeuer requireth you to leaue yͤ grace, requireth your losse. For let that once be takē from you, and you remaine very much disgraced. Yea were it so that the vse of scoffing and craking, and libertie of lying were vtterly denied you (lying I meane euery way, for in you it is of sundry sortes) then were you lefte very naked.

But

But M. Iewel, perge mentiri, (you know who saith it) lye on, ieast at me, mocke, raile, scoffe and scorne at me, while you list: assure your selfe, I shal not only not be grieued therwith, but contrarie wise by Gods grace, feele therein a great comfort, and inward ioye. If ye seeke to be reuenged on me for that I haue ben so bolde, as to answer your vaine Chalenge, and by this Reioindre to confute parte of your colourable Replie: either holde your peace, or speake so as you be not founde a lyer, if ye can. for truly by your euil speaking of me, you shal but increase the heape of my felicitie. Standing vpon a good grounde, as thereof I am assured, I shal drawe the wordes of Christe vnto my special comforte, who said, Blessed are ye when men reuile you, and persecute you, and say al manner of euil sayinges against you for my sake. Reioise and be glad, for great is your rewarde in heauē. For so persecuted they the Prophetes, which were before you. Math. 5

Neither can you say this saying is common, and serueth you no lesse then me. The case of vs both is not like pardy. I stay my selfe vpon the Church, the piller and sure stay of truth, as the blessed Apostle saith, and also vpon the Scriptures expounded by ẏ Church. You be departed from ẏ Church, & wander ye wote not whither, nor where to set sure footing. You impugne ẏ Church, I to my power defend the Church, against which hel gates shal not preuaile. You folow Luther, Zuinglius, Peter Martyr, Caluine, and Beza, men by sundry euidences knowen to be voide of the spirite of God: I folow and honour the Catholike Church, with which I am assured the holy Ghoste the spirite of truth by Christe is promised to remaine for euer. 1. Tim. 3. Math. 16. Iohn. 16. Esai. 59.

Now I come vnto your other point, wherewith as with a most hainous crime, you charge me, which is my departing frō your gospel as you say, This you obiect bitterly vnto me, not ōly in your Answer to my Preface, but also in very many places of your Replie, and specially in your Conclusion. You thinke by ofte rehersal of it, both to grieue me, and somewhat to discredite me, hoping so to bring preiudice vnto the cause, which I defende. In your Conclusion you spred abroade your winges as it were and take your ful flight at me. There you say, that of my person, as you promised, you wil say nothing. But how I may trust to your promise, as wel by this, as by your other dealing, you geue me to vnderstand. For there you say of me the worst you can, and more then you ought, and more then is true, and much lesse then you would say, in case you knew other euils by me. That you might haue the better oportunitie to vtter your spite, by a fiction you make a simple man to tel me your tale for you.

Vnder the vizard of your Simple man, you say, that *not long sithence I taught them of your side the Gospel, euen in like sorte and forme in al respectes, as it is taught novv,* for euen so be your very wordes. You remember (you say) *my vvordes, the manner, and courage of my vtterance.* You remember, I told you of the *Paper vvalles, and painted Fiers of Purgatorie,* that Rome was the *Sincke of Sodome,* that the Masse was a *heape of Idolatrie, and the Mysterie of iniquitie,* and, I can not tel what. Thus you say, I taught them the Gospel, whereby you do vs to weete, what ye meane by your Gospel and wherein it consisteth. And this you remember, you say, whereby it appeareth you haue a maruelous memorie. For if you can remember thinges, that were neuer said nor donne: what wil you not remember, that hath ben said or donne?

To answer to the mater simply and truly, as before God, I wil not here for my better excuse, accuse the wil of the Prince, in whose dayes I was brought vp in learning, the ernest endeuour of the Gouernours then being to satisfie his desires, the crueltie of the lawes, the peel-

ding

ding of al in general excepte a very fewe, the great silence of Preachers that then durst not teach necessaries, the common ignorance of men. Omitting al these, which I might bring for some parte of excuse, I am content for Truthes sake freely to accuse my selfe. In certaine pointes I was deceiued (I confesse) by Caluine, Melanchthon, and a fewe others, as you by them and sundry others are now deceiued in many.

In confessing this much, I remember the graue aduise geuen by S. Augustine in the like case. Qui primas non potuit sapientiæ, secundas habeat partes modestię: vt qui non valuit omnia impœnitenda dicere, saltem pœniteat, quæ cognouerit dicenda non fuisse. Who coulde not haue the first partes of wisdome, let him haue the second partes of modestie: that wheras he was not able to say al thinges so, as thereof a man should not repent him, at least let him repent him of those thinges, which he knoweth should not haue ben said. If any man thinke ẏ for my estimations sake, I should not so farre abase my selfe, as to confesse mine owne errour: take he it, as he wil, verely it behoued me to cōsider of that sentence of the Apostle, where he saith, Si nos ipsos iudicaremus, a Domino non iudicaremur, If we iudged our selues, we should not be iudged of our Lord. *August. lib. 1. retract. in prologo.* *1. Cor. 11*

Now as to confesse this much, truth requireth, so to acknowledge your false reportes, wisdome forbiddeth. Them would I also not let to confesse, if I wist God were delited with our lyes. Where then you say, I taught your Gospel *euen in like sorte and fourme in al respectes, as it is taught novv*: that I denie vtterly. In dede I hobde and roued somtimes, but your Prickes I euer tooke to be to farre for me to shoote at. Neither truely could I see the Marke, that you M. Iewel, and such as you are, shoote at, it was so farre of. And therfore I stood out, and shotte smaller game: wherat as my winning was lesse, so my losse also

(I thanke God) was lesse dāgerous. And as your Markes were far without my reach, so neither had I very great skil of ỷ *sort and forme*, which you your selfe now vse in this kinde of shooting.

As for your *Respectes*, to say truely, I neuer knewe what they were. At the gamening of your Gospel, you shoot to strike downe the true and real body of Christe out of the blessed Sacra-
In the. 5. Article. ment of the Aulter, with certaine Phrases of speach, with telling the people of your tropes and figures, with comparing the Eucharist to Baptisme, with making the presence of Christ like in both. You bende your force, to strike away the external and
In the. 17 Article, & other where. In the Replie. singular Sacrifice of the Church, with such a *forte and forme*, as I hitherto neuer vsed, and yet thinke to be very straunge. As for example, with teaching as you doo, that *a* Missa signifieth not the Masse, but your Communion. That *b* Eucharistia is to
a pag. 72 be taken not for the Sacrament consecrate, but for cōmon Bread
b. pag. 40. wherewith one Bishop did present an other. That *c* Melchi-
c. pag. 7. sedech, and Malachias, signified the Sacrifice of your Communion, whereat the people lifte vp their handes, and hartes (as you say) vnto heauen, prayeth and sacrificeth together, reioysing in the Lorde. That in the *d* Sacrament of the Aulter, there
d. pag. 623. is no vertue ne grace, but when it is vsed, nomore then in water after ỷ one is baptized. *e* That there is no difference betwen the
e. pag. 69. Priest and the people in the holy Ministerie of the Sacrifice, and that Laie folke men and wemen do make the Sacrifice, and be Priestes after the order of Melchisedech, that God is the author of euil, and driueth men to sinne. Many other such *fortes and formes* of shooting you and your companions vse at this day, with which I was neuer acquainted, as neither any man liuing can burthen me, and God is witnesse, wich to me is a sufficient discharge. wherefore you do me the greater wrong, in that you say I taught your Gospel *euen in like sorte, and forme, and in al respectes as it is taught nevv.*

The

Touching the other pointes of your Gospel, which you speake of, how so euer I spake once at Oxford of Purgatorie, and at an other time of the Masse, otherwise then now by Gods grace, & study of more mature yeares I haue ben instructed: yet that at any time I tolde you of the *Paper walles, and painted fiers of Purgatorie*, and that the Masse wa s a *heape of Idolatrie, and the Mysterie of iniquitie*: it is altogether false. Those Ministerlike termes of *Paper walles, and painted Fiers*, in good sooth I remember not, that euer I heard before your booke came forth. Neither of the Masse spake I at any time so blasphemously, as you report me. Nor in despite of Rome, euer entred I into such filthy talke, nor liked them, when I liked your Gospel best, that in their Pulpites empted their gorge of such stinking mater. In dede for that yere and halfe, in which onely now and then I occupied a Preachers place, and that by enforcement: of Rome, of the Pope, of Abuses, of thinges which then I thought to be amisse, of Ceremonies, and of certaine other pointes, being seduced by some of them that now seduce you, I talked otherwise, then (as now I iudge) was conuenient. And to say the truth, he that would not talke of such thinges at that time, how could he haue ben permitted in Pulpite to talke at al? And because in most places I spent the time with other maters, then either with these, or with such as they of your side were then desirous to heare, as it is wel knowen: they cōceiued a better hope of mee, then presently they saw any great thing, that to their iudgement semed to be liked in me.

What I should haue done, and how farre I should haue gone, in case Gods prouidence had not chaunged ẏ state: he saw, to whom nothing is vnsene. And perhaps in cōtinuāce of time, I should haue ioyned further wͭ you, except his special grace had called me backe, and seuered me from you. What so euer in those dayes I thought or said amisse, our Lorde forgeue and forgeue.

 Uery

Very like it is, had not the condition of that time ben altered, that I should haue thought & said worse then I did, & haue ben carried away further. But now I see what great cause I haue to reioice and thanke God, who vsed the chaunge of the time, as an occasion and meane, whereby to chaunge me vnto the better. For whiles I feared to suffer that I would not, by new condition of the time, I was compelled to seeke the Truth, which before I knew not, and willingly to holde that, which before I refused. And so now I may seeme to be of the number of them, whome Sainct Augustine in the like case maketh thus to speake. Nesciebamus hic esse veritatem, nec eam discere volebamus, sed nos ad eam cognoscendam metus fecit attentos, quo timuimus ne forte sine vllis rerum æternarum lucris damno rerum temporalium feriremur: Gratias Domino, qui negligentiam nostram stimulo terroris excussit, vt saltem soliciti quæreremus, quod securi nunquam nosse curauimus. We knewe not that the Truth was here (in the Catholike Church) neither had we wil to learne it, but feare made vs attent to know it, wherwith we feared, least perhaps without any gaines of euerlasting thinges, we should be striken with the losse of temporal things: Our Lorde be thanked, who hath driuen away our negligence with the pricks of terrour, that at least we should carefully seeke that, which being without al feare, we neuer tooke care to know.

Aug. ad Vincentiū, epist. 48.

Yet if I were so ernest & so vehement a Gospeller, as now to discredite me you say I was, why did I freely and without al compulsion geue ouer the Kinges Hebrew lesson, which was so good and so quiet a liuing, that I might not depart from that Catholike Colledge, in which I was brought vp, vnto Christes church in Oxford, where ye freshest Gospellers were then placed? If I were such as you make me, how happed it, I gote so litle fauour and preferment among the Prelates of your side? which of them al did ought for me? Yea among the meaner sorte, who ioyned frendship, or any inward acquaintance with me? With which of them was I great? Nay who was there of them, that did not loth mee for suspition of Papistrie (as you cal it) because they saw me dragge, and come nothing nigh the Gole, which they ranne vnto? were not the two Sermons which I made at Paules Crosse, very much misliked, because in the one I spake much for Charitie and good workes, and against the Maried priestes wallowing in their fleshly exercises, in the other of the great abuse of Gods worde, threatning that for euil life it should be taken from them, and be geuen to others that would performe it, and liue according vnto it? Remember you not how not long before king Edwardes death, Bradford, a your frend that was the distributour of the Merchantes exhibition at Oxford to the reliefe of such scholers as would frame them selues to your Gospel (you know whom I meane) once vtterly refused an Exhortation to be vttered to the Students, which with some difficultie they had caused me to draw forth in wryting, mynding I should in manner of a Sermon openly haue pronounced it, if they had liked it? The Theme I tooke for that purpose (if you remember) was the saying of S. Paule to Timothe, Attende tibi & doctrinæ. Take heede vnto thy selfe and vnto learning. Did I not there so exhorte a student to take heede first vnto him selfe, and then to the learning which he laboured to atteine, that they thought good, after they had heard me read it, to take heede of me, and of my learning, rather then to suffer myne Exhortation sounding so litle toward your Gospel, to be pronounced? was not I then misliked, as one not forewarde ynough for that purpose, and therfore dispatched of al, and therwith Sampson required to gete him vp into the pulpite? If you were not present when myne Exhortation was read, demaunding of the said mer- 1. Tim. 4.

chantes factour (if he can finde in his harte to tel you the truth) you may learne this much to be true.

What shal I speake of the sundry compasses and fetches, which they of your side vsed to bring me in, that I might be made a perfite Gospeller? What wayes and meanes did not Peter Martyr practise with me after my returne from beyonde the sea, to perswade me thorowly? To how many priuate Sermons was I called, which in his house he made in the Italian tongue, to Madame Catarine the Nonne of Metz in Lorraine his pretensed wife, to Syluester the Italian, to Frauncis the Spaniard, to Iulio his man, and to me? For al this I remained as before: and you know M. Iewel no man better, how far I was from his inward familiaritie whereunto you were admitted, and what strangenesse there continewed alwaies betwene him and me. I wil not say by whom, and how ernestly I was moued to become king Edwardes Chaplein, which was a deuise to set me further forward. Neither wil I here declare the secret practises, and large offers, with which the Brokers of your Gospel intised me to come on lustily, and to hasten me vnto the perfection in al respectes, which you be arriued vnto.

You shal do wel to beare the worlde in hand no more, that I was so great a Gospeller, least whiles you seeke to discredite me, you proue your selfe worthy of litle credite. That in some pointes I was deceiued with the common errour of the time, I confesse, and am right sory for it. But how farre I proceded in errour, and how neare vnto my harte I laid the loue of it, whether I mainteined it for any other purpose, then that for the time I knewe none other truth, whether I imbraced it with a simple, or a double harte, whether it grew in me from my youth by ignorauce, and continued through the same, or was affected afterward through ambition, and mainteined by malice: because hereas it is not your part to iudge, it shalbe best for you to leaue al to Gods iudgement, who seeth the secretes of al hartes.

If I may be beleued telling that of my selfe, which I my selfe and God know best: this is the truth. My errour was of ignorance, not of malice. My vnderstanding was obscured, my wil was not of selfe purpose peruerted. Wherein I offended, it was not so much through malice of wil, as through want of skil. I did not with animositie, as S. Augustine calleth it, mainteine what liked my priuate choise, but ignorantly I receiued, what gylefully the condition of the time obtruded. Though at the time when I made sute to our Lorde, I had conceiued an vndue opinion, though in knocking for him, I missed of the right doore, though in seeking him I streied out of the way into a bye path: yet because moued by his special grace I made sute and petition vnto him, because I knockte, because I sought him without any sparke of a malicious wil: it hath pleased his great mercie, to graunt my petition, to open vnto me, and to be founde of me. I trust I may truly and without offence of God say, that S. Cyprian reporteth to haue ben said by Maximus, Vrbanus, Sydonius and certaine other godly men, who had likewise ben deceiued by Nouatianus the heretike. Nos errorem nostrum confitemur. Circumuenti sumus perfidiæ loquacitate factiosa amentes. Videbamur quasi quandam communicationem cum schismatico homine habuisse. Syncera tamen mens nostra semper in Ecclesia fuit. We confesse our errour. We were begyled as men beside our selues by the busy babling of falshed. We semed as it were to haue ioyned with a Schismatike. Yet was our minde (that is to say our harte wil and intent) alwayes pure in the Church.

Math. 7.

Cyprian. lib. 3. epist. 11. ad Cornel.

That I proceded no farther in errour, it was the goodnes of God, who with his merciful hand staid me backe, from running to the extremitie, that you be ronne vnto. Why he suffered me to procede so farre, whether it were by the remembrance of such a fal to worke in me a more perfite humilitie, or to the intent I should thus be made for time to come the more stedfast & constant considering the danger I was in, or by my example to prouoke others to forsake these errours and heresies, & to returne vnto ẏ vnitie of the Catholique Churche, or thereby to moue my harte both to pitie those that are deceiued, and for some recompense to write against the errours of this time: al this I leaue vnto his secrete wisedome, which as the wise man saith, Reacheth from ende to ende mightily, and disposeth al thinges swetely, or (as the Greke text readeth) *profitably. Now say you what you wil, thus I am, and thus by Gods grace, wil I remaine to the ende.

*χρηστῶς

You seme to marueil how I became so perfite a Catholike in so shorte a time. As you say, I preached the contrary many yeres (wherein you say vntruly, for neither preached I ful two yeres, and that not many Sermons, neither was I priest before Quene Maries time): so you pretēd it to be an impossible thing, that in seuen dayes (for of that time you speake more then once) I should read ouer al the Scriptures, Councels, and Doctours: as though a man by Gods special grace, could not be turned frō errour to truth, whose harte was not stubbornly set to mainteine a parte, nor yet drowned in many errours, onlesse he first read ouer al bookes of Diuinitie. What meane you M. Iewel, wil you appoint God a tracte of time to worke in, when he toucheth the harte of man? S. Ambrose could haue taught you to iudge otherwise, where he saith, Nescit tarda molimina sancti spiritus gratia. The grace of the holy Ghost goeth not slowly to worke, when it goeth about good enterprises. And S. Leo, O quàm velox est sermo sapientiæ, & vbi Deus Magister est, quàm cito discitur, quod docetur? O how swifte is the worde of wisedome, saith

In the answer to my preface.

In the answer, & in the conclusion.

Ambros. lib. 2. in Lucam.

Leo ser. 1. de pentecoste.

saith he, and where God is schoolemaster, how soone is it lear- ned, that is taught? when Elizeus was called frō the plough, when S. Paul was striken down in the way, when S. Mathew was commaunded to come from his counting bourd to folow Christe, when the other Apostles were called from their nettes, wil you maruel, they obeied forthwith, before they had read ouer the Law, the Psalmes, the Prophetes, and the other bookes of the olde Testament? Standeth the mater necessarily in reading ouer many and great bookes?

3. Reg. 19. Act. 9. Mat. 9. Mat. 4.

And why do you charge me with the suddaine change of se- uen dayes? was it not one whole yeare after king Edwardes death, before I came in pulpite? And then did I not of myne owne accorde, without al compulsion or request of others, sim- ply and fully acknowledge and confesse my former ouersight and errour? was not al the Uniuersitie of Oxforde witnesse hereof? O M. Iewel, I doubt not but by that my voluntary and humble confession, I haue put the Deuil to silence, through the same he shal not haue power to obiect vnto me mine errour before Christe our Iudge in that dredful day. You I can not put to silence, your tongue and penne I can not staie. Doth not your malice then seeme to passe the malice of the Deuil? wel, say on here against me what you list, there litle shal you haue to say. I perceiue the saying of S. Cyprian to be true, Non possunt laudare nos qui recedunt a nobis. They can not speake wel of vs, that depart from vs. Our Lorde who can raise vp sonnes to Abraham out of stoanes, soften your stony harte, and open your blinded vnderstanding, to see the perilous and rueful state that you stand in.

Cyprian. Antoniano fratri. lib. 4. Epist. 2. Mat. 3.

BUt what meant you M. Iewel of al men, thus vncourteou- sly, and withal very falsly to deale with me? You might much better haue vttered this spite against me by meane of some

 of

of your frendes, or Ministers, one or other, then in your owne person. Now you haue geuen euident witnesse to the worlde, that you are not only spiteful and malicious, but also impudent and foolish. For who be you good Syr, that thus vpbraid me with the reproch of inconstancie? Are not you one M. Iohn Iewel that in S. Maries Church at Oxford, subscribed openly, before the whole Vniuersitie to the Articles by the Catholiques mainteined, by the Gospellers impugned, after the Disputatiōs there kept by learned men of both Vniuersities against Cranmar, Ridley, and Latimer, whereat you were present, and did the office of a Notarie, to reporte in writing, al that was there done and said, and after that you had heard the vttermost what could be said of your side? Subscribed you not to these Articles, That Christes true and natural body and bloud are verely and really present in the Sacrament of the Aulter vnder the formes of bread and wine? That the Masse is a Sacrifice propitiatorie for the quicke and dead? and to diuerse other Articles, which now you impugne?

M. Iewels subscription at Oxford

Sith you did this, as you can not denie it, what impudencie is it, to charge me as you do? Yea what folishnes is it? For inasmuch as your whole tale may iustly be returned vpon you, by this you haue much discredited both your self, and your learning in the iudgement of any reasonable man. You should haue been cleare your selfe, before you had thus vnto the worlde accused mee.

If I would compare both our doinges together, and with plaine truth at large set forth the oddes that is between them, when should I make an ende? Only this much your selfe may consider. whereas both we went from that before we held, you by Subscription of your owne hande, I by voluntarie Confes-

sion:

sion: sith you afterwarde fledde away, and returned to that you renounced, & I remained, and stil continew in that wherto with good aduise I haue cōmended my self: who seeth not, whether of vs both is either the more inconstant man, or the greater dissembler? What thought you when you subscribed, that you did wel, or otherwise? If wel, how were you so sone chaunged, I wil not say in seuen daies, but soothly in very fewe dayes in respect of so great a mater? If you thought you did euil, and yet wittingly woulde do it: then were you an euil man, yea a wicked man, a godlesse dissembler, a false lyer vnto the holy Ghost, a presumptious tempter of God. Remember you not the example of Ananias and Saphira his wife? Were you not afraid of Gods like iudgement to be excercised vpon you, and of his vengeance to light vpon you for the like wickednesse, and lying vnto the holy Ghost? Answere to whether parte you liste, you are taken and holden fast. Act. 5.

You do abscribe my chaunge to the chaunge of the Prince. I maruel you be so wel eyed in my doings, and so blind in your owne. What was it I pray you, that made you so suddainely to chaunge, and to subscribe? Was it not the chaunge of the Prince? Had the other yong Prince liued, would you haue subscribed to the Real Presence, to the Masse, to the Propitiatorie Sacrifice, and to the rest of the Articles, which now you denie? I thinke your selfe wil say nay.

Wel, then we see, the chaunge of a Prince may bring you also to a chaunge. What if God so dispose, that now also the harte of the Prince, detesting the lewdnesse of their liues who professe your Gospel, and seeing the vntruth of your doctrine, & lamenting this vniuersal decay of vertue proceding thereof, and the vtter damnation of so many soules: be wholy bent to restore the Catholique Religion of the Churche, and abandon al these wicked new diuises of Geneua? What wil you then do? Wil you subscribe once againe, or wil you not? Verely what you wil do, God knoweth. But your former actes be such, as I trow any wiseman wil hardly trust you.

How chaungeable your faith is according to the chaunge of euery Prince, to al them that euer knew you, it is not vnknowen. What King Henry would to be chaunged, folowed not you the same? Wherin he called backe with the lawe of the sixe Articles, such as to him seemed to runne forwarde ouer hastily, did you not retire, as it were, when his Trumpet blew the retrait? In King Edwardes daies, daunced you not after the Pipe of that time? When Quene Marie came to the Crowne, did you not frame your selfe to be a conformable man to the Religion of that state in euery respecte, and at length did you not subscribe as readily as any other man in the whole Uniuersitie? But after your Brethren had schooled you, did you not turne againe making a relapse? And because you coulde not abide their lookes remaining in that, whereunto you had subscribed, did you not flee away? In the raigne of the Quenes Maiestie that now is, haue you not folowed what so euer chaunge is propounded? And yet did you not once confesse to mee plainely in Sarisburie, when ye came thither in visitation, that you neuer liked the Supremacie of the temporal Princes ouer the Churche of England? Did you not tel mee, that it stood neither with Scripture, nor with Doctours, nor with the iudgement of the Learned men of Germanie, Geneua, and the parties where you had ben? And why then preach you not this Doctrine abroade?

Is this ỹ part of a cõstant man, at home to thinke one thing, a-broad to maintein an other? Do you not hereby much like ỹ Epicureans, who abroad speake of the Goddes, as other men do, at home beleue no Goddes to be at al? If vpon examination you wil denye this much, is not that also the parte of an inconstant man? whether you wil abide by it or no before your betters, I know not, certainely you letted not freely to tel me, that was your opinion then.

What fault so euer you finde with my chaunge, certaine it is al chaunges be not reprouecable. He chaungeth wel, that chaungeth from euil to good. It is a happy chaunge, that is made from errour to truth, from schisme to vnitie, frõ heresie to right faith, from contempt of Religion, to the loue of Religion, from darkenesse to light, from pride to humilitie, from pleasing men, to study how to please God. Who so euer maketh this chaunge, he is not to be accompted mutable, nor inconstant.

Some there be, that had rather suffer death, then be sene at any time to haue ben out of the way. Some least they should seme once to haue erred, do alwayes erre, and whiles they can not abide any smal portion of their reputation to be diminished, they cast away al together, liue with note of perpetual infamie, and fal into horrible heresies. Such, that they appeare not inconstant, be made obstinate. They be most proude that thus do, who wil seme Goddes, not men. We are men M. Iewel, and as men we haue erred, and may erre, let vs pray, that we do no more erre. so long as we folow the Catholike Church, we be sure not to erre. Let vs so liue, that errour be not punishment of our sinnes. Specially let vs beware, that with wil and hart, wittingly and stubbornly we neither choose vnto vs, nor defend any erroneous point by our iudgement, and in our owne knowledge condemned, as *Arius*, as *Macedonius*, as *Nestorius*, as *Eutyches*, and sundry other blasphemous heretikes haue donne.

Whether you do like as they did, or no, I leaue it to due cōsideration. Verely who so euer wil take the paines to reade this Reioindre, by diligent conference of both our treatises, he shal see your dealing to be such, as you may seme equal to them in malice, and farre to passe them in vanitie of lying.

Al they that mainteine vntruth, must nedes vse crafte and falshed. For vntruth can not be vpholden, but by vntruth. Hereof it commeth, that the mainteiners of the sundry sectes of our time be found so impudent liers. Yet of al that haue written sithens Luther began, for lying you deserue the garland. There neuer wrote any that within like quantitie of paper, hath vttered the like number of Vntruthes. As the Poetes faine, that what so euer Midas touched, it became golde: so may we truly say, that what so euer is brought against you for proufe of the truth, by one crafty sleight or other, if you passe it not ouer with silence, you put a false colour vpon it. And commonly what you bring for your owne parte, it is coyned with the same stampe.

I say not only, as you do in your Preface, but in this Reioindre I do manifestly proue in due place, Some Doctours by you to be vntruly alleged, Some corruptly translated, Some peruersly expounded, Some guilefully applied: Their wordes sometimes abbridged, sometimes enlarged, sometimes altered, sometimes dissembled. With these false sleightes you burthen me in worde, with the same I haue here charged you in dede. Sundry auncient Fathers which you denie, by good authoritie I haue auouched. Your owne childish Argumentes falsly and fondly by your self deuised, and fathered vpon me, I haue wholly contemned, and so returned them vnto you againe. For the 45. Vntruthes, which you pretend to haue noted in my Answer touching

touching your first Article, I haue returned vpon you. 225. noted in your Replie of the same Article. Those which you impute vnto me, be now already partly, and may shortly be iustified, and therefore proued not to be Untruthes at al. Yours you shal neuer iustifie: when you attempt it, you shal do it but with a multiplication of infinite other Untruthes.

Sith it is thus, the best aduise I can geue you, is, first, to consider better of these maters, and to cal to your minde what hath moued you to enter so farre: next, how faithfully you haue dealte in the same: then, what rewarde you may looke for in the ende. If your conscience tel you, that at the beginning you were stirred vp with vaine glorie, with the praise of the people, with hope of worldly promotion, with pride, with singularitie, with the opinion of your owne conceiued excellencie: that you haue proceded and folowed your purpose altogether without plaine and vpright dealing, with guile and crafte, with wresting and racking the Scriptures, with misalleging, misconstrewing, falsifying, and corrupting the holy and learned Fathers, with denying the autoritie of certaine who haue in olde tyme ben wel allowed, with counterfeit aduantages taken of patches and peeces of Doctours not folowing the Faith and intent of the Doctours, and with other the like suttel and deceitful sleightes: that after your parte is plaied, you shal be brought to iudgement, there to render a streight accompt of al your wordes, sayinges, wrytinges, thoughtes, desires, meaninges, and intentes, and for them to receiue the rewarde of euerlasting damnation, because they were altogether bent against the Catholike faith, to the defacing of the Church, and to the breach of vnitie: If your conscience vpō good, wise, & mature deliberatiō shal set these thinges before you, & as it were in a liuely paterne represent you vnto your self:

what is healthful for you to do in this case, but with meeke and humble submission to condemne your arrogant boasting, with sincere and simple truth, to reuoke your manifold craftes and falshed, with harty, ernest, and vnfained repentance, to turne away Gods vengeance from you, and doing the worthy fruites of penaunce, to procure vnto you pardon, fauour, and mercie?

If this counsel can not sincke into you, if neither this, nor any other the like aduise shal take place with you: what is my parte to do, but to leaue you to your selfe, and to the wil of God? If you wil in any wise write moe bookes, let them be such, as shal not pester vs so with infinite numbers of Untruthes. Use fewer wordes, you shal make fewer lyes: leaue nipping, hewing, hacking, and mangling the Doctours: leaue to take away what is against you, and to adde of your owne, what is for you. Alter not their sayinges by disordering their wordes, by false translation, by ouerthwarte and contrary vnderstanding. Leaue to do, as not only through your whole Replie, but also as in the first Article (which here specially I note) you haue donne. That is to say, proue not your Doctrine that is against the Church, by the autorities of them, who be enemies to the Church. Allege vs no more Gerardus Lorichius, and Georgius Cassander against the Masse, who are professed ennemies of the Masse as ẏ Church approueth it, and therefore be condemned of the Church. Bring vs no more the witnesse of a fewe Schismatike Grekes of late yeres, affirming Consecration of the body and bloud of Christ to be made by the Priestes Praiers, and not by the wordes of our Lord, against the catholike Church both Greke and Latine, specially whereas for the same errour they be manifestly reproued and refused, not only by the Latines, but also by the Grekes them selues.

Bessarion de sacramento Eucharistiæ.

Furnish not your selfe, as commonly you doo, with the

Obiecti-

obiections made by Schoole doctours by way of disputation against the truth, pretending that they so spake in declaration or resolution of the truth. When Innocentius tertius, S. Thomas, Scotus, and Bonauentura, propone the argumentes and reasons of Heretikes, to thintent by solution of them the truth may appeare the clearer: abuse not your vnlearned Reader with thẽ, bearing him in hand, they are the resolute sayinges, mindes, and censures of those Doctours. Where you see certaine errours and abuses condemned by Councels, leaue to alleage them, as thinges once generally vsed and approued by the Church.

If you intend to write against any of our Treatises, cul not out our sayinges forth of a whole heape, as your manner is, leauing what toucheth the point in controuersie, and taking parte that being put alone and besides the rest, semeth to haue lesse force. Deale plainely, lay forth the whole or the pith of the whole, dissemble not the force of your Aduersaries reasons. Vse no more the false, but very grosse parte, that thorowgh your Replie commonly you haue vsed. Which is this. You take by peeces my sayinges, you falsifie, alter, chaunge and frame them to your fansie, and when you haue made them weake and sounding litle to the purpose, for which they were first vttered, then you shew your worthy courage, then you geue your selfe the victorie, then you blow vp the triumph. Likewise you demeane your selfe with childish argumentes of your owne deuising, and make gay sport at them, pretending they are of my making. This childish practise argueth a childish witte, and a delight in light scoffing. If you wil nedes write more, amend wherein you haue offended. I meane not that you should amend what is amisse in your Replie, for that is altogether false and faulty, to amend that, is to new make it. For none other way wil serue but to throw al in the fier, and cast it in a new moolde againe.

Remember M. Jewel, it is the cause of God, you would seme to treate. God hath no neede of your Lyes. Leave wrangling, iesting, scorning, mocking, scoffing: Contēde not aboute wordes and syllables forsaking the mater, Obscure not ẏ truth with vaine Rhethorique, ouerwhelme it not with your abundance of wordes. Bring not confusion to the mater, when it is cleare of it selfe, make not shewe of victorie, where you are least hable to answer. Make not your reader to lawgh, where he would be taught. Affect not so much to be pleasant, seeke rather to be a true handler of Gods causes. Put not the hope of your victorie in the coldnesse of your Aduersarie, but in the truth of the mater. Refuse not to stande to their iudgemēt alleged against you, whose witnesse you bring for you. Allow not a writer in one place, condemning him in an other place.

If you wil vse the testimonies of the Schoolemen and Canonistes, consider it to be reason, that you subscribe to their faith. It is wel knowen vnto you, they be catholike in doctrine, as whom therfore you accompt for Papistes: Yet who euer alleged them so thicke as you haue donne (though to no purpose) in your Replie? It semeth you were desirous to shew al your wares at one market. Vse their testimonies and beleue them. If you beleue them not, what meane you to vse them? By this it appeareth you seeke not so much to set forth the truth, as to ouerbeare your Aduersarie. This is not to serue God: It is to gete prayse among light and deceiued men. Fil not vp your treatises with often and large handling of idle & superfluous Common places for shewe of learning, vttering much mater impertinent, which lieth not in question. Forsake your common fonde custome of putting away one truth by the proufe of an other truth. Leaue to fil your readers heades with vaine and false fables, whereof you vtter great store, reporting them in great sooth, some in

despite

despite of Gods Ministers, some in contempt of the most holy Mysteries.

Wheras you make so much adoo with me for one Visio of S. Basile, which neverthelesse is reported by men of good credite, remember your owne selfe are not hable so wel to iustifie your owne fables, which you tel at the beginning, as that Pope Gregorie, whom you had rather cal *Hildebrand, vvas a Necromancer and a Sorcerer:* that *Emperour Henrie vvas poisoned in the Communion bread,* that *Pope Victor vvas poisoned in the Chalice.* Take better heede fromhence forth, and beware you make not so many & so plaine Contradictions in your owne tale, and that you be not founde so contrary to your selfe, for that must nedes abase your credite among those that be most wilfully addicted vnto you. In the first Article of the Replie, & the first diuision.

Aboue al thinges haue better regarde to your honestie, that you impaire it not, I wil not say, with so many Vntruthes, of which some may seme to haue a colour of truth, but with so many, so notorious, and so impudent Lyes, for which you can haue no colour, nor so much as any shadow of colour at al. And least I should seme to sclannder you, I wil here put you in minde of three or foure, not pyked out of the whole heape of your Replie, but deprehended in your first Article. To put in al here that I finde in that Article, it were ouer long, and to reherse al ŷ I finde in your whole booke, it were to write an other booke.

You say of Albertus Pighius, that *he acknovvlegeth errours in the Masse.* This is vtterly false, he acknowlegeth no such thing, nor maketh any mention at al of any errours in the Masse. For the rest which I intend to note here, I wil not seeke farre abrode for them. They lye together (looke who wil) within the compasse of litle more, then one leafe of your booke.

You say that *S. Hierome by the reporte of Eusebius,* maketh Pag. 8.

mention only of one Epistle of Clementes, that he thought vvorthy to be receiued. This is controlled as vtterly false by S. Hierome him selfe, who maketh mention of an other booke of S. Clementes, which he translated himselfe into Latine at the request of Gaudentius a bishop, as S. Hierome writeth in the ende of Origens Commentaries vpon the Epistle to the Romaines, which he turned into Latine.

In Peroratione translatoris. Operum Origenis parte. 2.

You say further of S. Clementes booke which I alleaged, intituled Constitutiones Apostolorum, *that it vvas disallovved by Eusebius, and by S. Hierome, and condemned by Gelasius: that it vvas neuer heard of, nor sene before: and that it vvas laid vp in secrecie for the space of a thousand fiue hundred yeres and more.* Al this is vtterly false. Eusebius and S. Hierome neuer disallowed that booke, but the disputation betwen S. Peter and Appion. It was Itinerarium Petri, that Gelasius condemned, not this. Albeit if it were neuer sene, nor heard of before, how was it by Eusebius & S. Hierome disallowed? could they disallow that was neuer sene nor heard of? If it were disallowed, how was it not at least heard of? This booke was heard of, sene, and read before our time, of diuerse and sundry fathers of sundry ages. Of Athanasius by reporte of Zonaras, of Cyrillus Hierosololymitanus, of Epiphanius, of the auncient writer of opus imperfectum vpon S. Mathew, of Damascen, of Proclus, of Oecumenius, of Nicolaus Methonensis, of Marcus Ephesius, as I shew more at large in my Reioindre.

Pag. 8. You report Wolphgangus Lazius, whom you cal Zazius, to say, that *S. Luke the Euãgelist vvriting the Actes of the Apostles, borovved many vvhole stories vvorde by vvorde out of Abdias.* Lazius saith not so. He speaketh disiunctiuely, that it is to be thought, that either Abdias tooke certaine thinges out of S. Luke, or ỹ S. Luke tooke out of Abdias; seing both liued in one time, & were the Apostles scholers.

You

You say ẏ. *S. Augustine reporteth the fables of S. Thomas, of S. Matthevv, of S. Andrevv, of the Lion that slevv the mā, &c.* (euery mā may see ẏ place in your booke) *euē in such order, as thei be set forth by Abdias.* For proufe hereof by your note in ẏ margēt, you direct your Reader to S. Augustine cōtrâ Faustum, lib. 11. & lib. 22. cap. 80. Here you haue falsly thrust in the names of S. Mathew, and of S. Andrew, thereby to discredite the Sacrifice of the Masse reported in Abdias by them to haue ben donne. I chalenge you of a fowle lye, vntil yow shew vs out of the places by you quoted, or els where in those bookes, that S. Augustine reporteth any such fables, as you cal them, of S. Mathew, and of S. Andrew. Sure it is, that you haue belyed S. Augustine. He writeth no such thing of them, as Abdias telleth. Much lesse reporteth he the thinges which you reherse, *euen in such order as they be set forth by Abdias.*

In the same place you falsifie and corrupte S. Augustine beyonde al reason. You tel as out of him, what was written not by him, but in a false booke of one Leucius entituled the Actes of the Apostles, concerning *Maximilla vvife vnto Egetes, hovv she (being once Christened) vvould no more yelde dutie vnto her husband, but set Euclia her maide in her ovvne place.* Hauing rehersed this much, you say: *Al these and such like tales thus desallovved by S. Augustine, are reported by M Hardinges Abdias in great sooth.* This is a most impudēt lye. By Abdias Maximilla is reported to haue ben a very godly womā, & the disciple of S. Andrew. Of her denying dutie to her husbād, cōtrary to S. Paules wordes, & of that filthy placing of her maide Euclia in her owne stede, in al Abdias there is not so much as one worde. Neither is that maide Euclia, there so much as once named by Abdias. It may please the Reader to see, what I write vpon this mater in my Reioindre. If there be so many lyes founde with in lesse then one leafe and a halfe, the Reader may conceiue what a multitude is to be founde in the whole Replie. *1. Cor. 7.*

 For

For the rest of the first Article, I referre you to this Treatise, where you and the Reader shal finde good stoare of your lyes, Untruthes, corruptions, and falsifyinges, and of your other false dealinges, plainely laid forth, and clearely confuted. If men be not utterly blinde, and as I may say, so bewitched with the spirite of errour and lying, as to beleue what so euer you say, be it true, be it false: I doubt not but after they shal haue read my Reioindre, and what is written by others here of late: in their iudgement your Replie shal finde smal credite. Now to ende, If you feare not God, to whom of so many Untruthes you shal geue accompte, yet reuerence man, of whose worldly estimation you depende. For my parte, I shal pray, that either God moue your harte to repent and amende, or that he geue the people grace not to beleue you. At Antwerpe. In the ende of August. 1566. In which time your brethren of this low Countrie professours of that ye cal the Gospel, haue geuen euident testimonie to ẏ worlde, with what Spirite they be lead by their spoiling and robbing of Churches and religious houses, by destroying of Libraries, by threatning to fyer the places where they be resisted, & with other wicked outrages: through occasion whereof this Treatise could not be printed neither so spedily, nor so exactly, as in quiet times it might haue ben.

Thomas Harding.

Cyprianus Pupiano. lib. 4. epist. 9.

Habes tu literas meas, & ego tuas. In die Iudicij ante tribunal Christi vtrumq; recitabitur.

Thou hast my booke (of Answer) and I haue thine (of Replie). In the day of Iudgement before the iudgement seate of Christ, both shal be rehersed.

Faultes escaped in printing.

Leafe	Line	Faulte	Correction.
10.a.	2.	owin forme	how in forme.
11.b.	23.	more in the last	more in the. 8. & in y last.
20.b.	3.	Marcella	Marcellina.
23.a.	17.	the	put it out.
26.a.	20.	are	and
35.b.	2.	by report Abdias	by report of Abdias.
36.a.	15.	not of Abdias	not Abdias.
36.b.	4.	that he	that if he.
37.a.	2.	be pointes	be the pointes.
37.a.	31.	there	here.
46.a	31.	μοναςεάριον	μοναςήριον.
55.a	31.	for	from.
66.b	32.	Ceremonical	Ceremonial.
71.a	14.	vs not	vs as not.
100.b	1.	so	of.
103.b	9.	of	to.
104.a	13.	purhose	purpose.
123.b.	11.	Transubstantion	Transubstantiation.
131.b.		The.14.Diuision	The.12.Diuision.
134.b.	1.	and onely	not onely.
162.a.	13.	ye	he.
164.b.	21.	for he meane	for if he meane.
165.a.	13.	anthropophagia	anthropophagiam.
171.a.	2.	tme	seme.
173.a.	4.	his sole receiuing	this sole etc.
186.	19.	Abailardus de Brixia	Abailardus, Arnaldus de etc.
189.	18.	taked	taken.
190.	22.	salutation	saluation.

☞ Other faultes that may be espied should haue ben corrected, had not the troubles here begonne forsed vs to make an end.

A REIOINDRE TO M. IEVVELS REPLIE.

Ievvel.

There appeareth smal hope that M.Harding vvill deale plainly in the rest, that thus maketh his first entrie vvith a 1 cauill.

For vvhere as the mater is 2 knovven, and agreed vpon, it is great folie to pyke quarell vpon the vvoorde. Euery Masse 3 (sayth he) is common, and none priuate. If it be so, then hath he already concluded fully on our side. For if there be no priuate Masse 4 at all, then vvas there no Priuate Masse in the primitiue Church, vvhich vvas my first assertion.

But M. Harding, as may be gathered by his manner of proofes, is not yet vvell resolued, neither vvhat is Priuate, nor vvhat is Masse. For in the. 22. article of his booke, intreating 5 of the accidentes of breade and vvine, to the intent to auoyde the grosse absurdities that follovv Transubstantiation, he 6 sayth, These maters vvere neuer taught in open audience, but priuately disputed in the schooles, and set abroade by learned men in their priuate vvrytinges. There he calleth that thing priuate, that is disputed in open audience, in the hearing of fiue hundred, or moe, and is set abroad to the knovvledge of the vvorld: And here the thing that is done by the priest and his boye alone in a corner, he calleth common. Thus he maketh vvoordes to sounde vvhat him listeth, sometyme common to be priuate, sometyme priuate to be common at his pleasure.

And as touching Masse, sometime he maketh it the

The First Untruth. for it is no cauil, as it shall appeare.

The.2.vntruth. It is not knowē, nor agreed vpon.

The.3.vntruth. I say not so, but with addition, which maketh certaine limitation.

The.4. Untruth. It is not saide there is no priuate Masse at all. for there is Priuate Masse, as priuate is takē in an other sense.

The. 5. vntruth. In ŷ place I speake not hereof, but of M. Iewels.v. last Articles.

The. 6. vntruth. I say not so, but otherwise.

The. 7. vntruth. I neuer saide the Communion to be ẏ Masse

Sacrifice : sometyme the 7 Cõmunion: sometyme the prayers : and so seemeth not yet vvell to knovve, vpon vvhat grounde to stande.

His First reason is this : The Sacrifice of the Priest is common, therefore the Masse is Common. Here might be demaunded, vvho gaue the Priest authoritie, to make this Sacrifice ? and vvithout authoritie hovv can he make it ? But if his Sacrifice be common, vvhy 8 dothe he giue it these priuate titles, This for the liuing, This for the deade : This for a frende : This for him selfe?

The. 8. vntruthe. I giue not the Sacrifice these titles.

His second reason is this : It is a feast, and therefore it is common: and thus he salueth one 9 errour vvith an other. For if it be a feast, hovv is it receiued by one alone? If it be receiued by one alone, hovv can it seeme to be a feast? But he saith, it is prepared for al. Verely it is but smal prouision to serue so many. The priest him selfe knovveth this is vntrue. He prepareth for him selfe, and not for others : He speaketh to him selfe, and not vnto the congregation : He receiueth him selfe alone, and not vvith his brethren. Therefore in this respecte vve must needes say, the Masse is priuate and not common.

The. 9. vntruthe. It is no errour to say, the Communion which is in the Masse, is a feast

Harding.

HEREAS M. Jewel in the beginning of his Booke layeth to my charge, that in my Answere to his Chalenge I make my firste entrie with a Cauil, and would thereby remoue the Reader from hope of plaine dealing on my parte in the rest: how much my entrie reporteth no other thing but a Trouth, so much doth ẏ blame of an euil disposition cleaueth on him, thus quarclingly finding faulte where none is, and the Reader remaineth in hope notwithstanding, to see me in this mater to deale plainly.

The Cauil for which so hastily he reprouceth me at the first, is, for saying that euery Masse is publike, concerning both the Oblation, and also the Communion, and none priuate. which is true, as there I proue it. And in dede the Oblation which Christ made of him selfe once vppon the Crosse for remission of synnes, apperteining not to one person, nor to one Degree of men only, nor to one nation peculiarly, as Moyses lawe did to the Iewes, but to al right beleuers in general, euery one receiuing his saluation therof: that which is offered in the blessed Sacrifice of euery Masse being the selfe same, though the manner of Offering be diuerse: in that respect for good cause euery Masse is to be accompted Publike, and not Priuate.

In what respect is euery Masse Publike.

Psa. 147.

The Communion also of Christes body is a publike feast, by Christes Institution ordeined to be the foode of our soules. For that body, as it was borne not for one only, but for al, as it suffered not for one only, but for al: so it is geuen also to be meate, not for one only, but for al. Who so euer eateth of this bread, shal Liue for euer (saith Christ). In this consideration, the Communion of that Precious body consecrated of the Priest at the Masse by th'almighty power of our Lordes worde spoken in the Person of Christe, is duly called a Publike feast. And so in respect of the same, as wel as of the Oblation, the Masse is Publike. Though others beside the Priest, through negligence, and lacke of Deuotion forbeare to receiue: yet the thing to be receiued, ceaseth not to be Publike and Common, nor is it to be accompted for Priuate, because others refusing, one receiueth Sacramentally in one Place alone.

That the Communion is a Publike feast.

Iohn. 6.

The Priestes special Acte of Receiuing alone, sometime in respecte of place, I graunt is Priuate, without any offence of his

The Priestes Priuate receiuing, maketh not the Masse Priuate.

parte: but that maketh not the Masse Priuate. For the Hoste and Sacrifice considered in it selfe, which he receiueth, that not withstanding is Publike, neither therefrom is any excluded, that of the same sheweth him selfe worthy and willing. As a Conduicte builded in a Citie for the commoditie of the Citizens, is publike and common, though there be but one that fetcheth water of it at once: So is the Communion of our Lordes body by the priest at his Masse Consecrated, though others besides him, refuse to receiue it, a Publike and Common banket. And that it is so, it dependeth not of the receiuers parte, but of the thing it selfe.

But M. Iewel lacking proufe for his saying, only affirmeth it stoutely, pretending it to be graunted of all men. *VVhere the mater* (saith he) *is knovven and agreed vpon, it is great folie to pike quarel vpon the vvorde.* True it is. But why did he not proue it to be knowen and agreed vpon? First, knowen it is not, that euery Masse, at which the Priest hath not Company to Communicate with him Sacramentally, is Priuate. For knowledge is only of true thinges, and this is not true, as I haue now declared. Againe, agreed vpon it is not, for the Catholikes deny it, and M. Iewel auoucheth. Certaine it is, that before Martin Luther, no Auncient and Good wryter euer called the Masse Priuate, in respect of the Priestes Sole Receiuing.

After this Cauil, he twiteth me with foule ouersight and vnwarinesse, as though vnaduisedly I had vttered wordes concluding with the ennemies of the holy Sacrifice, and consequently with him against my selfe. Hereto he allegeth my wordes falsly, leauing out that which might answere the Obiection, and maketh me to speake otherwise then I do, as the place of my Booke lying before the Readers eyes, speaketh for me. For I say not simply, euery Masse is Common, and none Priuate, as he reporteth: but euery Masse is Publike concerning both the Oblation,

M. Iew. in the very beginning falsifieth my words *Fol. 9. a.*

lation, and also the Communion, and none Priuate. Whereby adding concerning the Oblation and Communion, I make a Limitation of Publike, and in that respecte exclude Priuate. This notwithstanding M. Iewel hoping to conuey him self safe away as it were in a cloude with a Sophisticall Argument, that in Schooles we cal Paralogisme, thus concludeth against me, that, *if it be so, then haue I already Concluded fully on his side.* Therevpon taking more, then before he imagined to be graunted vnto him, he proceedeth forth boldly, saying: *If there be no Priuate Masse at all, then vvas there no Priuate Masse in the Primitiue Churche, vvhich vvas my first Assertion.*

This is M. Iewels accustomed Sophistry. First he falsifyeth my wordes, and by Clipping, and Changing the Sentence, frameth them to his purpose, then he boroweth an Intche, after that he snatcheth an Elle. For neither was it by me Simply graunted, that euery Masse after any what so euer sense is common, and much lesse, that there is no Priuate Masse at al, that is to say, in no respecte. For within fewe lines after, the contrary by me is confessed. M. Iew. chiefe Sophistry stādeth in falsyfiing wordes & sayinges. *Fol.9.b.*

He that maketh this Argument, The Masse is not Priuate in respect of the Oblation & Communion, Ergo there is no Priuate Masse at al: reasoneth as wel, as if a man should say, M. Iewel is not a true man, concerning his Doctrine and manner of Wryting: Ergo he is no true man at al. The reason is naught. For though he be an vntrue man in that point, yet he may be a true man in an other point: As for Example, in confessing that with substantiall Lerning he shall neuer be hable to defende his insolent Chalenge. Who so euer hath learned Logike, can not forget Aristotles rule, that à secundum quid ad simpliciter, the Argument is naught.

Thus the reproch of a Cauil, with which M. Iewel beginneth

neth his Booke, is returned vpon him. And because he wil seme to play the good Auditor in making an exacte accompte of pretenced vntruthes noted in my Answere, least I shuld seme to remaine in his debte, and therfore to flie reckening with him: I wil that this be noted for the first vntruth, in that he would haue spotted my first entrie with the dishonestie of a Cauil, where none is.

The second vntruth is his secōd sentence, wher he saith, ÿ mater (whereby he meaneth that the Masse is Priuate) to be *knovven and agreed vpon,* for certainly it is not agreed vpon in the Catholike Church after Luthers sense. The third vntruth is the deceit of falsifying in the third sentence, where he falsifieth my wordes. The fourth vntruth is a false proposition taken in as graunted by me, which I graunt, not that there is no Priuate Masse at al, whereof he inferreth the false conclusion of his first Article. With these foure faire vntruthes within the space of vij. lines, hath M. Iewel garnished the first entrie of his Booke. Whereby he geueth the Reader to vnderstand, what flowers he is like to gather out of that garden. This noting of vntruthes, is odious I graunt, and beside the custome of learned men, neither would I haue vsed it at al, had not ÿ importunitie of M. Iewels former example compelled me therevnto.

M. Iew. piketh quarel for vse of certaine termes.

After this with like truth and like proufe, he obiecteth vnto me vncertaintie of Doctrine, as not being yet resolued, neither what is *Priuate,* nor what is *Masse.* For the first he reporteth him to a place of the .22. Article of my boke, where he saith that I treate *of the accidentes of breade and vvine, to the intent to auoide the grosse absurdities that folovve Transubstantiation.* Which being false, I recken it for the fifth vntruth. For in that place I speake not therof, but of the last fiue Articles of M. Iewels Chalenge to be considered altogether, terming them schoole pointes, whose dis-

cussion

cussion is more curious, then necessarie. But it liked him wel to saye somewhat that might sound in contempt of the miraculous Transubstanciation, though he said neuer so vntruly.

Here againe he falsifieth my wordes making me to say thus. *These maters vvere neuer taught in open audience, but priuately disputed in the schooles, and set abrode by learned men in their Priuate vvrytinges.* Thus hauing with his falsifying sleight framed my wordes to his aduauntage, he triumpheth ouer me, and concludeth a great absurditie against me, as though there I called that thing *Priuate, vvhich is disputed in open audience, in the hearing of fiue hundred or moe, and is set abroade to the knovvledge of the vvorlde,* and here *that thing common, vvhich is done by the priest and his boye alone in a corner. And thus I make* (saith he) *vvordes to sound vvhat me listeth, Common to be Priuate, and Priuate to be Common at my pleasure.* M. Iew. falsifieth my wordes

Now take the paines good Reader to vewe the place in my Booke, and there shalt thou finde these very wordes spoken of the subtilitie and curiositie of the Doctrine of M. Iewels fiue last Articles. Yet (say I) this mater hath not so much ben taught in open audience of the people, as debated Priuately betwene learned men in schooles, and so of them set forth in their Priuate wrytinges. Fo.182.b

Who compareth M. Iewels false allegation, and my wordes together, shal easily perceiue no smal diuersitie. And as I speake, what cauil can be made of them? I say not flatly as M. Iewel reporteth my wordes, that these *maters vvere neuer taught in open Audience,* but that the subtile pointes of those fiue Articles haue not so much ben taught in open audience of the people. Wherby my meaning is euident, that the vnlearned people were not taught that Doctrine out of the Pulpit. And why did M. Iewel in rehersing my wordes leaue out mention of the people?

Espied he not my *Antithesis* betwene *open Audience*, and *Schooles?* betwene *the People* and *Learned men?* betwene *Open* in respect of the Pulpit, and *Priuate* in respect of Scholastical debating? Yes verely, he could not but espye it, whose best sight is in the figures of Rhetorike.

Schoole points are priuate in cōparisō of maters set forth in Pulpits.

For truth of the mater, what man is there of any vnderstanding, to whose iudgement thinges debated among the Schoolemen in Scholastical disputations, and by such put in wryting, seme not to be Priuately treated, in comparison of those thinges, which be set forth in Sermons to al Christen people, and with such plainenesse of stile and Language committed to writing, as is fit for the capacitie of most men: whereas the Schoolelearning for the Subtilitie and Obscuritie of many high pointes, is not wel perceiued, but of such as haue their senses much exercised in that trade of studie? What learned man knoweth not, that Cicero oftentimes calleth the studie of Philosophie, Vmbram, Shadowe, and the exercise of Oratours and Lawyers, Lumen, Light: wherein he had consideration of the place, in which these Professions had their exercise? What difference he maketh betwene being Domi, and in Foro, the same we make betwene Schooles, and Paules Crosse, or generally the Pulpits. Thus I make good, that I haue vsed my termes Priuate, and Cōmon rightly, wherein M. Iewel wrangleth, and seeketh occasion to reproue me, where iustly none is ministred. Therfore let this be accompted for an other vntruth, where he saith, *I make vvordes to sounde vvhat me Listeth, so as Common be Priuate, and Priuate be Common at my pleasure.*

Now as touching the Masse, which he saith I am not yet resolued what it is, but make it *sometime the Sacrifice*, *sometime the Communion, sometime the Prayers:* true it is, that in the. 20. Article, where I treate of Opus Operatum, the better to shewe what it

is,

is, and whether it remoue synnes, whereto M. Iewels Chalenge leadeth me: I declare, that the terme Masse may be taken two waies. Either for the thing it selfe which is offered, or for the act of the priest in offering it. Which I haue not done altogether without skil, and the same could I here iustifie, if the place so required. As for the Communion considered aparte, I neuer make it the Masse.

The whole summe of prayers, lessons, psalmes, hymnes, inuocations. &c. called by diuers names, and distincted into diuers partes (whereby I vnderstand the whole seruice touching that blessed sacrifice) I do and may iustly cal, the Masse: as where I speake of S. Iames Masse, of S. Basiles Masse, of S. Chrysostomes Masse. So in olde time the first parte of it was called *Missa catechumenorum*, the later part, *Missa perfectorum*. Which is from the preface foreward to the ende, and in that sense the booke which conteineth that whole Seruice, is called the Masse booke.

The Seruice of the Masse is sometime called Masse.

Where I saye that no man offereth that dreadfull Sacrifice priuatly for him selfe alone, but for the whole Church in common, bringing that, as also that the Communion of the Sacrament is a publike feast, to proue the Masse to be publike, and not Priuate: Herevpon M. Iewel hauing mangled my wordes, & vttering thē otherwise then I do, maketh an argument as on my behalfe, to proue the Masse to be common. Then eftsones he saith, *It might be demaunded vvho gaue the priest auctoritie to make this Sacrifice, and vvithout auctoritie* (saith he) *hovv can he make it?* Hereto I saie.

Fol. 9. a

First, that how so euer he putteth forth my reason weakely, as I my selfe conclude, he shal neuer be able to disproue it, but that thereby the Masse is proued publike. Next, touching his surmised demaunde, *vvho gaue the priest auctoritie to make this Sacrifice*

crifice, the scripture telleth him it was Christe, who said to his
Luc. 22. 1. Cor. 11 Apostles, do, or make ye this in my remembrance. For this point let the Reader peruse that I wrote vpon the. 17. Article of M. Iewels Chalenge, and what shal be said hereafter, when I shal treate more thereof, and he shall finde his demaunde fully answered.

But if his Sacrifice be common (saith M. Iewel) *vvhy doth he geue it these Priuate titles, This for the liuing: This for the dead: This for a frende: This for him selfe?* Hereto I answer. First, the Sacrifice is not mine, as his scoffing sprite vttereth. It is the Sacrifice of Christe chiefly, offered by the ministerie of a priest of the newe testament, in the person of the Church, wherof Christe principally is the priest, the offerer, and the Oblation, saith S. Augustine.

Aug. de Ciuitate Dei lib. 10. cap. 20.

Then it may please him to vnderstand, that neither I, nor any other Catholike man, do geue to that most blessed Sacrifice, these Priuate titles, speaking properly and exactly. It is not a Sacrifice properly for any priuate thing, person, or persons, but generally for al: yet by the intention of the Priest, it may be applied to one more then to an other. Christe hath shed his bloud, and offered him selfe a bloudy Sacrifice vpon the Crosse for al. For al likewise, whom Christe admitteth to that benefite, is this vnbloudy Sacrifice, being the selfe same with that of the crosse in truth of the thing offered, and the sampler of that, in regard of the manner of offering.

The Sacrifice is Publique

In the celebration of this vnbloudy Sacrifice we praie, and do what in vs lieth, that by our deuoute intention the healthfull vertue of that bloudy Sacrifice may be applied to al in general, to certaine specially that liue, and to certaine that be dead, to our dere frendes, for whom we be most specially bound to praye, and to our selues. For these we haue special prayers in the Masse, and special remembrances. Neither for al that is the nature of that Sacrifice altered and made Priuate, but remaineth Publike and common, as our Lordes Praier is a common praier, though a man say it for him selfe, or for his special frende.

Whereas I cal the Communion of the blessed Sacrament a Publike feast, prouing the Masse in that respecte also to be Publike, and not Priuate: M. Iewel hauing set forth my reason so bare and naked as he could deuise, denieth the antecedent, saying, that *I salue one errour vvith an other. For if it be a feast* (saith he) *hovv is it receiued by one alone? If it be receiued of one alone, hovv can it seeme to be a feast?* Why Sir I praye you, can you not conceiue a feast to be a feast, except it be eaten of many gheastes? Is not the feast one thing, the gheastes an other? Neuer heard you one saye of a good Dynner, which is a feast, Dynner is ready, the gheastes be not come? If he saye true, who so saith, is there not then a feast, before the Gheastes come? And if they come not at al, shal not a feast be a feast? Saith not the king in the Gospel of the feast he had prepared at his sonnes wedding, Beholde I haue made ready my Dynner, whereas they that were bydden refused to come? Now if that were a feast whereof one alone receiued, why shal we not cal this diuine banket a feast, whereof one alone receiueth? Albeit in dede it is not at any time of one alone receiued, but sometimes in respect of place. For by this feast we vnderstand not one special peece of bread, or rather (after Consecration) the forme of one particular bread: but ye most pretious body of our Lord, into which by th'almighty power of the word of the Mystical benediction the bread is turned, which is the bread of life, sufficient to the sustenance of al. Which is eaten of many through the world, being euery where one and the same, and is not consumed.

A feast may be cōceiued without gheastes.

Mat. 22. Luc. 14.

And al they do Communicate together, be they in places neuer so farre distant.

The Cōmunion of Christes body, is called a feast.
δοχὴ.
Epulum.

If M. Iewel would not haue it called a feast, let him quarel with the holy Martyr S. Ignatius, scholer to S. Polycarpe S. Iohns scholer. who in his Epistle ad Smyrnenses, calleth it δοχὴν a feast. Let him quarell with the auncient and learned fathers, who cal it Epulum, that is, a solemne or Publique feast. Let him quarel with the whole Church, which in worship of it deuoutly singeth vnto it, O Sacrum conuiuium, O holy feast. &c. Had he not forsaken the faith of the Church, he would neuer haue denied this holy Sacrament to be a feast.

The want of prouision can not iustly be complained of.

I saye this feast is prepared for al. Thereat he scoffeth, because of smal prouision, as though it were none other but a belly cheare. If he meane the prouision of the material bread, to be to litle to serue al at one Masse, as by his captious answere he semeth to meane: he knoweth that neither al come to one Masse to receiue, and where any worthely require it, be they in any Church of Christendom neuer so many, they be admitted, and prouision is sone made ready. As for the bread to be vsed to that ende, when the priest vnderstandeth there is none disposed to receiue with him, he staieth not frō doing his owne dutie, and prouideth not in vaine for others, hauing notwithstanding a wil, and also an ernest desire, that others would dispose them selues, and be partakers with him of that heauenly foode, by Sacramental participation. This being so, there is no cause why M. Iewel shuld pike a quarel to vs, for that the prouision is so smal. Albeit how can it seme smal, sith none is vnprouided for, that duly requireth it?

Priuate vsage of a thing in it self cōmon maketh it not Priuate.

Al that M. Iewel here proueth is nought els, but the Priestes sole receiuing, which we graunt to be sole and priuate touching ẏ same place, when none els is wel disposed to be partaker with

him

him. which sole receiuing notwithstanding, the Sacrifice of the Masse is a publike sacrifice, and so is the Communion of our Lordes body a publike feaste. For if forebearing the vse of a thing that is publike and common, one only at certaine times vsing it, shuld alter the condition of the thing, and make it Priuate: then were the kinges high waye made Priuate, because somtimes there is but one that passeth through it. Then were a common welle or Conduict in a towne made Priuate, for that it happeth sometimes that one only person thereof fetcheth his water. whereof and of other the like thinges that might easily be brought for example, to say, that Priuate vsage of them at certaine times maketh them Priuate, it were very absurde.

Ievvel.

The thirde reason touching the vvil of the Minister, is very vncertaine. For neither can the priest by his vvilling alter natures, or make that thing common, vvhich is Priuate: nor can any man certeinely knovve, vvhat thing the priest vvilleth. For vvhat if his vvil be to vvorke
10 *Necromancie, or Sorcerie, as it is reported of Pope Hildebrande? Or vvhat if his vvil be to poyson some bodie, as Henry the Emperour vvas*
11 *poysoned in the communion bread:* 12 *Pope Victor in the chalice? Or vvhat if his vvil be to vvorke fained miracles, as* 13 *Lyra sayeth, many are vvrought in the open Churche by the priest*
14 *to mocke the people? Doubtles if the priestes vvil may be knovven, either by his vvoordes, or by*

The.10.vntruth. This is not reported by any graue & true writer, but by them that flattered the Emperour of that time.

The.11.vntruth, he was not so poisoned, but died otherwise.

The.12.vntruth. He died otherwise.

The.13.vntruth. Lyra saith it not. Dan.14.

The.14.vntruth. To mocke the people, is not in Lyra.

his doinges, or by his gesture, or by his prouision, or by the quantitie of his breade and vvine, or by his vvhole vsage and practise, it may soone be seene, his vvil is to make a priuate banket, and not a common.

These be very vveake foundations to buylde vpon. Of the same M. Harding might rather and farre better haue geathered the contrarie. For if it be the common sacrifice of the vvhole Church, it should be offered by the vvhole church, as S. Ambrose saieth: Vt multorum oblatio simul celebretur: *That the oblation of many may be made togeather.* False Translation.

If it be a common feast of the vvhole Church, it shoulde be receiued commonly of the vvhole Church. And therefore 15 S. Hierome sayeth, Dominica cœna omnibus debet esse communis. *The Lordes supper must be common to al, and that not for these simple shiftes that M. Harding and his fellovves haue diuised. S. Hieromes reason is this:* Quia dominus omnibus Discipulis, qui aderant, æqualiter tradidit Sacramenta. *Bycause the Lorde gaue the Sacramentes equally to al the Disciples that vvere present. These vvoordes be plaine, Equally, and To al the Disciples. Aud therefore saith S. Hierome, according to this example the Lordes supper must be common.*

The. 15. vntruth. For S. Hierome is not the author of those brief Cōmentaries.

Harding.

Where I say, the Communion of the Sacrament being common by order of the first Institution, and by wil of the ministers, ought to be reputed for common & not priuate: M. Iew. thereof

thereof taketh occasion by waye of wicked and false surmises, to talke his pleasure of the ministers wil, him selfe shewing a wil to bring the most holy thinges we haue in Christian religion, into contempt among the vnlearned people by his prophane lyes and false fables of Pope Hildebrandes Necromancie and Sorcerie, of Emperour Henries poisoning in the communion bread, of Pope Victors poisoning in the chalice, of fained Miracles wrought by the priest to mocke the people.

False fables wickedly sothed by M. Iew. to cause cōtempt of ẏ holy Mysteries.

But Hildebrandus (who being Pope, and named Gregorie the seuenth, for the bishoply libertie which he vsed towardes Henrie the fourth Emperour for his amendment, like to that which also S. Ambrose vsed towardes Theodosius, was much hated and persecuted, and euil reported of by such writers of that time as flattered the Emperour) was by report of the true histories of that age, not only farre from exercising Necromancie or Sorcerie, but also in al singular vertues an excellent man, and a worthy bishop. For better knowledge of him what manner a man he was, for what cause he susteined both the displeasure of that Emperour, and was without deserte reproued and slaundered of his adherentes, who refused to be brought to order: I remit the Reader to my Confutation of the Apologie, where he shal finde the mater partly touched, and be further aduertised whom to consulte for a large discourse thereof.

Pope Hildebrādus for what cause defamed.

fo. 187. b 189. a.

Likewise there shal he finde the true histories alleged, how Henry of Luxemburg the Emperour dyed not by poisoning, as M. Iewel here, and the author of the Apologie there reporteth, but otherwise: also that Victor the Pope died of a Dysenterie, as some haue witnessed, not of Poison receiued in the Chalice, as Martinus Polonus a vaine wryter amonge

Henry the emperors death. Fo. 183. b 184. a.

Pope Victors death.

other sundry his vntruthes hath fabled, which M. Iewel would to be taken for a truth, the rather to discredite the most blessed Sacrifice.

As for the fained Miracles, which M. Iewel would his Readers to conceiue, that the Priest hath a wil to worke, to the intent to bring priestes into hatred: I demaunde of him, where Lyra saith that which he fathereth vpon him: that many fained miracles are wrought in the open Church by the priest to mocke the people?

Ah Master Iewel wil you neuer leaue that falsehed and faitery of yours? wil you neuer ceasse to falsifie the Doctours sayinges that you allege? when truth is knowen, what winne you thereby, but the ouerthrow of your cause, and distrust of your credite?

Lyra hauing declared vpon the fourtienth Chapter of Daniel the manner how the false Idolatrous priestes of Bel, for gaines deceiued the people, and made them beleue, that Bel, which was but a Dragon was a great God, and wrought straunge thinges: speaketh thereupon of an abuse that sometime is committed in the Church. His wordes be these.

Lyra in 14.cap. Danielis.

Et similiter aliquando fit in ecclesia maxima deceptio populi in miraculis, fictis a sacerdotibus, vel eis adhærentibus, propter lucrum temporale. *Likevvise,* (saith he, *sometime it happeth in the Church, that the people be greatly begiled in Miracles fained by Priestes, or by their adherentes for vvordly lucres sake.* And to shewe that he spake this with a better spirite, then M. Iewel sheweth in alleging it, he concludeth thus. Et talia sunt extirpanda à bonis prælatis, sicut ista extirpata sũt a Daniele. And such things are to be rooted out by good Prelates, as these were rooted out by Daniel.

Lo

Lo M. Iewel, you may see, the Catholikes dissemble not the Faultes and abuses that happen to be in the Churche. They confesse them willingly, and admonish the Rulers of them, that they maye quite be rooted out. Sir Thomas Moore hym selfe that man of blessed memorie, so euil as they of your side reporte of him, both acknowlegeth and confesseth, the abuse of fained Miracles, and declareth how in times past, they were misliked and abhorred of all good Folke, whiche times you make, to be the times of Antichrist, of Superstition, and Idolatrie.

Sir Thomas More reproued fained myracles in his Dialogue.

Now good Sir, Lyra speaketh not as you make him to speake. He saith not, that *many fained miracles are vvrought*, but that the people be greatly deceaued sometime. He saith not, *in the open Churche*, but that it hapneth in the Churche: whereby he meaneth not the Materiall Churche, as you doe, where the Priest saith Masse, but the state of the Gospell, since Christes Incarnation, and therein he maketh a secrete Comparison of abuses betwen the Church and the Sinagogue of the Iewes. Neither saith Lyra such fained Miracles to be wrought by the Priest (by whiche wordes you do your Reader to conceiue such detestable practises to be done at the very Aulter in the time of the Holy Celebration) but by Priestes indefinitly, meaning some euil among the great numbre. Neither doth he ascribe the faining of Miracles to Priestes simply, but by way of correction, to them, or to their Adherentes, as Clerkes, Sextens, or such other Ministers of base condition, whose pouertie somtime driueth them to deuise shiftes to gaine wherwith to fill their hungry bellies. Lastly, Lyra saith not this Enormitie to be done, *to mocke the People* as You say, but Propter lucrum temporale, For Temporall gaine. Neither Priestes nor any retaining to them be noted of Lyra, to be so wicked, as to committe that Crime to mocke the People. That is your falsifieng to

Lyra truly declared

make Priestes and their ministerie more odious, it is not Lyras plaine saying.

To answere the mater it selfe obiected, I thinke verely, how litle so euer good wil M. Iewel beareth to Priestes, among a thousand he shall not finde one, who lacketh a wil to consecrate the Body of Christe, and to imparte it vnto any Christian person, that being duely examined and prepared therefore, desyreth to communicate with him. This being so, iudge no more M. Iewel of the Priestes vnwillingnesse, by his wordes, his doings, his gesture, his prouision, the quantitie of his Breade and wine, his whole vsage and practise, which you bring for a scoffing argument to proue, that his wil is to make a Priuate banket, and not a common.

the priests will is not to make ỹ Communion a priuate baket

That it be Publike and common, it is ynough that it be so by thinstitution of Christe, and that as touching the Priest, his wil be not to the contrarie. Albeit in my answere I spake not of the Communion, as it is receiued or ministred in particular, but in general. For though sometime it be receiued but of one man at once in one particular place, yet is the same receiued of many others aparte in sundry places, and remaineth whole and vndiuided, one and the same Body of Christe. Who so receiuing, communicate together, be they neuer so farre asunder. And thus alwayes the Communion of that holy Mysterie is a Publike and common feaste.

Wheras M. Iewel diuideth his treatises vpon euery Article into sundrie partes, naming euery parte a Diuision, wherein touching the placing of my mater, sometime he foloweth will, more then reason, and thorow the whole, his owne deuise, not mine: in the ende of his first Diuision, he bringeth that against me, which I do wel allow, so it be rightly vnderstanded. That is, that the Sacrifice of the Church, which we cal the Masse, be offered vp to God by the whole Church. True it is and therefore

The Sa-

fore

fore it is called also the Sacrifice of the Church. S. Augustine speaking of Christ, how in forme of God he taketh sacrifice with the Father, in forme of a seruant he had rather be a Sacrifice: saith, that he would the daily Sacrifice of the Church, of his Sacrifice to be a Sacrament, forasmuch as he is the head of that body, and she the body of that head, as well she by him, as he by her accustomed to be offered. But how it is offered by the Church, and how by the Priest, who is in this behalfe the common minister of the Church, by the Priest immediately, by the Church mediatly or by meanes of the priest: al this haue I plainely declared in my Answere to his twentith article.

crifice of the church is offered by the whole Church. August. De Ciuitate Dei. lib.10. cap.20.

If he meane, as it semeth he doth, that the whole Church, that is to say, the whole people should offer the Sacrifice in such wise and manner as the priest doth, consecrating it, making the oblation, and receiuing it none otherwise then the priest doth: that doctrine is erroneous and absurde, neither do S. Ambroses wordes which he allegeth, proue the same. For he speaketh not of the Sacrament, but of the feastes that were kept in Churches after the mysteries had ben receiued, which feastes were commonly called Agapæ, wherof more hereafter. Fo.175.6

If it be a common feast (saith he) *of the vvhole Church, it should be receiued commonly of the vvhole Church.* Sir we graunt you this, what cōclude you? But what if the whole Church, that is to say, euery Christen man and woman (beside the Priest) oftentimes be not disposed to receiue? Shal not the Priest do that he is commaūded to do by Christ, and celebrate the memorie of his passion by offering the vnbloudy sacrifice of the church, to wit, the body and bloud of Christ? which thing when soeuer he doth, shall he not receiue ỹ he hath offered? If not, how maketh he his oblatiō perfit? Thus he wout any offēce of his part, whē none wilbe induced to participate wͭ him, ought to receiue alone, sith in any wise ỹ is to be receiued which he hath offered: rather then to intermit the

Luc.22. 1.Cor.11.

memorie of our Lordes Death, which by the Sacrifice to celebrate, is the speciall dutie of a Priest of the New Testament, who is after the order of Melchisedech, to thintent thankes be alwaies rēdred to our Lorde, and the benefite of his Death be continewed in remembrance.

In 1. Cor .11. He allegeth a place (as he pretendeth) out of S. Hierome, that of necessitie all should actually receiue. Dominica Cœna omnibus debet esse communis. These wordes thus he Englisheth. *The Lordes Supper must be Common to all*, Then he addeth S. Hieromes reason, quia Dominus omnibus discipulis, qui aderant æqualiter tradidit Sacramenta. because the Lord gaue the Sacramentes equally to al the disciples that were there present. Here he vrgeth these wordes, and telleth that they be plaine, *equally*, and *to al the Disciples*. Hereupon he concludeth that *the Lordes Supper must be common to all*.

M. Iewel allegeth ā vnknowē writer vnder ẏ nāe of S. Hierome. To al this may be saide, first that these woordes be not S. Hieromes. That those briefe Commentaries vpon al the Epistles of S. Paule be not his, both the censure of Erasmus witnesseth, and the thing it selfe speaketh. There be probable coniectures they were writen by some Pelagian. Litle becommeth it M. Iewel of al men, to allege bastard writers for true & allowed Doctours, who is so peremptory in disallowing Doctours him selfe, and vseth the reiection and condemnation of so many Doctours for his chiefe defence. Then if the saing were allowed for S. Hieromes, yet M. Iewel may iustely be required to reuoke hys false translation. For the wordes reporte not, that our Lordes Supper must be common to al: but that it ought to be common to al. Your word importeth a necessitie, S. Hieromes word importeth but a dutie. And I denye not

Our lords supper is cōmō to all. but so it ought to be, and so it is common to al. For where it is denied to none, that without damnation may receiue it, and de-

siveth

streth the same: it may right well seme to be common to al. But M. Iewel would bring the mater so to an absolute necessitie (as it appereth by his translation (must (for) ought) that if the Sacrament be not receiued of al, it be not in remēbrance of Christes Death offered at al. And so bicause he is well assured, that hard, and more then vnlikely it is, to bring al the people to receiue together: he would cōclud, that vntil that be brought to passe, we haue no Sacrifice of the Masse, as hath alwayes ben accustomed in Christes Churche. wherein he sheweth him selfe a diligent seruaunt of Antichrist, who as Daniel prophecieth, at his comming for a time shal abolish that euer continewing Sacrifice. Dan 12.

But Sir, if you be so hote in this mater, and wil abide by it, that the Lords Supper must nedes be common to all, that is, that al receiue it, so oftē as we celebrate the memorie of Christes death: how commeth it to passe, that among you so Euangelical, so pure professours of the Gospel, and so exact reformers of the Churche, which in your iudgement hath ben deceiued these thousand yeares vntil of late dayes, that frier Martin Luther the man of God came to lightē our darknes, (how is it I say) that among you there be so many new Communions said and song, whereat of your owne sect, yea of the hotest Sacramentaries so few receiue?

Among ŷ hote Gospellers all do not receiue the Sacramēt at euery of their ministrations.

After that the first heate of your sudden deuotion was cooled, was not order by you taken, ŷ whereas ŷ lay people were weary of it, Priestes, Deacons, and Clerkes should be partakers of your the Lordes Supper, or els be punished? Then was it not brought to a mater of the holy lofe, & commaūded, they should resort to your Supper by course of houses? At length was not your Supper litle set by, and almost altogether lothed? In the Cathedral Church of Sarisbury, where you take vpon you more thē you are duly called vnto, how is it M. Iewel? do al ŷ people there

there come to your Lordes Supper? Nay, can you get them to come vnto it once in a month, or once in a quarter of a Yeare though you ring the great Bel out neuer so loude? I doubt not but within fewe yeares, wee shall see it shunned and forsaken altogether. Yet as ye vse it, it is no great paine for the People to come from their worldely busines to eate a piece of Breade, and drinke a draught of wine for your sakes, For your wil and Doctrine is, that more be not made of it. This being so, with what face make ye so much a doo for the necessitie of the whole Peoples receiuing together? Why vrge you S. Hieromes pretensed woordes so much, *Equally*, and *to all the Disciples?*

This may serue for Aunswere, in case Dominica Cœna, our Lordes Supper, be taken here for the Blessed Sacrament. But I rest more vpon this aunswere, that the Author vnderstoode thereby not the Sacramente of the Aulter, but the Feaste of common meates made for exercise of Charitie, after the Mysteries had been receiued. Whiche feast was called Agape, which ought to haue been common to all, as wel to the poore, as to the riche. And that is it your Doctor meant, whosoeuer he be. For the circumstaunce of the place declareth the same, and euen there mention is made expressely of the Common Supper. Hereof the Reader may finde more in the last Diuision of this Article. It was called Cœna Dominica, as there I shal declare. The place of S. Ambrose is likewise to be vnderstanded of the common Suppers, whereat, or rather before whiche, the holy Mysteries were wont to be receaued.

This much haue I saide (Gentle Reader) to M. Jewels First Diuision in his treatise of the first Article. Which as it seemeth to mee very much in comparison of that he saith in his First Diuision, which is contained in little more then twoo halfe

halfe sydes of his leafe: so am I very loth with like prolixitie to procede in confutation of the rest. For so both my labour should be infinite, and my time il spent, and the reading thereof to others neither profitable, nor pleasaunt. For as by this beginning thou maist perceaue, that hitherto he hath ministred no mater of substaunce or weight, whereby the Replier may haue occasion to shewe learning: suche is the rest of his huge booke, stuffed with many woordes to small purpose, with sundrye falsifienges of Places, with wrestynges of myne and other mennes sayinges, to a sense neuer thought vppon, with lyes and fables, and such other pelfe, rather to be contemned, then to be aunswered.

The stuffing of M. Iewels booke.

In confutation of this First Diuision I haue geuen thee a Taste as it were, what effect my labour should come vnto, if I woulde throughly examine euery Sentence, wherein he swarueth from reason, truthe, and learning. From hence forth I thinke it better, to passe by thinges of lesse weight, and staie at those thinges, the discussion whereof is of more necessitie. For better it is with conuenient breuitie to defende and teach the Truth, then with ouer longe and wearisome treatises, to withdrawe the Readers from due consideration of the truthe. Neyther let M. Iewel, or any of his syde thinke or reporte, what thinges I let passe vntouched, that either I allowe the same as true, being false, or can not confute: but that I hadde no list so often to trifle with a trifler, and esteemed more the profite of the mater, then multitude of wordes, and sought rather in deede to doe good to others, then with vaine shewe of a huge Volume to craue vulgare praise.

The Seconde Diuision.

The contentes of my wordes in the.2. diuision.

In the Seconde Diuision, as it liketh M. Iewell to diuide his booke and mine, is the conclusion of my former saying, that in respect of the Oblation, and of the Communion, forasmuch as bothe be Publike and Common, we doe not acknowledge any Priuate Masse, but leaue that terme to Luthers Schoole, where it was first diuised, and so termed by Sathan. &c.

This Conclusion M. Iewel letteth slippe, contenting him selfe with that he saide before, and forthwith leauing me, runneth very fiercely at Pighius, Hosius, and Staphylus, whom to wreake his malice vpon, he calleth a *Renegate*, I trowe because for Truthes sake and saluation of his soule, he forsooke Luthers wicked Schoole, and came to Christes Catholike Churche. Here he defendeth bothe Luther the chiefe Huisher of the Schoole of this new founde Gospell, and Sathan him selfe the Heade Schoolemaister. For he taketh vpon him to tel Sathans tale for him worde by worde, wherwith he imagineth Luther to haue been perswaded to say no more Masse, and commendeth both Sathan for telling it, and Luther for beleeuing it. *He savve* (saith M. Iewell,) *by the Testimonie and light of his Conscience, that all vvhiche Sathan saide vvas true, and therefore* (vpon Sathans motion) *confessed he had offended.*

M. Iewel defendeth Luther and Satan.

Iewel:

Who seeth not, that considereth the place, how freendlye these three Doctours ioyne together in league against the Masse, Doctor Iewel, Doctor Luther, and Doctor Sathan? *Remember M. Doctor Luther,* saith Doctor Sathan, as Doctor Iewel teacheth him his Lesson, *these many yeares thou hast said Masse, thou hast shevved vp Breade and Vvyne to be vvorshipped as God, and yet novv thou knovvest it vvas a Creature, and not God. Thereof folovved Idolatrie, and thou vvere the cause thereof.* Thus farre Doctor Sathan, or rather Doctor Iewel in the person of Doctor Sathan.

Three Doctours ioyned in league against the Mass. Satans tale to Luther by M. Iewels report.

than. Now Doctor Luther agreed vnto it, straight way desied the Masse, and became a new man, and beganne to set forth the light of this new Gospel, which Doctor Sathan taught him. Doctor Iewel commendeth wel both the Maister & the scholer for it. *For Luther* (saith he) *savv al these things to be true by the testimonie and light of his ovvne conscience.* Lo M. Iewel maketh Sathan a preacher of truth, whom the Scripture calleth a lyer, and the father of lying, a spredder of light, whom Gods worde maketh Prince of darkenesse. Is it not likely, that ye Masse is an il thing, sith that Doctor Sathan preached to his Nouice Luther so much against it? Wel, M. Iewel saith al was true, sootheth the Deuils tale, and ioyneth him selfe to his side. Thus by these three Doctours we are taught to abandon the Masse.

Iohn.8.

Ephes.6.

M. Iew. maketh Satan to be very simple in this case.

But would not a wise man thinke, that Sathan in this case had but a simple witte, & was nothing so crafty, as we at borne in hand he is? For if Luther by saing Masse did commit Idolatrie, and caused others to do the same, as M. Iewel on Sathans behalfe reporteth: what a simple and folish Deuil was he, to withdraw him frō it, and to perswade him to the contrarie? Can he haue any thing done by man, that liketh him better then Idolatrie? But M. Iewel making a commentarie vpon the Deuils Sermon, saith, that the Deuils purpose was to leade Luther to despaire. A man would maruel, how he should be so inward with that Deuil, as to know his purpose. What is he of his priuey counsell, that he vnderstandeth so much of his secretes? If he be, Gods people haue good cause to beware of him. And is it to be thought, that the Deuil had rather driue Luther alone to despaire, then kepe both him, and through him so greate multitudes of Christian people in Idolatrie? We may be sure his wit is not so simple, as to make so folish a bargaine.

M. Iew. is priuy to the diuels purpose.

Of al this it foloweth, that as M. Iewel, both in his

in the answere to my cõclusion in the third syde second line &c.

sermon at Paules Crosse, and in sundry places of his booke, layeth to my charge, (though vntruly and without cause) that I haue proued priuat Masse by wemen, boyes, children, laiemen, madmen, &c: so I may iustly and truly lay to his, & his felowes charge, that they haue abandoned the Masse, and professe enemitie against the Masse, with Sathan. To whether part more credite is to be geuen, I trust the very simplest of the people, whom they make iudges of their doctrine, may easily conceiue.

M. Iew. compareth Luthers conference with the Diuel, & tẽptacions of Christ, S. Paule and other Saintes.

Mat. 4.

2. Cor. 12

Because it semeth to al men a strange mater, and a thing that euery good christian man blesseth him selfe from, one thus to be schooled of the Deuil, and to haue cõferẽce with Sathan, least for that very cause the Masse of al good folke should be the better estemed: M. Iewel casteth a colour vpon it, that it might seme lesse hainous by alleging the examples of Christe, whom the Deuil was permitted to carie vp into an high mounte, of S. Paule, who had the angel of Sathan to buffet him, and of my portuise Saintes (so it becommeth Sathans frende to scoffe at Gods frendes the Saintes,) *vvhose Legendes* as he saith, *are full of visions of Deuils.* In dede this might seme to serue somwhat in defence of Sathãs schooling of Luther against the Masse, which mater M. Iewel goeth about to defend, if he could shewe, that either Christ or S. Paule, or any of the blessed Martyrs, Confessours, and virgins, (the memories of whose martyrdomes and holy liues in our Breuiaries or Portuises are set forth) euer yeelded and gaue place vnto the Deuils persuasions contrary to any article of our faith, as Luther dyd: who after that lesson taught him by Sathã, neuer worshipped the body and bloud of Christe, wherein M. Iewel foloweth him, though he acknowledged, and stoutly against the Sacramentaries defended, the same in the blessed Sacrament to be really present, wherein M. Iewel as all other the Sacramentaries, is at defiance with him.

As for visions of Deuils, wherewith Sainctes haue ben troubled, and vexed by Gods permission for their exercise, for that behalfe he hath no greater cause to scoffe at ye Legẽdes of Saītes mentioned in my Portuise, then at the life of S. Antony written by S. Athanasius, and of holy Hilarion writtē by S. Hierome, and sundry writings of other aunciēt fathers of most estimatiō, in whom not seldome is expresse mention made of such visions.

Visiōs of Deuils permitted by God to the exercise of his Saintes.

The Third Diuision.

IN the third Diuision I graunt vnto M. Iewel, that the name of priuate Masse is somtimes found in certain auncient Coūcels, in S. Thomas, & in other Schole Doctors but not in ye sense in which Luther with his Scholers calleth it priuate, but only as it is different from publike and solemne, in consideration of time, place, and other circumstaunces. For prouse thereof anthorities be alleged in the margent.

The contentes of the. 3. Diuision.

This is very true, as neither M. Iewel him selfe, nor any learned man can denye. Yet least he should say nothing to it, he saith much & to no purpose, neither proueth the contrary of yt I said. And herein I challenge him, & tel him that reason would he should haue disproued my saying, or not haue reproued it at al. Therei he sheweth ye disease of his mynd more thē any learning.

The wordes of S. Thomas be clere, which M. Iewel the better to wrest them to his purpose, somedeale falsifieth. For hauing graunted that at the solemne celebration of Masse, moe ought to be present for seruing the Priest, as in high feastes, and when a Bysshop doth celebrat with solemnitie, confirming the same by an old decre of Saint Soter the Pope: he saith thus. In Missis tamen priuatis sufficit vnum habere

part. 3. q. 83 art. 5. responsione ad arg. 12.

ministrum, qui gerit personam totius populi Catholici, ex cuius persona sacerdoti pluraliter respondet. Neuerthelesse in priuate Masses, it is sufficient to haue but one Minister, who beareth the person of the whole Catholike people, in whose person he answereth the Priest, plurally. In whiche place this worde tamen, that is to say, neuerthelesse, sufficiently admonished M. Iewel (but that he setled him selfe to wrangle) that somewhat was spoken by way of reuocation contrary, or at least different, to that whereof mention was made before, which is solemne Masse, whereat it is required that mo then one minister attend vpon the Priest, but at a Priuate masse, it is ynough there be but one to minister vnto the Priest, for thereto be S. Thomas words to be referred, and not onely to the presence of persons, as by M. Iewels falsifieng they be. By this place it appeareth plainly, that in S. Thomas, Masse is somtimes called Priuate, in respect of Solemne, and not onely of that the Priest receiueth the blessed Sacrament without companie, as M. Iewel would it to seeme, which is that I affirmed, and stil do affirme.

M. Iew. falsifieth S. Thomas by leauing out Tamen, whiche here specially perteineth to the pointe.

M. Iewel in his first Paragraphe of this. 3. Diuision, saith in spite of vs, that Albertus Pighius (whom he would faine make vile and contemptible by a light corrupting of the Orthographie of his name, not being able to disproue his Doctrine) *acknovvlegeth abuses and errours in the Masse. For trial of this, by the note in the Margent he referreth the Reader to the place. But reade Pighius in that place who list, or els where: and he shall finde no errours by him therein acknowleged. This therfore is a manifest lye. yet is this one of M. Iewels chiefe cômô places against the Catholiks. This hath he often times made the Pulpites to ring of, this hath he once or twise in his Challêging Sermô, so much & by so many now euidētly confuted. This is thundred out diuers times in the lying Apologie.

The. 16. vntruthe. he acknolegeth no errours in the Masse

In controuersijs de Missis priuatis, côtrouersia sexta.

Now

Now as errours Pighius acknowlegeth none to be in the Masse, so he complaineth of certaine abuses, that be crept into that most holy Seruice, geuing warning withal, to what man, and to what men the correction thereof belongeth. Touching these abuses, what manner ones we may thinke them to be, I haue sufficiently declared in my Confutation of the Apologie. Thither for answere hereto I referre the Reader. In the fourth part. Fol. 296.b & c.

In the last Paragraphe of this Diuision, M. Iewel at length commeth to agree with vs for the term Masse,* *although it be very seldome*, as he saith, *and almost neuer founde in the olde Catholike vvriters*, the contrary wherof it is easy to shewe out of S. Ambrose, S. Leo, and certaine auncient Fathers neare to the Apostles age, which if occasion so require, shal be done hereafter. Now is M. Iewel content speaking in the person of his Brethren, to *call that the Common or Publike Masse, vvhereas the Priest and people receiue the holy Communion together, vvhich vvas*, saith he, *the auncient order of the Apostles and Holy Fathers in the Primitiue Church*. Wel met, M. Iewel. I trust we shal be better aquainted with you & your fellowes. For if ye wil abide by that ye say here, ye will no more raile and barke at vs your poore persecuted countrie men of Louaine, as ye haue this long time done, for saying and hearing Masse: seeing that in these partes, very often times and commonly, we with the People, and the Priestes and ỹ people, receiue the holy Communion together. If that be the mater, for which ye can be cõtent to heare the Masse named, there is no iust cause why ye should so much abhorre vs, and the name of the Masse hereafter.

The. 17. vntruth. It is oftē founde in the olde Writers as it shall appeare hereafter, in the. 5. Diuision. M. Iew. confesseth & acknowlegeth a Masse.

I am glad we haue wonne so much of you, that your selfe confesse there was a Masse in the Primitiue Church. For if that be as it is by your owne graunt, a publike Masse, where the Priest and People receiue the Communion together, and the same was vsed by order of the Apostles and holy Fathers in the primitiue

Masse graunted to haue been in the Primitiue Church.

Primitiue Church: the publike Masse being a Masse, here of it followeth necessarily, that the Apostles and the holy Fathers had Masse in the Primitiue Church.

But Sir, you wil say perhaps, we haue not gained much at your handes, seeing that you graunt vs no more, but that to be called a *publike Masse, vvhereas the Priest and People receiue the holy Communion together*. In deede al dependeth vpon your meaning, which because we know not what it is, neither can we be certaine what ye graũt, more then the bare name of the Masse. If in your definition you referre your worde *Vvhereas,* to the whole auncient order of the Masse of olde time vsed in the Catholike Church, then as you call that a Masse which we do: so you vary from vs in that you make the receiuing of the People so to be of the necessitie of the Masse, as without that, there be none at al, but a Priuate Masse as you terme it, which in no wise you can allowe. But if you meane by your worde *vvheras*, the whole newe deuise of your *Communion*, we can not though ye woulde neuer so faine, suffer that to be called a Masse.

M. Iew. holy Communion a terme vncertaine.

Neither knowe we well what you meane by your *the holy Communion*, which being receiued of the people with the Priest, al that is there done, you seme to cal the Masse. If you meane by your holy Communiõ the peoples eating of bread, and drinking of wine together with the Priest (for more your selfe would it not to be) the Body and Bloud of our Lorde by no vertue of the mystical blessing or due consecration really made present: as that onely we do not acknowledge to be the true and holy communiõ of our Lords Body and Bloud, but rather a prophanation of the same, though you sende vp your sprite to heauen, and there feede on Christe by your faith, and imagination neuer so greedily: so much lesse doo we acknowledge it to be the Masse.

Let

Let vs I pray you M. Iewel set al contention aside, and seeke the truth with the feare of God, and so by preaching and writing deliuer it to ẏ people, as we may geue God an accompt in that great daye. In the Eucharist (the mater being so much spoken of the word may now be admitted) certaine we are by most cleere and plaine wordes of the Gospel, how stubbornly soeuer the Sacramentaries denye it, first that there is the very & true body of our Sauiour Christ, which I proue in the fifth Article, and now is very sufficiently proued by Doctor Saunders learned treatise: next, that it is there as a Sacrifice, as it was in the supper by Christes institution, which I proue in the. 17. Article, and also as a Sacramēt, which is by al the learned Fathers agreed vpon. As it is a Sacrament, it is receiued, as it is a Sacrifice, first it is offered, and afterward eaten. Christe at his supper by signes and outward tokens gaue signification of a Sacrifice. For he toke the Bread into his handes, he gaue thankes, he blessed it, and brake it. &c.

The Eucharist is a Sacramēt and a Sacrifice

Mat. 26. Luc. 22.

Now wheras you M. Iewel and the rest of your side, doe receiue the Eucharist, and do not also offer it, ye celebrate an eating and drinkīg, and make a supper of ẏ Lorde (I meane after your manner) the Sacrifice of the Crosse ye make not. And so hath Bucer him self one of your chiefe Doctours confessed with these words. In nostra eucharistia mors Christi tantū verbis, non etiam symbolis prædicatur. In our Eucharist (saith he) ẏ death of Christ is preached or set forth only by words, & not by signes. wherefore your eucharist, in which there is no signe nor tokē of an external sacrifice, is not ẏ Christiā Eucharist. For Christ commaunded vs not to saye these things in remembraunce of him, but to do or make. Do ye (or make ye) this in my remembrance, Therefore in the Mysteries the hoste or Sacrifice of Christe is not to be saide or spoken onely, but also to be done or made. And heereof it followeth that the memorie of Christes Sacrifice

The Gospellers in their supper celebrate an eating and drinking, they celebrate not the Sacrifice.

Bucer. lib. 2. de vera & falsa dominicæ cœna administratione.

Luc. 22. 1. Cor. 11.

Sacrifice be to be represented at the aulter by signes and tokens such as Christe at his Supper vsed, and not only by wordes. Els if there be an eating, and not an Oblation: there shalbe a sampler and image of the Supper, but sampler and image of the Sacrifice, there shalbe none at al.

Thus it is euident how ye abuse the holy Eucharist, and how ye breake and mangle the Institution of Christe. And as your the Lordes Supper is not only not our Lords true Supper for lacke of the specialst meate our Lords very body, hauing by your doctrine but only symbolical bread and wyne: so in the Eucharist of the Catholike Church, I meane in the holy Masse, the true body of Christe being first consecrated by the almighty power of the word, and so offered by the Priest to God in a Sacramēt vnbloudily, in remembrance of that bloudy Sacrifice offered vpon the Crosse: we do celebrate both the memorie of his Sacrifice, by which our sinnes are remitted, and also of the Supper. which Supper if the people at any time do not dispose them selfe worthily to receiue with the Prieste, for the same is he neither to be blamed, being desirous they examined and made them selues ready thereto, nor for that cause ought he to be debarred from celebrating Masse, wherein he may do that thing, which
Luc. 22. Christe commaunded Priests to do, saying, Do ye this in my remembrance.

The Fourth Diuision.

IN the Fourth Diuision M. Iewell aunswereth me reprouing him for that he shunned the accustomed name of Passion Sonday, chosing rather to call that day in the title of his Chalenge, the Sonday before Easter. which thing as it is not of great weight, so his aunswer to it is of of smal reason. *VVhat* (saith he very hotely) *thinketh he that all folke are Heretikes, that name the daies othervvise, then they be named in his Portuise?* Iewel.

You haue great spite at my Portuise M. Jewel, and so hath the Deuil too, J doubte not. J am as litle a shamed of my Portuise, or of any other order of prayer appointed by the Church of God, as you are busy to deface prayer, fasting, christiā discipline, and al other good meanes to bring the people to vertuous liuing. Jt is not my Portuise only that nameth that day Passion Sonday, but al Christen people of the west Church, in which you are borne, specially they of your Countrie. And to deuise new termes in religion, you knowe, it hath euer ben taken for a note of heretikes. J condemne neither you, nor others, as heretikes for this point, as you charge me: but for such affectation of noueltie, and for refusing the auncient name of the day vsed in the Catholike Church, J note you as being of affinitie to them, and as one that beareth them good fauour. Portuise / Passion Sonday.

Neither do J hereby condemne the Grekes, who for ought that you knowe to the contrary, may haue that name of the day in their Calender, or in their common vse of speaking. Though the day of Parasceue be of vs Englishmen called Good Fryday, and likewise of other nations in Christendom: yet J do not condemne them, as you surmise. But if any Englishman would vpon a newe euangelical spirite shunne the vsual terme of Good friday, and call it only by the Greke terme Parasceue in an English Sermon: if J called him a newe fangled foole for it, J thinke J should not greatly offend any wise man therby. Good Friday.

But the Italians (saith M. Jewel) *contrary to the Portuise, cal the first vveeke in Lente the Carneuale,* and then J should condemne them also. Here J am sore charged with one, that sheweth as great skil in the Jtalian tongue, as in the Grekes Calender. Iewel.

Carneuale. I wisse the Italians cal not the first weeke in Lent, Carneuale, at which time both the name and passetime of Carneuale is passed and gone: but the time of certaine weekes before the first weeke in Lent. And that could not he haue ben ignorant of, if euer he had ben in Italie in that part of the yere. Now he sheweth how litle he feareth to auouch thinges for truth, which he knoweth not.

He acknowlegeth that day to be called in the Portuise also the Sonday Iudica, and that name to be as catholike, as Passion Sonday. True it is, yet vsed he neither of them both, and if that day had fiue names moe, and euery one were appointed by the catholike church: he would rather deuise a newe of his owne head, then to be sene to vse any one of them.

In the ende of this Diuision, he praiseth much his vsing of the pulpite with sobrietie, and saith, *he spake of the abuses of Christes* Iewel. *last supper, hauing occasion therto of these vvordes of S. Paule.* The thing 1. Cor. 11. that I receiued of the Lorde, the same haue I deliuered vnto you, *vvho in his time seemeth to finde faulte vvith the Corinthians for the same.*

Of the Churche feastes mentioned by S. Paule to the Corinthians. That place of S. Paule M. Iewel both in his Chalenge, and in his Replie, sundry times abuseth much to the deceite of the people, wherein he foloweth Peter Martyr, as in many other false pointes. S. Paule in that place fyndeth not faulte with the Corinthians for the abuse of the blessed Sacrament directly, either concerning the Ministration of it, or the receiuing: but for that they abused their Church feastinges, whereat, or immediatly before which, they receiued also the Sacrament. For whereas in those feastes, which the fathers called ἀγάπας, they should haue shewed the fruites of vnitie, when they had now receiued the mysterie of vnitie: contrariwise they shewed schisme, and dissension. Likewise for charitie, humilitie, meeknesse, moderati-

on,

on, indifferencie towardes al, and other vertues, requisite to such holy bankets made in the church to the imitation and example of Christe, for which that kinde of feasting, was called Dominica cœna, our Lordes supper, euen of S. Paule in that Epistle after the minde of S. Ambrose, and of Theophylacte, who therin doutles foloweth the auncient fathers of ý Greke church: they shewed spite, pride, disdaine, dronkennesse, partialitie in admitting the rich to their table, and reiecting the poore, and sundry other great disorders. For these abuses committed in those Churchefeastes, whereof consequently folowed also the misprising of the blessed Sacrament, and not for any touching the celebration of that deuine mysterie specially, S. Paule rebuked the Corinthians. But hereof M. Iewel geueth me occasion to speake more hereafter in his. 8. and in his last Diuision.

In comment. in 1. Cor. 11.

The abuses of the Church feastes.

After this he would faine proue, that the supper of Christe (so he calleth the Sacrament) may be abused. Therto he allegeth once againe Albertus Pighius de priuata Missa, and sticketh not to say, *this appeareth to be true by the very confeßion of their aduersaries* (meaning the Catholikes,) *and that they deny not, but that there be abuses and errours cropen into the Priuate Masse.* What Pighius hereof hath writen, I shewed in the Diuision before this. Verely he acknowlegeth no errours to be in the Masse. This manifest untruth can not by any meanes be excused or coloured, yet hath he twise made it within the compasse of fewe lines. Thanked be our Lorde, that the ennemies of his Sacrifice can not impugne it, but with euident lyes, whereby they to the world to understand, how litle credite in doctrine of faith they deserue. What abuses Pighius complaineth of as cropen into the seruice of the Masse, I haue truly declared in my Confutation of their English churches Apologie, as is aboue noted.

Iewel.

A manifest lye of M. Iew. oftetimes reported.

Fol. 206.

The fifth Diuision.

IN the.5. Diuision M. Jewel hath laid together a great parcel of my answere to his first Article. To disproue the same he hath heaped together a farre greater parcel of stuffe such as it is. From which who so euer shal take away suche superfluous talke, bye maters not perteining to the point there treated, falsifyinges of Doctours, and specially a number of lies, which are the chiefe stuffing of his huge booke: he shal leaue very litle besides worth the reading.

The contents of M. Jew. Replie in the 5. Diuision.

First he maketh his entrie with a solemne prayer protestat-like, as if he were about to make a Sermon, and his fauorable hearers ready to sing a song. Then he accuseth thinflammation of my choler, because alluding to the wordes of Daniel, I glaunced at the name of the forerunners of Antichriste, therwith rubbing him and his holy companions, as it were on their gaul, for the Deuilish spite they shewe to the blessed sacrifice of Christe mystically represented, and truly continewed in the daily Sacrifice of the Church, now called the Masse. At length hauing with his Euangelical meeknesse compared my spirite with the spirite of those Pharisies, who stirred the Jewes to stone S. Steuen, and charged Christe with blasphemie vttered against God: full coldely and demurely he promiseth, that *he vvil not ansvvere heate vvith heate, but in that kinde of eloquence vvil geue place,* doing much like to one that crieth truce, after he hath geuen a stroke. which promise how wel he hath kept through his whole Replie, they can wel iudge, who sticke not to bestow the time so euil, as to reade it ouer.

Dan. 6.12.

Act. 7.

Mat. 26.

After this by a short Preface pretending to ioyne close with me, and to touch the mater, toward the which he made so great a pre-

preparation: he runneth out farre from the purpose ẏ my wordes import, to S. Gregories rebuking of Iohn the Archebishop of Constantinople, for his ambitious and vniust claiming of the name of Uniuersal Bishop, and there he hath vp his common pulpite bible bable, of the forerunner of Antichriste, of Lucifer, of his vaunting him selfe aboue his brethren, and of, I can not tel what. This place of S. Gregorie, and that of Pighius, where he complaineth of abuses crept into the Masse, be two of M. Iewels storeboxes, out of which commonly he storeth him selfe with multitude of wordes, when he is destitute of good mater.

Ad constã tiam August. lib. 4. epist. 78. ad Mauritiũ Imp. lib. 7. epist. 197.

Two of M. Iew. store boxes.

The mater of Uniuersal Bishop, because I haue already thereof treated in my Confutation of their Apologie, and occasion is geuen thereof to speake hereafter, and specially because it perteineth not to our present purpose: I thinke good with silence to passe ouer.

Fol. 55. a. Item. Fol. 204. a

Being charged with false doctrine against the mystical, Sacramental, and vnbloudy Sacrifice of the Church, wherein that very body that was once offered on the Crosse with shedding of bloud, and with sensible stretching forth of his most tendre membres, is now without bloude shedding, and beside visible manner also offered in a sacrament, and in a mysterie: he saith much of the Sacrifice of the Crosse, whereof is no question moued, and of the Sacrifice of the aulter, he speaketh neuer a word. As though by saying good of that, he should be borne withal for denying this.

Where he speaketh of a Sacrifice made by man, what he meaneth, wel I knowe not. If by that worde he minded to vtter some parte of his spite against the blessed Sacrifice of the Masse, vnderstand he, which he is not ignorant of, that sacrifice is not made by man, as the author and institour of it, but by our Sauiour Iesus Christ him selfe, who at his last supper first in-

How the sacrifice is made by man.

Luc.22. 1.Cor.11. stituted it, cōmaūding the Apostles, whō he thē created Priestes, and in the charge committed to them their successours, to do and offer the same in remembraunce of him. And for this commaundement of Christe, it is made and done by man, as minister, not as authour. Neither is this an other Sacrifice, as he pretendeth. It is the same that was offered vpon the crosse, there is no difference betwen this and that concerning the thing offered, the difference or diuersitie is only in the mãner of offering. This much must we oftentimes repete, yet these men make a wise, as though it had neuer ben tolde them.

The Sacrifice of ẏ Church is commonly called the Masse. He maketh much adoo with me, for that speaking of the Sacrifice of the Church, I said it to be commonly called the Masse. For these holy folke would faine, if they wist how, abolish not only the most blessed and healthful Sacrifice of the Masse, but also the very name of the Masse. Satan and they in no wise can abide it. But syr, I report me to al the worlde, is it not in dede commonly called the Masse? Is it not so called in England, Scotland, Ireland, Frāūce, Germanie, Pole, Hungarie, Spain, Italie, briefly al Christendome ouer, where so euer the Latine speach is knowen? what meant you to denie a thing so euident? O you say, that

Iewel. *neither the Hebrues in their tongue, nor the Greekes in their tongue, nor Christe, nor his Apostles, nor Tertullian, nor S. Cyprian, nor Origen, nor Lactantius, nor S, Hierome, nor S. Augustine, nor S. Clement, nor Abdias, nor Hippolytus in their bookes euer vsed the name of the Masse.* Syr what if I graunted you al this? what conclude you thereof? If the name of the Masse be not founde in the Hebrue, (wherein if one would stand with you, he might saye more for the affirmatiue, neither without auctoritie of very wel learned men, then you should be hable to refel) nor in the Greke, nor in the sayinges of Christe, or his Apostles, nor in the wry-

tinges

tinges of Tertullian, S. Cyprian, Origen, Lactantius, and of the rest which you recken: may it not yet be founde in others? wil you neuer leaue that peuish kinde of Argument deduced of negatiues, or, ab authoritate negatiue, as they terme it in schooles? what if neither I, nor any of vs here in Louaine, nor any other Catholike, or wise man wil cal you A bishop: wil you not replye for all that, and say, that so many the right reuerent fathers, your owne companions (fathers they be in dede) do commonly so call you? I make the comparison to shewe the weakenesse of thargument only, for touching the truth of thinges, be you neuer so much named bishop of Sarisburie, certaine it is, you are none, as none other of your order is. what if the Citie of Yorke be not so named in Hebrue, Greke, by Christe, the Apostles, Tertullian, Lactantius, nor by any other that euer wrote in Greke or Latine, but Eboracum, which is farre from the sound of Yorke: shal we thereof conclude that it is not commonly called Yorke?

M. Iew. cõmonly deduceth his argumentes of negatiues

If Missa be a Latine worde, as I beleue it is: what reason haue you against that it is so commonly called, out of Hebrue or Greke? Shall we not saye that bread is commonly called bread, because that worde is not founde in Hebrue, Greke, or Latine? Remember M. Iewel, you are borne in the Latine Churche. You ought not to shunne the names or thinges thereof, because you finde not them so named in the Hebrue tongue, or Greke wryters.

Seing that you dryue me to shewe some antiquitie of the name Missa, I fynde it recorded and mencioned by auncient Fathers of good auctoritie, euen within the compasse of your first six hundred yeres, whose auctoritie not without preiudice of the thousand yeres folowing, and of Christes premise of the

The name Missa founde in sundry old wryters, and Coũcels.

Iohn. 14.

holy ghostes remaining with the churche for euer, you seeme to allowe. S. Ambrose hath the expresse word Missa, in an Epistle, that he wrote to the noble woman Marcella his sister. Missam facere cœpi, that is, *I beganne Masse*, be his very wordes.

Ambrosi. Epist. 33.

Seuerus Sulpitius in vita Martini.

Seuerus Sulpitius a learned man of that age, in the life of S. Martine speaketh expressely of Masse, and nameth Missarum solennia, as much to say, as *solemne Masse*. The worde is oftentimes vsed of the auncient fathers in the plural number, because before al the people were come to the faith, that which now we cal the Masse, was then diuided into two, whereof the one was the Masse of the Catechumens, who were nouices and learners of the faith before they were admitted to baptisme, the other was the Masse of the perfite beleuers.

Missa Catechumenorum, & Missa perfectorum.

Epist. 81.

S. Leo that learned and eloquent bishop, writing to Dioscorus bishop of Alexandria, speaketh of the Masse by name. whose plaine worde Masse, M. Jewel in the Sermon of his Chalenge, turneth into ministring of the communiõ, putting Leo to schole as it were, and teaching him how to vse his termes, minister-like. Victor maketh expresse mention of Masse.

lib. 2. de persecutione Vandalorum.

Leauing out S. Alexander Pope and Martyr, nye to the Apostles age, and certaine other Popes, Martyrs, and holy Confessours of very great auncientie, who in their wrytinges haue made mention of the Masse by name, because these felowes with more stubbornnesse refuse their witnesses, then with reason are hable to disprone them: I wil now come to certaine Councels, euery one of good Auctoritie, and holden by learned and holy bishops within M. Jewels six hundred yeres.

The word Missa founde in auncient Cõcels.

Cocilium Carthaginen. 2. can. 3.

It was decreed by the fathers of the second Councel of Carthage, which was holden in the yere of our Lord. 407. after the computation of Marianus Scotus, *reconciliare quenquam in publica Missa presbytero non licere, that it should not be lavvful for a priest to re-*

concile any man in Publike Masse.

In an Aphrican Councel holden at Milenitum, where S. Augustine was present, it was ordeined, that such order of church Seruice, as Prayers, Masses, Prefaces, Commendations, &c. should be vsed of al, which was approued by a Councel, and none other, where the worde Missæ, is expressed. Can.12.

In the Councel of Agatha holden about the yere of our Lorde.400. it was permitted to men dwellig farre from parishe Churches, for ease of theire families, to builde Oratories or Chappels in theire owne groundes, and there to haue Masses. Prouided alwayes notwithstanding, that in the High and solēne feastes they should resort to ỹ towne and Parish Churches, to haue Masse and diuine seruice. In the same Councel secular folke are commaunded to heare Masse on the Sonday, and not to departe before they receiue the Priestes blessing, which is geuē at the end of Masse. In two Canons of this auncient Councell the expresse name of Masse is twise founde. Can.12. Can. 47.

At the thirde Councel of Arles in Fraunce, which was kept in the time of Marcian the Emperour farre within M. Iewels six hundred yeres, a decre was made, that if any Bisshop had promoted to ỹ holy orders of Priesthod or Deaconship any that was in publike penaunce, that had ben twise maried, or had ben the husband of a wydow: he should not presume to celebrate Masse for the space of a whole yere, for so be the wordes of the Canon. Anno integro Missas celebrare non præsumat. Concil. Arelate. Can.3.

Here might I allege other auncient Councels, as the first of Orleans, the Councel of Ilerda in Spaine, the Councel also of Gerunda there, in which the expresse name of Masse is founde.

To the auctoritie of these auncient Councels, I wil adde the authoritie of Epiphanius Scholasticus, who liued within the first six hundred yeares, as Henricus Pantaleon of Basile a Doctour of M. Jewels owne sect, maketh accompt. Who translating Sozomenus a Greke writer, where he speaketh of certaine that came to Church and hearde Seruice, turned his Greeke worde ἐκκλησίαζον, into these twoo Latine woordes, Missas celebrabant, that is, they celebrated Masse. Wherby he geueth witnesse that in his tyme the name of Masse was not straunge.

Tripar. hist.lib.3. cap.11.apud Sozomenū. lib.2.cap. 32.

Thus because M. Jewel was so importunate with me, as to demaunde whye I shewed not of what auncient Fathers the Sacrifice of the Church is called by the name of Masse, bearing his fauourers in hande, I had none at al to shewe: I haue thought it good to allege such numbre as might seeme to be sufficient to satisfie any man, that is not peruersly wedded to M. Jewels sayings, be they true be they false, and to beleue what so euer is taught by them which professe enemitie and hatred against the Catholike Church.

The cause wh y I alege testimonies for the worde Masse.

If the auncient authoritie of S. Ambrose, of Seuerus Sulpitius, of S. Leo, of Bisshop Victor, of Epiphanius Scholasticus the auncient Translatour, and of so many learned Fathers of Italie, Fraunce, Spaine, Afrike, and of sundry other Prouinces assembled together in Councels, the wordes of whose Canons be wel weyed and examined, before they be put in writing to stand for Decrees, if al these I saye, be not ynough to proue the auncient vse of the worde Masse: I knowe not what can be ynough. Verely it is euident by these testimonies, that at those dayes it was so called al Christendom ouer, where the Latine tongue was vsed.

Wherefore let M. Jewel marueil no more, that I would say the Sacrifice to be commonly called the Masse. Albeit

when

when I wrote so, my minde was not directed vnto antiquitie, so much as vnto the later age of the Church.

Now commeth M. Jewel to the chiefe point of this Fifth Diuision, wherein as by my wordes it appeareth, I geue the diligent Reader a warning, where to finde aucthorities for confirmation of his faith, concerning the Blessed Sacrifice of the Church, whether M. Jewel wil or no, commonly called the Masse. The auctorities I allege not at length, as they be vttered in their places, for that had been very long, neyther fitte to my purpose in that place. I thought best to direct the Reader vnto the view of them, where they be. And so much I signifie there. M. Jewel knowing wel ynough the force of those testimonies for the Masse, (so I cal with Christes Church the dayly and vnbloudy Sacrifice of the Church) and seing him selfe not able to aunswere them to the purpose: shifteth his handes of them so wel as his sprite serued him. but with shame ynough, as it wil appeare in the ende. The false and crafty sleightes he vseth, be these.

M. Iew. crafty sleightes, where mater of sufficient answere lacketh.

First, he reckeneth together my proufes, as it liked hym best for his purpose, geuing to them all, the name of Doctours, as though the Masse had no grounde of Scripture. whereas in my booke with due distinction, first I allege Scripture, then Doctours. For proufe of the Masse I referre the Reader to the figure of Melchisedech, to the Prophecie of Malachias, to the Institution of Christ, from him to the Apostles, from them to the Church, and so to the whole worlde. After this I bring the Reader to the Doctours.

Gen. 14.

M. Iew. annōbreth Christ, the Apostles, Melchisedech, and Malachias, for Doctours of the Church.

But M. Jewel to abase the auctoritie of the thing proued, accompteth Melchisedech the King and Priest, Malachias the Prophete, Christe our Sauiour, and his Apostles, for Doctours

Doctours. who though for some respecte maye so be taken, yet where mention is of ẏ Doctours of the Church, who haue treated of scripture, they are neuer accompted in that order.

What shiftes M. Iewel vseth feelig his parte to be the weaker.

After that he hath reckened them by name, he iesteth and scoffeth at the whole, and maketh prety sport, where the mater requireth grauitie, like as crafty Slaues in Comedies sōtimes shift them selues from their Maisters sadde reckeninges with a mery toye. And here haue we M. Iewels troupes, rankes, armies, camisados, Mummers, visardes, warlike and Christmas termes, for sporte mingled together. Then for shewe of some annswere to Melchisedech, Malachias, and the Institution of Christ, he maketh a ridiculous argument as on my behalfe, scoffingly concluding for priuate Masse, wheras I alleged them not for proufe of priuate Masse, but of the Sacrifice of the Masse in general.

Lastly he denyeth some Doctours whom I alleged, and findeth fault with their authoritie vpon light reasons, and false surmises, the more and better numbre of them he dessembleth, & answereth the point with silence touching them, and with many wordes vnnecessary touching things to the state of the present question impertinent. And thus in effect he dischargeth him selfe of the mater, which with reason, or any due colour of truth, he can neuer answere. But the weight of the mater is not with such light and slender leauers caryed away. Contemning therfore M. Iewels light scoffes, let vs weigh the graue authoritie both of the Scriptures, and of the holy and Learned Fathers.

Sacrifice how it is diuersly taken.

My purpose being to proue that we haue a Sacrifice in the Church, which is done, offered, & celebrated in ẏ Masse: to thintent ẏ mater may the better be vnderstāded, I require two thigs to be remembred, that the name of Sacrifice, is taken somtime for

for the thing which is offered vnto God, somtime for the acte it selfe of offering. For the thing it selfe, as where S. Paule saith, writing in his Epistle to the Hebrewes: Euery Byshop is ordained to offer giftes and Sacrifices for sinnes. For the acte, as where Jonathan to excuse Dauids absence from king Saules table, saide, that he was at a solemne Sacrifice of his Familie in their owne Towne. So Cicero taketh the worde, where he saith, Præbere hostias ad Sacrificium. To giue hostes to sacrifice. So are the wordes artificium, lanificium, and other the like of Learned men vsed.

Heb. 5.

1. reg. 20

The other thing to be remembred is, that as the Catholikes do speake of the Sacrament of the Aulter two wayes, so also of the Sacrifice of the Aulter two wayes. For it is a Sacrament onely, to witte, the outwarde formes of Breade and wyne, which do conteine in them the body and bloude of Christe: It is also the thing and the Sacrament, that is to saye, the Body and Bloud of Christe in and vnder the thoutwarde formes conteined. Likewise in the Oblation of the Church or Masse, there is an outward Sacrifice of the forms of bread and wine, which S. Augustine writing vpon the Psalmes, calleth the Sacrifice of bread and wine. There is also an inward Sacrifice, or a Sacrifice of inward things, to witte, of the body and bloud of Christe, which we offer vnto God in our Masse vnder those formes.

Sacramēt, and Sacrifice taken two waies.

in psal. 37

This much being said, let vs come vnto the places in my Answere alleged out of the olde Testament for proufe of our Sacrifice in the Masse. This is certain, that Melchisedech was a Priest, for he was the Priest of the highest God, saith the scripture. If he were a Priest, then he offered Sacrifice vnto God. For euery Priest is ordained to offer Sacrifice. But we fide not that euer he offered any other Sacrifice, then Breade and wine. wherefore

Gen. 14.

Heb. 5.

wherefore seing that after the same manner and order we offer vp the formes of bread and wine, it foloweth that we offer Sacrifice, verely and in dede. But where Melchisedech offered Breade and wyne onely, we by the commaundement of Christ and after the example of Christe, whose figure Melchisedech bare, and who ordained Priestes at his last Supper, which Priesthood doth continew after the order of Melchisedech for euer: we I saye, do offer vp vnder the forme of Breade and

The Sacrifice of ỳ Churche. Wine, the Body and Bloude of Christe, into which the bread and wine by thalmighty power of Christes woorde are really turned, for so him selfe said, This is my Body, this is my bloud.

Mat.26. Luc.22. Do this in my remēbraunce. And this Oblation of the Body and Bloud of Christe vnto God at the Aulter, is the Oblation and Sacrifice of the newe Testament, dayly offered by Priestes in the Sacrifice of the Church, which we cal the Masse, or the Sacrifice of the Masse.

Thus to vnderstande the figure of Melchisedech, and to thinke the Sacrifice of the Church therby proued, we are taught by the Blessed Martyr S. Cyprian, who writing to Cæcilius,

Lib.2. Epist.3. speaketh largely hereof. and among many other sayinges he hath this. In Sacerdote Melchisedech Sacrificij dominici Sacramentum præfiguratum videmus, &c. In the Priest Melchisedech we see the Sacrament of our Lords Sacrifice præfigured, ac-

Gen.14. cording to that the holy Scripture witnesseth and saith: Melchisedech King of Salem brought forth breade and wyne: for he was the Priest of the highest God, and he blessed Abraham. And that Melchisedech bare the figure of Christ, the holy Ghost declareth in the Psalmes speaking to the Sonne in the person of the

Psal.109. Father: before the morning sterre I begote the. The Lord hath sworne, and shall not repent him of it, Thou arte a Priest for euer after the order of Melchisedech. Which order is euery where here comming of that Sacrifice and descending from thence, that Melchisedech was the Priest of God the highest, that he offered breade and wine, that he blessed Abraham. For who is more the Priest of God the highest then our Lorde Iesus Christ, which offered Sacrifice to God his Father? And offered the very same that Melchisedech offered, bread and wyne, to witte, his Body and Bloud. Thus farre S. Cyprian. Who expressely saith the order of Melchisedech to be here on Earth euery where descending from that Sacrifice, because he offered Bread and wine, the type and figure of the Sacrifice of the Churche, that now is offered by Priestes of the Newe Testament ouer all the worlde, and to declare what Breade and wyne it is, he sayth, the Body and Bloude of Christe.

S. Augustine writing vpon the Psalmes allegeth this Figure of Melchisedech for the Sacrifice of Christ. Before the kingdom of his Father (saith he) he changed his countenaunce, and he let him go, and he went away, because he was there after the order of Aaron. And afterwarde he instituted a Sacrifice of his owne Body and bloud after the order of Melchisedech.

S. Augustine &c. In psal. 33 concione. 2.

But what reason is this, (sayth M. Iewel) *Melchisedech brought forth Breade and Wyne to banket Abraham, and his armie being weary of the chase,* Ergo there is a Priuate Masse in the Church.

Iewel.

I allege not, nor is there any auncient Doctour that allegeth the Figure of Melchisedech for priuate Masse, but for the Sacrifice of the Body and Blonde of Christe, which is offered in the Masse. And I denye not but that Melchisedech brought forth Breade and wyne vnto Abraham for refresshing of his armie, but whereas the Scripture forthwith sayth, for he was the Prieste of the highest God. except wee make it a foolishe cause, wee must beleeue, that he was wonte to offer the same things to God, which then he brought forth to Abraham, though to him for meate, to God for Sacrifice.

Melchisedeks sacrifice auouched by þ Fathers.

If M. Iewel wil not beleeue me, for witnesse hereof may it please him to reade S. Cyprian ad Cæcilium. S. Ambrose lib. 5. de Sacramentis. cap. 1. S. Hierome vpon the. 26. chapter of S. Mathew. Damascen de orthodoxa fide lib. 4. Cap. 14. S. Chrysostome in his Homilie De proditione Iudæ. S. Augustine in Psal. 33. concione prima. In all which places he shall fynde this mater of Melchisedeches Sacrifice plainely auouched.

The prophecie of Malachi referred to the Sacrifice of the Churche. Mala. 1.

Touching the Prophecie of Malachias, by the exposition in mãner of al the Fathers, it reporteth þ Sacrifice of the Body and Bloud of Christ dayly offered in þ Masse. I haue no liking in you (saith that Prophet in þ person of God to the Iewes) and no gift wil I take of your hand. From the rising of the Sunne to the going downe, my name is great among the Gentiles, and in euery place there is Sacrificed and offered to my name a pure Oblation. The Sacrifices of the Iewes being reiected and ended, which in comparison of the moste sweete and pleasaunt Sacrifice of the Body and Bloude of our Sauiour Christ, were both for the shedding of Beastes bloude base, and also to God of them selfe vnpleasant, as they which were but Figures of Christes most precious Sacrifice: what other special Sacrifice or Oblation can the Prophet iustly be thought to haue ment, that should be offered to God throughout al the world in euery place, and of him be reputed for pure and cleane, but the Blessed Sacrifice of the Church, wherein the Body and Bloud of Christe is offered vnbloudily to his Father by Priestes of the Newe Testament?

But

But M. Jewel, as they of Luthers schoole do, taketh this place of Malachias for spiritual Sacrifice which is common to al the faithful, for the Sacrifice of their holy Communion, where (as he saith,) *al the people dothe lifte vp their handes and hartes vnto heauen, pray and Sacrifice together, reioyse and praise the Lorde.* And when he hath said al that he could say in commendation of hys Communion, he can make but a spiritual Sacrifice of it. The sacrifice of the new Cōmunion. Iewel.

Which meaning squareth not with the saying of this Prophet for sundry considerations. First, whereas he speaketh of a pure Sacrifice, no workes of man can seme to be such, for as much as al our workes and doinges euen the very best and iustest of al, as Luther and his disciples do teach, be as Esay saith, tanquam pannus menstruatæ, like a defiled cloth. Wherefore they can not absolutly be called a pure Sacrifice or Oblation, specially of M. Jewel, if he wil stande to his great Maister Luthers doctrine, who holdeth opinion, that al our good workes and righteousnesse before God are synnes. *Esay. 64.*

Againe, to offer vp our worke as a pure Oblation and Sacrifice, that calleth M. Jewel and his felowes who haue ẏͤ sprite of this new gospel, Pharisaical. But this Prophete speaketh not of a Pharisaical Sacrifice.

Furthermore, forasmuch as spiritual Sacrifices, of which M. Jewel expoundeth this prophecie of Malachias, be they prayers, praises, reioysinges in the Lorde, or what els so euer: they be not the proper and peculiar sacrifices of the lawe of the gospel, vnder which we liue now, but they were common in al lawes, as wel in the lawe of nature, and the lawe of Moyses, as in the new lawe. Now this prophete speaketh of a sacrifice that is proper, special, singular, and peculiar to the newe lawe. Which is the pure sacrifice of the Aulter, of the holy Eucharist, in which the body and bloud of Christe purely vnder the formes of bread and wine is by Priestes of the new testament without shedding of bloud offered to God, thoroughout the whole world and in al nations, according to the commaundement and institution of Christ, saying, do this in my remembrance. wherfore it is clere that Malachies prophecie is to be vnderstanded of this Oblation and Sacrifice, which is offered to God in the Masse.

Thus vnderstode the auncient fathers that place of Malachias, for witnesse whereof the auctoritie of S. Iustine the holy Martyr may suffice in stede of many others, whom it were easy to allege. In the Dialogue which he had at Ephesus with Tryphon the Iewe, he saith thus, speaking of ẏ Christians & Iewes Sacrifices. Al the Sacrifices which Iesus Christ hath ordeined to be done in his name, that is to say, in the Eucharist of the bread and of the cuppe, which are made of Christen men in euery place, God vsing preuētion, witnesseth them to be acceptable vnto him. But those which are done by you and your Priestes, (he meaneth the Iewes) he disaloweth with these wordes, your sacrifices from your hands I wil not accept: because from the rysing of the sunne to the going downe, my name is glorified among the Gentiles.

Iustinus Martyr, in Dialog. contra Iudæos.

Mala. 1.

S. Irenæus in his bookes against the heresies of Valentinus, speaking of this Sacrifice, which he calleth the new Sacrifice of the new Testament, which (by his report) Christ taught the Apostles, and the Apostles delyuered to the Church, & the Church offereth it to God in the whole worlde: confirmeth that doctrine by the expresse place of Malachias, saying, de quo in duodecim prophetis Malachias sic præsignificauit: Non est mihi voluntas in vobis. &c. Malachias one of the twelue prophetes, of this sacrifice hath thus foresignified: I haue no lyking in you saith our lord almighty, and of your handes I wil not take Sacrifice, because frō the rising of the Sunne to the going downe my name is made glorious among the Nations. &c.

Irenæus. lib. 4. cap. 32.

Con-

Concerning the Institution of Christe, it is euident by the wordes of S. Luke the Euangelist, that Christe at his last Supper ordeined this Sacrifice which we speake of. Hauing taken bread saith the Gospel, he gaue thankes, and brake, and gaue to them, saying: this is my body, which is geuen for you. Do ye this in my remembrance. Likewise (he toke) the cup after that he had supped, saying, (after that he had geuen thankes, as before) this is the cuppe the new testament in my bloud, which is shed for you. That here Christe offered and sacrificed, if we had nothing els to proue it, the wordes of the scripture, and the circumstance of the place, do witnesse it. For one to render thankes to God, taking a cuppe in his handes, and lifting it vp, after the rite and manner of the Iewes, is a very act of one that doth Sacrifice. And so forasmuch as our Lorde said, Doo ye this, he commaunded the Apostles to do that which they sawe him do, that is to say, to offer vp the Sacrifice of thankes geuing, not only by geuing thankes in worde, but also by geuing and offering to God the body and bloud of his Sonne, which by thalmighty power of the worde made present, are inuisibly in the Sacrament vnder the formes of bread and wine, are really conteined. This was ẏ faith of the Primitiue Church, as we vnderstand by witnesse of S. Ignatius the Apostles scholer, whose wordes in an Epistle which he wrote ad Smyrnẽses, as Theodoritus allegeth, be these.

The institution of Christ. Luc. 22.

Eucharistias & oblationes non admittunt, quòd non confiteantur Eucharistiam esse carnem Seruatoris nostri Iesu Christi, quæ ꝓ peccatis nostris passa est, quam pater sua benignitate suscitauit. These heretikes admit not the Eucharistes and Oblations, because they wil not confesse that the Eucharist is the flesh of our Sauiour Iesus Christe, which hath suffered for our sinnes, which the Father hath raised vp againe by his goodnesse. Here haue we expressely the Eucharist to be the fleshe of our Sauiour Iesus Christ.

Theodorit. dialog. 3.

And what flesh? Euen that which hath suffered for our synnes, and hath risen againe, whereby al tropes and figures of the Zwingliãs, al enargies, vertues and efficacies of ye Caluinistes, al ouerthwarte and blinde phrases of M. Iewel, be defeited and quite put away.

Christes Sacrifice at his supper acknowleged by the olde Fathers.

lib.2. ep,3.

1.Cor.11.

Thus the Church vnderstode this mysterie in S. Cyprians time, who writing to Cæcilius, saith thus. The scripture saith, so oftentimes as ye eate this bread and drinke this cuppe, ye shal shewe forth the death of our Lorde vntil he come. Wherefore so oftentimes as we offer the cuppe in remembrance of our Lorde and of his Pasion, let vs do that, which it is euident that our Lord did. Againe likewise there within a litle. We are admonished and instructed of our Lorde (saith he) that we offer our Lordes cuppe with wine mingled, according to that as our Lord offered.

Irenæus lib.4. cap. 32.

To this agreeth S. Iræneus, who was so neare the Apostles time. The cuppe (saith he) likewise Christe confessed to be his bloud, and taught the newe oblation of the newe testament. Which the Church receiuing of the Apostles, offereth al the worlde ouer to God, which geueth vs foode. &c. And in an other place of the same Booke, he saith, We offer vnto him the Eucharist, not as to one that hath nede, but that we may geue thãkes for his gifte.

lib.4. cap. 34.

That the institution of Christe is rightly alleged for the sacrifice of the Churche.

Mat.26.

Luc.22.

1.Cor.11.

Here may M. Iewel be apposed in these questions out of S. Irenæus: when did Christe confesse the cuppe, that is to say that which was conteined in the cuppe, to be his bloud? was it not at his last supper? The scripture saith yes. when taught Christe the Apostles that newe Oblation of the newe Testament? If not at his supper, when and where els? No man liuing is hable to tel vs any other time or place. Then was it taught at his supper. what is that newe Oblation, peculiar to the newe Testament, which the Church hath receiued of the Apostles, and now offereth to God ouer the whole world? Can M. Jewel, or any of his companions name vnto vs any other, then the Oblation of the body and bloud of Christe in the daily Sacrifice of the Church? Name they what they wil beside this, and their errour wil plainely appeare. What so euer spiritual Oblation they name (for outward Oblation they acknowledge none) be it prayer, praise, thankes geuing, reioising in the Lorde, a contrite harte, or what so euer els: the same is neither new, nor peculiar to the newe testament. For al these were offered by them of the olde testament, and are common to al times and lawes.

By this it is euident how truly and rightly I alleaged the Institution of Christe, for this new Oblation of the new testament, as S. Irenæus calleth it, that is the Sacrifice of the body and bloud of Christe, which is daily celebrated by the Church in the Masse. Whereunto a longer treatise were requisite I confesse, but this is ynough to stay the Faith of a Christen man for this present, who being vnlearned might be deceiued through occasion of M. Jewels light scoffes. So now the indifferent Reader seeth more weight to be in the figure of Melchisedech in the Prophecie of Malachias, and in Christes Institution, for proufe of the Sacrifice of the Masse, then M. Jewel would his reader to beleue, by his light reasons, which for that purpose no man maketh but him selfe, going about to make it appeare none at al.

After the scoffing argumentes, wherby M. Jewel thought to abase the auctoritie of the figure of Melchisedech, the prophecie of Malachias, and the Institution of Christe: he commeth to denye the auncient Doctours, which I alleged as witnesses of the vnbloudy Sacrifice of the Church, and not for Priuate Masse, as he falsly & contrarie to his owne knowledge pretendeth. Of al them that I allege, he alloweth not one. Yet, as he is

M. Jew. denieth auncient Doctours for lacke of better answer.

is crafty, he durst not denye them al openly. Some he denieth flatly, condemning them *for fablers, for heretikes, for secrete vvryters, for suspect men. for vnknovven Doctours vntil this time.* Some he would faine discredite by light surmises, gheasses, coniectures, and supposinges. Some he letteth passe with silence, trusting to shoulder them out of credite by the contempt of the rest, whom he nameth.

Which be the doctours that M. Jew. denieth for witnessing the Sacrifice

The Doctours whom he vtterly denieth be these. S. Clemēt, Abdias, Martialis, and S. Hippolytus, S. Iames, and S. Chrysostome for their Liturgies. S. Dionyse, he would deface his auctoritie if he wist how. Yet to that purpose is *Erasmus* brought in, a man for many pointes now growen to be of smal auctoritie, and one *Iohn Colet,* who neuer wrote of S. Dionyse. And many others forsooth *graue and learned men.* which if he could haue named, they should haue put to their helping hande, to bolster vp this badde mater, sith that Erasmus writing contra Parisienses, and John Colet be alleged. Had it not bene for shame, he would haue named Peter Martyr, John Caluine, Illyricus, Bale, and such others of his syde, that be not yet canonizate for graue and learned men. If I had done so, he would haue said, I had brought in Mummers. But M. Jewel may pardon himself, and do as him listeth, so he please the people, and kepe his penne and tongue walking, least the plaiers of these new enterludes, should be hissed out of their stage for holding their peace.

Of the Auctoritie of S. Clements Constitutions.

M. Jew. reasōs for the discredite of S. Clements booke.

Phil. 4.

NOw let vs see, what good reason and arguments he bringeth for discredite of these auncient fathers. And first touching S. Clement, of whom S. Paule maketh mention to the Philippians, as of his worke felow, With Clement and with the rest of my worke felowes. The booke of his that I allege for the Sacrifice of the Church, is intituled Constitutiones Apostolicæ, the Constitutions of the Apostles. *But S. Hierome* (saith M. Jewel)

Iewel (*by the report of Eusebius maketh mention* * *only of one Epistle of Clementes, that he thought vvorthy to be receiued. One other Epistle of Clementes he speaketh of, but he saith, it vvas neuer alovved by the church.* For proufe hereof he referreth the readers by his note in ẏ margent to S.Hierome de Eccles.scriptoribus. To this I answere.

Iewel. The.18. vntruth, he maketh mention of more.

Although S.Hierome made mention but of one Epistle written by S.Clement, yet therof it foloweth not, that he wrote no more but that one Epistle. Other men might mention other his workes, as true it is. Now M.Iewel is so bold with S.Hierome in this place, as he is with me oftentimes. For S.Hierom maketh mention of an other boke of S.Clements, which he doth expressely acknowledge to be S.Clementes, and that he was earnestly moued by Gaudentius a bishop, to translate the same into Latine. This shal M.Iewel finde reported by S.Hierome him selfe, in the end of Origens commentaries vpon the Epistle to ẏ Romaines, which he translated into Latine, where he calleth S. Clemēt, Apostolorum Comitem, the Apostles folower or felow, wherof M.Iewel semeth to reproue me. That S.Hierome then maketh mention only but of one Epistle of S.Clement, if by his terme *onely* he exclude al other workes, it is one of the number of M.Iewels manifest and proued vntruthes.

In peroratione trãslatoris. Operum Origenis parte.2.

And further (saith M.Iewel) *S.Hierome saith, certaine other bokes there are reported to be abrode in the name of Clement, as. &c.* Where saith S.Hierome so good syr? you must be staid in your tale at ẏ first I see wel, for if you be let ronne, you wil tel mo lies thē one in a sentence. S.Hierome speaketh but of one boke, why speake you of certaine bokes? Can not your doctrine stand but wt lyes multiplied in the plural number? S.Hierome in dede saith, that the long talke betwen S.Peter and Appion was reported to be S.Clements, & that Eusebius reproued it. And al ẏ I graunt. But what is that to the reproufe of the booke which I alleged?

M.Iew. falsifieth S.Hierome.

Your gentle manner is to deuise weake arguments of your owne mery head, and report them as made by me. This may be sene through your whole Replie. I pray you geue me leaue to requitte you with an argument not deuised by me, but made by your owne selfe. It is euen this. The talke betwen S. Peter and Appion (Eusebius nameth it dialogues) was vntruly reported to be S. Clementes: Ergo, S. Clement wrote not the booke intituled, Constitutionum Apostolicarum. The argument is very folish, yet is it M. Iewels.

τοὺς διαλόγους. *Eccle. hist. lib.3.*

Iewel.

Novv vvhence then commeth M.Hardinges Clement? saith M. Iewel. Thereto he answereth him selfe with such truth as becommeth such teachers. *It vvas founde very lately in the Ile of Candie, by one Carolus Capellius a Venetian, vvritten in Greke, and in these countries * neuer heard of, nor sene before.* His author is Peter Crabbe the gray friere of Machlin. Here he triumpheth, as though he had wonne great honour at my hand, And would nedes the Reader to be iudge in the mater, *vvhether it be likelye, that the bookes of S.Clement being Bishop of Rome, so strange, so holy, of such vveight,* (thus it pleaseth him to scoffe) *vvere kept in an Iland in the Sea, so farre from Italie, and not at Rome. That they vvere vvriten in Greke, not in Latine, that they could be laid vp in secrecie * for the space of a thousand fiue hundred yeres and more, and no man misse them.* Al these thinges he would to be consydered by the Reader, be he neuer so simple.

M. Iew. disprouse of S. Clemēts boke

The. 19. vntruth, for it was both hard of, & sene before.

Iewel.

The. 20. vntruth. they were knowen to ỹ Fathers of most ages, as here it is auouched. where S. Clements booke of late yeres hath ben founde.

Now be the Reader neuer so simple, yet if he be not also wilfully disposed to beleue M. Iewel, when he is proued a lyer: he may easily vnderstand the truth. which touching this boke is this. That Carolus Capellius a Venetian founde a booke in Candie intituled the Constitutions of the Apostles, I deny not. That it was neuer in these countries heard of, nor sene before,

that

that I denye. For as that Venetian founde one booke, so before him other bookes of the same were in the libraries of other men. One hath ben founde of late in that parte of Italie, which is called Calabria, by the learned man Franciscus Turrianus. An other was founde in Cicilia by a learned man named Antonius Augustinus bishop of Ilerda in Spaine. And the same bishop bought an other for his money in Candie, which was a learned mannes booke there named Andreas Donus. which booke he gaue to F. Turrianus, as he taketh record of Zacharias Marapharas a learned Candiote of late Agent in Venis for Ioasaph the Patriarke of Constantinople, whose Greke verses be set before the booke printed in Greke at Venis by Iordanus Ziletus at the procurement of Franciscus Turrianus, who vewed and conferred these bokes together, as he declareth, and so with most diligence hath set it forth to the great commoditie of the church. As these three haue ben kepte in three sundry countries, so there is no doubte, but many moe be kept in other places.

F. Turrianus in Prolegomenis.

Now to M. Iewels substantial argumente.

S. Clement vvas bishop of Rome, ergo it is not likely that his bookes vvere kepte in Candie, and not in Rome. As though bookes made in Rome, or written by the bishops of Rome, were not subiect to fyre and violence of souldiers, at the sundry burninges and sackinges of that Citie, as other bookes and thinges were.

Iewel.

That this booke was laid vp in secrecie for the space of fiftien hundred yeres and mo, so as no man missed it al that while, And that it was neuer heard of nor sene before Carolus Capellius time: al these be false lyes. For the contrary is wel and sufficiently proued, as here the Reader may see, which is already declared by testimonie of S. Hierome before mentioned. The same wil I now proue by testimonies of other writers, which partly be already set forth in latine by Carolus Bouius a Bishop, but

but much more copiously by Franciscus Turrianus in his greke Prolegomena before S. Clement.

Testimonies for S. Clements booke of Constitutions.

First in the Canons of the Apostles alwaies much estemed of the Grekes, expresse mention is made of this very booke with these wordes. Constitutiones, (for so doth the Greke worde διαταγαὶ signifie) quæ vobis episcopis per me Clementem in libris octo nũcupatæ sunt. The constitutions (of the Apostles) haue ben set forth to you the bishops by me Clement in eight bookes. There these wordes folow immediatly. Quas omnibus publicare non oportet, ob quædam arcana quæ in se continent. These Constitutions (saith he) must not be made common to al, because of certaine secret thinges which be conteined in them. And this may be the cause, why this booke hath not ben so common as other bookes, that the mysteries of our religion should not be published to the infidels to be mockt, as our newe Gospellers mocke them at this day. If M. Iewel be loth to allowe the auctoritie of those Canons, as he is a great condemner of bookes, and loth to admitte any for good and authentical that make ought against him: for thapprobation of them, I remit him to Gregorius Haloander of Germanie the interpreter of the same: who sheweth good euidence for their auctoritie in the ende of his Translation. I trust his iudgement shalbe liked the better in this case, because he is no Papist, though in the race of the newe Gospel, he ranne not so farre, as M. Iewel and his companions.

Ad finem capitis. 84. Canonum Apostolicorum.

The cause why S. Clemẽts boke hath ben kept secret.

The auctoritie of these eight bookes conteining the Constitutions or ordinances of the Apostles, is acknowledged and very much vsed for the better disposition of churches, by the holy Martyr S. Ignatius, that was so nye to the Apostles time, as it appeareth by sundry places of his Epistles, which he wrote to sūdry Churches, as he passed forth in his iourney to Rome, there

Ignatius.

to be put to Martyrdom. In which places he letted not to put diuerse sentences of S. Clement, worde for worde, as he had found them in this boke. And though he name him not expresse-ly, as the manner of writers is in allegations, yet he sheweth good and clere euidence, that he meant this very booke of the Apostles Constitutions. To recite here the sentences, which he tooke out of S. Clement for his purpose, it were long and tedious, who is thereof desirous, in the preface of Carolus Bouius set before his Latine translation of the booke, he may see them, and conferre them together.

If M. Iewel denye that S. Ignatius wrote these epistles, as it is his commō shift to denye the Doctor with whose wordes he is manifestly conuinced: may it please him to vnderstand, they wil be auouched and approued by the testimonies of S. Irenæus, S. Athanasius, Eusebius, and specially of S. Hierome.

S. Athanasius that great pillour of the Church in his time, writing to one Ammus, hauing occasion to speake of holy bokes, diuideth them into two orders. In the one he placeth the bokes of the Canonical scriptures, in the other, such as be read and wel estemed, but not equal in auctoritie with the canonical bookes. Making special mention of these thus he saith. I adde this further also, that there be certaine bookes beside these (he meaneth the bookes of the holy Scriptures) which be not approued for Canonical, yet haue ben made of holy fathers like vnto these, and be reade of them that of late came to the faith, and be taught the doctrine of our religion. They be these. The wisedom of Salomon, Syrach, Hester, Iudith, Tobias, et doctrina quæ vocatur Apostolorum, and the boke which is called the doctrine of the Apostles. Whereby he signifieth the Constitutions of the Apostles written by S. Clement, as Zonaras the Greeke expositour of the Canons writeth many to haue said.

Athanasi. in Epist. ad Ammū monachū.

Among other the most auncient Fathers S. Dionysius Areopagita maketh mention of this Clement, calling him a Philosopher, libro de Diuinis nominibus.cap.5. where Pachymeres vnderstandeth him to meane S. Clement of Rome, and that after the minde of the olde interpreters.

Cyrillus Hierosolymitanus Catechesi. 18.

Cyrillus bishop of Ierusalem a Doctor of great antiquitie, in his boke intituled Catheche∫es, maketh mention of this boke of S. Clement, and vseth his auctoritie concerning the reuiuing of the byrde Phœnix for proufe of the resurrection. He letteth not to vse the wordes of S. Clement, as they be written in his fifth booke with very litle alteration. This is to be sene in Cyrillus, Catheche∫i.18.

If M. Iewel with his denying iudgement allowe not this Doctor notwithstanding his antiquitie, because he maketh very much for the veritie of Christes body in the blessed Sacrament: we may proue him by sufficient witnesses. Besides al these which make mention of him, Theodoritus, lib.5.cap.3. Socrates, lib.3.cap.29. Sozomenus, lib.4. cap.25. Epipha.lib.3.tom.1.hære∫. 73. Nicephorus, lib.9.cap.14.&.46. Beside these I say, Theodoritus in polymorpho dialogo.2. doth expressely alleage the Cateche∫es of this auncient Doctor. And so doth Damascenus, lib.3. Apologetico pro Imaginibus.

lib.1.hæres.45.

Epiphanius maketh mention of these Constitutions in diuerse places. In his first booke speaking against the heretikes named Seueriani, he saith thus. If the name of the vine be to be reproued, our Lorde would neuer haue applied vnto him selfe the similitude of that name. Sed etiam Apostoli dicunt in ea quæ dicitur Constitutio, catholica ecclesia est plantatio Dei et vitis. And the Apostles also in that booke which is named their Ordinance, say the Catholike Church is the planting of God and a vine. This is found in the beginning of the Constitutions set

In proœmio.

forth

forth by S. Clement.

S. Chrysostome, or who so euer els was the author of that vnperfect worke vpon S. Mathew, (that very auncient he was certaine it is) in the. 53. Homilie speaketh of this boke expressely, and allegeth the eight booke of the Apostles Canons. *Chrysostõ.*

Of this very booke mentioneth Damascenus, lib. 4. de orthodoxa fide, where he rehersceth the bookes of the holy Scriptures, and nameth S. Clement, as author of these very Canons of the Apostles in this booke conteined. Proclus also the Patriarke of Constantinople, speaking of the tradition of the diuine Sacrifice, acknowlegeth these bookes. Likewise doth Oecumenius in his commentaries vpon the first Epistle to Timothe, and Pachymeres, as is before noted, & Nicolaus also bishop of Methone in Grece, & Marcus Ephesinus, as Carolus Bouius partly allegeth, and the places be commonly knowen. *Damascẽ.* *Proclus.* *Oecumenius.* *Nicolaus Methonẽ.* *Marcus Ephesinus.*

Notwithstanding these proufes and witnesses of good auctoritie, who liued from the Apostles time to our dayes, in sundry ages, and in sundry partes of the world, M. Iewel most shamefully writeth in his Replie, that this booke of S. Clement was neuer heard of, nor sene before. If he may be magnified and accompted for a worthy Iewel of England, hauing made so many, so great, so notorious, so impudent lyes as this is, and as he hath stuffed his Replie withal: what wil he be either afraid, or ashamed to affirme stoutely both in writing and preaching, be it neuer so false? But though he deceiue the vnlearned people, though he be animated and clapped on the shoulders of them of his syde, though el be wel lyked that he doth, of them which would faine al were taken for truth, that is spoken against the Catholikes: yet hath he no regard of that byrde of his owne conscience, which daily singeth him a contrary song? of wise and learned men, who though they be not permitted to speake the truth, yet ful clerely see the truth, and wonder at the outragious impudencie of his lying? of the posteritie, that shal duly examine the pointes, wherin he goeth from truth and reason, and without feare setteth forth to ẏ world both his and his felowes manifold deceites? Verely he semeth to be so farre swallowed vp in ẏ gulfe of vaine glory, that to winne the praises of the light multitude, who measureth these thinges by their wilful phantasies, and to be taken for a worthy captaine of that bande , he sticketh not vtterly to lose the estimation of the grauest, wisest, and best learned, beside the dangerous state of his soule, which is brought into more then most terrible hazard , by deceiuing gods people redemed with so dere a price.

But who so euer they were, that found fault with this boke of S. Clement , yet may the graue iudgement of that auncient and holy Father Epiphanius be set against their opinion . For he denieth that any thing contrary to the faith is in S. Clemẽts bookes conteined . For disputing against the heretikes named Audiani, who fled to the auctoritie of these bookes, thus he saith of them. The Audians do bring forth the Constitution of the Apostles, (so he termeth S. Clementes boke whereof we speake) which by many is doubted of. But for al that it is not to be disallowed. For it hath nothing that is amisse touching faith and confession , neither touching the Ecclesiastical gouernement and rule. Loe by Epiphanius iudgement , there is nothing to be misliked in these Constitutions of the Apostles written by S. Clement, neither for doctrine, nor for Discipline. In which two thinges the Summe of true religion consisteth.

Epiphanius contrà Audianos. hæres. 70.

Thus is our booke of the Apostles Constitutions, that S. Clement wrote, by sufficient witnesses approued . Who is desirous to see further proufes for it , may it please him to read Car. Bouius in præfatione , and F. Turrianus in prolegomenis, there

there shal he finde whereby to be satisfied at large. To M. Iewel what may be said, who hauing a most manifest place for the vnbloudy Sacrifice of the Church laid before him out of this booke, not being hable by anye shifte or colour to auoyd it, thought it to be ẏ surest way to deny the boke? But how impudetly he hath denyed it, this much being knowen, who seeth not?

First whereas he auoucheth, that *S. Hierome by report of Eusebius maketh mention onely of one Epistle of S. Clementes,* there is one vntruth, as now we haue proued out of S. Hierome him selfe, in peroratione ad finem comment. Origenis in Epist. ad Romanos. That S. Hierome saith, *certaine other bookes there are reported to be abrode in the name of Clement, as the disputation of Peter and Appion, vvhich bokes vvere neuer in vse among our fathers, neither cōteine they pure and Apostolical doctrine:* for asmuch as it is alleged to the discredite of the boke of ẏ Constitutions, which is specially spokē of, and S. Hieromes wordes be not so written, * there is the vntruth of a falsifier. That this boke was neuer heard of nor sene before, there is the third vntruth. That it was laid vp in secrecie for the space of a M. v. C. yeres and more, and no man missed it: there is the iiij. vntruth. That it is disallowed by * Euseb. & by S. Hierom, there is the. v. vntruth, for they disallow only the disputatiō betwen S. Peter & Appion. That it was condemned by * Gelasius, there is the sixt vntruth. And beside ẏ dishonesty of a manifest lye, the argument which he maketh, is folish and very childish, which is this. Gelasius condemned itinerarium Petri, a boke falsly fathered vpon S. Clement conteining eight bokes: Ergo he condemned this booke of the Apostles Constitutions conteining also eight bookes. As good an argument as this: The church hath reiected a certaine Epistle reported to be written by S. Paule to the Laodicians: ergo it hath reiected S. Paules Epistle to the Romaines.

Seuen lies made by M. Iew. for disproufe of S. Clements booke.

The. 21. vntruth in falsifying S. Hierome.

The. 22. vntruth, they do not disallow this booke.

The. 23. vntruth. It is not condēned by Gelasius.

Dist. 15. Sancta Romana 1. part.

Lastly, that this booke was kept forth comming in close pryson for the space of. xv. C. yeres, there is the seuenth vntruth.

As for Bessarion, his age is to young, and his auctoritie to light (though otherwise and for his time a worthy mã) to be set in balance against so many fathers, so auncient, so learned, euer had in so much credite. Besyde this it perteined to the furtherãce of the point that there he treated of, to make the least he could of this bookes auctoritie.

But how hangeth this together, this booke was kept in close prison for the space of. xv. C. yeres, yea in these countries he was neuer heard of, nor sene before, as M. Iewel saith: and yet Bessarion who wrote that litle booke de Sacramento Eucharistiæ aboue a C. yeres past, had not only sene it him selfe, but signifieth also, that it was commonly knowen before his time? For so much his wordes doo importe speaking of a custome, which hath relation to the former times.

Commemorari soleant.

Againe if *M. Hardings Clement* (as M. Iewel speaketh) *be disalovved by Eusebius, and by S. Hierome, mystrusted by Bessarion, condemned by Gelasius:* how was he then in these countries neuer heard of nor sene before the late daies of Carolus Capellius the Venetian? Could M. Hardinges Clement be disalowed, mystrusted, and condemned before he was euer sene or heard of? If the booke were disalowed and condemned, then was the boke. For a thing is not condemned, that is not. If it be not, then neither is it condẽned. If then the boke was, in the times of those ỹ spake so against it, how is it true that M. Iewel saith, that it was neuer heard of nor sene? He should better haue remembred the old prouerbe, that requireth a lier to be mindefull.

M. Iew. fowly contrarieth him selfe.

All this being true, S. Clements boke standeth vnshakẽ in his auctoritie as before, notwithstãding M. Iewels. vij. lyes, peuish arguments, & vaine sleights, wherwith he goeth about to deface it,

S. Clemẽt being sufficiently proued to be no

it, specially because of ỷ place for ỷ Sacrifice out of him alleged. which place not being answered, I require him to yelde to the truth by S. Clemēt reported. The wordes be these. Pro Sacrificio cruento rationale & incruentum ac mysticum Sacrificium instituit, quod in mortem Domini per symbola Corporis & Sanguinis ipsius celebratur. For the bloudy Sacrifice (of the old lawe) Christ hath instituted the reasonable, and vnbloudy and mystical Sacrifice, which is celebrated in remēbrance of our Lords death by signes of his Body and Bloud, This Sacrifice can be no other, then the daily Sacrifice of the Church, the oblation of the Body and Bloude of Christ offered by the Priest in the Masse vnder the formes of bread and wine. And thus is al that M. Iewel hath brought against S. Clement either in his glorious Sermon at Paules Crosse, or in his Replie, clerely refelled and wiped away, and the Sacrifice remaineth proued.

counterfet writer, M Iewel is bound by his promise to yeeld and subscribe.

Clemens Constitutionum Apostolicarum lib. 6. cap. 23.

How vntruly and with what smal reason Abdias is reiected of M. Iewel.

What truth M. Iewel hath vsed to deface thautority of S. Clement, the lyke hath he vsed to disproue the booke of Abdias, in which the storie of the Apostles is conteined. First he reproueth me to haue said more of Abdias, then I said in deede, as my booke doth witnesse, which is a great vntruth. For neither say I * that he was conuersant with Christ, nor that he heard Christ preach, but that he saw our Sauiour in flesh, which I found so affirmed both in the preface of Iulius Africanus set before the booke, and also in the booke it selfe. But he belyeth the learned man wolfgangus Lazius much worse, whom he misnameth Zazius, who found this boke in two sūdry aūciēt monasteries. For he maketh him to say

The. 24. vntruth. I saye not so.

Lib. 6.

The. 25. vntruth. Lazius doth not so write.

Iewel. farre otherwise then he saith, * *that S. Luke the Euangelist, vvriting the Actes of the Apostles, borovved many vvhole stories vvorde by vvorde out of Abdias.* And therefore he concluding, as though it were so in deede, sayth, that *then S. Luke vvas vnthankeful, that neuer once made mention of his Author.*

M. Iew. belieth Lazius with an impudent falsifieng.

Now Lazius saith not thus, but speaking of a doubt, that might rise to the Reader, for that many things which be writen in the Actes, be rehearsed in the two first bokes of Abdias: saith that it is to be thought, that either Abdias toke those things out of S. Luke, or S. Luke out of Abdias seing both liued in one time, and were the Apostles Scholers. This is al that Lazius saith touching this point. And why might he not say so? But M. Iewel after his common wont of falsifying, with a shameless lye destroying the disiunctiue, and making a plaine mater of it, affirmeth Lazius to saye, *that S. Luke borovved many vvhole stories vvorde by vvorde out of Abdias.* Thus he belyeth both Lazius and me in the beginning of the disprouse of Abdias.

Abdias was found by three sundry men in three sundry places.

Touching the boke it selfe. Be it of that auctoritie it deserueth to be, and not otherwise. As I am not earnest to defend it, so neither see I any thing brought by M. Iewel for al his great triumph that he maketh thereat, why I should verely beleue that the boke is to be condemned. Neither was it founde out onely by Wolfgangus Lazius in two diuers places, but also by Sebastian Munster being in his company at the one place, who with M. Iewel ought to be a man of good credite, because he hath aduentured th'euerlasting state of his soule by forsaking the Catholike Church, and by going aside with him into Zuinglius sect concerning the heresie of the Sacramentaries. And as Lazius had found two bokes of Abdias, the one in Carinthia the other in Germanie: so long before that, Georgius Wicelius the learned man founde an other copie of the same boke in an o-

Sebastiā Munster

Georgius Wicelius.

ther

ther place, as he writeth in his Epistle dedicatorie to Albertus Archebisshop of Maguntia, which he set before his worke intituled Vitæ Patrum, printed in the same Citie of Maguntia. Anno. 1546. which copie agreeth with the bookes that Lazius founde, as by that which there he writeth, it appeareth. And like it is, the same boke may be founde in sundry other places, if it were with like diligence sought for. In consideration wherof M. Iewel hath to do about the denyal of Abdias, not with me onely, but also with Lazius, with his owne frende Munster, and with Wicelius.

But let vs see what great reasons he allegeth, to disproue Abdias. First, *he maketh many shamelesse lyes,* sayth he, *that he vvas present vvith Christ, and *at the most parte of the Apostles doings, vvhich could not be, they being dispersed abrode so farre asunder into diuers coastes of the vvorld. Againe vvhere he speaketh of Iphigenia, he saith that the people toke her brother Beor christened by S. Mathevv, and made him king, and that he reigned the space of lxiij. yeres. Furthermore he maketh mētion of Egesippus, that liued a hundred and threescore yeres after Christe. And it is not likely, that he liued so long. Therfore he can not be Abdias.* Iewel. The reasōs which M. Iew. bringeth against Abdias. The 26. vntruth. he sayth not so.

Al this is sone answered. That he saw Christe in flesh, M. Iewel saith it is a shamelesse lye. but rather he sheweth himselfe shamelesse so to saye, and not to proue it. Iulius Africanus writeth so of him in his Preface, and as yet M. Iewel bringeth no reason why I should beleue the contrarie. Is that a lye, because M. Iewel saith so? As he geueth to him selfe auctoritie to make lyes, so hath he also auctority to cōdemne whom it pleaseth him of lying? before we beleue this to be a lye, he must bring better proufe then his owne bare worde. Aunswere to the reasons.

That he was at the moste parte of the Apostles doings, I thinke it not true. neither is it necessary to beleeue, that Abdias saith so much of him selfe: neither sayth he so at al. It is a shamelesse lye of M. Iewel so to saye. It may appeare by the booke, that he was present at the death of S. Andrew and of S. Iohn, who died not farre asunder. For Ephesus is not farre from Patræ, as it is euident to those that haue meane skill in Geographie. And their death was so long one after ẏ other, that he had time ynough to be at both. At their deathes he might haue ben present, and at the doings of S. Simon and Iude, and thereof can folow no absurditie, what so euer M. Iewel saye. In dede the boke conteineth a storie of the Apostles actes and doings, but that Abdias was him selfe present at al, it is not so recorded. Yet if he reported more then he sawe, for truth of this mater, this much is to be knowen.

In the time of the Primitiue Church, when in sundry partes of the world great numbres of Christian people wer put to most cruel death by the persecution of Infidels, by common consent in euery countrie some of more learning then the rest, as Priestes and Deacons, were appointed to be publike Notaries, to put in writing and register the worthy fightes of Martyrs, their miracles at their death wrought, and their whole Martyrdomes. These recordes were sent from Church to Church, and diuulged abroad among the seruaunts of God, ẏ therby al might receiue comfort, be stirred to the like constancie by their examples, that those notable actes should be kept in memorie, and that the name of God should be magnified. That this was so obserued, it may be gathered of ẏ Eusebius writeth in the beginning of his fifth boke of the Ecclesiastical historie. So was the glorious death & Martyrdom of S. Andrew writen by ẏ Priests & deacons of Achaia, as Philactetus is reported to witnesse. So were ẏ things done in the cruel persecution of the Christians at Lions, and Vienna, regestred by the learned Notaries, & from the Churches of those cities, sent to the Churches of Asia, and Phrygia, as by Eusebius it is declared. The office of Notaries was instituted at

The office of Notaries in the primitiue Church was to recorde the actes of Martyrs.

lib. 5. hist. Eccles.

at the beginning by diuers Popes, as Damasus writeth in Clemente, in Fabiano, in Anthero. &c.

Such recordes made of the Apostles doings, miracles & deathes, by great probability we ar lead to beleue to haue come vnto the hands of Abdias, & that he made one volume of ẏ whole. In which volume where things are oftentimes reported in the first persō plural, they are not al of necessitie to be referred to Abdias, who was the gatherer of the boke, and so to be vnderstanded, as though he had therby auouched his owne presence at the things so declared: but they may be taken for some part as writen in the person of them that saw them, and were present at ẏ doing, and first registred them. which order of registring Abdias thought good not to alter, but suffered such publike recordes to remaine in the booke which he had compiled in that order reported, in which he founde them by the Notaries first written. As for example, whereas we finde these wordes writen in the fifth booke which is of S. John the Euangelist, where the raising of Drusiana from death is declared, Vidimus, we sawe, and audiuimus, we hearde: it is not necessarie hereof to thinke that Abdias was present at that miracle: (and whether he were or no I say not) but these may seme to be the wordes of the Notaries who wrote them, and were them selues presente, which Abdias in collection of the booke woulde not chaunge, but left them as spoken in their person. And so is Abdias cleered of the shamelesse lye, which he is charged with for that point, as one that of necessitie is not to be called to an accompt, how he could haue seene thinges done by the Apostles (as M. Jewel saith) *in Scythia, in India, in Asia minor, in Ethiopia, that be so many thousand myles asunder.*

That he noteth of Iphigenia, and Beor her brother, who reigned in Ethiopia lxiij. yeares: I maruel what thing therein

 he

he should accompt for a shamlesse lye. May not a man by course of nature lyue so long as by report Abdias Beor lyued? Haue we not in our time sene men of the age of lxxxviij. yeares? For of that age was Beor at his death, by accompt of Abdias. And it is likely that men lyued as many yeares then, as now, when nature is thought somewhat to be decayd from the cōmon strength of that age. If S. Simeon the sonne of Cleopas, and Bishop of Ierusalem next after S. Iames, lyued six score yeares, and notwithstanding ẏ age shewed him selfe to be of so great strēgth at his martyrdome, that all wondred at it, as Egesippus writeth alleged by Eusebius: why might not King Beor lyue lxxxviij. yeres, and raigne lxiij. yeres?

Hist. Eccle. lib. 3. cap. 32. in græc.

But Abdias (saith M. Iewel) maketh mētion of Egesippus which liued eight score yeres after Christ. And there he maketh a ioly triūph. *If he savv Christ, it is not likely that euer he savv Egesippus. If he savve Egesippus, it is not likely that euer he savve Christe.* This absurditie is sone auoyded. In al the booke it is not said, that he sawe Egesippus. Neither maketh he mention of Egesippus. That Egesippus is once in the sixth booke named, that is not to be attributed vnto Abdias, but to Iulius Africanus. Who finding the storie of the Apostles, which Abdias had partly writen in Hebrue him selfe, and partly had gathered into one boke out of the Registres made by the publike Notaries of diuers Churches, translated into Greke by Eutropius his scholer: tourned the same into the Latine tongue, as he saith him selfe, and disposed the whole into ten bokes. Wherin it is very euident, that he bound not him selfe to the scrupulous straightnesse of a translatour, but vsed his owne libertie by putting in, and leauing out at his discretion, what he thought good, so as he might best furnish the Churche with a perfit storie of the

Iewel.

Iul. Africanus in præfatione.

Africanus a [illegible] of Actes & monumē-

Apostles

Apostles. For which cause it may as iustly be accompted the worke of Africanus, as of Abdias. tes of the primitiue Church.

And the writing of such Actes and monumentes of the Primitiue Churche, was belonging to Africanus by profession. For so witnesseth of him Martinus an auncient Chronicle writer. Who describing the times of the Emperour Gordianus the first, saith thus. Floruit his temporibus Iulius Africanus, nominatissimus in Ecclesia scriptor, qui vnà cum alijs notarijs gesta martyrum scripsit, & multa in linguam Latinam traduxit. In these daies lyued Iulius Africanus a very famous writer in the Church, which together with other Notaries wrote the Actes of Martyrs, and translated many thinges into the Latine tongue.

Now if we say that Africanus spake of Egesippus, and not of Abdias, then hath this fierce accuser of Abdias nothing, wherewith to charge him as a lyer in that behalf. If M. Iewel, or who so euer vewed the booke of Abdias for him, had reade a fewe leaues farther, in the same sixth booke he shoulde haue founde the name also of Africanus him selfe, who though he be very auncient, yet lyued longe after Egesippus. And so he might haue made a more probable argumēt against Abdias in consideration of his age, and much better haue compared him with Ioannes de temporibus.

The mention of both may resonably be thought to haue ben put in by Africanus. Neither is it very straunge a writer of Stories sometimes to mention him selfe by name. Neither nameth he Egesippus onely alleging that he wrote touching Sainte Iames, but also Sainte Clement, and Craton, whose tenne bookes conteyning the Actes of Saint Simon and Saint Iude, he turned into the Latine speache speach, as there he saith.

That it was not impossible for Abdias to haue sene Egesippus.

And wheras M. Iewel would seme to conclude a great absurditie against Abdias, for saing that he saw Egesippus, affirming that he sawe Christe, it is not likely that euer he sawe Egesippus, and if he sawe Egesippus, it is not likely that euer he sawe Christe: If one would tel him, that Abdias might haue sene both Christ and Egesippus to, so farr as the likelyhod therof could be proued, then were he controlled, as one that maketh triumph before he acheue the victorie. That Abdias notwithstanding he had sene Christe in fleshe, might also haue sene Egesippus, thus it is proued. If S. James might haue sene Egesippus, thē why might not Abdias also haue sene him, specially wheras by report of Julius Africanus calling him ye Apostles scholer, he semeth to haue ben younger man then the Apostles. That S. James might haue sene him, it is proued by Egesippus owne wordes, who speaking of S. James, saith that he continewed from the time it selfe that our Lorde lyued in, vntil his time, for so be his very wordes, ab ipsis Domini temporibus perdurans vsque ad nos. But herein I stand not with M. Iewel, for I iudge that in dede Abdias neuer sawe Egesippus, specially as a writer of the thinges in the booke of Abdias alleged. Yet his rashnes is to be noted, that writeth so peremptorily of a thing, the contrary whereof may so probably be auouched.

Egesip. in quinto Cōmentariorū.

Touching the mater of the booke, if it be nothing els for the more parte of it, as M. Iewel saith, *but a vaine peuish tale, laid out vvith falshed, vvicked doctrine, and curious conference, and talke vvith Deuils:* Why was M. Iewel so peeuish as to condemne it hauing so great store of mater against it, without shewing reasō, learning or authoritie of some due allegation? If he accuse it of falshed and wicked doctrine, why did he not shewe to the world (specially seing that he made so much a doo about it at

Iewel. A heape of lies.

Paules

Paules Crosse in that vaine forerunning Sermon of his) what be pointes of falshed, and wicked doctrine that he noted? Is it ynough for M. Iewel only to say so? Thinketh he that men wil beleue him because he speaketh the word? May ought he not rather to thinke, that whatsoeuer he saith besides and contrary to other men, that it wil the lesse be beleued, because he saith it? verely if the vnlerned knew his custom of lying, as wel as lerned men see it manifestly: they would hardly beleue him, when he telleth truth.

For better commoditie of my vtterance, and to the intent al may the better be vnderstanded, euen there in the middes of the matter of Abdias, I craue leaue of the Reader to beare with me, if I alter some what the order of my talke, and from hence forth for the auoyding of the tedious rehersal of I say, and M. Iewel saith, put both our two names before both our sayenges. And euen here to beginne (oure former matter of Abdias being continewed) let it be consydered, what reason and authorities he bringeth for discredit of Abdias.

Ievvel.

*It may be gathered by S. Augustine in sundry places, that * some parte of this booke vvas vvritten by certain Heretikes named the Manichees, and auouched by them as the very true Storie of the Apostles.*

The 27. vntruth. S. Augu. hath no such thing of Abdias

Aug. contra Faustum. lib. 11. & lib. 22. cap. 80.

Harding.

It is not true that you saye M. Iewel. S. Augustine writeth not so much as one worde of this booke of Abdias, nor maketh he any mention at al of Abdias throughout his whole workes . And whereas you haue noted the margent of your booke, with this quotation, *August. contra Faustum. lib. 11.* reade ouer that booke who will , and he shal finde no worde spoken whereby it may be gathered this booke of Abdias after the opinion of S. Augustine, to haue been written by the Manichees . By this your vntrue dealing shal appeare to your vtter discredit. Now let the proufe of your saying be heard and discussed.

Ievvel.

The, 28. vntruth. The. 29. vntruth. He reporteth it not The. 30. vntruth. Not in such order

*For he reporteth the Fables of S. Thomas, * of S. Mathevv, of * S. Andrevv, of the Lion that slue the man that had striken S. Thomas, of the dogge that brought the same mannes hande vnto the table: of Maximilla vvife vnto Egis, and other like tales, * euen in such order as they be set forth by this Abdias.*

Harding.

Marke wel good Reader how reasonably M. Jewel proueth that he affirmed. Because he setteth forth in his Replie many folish arguments, fathering the same vpō me, which I make not, as by cōference of the place it may appeare: I thinke good here truly to put before thine eyes his argument, making it no worse then it is. The same is this.

S. Augustine reporteth the fables of S. Thomas, of S. Mathevv, of S. Andrevv, of Maximilla. &c: Ergo it may be gathered of S. Augustine, that some parte of this booke vvas vvritten by the Manichees.

Both to the Learned there appeareth smal Logike, and to a natural man smal reason in this argument. And yet is it M. Jewel that made it, who scoffeth so much at other mennes arguments. As great a Clerke as he is taken to be of his own deceaued brethren, yet in this point, as he sheweth him selfe weake in reason, so also slender in knowledge . For he findeth not in S. Augustine in the places by him alleged , that the Manichees, (who

M. Jew. sheweth his ignoraunce.

condemned

condemned the bookes of the Olde Testament, and receaued some partes of the new Testament, such as they liked, affirming the rest to be corrupted and falsified) leaned to the authoritie of bookes by them selues written, requiring them to be esteemed as equal with the Scriptures, or that they hadde written the bookes, which as S. Augustine saith, they preferred before the Scriptures, but that they had Scripturas Apocryphas, that is, such writings as were neuer brought forth into open light, and approued by authentical witnesse, written by others of olde time, which they alleged, and pretended to be as autentical as the true Scriptures, and would their Scholers to beleeue, that they were written by the Apostles. This much maist thou find good Reader in the. 22. booke of S. Augustine, Contra Faustum Manichæum, in the 79. chapter, and not in the chapter. 80. as M. Iewel hath falsely quoted.

Aug. de hæresib. ad Quodvultdeum hær. 46. de utilit. credendi ad honor. c. 2. Ad Quoduultdeum. Aug. cōtra Faust. lib. 11. cap. 2.

The summe of that I say, is this. By report of S. Augustine the Manichees had, and did read Secret & vnallowed scriptures, writtē vnder the name of the Apostles. That thei wrote such Scriptures or bookes them selues, this S. Augustine saith not. As for this boke of Abdias, or any part of it, that it should be written by the Manichees, and auouched by them, as the true storie of the Apostles: it can not be gathered by S. Augustine, that he did euer so much as once dreame of it.

Examination of M. Iew. vntrue sayings.

But by examination of M. Iewels sayings, his falshed is to be detected. First he saith, that *S. Augustine reporteth the fables of S. Thomas, S. Mathevv, S. Andrevv, of the Lion, of the Dogge, and of Maximilla, and other like tales, euen in such order, as they be set forth by this Abdias.* If this be true M. Iewel, I am content Abdias be taken for a fabler, which thing if it wer so, yet my answere to your chalenge standeth in force, and is not yet by you disproued. For I stande not vpon the auctoritie of Abdias, as I sayde before, neyther haue I alleged him for priuate Masse, but as you know for the Sacrifice in general.

Augustinus contra Faustum. lib.22.cap 79.& cõtra Adimantum. cap.17.

In deede S. Augustine speaketh of S. Thomas, how a Lion had killed a man whom he cursed, for that he had striken him on the head at a mariage dinner, and how a dogge brought that mannes hande vnto the table. And al this is but one mater which M. Iewel by putting in the names of S. Mathew, and of S. Andrew, hath so diuided, and otherwise dilated, as the Reader can conceiue none other, but that they are sundry narrations. That which S. Augustine telleth of Maximilla the wife of Egetes out of the Secrete Scriptures, is an other mater. To these two I haue to answere.

A false deuise put in by M. Iewel.

As for the fables of S. Mathew, and S. Andrew, I know not what fables he meaneth. It is a thing deuised of his owne fabling heade. Verely S. Augustine in those places reporteth no such thing. But where M. Iewel lacked good matter, he thought best to make vp a shew of somewhat though it neuer were done, nor imagined to be done. That false deuise I leaue to M. Iewel to answere vnto, and before al true men I charge him with the false inuention of it. By this shuffling in the names of S. Mathew and S. Andrew, he thought to discredite the Sacrifice of the Masse reported by them to haue ben done. He wil litle spare to belye me, I see wel, sith that he sticketh not to belye that most learned and holy Father S. Augustine. what manner of lye I shal cal this I wot not. But it is a very great falshed.

Contra Faustum lib.22.cap 79.

S. Augustine speaketh of

S. Augustine disputing against the Manichees, alleging certain Secret and vnallowed scriptures, writtẽ vnder the name of the Apostles (of which sort the storie of Abdias is not, for it beareth not the name of any Apostle, but of Abdias, and of Iulius Africanus the interpreter) telleth, that it is written in a boke of such scriptures, that S. Thomas the Apostle, at a mariage

riage feast cursed a seruaunt that had stricken him on the head, which seruaunt was slaine by and by of a Lion, as he went forth to a wel to draw water, and a dogge brought his hande being rent from the body to the table where ꝧ Apostle sate. But as the holy Apostle by his curse procured him outward punishment of his person, so he prayed for him to be forgeuen euerlastingly in the worlde to come, whereby a recompense of a greater benefite was made.

such bookes as beare the name of som of the Apostles of whiche sorte this booke of Abdias is none.

This is that which M. Iewel calleth a false fable. And because the same is found in Abdias, he wil neede haue al to be false, what so euer is conteined in that whole storie, touching the blessed Sacrifice of the Church. Now whereas M. Iewel allegeth S. Augustine for his purpose, reason would, he should folow S. Augustine, and not go beyond S. Augustine. This is a false fable saith M. Iewel, & to that purpose he calleth to witnesse S. Augustine. But S. Augustine refuseth so to say, Vtrū (saith he) illa vera sit aut conficta narratio, nihil mea nunc interest. whether it be a true or a fained tale, here I force not. Againe within fewe lines, he refuseth to determine, siue hoc verum sit, siue confictum, whether this be true or fained. If he had thought it had ben a false fable, he would not so haue spoken of it. he leaueth it as a thing neither to be taken as a written truth of Scripture, nor as a manifest vntruth. I doubt not but who so euer shal weigh this indifferently, he wil assone incline to the modestie of S. Augustine, as to M. Iewels rashnes, who condemneth that, which S. Augustine woulde not condemne, but rather semed to acknowledge for truth. For els whereto perteine those woordes, which he putteth there, Tenebat certe interius dilectionis affectum, & exterius requirebat correctionis exemplum, Verely S. Thomas inwardely kept the affect of loue, and outwardly required an example of correction? Fur-

S. Augustines modestie, M. Iew. rashnes. S. Augustine semeth to acknowledg this parte of Abdias storie to be true.

thermore there he saith, that by this example, the Manichees be compelled to acknowledge and graunt the vertue of patience to haue ben in the Apostle. It had ben vaine for S. Augustine to say thus, if he had thought al to be a lye, as M. Jewel doth.

Not what so euer is reported in Secret & vnknowen scripturs, is to be estemed as false.

The most ẏ he can say in reprouf of this thing, is ẏ it is reported in Secret & vnallowed Scriptures. This much I graūt. Yet is not ẏ an argument to proue it to be a false fable. for in the Secrete Scriptures also, which are called Apocryphæ Scripturæ, many thinges be tolde, that be true: as we find in Nicodemus Gospel and in the boke named Pastor, which was in the Primitiue Churche estemed for the instruction of the learners of our faith, almost equal with the Canonical Scriptures. Yea if al thinges were to be cōdemned as vntrue, ẏ be written in ẏ Secret Scriptures, then should we condemne the most and chief partes of the Gospel. Etsi (saith S. Augustine) in Apocryphis aliquā veritas inueniatur, tamen propter multa falsa aut suspecta, nulla est Canonica auctoritas. As much to say. Although in the Secret writinges some truth be found, yet becanse of many thinges which be false, or suspect, there is in them no Canonical authoritie. That Abdias be taken for Canonical scripture, therof I cōtend not. Things by him reported may be true, though his authoritie be not canonical, that is to say, of auctoritie as the Scriptures. Wherefore sith this storie reported of S. Thomas, by S. Augustins iudgment conteineth example of patience, and of charitie, and M. Jewel hath neither reason, nor learning wherby to proue it false: it is not against the dignitie of the Apostles, that it be thought to be true, and that, notwithstanding any thīg in the same reported, Abdias, or rather Julius Africanus, be admitted to be reade as a true writer.

Aug. lib. 1. cont. Aduers. legis & prophet. cap. 20.

That a Secret booke of the actes of S. Thomas was extant in olde time, it appeareth in that we finde by the Storie of his life. For whosoever was the author of it, he writeth of a booke wherein was declared his iourney into India, and his doinges there. But because the same was not receiued of some, for the superfluitie of wordes: he promiseth to omitte thinges that be of no effect, and to recorde those thinges, that be most certeinly true, and acceptable to the readers, and may edifie the Churche. Lib.9.

By this Author, what other thinges soeuer written in that booke were vntrue, yet this narration of S. Thomas, of the Lion, and of the mannes hande, is accompted true. Yet whether they be true or no, it forceth not greatly. I am content to suspende my iudgement therein, as S. Augustine doth. As I thinke not good with vehement asseueration to auouch it, so I dare not denie it. whether it be true or false, therby the Catholike doctrine concerning the Sacrifice is not impugned, for witnesse whereof amonge many others, Abdias was alleged. Now to the other tale of Maximilla and Euclia.

this story of S. Thomas auouched to be true.

Ievvel.

In an other place S. Augustine saith, Attendite qualia sint, quę scribuntur de Maximilla vxore Egetis, illam noluisse viro debitũ reddere, donasse & supposuisse Eucliam ancillam, & alias similes fabulas. *Behold vvhat thinges they be that be vvriten of Maximilla, vvife to Egis that she (being once christened) vvould nomore yeld dutie to her husband, but set Euclia her maide in her ovvne place, and other like fables. * Al these and such like tales thus disalovved by S. Augustine, are reported by M. Hardings Abdias in great sooth.*

Aug. de fide contra Manich. cap. 30.

M. Iew. falsifieth S. Aug. The. 31. vntruth. these tales be not reported by Abdias. let ye boke be trial.

Harding.

First M. Iewels quotatiõ is false. This tale of Maximilla

wife to Egetes (for so of S. Augustine he is called and not Egis) is not touched of him in his booke de fide contra Manichęos cap.30. but capite 38. Neither be these the wordes of S. Augustine, which M. Jewel here hath put, but other, and otherwise placed. Because if he had alleged the wordes as they be in S. Augustine, they wold haue disclosed his falshed and dasshed his cause: he thought it better to vse his accustomed sleight in falsifying the place, by chaunging the wordes, by cutting some awaye, and by putting in other of his owne, that so he might frame the whole to his purpose, then with plaine and vpright dealing to allege the Doctor as he speaketh.

S. Aug. findeth not fault with Abdias, but one Leucius.

S. Augustines wordes be spoken specially vnto the Manichees, who regarded certaine Secrete Scriptures more then holy Scriptures. And in that place he telleth expresly, who was the author of this tale of Maximilla and Euclia, not Abdias, but one Leucius. His wordes begin thus. Attendite in actibus Leucij, quos sub nomine Apostolorũ scribit, qualia sint quę accipitis de Maximilla uxore Egetis: &c. Consider ye (saith S. Augustine to the Manichees) in the actes of Leucius, which he writeth vnder the name of the Apostles, what things they are, which ye receiue touching Maximilla the wife of Egetes: which when as she would not render dutie to her husband, whereas the Apostle hath saide, Let the man render dutie to his wife, likewise also the wife to her husband: She set her maide named Euclia in her place, decking her, as it is writen there, with vnhousewifely trickes and trinkets, and placing her in her own stede, to the intent he not witting of it, should lye with her as with his wife. These be the very wordes of S. Augustine there, as also certaine other declaring very fond and vaine thinges to be writen in that vnlawfull and secret boke, called ỹ acts of Leucius, or rather of ỹ Apostles writẽ

Au. de fide cõtra Manichæos. cap.38.

1. Cor. 7.

of

of Leucius vnder the name of the Apostles, which the Manichees so much esteemed.

Now if M. Iewel or any man of his side finde this fable of Maximilla, and this bawdrie of her reported in al the booke of Abdias: I wil say that in this point he is a true man, and hath great aduantage against Abdias. But if there be no such thing, nor likelihod of any such thing there, as I am sure there is not: then must it folowe that Abdias is not hereby disproued, and that M. Iewel is a great lyer, for saying these wordes, *Al these and such like tales thus disalovved by S. Augustine, are reported by M. Hardinges Abdias in great sooth.* what is impudent lying, if this be not? *lib. 3. Abdiæ.*

By Abdias Maximilla is reported to haue ben a very godly woman, that she was a diligent hearer of S. Andrewes preachinges, that she buried his body after his Martyrdome, and that she continewed a faithful woman. Of Euclia her maid, and of denying dutie to her husband contrarie to S. Paules wordes, and of that filthy placing of her maide in her owne steede: in all Abdias there is not so much as one worde, nor is Euclia by him so much as once named. If any frende of M. Iewel beleue me not, let him peruse the storie of Abdias, and he shal fynde, whether of vs both is to be charged with this lowde lie. And if he be found a shamelesse lyer in this, why should he be credited in other pointes, wherein he goeth from the catholike Church? yet *al these* (saith he) *and such like tales thus disallovved by S. Augustine, are reported by M. Hardinges Abdias in great sooth.*

Maximilla what a womā she was by report of Abdias.

This is one of M. Iewels impudent lyes, that by no shift cā be iustified.

If Leucius were Abdias, or if Abdias whom I alleged, were Leucius, and had written the thinges which S. Augustine reproueth as fables: then had M. Iewel some truth on his side. But now sith it is, as it is, his lye is to shamelesse, and by no colour can be coue red, or excused. If he had me at this aduantage, both his booke should proclaime it to my discredite, and

Paules crosse should ring of it. But with him I trowe men beare the more, because he doth no otherwise, then he is wont to do, As it shal hereafter further appeare.

Ievvel.

The.32. vntruth S. Augustine can not seme to wryte thus of Abdias. *August. cōtra aduersar. legis & prophet. lib. 1. cap. 20.*

S. Augustine semeth in diuerse places to haue geuen his iudgement of this booke, vvriting against the aduersarie of the lavve and prophetes, he hath these vvordes. He hath brought forth vvitnesses out of Secrete scriptures vnder the names of the Apostles, Iohn and Andrevv, vvhich vvritinges if they had ben theirs, they had ben receiued of the Church.

Harding.

This place of S. Augustin speaketh of bookes set forth vnder the name of S. John, & S. Andrew, and therfore it perteineth not to M. Jew. purpose agaīst Abdias.

What meaneth M. Jewel to allege this place of S. Augustine? what maketh it against Abdias? would he men to thinke that S. Augustine meant, that Abdias hath brought forth witnesses out of Secrete Scriptures, or that the boke of Abdias is that, which S. Augustin calleth secrete scriptures there? If M. Jewel thought to make mē beleue that, thē should he haue vsed his olde crafte, and clipped away from the sentence, those wordes of S. Augustine, sub nominibus Apostolorum Andreæ Ioannisq; conscripta, wherby he doth al men to vnderstand, that those Testimonies which the heretike brought forth in his booke, were said to be written vnder the names of the Apostles S. Andrew, and S. Jhon.

Now neither the booke that beareth the name of Abdias, or rather of Julius Africanus the Translatour and disposer of it, as it appeareth, nor no parte of it, is set forth vnder the names of those Apostles S. Andrew and S. John. And therfore this place of S. Augustine serueth M. Jewel to no purpose, but onely

onely to dasel the eyes of them, that can not wel discerne his false sleightes.

For I graunt, if the thinges in that booke written, had ben written by S.Andrew and S.John, then doubtles the Church had receiued them as holy scriptures.

But as here M.Iewel alleged a peece of a Sentence out of S.Augustine, which he would seme to serue his purpose, and serueth not in deede: so would God he had alleged the whole Sentence, as it is written of S.Augustine, and would allow and beleue the same, which euidently ouerthroweth al his and his felowes false doctrine. The sentence is this.

Augustinus ibidem

Quæ si illorum essent, recepta essent ab Ecclesia, quæ ab illorum tẽporibus ꝑ Episcoporũ successiones certissimas, vsq; ad nostra & deinceps tẽpora perseuerat. &c. If these testimonies had ben theirs, (S.Andrewes and S.Johns) they had ben receiued of the Churche, which Churche contineweth by most certaine successions of Bishops, from their time to our time, and so afterward. &c.

By S. Augustin the church cõtinueth by moste certaine successiõs of bishops. wher thẽ is this new Geneuian Church?

In which wordes S. Augustine doth acknowledge the continuance of the Churche by most certaine successions of bishops, from the Apostles time foreward to the ende of the worlde. These wordes are wel to be noted, which being true, do proue these new Gospellers Doctrine to be false, and their Congregation to be no Church of Christe, but the Synagogue of Antichriste. For they are not hable to proue the continuance either of their Doctrine, or of their Churche, by successions of Bishops, which by S.Augustines iudgement ought to be most certaine.

But what continuance of successions of Bishops can they shewe for proufe of their Churche, who acknowledge it to haue ben begon by Martine Luther, and Huldrike Zwinglius about fifty yeres past, as in the Apologie of their church they protest, and haue no number of bishops to shewe, in whom and by whom their successions haue alwayes continewed? Of this mater I haue spoken in my Confutation of their Apologie: to the places where I treate thereof I remit the reader. But let nothing passe that M. Iewel bringeth for disprouse of Abdias, least he charge me with vntrue dealing, as I charge him. In his Replie thus it foloweth.

In the Confutation. fol. 15, b. 42. 57. a 129. b. &c.

Iewel.

*The like iudgement hereof semeth to be geuen by * Gelasius, vvho also saith that such vvritinges, according to an auncient custome, and by a singular prouision, vvere not reade in the churche of Rome, for that they vvere thought to be vvritten by heretikes.*

The. 33. vntruth. Gelasius meaneth no such thing touching Abdias.

Harding.

Seming and being is not one. If al were true, that to M. Iewel semeth true, then were many Heresies true doctrines, many lyes true reportes. Neither saith Gelasius, as M. Iewel allegeth him. He speaketh of certaine actes of Martyrs written by men, whose names be not knowen, which were thought to be written by Infidels, and there he nameth the passions of one Quiricus, and of Iulita his mother. Also certaine other thinges, as the passions of S. George, and of others, quæ ab hæreticis probantur conscriptæ, which passions are tried out (saith Gelasius) to haue ben written by heretikes. But seing that the boke of Abdias is neither thought to be written by Infidels, nor tryed to be wrytten by Heretikes, as neither Maister Iewel nor any of his syde can proue it: the place of Gelasius maketh nothing for his purpose. And so Abdias may be reade of catholike

Gelasius maketh no direct prouse against Abdias.

Distinct. 15 Sancta Romana.

like men, as Gelasius there would certaine writinges to be read with this caution and proviso, that when they come to catholike mennes hands, the sentence of the most blessed Apostle S. Paule goe before, Omnia probate, quod bonum est tenete, Proue ye al thinges, kepe that which is good. Here wil I put in M. Iewels conclusion touching Abdias, and then an ende of this mater. 1. Thes. 5

Ievvel.

*Thus is this Abdias a booke as it is apparent, ful of manifest lyes, and as it may be supposed * by S. Augustine and Gelasius, vvritten and fauoured by Heretikes, and refused of the churche: vpon such a one, good reader, M. Harding vvil haue thee to stay thy faith.*

The. 34. vntruth. A burthen of vntruthes, neither by S Augustin nor by Gelasius, is this supposed, as now I haue proued.

Harding.

Thus hath M. Iewel neither proued Abdias to haue written so much as one lye, much lesse to be ful of manifest lyes: nor can it iustly be supposed by S. Augustine or Gelasius, that the booke is written or fauoured by heretikes. Neither wil I thee good reader to stay thy whole faith chiefly vpon Abdias, nor to that purpose did I allege him: but only, for that he semed very auncient, by his testimonie, as by many others, to shewe vnto the studious Reader, where to finde mention made of the vnbloudy Sacrifice of the Church, and of the celebration of the holy Mysteries. which thing is otherwise so wel proued, that we nede not the witnesse of Abdias. whether his auctoritie be admitted or refused, to me it skilleth litle. Only I thought good to shewe, that for any thing M. Iewel hath yet said, who hath both in his Replie written, and at Paules Crosse scoffed much at him, he is not iustly disproued.

As for thy faith good reader, I aduise thee not to staie it vpon

Abdias, nor vpon M. Iewel, nor vpon me: but vpon the worde of God, that is to say, vpon that Doctrine which the holy Ghoste hath taught the Catholike Churche, and vpon those and other holy Fathers, so farre as their doctrine agreeth with the doctrine of the Catholike Churche, which Churche as S. Paule saith, is the pillour and sure staye of truthe. And this much hitherto of Abdias. Now let vs see what M. Iewel bringeth for disprouse of certaine other doctours by me alleged for the Sacrifice of the Church.

1. Tim. 3.

Of S. Martialis.

Ievvel.

The. 35. vntruth, It could be read, els how could it be printed?

*Martialis vvas lately founde in Fraunce in the Citie of Lemouica, in an arche of stone vnder the grounde, so corrupte and defaced, that in many places it could not * be reade, and vvas neuer sene in the vvorlde at any time before.*

Harding.

If S. Martialis booke of Epistles could not haue ben read, it could not haue ben Printed. M. Iewel found it thus writ-ten of those Epistles, præ nimia vetustate vix legi potuerunt, for very oldenesse they could scantly be reade: and by making a lye for aduantage, he had rather say it could not be reade. So by his profession oftentimes somewhat is made nothing, and no-thing is made somewhat. That it was neuer sene in the world at any time before, it is rather said then proued. Verely Grego-rius Turonensis an auncient writer recordeth, that S. Martialis was sent to be bishop to them of Lemouica, and that he lyued in great holinesse, and after that he had wonne many folkes to the Churche, and set abrode the faith of Christ, he departed this life in

In libro apud Henricū Petri Basileæ ædito, anno. 1555. Historiarum lib. 1. cap. 30.

in a blessed confession. In the booke intituled Orthodoxographa printed at Basile, where M. Iewels Sacramentarie doctrine was specially taught by Friere Oecolampadius commonly named Friere Huskin, the iudgement of a learned man concerning S. Martialis Epistles is declared with these wordes. The two Epistles of Martialis seme to be written at the imitation of S. Paule. Verely they be worthy to be reade, they are founde to sauer of the spirite of God. Who despiseth to see more of S. Martialis, may he reade Antonius Demochares. tom. 2. cap. 25. Petrus de Natalibus. lib. 6. cap. 29. Henricus Mauroy in prima parte Apologiæ pro Iudæis in Archiepiscopum Toletanum. cap. 34.

Of S. Dionysius the Areopagite.

Ievvel.

*Dionysius although he be an auncient vvriter as it may many vvaies vvel appeare, yet it is iudged by Erasmus * Iohn Colet, and others many * graue and learned men, that it can not be Areopagita S. Paules disciple, that is mentioned in the Actes.*

The. 36. vntruth. It is not so iudged by Iohn Colet.

The. 37. vntruth. There be no such graue and learned men.

Harding.

The wordes of S. Dionysius be so plaine for the blessed Sacrifice of the church, for which I alleged him, that M. Iewel not being hable by any shifte to auoide them, thought best to demnish his auctoritie. And therefore though he confesse him to be an auncient wryter, for which he is worthy no thankes, yet is he loth to take him for the Areopagite S. Paules scholer. *That it is not he, it may be iudged* (saith he) *by Erasmus, Iohn Colet, and others many graue and learned men.* If it be so, why did he not allege them? Why doth he not tel vs who they be, and where they pronounce such iudgment of S. Dionysius?

Here M. Iewel bringeth not forth his Mummers, but telleth vs of Mummers. Truly that is but a common shift of his, when authorities and euident proufes faile him, yet to pretende number, where one moe can not be named. As for Iohn Colet, he hath neuer a worde to shew, for he wrote no workes. If he said it at his table, or in a sermon, as M. Iewel perhappes hath heard saye: the proufe is of small auctoritie. we admit not the trial of hearesaies. As for Erasmus iudgement, we see it not greatly estemed among the best learned men, either for sundry his censures of wryters, or for any weighty point of learning besides touching Diuinitie.

Iohn Colet.

Erasmus.

But M. Iewel I suppose, by his graue and learned men meaneth Bale, Hooper, Cranmare, Caluine, Peter Martyr, and such others of that syde. For Peter Martyr would not this S. Dionyse to be the Areopagite S. Paules Disciple, but some other of later age. Neither is it likely (saith he) his workes to haue ben much estemed in old time, seing that beside Gregory a Latine man, none of the olde fathers euer alleged them. How true this is, ful wel it shal appeare vnto the Reader, that listeth to reade that auncient Doctor Origen. homilia. 2. in diuersos. where he is cited, and named Magnus Dionysius Areopagita, great Dionise the Areopagite.

Petrus Martyr in comment. in. 1. Cor. 15. fol. 413.

That S. Dionysius was the Areopagite, S. Paules scholer.

Origens wordes be these, after the Latine translation. In ipso enim vt os loquitur diuinûm, viuimus, mouemur, & sumus: & vt ait Magnus Dionysius Areopagita, esse omnium est superessentia, & diuinitas. In Greke thus. τὸ γὰρ εἶναι πάντων ἐστὶν, ἡ ὑπὲρ τὸ εἶναι θεότης. i. esse omnium est super essentiam diuinitas. These wordes are to be founde in S. Dionysius, Cælestis Hierarchiæ. cap. 4. The auncient Father Dionysius Alexandrinus wrote Annotations vpon the workes of S. Dionysius Areopagita, which be alleged by Maximus and Pachymeres, in their greke

briefe

briefe Commentaries. The learned Fathers assembled at the vi. Councel of Constantinople allege this auncient father, calling him S. Dionyse the Areopagite Bishop of Athens. Of him also speaketh Liberatus an olde wryter, Breuiarij cap.10.

So he is alleged of Damascenus de orthodoxa fide.lib 3. cap.6. where he is named by expresse wordes, Pauli discipulus, deifer, & circa diuina plurimus, Dionysius Areopagita. S. Paules disciple, the godly and great Diuine, Dionysius the Areopagite. Of S. Gregorie he is called, Dionysius Areopagita antiquus & venerabilis pater. Dionyse Areopagite, the auncient and reuerent father. In euangelia.homil.34.

And how can he seme to any man but very auncient, sith that he wrote certaine thinges to S. Timothe S. Paules scholer, to Tite and Caius, and to S. John the Euangelist? To proue his antiquitie, and that he was S. Paules disciple the Areopagite, If I thought it nedeful, and thereby should not to wise men seme ambitious, I would here allege no smal number of good authorities both of Greke and Latine wryters. These few now may wel suffice. So then is S. Dionysius Areopagita S. Paules disciple an vncontrolled witnesse of the blessed Sacrifice, and such as M. Jewel, nor any other Sacramentarie can take exception against.

Of S, Iames Masse, or Liturgie.

Ievvel.

S Iames Liturgie hath a special prayer for them that liue in Monasteries : and yet it vvas very rathe to haue Monasteries builte in al. S. Iames time.*

*The. 38. vntruth. There is no mentiō of such monasteries, as we cōmonly meane, when we speake of monasteries.

Harding.

A man can not wel tel, where to haue M. Jewel. For here he condemneth the auctoritie of S. James Masse or Liturgie, as a thing forged, and none of his, for that *he hath a special prayer*

M. Iew. both alloweth & disaloweth S. Iames Masse.

for them (as he saith) *that liue in Monasteries.* which he supposeth not to haue ben builte so rathe. And within a fewe sentences in the very same side of the leafe, as though he had forgoten him selfe, he alloweth S. Iames Liturgie, and allegeth it for proufe of the Cōmunion. Likewise in ÿ printed Sermon of his Chalēge he sticketh not to name it S. Iames Masse, and taketh ÿ same as of good auctoritie, wher he saith expressely, ÿ *S. Iames said his Masse in the cōmon tōgue, as the people might vnderstand him,* which is more thā he is able to proue, for it is writtē in greke, which was not ÿ peoples vulgare tōgue of Ierusalē. Item ÿ *S. Iames Masse vvas full of knovvledge.* That *vvhen S. Iames said Masse, the people resorted to receiue the sacrament.* That *S. Iames in his Masse had Christes Institution.* Al this saith he there. Yet here because I alleged it for witnesse of the Sacrifice, he reiecteth it, for hauing mention of Monasteries. Thus he admitteth and refuseth what him listeth, as any thing maketh for him, or against him.

M. Iew. is cōtrary to himself.

M. Iew. verdite of S. Iames Masse.

But if he be tolde, that S. Iames maketh no special prayer for them that lyue in Monasteries after his meaning, as truth it is that he doth not: what hath he then to say? what other shifte wil he deuise? For S. Iames Masse must not be admitted, what euer be said, because therby the vnbloudy Sacrifice is auouched. And not only that, but also prayer vnto our Lady S. Mary, and prayer for the dead. If he meane by the name of Monasteries, such houses of religious men and women, as the sprite of their newe gospel hath of late yeres throwen downe in sundry places of Christendome: as I graunt that such were not so rathe builte, I meane as they be considered with their rich endowmentes, landes, and all commodities, as we haue sene in England, so I affirme that S. Iames speaketh neuer a worde of them. Perhaps that he might seme to say somewhat against whatsoeuer is broght for proufe of the Sacrifice, he was content to abuse some

S. Iames Masse is quite contrary to the new Gospel.

Monasteries.

Latine

Latine translation, whereas the Greke original hath no suche thing at al.

In dede S. James in his Masse or Liturgie maketh a praier for them that liue ἐν ἀσκήσει, that is to say, in exercise. Neither prayeth he only for them in that special prayer, but also for them that liue in virginitie, in chastitie, in reuerend wedlocke, for them that liued hardly in hilles, in dennes, in holes of the earth, the holy Fathers and brethren.

What is meant by exercise, I trow M. Iewel is not ignorant, though he loue neither the thing, nor them that professe it. It signifieth that order of life, which they leade that sequester them selues from worldly affaires and cares, and applye their whole mynde and studie to the seruice of God. And because men may with grace so do, though they liue not in monasteries of welthy prouision, such as we haue sene Monkes of England liue in: therefore it is not necessary to understand the place of S. James Masse of them, that lyued in Monasteries, but of them, that liued (as Monkes then liued) solitarily, in the exercise of vertue, not hauing to do with the world. These were called ἀσκηταὶ the menne, ἀσκήτριαι the wemen, ἀσκητήρια the places, celles, or houses, where they liued.

Exercise what it signifieth.

How the place of S. James Masse is to be vnderstāded.

Yet am not I ignorant that in S. James time of whose Masse I speake, there were holy places called μοναστήρια Monasteries, but they were not such as M. Iewel would the vnlearned people to vnderstand, for the auoiding of S. James auctoritie alleged for the Sacrifice of the Masse.

Monasteries in the Apostles time.

For Philo the Iewe who wrote in the Apostles time, in his booke de vita contemplatiua supplicum, as Eusebius allegeth, speaking of the first Christians that lyued in Egypte, saith that in euery place where a companie dwelled together, they had a holy house, which they called σεμνεῖον καὶ μοναστήριον,

Histor. eccles. lib. 2. cap. 17.

as much to say in English, as a Church. which wordes properly as by Philo we are instructed, haue their sound of that men wēt a side from other worldly companie, where they exercised and kept the mysteries of chaste and holy life. Unto which places they brought neither meate nor drinke, nor any other thinges perteining to the seruice of mannes bodye, but bookes of the lawe and prophetes, of hymnes and prayers, and such others, whereby knowledge and godlynesse are encreased and perfited. If M. Iewel wil vnderstand the worde Monasteries which he founde in his Latine translation of S. James Masse after this sense, then I say it was not to rathe to haue Monasteries in S. James time.

Thus haue we cleered S. James Masse of M. Iewels slender Obiection. The auctoritie and credite of it is sufficiently auouched by the auncient father Proclus bishop of Constantinople, and specially by the sixth general Councel holden in Trullo. wherfore the Sacrifice of the Masse is approued by testimonie of S. James Masse, and so remaineth vnshaken, notwithstanding M. Iewels colourable Replie.

Sextæ synodi. cā. 32

Of S. Chrysostomes Masse or Liturgie.

Ievvel.

The. 39. vntruth. He praieth not for Pope Nicolas of Rome.

*Chrysostomes Liturgie prayeth for * Pope Nicolas by these vvordes. Nicolai Sanctissimi & vniuersalis Papæ longa sint tempora. VVe praye God sende Nicolas that most holy and vniuersal Pope a long time to liue.* But *Pope Nicolas the first of that name, * vvas the second Pope after Pope Iohane the vvoman, in the yere of our Lorde eight hundred fiftie and seuen, almost fiue hundred yeres after Chrysostome vvas dead. And likevvise in the same Liturgie there is a prayer for the Empier, and victorie of the Emperour Alexius. And the first Emperour of that name vvas in the yere of our Lorde a thousand and foure score, after the deceasse of Chrysostome seuen hundred yeres. Novv it vvere very much for M. Harding * to say, Chrysostome prayed for men by name seuen hundred yeres before they vvere borne.*

The. 40. vntruth. for there was no such womā Pope at al.

The. 41. vntruth. I say not this much

borne. I trovv that vvere prophesying, and not praying.

Harding.

As M. Iewel condemneth S. James Liturgie or Masse, so he condemneth also S. Chrysostomes, not being hable by other shifte to auoide the manifest testimonies for the Sacrifice of the body and bloude of Christ there mentioned. But the mater is sone answered. The Liturgie hath alwayes ben put among the workes of S. Chrysostome, and was neuer doubted to be his by any learned man. Erasmus hath translated it into Latine, and calleth it S. Chrysostomes Masse. The words ye M. Iewel allegeth, by which it semeth not to be his, be not found in the Liturgie, that is printed with the rest of his workes. In the translation of Erasmus there is put in no such mention of Pope Nicolas, nor of Alexius the Emperour. wherefore of good right, we ought rather to denye M. Iewels allegation, then S. Chrysostomes Liturgie.

S. Chrysostomes Masse, is not disproued by ought that M. Iew. saith.

But let vs graunt yt some Masse bokes or copies of that Liturgie, haue a prayer for Nicolas, & an other for Alexius. Let it also be graunted, yt they both lyued vij. C. yeres after S. Chryso. what inconuenience foloweth hereof? Is not the death of Moyses described in the bookes of the lawe, called of the number of fiue bookes, Pentateuchus? Yet is there no man so hardy as to denye, that Moyses wrote those bookes. And is it likely that a man should describe the order and manner of his owne death and burial? Answere me how this may be M. Iewel, and I wil answere you, how in the Masse or Liturgie of S. Chrysostome, a prayer might be made for Nicolas, and for Alexius, though they liued seuen hundred yeres after S. Chrysostome. Yea but (saith M. Iewel) *it vvere very much for me to say, Chrysostome prayed for men by name seuen hundred yeres before they vvere borne.* For he thinketh that to be prophesying, and not praying. That were much, and ouer much in dede for me to say, I graunt. Neither say I so. But that the names of men that were borne a thousand yeres after S. Chrysostome, were put in the Masse or Liturgie of S. Chrysostome, for me so to saye: it were neither much, nor vnreasonable. And who so euer at his Masse prayeth for such, whose names he fyndeth written in the Masse booke, though the Masse were first indighted by one a thousand yeres before, the same dothe praie, and not prophesie.

How it may be ẏ in S. Chrisosto. mes masse Nicolas & Alexius, ẏ liued long after S. Chrysosto mes time, were praied for.

Now whereas M. Iewel saith, Chrysostomes Liturgie prayeth for Nicolas and Alexius, if he meane that S. Chrysostome him selfe prayed for them at his Masse, he belyeth him, for they lyued long after him. But if he meane by the Liturgies prayer, the putting in of the names of Nicolas and Alexius into the booke of the Liturgie, by sight whereof the Priest that saith Chrysostomes Masse, is admonished to pray for thē: so Chrysostomes Liturgie may and doth pray for Ioasaph, that at this day is Patriarke of Constantinople, and no absurditie therein is graunted: for it may be, that his name is written in that place of the Masse, where the lyuing are remembred and prayed for, As I my selfe haue sene a Masse booke where king Henry the eight his name was written, and yet was the Masse made many yeres before he was borne.

Diptycha.

Such as be learned, be not ignoraunt of the auncient and long continewed custome of the Church, which was, that the names of the chiefe Bishops and Princes, both when they liued, and after their deceasse, were in all ages registred in rolles, bookes, or tables, which the antiquitie called Diptycha, to thintent they might be remembred and rehersed in the dredful Mysteries. Now according to the diuersitie of times diuerse names were put in. And in some places it is founde that S. Chrysostomes owne name was written in some auncient bokes of his

Liturgie

turgie,and was among others rehersed after his death. Now for that cause M. Iewel may not scoffe, and say it were much for me to say, that Chrysostome lyuing, remembred Chrysostome departed. This much if M. Iewel knewe, it was malice to ieast at Chrysostomes Masse, as he doth. If he knewe not, then is he very vnskilfull, and therefore ought not so much to presume of his owne part, nor be credited of others.

M. Iew. auoucheth an vntruth either of vnskil or of malice.

Neither was Nicolas, which is named in the Latine translation, that Claudius de Sainctes hath set forth, Pope or bishop of Rome first of that name, as M. Iewel ful ignorantly iudgeth. He was a Patriarke of Constantinople, at that time when Alexius the first was Emperour, as it appeareth by conference of the Registres of the Patriarkes and Emperours there. That he is called Papa, it maketh no argument, that he was bishop of Rome. For that name was common to other bishops, as euery where it is reade. The name Uniuersal, obteined by ambitious vsurpation of the Patriarkes of that See, and by flatterie of the Clergie. Neither is Nicolas only in that place of the Latine Translation named, but also the three other Patriarkes of the Orient. Eleutherius of Alexandria, Cyrillus of Antiochia, and Leontius of Ierusalem, who lyued in one time. The bishop of Rome is not named at al, because they of Constantinople at that time had diuided them selues from the Church of Rome, and lyued in schisme.

Nicolaus patriarke. and Alexius Emperour of Constantinople at one time.

Papa.

Vniuersalis.

The schisme of the East Church.

If M. Iewel had loked in the Greke Liturgie, he had not founde the names of Nicolas, and the rest expressed. But a signification geuen by ὁ δεῖνος, and by this rubrische ὅστις ἂν ᾖ as much to say, such a one, and who so euer he be. Wherby is meant that the Priest who saith Masse, put in and reherse such names, as his dutie, time, and place requireth.

The Latines in such a case vse to put the letter, N. which stādeth indifferently for any name, whose so euer it be.

That the names of Nicolas, and of the other three Patriarkes, and of Alexius, were put in the Latine translation, it is to be attributed to one Leo Thuscus, who being at Constantinople, turned the Masse of S. Chrysostome which the Grekes do vse, into the Latine tongue, at the request of a noble man named Rainaldus de monte Catano, who at the same time arriued there. Because he founde those names in the booke, out of which he made his translation, he left them also in the Latine: that his translation should not varie from his Greke exampler. If he had fallen vpon an other booke, that had had other names, he had put in other names, as he that purposed not to go from his exampler.

Leo Thuscus the translatour of the Greke Masse.

Pope Ioan.

Touching Pope Ioane the woman, whom it liked M. Iewel of his good deuotion here to name in the texte, and to place in the margent of his booke with great text letters, that euery mannes eye might thereby be moued to looke that waye: how vaine a fable it is, I haue declared in my Confutation of the English churches Apologie at large. By such fables they study how to lead the people from the loue and obediēce of the church, out of which Church they be assured to finde no other but euerlasting damnation. Thus thou seest Christian Reader, what so euer testimonie is alleged out of S. Chrysostomes Masse or Liturgie for prouse of the Sacrifice of the Eucharist, the same to be good, for so much as the auctoritie and estimation of it, is not any whit inpaired, by any thing M. Iewel hath brought to the contrary. And yet now he vpbraideth me, and craketh, as though he had made a great conquest. But of such bad fuel riseth more smoke then flame. Thou seest how iust cause I haue to require him to subscribe.

In the. 4. parte. fol. 164. a

Ievvel.

Ievvel.

*Thou seest Christian Reader, vvhat Doctors here be brought, as M. Harding saith, to grounde thy faith and * saluation vpon. If he could haue brought any better, I trovve he vvold haue spared these. But such doctrine, such Doctours. These doubtful authorities, I trust vvil set mennes consciences out of doubt.*

The 42. vntruth. I say it not.

Harding.

Fol. 11.

Read my woordes good Reader, and thou shalt fynde them to reporte no more, but that I gaue a taste as it were of proufes, without allegation of the wordes, for confirmation of of thy faith concerning the Sacrifice. Concerning the Doctors, they be so muche the more to be beleued, how much M. Iewel is farre from iuste reprouse of them. And what meaneth he? For any doctrine to be auouched, can better authoritie be brought, then the testimonie of the Scriptures, of yͤ Apostles, and Apostolike mē & of yͤ most aūcient & best learned Fathers? These Doctours I am not a shamed of. Moe could I haue named (for who speaketh not of yͤ Sacrifice of the Eucharist) but these I thought to be sufficient both for number of persones, and for weight of sentence.

Neither I trust wil any man yͤ feareth God, and is stedfast in the faith, chaunge his conscience touching this point, though Mysteries be of these Doctours treated and spoken of as becommeth Mysteries, that is to saye, not in moste plaine wise. Among all thinges perteining to Christian faith, the whole mater of this blessed Sacrament, hath euer of the fathers ben rather honoured with the holynesse of secrete conscience and silence, then with much and euident declaratiō set forth to the multitude. And the Doctrine of it hath ben kept by tradition, and custome, more then by expresse writing. Of very religiō yͤ Fathers forbare either to speake openly, or to write many words of it. S. Paule being

The doctrine of mysteries hath ben kept rather by secret tradition, then by publike writing.

ing about to speake therof, demeaneth him selfe very warely, and
prepareth the minds of the Corinthians to a depe consideratiõ, &
inuiteth them to thinke of it, rather then to talke of it, with these
wordes put for a pref ace, before he make expresse mention of it.
1.Cor.10 Vt prudentibus loquor. I speake as vnto them which be wise, iudge
ye what I say. Is not the cuppe of blessing, which we blesse, partaking of the Bloude of Christe? Is not the Breade, &c.

Likewise when the Fathers made mention of it, commonly
they added a short preface, thereby geuing warning, that they
Origenes spake of a Mysterie. Origen thus: He that is indued with the My-
homil.9.in steries, knoweth the Flesh and Bloud of the worde of God. wher-
Leuiticũ. fore let vs not tarry (saith he) in these thinges, which vnto them
that knowe, be knowen, and vnto them that knowe not, can not be
Chrysosto. open. S. Chrysostome thus. They that haue taken the Myste-
hom. de S. ries, vnderstand what thinges are spoken. The comparteners of
Philogonio the Mysteries knowe what is said. We that be Christened, let vs
homil.51. folowe, what thinges are spoken, the faithful knowe.
ad pop. An S. Gregorie Nazianzen hauing occasion to speake of this
tiochen.& thing sayth by way of complainct. Heu in quales sermones in-
61. cidere cogor? Alas what manner of talke am I driuen to fall into?
In prima Synesius that eloquent bishop, to signifie the secretnes of this
inuectiua Mysterie, calleth it τελετὴν ἀπόῤῥητον. as much to say, the holy vn-
in Iulianũ speakeable Ceremonie. To note the like sayinges out of S. Au-
Ad Hero- gustine, and the other Fathers, it were in manner infinite.
nem.

The notable worde of S. Paule is not to be passed ouer,
who hauing touched Christes Priesthod after the order of Mel-
Heb.5. chesedech, saith thus. De quo nobis grandis sermo, & ininterpre-
tabilis ad dicendum, quoniam imbecilles facti estis ad audiendum.
Whereof we haue many thinges to say, which are harde to be
vttered: because ye are weake to heare them.

Forasmuch then as it hath pleased the holy Ghost, that this
great

greate secrete should not be vttered in most euident and open manner, M. Jewel doth great wrong vnto these holy Mysteries, in that he doth with al his witte and cunning endeuour to withdrawe vnlearned folke from the faith in which the Churche hath alwaies continued to this time, concerning the Sacrifice of the Eucharist, because the Fathers haue not in theire writinges set it forth so plainly, as to their grosse senses it might appear manifest, without any doubtfulnesse or obscuritie. As for the authoritie of the Doctours by me alleged, how sufficient they are, it appeareth by that M. Jewel hath laboured to deface them, and hath shewed in disprouing them, but the vanitie of his witte, and the malice of his purpose, which is vtterly to abrogate the vnbloudy Sacrifice of the Church.

Ievvel.

Hovv be it, if al these be vvitnesse to the masse, vvhy speake they not? vvhy come they forth dumme? vvhat? haue they nought to say in this behalfe? Or is their vvorde not vvorth the hearing? Or are they so old, that they can not speake? Or must vve neds beleue M. Harding vvithout euidēce?

Harding.

Here be a number of vaine interrogations al tending to one meaning. One had ben ynough. And here to turne to you M. Jewel, sir vpon what confidence shew you al this malapertnes? Thought you with this courage of words to persuade your fauorable Readers, that the holy Doctours of the Churche be dumme, as much to say, out of whom no worde can be alleged for witnesse of the vnbloudy Sacrifice? Seing then by M. Jewels importunitie I am driuen to it, listen Reader, whether they be dumme or no.

M. Iew. malapert calling for the Fathers alegations for prouse of the Sacrifice.

Places vvitnessing the Sacrifice of the Aulter.

Saith not Sainte Clement, that Christe for the bloudie Sacrifice (of the Olde Lawe) hath ordeyned λογικὴν, a reaso-

λογικὴν *symbola* *Clemens Apostolic. institut. lib.6.ca.23* a reasonable, vnbloudy, and mystical Sacrifice, which is celebrate in remembraunce of our Lordes death by the signes or tokens of his Body and Bloude? What other Sacrifice is this then the Eucharist, which we speake of?

Saide not S. Andrew to Egeas the Lieutenant of Achaia, as Philastetus reciteth out of the recordes of the Priestes of Achaia, Immaculatum Agnum quotidie in altari sacrifico, I offer daily the vnspotted Lambe on the aulter?

In præfatione de traditione diuinæ Missæ. Sextæ Synodi ca.32 The Liturgie or Masse reported to be S. James by Proclus Patriarke of Constantinople, by the learned Fathers of the sixth Councel, by the Greeke Byshops Nicolaus of Methone, Marcus of Ephesus, Bessario Patriarke of Constantinople, saith it not: I am vnworthy to cast myne eyes vpon this holy and spiritual table, on which the onely begotten Sonne our Lorde Iesus Christ, to me which am a sinner, and al bespotted, is mystically set forth to be a Sacrifice?

Martialis Sayth not S. Martialis in his Epistle ad Burdegalenses, We offer the Body and Bloude of Christe vnto lyfe euerlasting? Againe, saith he not, We propone on the Sanctified aulter for cause of our health, that thing, which the Iewes haue offered, thinking to abolish his name quite from the earth?

Clemens Constitut. lib.8.ca.17 Doth not S. Clement set forth a forme of Masse not much different from the Masse commonly vsed in the Latine Church touching the substance of it? which as to rehearse here were long, so would it liuely declare the antiquitie of the chief partes of the Masse.

Cyrillus in Catechesi mystagogica.5. Do we not finde the like in S. Cyrillus Byshop of Ierusalem Catechesi Mystagogica.5? saith he not thus where he describeth the Consecration: We beseche God to sende forth the Holy Ghost vpon the thinges set forth, that he make the bread the Body of Christ, the Wine the Bloud of Christ? For what soeuer

uer the holy ghost toucheth, it is sanctified and changed.

Then after that that spiritual Sacrifice is made, and the vnblody worship vpon the hoste it selfe of propitiation, we pray to God for the common peace of the Church, for the tranquillitie of the Worlde. &c. **Againe saith he not there, that** the praier of the holy and dredful Sacrifice, which is layde on the aulter, is offered for the deade? **what Sacrifice is that but the Sacrifice of the body and bloud of Christ? Thus S. Cyrillus there, and much more for witnesse of this holy Sacrifice.**

Saith not S. Dionyse S. Paules disciple and Areopagite speaking of this Sacrifice, that the Venerable Priest or Bishop standing at the holy aulters, after praises of Gods workes, reuerently and according to his Byshoply office excuseth him selfe for offering that healthful Sacrifice, which is aboue his dignitie, First crying vnto him, (**he meaneth Christ**) thou hast saide, Hoc facite in meam commemorationem, Do ye this in my remembraunce? *Dionysius in Ecclesiast. Hierarch. lib. 1. cap. 3. part. 3.*

Saith not S. Iustine the Philosopher and Martyr, that God witnesseth al the Sacrifices, which Christe commaunded to be done in the Eucharist of the Breade and Cuppe, that are made in al places, to be acceptable vnto him? **Doth he not allege ye Prophecie of Malachie against Trypho the Iewe, for prouse therof?** *Iustinus in dialogo cũ Tryphone cõtra Iudæos.*

Saith not S. Ireneus that blessed Martyr, speaking of this Mysterie, that Our Lorde saide of the consecrated breade, it was his Body, and confessed the Wine to be his Bloude, and taught the newe Oblation of the newe Testament, which the Church receiuing of the Apostles, offereth to God ouer the whole worlde? *Irenæus cõtra hæres. lib. 4. cap. 32.*

Saith not S. Basile in his Liturgie, Receiue vs O God approching to thy holy aulter, according to the multitude of thy mercie, that we may be worthy to offer vp vnto thee this reaso- *Basilius in Liturgia.*

nable & vnbloudy Sacrifice for our sins, & the peoples ignorãce?

What shal I allege S. Chrysostome, whose testimonies for the Sacrifice gathered together, would fill a whole booke? Of many let one suffice. His woordes be these, which can not be vnderstanded, but onely of the Sacrifice of the Body and Bloud of Christe.

Chrysost. homil. 2. in 2. ad Timoth.

I wil tel you a certaine thing more, that in dede is marueilous, and marueil not at it, nor trouble your selues. And what is this? The holy Oblation it selfe, whether Peter offer it or Paule, or any Priest of what merite so euer he be: is the selfe same, which Christ his owne selfe gaue to his Disciples, and which the Priestes now also do consecrate. Nothing lesse hath this, then that. Why so? Because they be not menne, that consecrate this, but Christ, which consecrated that before. For as the woordes which Christe spake, be the same that Priestes now also doe pronounce: euen so the Oblation is one, &c.

4. thinges to be considered touching the Sacrifice. 1. The real presence.

In this saying of Chrysostome, Foure thinges are to be considered. First, that the Oblation which here signifieth the thing offered, is the Body and Bloud of Christe. For it is that which is consecrated by the Priestes pronouncing the same woordes that Christe did. But the woordes that Christe spake, were these, this is my Body, this is my Bloud, as the Euangelistes declare, and we ought to thinke that he spake truth: wherefore when the Priest duely pronounceth the same, which he doth at the Masse, he maketh and consecrateth that which Christe did, to witte, his Body and Bloud.

2. Christ offered him selfe at his Supper.

Secondly, that Christ made an Oblation of him selfe at his Supper. For els how, when, and where, gaue he the holy Oblation to his Disciples? This can not be vnderstanded of any spiritual Oblation, as of Prayers, thankesgeuing, praises, reioysing

sing in our Lordes death, lifting vp of heartes. &c. For such kind of Oblations Christe neuer gaue to his disciples externally eyther at his Supper, or at any other time: but rather it was their dutie to geue such Oblations vnto him.

Thirdly, that this Oblation is one, and of the same worthinesse, how diuerse so euer the merite of the Priestes be, that do consecrate: because it is consecrated with the wordes of Christ now, with which he consecrated before.

3. The Oblation of the Priest is ŷ same that christ offered at his supper

Fourthly, that the Priestes do offer this holy Oblation vnto God, which is the Body and Bloud of Christ, whereby that which we cal the Masse is proued. Which Oblation, and that Priestes haue auctoritie to offer, M. Jewel denyeth, but that vntruly he denyeth, partly by this, and more at large hereafter, it shal appeare.

4. Oblation of the body & bloud of Christe made vnto God.

Thus thou seest Reader, the Doctours, to whom I remitted the studious and learned Readers of my booke, for witnesse of the Sacrifice, be not dumme. And because M. Jewel beareth the worlde in hande, we are destitute of good recordes and autorities for this point: beside those I named before, now I wil name diuerse moe of such trust and estimation, as no Learned man hath euer taken exception against them. Neyther wil I onely name them, but also shew the place, where expresse mention of this blessed Sacrifice of the Church, which is the Oblation of the Body and Bloud of Christe, is made.

A briefe rehersal of such, who haue geuē witnesse for the sacrifice of ŷ Aulter.

To beginne with the aucthoritie of the Churche, it is needelesse. For to whom is it vnknowen that knoweth any thing, how often in the holy Canon, in sundry other deuoute prayers, and otherwhere the Churche reporteth, that shee offereth vnto God the pure and vnspotted hoste of the Body and Bloude of Christe? But the Churche which after Christe ought to be most regarded and hearde,

M. Jewel litle regardeth.

If Councels wil like him, the numbre of them is great, that for the Sacrifice haue geuen their sentence. The first Councel Toletane, cap.5. the eleuenth, cap.14. the twelfth, cap.5. The third Councel of Braccara cap.1. The third Councel of Carthage, the Cōucel of Nice, cap.14. of Antisiodorum, cap.8. To these might be added two later Councels, that of Florence vnder Eugenius the.4. in ye decree there made of the vnion of ye Armenians. And ye of Constantia, where wiklefes errour was condemned, who said it was not founded in the Gospel, that Christe ordained the Masse.

Councels

wiklef.

Auncient Bishopes of Rome.

As for the Bisshop of the See Apostolike, though M. Jewel, the Deuil, and al heretikes that euer were, beare endlesse hatred to that See, and to them whome God hath appointed to be gouernours thereof: because they were learned, holy, and of greate antiquitie, that beare witnesse to the Sacrifice: I should do them and the Church iniurie, if in this cause I refused their recorde. Of them therfore some here wil I name, as who do professe the faith of the Apostles and the Church, to be one. For the Sacrifice then, may be alleged S. Anacletus. de Consec. dist.1. cap. Episcopus. S. Alexander the first de Consecra. distinct.2. c. nihil. S. Eusebius, de consecrat. dist.1. c. consulto. S. Iulius de Cons. dist.2. c. cum omne crimen. S Felix, de Consec. dist.1. c. Sicut non alij. Soter in epist. ad episcopos Italiæ, Syricius ad Cumeriū Tarraconensem episcopum, c.1. Innocentius primus ad Exuperium Tolosanum episcopum. cap.1. Leo ad Dioscorum, epistola. 81. Al these be very auncient, and liued within the compasse of the firste six hundred yeares, when by M. Jewels owne opinion al was well.

The other Fathers Greeks, & Latines.

Of the other old Fathers of the Churche, if I would here allege so many, as might be alleged for this purpose, I shoulde with

with much tediousnesse encombre the reader. I wil admonish him of a fewe, that be the chiefe. Of the Greke fathers, byside those which my answere to M. Iewel reciteth, this Sacrifice is auouched by S. Athanasius in lib. quæstionum ad Antiochũ. q. 34. by S. Gregory Nazianzen in Apologetico, & in carminibus. by Eusebius Emisenus, sermone 5. de pascha. by S. Chrysostome lib. 6. de Sacerdotio. By Theophylact, in cap. 10. epist. ad heb. By Damascen. lib. 4. de orthodoxa fide. cap 14.

Of the Fathers of the Latine Churche, for this doctrine we haue the plaine testimonies of S. Cyprian. lib. 2. epist. 3. ad Cæcilium. Item Sermone de Cœna Domini. S. Ambros. lib. 1. Officiorum. cap. 48. S. Hierome. ad Hedibiam. quæst. 2. & aduersus Vigilantium. & ad Titum. cap. 1. S. Augustine. lib. 10. de ciuitate. cap. 20. & lib. 17. cap. 20. & lib. 20. Contra Faustum. cap. 18. Fulgentius, ad Monimum lib. 2.

The latin Fathers.

If M. Iewel not being hable with reason or learning to answer these holy fathers, vse his accustomed shift, and go about to auoid them with his common scoffes, saying they be but Mummers, but Visardes, but Dumme, and that al is but a Camisado, and I cannot tell what els: then I require the studious reader to resorte to the places here quoted: and assuredly he shall fynde them men of good vtterance speaking most euidently the truth concerning the vnbloudy Sacrifice of the Newe Testament, to haue faces, before which heretikes shal sone be confounded, armures & weapons, wherwith they shalbe vãquished and beatẽ downe. Here to alledge there wordes, it were to longe. wherefore let M. Iewel either denye these holy Fathers, or scoffe out the mater no more with his terme of Mummers, Visards, and Dumme. In dede perhaps his Serchers, waiters, and Promotours, may so handle our bokes, as they shal neither be seene, nor heard to speake.

Assure thy selfe good Christian Reader, there is no one thing more spokẽ of and witnessed by the holy Fathers and Cōcels, then the daily Sacrifice of the Churche, then ẏ vnbloudy Sacrifice & oblatiō of the body & bloud of Christ, thẽ the hoste of the vnspotted lambe, which Priestes of the new Testament after the order of Melchisedech do offer in the Masse. And that M. Iewel knoweth wel ynough. But now that he is ouer ẏ shooes he careth not, how farre he wade. Among whose other shiftes this is not to be dissembled, that whereas I alleged the names of a great nūbre of Fathers for witnesse of the Sacrifice: to such, as ouer whom some colour of disprouse might be caste, as to S. Clement, of whom he shooteth shorte, and to Abdias, against whom he bringeth no pith, he saith much: to S. Dyonisius, S. James, and S. Chrysostomes Liturgies, he saith a litle, and that is litle worth, as I haue declared. But to the testimonie of S. Iustinus, to the manifest place of S. Ireneus, to S. Basile, & to sundry places that might be alleged out of S. Chrysostome, and to S. Cyrillus of Ierusalem, who most plainly treateth of that special mater: to al these he saith nothing, thinking it a more policie, forasmuch as their authoritie is vndoubted, and their wordes euident, and their faith inuincible: to passe them ouer with silence, then with an insufficient aunswere to discredit his cause, specially whereas he had shewed some face of an answere, in that he had saide so largely in disprouse of S. Clement, and Abdias.

M. Iew. leaueth the manifest sayinges of certain Fathers vnanswered.

Ireneus lib. 4. cap 32.

in mystagogica catechese quinta.

Page. 5.

Yet in the margent of his booke, he wil seme to answere by prety briefe notes, calling sundry my allegations vntruthes. There in his. 6. vntruth, touchig S. Andrew, by him S. Andrew said the Communion, and not the Masse. An other where when the very terme of Masse is alleged, then must the Masse it selfe be a Communion. As where he bringeth in Abdias, saying cum Missam suscepisset omnis ecclesia. he englysheth it, *when the whole*

Churche

Church had receiued the Communion, whereas the worde Missa, in that place, signifieth not the Communion, nor the Masse neither, but leaue to departe, which likewise of ye Grekes is called ἀπόλυσισ, dimissio. So he enforceth both thinges and wordes to serue his turne at his pleasure. And when he is driuen to a narrow shift, the Masse it selfe, must be his Communion. Page 11. lin. 16.

But I doubt not euery learned man wil laugh at this, that S. Andrew should saye the new Communion. If he meane the Communion that was frequented in S. Andrewes time, which was the participation of the Body & Bloud of Christ, and was a thing that consisted in doing rather then in saying: as that I admitte to his smal aduantage, so I require him also to admit the Sacrifice, which then S. Andrew celebrated by saying and doing, which I vnderstand to haue been the Masse of that time. If he said not the Masse, as now it is saide, which I did not affirme: neither the Communion did he say, as the Sacramentaries say it, yet the Masse concerning the Substance of it, by report of my allegation, S. Andrew both said, and to God offered that holy Sacrifice and Oblation which I spake of.

In the. 8. vntruth, *There is no manner token or shevv of priuate Masse*, saith M. Iewel, whereas I alleged not S. Clement for priuate Masse at al, but for Masse or for the Sacrifice. With like vanitie in the other vntruthes vntruly noted, he aunswereth chalke for chese, as commonly they say, pretending contrary to his knowledge, as afterward he cōfesseth him selfe, *page.12.lin.29.* yt by those auctorities I would establish specially priuate Masse, wheras I brought them for witnesse of the Sacrifice onely, as my wordes declare, wherevnto for trial hereof I reporte me. Where in ye 10. vntruth, he auoideth ye graue autorities of S. Iustine, & S. Ireneus, wt this note in ye margēt, *a burthē of vntruthes:* who so euer wil cōsider ye places, he shal see M. Iewel further

Page. 5.

In my Answer fol.10. & 11.

Lib.4.c.32 burthened with the weight of their sayings, specially of S. Ireneus, then with al his light Rethorike and peeuish Sophistrie, he is hable to discharge himselfe of.

Among al other things, what meaneth he to note in his. 12. vntruth, that the order of the Masse or Liturgie vsed in Ierusalem declared and set forth by S. Cyrillus Byshop there, * *is the very expresse order of the Communion*. If by the woorde Communion he meane the Sacrifice of the Church, whereof we speake, as somtimes by the word Masse he meaneth the Communion: then that it is much agreable in deede to the Masse, as now we celebrate it in the Church, I graunt. If he wil needes vnderstand the Communion, what Communion meaneth he? Is there any better Communion then their owne, which is the freshest, and of the newest making? If he meane that, verely he deceyueth the worlde much, to say of that which S. Cyrillus declareth, that it is the expresse order of their Communion. For there after the Sacrifice is offered, mention is made of the Patriarkes, Prophetes, Apostles, and Martyrs, that God through their prayers and petitions receiue our prayers. Then also there is prayer made for ye Dead. And after the doctrine of S. Cyrillus, the soules of the departed haue great helpe, by the prayers made for them in that holy and dredful Sacrifice (for so he calleth it) that is laide vpon the aulter. But sith that in M. Iewels new Communion there is neither petition made for the prayers of the Sainctes, nor prayers for the Soules departed: how is that which Cyrillus treateth of, the expresse order of their Communion? Truely in this vntruth by M. Iewel imputed vnto me, he hath shewed him selfe not very true.

The. 43. vntruth. the masse set forth by Cyrillus of Ierusalem is not the very order of the English Communion.

In quinta catechesi mystagog. Praiers for the deade alowed by Cyrillus of Ierusalem.

After that M. Iewel hath shewed his final reasons, for which he reproueth and condemneth certaine of the Fathers that I alleged for the Sacrifice, and not for Priuate Masse: he commeth

in

in with a numbre of questions vttered by whatifs. And saith:

Ievvel.

*VVhat if neither Clement, nor Abdias, nor S. Iames, nor Basile, nor Chrysostome, nor any other in the ansvvere to the Chalenge alleged, speake one vvord of priuate Masse? VVhat if they haue not so much as the name of Masse? VVhat if they testifie * against M. Hardinges Masse? VVhat if thei testifie fully and roundly vvith they holy Communion?*

The 44. vntruth. thei testifie not so much as one worde against the masse.

Harding.

Al this needed not, you bestow many wordes in vaine, for I brought them not in for priuate Masse, & that your selfe knew ful wel, as by your owne wordes after, you confesse. what? lacked you better stuffe, that you folowed a lye in so long a processe? why deny you that with so many wordes, which I confesse not? why proue you so at large and length that, which I denye not? That those Fathers speake not of priuate Masse, as though the Sacrifice were priuate, and that they haue not the name of Masse, I graunt. That they testifie against the Masse, I denye it. You say it, and say it againe, but you proue it not. when come you to the very point, M. Iewel?

Though they testifie with the Communion, what maketh that for your purpose? May not the Sacrifice of the Masse, and the Communion stand together? I meane not your new deuised Communion of the English Geneuians: but that of the holy Fathers of the Primitiue Church receiued and distributed. Therfore leaue your common argument for shame, *These Fathers testifie vvith the Communion, Ergo they testifie against the Masse,* least men laugh at your simple Logike. For the argument is no better, then if a man should reason thus. M. Iewel breaketh his fast commonly with a couple of Egges, Ergo he drinketh no wyne at his dinner. which argument is foolish, for he may do both. Such is the reason you make for the affirmation

 of

of the Communion, to the denyal of the vnbloudy Sacrifice, or the Sacrifice of the Masse: This is your common manner, by one truth to exclude an other.

M. Iewels Buts.

Now I geue M. Iewel leaue to runne his rase freely without stoppe, from Butte to Butte, and to say his pleasure for one whole leafe, that is to say, from the. 36. line of the. 10. page, which is his first Butte, to the. 29. line of the. 12. page, where he placeth his second Butte. There he bestoweth great paines, and almost runneth him selfe out of breath, to proue that which no man denyeth, that is, the Communion. And forthwith of euery Communion he inferreth a conclusiõ against priuate Masse, which by these Fathers no man went about to proue. And so he is compelled to say, when he commeth to his second But. For there thus he speaketh.

M. Iew. bestoweth many wordes in prouing ÿ no man denieth.

Ievvel.

But he vvil say, he alleged al these Doctours by vvay of digression, to an other purpose to proue the Sacrifice.

Harding.

Looke in my booke who list, for proufe of the Sacrifice he shal see these Doctours alleged. And knew you that M. Iewel? why then haue you triumphed so much al this whyle? Do you not thus faine to your selfe monsters, such as you may easily ouercome? Al this whyle you haue fought with your owne shadow, and fiercely beaten the ayer. Thus some men with great courage let flee at their enemies absent, that dare not abide the skippe of a frogge present.

Of the authoritie of S. Hipolytus.

Ievvel.

Touching Hippolytus, the Bishop and Martyr, that, as M. Harding sayth, liued in Origens time, and is novv extant in Greeke, it is a

very

very litle booke, of smal price, and as smal credite, lately set abroade in print, about seuen yeares past.* before neuer acquainted in the vvorld, &c. The 45. vntruth. he was wel knowen before.

It appeareth it vvas some simple man that vvrote the booke, both for the Phrases of speache in the Greeke tongue, vvhich commonly are very childish, and also for the truth and vveight of the mater.

He * beginneth the First Sentence of his booke vvith Enim, vvhich a very childe vvould scarcely doo. &c. The 46. vntruth. he beginneth otherwise.

He saith and * soothly auoucheth, that Antichriste shalbe the Deuil, &c. And that he shal builde vp againe * the temple of Ierusalem, That S. Iohn that vvrote the Apocalips, shal come againe vvith Elias, and Enoch to reproue Antichriste. He allegeth the Apocalips of S. Iohn in steede of Daniel. Moreouer he saith that the soules of menne vvere from the beginning, vvhich is an Heresie. &c. The 47. The 48. vntruth. he saith not so.

Concerning the place of him here alleaged, Venite Pontifices, (Come ye Bishops) &c. If he vvil precisely builde vpon the vvordes, * then must al other Priestes stande backe and haue no place in heauen, but Byshops onely. For although they offer vp, as M. Harding saith, the daily Sacrifice, yet it is vvel knovven, according to the nature and vse of the vvorde, they are Priestes onely, and not Bishops. The 49. vntruth. it foloweth not.

Harding.

After this there foloweth in M. Iewel a reproufe of the auctthoritie of the blessed Martyr S. Hippolytus, whose special wordes I alleged for witnesse of the Sacrifice, as I did S. Clements: Yet he saith, I brought them in as Mummers, and dumme persons. That he was in Origens time, wherof M. Iewel semeth to doubt, S. Hierome affirmeth it. That his boke is litle, it is no argumēt of litle credite, as he would men to beleue. For the best Doctours of the Church haue writen bookes, M. Iewel setteth light by ẏ authoritie of the blessed martyr S. Hippolitus. *Hieronymus de Script. ecclesiast.*

 whereof

whereof some were of smal quantitie, yet of great authoritie and credit. The handling of that mater required no great boke. And S. Hippolytus besides this, wrote many other worthy bookes, which S. Hierome recketh.

Ibidem.

That M. Jewel quarelleth so with me for alleging S. Hippolytus, unawares he falleth out with S. Hierome, for he allegeth him in his Commentaries upon Daniel, and in an epistle to Lucinius. Wherfore I looke that he deale the more gentilly with me for S. Hieromes sake.

Hieronymus in Daniel. cap. 9.

If he were never before these last seven yeares acquainted in the worlde, as M. Jewel saith, How came S. Hierome by knowledge of him and of his so many bookes, among whom this very booke of late printed is one? This may iustly be annumbred amongst other untruthes of M. Jewels.

Neither saith S. Hippolytus, ye Antichriste shal build up againe the Temple of Jerusalem, as M. Jewel reporteth him to say: but only that he shal build a Temple in Jerusalem of stone, as Christ shewed his flesh as a temple. There is an other untruth reported of that holy Doctour. Certaine other I will let passe, as a thinge not worth the noting.

Whereas he noteth his misalleging of the Apocalips for Daniel, his saying that S. John the Evangelist shal come with Henoch and Elias at the later daye, and that Antichriste shalbe the Devil: al this he learned by the notes in the margent of the Catholike translatour Ioannes Picus. Who warneth the reader to reade those thinges with iudgement, and yet doth not condemne the Autour therefore, as M. Jewel for better defence of his bad cause, by the libertie of his Gospel doth. Who because he can pike some motes of smal errours out of the fathers eyes, thinketh it a sufficient reason to reiect them utterly, and to cloke the great beames of heynous errours in his owne eyes.

As touching our mater, that which I alleged out of S. Hippolytus, perteineth to a knowen point of doctrine of the Churche witnessed by him none otherwise, then the whole consent of auncient Fathers doth approue. But the thinges which M.Iewel hath piked out, were certaine particular pointes concerning the person, condition, and comming of Antichriste. wherein learned men haue said their myndes, not so much definitiuely, as probably, and as they thought. And therfore S.Hippolytus, where he writeth that Antichriste shalbe a deuil incarnate, a deuil in the shape of man, (not simply the deuil as M. Iewel reporteth him) he pronounceth his wordes so, as becommeth a modest man, speaking of a thing not altogether out of doubte. Hanc (opinor) dilecti carnis suæ substantiam phantasticam assumet organi vice. This phantastical substance (saith he) of his flesh a deuil shal take (I thinke) derely beloued, in stede of an instrument to worke by. Here we see, how this holy Martyr uttereth that point touching Antichriste, as his priuate opion only, not as a doctrine by consent of al determined, and generally to be beleued. Yet M.Iewel beareth the reader in hande that he saith it, and soothly auoucheth it, which is very vntrue.

To say that the soules of men were from the beginning, if S.Hippolytus so said, in that time it was no heresie, though it be so now, because the Churche, and consent of Christendome had not then defined it. For long after the time of S.Hippolytus, S.Augustin was doubtful touching the perfite knowledge of ẏͤ soule, as it appeareth by that he wrote to S.Hierome, desyring to knowe his mynde in certaine obscure pointes concerning the soules of men. M.Iewel therefore sheweth his ignorance in charging S.Hippolytus with the crime of heresie therein. Onlesse his diuinitie be such, as wil make euery opinion not defined by the Church to the contrary, to be an heresie.

M. Iew. bewraieth his owne ignorance

Vide Tho. p.1.q.118. art.3.

Augusti. epist.28.ad Hieronymum.

Among other thinges for which he goeth about to discredite the booke, he findeth fault with vnskil in the Greke tongue, in which the booke is written, and with childish phrases. As though M. Jewel could iudge of the greke tongue so exactly, and were worthy to buckell the latchet of the shooe to that learned bishop and blessed Martyr, in emulation of whom, Origen that most eloquent and learned man, was stirred to write bookes vpon the scriptures, as S. Hierome witnesseth. What maruel is it, if this man scoffe at me, and other catholikes, and finde fault with vs, seing that he spareth not such auncient fathers of famous learning, and alwaies so taken of the best learned?

M. Iew. findeth fault with S. Hippolytus phrases.

Hierony. de scriptorib. Ecclesiast.

Yet let vs weigh the defectes, for which he maketh S. Hippolytus to be but a simple man.

Enim.

He beginneth (saith he) *the first sentence of his booke, vvith, enim, vvhich a very childe vvould scarsely doo.*

Why syr haue you no more to say, then this? You spake of Phrases of the Greke tongue, which you said were childishe. And now haue you nothing to laye to his charge, but one poore worde, enim? I maruel that neither the Greke reader of Oxford, nor the schoolemaster there, with whom you conferred in making of your booke, nor any other of your felowes, whose conference was alwayes ready, would not, or could not haue better enstructed you. At your owne smal sight in Greke I wonder not, but that the Greke reader should be so euil eyed or rather blinde, I maruel not a litle. If S. Hippolytus had begon his booke in dede, with Enim, as you belye him, or with γὰρ, as by your wordes one may conceiue: you had some reason. For neuer was there booke nor sentence with either of these wordes begonne. But whereas S. Hippolytus beginneth with Επειδὴ, which in Latine signifieth not Enim, but postquâm, quûm, quoniam, quandoquidem, which manner of begynning is commendable,

dable, and before this time was neuer of any man reproued: he is cleared, and you M. Iewel founde very sawcy, so to controll the style and phrase of that excellent father.

If γὰρ, be the word, that you fynde fault with, which is added to garnish the Phrase, and standeth not in the first place: your cōferrers should haue remembred, that it doth not alwaies signifie, Enim. For sometime it serueth to an interrogation, as it is noted out of Eschines, σὺ γὰρ ἂν κώμην ἀποστήσαις; as much to say, art thou able to bring so much as a village to rebell? Furthermore many times γὰρ doth abounde, is vacant and superfluous. For example, where Cicero saith in his booke de Senectute, Sed tamen, Gaza in that eloquent translation, wherin he is reported much to haue folowed the elegancie of Plato, turneth it thus in Greke, ἀλλὰ γὰρ ὅμως. where γὰρ signifieth nothing, yet being superfluously put, bewtifieth the phrase. And so may it seme to doo in the first sentence of S. Hippolytus Oration, sometime it signifieth certè, quidem, verò, nempe.

Γὰρ, for what, and how it is takē.

Neither is it vtterly straunge or childish to beginne a booke with γὰρ, when it signifieth enim, being put after an other worde as his nature requireth. For so Aristotle, whom I trow, you accompt not for a childe, beganne his booke de Respiratione. περὶ γὰρ ἀναπνοῆς. &c. If you say, Aristotle might wel so begin, as hauing regarde of that went before: why may not the same be answered for S. Hippolytus? This much would haue ben learned M. Iewel of those that haue written obseruations of the greke tongue, before you had ben so rash, as to reprone so learned a Father for his speach.

Thus whiles you geue your selfe wholly to reprone others, specially such as teach otherwise then you do: you shewe your selfe most reproueable.

And with as much witte and good diuinitie you answer the place by me alleged , as with modestie and aduise you reproued the Doctor. Not being hable with truth to denye the plaine testimonie for the Sacrifice of the body and bloud of Christe, you would faine shift your handes of it with an impertinent wrangle. Because S. Hippolytus maketh Christe to speake to bishops at his iudgement, bidding them to come, who haue purely by day and by night offered vnto him Sacrifice, and haue daily Sacrificed his body and his bloud: thereof wil you conclude M. Iewel that Priestes must stand backe? I pray you what reason haue you therein? when wil you be ashamed of your folish negatiue conclusions? This is your peeuish argument.

> Christe at the last day shal cal Bishops vnto his kingdome. Ergo he shal not cal Priestes, but they must stand backe, and haue no place in heauen.

A man may as wel argue and saye thus. Christe at the last day shal cal bishops vnto his kingdome: Ergo, he shal not cal laye men. Or, he shal byd men come, ergo, he shal not byd wemen come, but they must stand backe and haue no place in heauen. who euer heard more childish reasons? Yet such be M. Iewels commonly, who so much scoffeth at other mennes reasons by his owne mery head falsified and set out of order.

But syr, why may not Christe I pray you at that day cal vnto him both bishops and priestes? clerkes, and laie? men and wemen? If Christe shall saye, come ye bishops only, then I graunt priestes must stand backe. But seing he shal say by report of my doctor, Come ye bishops, I besech you be not so hard to priestes, as to tel them, therby they are commaunded to stand backe, and so bereue them of that blessed expectation. Because you wil seme to leaue no parte of S. Hippolytus wordes, which I brought for witnesse of the Sacrifice vntouched, let vs heare further

further what you say, and how you auoide that auctoritie so, as with reason you may be iudged to haue answered thobiection.

Ievvel.

If he vvil make reckening of this vvorde quotidie, *daily, then vvhere shal the bishop of Rome and his Cardinals stande, that scarsely haue leasur to sacrifice * once through the vvhole yere?*

The. 50. vntruth. Sundry cardinals say Masse most daies in ẏ yere, and this present Pope euery day.

Harding.

What leasure the Bishop of Rome and the Cardinals haue, ẏ perteineth nothing to our presēt mater. Certain it is, you slaūder them. For it is wel knowen that oftentimes in the yere they say Masse, wherein they offer the body and bloud of Christe vnto God. And that doth the Pope ouer the bodies of S. Peter & S. Paule now, as the bishops there did in old time, by report of S. Hierome. But what nede al these delayes? Why trifle you thus, and kepe your self aloofe of, that you come not to the point? Leaue this wanton dallying M. Jewel in so serious a mater, and let vs heare your answere, if it be worth the hearing.

Aduersus Vigilant.

Ievvel.

If it be Christe him selfe, that they offer vp vnto the Father, as they saye, hovv is the same Christe offered vp vnto Christe him selfe? Hovv is Christe both the thing that is offred, and also the partie vnto vvhom it is offred? But there is no inconuenience to a man in his dreame.

Harding.

Marke reader, how this man proceedeth with howes, and questions, after the guise of Jewes, Turkes, and Infidels, *Hovv is Christe offered vp vnto Christe* (saith he,) *Hovv is Christe. &c.* as before. What M. Jewel tu es magister in Israel, & hæc ignoras? Beare you the name of a bishop, and knowe not this point of Diuinitie? Finde you not this in Caluine, Peter Martyr, Cranmare, Bale, Hooper, nor in any other of your diuines of the new trade? A meete question truly for a Turke, and some-

Ioan. 3. The ignorance of M. Jew.

what tolerable in an ignorant laie man, that would aske to learne, not to control. But one that in his booke calleth himselfe the Bishop of Sarisburie so many times (I trow that men should forgete the base name of M. Jewel) yea such a one as pricketh forth before al his felowes, for feare least some other should proclaime the Chalenge before him, and stand for the first game: such a famous Minister of the worde, to demaunde this question, if he were lawfully called to the charge of a Christian flocke, truly it were a mater to be lamented. O miserable flocke, that foloweth such a blinde guide.

If this fresh Minister disdaine to learne, or to be admonished at my handes, yet for thy good instruction Christian Reader understand, that our Sauiour Christe the true mediatour, in as much as he tooke the shape of a Seruaunt, as S. Augustine teacheth, he was made mediatour of God and men. And whereas in the forme of God he receiueth Sacrifice with the father, together with whom he is one God: yet in the forme of a seruaunt he had rather be a Sacrifice, then take Sacrifice. Hereby (saith S. Augustine) he is also a priest, him selfe the offerer, and him selfe the Oblation. Of which thing he would the daily Sacrifice of the Church to be a Sacrament, forasmuch as of the body it selfe, he is the head, and of the head she is the body, and as wel she by him, as he by her is accustomed to be offered. Thus S. Augustine. where expressely he saith, that Christe in the forme of God, and as he is God with the Father, so he receiueth Sacrifice. And so Christ in the forme of a seruaunt being the Oblation it selfe in the Masse, is offered to him selfe being in the forme of God.

August. de ciuit. lib. 10. cap. 20.

Christ as he is one God with the father, receiueth Sacrifice. And so he is offered unto him selfe.

Beware M. Jewel, how you wade farre in denial of this point, and say that Christe is not offered vp vnto Christe, least you fal into the heresie of the Arians. For if you wil not haue Christe consydered in the forme of a seruaunt to be offered vnto

M. Jew. maketh for the Arians.

Christe

Christe in the forme of God, and as he is God with the Father: then make you Christe lesse then the Father, as the Arians did. May it please you to read what the learned bishop Fulgentius of Africa hath written touching this point lib.2.ad Monimum, and if you wil beleue that auncient Father, herein you shal finde your selfe sufficiently resolued.

Be not ashamed hardely to reuoke this foule errour, as likewise your ouer presumptuous malapertnes, in that you twite ẏ holy and blessed Martyr S. Hippolytus with dreaming. For the saying, which semeth to you but a dreame, is his, not myne. Who by those words vttereth the same faith concerning the daily Sacrifice of the body and bloude of Christe offered vp vnto Christe, which S. Augustine, Fulgẽtius, other Fathers, and the whole Catholike church teacheth. But what shal it auaile me by writing to encountre him, who estemeth the doctrine and faith of the church witnessed by such Fathers, for a dreame?

Ievvel.

And if it be the Masse that Hippolytus here speaketh of, hovv is it offered both day and night? For Hostiensis saith, it is not lavvfull by the Canons to say Masse in the night season, sauing only the night of Christes Natiuitie.

Harding.

Yet more trifling delayes M. Iewel? when come you to the point? This is your rhetorike, with other impertinẽt mater, and vaine toyes to fill the head of your reader, that therewith being occupied, he be withdrawen from due and ernest consideration of the point, that is specially to be answered. Such dilatorie pleas lawyers do sometimes deuise, least by presẽt answer their bad cause should haue a foile.

But syr looke better in Hostiensis, and in other writers vpon the Canon Lawe, to whome nowe you runne for aide, though at other times you make gaye sporte of them:

and I warrant you, neither by him nor any other, shal you finde it to be vnlawful for a priest, to celebrate the Masse sometimes an houre or two before daye. And so you might haue vnderstanded S. Hippolytus, if it had lyked you. Albeit I vrge not so much the word λειτουργήσαντες, whereunto the mention of the day and night in the sentēce of S. Hippolytus perteineth, where by is signified that they did their seruice to God both daye and night: as that which there foloweth, pretiosum corpus & sanguinem meum immolastis quotidie, ye haue Sacrificed daily vnto me my pretious body and bloud, to which part of the sentence mention of the night doth not perteine. And so your Lawyer Hostiensis maketh no iote for you. Now at lēgth after that you haue wearied your reader with much mater impertinent, what say you to the point? You see, S. Hippolytus speaketh in moste plaine termes of the Sacrifice of the pretious body and bloud of Christe, daily offered by the bishops, which is that I went about to proue. What answer you vnto it?

The sacrifice of the body and bloud of Christ daily offered by bishops

Ievvel.

*But the meaning of Hippolytus * semeth to be this, that al faithful people in this respecte be priestes, and Bishops, like * as S. Peter also calleth them, and that euery of them by faith maketh vnto God a pure Sacrifice, and both day and night, as it vvere, reneuveth, and applyeth vnto himselfe, that one and euerlasting Sacrifice of Christes pretious body once offered for al vpon the Crosse. Thus are the vvordes of Hippolytus plaine, and vvithout cauil.*

The. 51. vntruth. It semeth not so.

The. 52. vntruth S. Peter calleth not the people by ŷ name

Harding.

Yea Sir? To whom I pray you semeth this to be the meaning of S. Hippolytus? To me it can not seme to be this, nor to any Catholike man I am sure, nor to any what so euer he be, that duly and indifferently weigheth the saying. Let the wordes be wel printed in memorie. Christ shal say to the bishops at the later daie, pretiosum corpus ac Sanguinem meum immolastis quotidie, ye haue daily Sacrificed or offered in Sacrifice, my pretious body and bloud. Semeth S. Hippolytus by these wordes to meane, that in this respecte al faithful people be priestes and bishops? why, construe them M. Iewel. How can you make this seeming? O you say, in this respecte al faithful people be priestes and bishops, and to them semeth Christ to speake by S. Hippolytus.

M. Iew. maketh ẏ people priestes & bishops.

Though the people were priestes and byshops as you say, yet in this place by report of this blessed Martyr, Christ is brought in thus speaking not to the people, for to them he speaketh afterward, but specially to bishops. For the order of the Doctor is an inuincible argument against you. First he maketh Christe to say, Venite Prophetæ. &c. Come ye Prophetes, then, come ye Patriarkes, nexte, come ye Apostles, after them, come ye Martyrs. Immediatly in order he placeth the calling of bishops, and saith, Come ye Bishops &c. After them he speaketh to the people in particular, Venite Sancti, come ye sainctes that lyued hardly in hilles and dennes, &c. Come ye young wemen, come ye that loued the poore, and so to others. Lastly he saith to al in general, Come ye blessed of my father, &c. Wherfore the name of Bishops here perteineth to a special calling, not to al the faithful people in general.

By the order of S. Hippolytus sayinges, the name of bishops in this place perteineth to a special calling.

And that he meant them which by special calling and consecration be bishops, and not the people, it is euident by S. Hippolytus him selfe, who is a litle before these wordes alleged, shewing that before the seate of Christe sitting in the last iudgemēt, they shalbe brought, who were once kinges, rulers, bishops, and priestes, (for these foure he nameth) he telleth wherefore, with these wordes, vt administrationis suæ & ouilis reddāt rationem, qui videlicet per negligentiam suam perdiderunt ouem de grege suo, to geue accompt of their gouernement, and of their folde, who through their negligence haue lost any Sheepe of their flocke. I trow M. Iewel you will not saye, that euery of the people, euery man and woman, poore and rich, young and olde, hath a folde of spiritual sheepe, and a flocke to kepe. Nay Sir, you knowe, the people be the shepe them selues, they be not the pastours, the herdmen, the shepherdes: they be fed by their bishops and priestes, they be not the feeders, they be lead, they be not the leaders, to be shorte in this respecte they be people, they be not priestes and Bishops. Of such Bishops meant S. Hippolytus. Of which sort and vocation, because euery one of the people is not, therefore the meaning of S. Hippolytus semeth not to be that, which you haue imagined.

Againe what meane you M. Iewel by *your respecte?* Be al faithful people, Priestes and Bishops in this respect, that they offer vp vnto God the body and bloud of Christe? For to any other respect you can not drawe your wordes in this place. If you meane so, you must tel vs where you learned that strange doctrine. The faithfull people in dede do offer vp Christ to God, by vowe, and deuotion. But the body and bloud of Christ properly and truly can not be offered or Sacrificed without consecration, which perteineth to the office of Priestes only, and not to the people. And therefore this kinde of Sacrificing belongeth not to the people.

And whereas you allege S. Peter, saying that he calleth the people priestes and bishops, that is a manifest vntruth.
1.Pet.2. Though S. Peter cal the beleuers a holy priesthod, meaning that euery faithful person is a Priest, in as much as he offereth vp to God spiritual Sacrifices, as prayers, thankes geuing,
Rom.12. praises, a contrite hart, &c. and specially in asmuch as he offereth him selfe a liuely hoste by mortification of him selfe: yet thereby

he

he meaneth not, that euery one may really and actually consecrate and offer the body and bloud of Christe. And how so euer
the faithful people of S. Peter be called Priestes, yet verely,
neither by him, nor by any other parte of Canonical scripture,
or by any of the Fathers, be they called Bishops. Now our place
of S. Hippolytus speaketh of Bishops, and not of Priestes. For
his worde is not ἱερεῖς, but ἱεράρχαι, whereby are signified the ἱεράρχαι
chiefe Priestes, or gouernours of Priestes, and by that name the
people are no where called. Wherefore this exposition of S.
Hippolytus meaning, deuised by M. Iewels new Diuinitie,
is vaine, false, and fonde, and is founded vpon no grounde of
scripture nor reason. For though a man apply to him selfe, as
he speaketh, the Sacrifice of the pretious body and bloud of
Christe neuer so much, yet is not that properly a Sacrifice of the
body and bloud of Christe offered vp vnto God. The apply-
ing thereof of a man to him selfe, is not the Oblation, or Sacrificing of it. Thus S. Hippolytus standeth fully on our syde, and
is not by M. Iewel answered, notwithstanding he hath said al
that he could, vtterly to deface his auctoritie.

The vij. Diuision.

HEre M. Iewel starteth aside altogether, staith him selfe in
bye maters, and commeth not to the point. Which is the
policie of them, that haue not what to say directly, and
yet are driuen to answer. For it semeth to them better in that
case to vse shiftes, and say somewhat, though impertinent to
the state of the present mater: then by yelding, or saying nothing, to seme ouercomme. And because a mannes yelding to
the truth, and acknowleging him selfe to be ouercome, procedeth
of humilitie, and humilitie stādeth not with the spirite of heresy:

thereof it commeth, that perfite heretikes seldom, or rather neuer geue ouer, and holde silence, though they be neuer so euidētly confuted. Euen so it fareth here with M. Iewel. And so wilt thou iudge Reader, if with good aduise thou consider both our sayinges in this place. Mary if thou bring not with thee an attent minde, he may happen to carrye thee awaye from the due consyderation of the mater, that is specially treated. Marke, and iudge.

There in effect I say this much. First, where as our aduersaries speaking of the priestes sole receiuing with great villanie of wordes, reproue Priuate Masse, because the people do not participate of the blessed Sacrament with him: if they might be stirred to such deuotion, as to dispose thē selues worthily to receiue their housel with the priest daily, as they did in the Primitiue Church: I aske, what these men should haue to say.

M. Iew. starteth from that he ought to answer vnto, and spendeth many wordes in thinges impertinent.

To this question M. Iewel, that maketh so long a Replie, answereth neuer a worde. But guilefully entreth into other matters impertinent, to lead the vnlearned reader from the question that is asked. which impertinent maters, as they be easy to be answered, so for auoiding of tedious prolixitie, (whereof there should be no ende, if I would treate of euery thing that he bringeth without iust cause or prouse) I wil let passe, and leauing the confusion he goeth about to bring me vnto in answering, I wil rest in the point not yet by him answered. Therefore I demaund of you once againe M. Iewel. whereas ye reproue the Masse, and raile so much at it, because the people receiueth not with the priest: If ye people were induced to receiue with him, what haue you then to say? As for example. we see in this Countrie, as also in other places we haue sene, certaine deuoute and wel disposed people, very oftentimes to receiue their housel with the priest at the ende of Masse, and that freely, and of their mere deuotion,

and

and not by compulsion of law as ye do. What say you to such Masse? Like you it? Or do you condemne it? Answer in fewe, of or on. If you like it, raile and scoffe no more at the Masse, but blame the people for their negligence, and lacke of deuotion. And if you wil blame the clergie for not warning the people of their duetie, I wil not therewith be offended, nor any good man els. Let negligence be reproued, and also duly punished.

If you like not the Masse, whereat many of the people do receiue, as I thinke verely you would be loth to see it said & done again in Sarisburie, as it was before you brought your new gospel thither, how many so euer receiued with the Priest: then tel vs for what other causes you accompt it vnlawful and contrary to the scriptures. And by gods grace we shal answere you, and withstand al your malice against the Masse, whether you fynde faulte with the priestes vestiments, with the gylted chalice, with the Latine tongue in which it is said, with the aulter, with ẏ adoration of our Lordes body, with lightes, or what els so euer it be, for which the deuil and you can not away with the Masse. If you tel vs this, then do you answere to the question which was demaunded of you, which yet you haue not done.

In case you could haue deuised a good and reasonable answer to this question, you should not haue had nede so farre to wander from the purpose, and to thrust into your booke such riffe raffe as you haue. When you were loth to disclose the weaknesse of your cause by making direct answer to my question, you thought good to leaue that vntouched, and to bring me into hatred with the readers, for saying, *the people be Dogges and Svvine.* *Wherein you reporte me falsly and vnhonestly. For read the place who wil by your owne selfe quoted, and he shal fynde you an vntrue reporter, and me cleere of that odious saying. For in that place is not so much as the name of Dogges.

The 53. vntruth. I say it not.

Likewise without truth or reason, you would father this vanitie vpon me, as though I held opinion, that the negligence of the people must be the rule of Christes religion. And thereat, * as though I had said so in dede, you make gay sporte: whereas no such thing can be gathered of ought that I said.

The. 54. vntruth. I say no such thing

And though I said, the people in the Primitiue church receiued their housel euery day, that when so euer they should be taken and done to death by the Infidels, they might not depart hence without their viage prouision: foloweth it thereof M. Iewel, that I haue confessed there was no Priuate Masse as you terme it in the primitiue Churche? If I had said expressely, that euery one had receiued the Sacrament with the Priest at churche in the Masse time, and that the Masse was neuer celebrated, but when the people receiued: you might haue had some colour of your false saying noted in the margent of your booke, and of your vntrue collection in the texte of your Replie. Remember you not, that ech person most commonly serued him selfe of the Communion secretly at home, because they might not safely do it in solemne assemblie for their cruel Persecutours?

Page. 14,

Now I pray you make your argument, and iudge how wise it is your selfe. Your aduersary saith, that the faithful people receiued the blessed Sacrament euery day by them selues secretly at home, hauing it consecrated at the handes of Priestes: Ergo he confesseth there was no Priuate Masse in the Primitiue churche. I denye your argument M. Iewel, how proue you it? Doth euery secret and Priuate receiuing of one in his house by him selfe alone argue, that there was no Priuate Masse? Why Syr, what if a man do now receiue at home, as sicke men do commonly, is there for that cause where this is

done

done no Priuate Masse? Verely Logike is good chepe, where such argumentes go for good.

I let passe many other thinges impertinent: As the bitter blame of the Clergie for that the people is no more preached vnto, and for taking vp their Tiethes, for that the people vnderstandeth not al that the Priest saith at Masse, and because he vseth certaine gestures that M.Iewel liketh not. Item that the Pope and his Cardinals do scarsely communicate once in a yere, but are as negligent and vndeuout, as the people: al these and many other thinges wherewith he stuffeth his booke in this seuēth diuision, I passe ouer, as not being worth the answering, and quite besyde the point presently treated.

One thing yet I thought good to note. What meant you to allege a Decree, whereby they were excommunicate in olde time, that being present at the reading of the scriptures, for negligence forebare to receiue the Communion? This was decreed say you by the Fathers of the second Councel of Bracara, and by your quotation you make it to be the. 84. chapter or canon, whereas of that Councel there be but ten in al, and among them that which you bring is none. This could I haue dissembled, were not that your selfe in your Replie to M. Doctor Cole, make much a doo with the Reuerend father of blessed memorie Steuen Gardiner, and triumphe at him as though he were a mā vtterly vnlearned, for that in alleging a saying of S. Augustine out of his treatise de Sermone domini in monte, he named the third booke for the second.

M. Iew. offendeth in that he blameth in others.

The Canon which you allege is to be founde in the collection of Chapters, that bishop Martinus made out of the Grecke Councels. Which as you allow to be of good auctoritie, so must you of reason allow the Masse also, whereof there is expresse mention by the name of Missarum solennia. Neither by that

In collectione capitū Græcarum synodorum. Can. 65.

that decree was any man excommunicate, that for negligence or wantonnesse withdrew him selfe from the Communion, as you do interprete the wordes: but for that he forebare to receiue the Sacrament pro luxuria sua, for cause of his lecherie, that is, because he had purposed to satisfie his vncleane luste, and rather then he would receiue with such a gilty mynde and intent, he would forebeare and not receiue at al. For so the word Luxuria signified in that age, specially among the Ecclesiastical wryters, who were much gone from the exactenesse of the Latine speach vsed in the former ages.

The other cause of excommunication, (for two causes in this case be there expressed) was, for that as some one turned him selfe away from the Sacramēt, so would he also decline and go from the discipline, which was then ordeined to be kept in the reuerend Mysteries. These be the causes of excommunication in that Canon truly reported. So that of that Canon it can not be iustly gathered, as M. Iewel doth, that who so euer had for negligence refused to receiue the Communion with the Priest, had therefore ben excommunicate. The fathers were not so straight, but a man might escape excommunication, though at sometimes he were not disposed to receiue.

That I and my felowes, as you cal them, do flatter the people, and fauer their negligence in this case, it is a false sclaunder. We neither flatter ẏ people forsloing their dutie, nor fauer their negligence, but wish with al our hartes, they would so liue and dispose them selues, as they might more often receiue that blessed Sacrament to their great benefite and increase of grace. And among other holesom lessons wherewith we taught them their duetie, before you and your felowes brake into our churches, and inuaded the pulpites: we forgote not to put them in mynde thereof, and to exhort them thereunto.

But

But that they should runne vnto it vnreuerently, as to a drinking, or an other prophane busines, without al former and due preparation, not being before purged by confession, and reconciled by the Sacrament of Penaunce, as we see they of your congregation do: from that wicked presumption, and contempt of the Body of Christe, by which we were redeemed: with al diligence we haue kept the people, and exhorted them to consider thoroughly, to whose table thei should go, whom thei should receiue, and to how great benefite if worthily, to how terrible damnation, if vnworthily. So both we taught, and they beleued, that safer for them and better it were, to receiue that heauenly foode more seldome and worthily, then often and vnworthily. Yet the oftener the better, if worthily.

In this Diuision, as M. Iewel answereth not the question demaunded, but carieth away the Reader to other impertinent mater: so neither saith he ought to my argument made in defēce of the Priest, but bestoweth many woordes in thinges at this time not specially treated. The argument is this, as it may be easely conceiued.

Where no fault is committed, there no blame is to be imputed. That often times the Priest at Masse hath no company to receiue with him, it proceedeth of the peoples vndeuotion, not of enuie or malice, or any other default of his parte: Ergo for that there is no blame to be imputed vnto the Priest.

Here the Maior, or first proposition M. Iewel wil graunt, I am sure. As for the Minor, if he finde fault with the Priest, because the people by due preaching is not persuaded to communicate with him: then let him be blamed for his negligence therein, not for saying Masse. And though he were worthily blamed for that, ye is there nothing shewed why he should be blamed for celebrating Masse without the people receiuing the Communion with him. And so is the Priest cleared of all blame for saying Masse without a company to communicate with him.

M. Iew. conueigheth him selfe away from the purpose by speaking thinges impertinent.

Al this doth M. Iewel passe ouer without worde of answer, vsing silence for a vantage, where woordes shoulde bewray the weakenes of his cause. And forthwith he addresseth him selfe to talke of other maters, as of the preparation and disposition of the heart, before we presume to heare or receiue any thing that toucheth God. And that point he proueth by Pythagoras, and by the manner that Paganes vsed in their Sacrifices.

After that he hath bestowed many wordes vainely in that common place, which semeth to haue been taken out of his note booke: he goeth to say, what he hath founde in al the Gospellers writinges alleged against Confession, which as to confute here were long, so very needlesse, forsomuch as I haue already proued the necessitie of Cōfession in my Confutatiō of the Apologie.

In the 2. parte *Fol.68.* a.& b.

This done he flieth fiercely at Priestes, and layeth forth what he hath gathered together in his note boke out of S. Bernard against the euil lyfe of Priestes, as though his fellowes were Angels, and he him selfe an Archangel. And here are brought in his golden cuppes, and treene Priestes out of Bonifacius. which place is euer at hande, when he is disposed to wreake his malice vpon Priestes. Now I thinke it better to confute that he bringeth for proufe of his First Article against Masse whereat the Priest receiueth alone, (albeit in deede litle it be, that he bringeth to that very point, and to the purpose directly) then to refel his impertinent digressions, wherein he wandreth for lacke of good groundes to stay him selfe vpon. Thus I note, that he neither answereth the question, what these fellowes of his syde would say to the Masse, if the people would receiue with the Priest, nor saith ought to ỹ argument, wherby

I proue the Priest to be blamelesse in case of the peoples negligence. wherunto it was requisite he should haue said fully.

As for the Popes and Cardinals rare saying of Masse, preparation to be made when we heare any thing concerning God, Confession of sinnes, ẏ Priestes saing of * many Masses in one daye, which is a manifest vntruth, if he meane the ordinary custome or any day beside the day of Christes birth, the euil lyfe of Priestes, the causes of the peoples loosenesse and negligence, the great multitude of Clerks in the Church of Rome: al these maters and many other bye thinges, that in this Diuision he talketh of, be quite beside the purpose. To al these idle pointes I intend to frame M. Iewel an answere hereafter, if I can not finde wayes how to bestow my time better.

The .55. vntruth. the priests say not many masses in one day.

The Eight Diuision.

The summe of this diuision.

TO declare briefly the summe of this Diuision, for so much as the wordes which M. Iewel hath taken out of my booke, and here laid together, do import: First I aske with what face he and his fellowes crye so busely for the Institution of Christe concerning this Sacrament, by whom in the chiefe pointes the same is violated. Therewithal I say, that in the Institution of the Sacrament three things are conteined which Christe him selfe did, and by his commaundement gaue the Churche auctoritie, to do, Consecration, Oblation, and Participation, by which Participation I meane the receiuing of the thinges offered, in which three consisteth the substance of the Masse. I say besydes, that they hauing quite abrogated Consecration, and Oblation, haue lefte to the people nothing but a bare Communion. In consideration wherof, them selues being breakers of Christes Institution, shew to the worlde their shamelesnes, in that they require it so exactly of others.

Then omitting to speake of Consecration, and Oblation, of Participation I say this much. That as it is in it selfe necessarie and of Christes institution: so the number of participāts together in one place is not of Institution. Thereof I conclude, that whether one or fewe, or but one in one place receiue: for that respect the ministration of the Priest, in that we call the Masse, is not made vnlauful. This is the briefe summe of that parte. The chiefe point that I stande vpon is this, that nūber of Participantes or receiuers together in one place, is Ceremonical, determinable by the Church, as many other Obseruaunces be, and not essential or of the substance of the Sacrament, or of the Institution of Christe.

Number of receiuers together is not of the substance of ỹ Sacrament, nor of Christs Institution.

Before M. Iewel commeth to this chiefe pointe, he wandereth farre abroade, and vppon light occasion taken of my wordes, maketh discourses against me. which discourses because therwith he impugneth ỹ truth, & goeth about to subuert ỹ Catholike faith, touching this weighty mater: litle esteming what he worketh against my person, for truthes sake here I intend to discusse. Such credite I require the Reader to geue vnto him, as by his doctrine here he shal seme to deserue.

Ievvel.

It liketh M. Harding to cal vs vvicked, and the ennemies, of the Sacrifice: and to say, vve iangle of the Institution of Christ, and yet our selues breake Christes Institution.

Harding.

Fol.12.a.b

Why M. Iewel doth your gilty conscience whisper you in the eare, that I meant you, where I named the ennemies of this holy Sacrifice? And take you peper in the nose, as thei say, because I meruailed, that they crye out so much for the Institution of Christ, by whom it is most wickedly broken? Loke in my

boke

loke, and you shal see that I speake indefinitely. If you confesse your selfe gilty, and iudge it meant of you & your fellowes: you may yet repent, and amend that is amisse. Verely by ought you haue therto answered, you haue not cleered your selfe.

That you are the ennemie of this blessed Sacrifice, euen here you confesse it for your selfe and for your fellowes: where you vtter rayling wordes of Satans prompting, calling that, against which you professe your hatred, errours, abuses, and sacriledge, maintained to the open derogation of the Sacrifice and Crosse of Christe. This is the vtterance of your malice, wherein you powre forth the cankred humour of your stomake, & bewraye the weaknes of your cause. For God be thanked, your serpentine tongue hisseth more agaist the Sacrifice of the Masse, then your venemous tooth byteth with dent of reason. As here it shal wel appeare.

M. Iew. blasphemouse rayling.

Ievvel.

As touching Christes institution, forgeat not good Christian Reader, that M. Harding confesseth, there are three thinges therein contemed, vvhich as he saith, Christe him selfe did, and by his commaundemẽt gaue auctoritie to his Church to do: the Consecration, the Oblation, and the Participation. Here he leaueth quite out the Annunciation of Christes Death, thinking perhaps it is no mater essential of Christes Institution. Of these three (he saith) vve haue broken tvvo, the Consecration, and Oblation: and so haue onely a bare Communion.

Harding.

I confesse these three things in dede to be cõteined in Christes Institution. forgeat it not Christian Reader eftsones I require thee. But I *leaue out the Annunciation of Christes death*, saith M. Iewel. what then? I exclude it not, saye I. He that of Foure thinges nameth three expressely, excludeth not the Fourth.

As touching Christes Institutiõ, although I name expressely Consecration, Oblation, and Participation: I except not the

That speaking of Conse-

That, speaking of Conse- cration, oblation, and parti- cipation, I exclude not the Annunci- ation of Christes death.

the Annunciation of Christes death. Yea I saye, that neither I leaue it out, as M. Iewel chargeth me, but how ignorantly he chargeth me, ẏ learned Diuines do wel vnderstāde. For these three do liuely shewe forth & preach vnto vs our Lords death in facte, so that ẏ worde of ẏ Annunciation is needelesse to ech of them, though ẏ word also be mentioned in the Masse. When we conse- crate, when we offer, when we participate, or receiue ẏ holy Ob- lation, what do we but signifie & shew forth the death of Christe?

Eusebius Emisen. Hom. 5 de Pascha.

Wil you haue this much M. Iewel to be confirmed by the witnesse of some good Doctour of the Churche? Heare you then first, what Eusebius Emisenus saith. Quia corpus. &c. Because (saith he) Christ would take his body from our sight, & bring it into heauen, it was necessarie that in the daye of his sup- per he consecrated vnto vs the Sacramēt of his Body and Bloud: that, that might be recorded stil by Mysterie, which was once of- fered for price. Next, what S. Ambrose saith touching this very thing, where he writeth vpon these woordes of S. Paule, Mortem Domini annunciantes donec veniat, Shewwing forth the Death of our Lorde vntil he come. Quia enim morte Domini liberati sumus, huius rei memores, in edendo & po- tando, Carnem & Sanguinem, quæ pro nobis oblata sunt, signifi- camus. For inasmuch as (saith he) we are diliuered by the Death of our Lorde, beīg mindeful of this thing, in eatīg & drine- king (he meaneth at the holy table) wee doo signifie and shew forth the Flesh and Bloud which were offered for vs.

Ambros. in 1. Cor. 11

Ibidem.

The same S. Ambrose saith againe there, He that com- meth to receiue the Body of our Lorde, ought to iudge this with him selfe, that it is our Lorde, whose Bloud in Mysterie he drinketh, which Bloude is witnesse of the benefite of God. Which if we receiue with discipline, we shal not be vnworthy

the

the Body and Bloude of our Lorde : for so we shal seeme to render thankes to our Redemer.

Lo M. Iewel if the Bloude in these Mysteries consecrated, offered, and receiued be a witnesse of Gods benefite towardes vs, as S. Ambrose saith: then what do we by Consecration, Oblation, and Participation or receiuing, but testifie, recorde, and shew forth to al, the benefite of God, that is the death and passion of Christe, whom God gaue and deliuered for vs, that we thereby should be redemed?

Neyther shal we after this holy Doctor, doing thus, onely testifie the benefite of God, which is the death of Christ: but also seeme thereby to render thankes to our Redemer. Now who so euer doth that, whereby thankes are rendred to his Redemer, the same thankefully signifieth and sheweth forth the Death of his Creator, by which he is redemed.

That the Annunciation of Christes death is set forth in this Sacrifice, it is most clearly declared by S. James in his Masse or Liturgie, where he maketh the Priest that sacrificeth, the Deacons that attend vpon the Priest or Byshop, and the people that is present, to confesse the same.

First the Priest saith thus. Hoc facite in meam commemorationem, &c. Do ye this in my remembrance. For as often times as ye eate this breade, and drinke this Cup, ye do shew forth the death of the Sonne of man, and ye confesse his resurrection vntil he come. Then say the Deacons. Credimus, & confitemur. We beleue it, and confesse it. Then saith the people. Mortem tuam Domine annunciamus, & resurrectionem tuam confitemur. We shewe forth O Lorde thy death, and thy resurrection we confesse. *Iacobus in Liturgia.*

S. Chrysostome declareth fully and plainely, that as the sacri- *Chrysost.*

Hom.83.in Mat. sacrificing and eating of the lambe in the olde Lawe, was a memorial and recorde of the miracles, which God wrought in the deliuerie of the people of Israel out of Egypte: so this Mysterie wherein the Body of Christ is sacrificed and eaten, is that, which alwayes bringeth to remembraunce and setteth before vs the great benefites, that we enioy by Christes death and passion.

Writing vpon S. Mathew, among other thinges apperteining to the proufe of this point, he saith, that, because the Hom.eadē time should come, when Marcion, Valentinus, Manichæus, and their folowers would denie that was donne by Christ in flesh (as specially his true passion and death) Christe doth continually bring vs vnto the remembraunce of his passion by this Mysterie: that no man which is in his right witte can be seduced. There he shutteth vp his whole tale with this Epiphonema, or conclusiō. Ita per Sacratissimam istam mensam & saluat, & docet: hoc enim caput bonorum omnium est. Thus through this most holy table Christe both saueth and teacheth: for this is the head of al good things.

Lo M. Jewel, heare you not that Christe doth the office of a preacher & teacher at these holy Mysteries, which S. Chrysostome signifieth by the name of this most holy table? which sometime is called a table, because Christes Body and Bloude are thence eaten and dronke, somtime an aulter, because theron they are offered and sacrificed? And how doth Christe the office of a teacher at this holy table, but by the ministerie of the priest, who not by expresse wordes so much, as by worke and act it selfe in the person of Christ, in the celebration of these Mysteries doth preach, teach, signifie, shew forth, and bring vnto remembrance the death of our Lorde? which shewing forth or Annunciation of our Lordes death being the principal ende of Consecration, Oblation, and Participation, and inseparably folowing the same, as the ende foloweth the thing whose ende it is: M. Iewel sheweth him selfe an vnskilful Diuine, in that he chargeth and blameth me hauing rehearsed those three, for leauing out the Annuntiation of our Lordes Death. For as he that saith, M. Iewel dranke a cuppe of wine, saith also that he swalowed it downe, though expressely he speake it not: So he that saith, Consecration, Oblation, and Participation be conteined in the Institution of Christe: doth not (as he saith) quite leaue out the Annunciation or shewing forth of his death. M. Iew. wrangleth through his owne vnskil.

The Scripture it selfe declareth this most euidently. For S. Paule describing to the Corinthians, how and what Christe did at his Supper, hath thus. Do ye this, so oftentimes as ye shal drinke for remembraunce of me. For as oftentimes as ye eate this breade, and drinke this cuppe: ye do shew forth our Lordes death, vntil he come. So I turne it after the Greeke text by the Present tense, which hath καταγγέλλετε, for so doth Nicolaus Gabasila, that learned Greeke vnderstand the place with other Greekes. Thus by S. Paule the eating and drinking, which I vnderstande by Participation, is an Annuntiation, and a shewing forth of Christes death, which M. Iewel very ignorantly pretendeth to be quite left out, wheras the doing of the other, is the most perfite performance of this. 1. Cor, 11.

I sayd the enemies of this Sacrifice haue broken the Institution of Christe, for that they haue abrogated the Consecration and Oblation, and haue left to the people but a bare Communiō, and that after their own manner. M. Iewel would seme herewith offended, & pretendeth that he and his fellowes haue both the Consecratiō and Oblation. But how wel he proueth it, let due examination trie.

Ievvel.

Concerning Consecration, he doth great vvrong to charge vs vvith the breach thereof, before he him selfe and others of his side * be *better resolued vvherin standeth Consecration.* The 56. vntruth. we are perfitly resolued herein

Harding.

I do you no wrong in saying, that ye haue abrogated the Consecration and Oblation. for very true it is, as in further processe it shal plainely appeare by sufficient prouse and by your owne confession. But you do me and Christes Churche greate wrong, by saying that I and they of my side, who be al that stand in the Catholike faith, be not wel resolued, wherein standeth Consecration. For truth it is, we are perfitely resolued according to the instinct of the holy Ghost, and doctrine of al holy Fathers of the Church, that the Consecration of the Body of Christ consisteth in these wordes of our Lord by a Priest duely pronounced, Hoc est corpus meum, This is my Bodie. Likewise we are resolued concerning the Consecration of the Bloud. By imputing vnto vs the contrary, you proue your selfe a false slaunderer. And here let your owne words be witnesse of your falsehed.

The.57. vntruth. they say it not.

Ievvel.

Bonauentura in.4. Sentent.

Bessarion de sacramento Eucharist.

*For Scotus and Innocentius tertius, and certaine others * say that this vvorde, Benedixit, He blessed, vvorketh Consecration. The common opinion is, that it is vvrought by these vvordes, This is my Body. Some thinke that Christ spake these vvords tvvise, first secretly to him selfe and aftervvard openly, that the Apostles might understand him. Cardinal Bessarion Byshop of Tusculum vvriteth thus. The Latine Church folovving Ambrose, Augustine, and Gregorie, thinketh that Consecration standeth in these vvordes, This is my Body. But the Greeke Churche thinketh the Consecratiō is not vvrought by these vverds, but by the praier of the Priest, vvhich folovveth aftervvard, and that according to S. Iames, S. Chrysostome, and S. Basil. By these * it appeareth, that they them selfe of that syde, are not yet fully agreed vpon their ovvne Consecration.*

The.58. vntruth. he writeth not so, but speaketh only of a fewe late schismatike Grekes.

Harding.

You make but a slender reason against the Catholike Church,

Church M. Iewel. For what if Scotus, and Innocentius Tertius, (as for your certeine others, you woulde haue named them if you had them) and some Schismatikes of the late Greke Church, thinke Consecration to be done, by other then our Lords wordes, is not the Catholike Church therfore herein resolued? Shal the diuerse opinion of so fewe, preiudicate the vniformitie and concord of the whole? Make your argumēt after your owne Logike, and the world shal easily see how peeuish it is.

> Scotus, and Innocentius, and a fewe schismatike Grekes thinke of Consecration otherwise then the Church holdeth: Ergo, the Church is not resolued by what wordes Consecration is made.

By such Logike it were easy to conclude against you many absurdities. But it is a very bad reason, you wil sticke to vse, rather then not to say somewhat against the Catholikes.

Now wherfore brought you in these fewe as Mumners? why speake they not for you? Discharge your credite, where teach they their doctrine contrary to that ye Church holdeth? wil you haue men beleue your bare worde? Verely then are they sure to be oftentimes deceiued.

Neyther Scotus, nor Innocentius Tertius euer sayd, as you reporte, that the worde Benedixit, He blessed, worketh Cōsecracion, as though we should thinke that the Priest doth consecrate the blessed Sacrament, when in ye holy Canon, and about ye words of the true Consecratiō he pronoūceth this worde, Benedixit. It semeth that you neuer read them, but folowed your note booke made out of some Gospellers treatise, or that you vnderstande them not, where they seeme to speake somewhat like to ye you reporte of them, there they speake not specially of

The obiection out of Scotus & Innocentius answered.

the forme of Consecration, which the Church vseth: but of that whereby Christ at his Supper consecrated.

In 4. sententiar. distinct. 8. quest. 2.

As for the wordes of Consecration of the Body, looke you in Scotus, and you shal finde him say, they be foure, which in order he reckeneth. the Pronoune Hoc, the Verbe est, & in apposito, corpus meum, as he speaketh. The Coniunction enim, saith he, is not of the essence of the forme. Of the forme of Consecration of the Bloude, he treateth also very exactly, and learnedly remoueth doubtes that might rise thereof, of which some be obiected to the Catholikes, by the Lutherans, and Zuinglians. Wherefore of al men that euer wrote, you had lest cause M. Iewel to bring Scotus against the Catholikes for shewe of any braul, cauil, or wrangling, to be made touching the doctrine of Consecration. But it is a signe you be neare driuen when you are faine to flee to Scotus for helpe, whom otherwise you litle esteme, because his doctrine in manner in al other pointes doth condemne you. But you care not what any be, so he seme to haue but halfe a worde against any thing that we saye, as in him yet you haue none.

M. Iew. is faine to flee to Scotus for helpe.

As for Innocentius, he doth not so determinatly pronouce sentence in this matter, as he declareth what certeine men haue said thereof. Whereas the Priest (saith he) at the pronouncing of these wordes, This is my Body, This is my Bloude, doth consecrate: it is iudged credible, that Christ also consecrated by speaking the same wordes. After this he rehearseth the opinion of certaine others. Of which some saide, that Christ consecrated, when he blessed, so construing the letter, as by blessing, they meant also the wordes, This is my Body, to be added. So benedixit, referred to Christe, signifieth this much, that Christe blessed with saying, This is my body.

Innocent. De officio Missæ. lib. 3. cap. 18.

Others haue saide (saith he) that Christe both consecrated the

the Sacrament, and instituted a forme of consecration after blessing, when he saide, This is my Body. These two opinions by him rehersed, he sheweth his owne, and that with such modestie, because it was not commonly holden, as I wishe M. Jewel would vse the like, when he vpholdeth any newe and strange doctrine contrary to that, the Catholike Church hath euer taught. Sane dici potest, Soothly it may be saide, saith he. And there telleth what may be sayde, and doth not determinatly affirme, what is to be saide. Wherein he sayde his owne opinion, that appeared to him probable, he pronoūced not a definitiue sentence, whereunto euery man should stande. The modestie of Innocentius in vttering his opinion.

Now this much you should haue considered, before you had spoken so rashly against vs not being resolued for Consecration: This smal diuersitie of Opinions is touching Christ, how and whereby he Consecrated, by that he blessed, as some fewe saide, or by his diuine power, as Innocentius thought, or by saying, This is my Body, which is the common and receiued opinion: but as touching the forme of Consecration, which Christe lefte to the Churche, & which ẏ Church vseth, & hath alwayes vsed, which is, This is my Body: therein al Catholikes be fully resolued. Yea although some susteyned a diuerse opinion from the rest, concerning that whereby Christe consecrated: yet they and al in general are resolued vpon this, that Priestes ought to Consecrate by pronouncing the woordes of our Lorde, This is my Body, and none other. So that this hath been agreed vpon by al, that the Churche consecrateth the Body of Christe, with these woordes, This is my Body. Thus it is proued, both that I haue here done you no wrong, and that you haue bely- The Catholikes be perfitly resolued with what wordes ẏ Body and Bloude of Christe is cōsecrated of the priestes.

ed vs, and haue shewed your selfe malapert in a mater, which you seme not to vnderstande.

In lib. 4. sentent. distinct. 8.

As for Bonauenture whom you allege, as you directe the Reader by your quotation, you haue fowly abused and falsified him. For whereas he reiecteth the opinion of certaine, and confuting it, as writing vpon the Fourth booke of Lombardus he is to be seene: it is no reason you shoulde take holde thereof, and laye it to our charge, as a thing mainteined by the Catholikes. For that place it selfe: is a witnesse against you. Is it not a shame to allege that against the Catholikes, which they reproue and confute?

M. Iew. allegeth ẏ obiections which the Schoolemen confuted, as doctrine mainteined by the catholikes

That Christe spake the wordes of Consecration, (some deceiued men said as Bonauenture there reciteth) *first secretly to him selfe*, (saith M. Iewel) Primo in occulto ad conficiendum, First in secrete to consecrate, saith Bonauenture reporting the erroneous opinion of others. *And afterwarde openly, that the Apostles might vnderstande him*, hath M. Iewel. Secundo in aperto ad formam institutam manifestandam, hath Bonauenture, that is to say, secondly (Christe spake) openly, to thintent the forme of Consecration instituted might be made manifest. What falsehed is this to turne, *Ad formam institutam manifestandam*, *that the Apostles might vnderstande him*? Is this the right englishing of Bonauentures wordes? Because you denye the forme of Consecration which the Churche vseth, therefore you were loth any worde should be seene in your booke thereof, though the Doctor you allege, speake of it neuer so plaine. You had done better, if you had neuer alleged neyther Bonauenture, nor Scotus, nor Innocentius, nor S. Thomas, nor Bessarion, for al these make moste euidently and expressely against you, as they shall

M. Iew. falsifieth Bonauenture.

M. Iew. allegeth doctors ẏ make most expresly & dyrectly

finde

kynde, who for tryal of the truth, wil take paynes to reade them.

against him.

Bessarion.

But let vs come to Bessarion, who was not onely Bishop of Tusculum, as M. Iewel noteth, but also Patriarke of Constantinople. Out of him he allegeth a long sentence, but so as falsifiers are wont to doo, leauing out a parte by mangling, and mingling his owne woordes with the Doctors, so making of the whole, a mingle mangle. For whereas Bessarion speaking of the Latines saith, that they affirme most manifestly those wordes, This is my Body, and, This is my Bloude, to be the wordes whereby the Body and Bloude of Christ are consecrate: that good peece hath M. Iewel cut of, which maketh for the truth: and putteth in of his owne, the name of *the Greeke Churche*, whereby the Reader myght thinke, the whole Churche of Greece to vary from the Latine Churche, touching Consecration: whereas Bessarion nameth not *the Greeke Churche*, but certaine Greekes, and them specially of late yeares, for so be his very wordes, Græci vero, præsertim recentiores, &c.

M. Iew. falsifieth Bessariō.

Concerning the thing it selfe, what prouse is that of disagreeing, and that the Catholike Churche is not reasolued by which woordes the Body of Christe is consecrate, because some Greekes of late yeares among other their errours, haue this also, that they thinke it to be Consecrate by the prayers of the Priest, which be made after that the woordes of our Lord, this is my bodie, be pronoūced? If we may not say, ỹ church is resolued in any thig, which by Heretikes haue ben gainesaid: what thing is there in our religion so sure & certaine, wherin it may be said to be resolued? wherefore we leaue ỹ singular opiniō of a fewe Late deceined Grekes, to the Schismatik Grekes, to whom M. Iewel now fleeth for helpe of his bad mater.

Take them vnto you M. Jewel if they like you: For where they forsake the Church, there also do we forsake them.

And forasmuch as they are holden for Schismatikes, and be diuided from vs for sundry other pointes, but specially for their errour touching the proceding of the holy Ghoste: you doo vs great wrong to burthen vs with their vntrue opinion of the Consecration. which you do, where you say after the falsified sentence of Bessarion alleged, *By these it appeareth, that they them selfe of that syde, are not yet fully agreed vpon their ovvne Consecration.* Those deceiued and schismatike Greekes be not of our syde M. Jewel. They of our syde, that is to say, al men that hold and mainteine the Catholike faith of Christes Church, be, and euer haue been fully agreed and resolued vpon this point, that the Mysteries are consecrate by the wordes of our Sauiour, This is my Body, This is my Bloud. And that of no man could you haue learned better the of Bessarion him selfe, whom you allege. who hath most exactly treated thereof in his booke De Sacramento Eucharistiæ written for the same purpose.

No man declareth the vniforme consẽt of ẏ church touching Consecration better then Bessarion.

There speaking of the late Greekes his countrie men, he saith, that as by the calamities of the times they haue lost many thinges that had their first beginning among them, (he meaneth ẏ knowlege of ẏ thiges ẏ belong to ẏ Sacramẽts) so they haue also forgotten these rites. But where he speaketh of ẏ olde learned Fathers of the Greeke Churche, namely of S. Basil, S. Chrysostome, John Damascen, and others: he sheweth plainely, that touching Consecration, they were of the same minde and iudgement, as the Latine Fathers be. The reasons whatsoeuer haue been obiected by Nicolaus Cabasila, Marcus Ephesinus, or any other late Greekes against the common consent of the learned Fathers of bothe Churches, there most learnedly and in good order he dissolueth, and in the conclusion persuadeth al

as

as wel Grekes as Latines, touching Consecration so to thinke and beleue, as the holy Romaine churche thinketh and beleueth. which is, that the body of Christe is consecrate by these wordes, of our Lorde, This is my body, and the bloud likewise by these, This is my bloud. That if you allow (M. Jewel) the auctoritie of that great learned man Bessarion, then you haue to beleue, that both these be the wordes of Consecration, and so agreed vpon by the whole Church of God: and that by vertue of them duly pronounced by a priest in the person of Christe, the bread is turned into his body, and the wine into his bloud. which would God, that for the saluation of your owne soule, and of many other ignorant soules that be caryed away vnto euerlasting damnation by your false doctrine and coũterfeit shewes of learning, you would truly beleue and professe.

Ievvel.

Hovv be it, by vvhat so euer vvordes Consecration is made, it standeth not in the abolishing of natures, as M. Harding teacheth: nor in precise and close pronouncing of certaine appointed vvordes: but in the conuerting of the natural Elementes into a godly vse: as vve see in the * vvater of Baptisme.*

The. 59. vntruth. I teach not so.

The. 60. vntruth. The consecratiõ of the Eucharist is far different from the consecration of water in baptisme.

Harding.

It is agreed vpon by al, beside the ennemies of the vnbloudy Sacrifice, that the Church hath the wordes of our Lorde for the consecration, and that our Lordes body and bloud are consecrate by these his wordes, This is my body, This is my bloud, duly pronounced by a Priest. Neither standeth Consecration in the abolishing of natures, as M. Jewel vntruly reporteth me to teach, but where Consecration is duly done, there by the almighty power of the word, the bread is verely conuerted into the body of Christe, and the wine into his bloud. which conuersion is not an abolishing of natures, as it liketh him to terme it,

See my Confutation of the Apologie Fol. 96. a.

(the authours of their lying Apologie call it *going to nothing*) but a change of substance into substance, of the substance of bread and wine, into the most excellent substāce of the body and bloud of Christe.

But what meaneth he to fynde fault with the manner of pronouncing the wordes of Consecration? would he haue vs after almost sixtien hundred yeres vniforme obseruation, by sundry miracles and otherwise witnessed to haue pleased God, alter and change the wordes, least the precise vse of them, as being certaine and appointed, should seme superstitious? But we wil geue eare vnto him, when he bringeth vs good proufe, why we should folow his newe deuises before the Institution of Jesus Christe the sonne of God. who at his last supper speaking these wordes, which the Church vseth for the forme of Consecration, consecrated his body and bloud, and commaunded his disciples to do the same. which they did, and taught the Church so to do, and shalbe done vntil he come againe, what so euer M. Jewel, his felowes, and al the wicked disciples of Antichrist shal worke to the contrary.

As for the manner of Pronouncing the wordes of Consecration, whether it be close, which M. Jewel liketh not, or open and lowde, as the Grekes sometimes vsed: it is not so essential, but a godly Christen man may beare good hart towarde either, and with al reuerence allow it, to what Church so euer he come. The auncient Church both Greke and Latine, pronounced the wordes of Consecration openly for encrease of Faith, the Latine Churche of later time hath pronounced them closely for the more reuerence, and to conserue the Maiestie of so high Mysteries. Of later time I saye, and yet when this custome began, I know not. Certaine it is that for. viij. C. yeres past, it was growen to be a custome, as appeareth by report of that learned and noble

Emperour Carolus Magnus. whom for proufe thereof I alleged in my answer to M. Iewels. 16. Article. where in his Replie without iust cause or reason, he triumpheth at me, as being contrary to my selfe, and hath put these wordes in the Margent, Printed in great text letters, that it might the more appeare, *M. Harding contrary to him selfe*: if he had vnderstanded me to speake as I did, of the Latine Church of later yeres, and not of the time of S. Clement, S. Ambrose, or S. Leo, of which time he would my wordes to be vnderstanded: he might haue spared much labour, and had lesse disclosed his owne euil disposition. In the replie. p. 550

But as M. Iewel vtterly denieth that Consecration, which the best learned & most auncient Fathers haue alwaies acknowledged, whereby as Eusebius Emisenus with these wordes setteth it forth, the inuisible priest by his secret power turneth bread and wine into the substance of his body and bloud, which is the special Cōsecration: so he admitteth none other, but ỹ whereby natural Elementes be conuerted vnto a godly vse. And that no mā should mistake him, *as vve see* (saith he) *in the vvater of Baptisme.* What see you M. Iewel in the water of Baptisme? See you Cōsecration? where see you it? Is the water in which you Baptise infantes, Consecrated or halowed in al England by the prayers of the Minister? Haue you not abandoned that Auncient obseruation, and sundry others belonging to thadministration of Baptisme, which were vsed in the Primitiue Churche? *Euseb. Emisenus in serm. de Corpore Christi.* M. Iew. new Consecration.

Yet you wil say perhaps, that in Baptisme common water is turned to a holy vse, and therin you acknowledge a Consecration. Yea syr, but that is a Consecration after the general significatiō of ỹ word. But the Diuines of the primitiue church, & of al ages speaking of ỹ mysteries, do acknowlege ỹ body & bloud of Christ to be cōsecrate by a special Cōsecratiō, which is far otherwise to be defined, thē here you teach: not whereby ỹ elemēts be cōuerted to a holy vse, but wher ther is by a maruelous chāge of Special Consecration.

 one sub-

substance into an other , the presence of a most holy and diuine thing made present, to witte, the body and bloud of Christe.

Cyprianus In serm. de cœna Domini.

Before those wordes be spoken (saith S. Cyprian meaning the wordes of Consecration) that was common meate conuenient only to nourrish the body, and gaue helpe to the corporal life. But after that it was said by our Lorde, Do ye this in remembrance of me, This is my flesh, and this is my bloud: as ofte as it is done with these wordes, and with this faith, this substantial bread and the cuppe consecrated with the solemne blessing, doth good to the life and saluation of the whole man, being both a medicine and a Sacrifice to heale infirmities, and to purge iniquities.

Thus S. Cyprian of this special Consecration. In which he speaketh not only of the conuersion or turning of a prophane thing vnto a holy vse, but also of the conuersion and change of the thing it selfe, so that of bread be made Christes body, of wyne his bloud: which he saith to do good to the life and health of a whole man, and to be a medicine and Sacrifice to heale our infirmities, and to cleanse our iniquities. Which great benefite to do, is aboue the dignitie of bread and wine of them selfe, be they put to an vse neuer so holy.

General or cōmon Consecration.

And that this be not taken only for the general Consecration, which turneth elementes to an holy vse, and that S. Cyprian speaketh not Sacramentally, so as the bread and wine be taken only for the signes of the body and bloude of Christe: his wordes in the same treatise do clearly witnesse, where he saith thus. Christe euen to this day doth creat, sanctifie, and blesse this his most true and most holy body. Which wordes can not be expounded of the common and general Cōsecration of prophane thinges to a godly vse, seing they report a making, and sanctification, to witte that of bread be made the body, of wine the bloud of Christe.

S. Ba-

S. Basile in his Liturgie or Masse setteth forth the effect of this Consecration with these wordes. Make me meete by the vertue of thy holy spirite , that being indued with the grace of priesthod, I may stand at this holy table, and consecrate thy holy and vndefiled body, and pretious bloud. For thou art he vvhich offrest and art offred, which receiuest and geuest, Christ our God. *Basilius in Liturgia.*

Here two thinges are to be considered. First, the greatnes of the thing that is consecrate, the body and bloud of Christe, next, the grace of priesthod, as therto being necessary, whereas by the general consecration, none so great a thing can be done, neither to the exercise thereof is requisite the grace of priesthod, whereby S. Basil vnderstandeth the degree of the visible Ministerie, whereunto Priestes be admitted by imposition of the handes of a bishop. For thinges may be conuerted and appointed to an holy vse by others then by Priestes only, as many thinges be by gifte and will of godly and deuoute lay persons. Hereof spake Arnobius that old writer, Quid tam magnificū. &c What is so worthie a thing, as to consecrate the diuine Sacramēts. And what is so pernicious, as if he do consecrate, that hath taken no degree of Priesthod? Psal. 139.

And whereas your common and general Consecration M. Iewel, by which thinges are conuerted to a holy vse, as with you the water is in Baptisme, and yet the same is not so much as by any praier of your minister halowed or consecrate: S. Ambrose speaking of the blessed Sacrament of the aulter, sheweth vs of a special Consecration, done by special wordes of our Lord him selfe, not only by wordes of a mannes prayer, by which the Elementes of bread and wine be not only conuerted to a holy vse, but into a holy thing, into an other most diuine substance of the body and bloud of Christe. Consecration then (saith he) with what wordes is it, and with whose sayinges? of our Lord Ie- By the special Cōsecration, thinges be not only conuerted to a holy vse, but also into a holy thing

 sus.

Ambrosi. de sacrament. lib. 4. ca. 4.

sus. For al the other thinges that be said, (he meaneth doutles at the holy Sacrifice of the Churche) be praise geuen to God, praier is made for the people, for kinges, for the rest. When the place is come vnto, that the reuerend Sacrament be Consecrate, now the priest vseth not his owne sayinges, but the sayinges of Christ. Therefore it is the saying of Christe, that consecrateth this Sacrament. Thus S. Ambrose. where he meaneth these sayinges of Christe, This is my body, this is my bloud.

Here is to be noted M. Iewel, that where other thinges what so euer be separated, appointed, or conuerted to a holy vse, it is done either by wil and order only without Prayers, as thinges are consecrate among them of your secte: or by prayers consisting of mennes wordes, as water, Bread, Oile, Salte, Vestimentes, Chalice, Aulters, Churches, and certaine other thinges are Consecrate in the Catholike Churche. But S. Ambrose speaketh of an other manner of Consecration, which is done by the sayinges of our Lorde Iesus, and by these only sayinges, This is my body, This is my bloud, whereby duly pronoūced by a Priest, the bread is conuerted not vnto a holy vse only, but into a most holy and diuine thing, the very body of Christe, and likewise the wine into his bloud. And this is the special Consecration that I speake of, which S. Ambrose calleth the diuine Consecration, because of the diuine wordes whereof it consisteth, the diuine power, which therein worketh the diuine effect that thereby is wrought. which diuine worke S. Hierome expresseth with a most significāt word conficere, saying of Priestes Christi corpus Sacro ore conficiunt. with a holy mouth they do Consecrate or make the body of Christe.

Ambrosi. De ijs qui initiantur cap. 9.

If so be (saith S. Ambrose in an other place) humain blessing or the blessing of a man could do so much, as to change nature, what say we of the diuine Consecration, where the wordes of our

Lorde the Sauiour do worke? How say you M. Iewel, can you reasonably, and according to faith, draw this diuine and maruelous Consecration, wherby such a diuine worke, by gods special power is miraculously wrought, to the limites of your General Consecration, so as nothing of more excellencie be done in this, then in that, and in other vulgar Consecrations?

Let vs heare S. Chrysostome. Euen now also (saith he) is that Christe here present, which dighted that table. He him selfe doth Consecrate this also. For it is not man, which maketh these giftes that be set forth, the body and bloud of Christe, but it is Christe who was crucified for vs. The words be pronoũced by the mouth of the priest, and (the thinges setforth) be consecrated by the power of God and grace. This is my body saith he. With this worde the thinges laid forth be cõsecrated. And as that voice which said, *Gen. 1.* Grow ye, and be ye multiplied, and fil ye the earth, was once vttered, but yet in al times feeleth the effect nature working to generation: euen so that voice was once spoken, but it geueth strength and performãce to the sacrifice through al the tables of the church vntil this present day, and vntil the comming of our Lorde.

Thus S. Chrysostome. In Baptisme M. Iewel which you bring for example, you haue no such change of the water, though spiritually maruelous things be in ẏ holy Sacrament wrought: nor in any other thing by your conuerting to an holy vse, or otherwise by prayer consecrated.

Of this special Consecration speaketh S. Augustine. We (saith he) in the forme of bread and wine which we see, do honour thinges inuisible, that is to say, flesh and bloud. Neither do we likewise take these formes, as we tooke them before Consecration, seing that we graunt faithfully, that before Consecration it is bread and wine, which nature hath formed, but after cõsecration the flesh and bloud of Christ, which blessing hath cõsecrated. *Augustin. in lib. sent. Prosperi.*

I trow M. Iewels general definition of Consecration wil not wel be stretched to that special consecration which S. Augustine speaketh of here. Verely water after it serueth for Baptisme, is both named, and taken to be water stil, neither is it honoured as the inuisible thinges of the Eucharist are, neither is it changed into any thing that it was not before, nor any terme of trãsmutation, transelementation, conuersion or mutation is applied by any Doctor to the very water of Baptisme. Neither is there any such change made at al in any other thing, how so euer it be consecrated and conuerted to an holy vse, as according to the sayinges of these auncient Fathers, is made in ẏ bread and wine, set forth for the vnbloudy Sacrifice. For in this Sacrament of the Eucharist only, the mater it selfe is changed into an other more pretious substance. In other sacramentes the vse of the Elementes only is changed to an holier vse, the Elementes them selues remaining vnchanged.

But it appeareth, that M. Iewel as good a clerke as he would seme to be, hath not yet founde in the fathers, that Consecration is not al of one manner, and that he hath not reade what S. Augustine writeth thereof. whose wordes these be.

Consecration is not of one mãner. *Augustin. De peccatorum meritis et remiss. ca. 26* Holy bread.

Sanctification, (wherby he meaneth the conuerting of prophane thinges or natural elementes vnto an holy vse) which is al M. Iewels consecration, is not of one manner. For the catechumens (who were the learners of our faith not yet Christened.) I thinke them to be sanctified after their certaine manner by the signe of Christe, and praier of laying on of handes. And that which they take, although it be not the bodie of Christe, yet is it holy, and holier then the meates with which we are nourished. Because it is a sacrament. Yea the verie meates with which we are fed to susteine the necessitie of this life, S. Paule saith, they be halowed or sanctified by the word of God and praier, with which we pray

1. Tim. 4.

when

when we are about to take refection for our poore bodies. Thus S.Augustine.

Hereby we understand M.Iewels doctrine concerning Consecration, defined by his general and confuse description, which only and none other he admitteth, to be contrary not only to the faith of the church witnessed by so many auncient fathers, but also to confounde the degrees and specialties of sanctificati-on, which partly by S.Augustine are touched here, and may o-therwise at large be declared.

Ievvel.

Christe said not, Say ye this: or by these vvordes goe and transubstan-tiate, or change natures: But thus he said. Do this in my remembrance.

Harding.

As though Christe commaunding his disciples to do that he had done, would not them also to speake the wordes of Conse-cration, which at his supper he spake, the same being comprised vnder the signification and precepte of doing, which being done, transubstantiation forthwith foloweth. What Christe did, that be Priestes bounde to do, who in this respect be the successours of the Apostles. Christe as the Euangelistes and S.Paul do de- Mat 26.
clare, tooke bread, gaue thankes, blessed, brake, gaue to his disci- Luc.22.
ples present, and said, take ye, eate ye, this is my body. &c. And I.Cor.II.
so of the cuppe. Now if M.Iewels reason be admitted for good, who may not make this argument? Christ said not, take ye bread and wine, but do this in my remembrance: Ergo, to the administration of the blessed Sacrament, it is not necessary to haue bread and wine. And then why may not an apple, and a cuppe of biere serue? Christe said not, when so euer ye celebrate my supper, goe and gete you a companie, at least three together, how smal so euer the parish be: Ergo, the priest or any other per-son may go and take it alone. If so, then why make you so much

What wil folow, if what so e-uer Christ said not, it may be done.

a doo with the priest for receiuing without companie?

Christe said not, looke that ye haue a Communion song or said, when so euer ye kepe my supper: But thus he said, Do this in my remembrance. Christe said not, let the holy Communion be said by a Priest or Minister, let the bread and wine be consecrate by a Priest, let it be done in ye Hebrue, Greke, Latine, Vulgar, English, or in any tongue at al: But thus he said: Do this in my remembrance. Ergo, why may we not ech man and woman receiue when we list, besides and without any Communion, without Priest or Minister? what nedeth any consecration? what skilleth it what wordes or what language be vttered? To conclude, Christ said not to his Apostles at his supper, see that ye make Priestes, by whom the celebration of my supper may hereafter be kept and continewed, and cause your posteritie to do after you, as now ye see done: Al this Christe said not: but thus he said. Do this in my remembrance. Ergo, there is no cause wherefore now we should do, as we do at al.

These argumentes M. Iewel, wel may they become your tinkers and tapsters, your fidlers and coblers, and such other the rascals of the people, whom you and your felowes folowing
3. Reg. 12 the example of Ieroboam, Herod and Antiochus, haue made your Ministers, and haue committed to them charge of soules, (but O miserable soules): verely such a famous Superintendēt, and such a ringleader of this new Gospel as you are, they becomme not. They shame your Logike vtterly, be it neuer so loose, neither procure they great praise to your open Rhetorike, which it doth your hart good to see so much praised of the vulgar and vnlearned sorte. Yet this is the forme of argument, wherewith you and your companions begile the simple people, with none more: Christe said that, ergo he said not this. Christe

and

and his Apostles did so and so: Ergo, not thus and thus. Ergo, neither must we do thus and thus. By which peuish but wicked argument, ye withdraw Christen people from a great parte of Christian Religion. In stede whereof ye set vp your vnreligion, which now is the canker, and within fewe yeres, where God for plague letteth it ronne, shalbe the ruine and extirpation of all godlinesse and true religion.

Ievvel.

*This is vvel noted and opened by * S. Augustine. Put the vvordes of God (saith he) vnto the element, and it is made a sacrament. For vvhat povver is there so great of the vvater (in Baptisme) that it toucheth the body and vvassheth the harte, sauing by the vvorking of the vvorde? Not bicause it is spoken, but bicause it is beleued: and this is the vvord of faith, vvhich vve preach. The vvord of faith vvhich vve preach * saith S. Augustine, not the vvord, vvhich vve vvhisper in secrete, is the vvord of Consecration.*

The 61. vntruth. This is not there opened by S. August.

Tractatu in Ioan. 80

The. 62. vntruthe. S. Augustine saith not so.

Harding.

I am content here to dissemble and let passe with silence, your false Englishing of S. Augustines wordes. I wil not stay at trifles. But syr I pray you, where you say, this is wel noted and opened by S. Augustine: which *this* meane you, or what vnderstand you by this word *this?* Remember you where of you spake? A line or two before spake you not of the Consecration of the Eucharist? Said you not, that it standeth not in the abolishing of natures, nor in precise and close pronouncing of certaine appointed wordes: but in conuerting of the natural Elementes vnto a godly vse, as you see in Baptisme?

M. Iew. confoundeth the special consecration of the Eucharist, & the cōmon consecration of water for baptisme together.

By so saying seme you not either to confound the consecration vsed in baptisme and in the Eucharist together, or to make a Cō-secration where no wordes be spoken at al? And how frame you S. Augustines wordes to your purpose, that you haue here so at large alleged?

In this place S. Augustine speaketh not so much as one word of the Consecration of the body and bloud of Christ, wher-of I spake in my Answer, but of faith and of the Sacrament of baptisme. And that vpon iust occasion ministred vnto him by the wordes of Christe, which he tooke in hand to expounde. Only you say, *this is vvel noted and opened by S. Augustine.* But how it is noted or opened to your purpose, who can see, sith that S. Au-gustine speaketh not of our water, but of an other? Yet you adde for the song of your triumph, after the rehersal of his wordes, as though they had serued you to good purpose, and proued your strange doctrine thus.

M. Iew: fouly abu-seth S. Augustin.

The vvord of faith, vvhich vve preach saith S. Augustine, not the vvord vvhich vve vvhisper in secrete, is the vvord of Consecration.

Yea M. Iewel? where saith S. Augustine so? verely in this place he saith it not, as you allege. Are you not ashamed to make so open a lye of S. Augustine? He speaketh of the wonderful vertue wrought in baptisme. From whence (saith he) is so great vertue of the water, as that it toucheth the body, and washeth the hart, nisi faciente verbo, but by the word that doth it? This great vertue wherby the hart in Baptisme is cleansed, when the water toucheth the body, is specially attributed to the word, not to the natural element. And yet in Baptisme both must concurre.

Augustin. in Iohan. tract. 80.

Why said not Christe (saith S. Augustine) ye are cleane for cause of baptisme, wherewith ye are washed, but saith for cause of the word, which I haue spoken vnto you: but for that the word cleanseth also in the water? Take away the word, and what is the

Ibidem.

water,

water, but water? S. Augustines purpose is in that place to declare, that in baptisme the word, that is to say, the word beleued, or faith in the word of Christe, is that wherby we haue most benefite in baptisme. Of faith speaketh he there, of Consecration of this blessed Sacrament, he speaketh not.

And wil you vnderstand M. Iewel of what word he meaneth? he declareth it there him selfe saying. This is the worde
of faith, which we preach, saith the Apostle. For if thou confesse Rom. 10.
with thy mouth, that our Lorde is Iesus, and beleue in thy harte, that God hath raised him from the dead: thou shalt be saued.
The word of Faith here specified, is the general word of faith, which word conteineth the whole Faith. And if this word come to the Element, that is, if any person of ful and perfite discretion: (for of such one speaketh S. Augustine in that place) professing this faith, be Baptized in water, with the Inuocation of the blessed Trinitie: by this word, because it is beleued, and not because it is spoken, he receiueth both Baptisme, and the effect of Baptisme. And that is it S. Augustine meant by his Phrase, consecratur Baptismus, whereas he saith thus, verbo fidei sine dubio, vt mundare posit, consecratur & baptismus. By the word of faith without doubt is baptisme consecrated to this ende that it may cleanse. By this word then is baptisme after S. Augustines mynde, consecrated to this ende, that it may washe and cleanse the receiuer.

To what purpose M. Iewel hath brought in al this, it doth not wel appeare, onlesse it be to this end, that there be none other word whereby the body and bloud of Christe in the Eucharist are consecrated, but the general word of faith, that is to say, preaching of the gospel. That he semeth to meane, where he denyeth the Consecration to stand in precise words. So that where so euer there is bread and wine layd on a table, the word of faith

The Lordes Supper of this new Gospel. preached, beleued, and the Elementes receiued: by this doctrine, there is the Eucharist consecrated, and the Lordes supper made and kepte. Likewise as touching Baptisme, if the word of Faith be preached, and one beleue it, and haue water cast vpon him, though the precise wordes as M. Jewel calleth them, be not at al pronounced, which are the wordes of the inuocation of the Trinitie, spoken by the minister, I baptise thee in the name of the father, and of the sone, and of the holy ghost: though these be left out, by this doctrine of M. Jewels, the partie is baptized & safe.

Baptisme after M. Jewels doctrine.

And least any man should thinke, this word of Faith, whereof S. Augustine speaketh, were of necessitye to be beleued on the behalfe of euery one that is Baptized, as though the effect of Baptisme, which is cleansing from sinne, were to be obteined by the faith of the receiuer, and not by vertue of the sacrament ministred in the faith of the Church: S. Augustine in that place auoucheth this effect to be acheued of infantes, who be not yet able neither to beleue this worde of faith with hart, nor to confesse it with their mouth. His wordes be these. Hoc verbum fidei tantum valet in Ecclesia Dei, vt per ipsam credentem, offerentem, benedicentem, tingentem etiam tantillum mundet infantem, quamuis nondum valentem corde credere ad iustitiam, & ore confiteri ad salutem. This worde of faith is so much vaileable or of so great force in the Church of God, that through the Church beleuing, offering, blessing, baptizing, it cleanseth euen so litle an Infant, though not yet being able with harte to beleue vnto righteousnes, and with mouth confesse vnto saluation.

Tractatu In Ioan. vt supra.

If M. Jewel meant not so, as I haue now declared, why should he scoffe so at the precise pronouncing of certaine appointed wordes, and allow only the conuerting of the natural Elementes vnto an holy vse? Haue not these holy Sacraments certaine precise (as I may so cal them,) and appointed wordes for their

Precise wordes.

their forme, as wel as certaine precise and appointed Elementes for their mater? Is it not to be thought that he agreeth with his brethren of Geneua? In the Communion of the English church at Geneua, the wordes of Consecration be omitted, least the people by rehersal of the wordes should be moued to thinke, that there is alteration made in the bread and wine.

The communion of the English church in Geneua without ẏ wordes of Consecration. Printed in Geneua

But here me thinketh I smell, where about M. Iewel goeth. Yet if I should vtter it, doubtelesse he would charge me bitterly with gheasses, as in his Reply he doth oftentimes, though without iust cause. Cofte out M. Iewel the vile poison that you haue receiued of Caluine and swallowed downe, touching this blessed Sacrament, which yet you and your felowes dare not vtter plainely. why speake you so as it were vnder a cloude that, which your Euangelist Iohn Caluine of Geneua speaketh so openly in his Institutions, where he treateth de cœna Domini? where he teacheth these wordes, This is my body, which is geuen for you, to be wordes of promise in way of preaching at Christes supper, being in dede wordes of performance in way of working. That this is your opinion, I may gather partly, by that you say here, partly by that I finde in the booke of your English homilies which are read in your congregations, wherunto you haue geuen your consent and aduise I doubt not. Of this new, vaine, phantastical, and heretical doctrine, I thinke nedelesse to say ought here, ẏ same being very sufficiently confuted already by D. Sanders in his first boke, of our lordes supper.

Caluins straunge doctrine cōcerning the wordes of Consecration.

Iewel.

With what honest countenance then can M. Harding say, that we haue no Consecration?

Harding.

With what countenance I said before in my Answer, with the same I say here again, not ẏ ye haue no consecration: but that ye haue not the Consecration. A consecration after your manner ye haue, I graunt, such as your Communion is: Schismatical Communiō, schismatical Cōsecration. What say you now to the honestie of my countenance?

Ievvel.

Vve pronounce the same vvordes of Consecration that Christ pronounced.

Harding.

It is not euery pronouncing of the same wordes, that maketh the Consecration. A gyrle, a boye, a woman, any lay person, a Minister of your congregation that is no priest, as ye haue no auctoritie to make any priest by lawful imposition of handes for that ye are no bishops, againe you or who so euer besides hath not the general intent to do that the Churche doth in the consecration of the blessed Sacrament, but vtterly a contrary intent: al these, pronounce they the wordes of Consecration neuer so much, do not, ne can not consecrate. As for you, when ye pronounce the wordes, ye do but as one that telleth a tale, or readeth a lesson, not directing them to the bread and wine, in the time of pronouncing. Certain other thinges be requisite besides to due consecration, which they of your sect obserue not.

Euery pronouncing of the wordes of consecration maketh not consecration.

Ievvel.

Vve do the same that Christe bad vs do.

Harding.

Would God ye did. Then would ye not do, as ye do. Which because ye do not, nor wil not do, the more greuous shal be your condemnation. Christe commaunded his Institution to be kept, and that to be done, which he himself did. He at his supper ordeined Priestes to be Ministers of this high mysterie, as him selfe was a Priest after the order of Melchisedech, and prince of al Priestes. Ye for the more parte are no Priestes, nor none would be, for ye denye the outward Priesthod, and Sacrifice of the new Testament. Christ at his supper offered him selfe, ye offer him

not,

not, but thinke no man able nor of aucthoritie, so to doo. Christe tooke Breade, and blessed it. Ye take not the bread but let it lye on the Table. Christ directed his intention to the Breade, which he shewed by taking of it into his handes. Ye as ye take it not into your handes, so ye turne your whole minde and intention from that which Christe did, and which the Church doth.

Ievvel.

VVe proclaime the death of the Lorde. VVe speake openly in a knovven tongue, and the people vnderstandeth vs: vve Consecrate for the Congregation, and not onely for our selfe: vve haue the Element: vve ioygne Gods vvorde vnto it: and so it is made a Sacrament. Yet saith M. Harding, vve haue no Consecration.

Harding.

Foure thinges be necessarily required to the due Consecracion. The mater, forme, minister, and intent. The necessarie mater is bread of wheate, for the one kinde. And wine mixt with water for the other kinde. which mixture of water ye refuse, contrary to the auctoritie of S. Cyprian, of S. Iustine the Martyr, and of the whole Catholike Church. And so ye reuiue the olde buried Heresies of Fermentarij, and Armeni. The forme, is the wordes of our Lorde, This is my bodie, This is my Bloude, duely pronounced ouer the bread and wine. The Minister ought to be a Priest, and none other, consecrated and ordered accoording to the rite and order of the Catholike Church. Lastly, the intent to do that thing which the Church doth is allso necessarie. For if a man do it in mockery, or by way of dissimulation, or with a contrary purpose, or without mind and intent to do that Christe ordeined to be done, and the Church doth: the Sacramente is not consecrated at al. This intent and minde, you M. Iewel and your Fel-

Fowre thinges are necessarily required to Consecration.

Y i lowes

In the English Cõmuniõ they desier that by receauing bread and wine, they may be made partakers of ẏ body and bloud of our Lord.

lowes do lacke, and at the Communion that ye celebrate in your congregations, denye vtterly to consecrate or receiue the very Body and Bloude of Christe vnder the formes of Breade and wine: that make your petition, that receiuing the creatures of Bread and wine, ye may be partakers of Christes Body and Bloude, therein declaring your selues to be the professours of the Sacramentary heresie. For euen so be the wordes of your inuocation in your Communion booke. In which inuocatiõ ye pretend and say it to be according to the Institutiõ of ẏ sonne of God, whereas in deede any such Institution of the sonne of God was neuer hearde of, and through all the Scriptures can not be founde, nor is it by any auncient and allowed Doctor of the Church mentioned, that by receiuing the creatures of bread and wine, we should be made partakers of the Body and bloud of Christe.

Now M. Iewel vntil you proue vnto vs, that ye the Sacramentaries, who beare the swaye in England touching maters of Religion, admitte and vse these foure things necessarily required to the due Consecration of the blessed Sacrament: I wil say stil as before, that ye haue not the Consecration, though ye make your proclamation (as you cal it) of our Lords death, neuer so loude: though ye speake at your new Cõmunion neuer so plaine & fine english: though ye make a mocke Consecration for neuer so greate a congregation besides your selues: though ye haue Bread Gods plentie, and tankardes of wine of the largest sise: to conclude, though ye preach the word neuer so busily. For it is not such proclaiming, such speaking of ẏ vulgar tongue, such a new found toye as ye vse, such bestowig of your bread and wine, such prating of the Scriptures, that maketh the right and due Consecration wherof I spake, and wherof the best learned Fathers of the auncient Churche haue most

plainely

plainely spoken, as of them some here before I rehearsed.

Ievvel.

*And vvhereas he * saith further, that vve haue no manner Oblation in our Communion, he should not him selfe speake manifest vntruth hauing taken vpon him, as he * saith, to reforme falshed.*

The. 63. vntruth. I say not so.
The. 64. vntruth. neither do I say.

Harding.

Where say I, that ye haue no manner Oblation in your Communion? Looke vpon my wordes againe, reade them diligently, and if I say so, then your Replie standeth in force against me. If I say it not, what shal I then say, but all is false that you say? But what els should you say, being determined rather then to subscribe, to gainsay me, though you damne your soule for it, but that which is false? Therefore truth being farre remoued from you, on lyes you take holde, and set them forth al your booke ouer, yea almost in euery sentence, to serue your turne at least way for some shewe. I say then in my Answere, as in your owne booke it is to be seene, that the enemies of this blessed Sacrifice, haue quite abrogated the Consecration and the Oblation. By which who seeth not, that I meane the vnbloudy Oblation of the Body and Bloude of Christe, which the Church of God doth dayly frequent in the Masse? I saide not that ye haue no manner Oblation. As neyther that ye haue no Consecration, which falsely ye impute vnto me. Neyther doo I saye in al my booke by these expresse termes, that I take vpon mee to reforme falshed. With which also, as with other shamlesse vntruthes, you burthen me here.

But let vs see whether you can proue that you haue the Oblation that I spake of. Or if you be not able to proue that, as I am wel assured you be not: tel vs what manner of Oblation ye haue.

Ievvel.

*For he knovveth vve offer vp vnto God in the holy Communion our selues, our soules, our bodies, and almes for the poore: prayses, and thankes geuing vnto God the Father for our Redemption: and prayer from a contrite hearte, vvhich, as the olde Catholike Fathers * say, is the Sacrifice of the Nevve Testament.*

Thi.65. vntruth. they say not so.

Harding.

I denyed one thing, and you affirme an other. These be your Oblations you say, which you offer to God in your Communion. Be it so. As these be the thinges, which ye ought to offer to God in dede: so whether ye do it or no, ye doo them vnfruitfully, yea being in heresie, after the minde of S. Augustine, ye do them to your perdition. If ye offer none other Oblatiō then such as these be, what difference in offering is there betwene you & them of ẏ Old testamēt? Al these ẏ Iewes offered before the comming of Christe into fleshe, no lesse then ye. Againe al these Oblations be offered by Lay men, by women, briefely by al sortes and degrees of people. It is a peculiar Oblation, & a singular Sacrifice that I spake of, as you know wel ynough, and such as is to be offered not by euery one of the people, but by special Ministers thereto appointed and ordeined

The Gospellers acknowledg no other Oblation, then the Iewes had in the olde lawe.

If because the Priesthod of the Olde testament is translated, it be necessary there be a translation of the Lawe also, as S. Paul saith: Now that ye claime the benefite and right of the Newe lawe, ye must acknowlege a new Priesthod, and a new Sacrifice belonging to the same. Where is your Priesthod? which is your Sacrifice? These Sacrifices and Oblations, which here you recken, be not peculiar to the new Lawe, but are common to al Lawes. For they that serued God in the lawe of Moyses, and in the lawe of Nature, offered the Oblations

Heb. 7.

that you tel vs of vnto God, as wel as you or any of your secte do. Onely they offered prayses and thankes geuing vnto God for Redemptiō to be wrought, whereas now these are offered vnto him for Redemption already wrought. Otherwise there is no difference.

Wherfore if ye haue not the Peculiar Oblation and Sacrifice of the newe Lawe, which is the vnbloudy Oblation of the Body and Bloude of Christe, that he instituted at his last Supper: then ye proue your selues not to be of this Lawe. And therefore are ye to be turned ouer to Moyses lawe, or to the law of Nature, or some other what so euer: for of Christes lawe ye be not.

Where you say of prayer from a contrite hearte, that it is the Sacrifice of the Newe testament: You see it is no more the Sacrifice of the New testament, then of Moyses law, then of the lawe of Nature. For in al lawes and in al times some haue made their prayers to God from a contrite hearte. Speaking thus, you speake vnlearnedly, and saying that the Olde Catholike Fathers haue so said, if you meane of the peculiar Sacrifice which S. Ireneus calleth the newe Oblation of the new testament: you speake vntruly. You should haue done wel to haue named them, and to haue alleged their owne woordes for your credites sake, or wherin you had done better, to haue said lesse. *Irenæus. lib. 4. cap. 32.*

Ievvel.

*To couclude, vve offer vp * as much, as Christe commaunded vs to offer.* The. 66. vntruth. ye offer not the Body & Bloude of Christe.

Harding.

What ye offer vp, you haue now declared at the vttermost, and I dare say more then ye do in dede. But ye offer not that which Christe offered at his Supper, which he taught and commaunded his Apostles, and in them their successours Priestes of the Newe testament to offer. Who after that he had Consecrated his Body and Bloude with his owne wordes, and had made his Oblation to his Father: said Doo ye this in remembrance of me. To confirme this with good witnesses, ye scripture saith (as writeth S. Cyprian to Cecilius) yt, so oft as we offer vp the Chalice for remẽbrance of our Lorde & of his Passiõ: we do that, which is certeine our Lorde did. And after that a litle. We be admonished and instructed of our Lorde, that we offer vp our Lordes Chalice mixte with Wine, according as our Lorde hath offered. The chalice or cuppe likewise (saith S. Ireneus) he confessed to be his Bloud, and taught them the new Oblation of the new Testament. Which the Church receiuing at the Apostles handes, ouer the whole worlde offereth vp to God. &c.

De consecra dist. 2. cap. scriptura.

Irenæus lib. 4. cap. 32.

These be good and authentical witnesses, what Christe him selfe offered vp at his Supper, and what he taught, admonished, and commaunded his Apostles to offer, and what of them the Churche hath receiued, and now offereth ouer the whole worlde. This is the Body and Bloud of Christ vnder the formes of Bread and wine mixte with water, the daily and perpetual Sacrifice of the Masse offered vp to the Father, to the Sonne, and to the holy Ghost, as the auncient Father Fulgentius saith. Which because ye offer not, but haue vtterly abandoned, the same being thus commaunded, ye offer not vp so much as Christe hath commaunded to be offered.

Fulgentius ad Monimum lib. 2. q. 25.

Ievvel.

In deede vve offer not vp Christes Body to be a Propitiatorie Sacrifice for vs vnto his Father. For that Sacrifice is once vvrought for al vpon the Crosse, and there is none other Sacrifice left to bee offered

offered for Sinne.

Harding.

Ye offer not vp Christes Body at al. And therefore ye saye true, as he doth, who saith, he doth not good workes to merite by them, when he doth no good workes at al. But if ye were Priestes duely consecrated by a Bishop after the rite and order of the Catholike Church, and would offer vp the new Oblation of the new Testament according to thinstitution of Christe, and as the Churche hath receiued of the Apostles: then shoulde ye offer vp the Body and Bloud of Christe in Sacrifice. For doing whereof ye are assured by the auctoritie of the Catholike Churche, and by the doctrine of al the Fathers. Christus (saith S. Augustine) de Corpore & sanguine suo instituit Sacrificium secundum ordinem Melchisedech. Christe hath ordeined a Sacrifice to be made of his Body and his Bloude after the order of Melchisedech. And in an other place. Now (saith he) the Christians doo celedrate the memorie of Christes Sacrifice that was done on the Crosse, by the holy Oblation and Participation of the Body and Bloude of Christe. For this it were not harde to allege a greate number of Testimonies out of the moste auncient Fathers. Let this of S. Augustine onely suffice in a mater not doubtful.

Aug. in psal. 33. Concione. 2.

Contra. Faustum Manichaeum. lib. 20. cap. 18.

If then ye would thus doo, as by commaundement of Christe, by continual practise of the Churche, by the doctrine of the holy Ghoste vttered by the Fathers, being priestes duely ordered ye ought to doo: then might ye truely say, that ye offered vp a Sacrifice Propitiatorie. For how saye you good Sir, as concerning the thing it selfe which is offered, wil you denye, that Christes Body is a Sacrifice propitiatory? Saith not S. Iohn, Ipse est propitiatio pro peccatis nostris,

Sacrifice propitiatorie.

1. Ioan. 2.

He is the propitiation of our sinnes? Saith not Oecumenius, Caro Christi est propitiatorium nostrarum iniquitatum, The flesh of Christe is the propitiation, or the thing that obteineth forgeuenesse for our iniquities? Said not Christ him selfe of his body, This is my body which is geuen for you? and of the Cuppe likewise, which is shed for you? Doth not the forme of Consecration reporte, that the Blonde of Christe is shed for remission of sinnes? what els meant S. Dionyse, when he called it Hostiam salutarem, The healthful hoste, or the hoste that procureth saluation vnto vs? Euery Priest (saith S. Paule) is ordeined to offer giftes and Sacrifices for sinnes. Thereof it foloweth, that either we haue no Priest, or that we haue Sacrifice propitiatory. For that Sacrifice which is offered for sinnes is Propitiatorie. what els meant S. Cyprian, where he saith that It profiteth to the life & saluation of the whole man, and that it is Holocaustum ad purgandas iniquitates, a Sacrifice to purge iniquities, and a medicine to heale infirmities?

Ocumenius in cap.3 ad Rom.
Luc.22.
Dionysius Ecclesiast. hierarch. part.3.c.3.
Heb.5.
Cyprian. de Cœna Domini.

Now though this which we celebrate and do in the Church be an image and sampler of that which Christ did on the Crosse, in respect of the meane whereby it is done: yet notwithstanding we offer vp now the same bloud, which Christe did shedde vpon the Crosse, nolesse then if it were presently shed. Wherevpon S. Augustine said, Semel immolatus est in semetipso Christus, & tamen quotidie immolatur in Sacramento. Christ hath once been Sacrificed in him selfe, and yet is he euery day Sacrificed in the Sacrament.

De Consec. distinct.2. cap. semel.

And though this Sacrifice was once wrought for al vpon the Crosse, as you saye, which is true as concerning the outward shedding of Bloud: yet doth the same before God continew. and because nothing to him is so acceptable, and to man so healthful: to him of the Church it is offered dayly, and to man applied vnto remission of sinne, as though very now Christe were dying on the Crosse, and freshe bleeding. That there is none other Sacrifice left for sinne, as you say, we graunt. For this is not another, it is the same, which continueth in truth and substance of the thing offered, though diuerse for the manner of offering.

Ievvel.

*But * saith M. Harding, vve make no mention of any Sacrifice in al our Ministration: Therefore vve breake Christes Institution. This reason impeacheth Christ him selfe as vvel as vs: For Christe him selfe in his vvhole Ministration spake not one vvorde of any Sacrifice, no more then vve doe. Therefore by M. Hardings Logike, Christ him selfe brake his ovvne Institution.* The. 67. vntruth. I say not so.

Harding.

Who so euer conferreth my sayings M. Iewel and yours together, shal sone take you with an vntruth. God be thanked that you can not bring a true conclusiō against me, deduced of true premisses, no not in the smallest trifles, that you charge me withal. Syr, where I pray you say I, that ye make no mention of any Sacrifice in al your Ministration? This is like the other vntruthes you reported euen here before concernig the Consecration, and the Oblation. As I might answer the most parte of your booke, yea in manner al, by saying, al is false, wherein I should say truely: so I answere here, that which you say is false, therefore it is not to be regarded, what thereof you conclude. Of the Oblation wherby I meane the vnbloudy Oblation of the Body and Bloud of Christ, ye make no mention in your Communion booke, I am sure. And that you knowe your selfe, how so euer you be disposed to gainsay me, say I neuer so truely. But where true mater wanteth, and a great booke is intended, lyes must serue in stede of good stuffing.

Ievvel.

The.68. vntruth. It is not Christes ordinance, it is your owne deuise.

*But vvhat should moue this man thus scornefully to ieast at the holy Ministration, and to cal * Christes ordinance a bare Communion?*

Harding.

I assure you M. Jewel, you are foule deceiued. I ieasted not, but spake in so good earnest, as so weighty a mater requireth. Reade my wordes againe, and tel the worlde wherein I ieast. I called your Communion bare, conside-ring the lacke of Consecration and Oblation. For wher-as eating is the consūmation of a Sacrifice, which foloweth the outward Oblation of the Sacrifice, and Oblation is of thinges consecrated: ye hauing neither Consecration, nor Ob-lation, what haue ye more then a bare Communion? Yea bare I say, not onely for lacke of these thinges rightly done, but also, and that most chiefly, because by your wil and intent and according to your Sacramentary doctrine, ye minister to your congregations (our Lorde deliuer his people from your damnable deceit) nothing but bare breade from the Ouen to eate, and bare wine out of the potte to drinke. I ieast not M. Jewel at any holy Ministration, neither cal I Goddes ordinance a bare Communion, God forbid I should be so void of grace, as therein to followe you, who ieast at Gods holy ordinaunces and thinges, more then any the blasphemoust wri-ter of our miserable dayes, that for our countrie of England, you are most worthy to be named the Lucian of our time. In deede your new toyes, that you cal your holy Ministration, I vtterly reproue, your Schismatical and wicked Communion which is no Christian Communion, I detest. Loe I speake plaine, say not that I ieast.

The Sacramentaries Communion is a bare Cōmunion.

Ievvel.

A litle before M. Harding said, in Christes Institution three things

are.

are conteined: Consecration, Oblation, Participation.

Harding.

Adde the Article The, to these three, as I did, and I acknowlege it to be my saying, falsifie not my woordes. What inferre you?

Ievvel.

Immediately after, as a man that had sodainly forgotten him selfe, he saith, The number of Communicantes together in one place, that they iangle so much of as a thing so necessary, is no parte of Christes Institution.

Harding.

I remembred wel what I said, the same I say here againe. How are you hable to shewe, that I forgote my selfe, which both you saye in the Text, and also note in the Margent?

Ievvel.

*It is no maruel though hee can so il agree vvith the olde Catholike Doctours, that * falleth out so sodainely vvith him selfe.*

The. 69. vntruth. I fal not out with my selfe at al.

Harding.

Here is much a doo. I require your prouse. Would God you would vtter fewer wordes and more truth, more pith of reason, lesse railing and depraning of him, whom you would faine confute, if you could. Nay Sir, because I agree so wel with the old Catholike Doctours, therfore you and your fellowes fal out with me. And that ful wel doth appeare in their mad fretting writings. But them God wote, litle do I esteme, as neither you very much. Neither would I vouchesafe to answere your lying Replie, were it not for the vnlearned Peoples sake, whom (good soules) it greeueth me so

 dangerously

dangerously by you to be seduced. But how proue you that I forgote my selfe?

Ievvel.

For if Participation be not necessary, hovv is it a parte of Christes Institution, If it be a parte of Christes Institution, hovv is it not necessary?

Harding.

When come you forth with proufe of my forgettig of my selfe? Me thinke you haue forgotẽ, what you toke vpon you to proue. Participation is of Christes Institution, and therefore it is necessary. Thus I sayd, and thus I say againe. What conclude you?

Ievvel.

He vvould faine conuey Christes Institution, and his Masse, bothe vnder one coloure. But they are contraries, the one bevvrayeth the other.

Harding.

These be but wordes and proue nothing.

Ievvel.

As for the Priest he taketh no parte of the Sacrament vvith others vvhich is the nature and meaning of this vvorde Participation, but receiueth al alone.

Harding.

Participation what it signifieth.

Let the nature and meaning of this worde *Participation* be, ỷ one take parte of a thĩg with others, as you say. Yet in dede ỷ there be a Participation, it is inough, that one take parte with an other. And where two alone be parteners, there properly is Participation, and they are called Participes, Partakers, as of Cicero, Iuno was called Particeps cõnubij, Partaker of wedlocke in respect of her husband Iupiter. Neither is it necessarie that where there is a Participation, there be a Diuision of the thing participated into partes. For there is a Participa-

tion

tion of counsel betwene two frendes, where the whole counsel is imparted in common vnto both, of the one to the other. The worde Participation, hath his name in respect of parts, not alwayes of the thing participated, but of the participantes, who being diuers, make partes. And truth it is, who so euer receiueth the blessed Sacrament, he receiueth not a parte of Christes Body, being the thing imparted in the Sacrament, but the whole Body. For now as it is impassible, so it is indiuisible. Therefore it is not taken in parte, but wholy.

In deede through that body we do participate the Godhed of Jesus, as saith Damasceen, which because it is imparted vnto vs according to such measure of grace, as it pleaseth him to geue: therefore it is of him called μετάληψις participatio, and they that receiue be participantes, because one thing is imparted vnto them, be they in one place together, or a sunder, it skilleth not: the Sacrament is participated, and so there is a Participation notwithstanding. As there may be a participation of counsel, or some other thing betwene diuerse being aparte and diuided. And because the Sacrament is not receiued of one alone, but of many, the thing being the common benefite of al Christian people: therefore the receiuinge of it is called a Participation, though the receiuers be in sundry places.

Damascenus lib. 4. cap.14.

Participation of one thing may be attributed to those that be not together in one place.

When Dauid said, Particeps ego sum omnium timentium te, I am partaker of al that feare the, He meant not that he was in one place with al those that feared God: yet betwene him and them there was a participation. We being many are one bread, one body, for al we do participate of one breade, saith S. Paule. Yet his meaning is not so vnreasonable, that al beleuers participate together, to witte in one place. Lo I am here, sayth Christe in S. Paule, and the Children whiche God hath geuen me. Forasmuch as the children be partakers of flesh and bloud.

Psal.118.

Μετέχομεν.

1.Cor.10.

Heb.2.

he also him selfe likewise did participate of them, μετέσχε αὐτῶν, yͭ is to say, was made of flesh and Bloud likewise as the children. He tooke parte of them, not with them, so as it be referred to the Children, as the English Bible hath, but not so wel: For αὐτῶν, them, is not to be referred to Παιδία Children, but to flesh and bloude there mentioned. Now where as S. Paule saith, Christe did participate of flesh and bloud, there must be graunted a Participation. For he tooke flesh and bloude in the pure wombe of the Virgine Marie, and there he was conceiued of the holy Ghoste, incarnate and borne out of her, and so was participant of flesh and bloude: yet I trow, none wil be so blasphemous, as to acknowlege any other partaker thereof with our Sauiour in the same place. So the Priest at Masse receiuing the blessed Sacrament, doth participate, and there is a Participation, though he receiue not with others in the same place. As Christe did participate of flesh and bloud with others, but not together in the same place. Thus M. Iewel by this word Participation, you proue nothing at al against me, much lesse that I forgote my selfe.

Ievvel.

This is a very simple argument, Certaine circumstances may be altered: Ergo the Priest may receiue alone.

Harding.

It is a simple shift for M. Iewel, when he is not able to answere mine argument, to deuise a weake reason of his owne head, and to scoffe at it, as though it were by me set forth. Seeing that you father so many peeuish argumentes vpon me M. Iewel, which I make not, nor no man of any meane wit would make: I thinke it good to frame you hereafter certaine argumentes, which I wil acknowlege to be mine owne, & demaund your answer to them, or require you to subscribe. Hitherto

you

you haue sought occasion to wander abroad in maters either altogether impertinēt, or of lesse weight. Now by very order of my Answer to your Chalenge, you are brought neare to the point, wherein the pith of the first Article consisteth.

Your large talke of Common and Priuate, your simple disproufe of the auncient Fathers, whom I brought in for witnesse of the Sacrifice, your feble answers to certaine auctorities by me alleged, your scoffing at the sequel of the Peoples negligence, your false slaundering of the Pope and Cardinals, your vnnecessary cōmon place of Preparatiō, ye prouf of your general Consecration & Oblation, the handling of these and the like idle maters, hath thus farre serued you for stuffing of your booke. In folowing the course of your talke in these superfluous digressions, you haue kept your selfe, your Reader, and me your Confutour, aloofe from the chiefe purpose.

Maters impertinēt partly touched, wherein M. Iew. hath to no purpose spent time hitherto.

But now that we draw so nigh to the marke that you ought to shoote at, let vs so ioigne in discussion of the chiefe point of this Article, that as S. Augustine saith, mater with mater, cause with cause, reason with reason may buckle together.

The mark that M. Iewel ought to shoote at. *De vtilitate credendi ad Honnorat. cap.1.*

Concerning the first Article of M. Iewels Chalenge, which is of priuate Masse, as they of Luthers schoole terme it, two thinges are specially to be considered. whether the vnbloudy & Mystical Sacrifice of ye Church, which cōmonly we cal ye Masse, may be done without a number of cōmunicantes with the Priest in ye same place, which after their sēse maketh it priuat, or whether any such was done withī vi. C. yeres after Christes being on earth. The First is Quæstio iuris, ye Second is Quæstio facti. If ye First be proued, it forceth not greatly, whether ye Secōd may be proued or no. For if a thīg be lawful, thē it might haue ben done, and it may be done. And for our case that is inough.

whether it haue been done, the prouse thereof for the most parte is not so easy, because it dependeth of circūstances of time, place, and person, which seldom by euident witnesse of writers be recorded.

In my Answere to M. Iewels Chalenge I haue brought prouses for the one and for the other. The same hath he endeuoured in his long Replie to refel. But how sufficiently, I leaue it to the skilful Readers iudgement. By comparison of my prouses & of his refutation together, it may best appeare, on whether side the truth resteth. which prouses how much he faileth of refelling, so much right he leaueth vnto me to chalenge him of his promise, and to require him to yelde to the truth, and to subscribe.

Fol. 12. b. &c.

Number of Communicāts with the Priest in one place is not necessarie.

In that parte of my booke which he hath laid forth in his 8. Diuision, I affirme, that a number of communicantes together with the Priest in one place, is not of necessitie required to the right vse of the blessed Sacrament. which if it be true, then it foloweth by good reason, as there I saye, that although there be not others at al times ready and disposed to receiue the Communion with the Priest in the same place, yet for that respecte, the ministration of the Priest is not made vnlawful. That thing then remoued for which of these men Priuate Masse is condemned, it standeth in force as before, notwithstanding his Replie, that he hath made notable with multitude of Vntruthes, rather then commendable for weight of mater. That al ambiguitie be auoided, and that by plainenesse the truth may appeare, Let mine argument, which in my Answere I made, thus be fourmed.

An argument prouing priuate masse to be lawful.

It is neither of Christes commaundement, nor of the substance of the Sacrament or Sacrifice, that there be a number of communicantes receiuing together with the Priest in in the same place at the celebration therof: Ergo the priest may without synne or offence, receiue by him selfe alone at the celebration. If a priest may so lawfully do, then is priuate Masse proued.

This is my argument, not that which M. Iewel maketh for me. Hereto he answereth thus.

Ievvel.

Christe him selfe hath already determined the case. For al be it Christe haue appointed no certaine number of communicantes, yet hath he by special vvordes appointed a number. Replie page. 20. paragr. 3.

Harding.

I denye, that Christe hath by special wordes appointed a number of communicants to receiue with the priest in the same place. Come to the point M. Iewel.

Ievvel.

For these very vvordes, Take ye, eate ye, drinke ye al, Diuide ye among your selues, do ye this in my remembrance, ye shal set forth the Lordes death: these very vvordes I say, can not be taken of one singular man, but necessarily importe a number. Mat. 26. Luc. 22. 1. Cor. 11.

Harding.

Christe speaking to his twelue Apostles, knewe that he spake to moe then one, and therefore he disposed his speach accordingly, and spake in the plural number, Take ye, eate ye. &c. But that a number should alwaies receiue with the priestes of necessitie, when they celebrate the Oblation: that is not imported by the wordes. Neither at his whole supper vttered he any special wordes to that purpose.

For if vpon this place you grounde a necessitie of nūber alwaies to receiue with the priestes at one time and one place, because Christ spake in the plural number, then likewise we may require you of no lesse necessitie, to haue a number of priestes or

Ministers as ye cal them, to distribute the Sacrament to any companie of Communicantes that are to receiue, at one time and place, or els to haue no Communion at al. And furthermore by this conclusion, no one bishop of the world shal haue auctoritie to make Priestes or geue holy orders, onlesse there be a number of bishops at one time & place together to do the same, because of Christes worde, hoc facite, do ye this. Of which thinges the two later to be absurde, the practise of your owne congregations do euidently declare.

If because Christe speaking to twelue, said in the plural number take ye, eate ye, when so euer the Communion is receiued, it must of necessitie be receiued of a number together: then by like Argument, because Christe said to his Apostles, go ye,
Mark.16 and teach ye al nations, baptizing them in the name of the father, and of the sonne, and of the holy ghoste: no man being neuer so duly called, may go and preach to any one alone, but must holde his peace vntil a number be gathered together, to heare the preaching.

Also by this argument the Minister may not Baptise, except there be a number together ready to be baptized. By
Act.8. this Argument M. Jewel condemneth S. Philip, who both preached to the Enuche alone, and baptized him alone without other companie.

Iohn.20. When Christ said to his Apostles, Receiue ye the holy ghost, whosoeuers sinnes ye remitte, they are remitted vnto them. &c: Did he limite vnto thē the power of the keyes, so as they might not exercise the same, remitte, or retaine, onlesse there were a number together both of Priestes to remitte or retaine sinnes, and a number of penitentes, whose sinnes were to be remitted or retained? which if it be true, then neither one Priest alone can exercise his autoritie, nor any one penitent, can receiue absolution alone.

Absurdities folowing of M. Jewels fond kinde of arguing.

When

when he said, forgeue ye, and ye shalbe forgeuen, would he put vs in despaire of forgeuenes, except there be a number of vs together, that would be forgeuen? Luc. 6.

When he said, Vigilate, & orate, watch ye, and pray ye: ment he that we should neuer watch nor praye, but when there were a companie of vs together? Mark. 14

When he said, If they persecute you in this citie, flye into an other: was it his meaning that no man should saue him selfe by flight in time of persecution, except he had a number of felowes to flye with him? Mat. 10.

When he said, Come ye al to me, that trauaile and be laden: forbad he any to come vnto him alone, whose harte he moueth, except he gete moe to come with him, or rather al to come with him, because it was said, Come ye al? The like absurdities might be alleged against your peeuysh proufe of number in receiuing the Communion together M. Iewel out of innumerable places. Wherfore you were best to geue ouer your arguing to proue this mater, and returne to your accustomed reprouing of vs the Catholikes, and disprouing of our proufes, wherein you spende your time and learning, though with smal honestie, and litle gaine of estimation among the discrete and learned iudges. The farther you wade in this your argument, the more shal you fynde your selfe graueled, and worse encombred. Yet it semeth you geue not ouer. You make a smoother before your flight out of the feelde. For in your twelfth Diuision you say touching this mater. Mat. 11.

He moueth talke of place, vvhereof vve had no question. But the number of Communicantes, vvhereof S. Paule so plainely speaketh, he thought best to salue vvith silence. Page. 33. Paragr. 5

Talke of place and of number receiuing the sacrament together, is coincident. For when a number receiueth together, they receiue in one place. If not in one place, then neither together, onlesse you referre the terme *together,* to time, and not to place. which I trow you do not. For that should make litle with you.

The lacke of number of Cōmunicantes ought not to stay the celebratiō of the vnbloudy sacrifice.

But syr, the number of Communicantes I salue not with silence. For I know it not to be sore, that it nede the salue of any leach. I meane, it maketh no woonde, nor so much as a raze in the countenance of the Catholike doctrine. For as we wish hartely that the whole number of Christen people would dispose them selues worthily, and be partakers of our Lordes body with vs at the Masse, to our vnspeakeable comfort, and their inestimable benefite: and do oftentimes both in Sermons openly, and in Confession secretly exhort them therto: So if for lacke of deuotion, or for any other cause they do it not: we knowe it to be our dutie in this case, to celebrate the memorie of Christes bloudy Sacrifice in the vnbloudy Sacrifice of the Church, receiuing that which is offered, without other number of communicantes without any our default: rather then contrary to his commaundement to suffer his death in such manner as he him selfe hath ordeined, not to be set forth for remembrance.

Ievvel.

Yet saith M. Harding, S. Augustines vvordes be plaine, Saluator non praecepit. &c. Christe gaue no commaundement, in vvhat order it should be receiued: to the intent he might leaue that mater to his Apostles, by vvhome he vvould dispose his churche. Therefore saith M. Harding, the number of communicantes is at libertie, and the priest may receiue alone. S. Augustine in that place speaketh not one vvorde of any number, but only of the time of receiuing. &c.

Harding.

I would be loth to hier you M. Iewel to tel my tale for me in any weighty mater, sith that you report my wordes so vntruly

truly in a mater that should be handled with al truth and sincerities. The manner of learned men is, to set forth the argumentes of the aduersaries to the most aduauntage, and to hide nothing, wherein any force against the parte which they defende, may appeare. Your manner is quite contrary. You mangle my wordes, you disorder my sentence, you leaue out the synowes and iointes of my reason, and bring as it were only bare skynne and loose bones. If of it selfe it be good and probable, by your falsifying, and contrary framing, you labour to make it appeare weake, childish, ridiculous, and altogether besyde the purpose. And as you play this false parte in missereporting my sayinges, so you deale much worse with fond argumentes, which you father vpon me. But to neuer a good argument do you answer as becommeth a learned man, as nothing els do you proue by any substātial discourse in your whole great boke, but with scornful scoffes, bitter tauntes, and borowed phrases, do only disproue. I require the reader who is loth to be deceiued, at al times to haue recourse to my sayinges, and with good diligēce to examine, whether they be iustly impugned by M. Iewel or no.

M. Iew. manner in reporting his aduersaries sayinges and argumēts quite contrary to the mãner of learned men.

As touching the celebration of the blessed Sacrament, to the intent I speake of it clerely and without ambiguitie: some thinges be of precept, some of example only. It is of precept, that it be consecrated, offered, and receiued. Of example only that it be done after other meates, in the euen, with number together, with sitting at the table. &c. The thinges that be of precept, be of the substance, and al such be inuariable. The thinges that be of example only and not of precept, be of order: and they are to be disposed by the Church, as S. Augustine saith in his Epistle to Ianuarius. Our Sauiour hath not commaunded in what order the sacrament from that time foreward should be receiued, to the intent he might leaue to the Apostles that mater, by whom he

Touchig the blessed sacrament somthings be of Precept, some thinges of example only.

Augusti. epist. 118.

would dispose his Church. In which place although S. Augustine speake not of number expressely, but of the time: yet in that he speaketh of order in general, he meaneth al such thinges, as be not of the substāce. If he had meant to haue spoken in that place of the time of receiuing onely, as M. Iewel saith: then would he not haue said, *Christe gaue no commaundement in vvhat order it should be receiued,* but rather *in vvhat time it should be receiued.* For Order is a general terme, perteining to al that is not of the substāce, as time, number, place, sitting, standing. &c. Time is special.

Order.
Time.

Now that a number of communicantes alwaies receiue together with the Priest, it is not commaunded either by Christe, or by the Apostles, or vniuersally so vsed in the whole Church. Therfore when a number wanteth, the Priest may lawfully offer, (whereof S. Augustine speaketh specially in that place) and receiue alone. Wherewith these men, specially M. Iewel, ought to be offended the lesse, leaning to S. Augustines auctoritie as he doth: forasmuch as in that very place he saith, quod per totū orbem frequentat ecclesia, hoc quin ita faciendum sit disputare, insolentissimæ insaniæ est. To dispute whether that as the Church commonly vseth to do thorow the whole worlde, be likewise to be done or no, is a point of a most proud madnes. By which rule M. Iewel semeth to S. Augustine to be distract with most insolent madnes, as he that neuer ceasseth barking against the blessed Sacrifice of the Church, as it is generally vsed and frequented through the whole Church, where so euer God is rightly honored in the worlde.

August. ibidem.

As for Christes commaundement, I may say that concerning number, which S. Augustine in that Epistle to Ianuarius saith concerning time. Si hoc ille monuisset, vt post cibos alios semper sumeretur, credo quód eum morem nemo variasset. If Christ had com-

commaunded that the Sacrament should be receiued euer after other meates, I beleue no man would haue changed that manner. So if Christe had commaunded that it should alwayes be receiued with a number of other Communicantes at the same time and place: I beleue no man would haue ben so hardy, as to change that order.

Touching the number of communicantes, wherof S. Paule speaketh so plainely, as you saye: I assure the discrete Reader that shal peruse your wrytinges and myne, that by S. Paule he shal finde you able to proue no better that of necessitie manye ought to Communicate together, then now you haue proued it by the wordes of Christe spoken to the Apostles then present, in the plural number. Albeit I know M. Iewel, what you haue alleged already in your chalenging Sermon, and otherwheres to proue that point. But verely in alleging those wordes, inuicem expectate, waite ye one for an other, you misse the marke, and shew your selfe either to mainteine that errour stubbornly, or to be deceiued ignorantly by geuing credite to your false schoolemaisters, Peter Martyr, Ihon Caluine, Thomas Cranmar, and such others of that syde, whom you folowe blindly and affectionatly, not hauing weighed the text it self, nor the auncient Fathers wryting vpon that place. 1. Cor. 11. In commentar. in 1. Cor. cap. 11.

Syr rightly to vnderstand the Apostle there, you must not missconstre him, as finding fault with the Corinthians for the forme and order of the administration of the Communion vsed among them, (for he findeth no fault therewith specially) but with the abuse of their publike Churchfeastes, which of the Fathers are oftentimes mentioned, and of some called ἀγάπαι. If you consyder the place wel, you shal not thinke your selfe furnished with any Argument at al out of that Epistle, for prouse ἀγάπαι.

 of

of the necessitie of your number receiuing the Communion together. Your errour of the necessitie of number you may not salue with an other errour. Yet let vs heare what you haue to say.

Ievvel.

Page.21. line.1. *That S. Augustine requireth a number of Communicantes, it appeareth by that immediatly in the same place he allegeth the vvordes of S. Paule, Quapropter cum conuenitis ad manducandum, inuicem expectate.* wher-

1.Cor.11. fore brethren when ye come together to eate (*the Communion*) waite one for an other. *Vvhich vvordes M. Harding thought best cunningly to dissemble.*

Harding.

No, no M. Jewel, I haue not with any great cunning dissembled those wordes. You haue with more falsehed then cunning added to the Scripture, by putting in of your owne with a parenthesis these two wordes (the Communion) to the intent that where S. Paules wordes make not for you, your owne wordes being put to his, might supply that you would faine proue. If this sleight may be borne withal to serue your tourne, you wil sone proue what you list.

M. Jew. addeth to S. Paule wordes of his owne, to helpe a bad mater

If I had thought, those wordes of S. Paule had vndoubtedly made for proufe of your number of Communicantes together with the priest, and then had dissembled them: I had not done so cunningly, as falsly and wickedly. But because you vtter them for confirmation of your necessitie of number, thereby you shewe your selfe to handle your mater more boldly, then cunningly. For in dede those wordes of S. Paule serue nothing to your purpose. For trial whereof I referre me both to thexact construing of that texte it selfe, and to the auncient Fathers who haue expounded the same, namely Eucherius, de difficilioribus quæstionibus veteris & noui testamenti. Theophylacte, the wryter

ter of the tripartite historie lib. 9. cap, 38. Sedulius, S. Ambrose the author of the briefe Commentaries vpon S. Paules Epistles set forth vnder the name of S. Hierome, and chiefly of al others S. Chrysostome.

The scope and purpose of S. Paule in that place, is not specially to deliuer to the Corinthians a doctrine concerning the celebration of the Sacrament, for that had he performed before. But now his special intent was to correct the great disorder that was cõmonly vsed amõg thẽ in their Churchfeastes, by putting them in minde of the supper, which our Lord kept the night that he was betrayed. For what cause (saith S. Chrisostome) doth he make mention of the mysteries in this place? Because (he answereth) this talke was most necessary in the present case. wherby he sheweth that this mention of the Sacrament is brought in by S. Paule as a bye mater, yet to a very good purpose. His meaning is, that this mention is made, because the Apostle thought good to allege thexample of Christes charitie and humilitie for ẏ amendment of the pride, contempt, and disdaine, that was vsed among the Corinthians, who at their Church feastes diuided thẽ selues from the companie of the poore, & taried not for them, but went to their meates alone, and despised them, and so shewed great abuse, not in the order of ministring or receiuing the Sacrament, but in their breach of vnitie, wherof the Sacramẽt was a mysterie, and in other their manifold disorder.

Chryso. in 1. Cor. 11.

That at such feastes they receiued the Sacramẽt, either before other meats after S. Chrysostomes mynde, or after other meats as thopinion of some is, I deny not. But by the words, waite ye one for an other, it is not meant that the Corinthians should not receiue the sacrament without a number of communicantes, but that they should not go to their banket, and eate vp their cõmon meates by seueral companies, the richer and nobler sort by them selues, but waite and tarye for the poore, and admit them charitably

The meaning of S. Paules wordes, waite ye one for an other.

rably and humbly to be partakers of their table, as Christ admitted al his Apostles to be partakers of his table indifferently. To be short S. Paule there doth not exhort or stirre the Corinthians to a publike Communion, or to the receiuing of the Sacrament wt a number, but to charitie, indifferencie, meeknesse, equal regard of their poore brethren, humilitie, moderation & sobrietie. As for the Sacrament, he speaketh of it, but biely, and as it were by the waye, that by thexample of Christes supper, wherin he gaue the Sacrament to al, & admitted al to his table indifferētly, he might bring the Corinthians to the like vertue & indifferencie, to be vsed in their accustomed Churchfeastes, where specially vnitie, the fruite obteined by the worthy receiuing of the Sacrament the mysterie of Vnitie, was to be exercised.

Ievvel.

In other places S. Augustine like as also S. Hierome and others, vvitnesseth, that the vvhole people daily receiued together, and generally intreting of the holy Communion, he speaketh euermore of a number, and neuer of one alone.

Harding.

The state of this whole Article.

We dispute not now what was done, but whether number of Communicantes together Sacramentally be of Christes precept or Institution, and so of necessitie: whether if others fail, the priest may not be suffred to receiue that common benefite the vitaile of life. If he may, thē is our case cleare, that in S. Hieromes & S. Augustines time many commōly, & al the people sometimes receiued together, I denie not. The same deuotion we wish hartely it were in the people now. And if it were, yet would ye not be content therewith, such a desyre ye haue to vndoo that the Church holdeth for good, and to preferre your new fangled fansies. And whereas oftentimes you allege the places of the Fathers, that make mention of the Sacrament receiued by ỷ whole people, why do you not bring your whole people to your Communimunion? why admitte you that to be a good and lawful Communion, whereat three only receiue? Either bring al to it, or allege no more the Fathers speaking of al, or blame your owne sect, as wel as the catholike Church. For if al the people be requisite to a right and due Communion, then are they of your congregations to blame, among whom three receiuing together be allowed. Reason it is, ye amend your owne faultes, before ye reproue others.

the whole people do not Communicate together amōg the gospellers

That S. Hierome speaketh of some, who in his time at Rome receiued alone in their houses, I do most plainely shewe in my booke out of his owne wordes. Though S. Augustin speake neuer, (likewise) which I graunt not, yet thereof you can not conclude, that it ought not to be receiued of one alone, as you seme here to conclude. For this is a simple argument, you knowe, S. Augustine neuer speaketh of sole receiuing, ergo it is not lawful to receiue alone. I maruel, that you were so much ouerseen, as thorough your whole Replie to make such loose reasons. As for that which foloweth in the next Paragraph, I nede not to answer it, seing that you charge me vntruly with that I say not. Your seeming and surmising there of that which I touch not, serueth you only for stuffing towardes the heape.

In apolog, aduersus Iouinianū Fol, 20. a

Ievvel.

But if the Churche haue determined this mater for Priuate Masse, as M. Harding saith, in vvhat Councel, at vvhat time vvithin vi. C. yeres after Christe, and in vvhat place vvas it determined? Vvho vvas vvitnesse of the doing? VVho vvas president, vvho vvas present? This is that the Reader vvould faine learne. And M. Harding thinketh it best to proue it by silence. Hovv be it, it is confessed, that Priuate Masse came in, not by Christe, or by any of his Apostles, or by the auctoritie of the Churche, but only by the vndeuotion and negligence of the people.

Harding.

Here is much adoo, and many idle questions demaunded.

It hath ben not without cause commonly said in Schooles, an Asse may aske moe questions, then Aristotle is hable to answer. If I were disposed so to appose you M. Jewel, it were easy to requit you with no smal number of questiōs touching your new deuised Gospel, whereunto I am wel assured you can not with any colour of reason or learning answer. Albeit I nede not to repete them here againe. You be not vnmindful I dare say of the questions, which by way of your owne chalenge M. Rastel hath proponed vnto you, and requireth your Answer vnto them, in the ende of his Confutation of your Sermon. It stādeth you vpon, and vpon the estimation of your whole Gospel, that you satisfie the world with some reasonable Answer thereto. Els you shal cause al men to suspect your whole doctrine and preaching. For shame defende not your cause so with silence, and with putting good men in prison for hauing our treatises. Until you answer those Articles, ye are like to be on the losers syde.

M. Rastels Chalenge to M. Jew. not yet answered.

But as concerning your questions, I wil not altogether folow you. To them al thus I answer. Priuate Masse, that is to say the Priestes sole receiuing, we acknowledge. But that Masse is priuate, being takē for the Sacrifice, we do not acknowledge. As touching that you cal Priuate Masse, to wit the Sole receiuing of the priest, it is sufficiētly determined by the long practise of ẏ church, and why it ought not so to be done, there is no prohibition in the scripture to the contrary. The Sacrifice of the Masse, which we defende, that is to say, the vnbloudy Oblation of the body and bloud of Christe, is by our Sauiour Christe him selfe determined. Who as I haue sufficiently before proued, at his last supper after he had taken bread and wine into his handes, geuen thankes, blessed, and consecrated his body and bloud, and deliuered to them which were present: said to his Apostles, and in them to their successours priestes of the new Testament,

ment, Do ye this in my remembrance. And thereby he taught (as S. Ireneus saith) the new Oblation of the new testament. *Irenæus lib.4.ca.32*

This the Apostles receiued of him, the churche of the Apostles, and (as that blessed Martyr S. Ireneus reporteth) offereth it to God in the whole world. For this I haue no nede to allege any Councel. The time was the night when he was betrayed. The place was the chamber in Ierusalem, where he kept his Maundy. The witnesses of the doing were the three Euangelistes. S. Mathew, Marke, and Luke, and S. Paule. Christ him selfe was President, the Apostles were present. Thus you haue the mater for the blessed Sacrifice determined, and your questions answered.

That we distribute not the Sacrament to a nūber of others, as Christe did, that is of the imperfection of them, who refuse to frequent that benefite, not of any default of our parte. which vndeuotion of others & not receiuing, maketh not Priuate Masse, but is cause that the Priest at Masse receiue alone, and make no distribution, which ye cal Priuate Masse. You beare the people in hande, that Priuate Masse as ye cal it, came in, not by Christe, nor by the Apostles, nor by auctoritie of the Church, but only by vndeuotion and negligence of the people. And so ye would haue it seme euil, because as you pretende, it procedeth of euil.

But this is wicked and false sophistrie, whereby you begyle the vnlearned people, neither is it confessed, that Priuate Masse proceded of the peoples vndeuotion and negligence, neither in dede therof proceded it al. Christe is the author of the blessed Masse touching the substance of it, as now I haue declared. But the lacke of others to communicate with the priest, and that none oftentimes be disposed to receiue with him, that procedeth of vndeuotion, and negligence. Of this imperfection or negligence the Masse taketh not his name, much lesse his being, *The masse taketh not his name of the imperfection of the people, yet through it the priest sometime receiueth alone.*

ing. In dede because other be negligent, and do not Communicate with the Priest, for that cause the Priest receiueth alone, which the Gospellers cal Priuate Masse: but that is not ẏ cause of Masse, be it named Priuate, or how so euer it be named. That it is Masse, it is of Christes Institution, that it is priuate, or rather that the participation or receiuing of the Oblation is priuate, or singular to the Priest, that is through the occasion of the peoples vndeuotion and negligence.

In what sense it may be said, the negligence of the people is cause of priuate masse

To make this plaine by an example. It may be said, Lacke of tribute maketh a poore king. Shal we hereof conclude that a king commeth to his Crowne by his subiectes withdrawing of tribute? The French king of late yeres had not his tribute, custome, and rentes, duly payd and leuied, through the rebellion of the Huguenots, and thereof grewe poore. Shal we in consyderation hereof say, that rebellion made a poore king? No, rebellion made not a poore king, for then had it made a king: but rebellion made the French king poore. For the king was made of God. Neither came he in by rebellion, but by right of succession and inheretance. yet by a manner of common speach we may say, that rebellion maketh a poore prince. wherby is meant that it bringeth pouertie, not a kingly state to a king. Euen so though the vndeuotion and negligence of the people be a cause, why the Priest at Masse many times receiueth the blessed Sacrament alone, (for which cause the Gospellers cal the Masse Priuate, whereas they should cal it rather Priuate receiuing, for the Masse that notwithstanding is both for the mater, and for the Minister publike and common): yet is not that the cause of Masse, but only that the Masse is celebrated without a companie of communicantes together. It maketh not Priuate Masse, but it maketh the Masse after their terming, to be Priuate. So that Priuate Masse as they cal it, proceded not, ne came not in

by

by the negligence of the people, as M. Iewel goeth about with his sophistrie to perswade the vnlearned, but by Christe, as I haue said, whose example is witnesse of a number Communicating together in one place, to whome then he delyuered a forme of administration, which they should afterward folowe, but the same touching number, was not a commaundement. For as the hauing of number to receiue with the Priest, maketh no part of the substance of the Masse, nor bettereth the same: euen so the lacke of receiuers marreth not the substance, nor any whit impaireth the same. For the substance is both in one.

Here I omitte the great adoo and scoffing that M. Iewel maketh at the Catholikes, for the constructions, which they make (as he belyeth them) of these wordes of S. Paule, cætera cum venero, disponam, Touching the rest, I wil take order when I come. There he beareth men in hand that vpon these wordes we build Priuate Masse, and maketh S. Paule to tel a foolish tale, as though he were a Vise in an enterlude, made by some Minister of their Gospel. which I contemne, as almost al the rest of his vaine babling Replie, and thinke it not in dede worth of answer. Page.21. paragr. 2. f.4. 1. Cor.11.

Ievvel.

I may not novv dissemble the value of M.Hardinges argument. Christe (saith he) ordeined the sacrament after consecration and oblation done, to be receiued and eaten. Ergo the number of Communicantes together is no parte of Christes Institution. Vvhat thought M.Harding that none but children and fooles should read his booke? For hovv loosely hang these partes together? The sacrament must be receiued after Consecration: Ergo, The number of Communicantes is not necessary. There is not * one peece hereof that either is true in it selfe, or agreeth vvith other.* The.70. vntruth. It is not my argument. The.71. vntruth. For some parte is proued to be true.

Harding.

What say you M. Iewel? Is there not one peece of that I

M. Iew. speaketh like a man that is out of his wit.

haue here said true in it selfe? Be you wel aduised what you say, or hath the spirite of malice against the catholike Church caried you out of your witte? Is not this true, Christ ordeined the Sacrament after consecration and oblation done to be receiued? Do you not allege Gabriel Biel your selfe for proufe thereof within fewe lines?

When you come to your right minde again, you wil reuoke this, I am sure, and say it was spoken vnaduisedly. For els let manducate and bibite, eate ye, and drinke ye, be taken out of the Gospel. Wel this peece then is true. Now let vs see, how the argument that may be gathered out of my wordes, holdeth together. Let M. Iewel loose it if he can. My argument I wil make my selfe. It is easy for a scoffer to scoffe at argumentes framed of his owne scoffing head. Take none other but mine owne argumentes M. Iewel, and handle them, as your scoffing head thinketh best, I geue you leaue. But to deuise peuish arguments of your owne, and to father them vpon me: it shal appeare a peuish practise, to al that shal perceiue it. For thinke not good Sir, that al be childrẽ, or fooles, or fond fauourers of your owne pleasant gospel, that shal read your booke. Some wise men may happen to see your vneuen dealing, your immoderate lying, your ambitious affectation of learning, your wilful peruerting of truthe, and your other euil demeanour, in whose iudgement you shal neuer recouer credite.

An argument proponed to M. Iew. to be considered.

My argument then is this. Touching the blessed Sacramẽt due mater, forme, minister, and intent presupposed, what so euer is beside Cõsecration, Oblation, & receiuing, which I vnderstãd by Participation: is no part of Christes Institutiõ, but is left to the disposition of the church. The number of Cõmunicantes together in one place, is besyde these three fornamed: Ergo the nũber of Cõmunicants together is no part of Christes Institutiõ.

Thus

Thus you haue that by due argument concluded, which you so often haue denyed M. Jewel. Scoffe no more at my argument. If the conclusion like you not, the argument being good: what haue you here to denye, but the *minor* or second proposition? That the number of Communicantes together in one place, is a parte of Christes Institution, which is denyed in the *minor*, in this very Diuision you take vpon you to proue, for that these wordes, take ye, eate ye, drinke ye al, &c. importe a number. But how weake that proufe is, I haue now sufficiently shewed. You must get you better proufe then Christes speaking to many in the plural number, or els yelde to the truth, and admitte the conclusion of my Argument. At least vntil you proue it, which you shal neuer do, stint your railing and barking at the blessed Sacrifice of the Churche, and so yelde by silence, where speaking or writing auaileth you nothing. If you presse vpon ẏ number, consider to whom and to how many it was spoken. It was spokē to the Apostles being twelue in number, wherfore it must be deliuered to such, and to no moe. And so the Laitie by you is cleane excluded, and the Churche driuen to a vaine precisenesse of number. *Page.20. par.3.*

Now (that I may folow M. Jewels kind of eloquence) I may not dissemble the valew of M. Jewels argument.

> These wordes (saith he) Take ye, eate ye, drinke ye, &c. can not be taken of one singular man, but necessarily importe a number: Ergo Christ hath by special woordes appointed a numbre (of Communicantes together). so much is to be vnderstanded, els we agree. For that so many as be worthily proued and disposed, should Communicate, we graunt and wish. But that they should Communicate together, that is to say in one place, that we denye Christes wordes to inporte. For by like reason (as I haue before declared)

M. Jewels argument for necessitie of a nūber to receiue the Communion together.

declared.) Christes other commaundementes geuen to the Apostles in the plural number, importe also signification of number together. And so one might not preach alone, baptise alone, absolue alone, nor do any thing geuen in commaundement by Christe in woordes of the plurall number: except moe were alwayes together, in the same place. Which is very fonde and absurde, and the Apostles neuer obserued it, who at length were diuided a sunder into diuers coastes of the worlde, and didde preach, baptise, remitte sinnes, and other dueties apperteining to their vocation, when none els in those functions made vp a number with them.

What thought you M. Iewel, when you made this Argument, that none but Children and fooles should reade your booke? How hang these partes together? Christe said speaking to moe then one, Eate ye, drinke ye: Ergo, one may not eate and drinke the Sacrament alone. By like Logike, *Mat.11.* a man may reason thus, Christe said to al, Venite ad me omnes, Come ye to me al, Ergo no man or woman may come to Christe, except al go together with him. And so no one person may euer go to Christe, because he shal neuer finde al ready to go with him. I woulde not thus trifle with you, if I sawe any better mater then very trifles in you. And how can it be otherwise, sith that your grounde is not truth? And how can falshed be vpholden and mainteined against truth, but with Argumentes of vntruth, and with groundlesse trifles?

Ievvel.

Concerning the force of M. Hardings Argument, it concludeth directly against him selfe. For if Christe instituted the Sacrament to the

the intent it should be first consecrate, and then receiued of a company: it must needes follovv, that receiuing vvith companie is parte of Christes Institution.

The,72, vntruth, this is a very grosse falsifying of my saying.

Harding.

Lorde what impudencie is there in this man? He hath caused his Printer to put into his booke my wordes by sundry Diuisions, and yet in the same place, where he commeth to replie against them, he falsifieth and misreporteth them. Take lying and falshed from his booke, and truely the rest may seeme a smal deale. Contrarywise let him followe the vaine of his accustomed impudencie in Lying, and what number of Paper may not he blotte? where say I, *that Christe instituted the Sacrament to the intent it should be first Consecrated and then receiued of a companie,* or with a companie together in one place? for so he meaneth & so he maketh his conclusion. Say not I expressely the contrary? Be not these my woordes? The number of Communicantes together in one place, that they iangle so much of, is no parte of Christes Institution. Item, Christe ordeined the Sacrament after Consecration and Oblation done, to be receiued and eaten, and for that ende he said, Accipite, manducate, bibite. Take, eate, drinke. Herein consisteth his Institution.

This falshed of M. Iew. can by no colour be excused.

In my answere fol.12.b.

Now where is the necessitie of your companie by me spoken of in al these wordes? If it be not, but if the contrary be spoken, why had you rather to seme impudent in lying, then not to reproue me for my Argument, or rather for your argumēt? for mine it is not as you report it. And here must ẏ margent of your booke be painted al ouer with my poore name, to bring it into hatred & contempt. *M.Harding cōcludeth against him self. M.Hardings*

A burden of lyes.

 argument.

argument. M. Harding hath forgotten him selfe. M. Harding ieasteth at the ordinaunce of Christe, &c.

Uerely M. Iewel you are iustly annumbred among them, of whom the Prophete Esay speaketh. Posuimus mendacium
Esai.28.
spem nostram, & mendacio protecti sumus. We haue put our trust in lying, and lying is our Protection. If you had forborne lying, your booke had growen to a smal quantitie. Yea you might haue holden your peace. But this is that smoke and smoder I forsawe and spake of in my Conclusion to you.
Fol.191.
which by Gods grace shal sone vanish awaye, the light of the Truth driuing awaye the darkenes of your Lyes. To conclude, I saye, the Sacrament ought to be receiued, and would God that alwaies a number were worthily proued, examined and disposed to receiue. But that a number be alwayes together in one place to receiue, that is not of Christe expressely commaunded, nor is conteined in his Institution. The contrary whereof if you proue not M. Iewel, leaue your barking against the Churche, for that the Priest receiueth alone, when others be not disposed to receiue with him.

The Ninth Diuision.

The effect of my wordes in the.9.Diuision.

THe effect of my woordes, which M. Iewel hath placed in his.9. Diuision, is an answer to the common obiection of Christes example, that we ought to deliuer the Sacrament to a number together, because Christe so did at his Supper. Whereto I say there, that we are bounde to followe the example of Christe, for so much as concerneth the substance of of the Sacrament, not the outward ceremonie, to which number perteineth. Also that, in case of the peoples slackenes, the Priest notwithstanding, ought to do his duetie.

M. Iewel in his Replie to this, would seme to touch the very point, but in dede he shooteth at randon, and commeth nothing nigh the Butte, where the scope and marke of our mater is. And because he bestoweth many woordes to litle purpose, to confute them, I entend not to bestow long time, reseruing my labour for pointes of more pith and substance.

Ievvel.

The question that lyeth betvven vs, standeth not in this point, vvhether vve ought to do euery thing that Christe did: but vvhether vve ought to do that thing, that Christe both did him selfe, and also commaunded vs to do, &c.

Harding.

Now that you are come to the question it selfe, I trust you wil not roue abroade as you haue done hitherto, but speake to the purpose, and auoide al superfluous talke. Wel, then what say you to it?

Ievvel.

Christe said not, Do this in Ierusalem, or in this Parler, or after Supper, or at this table, or being so many together, or standing, or sitting: but he said thus, Do ye this, that is, Take ye Breade, blesse it, breake it, geue it in my remembrance. This is not a Ceremonial Accident, but the very ende, purpose, and substance of Christes Institution.

O intollerable corruption. where is, this is my body? etc.

Harding.

Here commeth me in this newe Euangelist, I watte not from whence, and forsooth pareth away al the cerimonial accidentes of the Supper, and setteth forth nothing but the very ende, purpose, and substance of Christes Institution. A substan-

 tial

cial Doctor, I warrant you Christian Readers, ye may beleeue him, if ye wil. For he goeth to the substance of the mater.

Christe (saith he) said not thus, but he said thus, *Do ye this in my remembrance.* And what *this*, meant he, we should do? Mary saith this new Euangelist, that we *take Breade, blesse it breake it, and geue it.* Why Sir by your fauour, shal we fare no better at your Supper? If this be al the substance of your banket, and of Christes Institution, as you tel vs, we thinke it a smal pitaunce, to haue nothing but Breade. O saith he, this now is not common Bread, it is holy Bread, for it is conuerted to an holy vse, it is Sacramental breade, it is tokening breade, for it is a token, a signe, a figure, or a signification of the Lords Body that is in heauen. &c. O M. Iewel, begile not the people of God, for whom Christ gaue his Body. Serue them not with signes and tokens, which can not fede their hungry soules, but with the thing it selfe. Ye bereue them of the best dish, the body of Christ, without which your symbolical, tokenīg, & figuratiue bread profiteth them nothīg. And Sir I pray you, is this the substance of Christes Institution? Nay haue you not falsified, corrupted, and belyed his blessed Institution? Where is the chiefe grace and gift, Hoc est corpus meum, This is my Body?

M. Iew. pretendīg to speake of the substance of Christes Supper, leaueth quite out ye body and bloud of Christe, & setteth fourth bread, and thereof maketh ye whole banket.

You blame me (though without cause as I haue before proued) that reckening the essential partes of Christes Institution, I spake not of the Annuntiatiō of our Lords death, which in deede is done by speaking of Consecration, Oblation, and Receiuing. And shal you escape blame for leauing quite out the Body and Bloude of Christe, where you speake of the substance of his Institution? What haue you there, if you haue not the substance of his Body and Bloud? Do these wordes, Do ye this, importe nomore but a request, to take Bread, blesse it, breake it, and geue it? Why then three or foure good felowes

Supra fol.

of your Congregation hauing a cake or a crackenel before them in a Tauerne, may celebrate your Cōmunion whiles the Tapster is filling a quarte of wine. For what let is there? who can not take bread? who can not breake it, and geue it to his companions? As for blessīg, if you meane no more but saying of a praier, (for the Consecration of ẏ Church you allow not) they may sone geate a Ladde or a girle to say grace at the table.

O M. Iewel, that you restraine Christes commaundement Do ye this, to taking, blessīg, breaking and geuing bread. Where is the word of Consecration, This is my Body, this is my bloud, by which he consecrated his body and bloud? Are not they conteined vnder Do ye this? If ye do not consecrate, and by the almighty power of the word, the bread and wine chaunged into an other most excellent substance, make really present the Body and Bloud of Christe, as he did him selfe at his supper: how do you performe and fulfil this commaundement, Do ye this? If you thinke it necessary to be done, what falshed, what malice, what Deuilish wickednesse is it for you to obscure it, to hyde it, to put it out of memorie, to abolishe it by wilfull omission? In M. Iewels description of Christs Supper ẏ chiefe substance is put away.

By like your aduise was geuen to the framing of the English Churches Communiō at Geneua, which was printed there. Wherein the woordes of Consecration be omitted, least the people by rehearsal of them should be moued to thinke, that there is some alteration made in the Bread and wine. So ye haue put away and made voide the commaundement and Institution of Christe, to set vp and establish your owne Traditions. The Cōmuniō of the English Churche at Geneua leaueth out the wordes of Consecration.

Ye charge vs with robbing the people of the one kinde in the administration of the Sacrament. How much more iustly may we charge you for robbing them of both kindes?

For if in Chriſtes commaundement and wordes of his Inſtitution, ye include not the Conſecration of his Body and Bloud, whereby they are made preſent through the omnipotencie of his worde: then geue ye to the people in ſtede of the moſt precious gifte of his Body and Bloud, nothing but Breade and wine. God ſende you to Geneua againe (I feare me he wil ſende you to Gehēna) with ẏ doctrine, if ye mind not to change your opinion. Verely the holy Ghoſt neuer taught it, the Church neuer receiued it of the Apoſtles, in al the holy Fathers we finde the contrary.

But Sir, if we would admitte your expoſition of Chriſtes wordes, Do ye this, (as we do not admitte in no wiſe) what conclude you? We take Bread, we bleſſe, we breake, we geue. What more wil ye haue of vs? If this be the very ende, purpoſe, and ſubſtance of Chriſtes Inſtitution, as you ſay, it is: ſith we do al this at our Maſſe, why profeſſe you ſuch opē hatred againſt it? Why worke you al the ſpite you can, againſt it? Why do you deſpiſe it worſe then any Turke, Saracen, Iewe, or Infidel? Why barke you at it with woordes viler then the barking of any Dogge? Why do you abhorre it no leſſe then the Angels of Satan? From whence bloweth this wicked and blaſphemous ſprite?

But ſay you, we geue it not. Yeas forſooth Sir, we are alwayes willing, deſyrous, and ready, to geue it to al faithful perſōs being in caſe worthily to receiue it with vs and demaunding the ſame, and ſometimes we do actually geue it to certaine being wel diſpoſed. And when none is diſpoſed, wee receiue alone, and geue it eche one to our ſelues in the dreadful Myſteries. And of our parte touching this behalfe, this is inough. And thus is the Inſtitution and commaundement of Chriſte, who ſaid, Do ye this, kept and obſerued.

If you say, it is broken, because we receiue it not with a number, I tel you againe once for al, a number were to be wisshed in dede at al times, yet is the same ceremonial, not essential. I meane, it perteineth to the ceremonie of eating, and to further honour of the Sacrament, but it is not so of the Institution, as it may not be at any time receiued of the Priest without number of Communicantes together with him in one place, vnder paine of deadly sinne. You say, the number is of the substance of thinstitution, and of necessitie: but you proue it not. Say it no more so often, but proue it once, least you seme stil to repeate one song like a Cuckow.

Ievvel.

*Yet saith M. Harding, vve are bound to follovv Christes example in thinges that be of the substance of the Sacrament, not in things, that be of order and congruence. Here vnavvares he * semeth to confesse, that his Masse vvhat so euer substance it beare, yet is voide both of good order, and also of congruence.*

The. 73. vntruth. I seme not to confesse any such thing

Harding.

You wrangle M. Iewel. You seeke al the occasion you can, to speake euil of me, and blasphemously of the blessed Sacrifice of the Masse. This to do, at least in some shewe, you falsifie my wordes, and hauing made me to speake as is for your scoffing purpose: you handle me as it liketh you. And this is your custome through al your booke, to reporte my woordes otherwise then I do, and then to carpe them. But what should I complaine of priuate iniurie? Your vntruth and falsifying is not extended to my wordes onely, but also to the wordes of the auncient and holy Fathers of the Churche, yea to the wordes of our Sauiour Christ him self, as euē here a litle before I shewed.

But sith there is no plainenesse nor sinceritie in you, I report me to the discret Reader, whether it may be gathered of my woordes that I confesse the Masse to be void of order and so congruence. Speaking of Christes example touching the administration of the blessed Sacrament, I say, we are bounde to follow it, for the substance, not for the outwarde ceremonie, to the which perteineth number, and other rites. Then I say further by way of explication: Christes example imporreth necessitie of receiuing onely, (I meane after Consecration and Oblation done) the other rites, as number, place, time, &c. be of congruence and order. I would faine vnderstande what be the woordes here, whereof M. Iewel gathereth his scoffing conclusion, that I seeme to confesse, that the Masse, (which in spite he calleth my Masse) is voide both of good order, and also of congruence. But common scoffers and iesters chalenge to them selues a libertie, to speake what they liste without control.

Fol.13.a.

And Sir if I say, we are not bounde to followe the example of Christe in thinges, which then were of order and congruence: do I confesse that the Masse is voide both of good order, and also of congruence? That Christe at his supper after he had consecrated his Body, gaue it to a number, it was of order and congruence. For if he had geuen it but to one only, as to S. Peter, or S. Iohn: the rest might haue thought them selues litle regarded. If he had geuen it to some and not to al, there should haue appeared parcialitie, and grudge therof woulde haue folowed. And where as they were al made Priestes at that Supper, and were taught a forme of the administration of the Sacrament: it was of order and congruence, that they shoulde al be partakers, yea they onely without the companie of any women.

That the Supper was kept in the Citie of Ierusalem, in a semely eating chamber dressed vp for that purpose, that the true

Lambe

Lambe which taketh away the sinnes of the worlde, was offe-red & eaten after the typical or figuratiue Lambe of the Old law, that the Sacramentes of both Lawes so mette together, that this precious deinty was last of al geuen, after Supper, a litle before Christe was taken away from their presence: al this was of order and congruence. To these obseruances the example of Christe doth not binde vs. And shal we say therefore, that ẏ Masse is void both of al good order & also of congruence? Now weigh this argument good Reader, which M. Iewel for lacke of honest Logike, maketh here with his scoffing Rhetorike.

M. Iew. argument in effect.

That we celebrate Masse duely, we are not bounde vnder paine of deadly sinne to the ceremonials of Christes example at his Supper: Ergo the Masse is void of al good order and congru-ence. Such Logike becommeth such a cause. Like doctrine, like proufes. Thus falshed is best defended by falshed.

Now M. Iewel you haue said al that euer you could say, for that a number ought alwaies to communicate together with the Priest. And yet you haue not proued it. If you wil needes holde that opinion, and not geue ouer: remember that you seke new proufes, for al that you haue yet brought, serueth not your turne. Conferre with your brethren, and learne, whether any better reasons may be founde for proufe thereof, then hitherto you haue made. Hereon dependeth the whole case. You should haue debated this point more piththily & more at large. Your bare worde, and bolde affirmation without iust proufe, wil no more be taken for the Gospel. And if you faile of suf-ficient proufe for this pointe, then may we iustly require you to yelde and subscribe.

What is that M. Iewel hath to proue, and proueth not.

That both you may beare it away, and others deeply thinke of it, the thing ẏ stādeth you vpō clearly to proue is this.

That a number of Communicantes together in one place is so absolutely necessary, that a Priest after Consecration and Oblation done, may not in any wise receiue the blessed Sacramente except there be a number to communicate Sacramentally with him in the same place. Until this be proued, priuate Masse as you terme it, is not disproued. That is to say, this remaineth lauful and godly, that a Priest do consecrate & offer vp to God the Body and Bloud of Christe in that order as the Churche vseth, and receiue it alone, when others be not disposed to receiue it with him.

This much belongeth to you clearly and euidently to proue both for your owne priuate credites sake, and for the credite of your Gospel. Which if you do not, and that substantially, farre otherwise then you haue done in your vaine babling, & lying Replie: you shal cause as wel that parte, as the rest of your newe doctrine, generally to be suspected.

After this M. Jewel being loth to tary long in the weightiest point, which required most learning and best discussiō, conueieth him self away to rayling and finding fault with ye Church for other thinges not specially by me spoken of in my Answere to his First Article: The Latine tongue, the Priestes turning of his face from the people, Ceremonies, which he termeth infinite and childish, al these he reproueth, saying that al these be holden for thinges substantial, but falsly he saith it, as likewise most lyingly and impudently, that we haue power to change accidence into substance, and substance into accidence, when we liste. These, and the like vaine railings and lyes, wherewith his booke is stuffed, if I would passe ouer vnanswered, I might sone make an ende. Of them al, leauing aparte the lightest, faine woulde I see, of what value be his sayinges of most weight.

In this Diuision as it foloweth, he cryeth out O miserable vpon the Church of Rome, and the whole Colledge of Cardinals, for that they be not disposed to receiue the Communion, so often as the Priestes say Masse. I would he went to Rome, and tolde them that, whereby he might amend al that is amisse.

As he goeth forth, he sheweth his wil to be, that receiuing of the Cōmunion be, as common as prayer. *Whosoeuer is a member of Christe* (saith he) *and may boldly cal God his Father, may also be bolde to receiue the Communion.* As though through occasion of such bolde preachers and teachers, many toke not themselues for the members of Christ, which be the members of Antichrist, and many ful boldly called not God their Father, to whom God may say, as he saith by the Prophete Malachias, Si ego sum pater, vbi honor meus? If I be your Father, where is my honour? But how boldesoeuer M. Jewels companiōs be oftenties to receiue ye Communion, the godly & deuout Catholike people tremble and feare, when they come to that most holy table, to receiue the very body of their maker in forme of Bread, and make an ernest and careful preparation long before, that they come not vnworthily. They proue them selues most diligently before they presume to eate of that diuine Bread, least they should eate it to their condemnation. And this is the cause why they be houseled more seldome, then they were in the Primitiue Church. Yet yt they be in many places ouer slacke & cold herein, I denye not. Neither do I wholy excuse them, by whom thei should be stirred to receiue that greate benefite oftener. But what is that to the abrogation of the Masse? Among other thinges I maruel what he meaneth, where speaking of the daily Sacrifice of the Church, wherein the Priest offereth vp Christe vnto his Father, he calleth it a wanton Folie, and saith thus.

Malach. 1.

The cause why they receiue more seldōe now, then they did in the Primitiue Church.

Ievvel.

Ievvel.

The. 74. vntruth. It hath ben throughly beleued.

*The mater being so vveighty, and not * yet throughly beleued, it had ben good for M. Harding to haue made proufe thereof by the auctoritie of S. Augustine, S. Hierome, or some other olde Catholike Doctor, vvithin the compasse of six hundred yeares.*

Harding.

As though I had not done this already in my Answere ot the .17. Article. But it semeth M. Jewel, you care not what you say, so you say that is il, and false of me. *The mater is vveighty and not throughly beleued* you say. The weightier it is, the more danger is to them that beleue it not. Whom you meane I know not: but if your selfe be he, that beleueth it not, as I may easily beleue that: You should not haue said, *not yet throughly beleued*, but not now throughly beleued. For once you beleued it, as al the Catholike Church beleueth, but now that belefe you haue forsaken, and at this present beleue it not. If you wil beleue the auncient Fathers, who both beleued it, and spake most plainely of it: them you may see and read by me alleged vpon your seuentienth Article, & in this present Treatise here before.

But touching this Article, you wil not beleue me, nor the Fathers, nor þe whole Church, nor Christe him selfe: who by verdite of al þe Fathers, both by his exãple at his last supper, and by these expresse wordes, Do ye this in my remembrance, commaũded his Apostles, and in them their successours to offer vp vnto God his Body and Blond in the holy Mysteries, and taught as S. Ireneus saith, The new Oblation of the new Testament. Wherefore though I make proufe of the vnbloudy Sacrifice neuer so sufficiently, though for witnesse and declaration of the Churches faith therein, I allege neuer so many Doctours, as it is easy to allege in manner al that euer wrote: al this wil not

Irenæus lib. 4. c. 32.

help

helpe you, it is not I, nor the authoritie of any Father, that can bring light or wisedome into your darke and malicious soule, malicious I meane against the Church, but it is onely he that first diuided light frō darkenes, the Creator of light, and iudge of the workes of darkenesse. If he do it not, it is vaine labour for men to trauail with you. To his merciful iudgemēt I recommend you. I had rather pray for you, then haue to do with you. Onely for the deceiued peoples sake, I do that I do.

Because I say, the vnbloudy Sacrifice is to be celebrated daily, to the intent the bloudy Sacrifice once made on the Crosse for redemption of mankinde may be kept in memorie: herof M. Iewel taketh occasion to enter into a common place, concerning these wordes daily Sacrifice. wherin hys purhose is to abolish the memorie of that, which the Church calleth as the fathers do, the daily Sacrifice, meaning the blessed Sacrifice of the Masse, wherein the memorie of Christes death is dayly renewed. To this purpose he allegeth certaine places out of Doctours, in which a continuance of the benefite of Christes death and resurrection is signified. By which places he concludeth nothing against the Daily Sacrifice. His wordes be these. Daily Sacrifice.

Ievvel.

*The olde Fathers * cal that the Daily Sacrifice, that Christe made once for al vpon the Crosse: for that as Christ is a Priest for euer, so doth the same his Sacrifice last for euer: not that it is daily and really renevued of any mortal creature, but that the povver and vertue thereof is infinite in it selfe, and shal neuer be consumed.* The.75. vntruth. The fathers cal not the Sacrifice of ỹ Crosse the daily Sacrifice.

Harding.

That the olde Fathers cal the Sacrifice, once made vpon ỹ Crosse, ỹ Daily Sacrifice, I heare you say it, but I heare you not proue it. That which you bring for proufe, reporteth it to be of time euerlasting, and of vertue infinite, which no man denyeth. Yet here are two thinges to be considered touching this worde Sacrifice, The thing Sacrificed, and yͤ act of Sacrificing. The thing Sacrificed is Christe, as he was man, or the Body of Christe. The same is of power and vertue infinite, of time euerlasting. The act of Sacrificing is Christes Passion, wherby is wrought our Redemption. This act and real Passion, was done but once vpon the Crosse: and therfore can not properly be called dayly. For it began & ended within compasse of a certaine place, and certaine time. Yet the vertue of it lasteth for euer. Both are called by the name of Sacrifice.

In Sacrifice two thinges are to be considered

Now the Body of Christ is called of the Fathers, the daily Sacrifice, not in consideratiõ that it was once sacrificed vpon the Crosse, but for yͭ the commemoration & memorie of it is daily renewed in the Masse, and it selfe mystically Sacrificed. For in the Masse the same thing, that is to say, the same Body, is offered, but after an other manner of offering, then that was vpon the Crosse. S. Augustine speaketh distinctly and plainely of both these Sacrifices. Nõne semel Christus Oblatus est in semetipso, & tamen in Sacramento, non solum per omnes Paschæ solennitates, sed omni die populis immolatur? Was not Christe offered vp once in him selfe, and yet in the Sacrament he is sacrificed for the people, not onely at euery Easter feast, but euery day? The Sacrifice once made vpon the Crosse, S. Augustine calleth Christe once Sacrificed in him selfe, that is to saye, in his visible and passible Body with shedding of his bloude. The Sacrificing of the same Christe for the people, in the Sacrament, he calleth Quotidianam immolationem, The daily Sacrifice. And this is that I named the daily Sacrifice, as S. Augustine and al other Catholikes do.

August. Epist. 23.

O

Of this daily Sacrifice S. Augustine speaketh very plainely in an other place, by whom we may vnderstand what it is. The Hebrewes (saith he) in the sacrifices of beastes, which they offred to God, by many and sundry wayes, as it was meete for so great a thing, did celebrate a prophecie of the Sacrifice to come, which Christe hath offred. Wherefore now the Christians do celebrate the memorie of the same Sacrifice done, by the holy oblation and participation of the body and bloud of Christe.

Contrà Faustum Manich. lib. 20. cap. 18.

Consider this wel reader. That Sacrifice which was made vpon the crosse, in the place before alleged of S. Augustine is called, Christe offred in him selfe. Here it is called in respecte of the olde Hebrewes, the Sacrifice to come, in respect of the Christians that be now, the Sacrifice already done. But that Sacrifice whereof the controuersie is betwen the Sacramẽtaries and vs, there of S. Augustine is called the daily Sacrifice of Christe in the Sacrament: Here the celebration of the memorie of the Sacrifice already done. And least any man should thinke this Sacrifice to be a memorie only, or a celebration and keping of that memorie only, without the thing whose memorie is kept, to put that quite out of doubte: S. Augustine addeth, sacrosancta oblatione & participatione corporis & sanguinis Christi, with the holy Oblation and Participation of the body and bloud of Christe.

In the Masse then that which we speake so much of, which M. Iewel impugneth, by S. Augustines description, is the celebration of the memorie, or a solemne commemoration of the Sacrifice once done vpon the Crosse, made with the holy Oblation and partaking of the body and bloud of Christe. This Sacrifice for that it is Daily made, is named the Daily Sacrifice, And it is a Sacrament of the bloudy Sacrifice, a sacrifice commemoratiue or representatiue of the Sacrifice done vpon the crosse, and

What is meant by the daily Sacrifice of the Masse.

yet a true Sacrifice, because the thing it selfe, to witte, the body and bloud of Christe, is no lesse present here, then there, no lesse offred here, then there, though here in Sacramento, in a Sacrament, there in seipso, in him selfe, as S. Augustine speaketh.

S. Chrysostome hauing declared S. Paule affirming that Christe offered him selfe once to the destruction of sinne, forthwith saith of the daily Sacrifice offred vp by christian Priestes. Quid ergo nos? Nonne per singulos dies offerimus? &c. Then what do we? Do we not offer daily? yeas verely we do so, but that we do, we do it for the remembrance of his death. And this is one hoste, or one Sacrifice, not many. Beholde reader, to thee I speake, for M. Jewels eares can not away with this doctrine. S. Chrysostome saith, the Sacrifice which we offer at the Masse, and that which Christe offered vpon the crosse with suffering death, is one hoste, one Sacrifice, verely the selfe same one body of Christe. The difference that is, is only in the manner of Offering.

Chrysosto. in Epist. ad Heb. 10.

The hoste of the crosse, & of the Masse is one.

That holy Oblation, saith he an other where, whether he be Peter, whether he be Paule, or a priest of what so euer merite, that offereth it, it is the same that Christe him selfe gaue to his disciples, and that Priestes do now consecrate. Why so? Because they are not men that Sanctifie or Consecrate this, but Christe, which before consecrated that. Euen as the wordes, which Christ spake, be the same, that the priestes do also pronounce, so the Oblation is the same. &c. And he that thinketh this to haue ought lesse then that, knoweth not that it is Christe, who now also is present and worketh.

Chrysosto. hom. 2. in 2. ad Tim. 1

It is one oblation y Christ offered, and that the priest offereth.

If I thought these Testimonies were not ynough, and sufficient to proue that the Sacrifice of the Masse is a true and Real Sacrifice, forasmuch as we haue the same body of Christe, that was Offred vpon the crosse: I could easily here reherse no

smal

smal number out of the auncient Fathers, by whom with one consent the body of Christe is auouched to be present in the Sacrifice of the aulter, and in a Sacrament to be Offred vp vnto God.

But let vs consider the weight both of M. Iewels reason, and of his Testimonies, whereby he would proue, that the Sacrifice of the Crosse is the Daily Sacrifice, so as the Sacrifice of the Masse be not the Daily Sacrifice. For if he would graunt both, which differ not in the thing Offred, but in the manner of Offering, to be the Daily Sacrifice, so the Sacrifice of ye Church, which he inpugneth be not excluded from that name: in a right sense I would agree therto. But his discourse hereof is such, as he semeth by thaffirmation of one truth to denye an other truth. *As Christe* (saith he) *is a priest for euer, so doth the same his Sacrifice last for euer. For the vertue of it is infinite, and is neuer consumed.* What conclude you M. Iewel? Ergo that Sacrifice is daily, or the daily Sacrifice? Nay you should rather conclude thus. Ergo it is perpetual or euerlasting.

For as Christes Priesthod is euerlasting, so is his Sacrifice euerlasting. And the thing that lasteth for euer, is not in respect of euerlasting continuance properly called quotidian or daily, though what thing is euer, be also Daily. As the Priesthod of Christe is no where called, Daily Priesthod, nor Christe him self, Daily Christe, or the daily sonne of God, but the eternal or euerlasting sonne of God. Passe you through other thinges that be euerlasting, and you shal not fynde them for their infinite vertue or continuance, properly named daily. Of S. Cyprian this Sacrifice is called Perpes Sacrificium, & semper permanens holocaustum. An euerlasting Sacrifice.

The thing which is called daily, hath that name in consideration of often renewing, repetition or frequenting.

Differēce betwen euerlasting and daily.

An euerlasting Sacrifice.

Cyprian. de Cœna Domini.

Daily sacrifice, wherof it is so called

As this sacrificing of Christe in the Sacrament is daily repeted and frequented, whereas the sacrifice made vpō the crosse, which Christe made in seipso, in him selfe, as S. Augustine speaketh, is not iterated, repeted, and done oftentimes. In dede in this Sacrifice of the Church, which is done in Sacramento, it is daily recorded and set forth, and for this, and in this it is daily, because the hoste is one, and no otherwise.

Aug. de uerbis domini in Lucam serm. 23.

The wordes that you allege out of S. Augustine, (Tibi hodie Christus est, tibi quotidie resurgit, to thee Christe is to day, to thee Christe daily ryseth againe) do signifie, that if worthily you receiue Christ daily in the Sacrament of the aulter, for therof he speaketh there, then you receiue and enioy daily the benefite of his resurrection. Loe of the daily receiuing, and repetition of the blessed Sacrament, Christe is said daily to rise againe to vs. So because he is daily offred in the same Sacrament by priestes vnto God, therof commeth the name of the daily Sacrifice. Of which sacrifice in the same place immediatly before S. Augustine speaketh with these wordes. Thou hearest, that, how oftentimes so euer the sacrifice is offered, the death of our Lorde, the resurrection of our Lorde, the lifting vp of our Lorde is signified, and remission of sinnes, and takest not this daily bread of our life?

Wherof is the name of daily sacrifice.

There haue you mention M. Iewel, which you were loth to see, of the daily sacrifice of our daily bread, of the daily enioying of Christes resurrection. Which place serueth vs for proufe of the daily Sacrifice, it serueth not you for proufe, that ẏ sacrifice once done vpon the crosse is of the old Fathers called the daily Sacrifice. Whereby you labour to abolish the memorie of that sacrifice daily offred in the Sacrament.

Daily bread, daily sacrifice daily resurrection.

Neither maketh any more for you the place you allege out of the briefe Cōmentaries vpon the Epistles of S. Paule printed among S. Hieromes workes, & be not S. Hieromes, which

you

you for your aduantage wil here nedes once againe, haue to be S. Hieromes. For what if it be said by an allusion to the old custome of the Hebrewes, that, if we haue no leuen of malice and wickednes in vs, (which wordes falsly you suppressed) the lambe (who is Christe the lambe that taketh away the synnes of the worlde) is daily killed to vs, and we celebrate our Easter daily? which is true, because then the vertue of Christes death is effectual in vs, as contrarywise it is not, if we haue in vs remaining the leuen of malice and wickednesse. But what cōclude you hereof, that therfore the Fathers called the sacrifice once done vpon the crosse the daily Sacrifice, and not rather the sacrifice, wherin a memorie of that sacrifice is daily celebrated with the Oblation, and participation of the body of Christe, as S. Augustine speaketh?

In. cap. 5. 1. ad Cor. nō in cap. 6. vt Iuellus notat.

But seing you allow these commentaries for S. Hieromes, we require you to approue the doctrine which you finde contrary to that you teach, in the sixth chapter which you allege in stede of the fifth. There your onely faith, for which your felowes haue made so much a doo, is accompted insufficient to saluation. For this is the saying. Nolite errare, putantes vobis solam fidem sufficere ad salutem, cum omne peccatum permanens, excludat a regno. Be ye not deceiued, thinking onely faith to be sufficient to saluation, whereas euery sinne continuing excludeth vs from Gods kingdome. By this you may see, your onely faith founde insufficient to saluation, and that your faith may stād with synne remaining. How much surer and sounder is the doctrine of the Catholikes, who teach penaunce, and workes of charitie to be necessarily required to the Iustification of a synner?

That only faith sufficeth not to saluation.

Your place of Germanus a later writer, proueth as the other do, the vertue of the Sacrifice made vpon the crosse, to be euerlasting, which I denye not. But our spiritual sacrifices of praises and thankes geuing do proue your assertion very childishly. For what a folish argument is this? we do daily offer vp vnto God praises & thankes geuing for our redemption: Ergo, the Sacrifice once done vpon the crosse is of the Fathers called ẏ daily Sacrifice. So simple is your logike both here & in manner through your whole boke, and yet who scoffeth so much at other mens arguments, as you? Nay you do not so much scoffe at my argumentes, as at a number of peeuish and childish reasons diuised by your owne mery head, & by you fathered vpon me. But God be thanked, though your malice be great, your power and cunning is smal, in their iudgement, ẏ see you. In dede the simple people you deceiue pitifully. As for the learned, the more they reade your doinges, the more they espie your weakenesse and falshed, and abhorre your whole doctrine.

A foolish argument of M. Jewels making.

The authoritie that you bring out of S. Irenæus, lib. 4. cap. 34 is vtterly to no purpose, being so falsified. For you put in your booke quotidie, in stede of quoque. Looke better to your booke, vse more truth, we wil looke better to your fingers. You ought to be ashamed to haue alleged that chapter, in which S. Ireneus speaketh so plainely of ẏ veritie and real presence of Christes body in the Eucharist, and of the Sacrifice, which we now treat of.

M. Jew. falsifieth S. Ireneus.

After this number of authorities alleged to defeit the blessed Sacrifice that we offer vp in the Masse, of the name of the daily Sacrifice: M. Jewel commeth in with one of his phrases, wherof (as I suppose) he hath made him a notebooke: And al to haue in a redinesse, whereby to make some shewe of an answer to any thing alleged in defence of ẏ Catholike doctrine, which he liketh not. *That sacrifice* (saith he) *once offred vpõ the crosse is rightly called our daily sacrifice, in like phrase of speach, as is this of Tertullian. VVe keepe the sabboth not euery seuẽth day, but euery day.* This he saith, and proueth it not, but he must be beleued because of ẏ phrase of Tertullian.

Tertul. aduersus Iudæos.

Syr, and wil you nedes haue this to be a phrase in Tertullian, to serue your turne against the Sacrifice of the church? what phrase make you of it? Sabbatum signifieth in the Hebrue tongue, rest and quiet. The keping of the sabboth day in ẏ olde law, was a figure of our rest from synnes, and fleshly workes. The figure is past, the truth taketh place. Now saith Tertullian, we keepe the sabboth not euery seuenth day, as the Hebrewes did in the figure, but we kepe it euery day, that is to say, we rest frō synnes, and the dead workes of the body, and make euery day, as it were holy day. What can you conclude of this phrase? Because Tertullian said so truly, wil you say falsly, that there is now no daily Sacrifice in the Church, wherein the body and bloud of Christe is offred vp vnto the father vnbloudily, but that the Sacrifice which was once made vpō the crosse, is the only daily Sacrifice, and not the same after an other mãner daily offred vp of priestes of the new testament? your phrases be to weake M. Iew. for you by thē to peruert ẏ faith of Christes Church, which hitherto hath continued so many C. yeres, notwithstanding the manifold assaultes ẏ Satan hath made vnto it, by the violence of tyrauntes, and malicious fraude of heretikes.

Least any shift should be omitted, that might seme to haue any shewe or colour against ẏ daily Sacrifice, M. Iewel toward the ende of this Diuision obiecteth, that on good Friday there is no Consecration made: that the Greekes consecrated not in the Lente, but only vpon Saturdayes and Sundayes: that S. Ambrose mentioneth twise offering euery weeke.

M. Iew. obiections against the daily Sacrifice.

Sexta synod. ca. 52.

Cōcil. Laodicē, ca. 49

Ambros. in. 1. ad Tim. cap. 3.

These Obiections may sone be answered. The forbearing of Consecration vpon good Friday, which procedeth of great reason, letteth not, but that the blessed Sacrifice ought to retaine the name of Daily Sacrifice. For as one swallow maketh not a Springe tide, as Aristotle saith, so neither the intermission of one day, taketh away from this Sacrifice the name

Vna hirūdo nō facit ver. In Ethicis.

name of Daily, being els euery day offred. What if some for deuotion or sickenesse do not eate bread vpon some one day in the yere, as many there be that eate nothing vpon that day, is not the foode therfore, where on they liue, to be called their daily foode?

That *the Greekes neuer vsed to consecrate in the Lent, but vpon Saturdayes and Sundayes,* as M. Jewel saith, it is more then euer he founde written. It was decreed in the second Councel of Constantinople, that vpon al other daies of Lent beside Saturdaies, Sundaies, and the daye of the Annunciation, a holy Sacrifice should be made of the thinges before consecrated, for so be the
Ca.52. wordes, Fiat sacrum præsanctificatorum sacrificium. A certaine manner of Oblation there was of the sacrifice already done and consecrated. Because the other dayes of the Lente were dayes of fasting, wailing, and compunction for their synnes, and to celebrate the vnbloudy Oblation, and to offer vp the sacrifice vnto God, was as much as to celebrate a feast: in token of their sad penaunce, the Greeke fathers of that age, forbad Cōsecration to be made but vpon the forementioned dayes, that so they might the more be put in mynde of their fasting and mourning. This much in effect we finde reported hereof by Theodore Balsamon. That this was euer the custome of the Greke church, which M. Jewel saith, neither by this councel, neither by the councel of Laodicea may it be proued. By S. Chrysostome in sundry places the contrary rather appeareth, that the sacrifice was dailye offred, for which cause of him, as of the other Fathers it is very often called the daily Sacrifice.

But admit, this was a general custome among the Grekes obserued in Lente. At other times they offered the sacrifice daily after the custome of other Churches. And in respect thereof it might iustly haue ben called the daily Sacrifice.

wil M. Jewel take the worde *Daily* so streightly, that if a thing be left vndone a fewe dayes in respect of the other cōtinual time, it must not be called Daily? Saith not Christe in the gospel to them that came out with swordes and staues to take him, I sate daily among you in the Temple teaching, and ye tooke me not? wil M. Jewel be so exact in taking this word daily, as no day might be excepted? If he be, doth he not charge Christe with a lye for saying, he sate daily in the Tēple? For it is certaine by report of the gospel, that oftentimes he was forth of Jerusalem where ŷ Temple stoode, at Capernaum, at Hierico, at Bethsaida, at Nazareth, in the coast of Tyre and Sidon, in Samaria, in Galilea, in Decapolis, and in many other places farre distant from the citie of Jerusalem.

A thing may be named daily, though it be not don precisely euery day. Mat. 26.

When Dauid complained of his ennemies, & said of them, ŷ they vpbraided him daily, saying, vbi est Deus tuus? where is thy God? Must we thinke, that Dauid lyed, and wrote false in his psalme, if some fewe daies he escaped clear without hearing such cursed speach, vttered against him? There is no reason why M. Jewel should exact such a preciseneſſe in taking this word *daily*. That may be wel said to be done daily, which is commonly and continually done. M. Jewel sheweth him selfe destitute of good mater, when he is dryuen thus to hunte after wordes. Which kinde of trifling vsed of him through his whole booke, the learned Fathers were wont to cal, Aucupium verborum.

Psal. 41.

S. Ambrose speaketh not of the custome of the whole latine Church, but of his Church of Millan, and of his owne time. For S. Augustine who was his scholer, witnesseth this Sacrifice to be daily with these most plaine wordes, which can not be takē of the Sacrifice once made vpō the Crosse, but of this which is daily made in a sacrament, whereof we speake. In forme of a seruaūt he had rather be Sacrifice, then take Sacrifice. Hereby he is also a

De ciuitate Dei. lib. 10. cap. 20.

priest, him selfe the offerer, him selfe also the Oblation. (Hitherto he meaneth the Oblation once made vpon the crosse. Now he speaketh of our Sacrifice) Cuius rei Sacramentum quotidianum esse voluit Ecclesiæ Sacrificium. Of which thing, (to witte of his bloudy Oblation vpon the crosse) he would the daily Sacrifice of the Church to be a Sacrament, whereas of the body it selfe he is the head, and of the head she is the body, and as wel she by him, as he by her is accustomed to be offred.

What is the daily Sacrifice according to S. Augustine.

Here haue you M. Iewel first, ỷ Christ in forme of a seruaũt,
1. that is to say, as being man, was a Sacrifice, in making which
2. Sacrifice he was both the priest, and the Oblation. Secondly,
ỷ the Sacrifice of the Church, which is a sacrament of the Oblation ỷ was offred vpõ the crosse, is the daily Sacrifice, which we treate of, and you deny. Which daily Sacrifice can not be vnderstanded of ỷ, which was once done vpon the crosse, as you would haue it, because it is a Sacrament thereof, and so is different from that, only in the way and manner of offering. Thirdly, you
3. haue here, that in this Sacrifice the Church is offered vp to God by Christ, forasmuch as she is the body, and he the head. Fourth-
4. ly, that likewise Christe the head is accustomed to be offred vp to God by the Churche, without doubt spiritually by euery faithful persons deuotion, but Sacramentally by the Ministerie of the Priest, the Churches publike Minister in that behalfe. Which power you M. Iewel do denye to be in the priest, both in this and in your. 17. Article, but how ignorantly and contrary to S. Augustine you deny it, by this it may appeare.

One saying of S. Augustine I can not here let passe, ỷ both witnesseth ỷ Sacrifice to be daily offred, against which M. Iew. cauilleth, and sheweth the custome of the Greke Church ratified by decree of the. vj. Councel before mentioned, to be particular to that country, (as likewise the testimonie of S. Ambrose is to be vnderstanded of his owne church) not general through ẏ whole Church. wryting to Ianuarius he saith thus. Alibi nullus dies intermittitur, quo non offeratur, Alibi Sabbato tãtum & dominico, Alibi tantum dominico. One where, there is no day let passe, in which the Sacrifice is not offred. Other where it is offred only vpõ the Saturday and Sũday. An otherwhere vpõ the Sũday only. Lo M. Iewel, seing that you are so precise in the word *Daily*, I bring you S. Augustine to witnesse on my behalfe, that in some places of Christendome no day was intermitted, in which the Sacrifice was not offred. *August. epist. 118.*

By your owne learning and iudgement I may better allege S. Augustine, who of many is thought to be ẏ best learned doctor that euer wrote in Christes churche, and lyued farre within ẏ terme of your first vj. C. yeres after Christe: then you may allege the authoritie of the vj. Councel at Constantinople, which was holden after those yeres, in the time of Iustinianus the Emperour sonne of Constantinus about the yere of our Lorde. vi. C. lxxx. and besides that, semed to allow the olde Councel of Africa holden in S. Cyprians time, wherein it was decreed that such as were baptized of heretikes, and returned to the Catholike Churche, should be baptized againe. which I trow you wil confesse to be erroneous.

Item that Coũcel decreed that bishops, after that they were promoted to the order of bishops, should depart and absteine frõ companie of their wyues, which they were maried vnto before they came to be bishops. Neither that wil you allow (I am sure) for vpright and sounde doctrine. You wil rather I trow, admit a councel, that should licẽce your bishops, who neuer had wiues of their owne, to take systers vnder the name of wyues vnto them, and cal it holy wedlocke, which Canon our holy prelates of this new English Churche haue founde in your new Gospel, as sundry others of like austeritie. *Can. 12.*

But if you wil nedes approue this Councel, notwithstanding these erroures, and that it was without the compasse of the yeres of your owne allowance, that the canon which you allege to proue the Sacrifice of the Church not to be daily, may be takẽ to be of good auctoritie: then how say you to Reseruation of the blessed Sacrament in the very canon, which you allege euidently mentioned? For where as the wordes of that Canon be, Γινέσθω ἡ τῶν προηγιασμένων ἱερὰ λειτουργία, fiat sacrum præsãctificatorum Sacrificium, Let a holy Sacrifice be made of the thinges before Cõsecrated: what thinges were they which were before consecrated vpon the Sunday or Saturday to serue for a kinde of Sacrifice in the weeke dayes, but onely the body and bloud of Christ, reserued to be receiued vpon other daies in Lent beside Saturdaies and Sundaies? Therefore admitting the Canons of this Councel, you must recante your false doctrine touching Reseruation, which you impugne in your. 9. Article.

Reseruation of the blessed Sacrament vsed in the Greke Churche.

And what shal I cal this, impudencie, or great blindenesse in you, that you allege the place of S. Ambrose? For as it proueth not the Sacrifice not to haue ben daily, for which purpose you bring it, but only that in his Church it was at least twise in the weeke offred, whereby he denyeth not but it might be daily offred in other Churches, which I shewed before out of S. Augustine: So it geueth an euident witnesse for the Sacrifice, which you M. Jewel, & they of your sect haue abandoned. His wordes be plaine, the sense whereof you haue corrupted by your false translation. For offerre, is not to celebrate the Oblation, as you turne it, but to offer or to make the Oblation. Omni hebdomada offerendum est, etiamsi non quotidie peregrinis, incolis tamen vel bis in hebdomada. Euery weeke we must offer vp (the Sacrifice) although not euery day for strangers, yet for the inhabitantes at least twise in the weeke. These wordes haue you

M. Jew. allegeth S. Ambrose, making al together against him & witnessing the sacrifice.

M. Jew. corrupteth S. Ambrose with false translatiõ.

Ambros. in. 1. ad Tim. cap. 3.

you thus turned, but how vntruly, I would it to be iudged by the learned. *Euery vveeke vve must celebrate the Oblation, although not euery day vnto strangers, yet for the inhabitantes, yea some times tvvise in the vveeke.*

See Reader the true dealing of this man. whereas S. Ambrose saith, we must offer or do Sacrifice euery weeke for strangers, whereby doubtlesse he meaneth, as al other holy Fathers do, the vnbloudy Sacrifice of the Churche: to remoue the mynde and vnderstanding of the reader from that sense, because he can not away with that Sacrifice, by his false translation he maketh him to say, we must celebrate ẏ Oblation euery weeke vnto strāgers. wherby he excludeth vtterly ẏ Oblatiō & Sacrifice it selfe, for that can not be done ne offred vnto strangers, but vnto God onely. But he maketh no better thing of it, then that which is to be done not for strangers, but vnto strangers. Now as strangers be not God, so neither is the Sacrifice that S. Ambrose saith must be offred weekly, to be made vnto strangers. The other falshed vsed in the translation of this sentence, as the diuiding of that which S. Ambrose ioyned together, by making a new point, and the putting in of the word *sometimes*, to euil purpose, I am content to couer with silence. For if I would note al the false partes that M. Iewel hath plaid in his Replie, there should be no ende.

To conclude, I maruel M. Iewel, that your shamefastnesse suffred you so much as once to touch this place of S. Ambrose, in which he sheweth that Deacons, Priestes, and Bisshops must not only not mary wiues, but also wholly forebeare the companie of a woman, and be purer then the laye people, because they be the agents of God. Verely this doctrine of S. Ambrose squareth euil with the doctrine of your Gospel, which, as ye of that syde both by word, and practise of life declare, permitteth not only

S. Ambrose is quite contrary to the doctrine of this new Gospel.

Actores Dei

ly your new (what shal I cal them) Ministers of the worde, but also deacõs, priestes, and bishops, that by solemne vow haue promised to God the contrary, yea also monkes, frieres, and Nonnes to marrye, and to tame the rebellion of their flesh with satisfying the lustes of their flesh.

The argumentes, which in the ende of this Diuision M. Iewel diuiseth of his owne head, and pretendeth to be made by me, because they be not myne, I do not vouchesafe to answer. I wil not let such a mery head of his pastime. Yet amõg his scoffes he putteth in as poison, many droppes of vntruth and lying. As (for example.) That, if the vnbloudy Sacrifice be necessarily to be frequented, then may it by the priest be done, though he him selfe receiue not.

This would he proue, because the Sacrifice, and the receiuing be diuerse, as he noteth out of a Councel holden at Toledo in Spaine. In which Councel priestes be expressely forbidden at any time to offer Sacrifice, but when also they receiue. This Councel because it maketh against him in sundry pointes, he reiecteth, fynding no greate fault with it here, but that it was a late Councel. And yet was it holden within.lxxx.yeres after his vj.C.yeres, within.v.of.ix.C.yeres past. But because it maketh against M. Iewel, it must be accompted a late Cõucel, and.ix.C yeres agon, was but yesterdaye.

Concilium Toletanũ 12.can.7.

Again, that, touching number of communicantes together, though it be no part of Christes Institution, yet neuerthelesse *vve are bounde to his example, because he hath commaunded vs so to do.* which is very false. For Christ commaunded vs not to do so, but to do that, or rather not thus, but this. Doo ye this (saith he) in my remembrance, we are bõude to the thing that Christ did, not to his whole example. For then we should haue.xij.men, and no woman, and obserue many other thinges that Christ did, which we can not do.

The. x. Diuision.

In the summe of my wordes in the. x. Diuision, ye argument deduced of the word Communio, to the denial of Priuate Masse, is reported to be weake and vnlearned, as that which procedeth of ignorance. M. Jewel, who vseth the same for the chief & best of al other, & maketh it very commonly in his Chalenge, goeth about to iustifie it: but how directly, and how substãtially, I report me to the iudgement of the Learned. In dede much paines he taketh about it, and faine would he make it good, as he that thinketh his estimation therin very much touched. And whereas he noteth me for a mã wel brooking myne owne learning, what so euer he iudgeth of me, it was his parte to haue proued his argument with more learning, then yet he sheweth.

That the mater appeare plaine to ye reader, it shalbe nedeful he peruse both our sayinges: so shal he be hable ye better to iudge. Here to reherse the whole, it were to long, and the Replie in this as in other places, is enlarged with much stuffe impertinent.

The point we varye in, is touching the word Communio. M. Jewel, as it appeareth euidẽtly by the Sermon wherein he made his Chalenge, thinketh the Sacramẽt to haue the name of Communion, in cõsideration of many receiuers together in one place. Therfore where so euer he findeth Cõmunion mentioned, of the same he deduceth an argumẽt against Priuate Masse as he calleth it. This is to be sene in his sermon in sundry places, set forth not wout insolẽt insultatiõ. But because I said, which I say again, yt it had this name of an other cõsideration, and yt this argumẽt proceded of ignorãce: therfore he hath made no litle a doo. Wherof is Cõmunio so called.

Now so farre as I proue the blessed Sacrament to be called Communion, not because many, or as M. Jewel saith, ye whole Cõgregation receiueth together in one place, but in cõsideration of the effect of it, for yt by the same we are ioyned to God, & many that be diuerse be vnited together, and made one body, whether In his Sermon fol. 41.

they receiue together or a sundre : so farre I say is M. Iewels argument founde weake and vnlearned.

That the Sacrament is so called specially and singularly aboue other Sacramentes for ẏ effect it worketh in vs, for prouse thereof I alleged S. Dionyse the Areopagite. And that it worketh such effect in vs, no man can speake it more plainly then S. Chrysostome writing vpon S. Paules first Epistle to the Corinthians. And likewise Cyrillus vpon S. Iohn. lib. 11. cap. 26. But let vs heare M. Iewel tel his owne tale.

Dionysius Ecclesiast. hier. p. 1. c. 3 Chrysosto. homil. 24. in 1. Cor. cap. 10.

Ievvel.

Of the nature of this vvord Communio, I tooke occasion to say, that the priest ought to communicate vvith the people, for that othervvise it can not iustly be called a Communion.

Harding.

And I say, that Communio may be, though the priest receiue not the Communion together with the people in one place, and that when the people fyndeth them selfe not worthy, proued, and disposed to receiue, the priest may receiue without the people, as I haue before proued. The thing ẏ I denyed was this, ẏ the Sacrament is called Communion because many receiue together in one place. For it is so called chiefly, because al Christians receiuing one thing, to witte one body of Christ vnder forme of bread it worketh vnitie, and maketh vs one wᵗ Christe, and one within our selues, so that therby we and Christ be made one body. This was your part to disproue M. Iew. which if you do not, thē my denyal stādeth, & so is not priuate Masse as you cal it, or rather ẏ priestes Priuate receiuing disproued. But let vs see, how you proue Cōmuniō to haue ẏ name of ẏ peoples receiuing together wᵗ the Priest, or of that that many receiue together in one place.

What is meant by Communion.

Ievvel.

Here to leaue al contention of learning, and onely to haue regard vnto the truth, If the very nature of this vvord Cōmunio, import not a thing to be cōmō, as it is supposed, much les may it, as I iudge, ĩport a thĩg to be priuate.

Harding.

How you leaue al contention of learning, ỳ world seeth, what regard you haue onely vnto the truth, let vs examine. The nature of the worde Communio, importeth a thing to be common, I graunte. For through Communion the Body of Christe is made common and one with al that worthily receiue it. But you mistake your woordes Common and Priuate. The Communion is common, not for the receiuing of many together in one place, but for the thing communicated, and imparted to the receiuers, so as it and they be made one thing, whether there be many, fewe, or one in a place. Priuate in this case properly it is not in respect of the thing receiued, nor of the effect, but onely in respect of receiuing. For if a man receiue alone, it may be called single or priuate receiuing in respect of place where he receiueth, and priuate Communion also, as it is referred to the act of receiuing concerning the place.

How is the Communion common.

Priuate Communion.

Ievvel.

It is named Communion, saith M. Harding, of the effect that it vvorketh in vs, because by the same vve are ioined vnto God, not because many Communicate together in one place. And for proufe hereof he allegeth the authoritie of Dionysius: vvherin he doth great vvrong to that good olde Father, alleging his authoritie for the Masse, that neuer spake vvorde of the Masse.

Harding.

Is this the truth M. Jewel, that in the next sentence before you promised onely to haue regard vnto? Do I allege the authoritie of S. Dionysius for the Masse in that place? Or thinke you that S. Dionysius spake not of the Masse, whereas he wrote ỳ whole order of ỳ Liturgie or Masse? Hath he not ỳ thig? what sticke you so in the name, which the Greeke Fathers haue not? What vntruth is this? Yea what folly is it so to

M. Jew. promiseth truth, and performeth vntruth.

say, specially my wordes being laide before the Reader in your booke, that he may sone espie the contrary? Againe how hangeth your owne tale together? *for proufe hereof, &c*, say you. Whereto hath your word *hereof* relation, but to the effect which the Communion worketh in vs? Immediately you say, *vvherin he doth great vvrong to that good olde Father, &c.* To what referre you, *vvherin*, but to that is comprised vnder your former word *hereof*? Then with what reason follow those wordes, *alleging his authoritie for the Masse, that neuer spake vvorde of the Masse?* It seemeth your wittes were troubled with other cares, when ye wrote thus. But when proue you Communion to haue that name specially of the peoples receiuing with the Priest, or of the receiuing of many together in one place?

Ievvel.

It is graunted of al vvithout any contradiction, that one ende of al Sacramentes is to ioigne vs vnto God. &c. An other ende is to ioigne vs al together. &c.

Harding.

What nede many wordes, if it be graunted of al? I alleged S. Dionyse speaking of the effect of the Sacrament, to thintent it might appeare, that thereof it hath the name of Communion, and not onely of many receiuers together. You speake of two endes: but to what purpose? When come you to proue your chiefe point, that the Cōmunion is so called chiefly because many receiue together in one place?

Ievvel.

The. 76. vntruth. I do not concele y other, as my boke witnesseth

*And notvvihstanding Dionysius speaketh plainely of both these endes, yet it pleaseth M. Harding in his allegation only to name the one, and * to concele the other: and by the affirmation of the one, vntruely to conclude the denyal of the other.*

Harding.

What soeuer you talke of your two endes M. Jewel, I reported

Ported my allegatiō truely as ỹ Doctor wrote it. If I had done otherwise, I perceiue your good wil towardes me to be such as I had ben like to haue hearde of it. Neither in dede speaketh S. Dionyse in that place expressely of the other ende, for which you make so much a doo. What? would you haue me to adde and put vnto the Doctor of myne owne, more then I finde in the Doctor? That false demeanour we leaue to you, which very often you vse for bad shiftes. If he spake of it in an other place farre distant from that, it was not my duetie to lay it to ỹ words that I alleged, & to ioyne ỹ together, which I found separate.

But how farre I am from conceling the one of your endes, and from concluding the denyal of the one, by the affirmation of the other, which you lay to my charge: myne owne woordes as they be laide forth in my booke, and as they be put into your booke also of Replie, may witnesse. If such wordes, wherby the ioyning of vs together wrought through the Communion, as one effect of the same is signified, be to be found in my booke: then remaine I cleare of the blame, wherewith you charge me, and you are deprehended in a manifest vntruth.

For trial hereof I require the Reader, and your selfe also M. Iewel, to peruse the place. There I say thus, Folio. 14. 2. lin. 1. The Sacrament is not called Communio, because many or as M. Iewel teacheth, the whole Congregation communicateth together in one place: but because of the effect of the Sacrament, for that by the same we are ioyned to God (Lo there is one effect) and many that be diuerse, be vnited together, and made one mystical Body of Christe, which is the Churche, of which Body by vertue and effect of this holy Sacrament, al the faithful be members one of an other, and Christe is the head. Lo there is the other effect, or as M. Iewel termeth it, the other of his two endes.

Againe in the same side of that leafe I say thus, after the

allegation of S. Dionysius. By which wordes, and by the whole place of that holy Father, we vnderstand that this Sacrament is specially called the Communion, for the special effect it worketh in vs: which is to ioyne vs nearly to God, so as we be in him, and he in vs, and al we that beleue in him, one Body in Christ. Lo there is your other ende spoken of againe. Can there any ioyning be nearer, then that we be made together one body, and members one of an other? Yet wil you say, that I concele it, and that by the affirmation of our ioyning with God, I do vntruly conclude the denyal of our ioyning together?

M. Iew. speaketh without sense or reason.

But M. Iewel if you be not ashamed of your lye, yet how can you cloke your follie? For the one the world wil take you for a Lyer. For the other wisemen wil accompt you for a foole. For how foolishly do you speake, how farre beside sense, witte, and reason saying, that *in my allegation by the affirmation of our ioyning vnto God, I conclude the denyal of our ioyning together?* Be not they which be ioyned vnto God, ioyned also together? In sensible thinges, what two thinges be ioyned in a third, the same be ioyned together: and shal we say, they that be ioyned vnto God, be not also ioyned together? Doth not God knitte, fasten, and binde together al those that be ioyned vnto him? How then can they be sundry and separate? Haue you forgoten the cōmō principle which you learned in schoole at Oxford, Quæcunque conueniunt in aliquo tertio, & ipsa inter se conueniunt? Whatsoeuer thinges agree together in any third, the same do also agree within them selfe. Wherefore recant that for shame, that *by the affirmation of our ioining vnto God, I conclude the denial of our ioining together.* But when come you to the point, that it standeth you vpon to proue, that the Communion is so named for that many or the whole congregation doth receiue together in one place?

Ievvel.

As touching the later of these tvvo endes, the same Dionysius in the same chapter that M. Harding here allegeth, vvriteth thus: Sancta illa vnius & eiusdem panis, & poculi Communis & pacifica distributio, vnitatem illis diuinam, tanq̃ vnà enutritis præscribit. That holy Communion, and peaceable distribution of one breade, and one cuppe, preacheth vnto them a heauẽly vnitie, as being men fedde together. And Pachymeres the Greeke Paraphrast expounding the same place, hath these vvordes, τὸ γὰρ ὁμοδίαιτον &c. For that common diete and consent farther bringeth vs vnto the remẽbrance of the Lordes Supper. Vvhat so euer M. Harding haue said, I reckẽ it vvil hereby appeare vnto the indifferẽt Reader, that these vvordes do sufficiently declare, both the common receiuing of the Sacrament, and also the knitting and ioyning of many together.

Harding.

By your last sentence I perceiue to what purpose you bring al this. to proue common receiuing, and ioyning of many together. That by the worthy receiuing of the blessed Sacrament many, yea so many as do receiue be ioyned together, there was no cause why you should proue it, no man denyed it, and I in my booke in this very place whereupon you make this parte of your Replie, affirmed it most plainely. But when you are not able to proue that is denyed, then your sleight is, craftily to conuey your selfe from speaking thereof, and to shew your copie in a mater, that no man doubteth of. So you seeme to the ignorant to say much, and to proue that you tooke in hand, like a Clerke.

And yet Sir, if I had denyed, that by the Communion men are ioyned together, me thinketh you would proue it very weakely, if you haue no better proufe for it, then this saying of S. Dionysius, and of Pachymeres, which here you haue alleged. For what if the distribution of one bread and one cuppe preach vnto the receiuers, as you english it, or prescribe vnto them as a lawe which the Greke worde νομοθετεῖ signifieth, heauenly vnitie? wil it follow thereof, that they be therfore ioyned together? Nay you may argue, that therefore they should be ioyned together. ẏ they be ioyned, these wordes proue not. Neither can you build ought vpon the Greeke woorde ὁμοτρόφοις, which your Greke frend of Oxford and you, haue turned vnà enutritis. For false translation maketh no good Argument. You should haue turned the woorde thus, Eodem cibo alitis, that is to say, fedde or nourished with one foode, not fedde together as you turne it. The Greke word in that place of S. Dionysius signifieth the vnitie of the foode of diuers receiued, not vnitie of place in which they should receiue.

M. Iew. helpeth his cause with false translatiõ.

To what purpose you alleged the words of Pachymeres, I see not. Verely they proue neyther the ioyning of many together by receiuing the Sacrament, nor that it must alwayes be receiued of a number together in one place. The meaning of it is, that forasmuch as they that receiue worthily eate of one meate, and maintaine mutual loue and concorde among them selues, (for so the two Greke wordes ὁμοδίαιτον and ὁμότροπον do signifie) Thereby they are euen at this day brought to remẽbrance of our Lordes Supper. This saying sheweth ẏ the receiuers ought to be in concorde, it proueth not the special ioyning together, which by receiuing the Body of Christe worthilye in this Sacrament is caused.

In Hierarch. eccle. part. 1. cap. 3. ἔτι

Of like M. Iewel wil proue the chiefe point, which is his parte to do, substantially, when he commeth vnto it, that tarrieth so long from it. Forgete not Reader, what he hath to proue, that this worde Communio, hath his name not specially of the effect, which is the vniting of vs vnto God, and of our selues together: but of that that many receiue with the Priest together in one place. This much standeth him vpon to proue, els

What hath M. Iew. promised to proue.

els is priuate Masse as they cal it, no whit disproued. But before he come to his proufes, he mindeth to stuffe his Booke, which at ỹ first for shew of learning he purposed to make great, with other prolixe talke, though to litle purpose. Loth I am thus to spend my time in answering his trifling Obiections. And yet least he should make his vnlerned Disciples beleue, that he were not confuted: I wil leaue nothing that semeth to haue any colour of learning or truth vnanswered. The most that I am troubled withal, is his common custome of belying mee, which were easyly perceiued, if the Reader would but retourne to my sayinges set forth in his Booke, and marke them wel, after the reading of his Replie. Whereof this may be an example.

Ievvel.

*Novv let vs examine this reason. The Communion hath his name of the effect, for that it ioyneth vs vnto God: Ergo * saith M. Harding it signifieth not the Communicating of many together. Surely this Argument is very vveake: I vvil not say, It is vnlearned, or procedeth of Ignorance. He should neede a nevv Logique, that vvould assay to make it good.*

The. 77. vntruth. I say not so.

Harding.

What so euer this Argumente be, learned or vnlearned, surely it is not mine. It procedeth out of M. Iewels owne forge. Many such he forgeth, and yet displayseth the diuise of his owne head. Wherein he followeth Children, that oftentimes blame, and chyde, and beate the babies which they make them selues of clowtes.

M. Iew. forgeth vaine argumentes of his owne, and with the same burtheneth his aduersary.

I say leaning to the auctoritie of S. Dionysius, that this Sacramente is specially called the Communion for the speciall effecte it woorketh in vs, whiche is to ioygne vs vnto

God, so as we be in him, and he in vs, and al we that worthily receiue Christ in the Sacrament, be made one body with Christ. what haue you to replie agaist this M. Iewel? If you haue nothig, leaue your childish Argumẽts, forge no more such poppets & vaine toyes. Eyther yeld to the Truth, or leaue to scoffe at the Truth.

Ievvel.

Nay it may much better be replied: Vvhat effect can this Sacramẽt haue, or vvhom can it ioine to God, but onely such as do receiue it? Or vvhat effect can the Sacrament of baptisme vvorke, but onely in them, that receiue Baptisme?

Harding.

What vaine iangling is this? who euer said, the Sacramentes, as they be Sacramentes, can worke their effect in any other persons, then in them who receiue them? If no man euer said it, wherat shoote you? whom strike you? whom burthen you with suspition of vntruth?

Ievvel.

Vvithout al question, the effect that Dionysius meant, standeth not in this, that one man saith a Priuate Masse, and receiueth the Sacrament a lone: but in this that the people prayeth, and receiueth the holy Communion together, and thereby doth openly testifie, that they be al one in Christ Iesus, and al one amongest them selues.

Harding.

Without al question the effect that S. Dionysius meant, what so euer the Deuil and his Ministers meane, is to be gathered of his owne wordes, not of a gainsayers peruerting. And His wordes report, as is before said, this blessed Sacrament to worke an vnion and ioyning of vs vnto God, and to gather vs being diuided, and with a diuine folding or wrapping together (θεοειδεῖ συμπτύξει is his word) to bring vs so vnto God,

as

as we be one with him. which ioyning of vs to God, and of our selues together, is both more largely, and also more plainly set forth by other Fathers, specially by S. Chrysostome. who writing vpon S. Paules first Epistle to the Corinthians, saith, that We do not cōmunicate together onely in Participatiō and receiuing, but in vnitie, or if it were lauful so to speake, in onenesse. For as that Body is vnited vnto Christe, so by this bread in an vnion we are ioyned together. And as (saith he a litle after) Bread is brought into one of many graines, so as the graines appeare not, but yet they be graines, ioyned together by vncertaine seuering: so we are ioyned both within our selues one to an other, and also vnto Christe.

Chrysostomus homil. 61. ad pop. Antiochen. in. 1. Cor. 10.

This doubtlesse is the effect of the Communion which S. Dionysius meant, and the Fathers haue taught. But in M. Iewels opinion, without al question this effect is the prayer of the people, and their receiuing of the Communion together. But wote you what you say M. Iewel, and wherof you affirm? Is this the effect of the Communion, that the people pray, and receiue the Communion together? As touching the first, if that be the effect, then when two or three communicate, the people prayeth. which is not alwayes true. For many times they be worse occupied, when that is done. For the second, how is the peoples receiuing of the Communion theffect of the Communion? Is the Communion the effect of the Communion? How can any effect be ẏ effect of it selfe? As for example, is my eating the effect of my eating? The effect of my eating, is the sustenance of my body, and is not the effect of my eating. Effect is produced of an action, and is caused thereof. It can not produce, nor cause the same action. A house is the effect of building. For by building a house is made. But how absurde and beside reason is it to say on the other side, that building is the

It appeareth by M. Iewels vnsauoury talke, that he knoweth not what he speaketh, nor wherof he affirmeth.

the effect of an house, or that an house effectually bringeth forth building? The Childe is the effect of generation: the Childe engendred worketh not that generation. A thing is not the effect of it selfe. What reason is in this? What idle head euer so dreamed? Yet he woulde seeme to proue his dreame by S. Chrysostome. For thus he saith.

Ievvel.

Chrysost. ad pop. Antiochē. hom.61. *And therefore Chrysostome saith, Propterea in Mysterijs alter alterum amplectimur, vt vnum multi fiamus. For that cause in the time of the Mysteries, vve embrace one an other, that being many, vve may become one.*

Harding.

For auouching thaucthoritie of this saying, you haue directed the Reader to S. Chrysostome Ad popul. Antiochen. homil.61. For so we finde the margent of your booke quoted. But there S. Chrysostome hath no such saying. Wherefore it resteth that men beleue it to be an auctoritie brought out of your owne forge, from whence you haue sent forth much counterfeit stuffe. And though S. Chrysostom said so, yet it proueth not your purpose. But I maruel when we shal heare your prouses, that the Communion is so called, for that many or the whole people receiue it together with the Priest in one place.

Ievvel.

The.78. vntruth. for the worthy receiuing of the Sacrament worketh this effect Rom.4. *Hovv be it, in plaine speach * it is not the receiuing of the Sacrament, that vvoorketh our ioyning vvith God. For vvho so euer is not ioyned to God before he receiue the Sacramentes, he eateth and drinketh his ovvne iudgement. The Sacramentes be seales and vvitnesses, & be not properly the causes of this coniunction. Otherwise our Children that departe this lyfe before they receiue the Communion, and al the godly Fathers of the olde Testament should haue no coniunction vvith God.*

Harding.

Harding.

We be ioyned vnto God two wayes, by charitie and in very dede. Who so euer is not ioyned vnto God by Charitie, and presumeth notwithstanding to receiue the blessed Sacrament: he receiueth it to his iudgement. But who so euer is ioyned vnto God by charitie, & receiueth the Sacrament worthily: the thing of the Sacrament which is the Body of Christ, so receiued, worketh his ioyning with God, truely and in deede. And marke M. Iewel, how plainely this doctrine is taught by S. Chrysostome in the Homilie out of which you fayned your self to allege a testimonie a litle before. His wordes be these. Vt non tantum per Charitatem hoc fiamus, verum & ipsa re in illam misceamur carnem, hoc per escam efficitur, quam largitus est nobis, uolens ostendere desiderium, quod erga nos habet. That wee be made this (that is to say, one body and members of Christes flesh and of his bones wherof he spake there) not onely by charitie, but also that by the thing it selfe, we be mingled into that flesh: this much is done by the meate, which he hath geuen vnto vs, hauing a desire to shewe the good wil that he beareth towardes vs.

Our ioyning vnto God is two waies, by charitie, & in dede.

1.Cor.11.

Chrysostom. homil.61. ad popul. Antioch.

It behoued (saith Cyrillus) that not only the soule should ascend into blessed life by the holie Ghost, but also that this rude and earthly bodie should be reduced to immortalitie, by taste, touch, and eating of that thing that is of cousinage with it. Wherby he meaneth the real eating of Christes precious flesh in the blessed Sacrament of the aulter. Thus by the Sacrament, we haue a further benefite, and greater coniunction with Christe, then by Charitie onely.

Cyril in Ioan lib. 4.cap. 14. Cognato sibi gustu, tactu, cibo

Wheras M. Iewel telleth vs in plaine speach, it is not the receiuing of the Sacramẽt that worketh our ioyning with God, it must by vs be tolde him againe in plaine speache, that that doctrine is false and heretical. For if the due and worthy receiuing

The worthy receiuing of ỹ blessed Sacrament worketh our ioyning with god.

receiuing of the Sacrament worke in vs the sanctification of the sonne of God, then are we ioyned with God. But that is by receiuing the Sacrament wrought in vs: Ergo, therby we are ioyned with God. The minor or second proposition wherof the proofe of this doctrine dependeth, is thus proued. Cyrillus saith, Ipsum domini corpus coniuncti virtute uerbi sanctificatur, & ad benedictionem mysticam adeo actiuum fit, vt posit sanctificationem suam nobis immittere. Our Lordes Body it selfe, by vertue of the word ioyned with it is sanctified, and is made so actiue to the Mystical blessing, (whereby is meant the Sacrament) that it may put into vs his owne sanctification.

Cyrillus. In Ioan. lib. 11. cap. 22.

And as the flesh of Christe receiued in the Sacramente putteth into vs the sanctification of the sonne of God, whereby we are ioyned vnto God: so it putteth also into vs lyfe immortal, whereby likewise we be ioyned vnto God. For inasmuch as (saith Cyrillus) the sonne of God that geueth or maketh life dwelt in flesh, he reformed it vnto his owne good, that is, to lyfe, & beīg by an vnspeakeable meane of vnion, whole ioined vnto the whole, made the flesh it selfe, quickening or lifemaking: because by nature it is quickening, therefore this flesh quickeneth the partakers or receiuers of it: for it casteth out death from thē, and quite expelleth destruction.

The great benefite of Christes flesh worthily receiued in ẏ sacrament. *In Ioan. lib. 4. c. 12.*

He that eateth the flesh of Christe (saith the same Cyrillus in an other place) hath life euerlasting. For this flesh hath the worde of God, which naturally is life. Therefore he saith: For I wil raise him vp againe in the last day, I, saith he, that is my bodie which shalbe eaten, wil raise him vp againe. How then doth not this Sacrament worke in vs the ioyning of vs vnto God, in which we receiue that flesh, which is lifegeuing for the inseparable vnion of the Worde?

Lib. 4. in Ioan. c. 15.

And as we are ioyned vnto God spirititually by faith

and charitie, so after the teaching of Cyrillus, by meane of Christes Body receiued in this Sacrament, wee are ioyned vnto Christe corporally or according to the flesh. Disputing with an Arian heretike, who acknowleged that we are ioyned vnto Christe spiritually by faith and charitie, he declareth that we are ioyned vnto him also according to the flesh. His woordes be these. We denie not but that we are ioyned vnto Christe spirituallye by right faith and sincere charitie. But that there is no coniunction betwen vs and him according to the flesh: that truly we deny vtterly, & we say, it is quite beside the Scriptures. Heare Paule saying: that we are al one body in Christe. For although we be many, yet in him we are one. For we do al participate one Breade. Doth he (the Arian heretike he meaneth) perhaps thinke, that we know not the uertue of the Mystical blessing? Which when it is in vs, doth it not cause Christe to dwel in vs also corporally by the receiuing of the flesh of Christe in the Communion? For why be the members of the faithful the members of Christe? Do ye not know saith he, that your members be the members of Christe? Shal I then make the mébers of Christ the members of an Harlot? God forbid. Our Sauiour also saith, He that eateth my Flesh, and drinketh my Bloude, dwelleth in me, and I in him. Wherfore it is to be considered, that Christ is in vs, not by habitude or spiritually onely, which is vnderstanded by Charitie, but also by natural Participation. For as if one mingle molted waxe to other waxe likewise molted, it shal seeme that of both is made one thing: so by receiuing of the Body and Bloud of Christe in the Communion, he is in vs, and we be in him.

In Ioan. lib. 10. c. 13.

1. Cor. 10.

The vertue of the blessed Sacrament.

1. Cor. 6.

Ioan. 6.

Of this Union and coniunction of vs to Christe, and of our selues one to an other, he speaketh also very plainely in his eleuenth booke, vpon S. Iohn, chapter. 26. In that he blesseth (saith he) them that beleeue with his owne Bodie through the Mystical Communion, he maketh vs one Bodie both with him selfe, and also betweene our selues. In which place he calleth this vnion made by receiuing Christes Body in the Sacramēt, a natural vnion, to exclude the onely spiritual vnion. Of this likewise very much and very plainely speaketh S. Chryso-stome vpon S. Paule. 1. Cor. 10. Homil. 24.

As touching that which is said here concerning the Sacra-mentes, neither be the Sacramentes onely seales, witnesses, markes, tokens, badges, pledges, printes, &c. as M. Iewel and the authors of the Apologie according to the doctrine of Caluine, do teach: but also they conteine grace, and through them grace is geuen. The thing of this Sacrament which we speake of, being the true Body of Christe, is not a seale or witnesse of our coniunction with God, but in dede (if we receiue it worthily) is the cause of our ioyning with God, forasmuch as to it is ioyned the Sonne of God, which consubstantially is life, as Cyrillus saith. And because the actual receiuing of
Lib. 4. the Sacrament, is not the onely meane and way whereby we
cap. 24. may be ioyned vnto God, therfore M. Iewels obiection of his Children, and of the Fathers of the Olde Testament, is voide and vaine. But he would faine persuade, that we haue in this blessed Sacrament no better thing, then Manna was, which is both false and plasphemous.

Whereas vpon occasion of that S. Dionysius wrote con-
Fol. 14. b. cerning this blessed Sacrament, I said in my booke that it is specially and peculiarly called the Communion, for the special effect of it, which is to ioyne vs to God and our selues toge-ther, so as with Christe our head we be one body: hereof I in-ferred that in consideration of this vniting of vs and ioyning together, we do not communicate alone: but that as the Lambe

of

of the olde Lawe was eaten of a companie in one house, so the Church being as S. Cyprian saith, one house, who so euer eateth this our true Lambe worthilye, they do Communicate with al other faithful persons of al places that be of this house, and do the like.

Exod. 12.
Sermone de Cœna Domini.

There I alleged S. Hierome calling S. Augustine a Byshoppe of his Communion, prouing thereby them to be of one Communion, and to Communicate together, though they were farre a sunder, and Communion to be, though the Communicantes be not together in one place. Which is true, and may right wel be said againe in ẏ same termes: if by the worde Communion, be vnderstanded a Participation or partaking of that which is euery where one and the selfe same, neither can be diuided by any diuersitie of places or receiuers, the Body of Christe in the Sacrament really conteined, and not the bodily receiuing of the formes of Breade and wine. The receiuing of the outward formes (I confesse) is diuerse, but the Communion is one, because it is but one Body that is communicated and imparted. The vnitie or the onenesse of that precious meate, maketh al one that receiue it worthily, and so the Communion is one, though ech Consecration be diuerse from other, though the outward celebration be diuerse, though the receiuing be diuerse in diuerse places. In this respect no Catholike Priest doth Communicate alone, but with other Catholike persons where so euer they be. At his Masse oftentimes for lacke of companie, he receiueth alone touching place, none receiuing with him in the same place. For which ẏ Masse ought not to be called Priuate, ne can not at al be priuate, how so euer ẏ receiuig may be called in respect of place, sole or priuate.

Inter epist. Augustini epist. 14.

In ẏ sense is ẏ Communion one betwene diuerse being asunder.

Hereat M. Iewel inueyeth, scoffeth, sporteth, spendeth his Diuinitie, Rhetorike, and Sophistrie, maketh ridiculous

Argumentes of his owne ridiculous head, reporting them for mine, and doth al that he can deuise, as it were a vice in an Enterlude to laugh one out of his cote. But when he hath al said, he hath al done. The thing remaineth as before. Al that he goeth about to proue, faileth him, because he worketh vpon a false grounde, which is, that the worde Communio signifieth the outward and corporal administration of the Sacrament, in which sense I tooke it not, as I haue declared.

After that he hath sported and taken his pleasure with his owne foolish Argumentes, that no man of any witte or learning would make: at length he commeth to that, he should long before haue proued, or geue ouer: that the Cōmunion hath his name for that many receiue together in one place, or for that (as he saith) the Priest receiueth together with the people.

Ievvel.

I vvil note one or tvvo and such as M. Harding can not denie but they speake directly to the mater. Pachymeres a Greke vvriter, the Paraphrast vpon Dionysius, hath these vvordes: ταυτὴν δὲ καὶ κοινωνίαν λέγει, διὰ τὸ τότε κοινωνεῖν τοὺς ἀξίους πάντας τῶν μυστηρίων. *Therfore (saith he) hath this Father Dionysius called it the Cōmunion, for that then they that vvere vvorthy, did communicate of the holy Mysteries. Thus Pachymeres a man of late yeares vvrote vpon the same boke of Dionysius: and vvee may safely thinke, he vnderstoode his Authors minde as vvel as M. Harding. He saith Communio is so called of that*
The.79. vntruth. he saith not together. *vve doo Communicate * together. But M. Harding thinketh other-vvise, and constantly saith it is not so.*

Harding.

M. Iew. proueth ỷ I denied not, and ỷ I denied, he proueth not at al. Remember Reader what I denyed, and what M. Iewel hath here to proue. I denyed Communio to haue this name chiefly, not of that many do receiue, but of that many do receiue together in one place, for so be the wordes of my booke. And though M. Iewel crake of those he allegeth for his purpose, and

say

say they be such as I can not denie, but they speake directly to the mater: because they touch not the principal point wherein we varie, I must tel him, that his Doctours speake not directly to the mater.

Pachymeres expounding S. Dionysius calling the Sacrament by the name of Synaxis, vttereth the wordes by M. Iewel recited. This Sacrament (saith he) S. Dionysius nameth also Communion, because at that time al that were worthy did communicate of the Mysteries. That they communicated of the Mysteries I graunt: that is to say, that by worthy receiuing of the Sacrament, they were made one body with the body of Christe, flesh of his flesh, bone of his bones, as S. Chrysostome and Cyrillus do most plainely affirme.

Pachymeres in eccl. hierarch. p. 1. cap. 3.

S. Chrysostome hauing alleged those wordes of S. Paule, The bread which we breake, is it not the Communion of the body of Christe? saith thus: Quare non dixit Μετοχή? &c. Why said said he not partaking? Because he would signifie a certaine greater thing, and shew a great agreing together betwen these thinges. For we do not Cōmunicate only in participation and receiuing, but in vnitie or onenesse. For as that body is vnited to Christe, so we also by this bread be ioyned together in vnion.

1. Cor. 10 What is meant by Communion.

Againe within a sentence or two. Because many of vs be one bread, and one body: What do I cal (saith he) Communion? We are the selfe same body. What is that bread? (Est, is, hath ye greke not significat, as M. Iewel noteth) the body of Christe. And what are they made, which receiue? The body of Christe. Not many, but one body. Thus S. Chrysostome. Of this effect of the Sacrament, that thus we Communicate in vnion, and are made one body with Christe and within our selfe, it hath the name of Communio, and this is that Pachymeres meant.

Est, not significat

But that it is called κοινωνία in Greke, Cōmunio in Latine,

because many receiued ỹ Sacramẽt together in one place, which was M. Iewels part to proue: Pachymeres mẽt no such thing. The contrary as I haue now declared, he semeth to meane in plaine wordes speaking in the same chapter that M. Iewel alleageth, of the other worde Synaxis. For this is to be cōsydered, that where as of S. Dionysius this blessed Sacrament is called by two names, Communio, & Synaxis: Pachymeres sheweth wherof eche name procedeth. The signification of both tendeth to one ende. And what he said of Communio before, the like and ỹ same in effect, he saith afterward of Synaxis. His wordes be these. Σύναξιν δὲ νοητέον, οὐ τὴν τοῦ λαοῦ, καθὼς τὴν λέξιν τινὲς σήμερον ἐκλαμβάνονται, ἀλλὰ τὴν πρὸς θεὸν συναγωγὴν καὶ κοινωνίαν. Asmuch to say, By this worde collection or gathering together, (for so Synaxis one of the names of the Sacrament signifieth) we must vnderstād, not the gathering together of the people, as some now a daies do expounde, but the gathering together and Communion which is to Godward.

The blessed sacramẽt is called by two names, *Cōmunio & Synaxis*

What is meant by *Synaxis.*

Lo reader Pachymeres saith in expresse wordes, that the Sacrament is not called Synaxis, which is the same as Communio is, of that the people be gathered together (to receiue with the Priest as M. Iewel teacheth) but of that they are gathered together and made one with God, because they are compact and gathered together into one body with Christe by worthy receiuing of this Sacrament. We may safely thinke he vnderstode his authours mynde as wel as M. Iewel. He saith, as some now a daies do expound, of which number M. Iewel is one at this time. And so he is expresly confuted by Pachymeres his owne Doctor. Thus by Pachymeres, as the Sacrament is called Synaxis, not because ỹ receiuers are gathered together to receiue in one place, but because they are gathered to God, & in him ioyned together: so by his interpretation & meaning, it is called κοινωνία ỹ is Communio, chiefly, because through the blessed Sacrament & the

One thing is ment by *Syanxis & Cōmunio.*

the participation of the Mysteries, we are made one body with Christ, & cõsequently one wt God. Now as to be made one with God, wheras before we were diuerse & sundry from God, & to be gathered to God, is one thing: so is Communio and Synaxis one thing, though diuerse names. Therfore as Synaxis is so called of yt we be gathered together to God, not of the peoples gathering together into one place: so is Cõmunio likewise, of yt we are by the Sacramẽt made one with God, and ioyned together in God. Which is that I said, and is not disproued, but rather wel approued by Pachymeres, whom M. Iewel allegeth.

But what if I graunt, the Cõmunion to haue that name, for yt the worthy do cõmunicate of ye mysteries in the sense yt M. Iew. can iustly cõclude of Pachymeres wordes? It is called Cõmunio because many did cõmunicate. What thẽ? Ergo together? I graũt together spiritually, as S. Dionysius & Pachymeres ment, yt so they be made one body wt Christ, & within them self brought together into one body, & into one with God, but yet not into one place. Of euery priest yt saith Masse the blessed Sacramẽt is receiued, & so he cõmunicateth of the flesh of Christ, & is made one body wt al those yt worthily receiue any where els, and doth not cõmunicate alone, though in respect of ye place he is in, he receiue ye outward formes alone. That it be a Cõmunion, it is ynough the Sacrament be worthily receiued. And who so euer doth so receiue, though he receiue alone concerning the place, yet he doth Communicate with al others doing the same. For thereby al are ioyned together and made one body, be their outward persons neuer so farre a sunder. And so in the Primitiue Church the faithful receiued the Communion daily, yet very seldome together in their Publike assemblies, but most commonly at home Priuatly in their houses, for feare of the Infidels, of whom they were persecuted. M. Iewel proueth no more but that the Communion was receiued, which no man denieth,

Who so euer receiueth the sacrament alone worthily, doth cõmunicate with al others doing the like, though when they receiue, they be a sũder.

The point that M. Iewel ought to proue.

and that it were wel done to receiue it altogether, or in companies, it is not denyed. But that of necessitie it be alwayes receiued of a companie together in one place, or els not at al: that is denyed, and that is the point which M. Iewel hath to proue, and yet through his great booke hath not proued, nor shal neuer be able duly to proue. For lacke of proufe of this point, al is void what so euer he bringeth against the Masse, which he calleth Priuate.

M. Iew. falsifieth Pachymeres, by puttig in this worde *together* of his own

This being so, the more euident is your lye M. Iewel, that you make vpon Pachymeres, where you say thus. *He saith Communio is so called of that vve do Communicate together.* For he saith not so, the word *together,* is of your owne putting in more then you founde in your Doctor. That we who are Priestes, are bound to communicate when so euer we celebrate the vnbloudy Sacrifice of the Church, we graunt, and so we do: but that we must of necessitie do it with al the people, or with a number together in the same place: that we deny vtterly, and vntil you proue it, we shal require you to subscribe according to your promise. Now that Pachymeres serueth not your turne, let vs see what auncient Fathers you haue.

Ievvel.

In 1. Co. 10.

Haimo vvriting vpon S. Paules Epistles saith thus, Calix appellatur Communicatio, quasi participatio, quia omnes Communicant ex illo. *The cuppe is called the Communication, vvhich is as much as Participation, because al do Communicate of it.*

In speculo ecclesiæ.

Hugo Cardinalis saith thus: Post hoc dicatur Communio, quæ appellatur, vt omnes communicemus. *Aftervvard let the Communion be said, vvhich is so called, that vve should al Communicate. And he saith further.* Vel dicitur Communio, quia in primitiua ecclesia populus communicabat quolibet die. *Othervvise (saith he) it is called the Communion, for that the people in the Primitiue Church did Communicate euery day.*

Harding.

Harding.

It is an euident tokē your mater is euil, that you haue not one auncient Father on your syde. For those which you allege be farre without the compasse of the first six hundred yeres after Christe. Haimo maketh no more for you, thē Pachymeres doth. For what if the cuppe be called Communication, because al Cōmunicate of it, as peraduenture in Haimos time, and in the coūtrie where he lyued, the people receiued the bloud of our Lorde in forme of wine: wil it thereof folow, that Communion is so called specially for that many receiue together in one place, and not rather because through the Sacrament they are made one body with Christ? And who so euer doth Communicate of Christes body, is he not also made partaker of his bloud?

M. Iew. hath not one auncient father for proufe of his assertion.

But in alleging Haimo, why did you not reherse his wordes wholly, as you founde them? The cuppe of Haimo is called Calix benedictionis, qui benedicitur a sacerdotibus in altari, the cup of blessing, which is blessed or consecrated of priestes at the Aulter. Was that soppe to hote for you? What is that you misliked, the Consecration, or the blessing, the Priestes, or the Aulter, or the blessing at the Aulter, or altogether? This was your wisedom, where you impugne the Masse, to cut awaye al wordes, that may make for the Masse. Verely therein you do but your kinde. Al of your professiō haue euer vsed the like falshed. Wherin the fauourers of your sect, must beare with you, as doubtlesse they do, or require you to hold your peace. For how can vntruth be bolstered, but by vntruth.

Haimo falsified of M. Iew. by leauing out wordes of great importance.

And Syr, seing ỷ you were not ashamed to allege Haimo for you, though in dede to no purpose: it is reason you admitte his authoritie as good and lawful. With euen dealing you can not take his witnesse in one thing, and refuse it in an other. How say you then to the real presence by him most plainely auouched in

Haimo maketh wholy against M Iewels doctrine touching the real presence, & transubstantiatiō,

in these wordes? Caro quam verbum dei patris assumpsit in vtero
1.Cor.10 virginali, in vnitate suæ personæ, & panis qui cōsecratur in ecclesia, vnū corpus Christi sunt. Sicut enim illa caro corpus est Christi, ita iste panis transit in corpus Christi, nec sunt duo corpora, sed vnum corpus, The flesh which the word of God the Father toke in the virgins wombe in vnitie of his person, & the bread which is Cōsecrated in the Church, are one body of Christ. For as that flesh is the body of Christe, so this bread goeth into the body of Christe, neither be they two bodies, but one body.

If I had alleged this place for the Real presence, and for Transubstantion, you would haue founde fault with his age, and would haue said, he had ben out of your compasse. Now that you allow him, we require you to yelde and subscribe to the Real presence, and to the breades going into the body of Christe, which is a Transubstantiation. Yelde you wil not, yet answer you can not.

Hugo Cardinalis alleged by M. Iewel, is a late wryter.

Hugo Cardinalis a late wryter, who liued about three hundred yeres past, in these wordes saith nothing that proueth the Communion so to be called, because the Communicantes receiue the Sacrament together in one place. Let it be, as he would haue it, if the wordes be truly alleged, that it is called Cōmunio, that al we should communicate: yet it is not necessary that al come together into one place to Communicate, neither that there be no Communion at al, except al in a parish, or at least a good number receiue together.

Were not M. Iewel driuen to narrow shiftes, he would not cal Hugo Cardinalis to helpe him. For it is wel knowen, that if he committe his cause to his arbitrement, he is condemned. If he permitte vs to vse the testimonies of the later wryters, as he vseth them him selfe for his aduauntage very ofte: he were sone oppressed both with number, and also with weight of testi-

testimonies, condemning euery parte of his doctrine, wherin he varieth from the Catholike Church. But iudge Reader whether this be euen dealing or no. M. Iewel admitteth no authoritie alleged by vs out of any writer, that lyued after the first. vj. C. yeres after Christe. Yet he him selfe boldly vseth to bolster vp his new doctrine by late wryters, by Schoole men, whō in dede he vtterly contemneth, and by who so euer semeth to say ought sounding to the sense he would bring the world vnto. Yea he wil not let to allege the very obiections of the Schoolemen dissembling their answere, which obiections they make in their disputations against the truth, to thintent by assoiling the same, the strength of truth might appeare the better: as though they were in earnest, and of purpose written of them in defence of the truth.

The vneue dealing of M. Iewel. M. Iew. bindeth vs for proufe of the Catholike doctrin to the Fathers of the first vj. c. yeres and he him selfe vseth for his help, the writers of al ages.

After Pachymeres, Haimo, and Hugo Cardinalis, he allegeth one Gerardus Lorichius, and Georgius Cassander bringing in with him an obscure booke named Micrologus, men of our time, and in many pointes addicted vnto them that haue diuided them selues from the Catholike Churche. whose doctrine is condemned by the Church, and therfore we admit not their authoritie, nor esteme it no better, then the authoritie of Peter Martyr, Caluine, Cranmare, Frier Couerdal, Frier Bale, Monke Hooper, or any other the like Apostates doctours of this newe founde Gospel.

The. 80. vntruth. It is no decree, nor canon Ecclesiastical

Ievvel.

*S. Basile reporteth an *ecclesiastical Decree or canon, that at the receiuing of the holy Communion, vvhich he calleth mysticum Pascha, there ought to be tvvelue personnes at the least, and neuer vnder.*

Exercita. ad pietat. serm. 4.

Harding.

This is false, as the rest before is. There was neuer any such ecclesiastical Decree or Canon made. Neither doth S. Basile

M. Iew. reporteth S. Basils woordes falsly.

reporte the necessitie of twelue persons at euery Communion, for that were absurde, and your selfe M. Jewel do not allow it, I am sure. S. Basile onely proponeth the example of the number, which it pleased the holy Ghost to be present at Christes last supper, where the mystical Lambe after the typical or figuratiue Lambe of the olde lawe was first eaten: By that example requiring the Monkes of his Institution not to liue solitarily, but ten together at least. Neither reporteth he by way of an ecclesiastical Decree or Canon, what the holy ghoste would for time to come to be obserued in the Communion touching the number of them that should receiue together in one place: but what he would to be done at the first Institution of the Communion, where their presence was requisite, who then were to be instructed, how to do the same, & to deliuer it to the Church afterward. More thereof for number of Communicantes together in one place, can you not conclude. Abuse not the simplicitie of the vnlearned reader M. Jewel, whom for lacke of knowledge it is easy to deceiue, specially for him that by outward shewe of such calling hath goten him selfe some credite.

The place of S. Basil declared.

The. xi. Diuision.

My wordes placed by M. Jewel in his. xj. Diuision, perteine to that goeth before. By diuiding them a sundre, he would haue them seme to conteine a newe mater diuerse from that was treated before. In that place I say, there may be a Communion, though the Communicantes be not together in one place: which be my wordes immediatly before the first sentence of this diuision. There I demaunde a question: whether, if a Priest after his dyner deliuer the blessed Sacrament

The effect of my wordes in M. Jewels. xj. Diuision.

In the Answer. fol. 14. b.

crament to.iiij.or.v.sicke persons in sundry houses, requiring to receiue their rightes before they depart this life, when no other person is ready to receiue with them: he do not communicate with them hauing receiued at his Masse that day, and whether they do not communicate together, though they be not together in one place. If this be not a Communion, and if so to do it be vtterly vnlawful for lacke of a number to receiue with ech of thē in the same place: then should the sicke be defrauded of their viage prouision, which were a cruel iniurie, and wheras by sundry olde canons they that were excommunicate were admitted to receiue their rightes before their departure, it were beside reason other christian folke, who had not deserued the like punishment, at their ende to be denied that necessarie vitaile of life. If then this be admitted for a good and lawful Communion, why is not that which the priest receiueth at his Masse likewise a Communion, specially why shal we not say, he doth Communicate with others doing likewise, though not in one place? This is the effect of my wordes there.

To this M. Iewel replieth with mo scoffes, then learned reasons, and turning away from the principal question, he speaketh most of thinges by me not mentioned. And to haue the better occasion to make sport with argumentes of his owne forgerie, he surmiseth that al this was said for proufe of priuate Masse directly, whereas I speake it onely to this ende, to declare that communion is among them, who be in places distāt, as by view of my booke the reader may iudge. And when he hath altered the state of the question, and borne his reader in hande, that I say, as he would haue me say for his better aduauntage to replie: then he triumpheth and maketh gay sporte at me, as though his minde were to make a fitte of mirth for Prentises, rather then to satisfie the expectation of the graue reader. Among his scoffes he mingleth certaine vntruthes worthy to be noted, as for example.

Ievvel.

If the priest notvvithstanding his diner, communicate vvith the sicke, then
The 81. vntruth. It appeareth not. *hath M.Harding yet founde no priuate Masse. And it *appeareth by S. Augustine and certaine olde Canons, that in the primitiue church both the priest and people sometimes communicated together after supper.*

Cōcil. Carthag.3.c.6

Harding.

Whether the priest after his diner receiue the Sacrament with a sicke mā or receiue not, therein consisteth not priuate Masse. And *Augustin. ad Ianua. epist.118.* what if it appeare by S. Augustine, that certaine were delited with a probable reason (as he saith) that the body and bloud of our Lord might be offred and receiued after other meates, as for a more notable Commemoration vpon one certaine day in the yere, in which our Lord gaue his Supper? And this is al that he saith touching that mater. Wil you hereof conclude as though it were so at other times vsed? Verely you can not. Why then do you falsifie S. Augustine, & faine certaine olde Canons, as mencioning that the priest and people sometimes communicated together after supper? He ỳ saith sometimes, meaneth he not more then one certaine day in the yere? And what olde Canons cā you allege for it? What Canons you haue, it appeareth ful wel by that you haue noted in your bokes margent, where you referre your reader to the third Councel of Carthage, Can.6. And there is no worde of any such thing. In the.29. Canon of that councel special charge is geuen, that the Sacramēts of the aulter be not celebrated but of men that be fasting, except Maundie Thursdaie.

M. Iew. manifestly falsifieth S Augustine, and faineth old Canons.

But what pleasure had you thus to saye? Or why said you this much, but to bring the blessed Sacrament in contempt by perswading the people, it might as wel be receiued after diner and supper, as before when they be fasting? Saith not S. Augustine in that very Epistle to Ianuarius the contrary? That the

Sa-

Sacramēt is through ẏ whole Church alwayes taken of them ẏ be fasting? That it hath pleased the holy ghost, that for the honor of so high a Sacrament our Lordes body shuld enter into the mouth of a Christian before external meates? That this custome is kept through ẏ whole worlde? And that although Christ gaue it after supper for great cause, yet now it ought not so to be? *Augustin. ad Ianua. epist. 118.*

Ievvel.

And vvhy is this prouision thought so necessary? Or vvhy is it counted so cruel an iniurie, if the sickman passe vvithout it? Shal no man be saued that so departeth? In dede that vvere a cruel iniurie. Infinite numbers of childrē and others depart this life in goddes mercie vvithout that vitaile.

Harding.

The Sacramental eating of this heauenly foode, is not to euery one absolutly and simply necessary, so as without it there be no hope of saluation besides. The benefite of it, if it be worthily receiued, is so great, as no other thing can seme to profite vs more, specially if it be receiued at our departure hence. For wheras the thing which we receiue is ẏ body whereunto the worde is ioyned, which by nature is life, and thereby that body is made Viuifical, quickening, or lifemaking: how can it be thonght, but that it is an inestimable benefite, when death approcheth, a man to be made partaker of life, and to receiue that whereby death (as Cyrillus oftentimes saith) is driuen away, & quite expelled frō vs? *The benefite of the blessed Sacrament worthily receiued.* *Viuificum* *In Iohan. lib. 4. & lib. 10. & lib. 11.*

This great profite S. Basile commendeth very much, calling it the participation of life. To communicate euery day (saith he) and to receiue the holy body and bloud of Christ, it is a goodly mater, and a thing very profitable, as he saith him selfe: he that eateth my flesh, and drinketh my bloud, hath life euerlastīg. Quis enim ambigit, quin frequens vitæ participatio, nihil aliud sit, quá pluribus modis viuere? For who doubteth, but that the often participation of life, is nothing els, but a man to liue by many waies? *In epist. ad Cæsariam patritiam quæ græcè extat.* Ioan. 6. S. Basile cōmunicated foure times in a weeke.

we therefore do communicate sometimes euery weeke, the Sunday, Wenesday, Fryday and Saturday, and other dayes also, if there happen a memorie of any Sainct.

Hereof we finde a notable testimonie in S. Chrysostome de Sacerdotio, lib. 6. which I trust M. Iewel wil not ieast at, as he doth at the like visions of holy mẽ, for the graue auctorities sake of S. Chrysostome. Quidam mihi narrauit. &c. One tolde me (saith he) who was not tolde it of an other, but was accompted worthy, both to haue sene it him selfe, and to haue heard it: that they who depart out of this life, if they be partakers of those mysteries with a pure and cleane conscience when they be at the point to yelde vp the ghost, are carried away from hence streight into heauen by Angels beset about their bodies in manner of a garde. For these causes to denye a man his rightes at his end, I might wel cal it a cruel iniurie.

Chrysosto. lib. 6. de Sacerdotio.

Concerning necessitie, it is in a certaine degree necessary, for that the Church of Christe hath ordeined, that sicke persons be not denied their viage prouision. Againe, because it is a cruel iniurie, that any mans good affection and deuotion in that case, & at that time should be denied: necessary it is that such a deuoute request be satisfied. Who wil not say, it is necessary euery christen person at his departure hence, be fensed against the common ennemie of mankinde? Of al thinges what can be a better fense against our mortal ennemie the deuil, & against euerlasting death it selfe, then the body of Christe, which conquered the deuil, & being vnited to the worde is by nature viuifical, quickening, & life geuing, and therfore dryueth away the death, and procureth life for euer, of whom so euer it is worthily receiued? The Eucharist (saith S. Cyprian) is made to this ende, that it may be a safegard vnto them that receiue it: whom we wil to be safe against the ennemie, thẽ we arme with the armour of our Lordes fulnesse, Dominicæ

De consecrat. dist. 2 Presbyter Eucharistiam.

The necessitie of houseling in time of sicknesse.

Cyprian. lib. 1. epi. 2.

minicæ saturitatis, that is to say, of our Lordes body in ẏ blessed Sacramēt, wherwͭ their spiritual stomake is filled & refreshed.

In cōsideration of this great benefite the Fathers euer moued the sicke persons hereunto. Refuse not my sonne (saith S. Augustine) to receiue that body of our Lorde which supplieth life: yea rather see that thou seeke for it most greedily, and eate it faithfully. That incomparable and vnspeakeable meate shalbe vnto thee a most holesom wayfare or viage prouision, and price of thy redemption.

August. de visitatione infirmorū. lib. 2.

Ievvel.

*In the primitiue church, this order vvas thought expedient, * not for the sicke, for they in their health receiued * daily, and in their sicknesse had the Sacrament ordinarily sent home vnto them: but for personnes excommunicate, and enioyned to penaunce.*

The. 82. vntruth.

The. 83. vntruth.

August. de Serm domini in mōte. cap. 12. Iustin. martyr.

Harding.

What say you M. Iewel? was it thought by the Fathers of the Primitiue Church ẏ this heauenly vitaile was expedient for the excōmunicate persōs only, & not for ẏ sick? sothly it was thought expediēt for both, albeit ẏ excōmunicate persōs were not permitted to receiue but at their end, onles they had before ended their penāce enioyned, & had ben absolued, & al others might receiue, whēsoeuer they required ẏ same. And how folish a thing is ẏ you say, the Sacramēt was thought expedient not for the sick, but for the excommunicate persons in the primitiue church? for (say you) the sicke in their health receiued daily. If they receiued in their helth, then were they not sicke. But to leaue that to some excuse, If they receiued it daily in health, why should they not receiue it in sickenesse, being accordingly disposed? was it profitable in health, yea being daily receiued, and not profitable in sicknesse, and at the departing out of this life? wil you haue a man receiue life when he is hole, and to be destitute of life, when he is sicke? Hath he not rather at that time most nede of life?

M. Iew. tale hangeth not together.

And how standeth this together, the Sacrament was not

M. Iew. fighteth against him selfe with cõtradiction. thought expedient for the sicke, & yet in their sicknesse they had it ordinarily sent home vnto them? If it were ordinarily sent home vnto them, then was it thought expedient. For had it not ben thought expedient, then to haue sent it vnto them, it had ben superfluous. The ordinary sending argueth, that it was thought expedient as wel for them, as for the Excommunicate persons. For what was done more for the excommunicate, concerning the Sacrament, but that it was sent vnto them being at poinct of death? If the sending of it to both were equal, why was it thought expedient for the one, and not for the other? How hangeth your tale together?

Here let vs cõsider how many vntruthes you haue vttered in one short sentẽce. That the Sacramẽt was not in the Primitiue Church thought expediẽt for the sick, it is vntrue. For ye Fathers of the Nicene Councel geue great charge to Bishops, to deliuer the Cõmuniõ to al them that depart out of this life. For the sick, & for the pilgrimes & strãgers it was kept in readinesse alwaies as it appeareth by sundry histories. That the sicke in their health receiued daily, for so you say, if you meane it of the East church, it is also vntrue. For S. Chrysostome complaineth vehemently of the peoples negligence & slacknesse in that behalfe. S. Ambrose likewise noteth a great slaknes in the people of the East church, for that they had a custome to receiue but once in the yere. S. Augustine in his Epistle to Ianuarius reporteth, that some cõmunicated of the body and bloud of our Lord euery day, some receiued but certaine daies. And in the place it selfe which you allege here for you, he saith, plurimi in orientalibus partibus non quotidie cœnæ dominicæ communicãt, very many of the East partes do not communicate of our Lordes supper daily.

And whereas he saith there of the Sacrament, quotidie accipimus, we receiue daily, he meant indefinitely of Christẽ folke, amõg whom some euery day receiued in one place or other. But that

Can. 13

Chrysosto. homil. 61. ad popul. Antiochẽ. Ambrosi. de sacramentis. lib. 5. cap. 4. August. epist. 118. August. de sermone Domini in monte lib. 2. cap. 12.

that al receiued daily that were in helth, or that any certain and determinate persons receiued daily, that S. Augustine saith not. Therefore you alleged S. Augustine vntruly for daily receiuing of the Sacrament.

That you allege S. Iustinus for the sending of the Sacramēt ordinarily home to the houses of sicke persons, it is also vntruly done, for in the place of his second Apologie, he speaketh neuer a word of any sicke persons, but only of such as remained at home. *Iustinus in 2. Apolo.*

Ievvel.

*At last (the geuing of the viage prouision) grevv to such superstition, that it vvas*thrust into mennes mouthes, after they vvere dead, as vve may see by *the Councel of Carthage forbidding the same.* The. 84. vntruth. The. 85. vntruth. It is not so to be sene.

Harding.

Seldom say you truth M. Iewel. where finde you ÿ the blessed Sacrament was thrust into mennes mouthes after they were dead? That it was geuē to the bodies of some ÿ were dead, it appeareth by the. vj. Canon of ÿ third Coūcel of Carthage forbidding the same, which you allege, but that it was thrust into their mouthes, you say it, for more contēpt of the Sacramēt, but without witnesse, without proufe, and vntruly you say it. So you say in your chalēging sermon wt like libertie of lying, and with like wickednes of desire to bring that holy Mysterie into further cōtempt, that S. Benet ministred it vnto a dead woman. The Sacrament was geuē to the bodies of some that were dead not thrust into their mouthes. A notorious lye, made by M. Iew. vpon S. Benet.

Al which be vaine lyes. And no such thing was euer reported by any graue authour to haue ben donne by any Saint. In dede S. Gregorie writeth ÿ S. Benet gaue with his owne hand a singing cake (as we cal it) to be consecrated, & so to be offred in Sacrifice at Masse for two noble religious wemen, to the intēt they might be reconciled & absolued, who after their death by Gods secret disposition were permitted to shewe, ÿ they remained in state of excommunication, with which S. Benet had threatened thē being a lyue, onlesse they would amend certaine faultes they had committed, which they amended not. *Dialogorū lib. 2. cap. 24.*

He writeth also that the same S. Benet caused the Sacramēt to be laid vpon the breast of a Ladde, whose dead body rested not in the graue it was buried in, but sundry times was cast forth againe, vntil that was done by S. Benetes commaundement. Now as if others had presumed to do ẏ like, it had ben an abuse, and therefore the thing being growen vnto an abuse, it was forbidden by the third Councel of Carthage: so forasmuch as it was done of so holy a man as S. Benet was, and good thereof proceded: it is rather to be wondered at, and God to be praised for it, (who by special dispēsation of his mercie worketh such grace by men) then to be reproued, scorned, & mocked. But al this is besides our purpose. why come you not to the question M. Iewel? why bestow you so many wordes in a mater impertinent, and touch not the special point, that here is of you demaunded?

Dialog. lib. 2. cap. 24.

Ievvel.

But let vs graunt M. Harding his vvhole request: Let his priest come and minister to the sicke.

Harding.

Sir I make no request nor sute vnto you. Only for further declaration of ẏ I said before, I demaund a question, whereunto you are loth to make direct answere I perceiue. My question is knowen, and set forth before, therto what answer you? whē the priest after he hath said Masse and dined, geueth the Sacrament to certaine sicke persons at the point of death in sundry houses without other companie to receiue with ech one, is it a lawful Communion or no? Doth the Priest and they communicate together or no? If such communion be vnlawful for lack of others to communicate in the same place, then shal the sick be defrauded of that necessary vitaile of life through others default, which is not reason, and great iniurie it were to denie that benefite to any Christian person at his departure, that requireth it, and contrary to Decrees of holy Councels.

Neither

Neither is the Priest in that case bound to kepe him selfe fasting to receiue at al callinges with a sicke man, nor after common meates being in helth may he receiue, for al these are forbidden by decrees of auncient Coūcels. If this be a lauful Communiō, notwithstanding theire being aparte in sundry places: why is not that also a lauful Communion, which the Priest frequenteth at his Masse, hauing no company disposed to receiue with him in the same place?

Ievvel.

*Vvhat maketh al this for his Priuate Masse? The members of these * Argumentes hang together like a sicke mans dreame, not one piece like an other. For if there be a Masse, vvhich of the tvvo is it, that saith this Masse? Is it the sicke man or the Priest? The Priest hath dined, and therefore may not: the sicke man is no Priest, and therefore can not. Here * vvould M. Harding faine finde a Masse: but he can find no man to say his Masse, and so hath hitherto found no masse at al. And thinketh he to proue his Masse by the thing that is no Masse?*

The. 86. vntruth. I make no argumentes in this place.

The. 87. vntruth. here I seeke not for the Masse.

Harding.

What this maketh for priuate Masse, you see. Albeit I said not this, therby to proue priuate Masse directly, but by way of a question to declare that priuate or sole receiuing is not vnlauful, for which your fellowes and you speake much vilanie against the Masse. And this is said to thintent that if Communion receiued by one alone be not vnlauful, the Masse wherat the Priest receiueth alone, for which cause ye cal it Priuate, be no more impugned, as for that respect vnlauful.

But what meant you to find so great fault wͭ my arguments? which be the Argumēts that you reproue? Or made I in this place any arguments at al? Verely I made none. Yet you beare your Readers in hand I do, ỳ you may take occasion to say your pleasure. And this is your common custome through your whole booke, to go from the point that is specially treated, to

M. Jewels comon custome through his Replie

by things, and to scoffe at your owne fained Arguments, pretending them to be mine. Wherewith you please your Prentises and other good fellowes perhappes, whose lippes like wel such Letise: wise and learned men I am sure you please not, and time shal trie your Replie, to be but a smoother, that geueth no light, and casteth no heate. Now Syr touching your long scoffing tale, if I tel you, that when a sicke man receiueth his rightes alone at a Priestes hande, as the manner is in the Catholike Churche, there is no Masse: what haue you to say? This being tolde you, your gaye sporte whereof you are ful in this Diuision, is altogether disgraced.

Ievvel.

Againe, graunt vve this action of the Priest not onely to be a Priuate Masse, but also the necessitie of the sicke considered, to be lauful. Yet coulde not this president make it lauful to be done openly in the Churche, vvhereas is no such case of necessitie. The circumstances of place, of time, of cause, of ende, of manner of doing be not like.

Harding.

M. Jew. within fewe lines gainesaith him selfe, by a manifest contradictiō making one thing necessary & not necessarie.

Pag. 31. in

This action of the Priest is not onely lauful, but also due, whether it please you to graunt it or no. But if you graunt it to be a Priuate Masse, it is more then I require, and more then truth acknowlegeth. But you speake of a case of necessitie, as though it were lauful onely in consideration of the sicke mannes necessitie, not otherwise. What M. Jewel haue you so sodainely forgotten your selfe? Is that now become necessarie, which euen now you said, was not necessarie? Go backe againe a fewe lines, and reade your owne wordes in this verye Diuision, reporting the

blessed

Blessed Sacrament, neither to be necessary, nor expediente for the sicke, nor any iniury to be done vnto him, if he departe without it. There it serued your turne better to denye the necessitie of it, here to confesse it. So rather then you woulde lacke woordes, and yeelde to the truth, you thought good for your aduauntage to saye, and vnsaye, to make one selfe thing necessary, and not necessary.

And what speake you of circumstances of place, time, cause, ende, manner of doing? Shal any Circumstance, change or take away the Institution of Christe? Say you not before in your viij. Diuision, that touching the number of Communicantes together, Christe hath determined the case? Say you not (though vntruely as here I haue proued) that, *albeit Christe haue appointed no certaine number of Communicantes, yet he hath by special vvoordes appointed a number? For these vvoordes* (saye you) *Take ye, eate ye, drinke ye.&c. necessarily importe a number.* Wherefore it were best you agreed with your selfe, ere you go about to bring other men to agree with you. For if number be necessary, and appointed by special woordes of Christe, as you saye there, then is it not lauful for a sicke man to receiue alone, as you say here.

An other contradiction of M. Iewels.

Pag. 20.

Let it be considered what inconuenience followeth of your doctrine. That there be a number of partakers together at euery Communion, by you it is necessarie. That a sicke man at his departure receiue the Communion, by you also it is necessarie. But what if in that case a number such as you require to be, bee not alwayes readye to receiue? what then remayneth, but that either he passe without it, and so that be not done which is necessary; or that he

The ineuitable incōuenience of M. Iewels doctrine.

receiue alone, and so Christes necessary commaundement to be broken? whereof it must follow, that Christe was not a wise Lawmaker, who prouided nothing for the auoiding of such inconuenience, and bindeth a man to that which in some case can not be perfourmed. Thus euery man may see, to what contradictions and absurdities through the sprite of Contention, and gainesaying M. Iewel is brought.

But saith M. Iewel, although the case of necessitie make single receiuing lauful in the sicke man, yet can not this presidẽt make it lauful to be done opẽly in the church, wheras is no such case of necessitie. Herunto I say: If it be necessitie that maketh single or rather sole receiuing of the Sacrament lauful in the sicke man: the necessitie of the Priest at Masse when others be not disposed to receiue with him being no lesse, yea much more: the case of necessitie maketh it lauful to be done also by him opẽly in ẏ church. For when he hath Consecrated the Body of our Lorde, he is bounde to receiue it, for that is the consũmation of the Sacrifice. And to that, is alleged by some the scripture, Sacerdos qui offert hostiam, comedet eam in loco sancto, The Priest that offereth the hoste, shal eate it in the holie place. Therefore S. Dionysius saith, this to be ẏ most semely order of diuine things, that first the Priest do Communicate of the holy giftes, for so S. Chrysostome witnesseth, that Christ him selfe did, likewise S. Hierome in his Epistle Ad Hedibiam, and S. Augustine, De doctrina Christiana lib. 2. cap. 3. That so it ought to be the Fathers of the twelfth Toletane Councel doth both proue, and commaund very streightly to be euermore obserued. The Priest then being bound to receiue after that he hath consecrated and offered the Sacrifice, whẽ as there be none to receiue with him: why he may not receiue alone, you haue yet shewed vs no cause, nor euer shalbe able to shewe.

Leuit. 6. *Ecclesiast. hierarc. part. 3. c. 3.* *Chrysost. in cap. Mat. 26.* *Can. 7.*

M. Iew. hath no cause to shewe, why the Priest may not receiue alone, in case of others refusal.

You wil say perhaps, what neede is there at al, that the Priest at Masse celebrate the Sacrifice? Yeas Sir, there is neede. Els Christ would not haue said, Do ye this in my remembrance. By this Oblation we renew, and continue the memorie of Christes death, and render thankes to God the Father, that by the death of his Sonne, whose Body is offered in this Sacrifice in a Mysterie, he hath redemed vs. And how so euer this memorie may be renewed, and thankes geuen to God by other meanes: yet this is a special meane, and specially commaunded by Christe. And forasmuch as the memorie of man is fraile, and this is commaunded to be done in remembrance of Christ: if it should not be frequẽted, but for a long time be intermitted, we for our parte should seme vnmindeful of so greate a a benefite, and Christes death should not according to his owne Institution be recorded.

Wherefore is the Sacrifice to be celebrated. *Luc. 22.* *1. Cor 11.*

Ievvel.

In case of necessitie a dispensation vvas graunted to the Priestes of Norvvey to consecrate the Mystical cuppe vvithout vvine: for that vvine being brought into that Countrie by meane of the extreme cold can not last. Yet vvas it neuer thought lauful for al other Priestes, in all other Churches generally to do the same.

Volaterrã. Lib. 7.

Harding.

That which you allege here of the dispensation graunted to the Priestes of Norwey to consecrate the Mystical cup without wine, I denye it vtterly. There was neuer no such thing graunted. Whether by permission of Innocentius Octauus they celebrated the Sacrifice without wine for cause by you alleged, I affirme nothing: but that they were dispensed with to consecrate the Mystical cuppe without wine, I denie it, and you shal neuer sufficiently proue it. And what so euer Raphael Volaterranus writeth hereof, it may as sadly be contemned, as of of him it is lightly reported. He liued in our age, and might therein be deceiued by others, as sithens others haue ben deceiued by him. his authoritie is of smal credit in such a mater. Wherefore your Argument depending thereof is of litle force.

As bread and wine are the necessarie mater of ẏ most blessed Sacrament by Institution of Christe, and can not be changed by man: so if a number of communicantes or receiuers together in in one place be of his Institution, as you say it is: no such humaine necessitie can happen, for which his diuine ordinance may lawfully be broken. But the sicke person receiuing the Communion alone, Christes Institution is not broken, because the number which is spoken of is not of necessitie alwayes required: therefore neyther by the Priestes sole receiuing at Masse, is it broken, when there are no others worthily prepared to receiue with him. Els must you shewe some weighty cause for which our Lords Institution is kept in the sicke, and broken in the Priest.

The. 14. Diuision.

BEcause it were a lẽgthening of my boke, which I couet to be short, to reherse my wordes which M. Iewel hath put into his. 12. diuision: I require thee good Reader to peruse them, as they are set forth in my Answer to his Chalenge. wey
Fol. 15. a. them there as thei be vttered, not as he hath mangled them, & as vntruly he reporteth them in his Replie. The sũme of them tẽdeth to this, ẏ if no faithful person might at any time receiue the blessed Sacramẽt but with moe together in one place: then for ẏ

enioying

ioying of that necessary benefite, we were bounde to the condicion of a place. And so the Church delyuered by Christ from al bondage, and set at libertie, should notwithstanding be in seruitude and subiection vnder those outward thinges, which S. Paul calleth infirma & egena elementa, weake and poore elementes. So might we be blamed for obseruing places, as the Galathians were blamed of S. Paul for obseruing dayes, monethes and times. so should we seme Iuishly to returne againe to the elementes of the worlde, from which, S. Paul saith we are dead with Christ. &c.

Conditiō of place.

Galat. 4.

Here M. Iewel first of al piketh a quarel, for that I mencioned euery other Christen man or woman, saing, if either the Priest, or euery other Christen man or woman, might at no time receiue the Sacrament, but with moe together in one place: then &c. as is before recited. his Replie is thus.

Ievvel.

*Here these vvordes, euery other Christian man, or vvoman, that he hath taken in by the vvay, are an ouerplus, and * quite from the purpose.*

The. 88. vntruth. these wordes are not quite frō ẏ purpose.

Harding.

These wordes I graunt, and the thing by them signified, be quite from your purpose, but not from our purpose. For if any other Christen man or woman may lawfully receiue the Sacrament alone, what religion haue you, why the Priest may not receiue it alone? where you make the Masse vnlauful specially for the Priestes sole receiuing, the same being founde lauful in others, the Masse is proued lauful, and defended from your wicked reproufe.

Ievvel.

The 89. vntruth.

*For the * question is moued, not of any other Manne or Vvoman,*

but

There was no such question moued.

but of the Masse, and onely of the Priest that saith the Masse.

Harding.

Who moued that question, I pray you Syr? A vaine foolish Chalenge you made, for which you haue no thanke of God, you may be sure, nor commendation of men (I thinke verely) which you looked for, no not of the wiser sort of your owne sect, as partly it appeareth by your owne confession. Question you moued none. But because here you seeme to be driuen to allow sole receiuing in an other Christen man or woman, which you can not away with in any person in your Chalenging Sermon: it remaineth you shew vs a better cause then you haue hitherto, why you condemne it in the Priest, when he hath consecrated and offered. If you can not, reuoke your wicked and foolish Chalenge, leaue rayling at the Masse, and subscribe.

Page. 33. The accustomed sleight of M. Jew. when he hath not what reasonably to answer.

Here M. Jewel vseth his accustomed sleight. Not being able to answere that I bring against his precise necessitie of a nūber of Cōmunicāts wͭ the Priest together in one place, the better to be able to say somwhat, or rather that he might seme to the ignorāt to haue some colour of a iust Replie: he telleth my tale for me, & reporteth my words far otherwise then I vttered them my selfe. After that vntrue dealing vsed to ỿ aduātage of his cause, he pretendeth to doubt, whether I scoffe and dally for my pleasure, or speake soothly as I thinke. Wherof I maruel why he should so doubt. For who so euer reade my wordes, which the Printer hath in his booke laid together truely, though M. Jewel by his vntrue report do falsifie them: shal sone iudge, I speake them in good sooth, as being such, that haue not so much as any shadow of scoffing.

That flower willingly I leaue to you M. Jewel, the pleasauntst of al other in your garland in ỿ sight of your owne light sorte, and most vnpleasant in the sight of the graue and wise. And as you say here, to scoffe and dally becommeth not the mater, wherein you say truly: so with your owne testimonie you condemne your selfe, who vse it so much without regard of the person you haue put vpon you, and of the sad mater, you haue taken in hande to treate.

At length you resolue in this, That if I spake soothly and as I thinke, then I haue not wel aduised my selfe, neither from what seruitude Christ by his bloud hath deliuered vs, nor of what libertie S. Paule speaketh. This being so, that is to say, if I were not wel aduised, but ouersene therein: you haue the more aduantage to replie. Let vs then see your rare cunning, great learning, and high deuise.

Ievvel.

Certain it is, Christ hath not deliuered vs from honest Ciuile Policies, vvithout vvhich no state neither Ecclesiastical nor Ciuile can be maintained: but from the curse of the lavve, vvherein vve reasted vnder sinne: and from the ceremonies and ordinances geuen by Moses, vvhich for that they vvere vveake according to the imperfection of that time, therefore S. Paule calleth them the Elementes of this vvorld.

Harding.

Three thinges you speake of, honest Ciuil policies, the curse of the lawe, Ceremonies and ordinances geuen by Moses. Frō the first you say, Christ hath not deliuered vs, but from the other two: of which the last S. Paule calleth Elements of this world. Now because place, which is vnderstanded when many communicantes be together, that you binde vs vnto, is conteined vnder the Ceremonies and ordinances geuen by Moses: therefore if for the enioying of the benefite which we attain by receiuing the Communion, we must nedes be together with many in one

 place:

place: I might wel say as I said, that we should notwithstanding the libertie which Christe hath set vs in, remaine in seruitude and subiection vnder the weake and poore elementes.

That condition of place is of the Ceremonies of the olde Lawe.

Exod. & Leuit. &c.

That Place is one special thing required by the Ceremonies and ordinances of the olde Lawe, and belonging vnto the same, it is euident by the bookes of the olde Testament. For there we finde, that some thinges were commaunded to be done in the court of the Tabernacle, some at the doore, some in the entrie of the Tabernacle, some within the Tabernacle, some at ẏ Aulter where beastes were sacrificed, some at ẏ Aulter of the sweet perfume, some within ẏ Vaile, some without ẏ Vaile, some in ẏ Tent, some in Sancta Sanctorũ, Finally, at lẽgth they might not sacrifice but in the Temple, and three times in the yeare they were bounde to come to Ierusalem there to make their Oblations. To the like seruitude of place, M. Iewel would driue vs, who doth forbidde vs to receiue the Communion, onelesse there be a number of Communicantes together in one place. In consideration whereof, as S. Paule rebuked the Galathians for obseruing times, so he might rebuke vs for obseruing places. Thus is the necessitie of his number receiuing together in one place displaced, as a thing Iewish, if Place be conteined vnder the Ceremonies, and ordenaunces of the Lawe appointed vnto the Iewes.

Galat. 4.

That nũber of com municãtes be together in one place is by M. Iewels graunt but a Ciuile policie

But you say, that your number of Communicantes together in one place, is but an honest ciuil policie. And this semeth here to be your resolution. Very wel. The same wee accept. But then must you vnderstand, that if it be a ciuil policie, it may be altered and changed, as the gouernours of the state thinke it conuenient, to whose commoditie that ciuil policie serueth. And euen so it is in very dede. For somtimes the people receiueth with the Priest, as at Easter, and at other high feastes,

and

and when els any be disposed : some times when none are disposed, he receiueth alone, for in any wise receiue he must when so euer he consecrateth and offereth. That diuersitie (we see) the custome of the Churche hath of longe time approued. And so though the people be seldome ready and worthily proued to Communicate Sacramentally with the Priest, yet is the vnbloudy Sacrifice of the Churche by the Prieste the Churches publike Minister in that behalfe oftentimes to be offered, and Masse to be celebrated according to Christes commaundement geuen to Priestes at his last Supper.

Ievvel.

Here M. Harding semeth by the vvaye, to touch the Englishe Translation of the Bible, vvhich calleth such Elementes Beggarly Ceremonies, *him selfe being not able to translate it better. And yet if he vvere vvel apposed, I thinke he vvould hardely yeelde any great difference betvvene the Greke vvorde* πτωχὰ, *and the Latine vvoorde* Egena, *and this English vvoorde* Beggarly. *Vvhich vvoorde if it seeme to homely, yet S. Hierome in his exposition is as homely, calling * it* Vilem intelligentiam Traditionum. *And yet the Prophetes abase it further. Hieremie calleth such Ceremonies so abused, and others diuised by Men, Chaffe, Svvill, Drosse, and Dreames: Esaie, Filth: Zacharie, Curses: Ezechiel, Mans doung. And other like.*

The.90. vntruth. S. Hierō calleth not the ordinā ces of Moyses Law so.

Harding.

I must looke for smal curtesie at your handes, I see wel M. Iewel, sith that you are disposed to reproue not only what I saye expressely, but also what I seeme to touch by the waye. where you can not abyde any thing of your Gospelling procedinges so much as to seeme to bee touched by mee, and that but by the waye, not of professed purpose: Howe will you abyde to see the Chiefe partes of your new Gospel, partly by me, but much more by others, and onely touched, but also launced, cutte, pearced through, hewed, and quite throwen downe to the grounde? what? you are very nice and tender, that could not beare with me reporting S. Paules wordes, infirma & egena elementa, to signifie weake & beggarly Ceremonies after the English Bibles translation. Are you come of their race, who are called, you know by whom, Genus irritabile vatum? Are you so waspish?

M. Iew. nice tendernesse.

But touching the thing it selfe, why semed I to you, to touch your English Bibles translation for turning the Apostles word πτωχὰ in Greke, Latined egena, into this worde beggarly, rather then for turning the other word στοιχεῖα, elementa, elementes in english, into this worde Ceremonies? Thinke you not, that the one is with as litle reason called in the translation Ceremonies, as the other is with semelinesse englished beggarly? If the terme beggarly liked you and your fellow Gospellers wel, whereof I striue not much with you: wherefore chaunged you the most conuenient worde in that place Elementes, into Ceremonies? why would you not egena elementa, to be englished beggarly elementes?

Elemēta englished Ceremonies.

Doubtlesse that ye might the rather bring al holy Ceremonies into contempt and despite, against which you beare endles hatred: you liked better for poore or needy Elementes (for so S. Paules owne wordes do signifie) to put in your publike translation, *beggarly Ceremonies*, that the sound of so vile a word oftentimes falling into ŷ peoples eares, might driue into their hearts a vile estimation of al Ceremonies of holy Church. For this your vntrue Translation I am sure your defence is but beggarly. But let vs see, first what good reason you haue to turne πτωχὰ, egena, paupertina, as S. Hierome termeth, into beggarly, and not rather into poore, or nedy: Next, why ye turne στοιχεῖα

In cōment in 4. caput ad Galat.

elementa

elementa, into *Ceremonies*, rather then into Elementes, or Beginninges, for so S. Hierome also sheweth it to signifie.

There is no great difference (say you) betwene the Greke and Latine worde, and the English woorde Beggarly. Yeas Syr by your fauour, there is so great difference, that whereas the one is applied to our Sauiour Christe, the other may not so be applyed without offence of godly eares. S. Paule saith of Christe, Propter vos egenus factus est, cum esset diues: vt illius inopia vos diuites essetis. Though he were rich, yet for your sakes he became poore, that ye through his pouertie, might bee made rich. The Greke hath the same worde, which you haue turned into beggarly. Now I report me to the Christian eares, whether they would not glow and be offended, if any would be so impudent, or rather impious, as to say, that Christe was beggarly, and that we are enriched by his beggarlines. Aske M. Iewel of any poore body that requireth your Almose, what he is, be it man or woman: and you shal heare answered I warrāt you, I am a poore man, a poore woman, or a poore creature, and not I am a beggarly mā, a beggarly womā, a beggarly creature. The worde being such as importeth a contempt, and soundeth not grauely in so sadde a mater: the translation had been more conuenient, if for egena, ye had put Poore, and not *Beggarlye*, specially the Greeke worde being πτωχὰ, not πτωχικὰ, which rather soundeth your terme Beggarly.

Of the terme Beggarly

2. Cor. 8.

πτωχὰ, πτωχικὰ

And seing that Heretikes, as S. Hierome saith, of that we cal Moyses law weake and poore Elementes, take occasion to say euil of the Creator, because he hath created the worlde, and made the lawe: we should rather cal the lawe poore Elements, then Beggarly Elementes, for that so we should minister further occasion to the Heretikes to blaspheme our Creator.

In cōment epist. ad gal. cap. 4.

A reason why we should turne the Greeke woorde πτωχὰ, Poore, rather thē Beggarly.

That this worde should not seme to vs ouer homely, you allege S. Hierome, saing that he in his exposition is as homely, calling it, (whereby you meane Moyses lawe) vilem intelligentiam Traditionum. But you falsifie S. Hierome after your cōmon manner. S. Hierome in that place speaketh not of the ceremonies and ordinances geuen by Moyses, where of you speake: but of the Iews Traditions, and of their wrong vnderstanding of the lawe according to the letter. which Iuish vnderstanding of the law according to ỹ outward letter, he calleth vile. You haue altered the words of S. Hierome to frame a sētence to your purpose, wheras he hath no such order of words as you allege, vilem intelligentiam Traditionū, but otherwise. Neither calleth he the law it selfe vile and beggerly, as you do, but the misse-vnderstanding of the lawe according to the letter, he calleth vile in comparison of the spiritual vnderstanding.

Ibidem.

M. Iew. falsifieth S. Hierō.

Why the translatours of your English Bible haue turned the Greke worde στοιχῖα, elementa in latine, into *ceremonies*, you shewe no reason, nor in deede none haue you to shew, for which, as wel as for your vnsemely woorde beggerly, I might haue noted the translation. First although the ceremonies of Moyses lawe were elementes, yet elementes signifie not ceremonies, the worde is more general. And seing that the Apostle calleth the thinges here weake and poore elementes, after the minde of S. Hierome, which in the first parte of the chapter he calleth the elementes of this world: whereof mention also is made in the epistle to the Colossians: what reason had the Translatours, here to turne the worde *Ceremonies*, and there, *ordinances*? Verely by good reason they should not haue turned the woorde neither ordinances nor ceremonies. For beside that the Greeke worde doth not properly so signyfie, the place being this in

στοιχῖα, elemēta, not wel englished *ceremonies.*

Coloss. 2.

S. Paule,

S. Paule, quomodo conuertimini iterum ad, &c. how is it that ye turne againe to the weake & poore elementes: ẏ Galathiās could not turne againe to the ceremonies of Moyses law, because they had neuer ben accustomed vnto them. For they came to the faith from Paganisme, and not from Iudaisme. Galat. 4.

But because before their conuersion to the faith of Christe through S. Paules preaching, they worshipped the Sunne, the moone the Goddes of the hilles and ẏ woddes, and other vaine thinges of the worlde after the superstition of the Heathens: S. Paule might wel saye vnto them, howe is it, that ye turne again vnto the weake and poore Elementes? Thus is that place to be expoūded, if by the word elementes, such Ethnicke superstitions be signified. Els if the lawe of Moyses be signified, then is the word taken metaphorically, & beside his special proprietie, and signifieth Rudimentes, principles, and beginnings. which signification of the worde lyketh your one Maister Caluine better, then an other. In cōmēt. Neither is that beside the minde of S. Hierome. For God whose fore purpose was at the time by his wil appointed to cal the worlde vnto perfite knowledge of the truth, would in the meane time instruct and teache men with these rudimentes and principles as it were of Moyses lawe, and for that purpose he vouchesaued to set vp a schoole in one only corner of the worlde.

The lawe of Moyses and the Prophetes saith S. Hierome, may be taken for the elements of letters. Ibidem. For as we learne the letters not for any profite of them only, but of an other thing: to thintent by ioyning syllables and wordes together, we may come to the reading and vnderstanding of speaches, sentences, orations and bookes, in which the sense and order of wordes is more considered, then the beginninges and order of letters: Right so by Moyses Lawe, by the Ceremonies and ordinances thereof, and by the Prophetes, men were lead vnto the knowledge of Christ, and learned a further lesson by the law, then was founde in the outwarde letter of the lawe. In this sense where the elements of this world by the interpretation be the lawe and the Prophetes, this worlde is taken for them that

2.Cor.5. be in the worlde, as in S. Paule, God was in Christ reconciling

Iohan.1. the world vnto him selfe: and in the Gospel, the world was made by him, and the worlde knewe him not. Thus you see M. Iewel, what good occasion I had to touch by the way your English Bibles translation, which hath for poore or needy Elementes, *beggerly Ceremonies.* which you might ful wel haue dissembled, but that your gilty conscience would nedes bewray the offence.

The Prophetes whom here you allege without notice of place, applied not those wordes of vilenes, to ẏ cotempt of Moyses lawe and ordinances whereof mention was made: but of mennes inuentions, fantasies, and traditions contrary to Gods ordinances, whereof the place treated conteineth no mention. And therefore is your reporte of the Prophetes wordes of reyling, quite beside the purpose.

Ievvel.

To condition of a place, saith M. Harding, vvere mere Iuish: for as S. Paule saith to the Galathians, ye obserue monethes, and daies, *so might he say vnto you, ye obserue places. Thus he saith, as though he him selfe had no choise of place to say his Masse in.*

Harding.

Choise of place to say Masse in, is of Ecclesiastical order.

Let my wordes be considered, as I vtter them, not as you disorder them: and then replie against them what you can. Here you say nothing, that is worth the answering. That we haue choise of a place to say Masse in, I graunt, what conclude you thereof? So haue you choise of a place to dine and suppe in, and choise of a place to slepe in. But this haue you by ciuile order, and

and that other haue we by ecclesiastical order. That we haue a certain place appointed for the celebration of the Masse, it is not of Christes Institution, but of mans ordinance. And therefore we thinke not our selues bounde so straightly in this case, but that when occasion so requireth, by licence ordinarily obteined, we may change the ordinary place, which is a consecrated aulter in a consecrated Churche or Chappel, and hauing that by order is requisite, may say Masse in a priuat house or chamber, in a tente or pauilion.

If you acknowlege your number of communicantes which you require to be together to receiue the Sacrament with the Priest in one place, to be likewise not of Christes Institution, which may not at all be broken, but of mans ordinance, and so to be of mere ciuile policie: then we agree wyth you so farre. For so is it not of necessitie and invariable, as Christes commaundementes and Institutions be: but of congruence, and so as in certaine cases it may be changed. Therfore there is no offence committed touching thys point on the priestes behalfe, when lacking a number to receiue wyth him in the same place, at hys Masse he receiueth the oblation alone, though so he cōmunicate not alone, which thing being graunted, as you M. Jewel haue here before graunted, in that you referre the place to Ciuile policie: it remaineth that you reuoke your first Article, and inueigh not so much agaynst priuate Masse. Els if you bynde the priest neuer to receiue, but when he hath a number to receiue with him: thē because many can not receiue with him but in the same place, you bynde him to necessitie of place for the enioying of the benefite, which we receiue by taking the blessed Sacrament.

Marke wel the point M. Jewel that we agree in, and that other point in whiche we dissent. That there bee a number of Communicantes, and that many do communicate, I graunte. *The point wherein M. Jew. and we dissent.*

But that the Sacrament be not receiued of one alone in a place but that many come together into one place to receiue, as though els it were no communion: that I denye. That a number of communicantes was at Christes supper, it is graunted. That a number should alwayes receiue with the priest, that is denied & can not be proued. Idētitie of place for Cōmunicantes to receiue together in, is denied to be of Christes Institution, or otherwise of precise necessitie: to be of great congruence, it is not denyed. When so euer you replie, if you proue not this, and that substantially, and clerely: you proue nothing. Which if you proue not, then ought you to subscribe vnto the approbation of the blessed Masse. You nede not for this to trouble the worlde with bookes of much talke, of which sorte your Replie is, ful of wordes for shewe to the simple, and emptie of iust proufes. A sentence or two, or three at the most, wil serue your turne, if you haue them.

Ievvel.

He moueth talke of place, vvherof vve had no question: but the number of Communicantes, vvhereof S. Paule so plainely speaketh, he thought best to salue vvith silence.

Harding.

How much it is necessary that they who receiue the Sacrament together, be in a place together: so much perteined the talke of place to the purpose. Touching the number of communican-
1. Cor. 11. tes, & what is to bee thought of the saying of S. Paul to the Corinthians, and how those wordes, expectate inuicem, *Waite ye one for an other*, be to be vnderstanded of the church feastes, and not of receiuing the Sacrament specially: hereof I haue spoken before in the 8. Diuision.

See the last diuision.

Page. 34. Lin. 1. After this M. Iewel entreth into a common place of rayling, and cryeth out after his preaching maner *O good reader*: & vttereth grieuous mater against vs, that we haue defiled the Lordes Sacramentes

cramentes with superstitious ceremonies, that we burthen the peoples cōsciences with choise of meates, that we kepe Priestes, Monkes, Frieres, and Nonnes, from Mariage, and lay an intolerable yoke vpon them, that we teach the doctrine of deuils, & many other deuilish maters, that I liste not here to reherse. For answere wherunto I remitte the Reader to my Confutation of their Apologie. The most pointes and in maner all here so bitterly cryed out vpō, there haue I sufficiently answered. Now let vs see what fault els he findeth with vs.

Ievvel.

Hovv be it M. Harding hath vvel disclosed him selfe herein, that this libertie is nothing els, but to do vvhat him listeth: & his bōdage nothīg els, but to be subiect vnto God. For he addeth immediatly, that the mingling and blinding of vvater and vvine together, & thintentiō of the priest, are thinges necessarily required to the Consecration of this Sacrament.

Harding.

Do you not see M. Iewel, what a foolish argmēt you make? He that answered your Chalenge saith, these thinges be necessarily required to this Sacrament by Christes Institutiō, either declared by written Scriptures, or taught by the holy Ghost, bread and wine mingled with water for the mater, the due wordes of cōsecracion for the forme, and the priest rightly ordred hauing intention to do, as the Churche doth, for the ministerie, for these be the wordes there: Ergo he hath disclosed him self herein, that thys libertie is nothing els, but to do what him listeth. In my Answer. Fol. 15, b

How proue you this argument good sir? How hange the partes together? where lay your Logike, when you laid forth this simple Rhetorike? You shoulde haue spoken better reason, or haue holden your peace. Your owne Prentises, who are your chiefe fauourers, can not but mislike this your vnsauoury talke.

Wel syr, of the foure thinges requisite to this Sacrament, you take vpon you to deface the estimation of two, the mixture, and the priestes intention. Therof specially of the one thus you say.

Of mingling vvater vvith the vvine in the Sacrifice.

Ievvel.

The.91. Untruth. Thys is false, for yͤ olde fathers make accōpt of it.

*Of the first hereof (that is to say of mingling vvater vvith the vvine) the superstition only excepted, *no man maketh any great accompte. In dede S. Cyprian and certaine olde fathers speake of it, and force it much: and Iustinus Martyr calleth it* ποτήριον ὕδατος καὶ κράματος, *the cuppe of vvater and mixture.*

Harding.

Cyprian. contra Aquarios. Iustin. in Apolog. 2. M. Iew. cōtrarieth him selfe.

Why do you except superstition? Who euer complayned of superstition committed, in that the wyne is tempered with water? But Syr, wrote you this in your dreame? Hange your sainges together beter then a sicke mans dreame? *S. Cyprian in dede* (say you) *and certayn olde fathers speake of it, and force it much: yet no man maketh any great acccompt of it.* Is S. Cyprian no mā? Are the olde fathers no men? Yea they speake of it, (and o Lord how ernestly speake they of it, specially S. Cyprian) and force it much: yet will you say, they make none accompt of it? He that speaketh of a thyng so seriously, and forceth it so much, as S. Cyprian doth thys, maketh he no great accompt of it? What make you the blessed Martyr and learned Bishop S. Cyprian a dissembler? An Hypocrite? a double man? Wyll you haue vs beleue, that he vttered all the force he coulde to persuade thys mater of mingling water vnto yͤ wyne for yͤ holy oblation, & yet cared not greatly whether it were obserued or no? Made he not any great accompt of it? How could he otherwise signifie yͤ great accompt accōpt he made of it, thē so to write of it as he wrote to Cecilius? Saith he not that our Lord him selfe both so did at his Supper, & commaunded so to be done? Saith he not, Non mane, sed post cœnam mixtum calicem obtulit Dominus, That not in the morning, but after Supper, our Lorde offered the mingled cuppe? Saith he not also there, that he was admonished of our Lorde, that the cuppe which is offered vp in commemoration of him, be mingled with water? To proue that, doth he not shew by many similitudes of the Fathers of the olde Testament, and by testimonies of the Prophetes, the same to haue ben before signified? Briefly is there any thing more earnestly treated and persuaded of S. Cyprian, then this mixture of water with the wine in the celebration of the daily Sacrifice? Yet saith M. Jewel, no man maketh any great accompt of it. What is a manifest Contradiction, if this be not? Beleue him good Reader in the rest of his doctrine, as thou seest cause to beleue him in this.

Cyprian. li. 2. epist. 3

Contradiction.

Ievvel.

*But neither *Christ, nor any of his Disciples, euer gaue commaundement of it: neither vv is it at * any time in the Church vniuersally receiued, or accompted necessary. For Scotus and Innocentius vvitnesse, that the Greke Church in their time vsed it not. Vvherefore it can not be iudged Catholike.*

The. 92. Untruth both christ and the Apostles ordeined it, as here it is proued.

The. 93. vntruth. the contrary is reported by the 6. general coūcel.

Harding.

That it is not expressely written in the Gospel: I graunt. That Christ commaunded it S. Cyprian semeth to say. For he calleth it our Lordes Tradition, and Diuinitus institutū, a thing instituted by God, he saith that our Lorde both did it, and also taught it. He seemeth to recken it among those commaundementes, which he calleth in comparison of the least, Tam magna, tam grandia, tam ad ipsum Dominicæ passionis & nostræ redemptionis Sacramentū pertinentia mandata: So great, so weighty,

Mixture of the chalice, is our Lordes Traditiō.

 com-

Synod 6. Can.32. comaundements, & so much perteining to ẏ Sacrament of our Lords passion & of our redẽption. The learned Fathers of ẏ vi. general Cōucel cal it, Ordinem diuinitus traditum, An order deliuered to the Church by God. They saye also that it was a Tradition of ẏ Apostles, & that it was obserued in al the Church, where spiritual lightes haue shined. You must beare with vs M. Jewel, if we esteme S. Cyprians aucthoritie, and that general Councel more then your bare saying.

A tradition from God. A tradition of the Apostles. The mixture of the chalice obserued in al the Church.

If it be a Tradition of our Lord, as S. Cyprian saith it is, if it be deliuered by God, and by the Apostles, as the sixth Councel reporteth: then may we reasonably thinke, that the Apostles, when they offered the diuine Oblation, vsed to mingle water ŵ the wine, as Christ taught them both by his example, and by his tradition, and that they deliuered the same to their posterite. Verely S. Clement declaring the manner how Christ offered at his Supper, saith thus. Likewise mingling the cuppe of wine and water, and cōsecrating it, he gaue it vnto thē, saying, drinke ye al, &c. S. James mentioneth the same in his Liturgie: S. Basile likewise in his Liturgie, and S. Chrysostome also in his.

Clemens Constitut. Apost. lib. 8. cap. 17. Liturgiæ Iacobi. Basilij. Chrysost.

Neither vvas it at any time saith M. Jewel, *in the Church vniuersally receiued, or accompted necessarie.* This we deny. How can he proue it? *For Scotus and Innocentius* saith he, *do vvitnesse that the Greeke Church in their time vsed it not.* I marueil how he can be so bold, as to scoffe so cōmonly at other mens Arguments, ẏ maketh such peeuish Arguments him self. what Child would reasō thus? Scote and Innocentius do witnesse, that mingling of wine and water in the Oblatiō was not vsed among the Greeks in their time, which was of late yeares: Ergo it was not at any time in the Church vniuersally receiued.

Io. Scot. in 4. sentent. dist. 11. quest. 6. Innocent. de officio Miss. part. 3. c. 4.

Although it were not vsed of the Greekes at that time, might it not haue ben vsed generally at other times before?

If he had inferred, Ergo it was not vniuersally receiued and vsed of the Church at that time, he had wel concluded, this being supposed, that the Grekes were not by schisme departed from ye church: but now yt he cōcludeth, ergo it was not at any time vniuersally receiued, he sheweth him self to vse very simple Logike.

What so euer Scote saith hereof touching the Grekes, it is of no better auctoritie then yt is which Innocentius reporteth, for him doth Scote allege. Now Innocentius saith no more but this. Græcorum Ecclesia dicitur aquam non apponere Sacramento. The Greeke Churche is said not to put water vnto the Sacrament. Whether it were so or no, he doth not affirme it, onely he telleth what is reported. Now if this report were not true, as many such made of Countries farre of be vntrue: then M. Iewel beside the losse of his best Argument, hath lost his whole cause touching that point.

Answer to Scotus & Innocentius.
De officio Missæ. lib. 4. cap. 6.

But what forceth it what the Grekes did for three hundred yeares past, who were then fallen into schisme and heresie touching Procession of the holy Ghoste? The example of Schismatikes and Heretikes ought not, ne may not be alleged to the preiudice of any doctrine, ordinance, or custome of the Catholike Churche. And here it is to be considered, how litle good reason M. Iewel vseth for maintenance of his vaine Chalenge, that bindeth vs to the compasse of the first six hundred yeares after Christe for prouse of the Catholike doctrine, and he for disprouse of it, vsurpeth helpes of al ages and al writers, be they neuer so litle worthy to be estemed. Therefore notwithstanding the Grekes contrarie schismatical vse, the mingling of the sacred cup may wel seme to haue ben vniuersally receiued in ye Church, and that it was Catholique.

M. Iew. runneth to schismatikes and heretikes for helpe.

Witnesses prouing the mingling of wine and water to haue been vniuersal.

For good prouse herof, we are wel able to shew, yt this was receiued in the west Churches, first in Europa, by ye testimonies of S. Clement, who liued with the Apostles, and was bishop of Rome:

Clemens. lib. 8. c. 17

Alexāder Papa. Rome: of S. Alexander Pope and Martyr neare the Apostles time: of S. Ireneus lib. 5. who came to Lions in Fraunce, and was Byshop there: of S. Ambrose Bishop of Millan, lib. 4. De Sacramentis, cap. 5. & lib. 5. cap. 1. Of the Councel Arausican holden in Fraunce, Can. 17. of the thirde Councel of Braccara in Spaine, Can. 1. Then in Africa by the testimonies of S. Cyprian ad Cæcilium aboue alleged: of S. Augustine De dogmat. Ecclesiast. dogmate. 75. of ye third Councel of Carthage. can. 24.

Iræn. lib. 5. Ambrose. Cō Arausi. Concil. Braccarē. Cyprian. August. Cō. Car. 3.

Then in the East Churches, as in Hierusalē, and Syria, by the testimonies of S. James Liturgie: of S. Iustinus the Martyr, in Apologia. 2. of Eusebius Emisenus, Homilia. 5. de pascha: of Damascenus. lib. 4. cap. 14: In Asia the lesser, by testimonies of S. Basile in Liturgia: of Gregorius Nyssenus, in Sermone Catechetico, as it is alleged by Euthymius in Panoplia. lib. 2. titul. 21: of the Chapters of the Greke Synodes. cap. 55.

Iacobus in Liturgia. Iustinus. Euse. Em. Damascen Greg. Nys.

In Grece, and other countries of the East Church, by testimonies of S. Chrysostome, in Liturgia, Homil. 84. in Iohan. & Homil. 24. in 1. Cor. Of the sixth general Councel, where there was a special decree made therof against the Armeniās: can. 32. of Theophylactus in Iohan. cap. 19. I trow these are testimonies sufficient, to counteruaile the vncertaine hearsaye of Innocentius tertius alleged by Scote, for proufe that the custome of mingling water and wine together in the Sacrifice, was generally receiued.

Chrysost. Concil. 6. Constant. Theophylactus.

The 94. vntruth. Neither I say so.

Ievvel.

And touching the necessitie thereof, Scotus saith in plaine vvordes. Huic vino apponere aquam non est simpliciter necessarium de necessitate Sacramenti. *Here vve see these Doctours agree not. M. Harding *saith, this mixture is necessarie to the Sacrament, *Scotus saith it is not necessary.*

The 95. vntruth. nor Scote saith so. M. Iew. hath falsified both our saings

Harding.

If you had englished Scotes wordes, your falsifieng would haue

haue appeared. He saith not, this mixture is not necessary: but, is not necessary simply or absolutely of the necessitie of the Sacrament.

In 4. Sent. dist. 11 in fine.

M. Iew. falsifieth Scotus by nipping away the wordes that make directly against him

Scotus and I agree. For although he say, to put water to the wine, it is not simply necessary, that is absolutely and without any exception, so as it be not a Sacrament, if in some case the water be omitted: yet he saith in ye same place, which beside al plaine dealing you dissembled and leaft out: est tamen de necessitate ministri, it is necessary on ye behalf of the Minister, for that it is cōmaunded by the Church, & because Christ consecrated the cuppe wherein water was mingled with wine, as S. Cyprian in his Epistle to Cecilius, and Damascenus do say. And I say that to this Sacrament are necessarily required, bread and wine mingled with water for the mater.

Damascenus lib. 4. cap. 5.

Now wil you see how we agree? Scote saith the mingling is not simply necessary of the necessitie of the Sacrament. I say the same. For so I learne of S. Cyprian, who saith thus. If any of our predecessours by ignorance or simplicitie haue not obserued that, which our Lorde both by example and instruction hath taught vs to do: his simplicitie may be pardoned by our Lordes fauour. But we can not be excused, who now be taught of our Lorde to offer the cuppe mingled, as our Lorde offered. S. Cyprian would neuer so haue pardoned ye omitting of that which he had knowen simply and absolutly to be necessary of the necessitie of so great a Sacrament.

Scotus and I do agree.

Cyprianus epist. ad Cæcil.

Scote saith, it is necessary, de necessitate ministri, on the behalfe of the Minister, that is to say, it is necessary, that the Minister offer so, and none otherwise. I say so also. And to that pertaine these my wordes, necessarily required to the Sacrament for the mater, I say not, absolutely of the necessitie of the Sacrament, but necessarily required to the Sacrament for the mater, because, that the Sacrament be so consecrated and offered, it is, required on the Ministers behalfe. And if he do not mingle water with the wine, he synneth deadly. And therfore I might wel say therof, that it is necessarily required to the Sacrament. For I say not, as M. Iewel falsifieth my wordes, this mixture is necessary to the Sacrament, but speaking of thinges that be necessarily required to the Sacrament, I name bread, and wine mingled with water for the mater. A thing may be necessarily required to a Sacrament, because of the precept of the Churche, wherunto the Minister is bounde, and yet the same not simply of the necessitie of the Sacramēt: As certaine things be to be vsed at the Sacrament of Baptisme, which among the Gospellers we see lefte vndone: yet that notwithstanding it is a Sacrament in it selfe perfite. This had M. Iewel acknowledged, and therfore had not noted any disagreing betwen Scote and me: if he had ben so desirous to vtter the truth, as he was disposed to gainesay me, and to control my sayinges.

M. Iew. falsifieth my words In my boke, page 15.b.

Iewel.

The .96. vntruth. The powring of the water on the groūd is no part of our mysteries.

Novv to reuele the secretes of M. Hardinges Mysteries touching the same: that one droppe or tvvo must be poured on the grounde. &c.

Harding.

What wise man wil not thinke a fooles coate and a babul fitter for this Hicke Scorner, then a sad answere? But syr, remember, you scoffe not at me, nor at my Mysteries, but at the Church the spouse of Christe, once your Mother, now as you vse her, your icasting stocke, whom you haue wickedly forsaken, & now do dishonor with much worse villanie, that euer did Cham his Father, or Iudas his Maister. You belye our Mysteries, the powring of one droppe or two on the grounde, is no parte therof. As some haue so done for a cleanesse, so of the most sorte it is

Gen. 9.

not

not done. But thus it appeareth what litle good mater you haue to charge vs with al, that for stuffing of your booke, you are dryuen to fynde fault with a droppe of water poured on the groūd. were you in these parties, you should not see that to scoffe at, but the water reuerently taken out of a cruet with a litle syluer spoone. Thereof you may iudge how litle accompt is to be made of that, whereat you make such a prety sporte. The rest of your foolish scoffes wherwith you haue made your selfe mery in this Diuision, I contemne. Beware you meete not with such one day, as shal ieast you out of your coate.

M. Iew. leueth not without a scoffe so much as a droppe of water poured on the grounde.

Here, as this Bicke scorner goeth forth in his scoffing at holy thinges, so he vttereth good store of lyes. whiles he scoffeth at the Intention of the Priest, among other vayne toyes he saith thus.

Ievvel.

*Novv it *appeareth, that the Church is not yet resolued vpon one Intention. For the Intention of the Church of Rome, is to *vvorke the Transubstantiation of Bread and Vvine: The greke Church had neuer that Intention, as * is plaine by the Councel of Florence. The Intention of the Churche of Rome is to consecrate vvith Christes vvordes: The Intention of the Greke Church is, to *consecrate vvith prayers. And vvhether of these churches the priest shal folovv vvith his Intention? This is the very dungeon of vncertaintie.*

The. 97. vntruth. No such thing appereth, for herein the church is resolued. The. 98. vntruth. The. 99. vntruth. There is no such thing ther made plaī. The. 100 vntruth. That is not the Greke churches intention.

Harding.

As this ieaster hath said what his scoffing head could deuise against the mingling of water with the wine, that ought to serue for the mater of the Sacrament: so here also with like malice he saith what he can against that the Catholike Church teacheth touching the Intention of the Priest. But altogether vntruly, and so as becommeth a prophane mocker of the holy Mysteries.

It appeareth saith he, the Churche is not yet resolued vpon one Intention.

Yeas Syr, it appeareth right wel by the common custome, doctrine, consent, and publike profession of the whole Catholike Church, that touching the blessed Sacrament of the aulter, it is resolued vpon one vniforme Intention. Which is to do that Christe at his supper did, and commaunded his disciples, and their successours likewise Priestes of the new testament to doo, vntil his comming. That is, due mater had, with the wordes of Christe to consecrate his body and his bloud. What haue you to say to the contrary?

the church is resolued vniformly vpon the Intētion of ẏ priest.

Iewel. *For the Intention* (say you) *of the Churche of Rome is to vvorke the Transubstantiation of Bread and vvine. The Greke Church had neuer that Intention, as it is plaine by the Councel of Florence.* Do you scoffe and dally M. Iewel herein after your common manner? Or speake you soothly, and as you thinke? If you dally, it becommeth not the mater, if you speake in sooth, and as you iudge: then are you of the number of them, whom S. Paul reproueth, who vnderstand not neither, what thinges they speake, neither whereof they affirme. The Intention of the catholike Church, which for spite you cal the Church of Rome, is not by any vertue or power of man to worke the Transubstantion (as it liketh you to terme it) of bread and wine. It intendeth not so to do, that of it selfe it can not do.

1. Tim. 1.

The work of Transubstantiation is to be ascribed only vnto God.

To worke the transubstantiation of bread and wine principally, or to change the substance of any thing in to an other substance, it passeth mans power of him selfe. It is God only that both createth substances, and turneth the substance of one thing into the substance of an other thing. What man doth herein, he doth it onely as the Minister of God. The Intention of the Church is to consecrate the body and bloud of Christe with the

wordes

wordes of Christe pronounced by a Priest, by vertue of which wordes the substance of the bread is changed into the substance of our Lordes body, and the substance of the wine is changed into the substance of his bloud. The worke of this marueılous and diuine Transubstantiation is to be abscribed to the power of the holy Ghoste working by the worde as the author, and to the Priest pronouncing the worde as the Minister. Hereof S. Chrysostome speaketh notably saying. Non sunt humanæ virtutis hæc opera, quæ tunc in illa cœna confecit: ipse nunc quoq; operatur, ipse perficit, ministrorum nos ordinem tenemus: qui verò hæc sanctificat, & transmutat, ipse est. These workes be not of mans power, which Christe wrought at that supper: he it is that now also worketh, he performeth, as for vs, we do but holde the order of Ministers: but he it is him selfe that sanctifieth & chaungeth these thinges.

Chrysosto. hom. 83. in Matt.

Whereas you say, the Greke Church had neuer that Intention, if you meane Intention to consecrate the body and bloud of Christe: it is starke false, and you belye the Greke Church. It hath euer intended in the celebration of the dredful Mysteries (so S. Chrysostome and others cal them) to do as the Latine church doth, that is to say, to consecrate the body and bloud of our Lord. Which thing appeareth euidently by the Liturgies of S. Basile, and of S. Chrysostome, and by sundry places of S. Chrysostome, and the other greke Fathers workes, as partly I haue before declared. In dede the worde of Transubstantiation (I graunt) is not common to the Greke church, as neither was it to the Latine church before the Councel of Laterane: but the faith and doctrine which the worde or terme implyeth, hath euer from the begynning ben common to both Churches: that is, when these wordes of our Lorde, This is my body, this is my bloud, be duly pronounced by a Priest: that then the bread is changed and con-

The faith of Transubstantiation generał to al times, and places.

 uerted

uerted into the body, and the wine into the bloud of Christe.

M. Iew. reporteth a great vntruth of the Councel of Florence.

But that the Greke church had neuer that Intention, you say, it is plaine by the Coũcel of Florence: and that al men might be witnesses of your vntruth, you referre the reader vnto the last Session of that Councel. Read the last Session, or the whole Florentine Councel, who wil: he shal fynde nothing, wherby it may appeare, that the Greke church had neuer this Intention. This much we fynde there in dede, that, when the Grekes had accorded to the Latines touching the Procession of the holy ghost out of the Sonne, for which spetially that Coũcel was assembled, also touching the Popes Supremacie, Purgatorie, and the indifferencie of bread for the Sacrament, whether it be leuened or vnleuened, so it be of wheate, to thintent the one church should not condemne the other for the diuersitie of bread: after al these maters ended and agreed vpon, the Pope there present required, the question of the diuine Transmutation of the bread to be debated in the Councel.

The question of Transubstantiatiõ was moued to be debated in the Councel of Florence, but not treated of at al.

To this demaunde the Grekes made answere, that they had no auctoritie to treate of any other question, without a Commission of the whole East churche. Yet they promised to referre it to Palæologus their Emperour of Constantinople at that time present in Florence. But both he and the Greke Bishops being weary of their long tarying from home, and desyrous to returne to their countrie, fearing that if they entred once into reasoning of that question, they should tarry there longer then they would: hauing after mature disputation graunted and agreed to the other foure pointes that were proponed: they refused to dispute and treate further of any other point. And so was the question of Transubstantiation left vntouched in that Councel. And this is al that is reported thereof in the

last

last Session of the Florentine Councel. Uerely of this, or any thing that there is said, M. Iewel can not with any reason conclude, that the Greke Church had neuer the Intention, of which I haue now spoken.

And whereas he sayth, that the Intention of the Greke church is to consecrate with Prayers, if he meane that the Grekes consecrate not with Christes wordes: this is as false as that he said before. Touching this mater, it is plainely declared in the last Session of that Florentine Councel, that when the Latines had demaunded of the Grekes, why after the wordes of our Lorde by which Consecration is beleued to be made, they vse to say also this prayer: Et fac panem quidem hunc. &c. And make this bread the honorable body of thy Christe, and that which is in this cuppe the honorable bloud of thy Christe, thy holy spirite changing them: They answered, that they beleued stedfastly, the Sacrament to be made and consecrated with the wordes of our Lorde: But as the Latines after that the Sacrament is Consecrated, vse to say this Prayer, Commaunde O Lorde these thinges to be borne vnto thy highe aulter by the handes of thy holy Angel: Euen so, the Grekes (said they) be wont to pronounce those wordes, that the most holy body and bloud of Christe may be made to the remission of our synnes, and saluation of our soules. Thus farre be the wordes of the Councel.

Whether the Greke church do consecrate with prayers, as M. Jewel meneth, or with our Lordes owne wordes.

Sessione vltima Concilij Florētini.

Loe M. Iewel, they answered, that the Greke church stedfastly beleued the Sacrament to be made, and Consecration to be perfited by the wordes of our Lorde, this is my body, this is my bloud, pronounced by the Priest. This then being true, as for trial of it I referre me to the Councel it selfe, as it is set forth:

what remaineth but that you recant your notorious lye made vpon the Greke church, that their Intention is to consecrate with Prayers, and not with Christes wordes?

Can you haue any better witnesse hereof, then the Councel it selfe? If you replie for some colour of your defence, that Nicolaus Cabasilas, and one or two moe besides were of that opinion, what is that to your purpose? what are two or three to the whole Greke church? If singular errour were in some, what proufe maketh that against the whole? Neither speake you of a fewe deceiued Schismatikes, but of the Greke church. And what so euer they haue said for thauouching thereof, it is very sufficiently and substantially confuted by the learned Greke Cardinal Bessarion. For your parte therefore M. Iewel, I must here be so bolde as to tel you, that lyes make no proufe. If they could iustly serue to that purpose, then were my booke by your Replie amply confuted. Use more truth, when so euer you intend to write hereafter, els you are like to go vnanswered, and so running by your selfe alone, you may soone winne the game.

Nicol. Cabasilas.

Lib. de Sacramento Eucharistiæ.

lies make no proufe.

The remnaunt of this Diuision, I thinke not worth the answering, wherein you make sport with argumentes of your owne forging, and with this absurditie, as though I had said, that Christe had delyuered vs from the creatures of the worlde, which I say not, but from the Iewish seruitude of Elementes, where the Institution or commaundement of Christ maketh not their vse necessary. I doubt not but the reader shal see al sufficiently confuted, and be satisfied, for ought that you say to the contrary, if he take the paynes, after that he hath reade the wordes of your Replie, but to peruse againe with good aduise, what I haue said in my booke.

The xiij. Diuision.

BEcause M. Iewel findeth fault with the Masse specially for the single Communion, and for that the Priest doth Communicate alone: in my Answere I say, that ye Priest doth not communicate alone, when he receiueth the Sacrament at Masse alone, but with al others that receiue els where, though they be as touching place, neuer so farre distant. For the proufe of this in the xiij. Diuision I allege a saying of Cyrillus. who writeth, that our Lord blesing vs that beleue, with his owne bodie through the mistical Cõmuniõ maketh vs one body both with him selfe, and also betwen our selues. The Body of Christ in the Communion receiued, he calleth a meane deuised by our Lorde, wherby to vnite and ioine vs to God, and our selues one to an other, though we be distant in bodie and soule. For this cause the Priest doth not Communicate alone. The cause then remoued for which M. Iewel reproueth the Masse, it remaineth, that he yelde & subscribe according to his promise. The whole place which in this Diuisiõ is to be read more plainly and more at large, M. Iewel would faine auoide, if he wist how. The best shift he could deuise, is this.

Fol. 16. a.

Cyrillus. lib. 11. in Ioan. c. 26.

Ievvel.

*If M. Harding can proue that this same Cyrillus euer said priuate Masse, or in any of al his vvorkes once vsed the name of Masse, I vvil gladly yelde to the vvhole. But if Cyrillus neuer spake vvorde of the Masse, hovv is he here brought in *to proue the Masse.*

The .101. vntruth. Cyril. is not here brought in specially to proue the Masse.

Harding.

Why Sir beare you such malice to the Masse, that for ye Masses sake, except I proue vnto you (and that so as your selfe wil alow it to be sufficiently proued which I beleue you neuer mind to do what so euer I bring) that Cyrillus said Masse, you wil not yelde to a point of true doctrine, auouched by many other Fathers besides? what reason haue you herein? what if you and I varied about the doctrine of Baptisme, and I for confirmation of the Catholike faith therein alleged Cyrillus: would you not yeelde vnto it, onelesse I coulde proue, that hee in his time ministred the Sacrament of Baptisme? As for the name of the Masse, how absurde and foolish a thing is it, to require it to be shewed in the writinges of Cyrillus, who wrote not in Latine, but in Greke? But it is an easy thing for you to mocke the ignorant, and by wordes to make shew of an answer, when in dede you haue nothing reasonably to answer.

The communiō ioineth vs together, though we be in sundry places.

Neither was Cyrillus brought in directly and chiefly for proufe of the Masse, but against the necessitie of the Communicants comming together or being together in one place. whom, though they be distant in body and soule, and therefore also in place: yet Christ blessing them wᵗ his owne body through ẏ Mystical Cōmunion (as Cyrillus saith) maketh one body both with him selfe, & also betwen them selues. wherby it is proued ẏ the Priest receiuing alone at the Masse, for which cause of Luther, it was first called Priuate, doth notwithstādīg communicate with others. And therefore the Masse is defended from that, for which the Gospellers of these dayes, specially condemne it, inasmuch as the Priest though the people be not disposed to receiue with him, doth not yet communicate alone.

You M. Iewel hauing a desire to reproue & deface al that I say, be it neuer so true: and being loth I should seeme to your disciples to say any thing in defence of the Masse, that were not by you controlled: for colour of some maintenance of your glorious Chalenge, not being able otherwise to impugne the doctrine which in this place I confirmed by the aucthoritie of the auncient and learned byshop Cyrillus: you thought it ye best policie, to make your Replie against ye truth by me auouched, with an other truth. wherein you laye forth a shew of disprouse of my sayinges and in dede disproue them not at al. For a truth can not be disproued by an other truth, neither can one truth putte away an other.

M. Iew. would disproue one truth by an other truth.

As you procede, you take greate paines to proue, which no man denyeth, that by faith wee are incorporate and made one Body with Christ. Truth it is, through Faith, Christ and we are one Body Mystical, he the head, we the members. This is so wel knowen and so thorowly agreed vpon, that there was no neede, why you should vtter a sentence of your owne, and, that it might be of better aucthoritie, to father it vpon Cyrillus. For where you say thus, *Cyrillus saith that as many as beleue in Christ vvhether they be farre or neare, Ievves, or Gentiles, free or bond: they are al one body in Christ Iesu:* although this be true in it selfe, yet is it false that Cyrillus saith so. For the wordes be yours and not his.

Iewel.

Likewise where you say, that *Christ by the Sacrament of regeneration hath made vs flesh of his flesh, and bone of his bones,* and impute it vnto S. Chrysostome, though the saying be true in a right sense: yet is not that said by that holy father with the same termes as you allege. You might be borne withal for vsing such libertie to the prouse of a truth, were not that you abuse it oftentimes to the prouse of sundry vntruthes.

In Epist. ad Ephes. Homil. 20.

Forth you procede & bring in the wordes of Paulinus, and of S. Augustine witnessing ye by faith we are incorporate & ioyned vnto Christ, which is not denyed. At length you come to vtter those wordes, wherby you would confirme your Sacramētarie heresie, hauing intent to proue, ye we receiue not ye body of Christ in the Eucharist verely and in dede, wherby we are vnited vnto him according to the flesh: but onely by faith and in spirite.

In epist. 31. ad August.

we are vnited and ioyned vnto Christe ij. wayes. spiritually onely, and according to the flesh

Here this much is to be considered. That we be vnited and ioyned vnto Christ, two wayes, spiritually or according to the spirite onely, and according to the flesh. This is of the Fathers called, vnion, vnitie, coniunction, Communion, in corporation. Spiritually we are of the auncient and best learned Fathers reported to be vnited, knitte, and ioyned together, by faith, by charitie, by wil, by grace, by obedience of Religion: this coniunction is named Spiritualis vnitas, Spiritual vnitie, or the vnitie of wil.

Spiritual vnitie.

Natural & perfite vnitie.

An other way we are ioyned and vnited vnto Christe, as Cyrillus and S. Hilary say, Secundum carnem, according to the flesh, non habitudine solum, but also by natural Participation. This vnitie or cōiunction is of the Fathers called a natural vnitie, a perfite and consummat vnitie: and the same is wrought by receiuing the flesh of Christe in the Mystical Communion.

You M. Iewel do exclude the natural vnitie, and that cōiunction which we haue with Christe according to the flesh, and harpe onely vpon that string, which soundeth altogether the spiritual vnitie. But sith we are ioyned vnto Christ, and made one Body with him, both Spiritually, and Corporally: you labour in vaine by prouse of the one coniunction, to exclude the other.

Cyril in Ioan. lib. 10. cap. 13.

We denie not (saith Cyrillus, as before I haue alleged) that wee are ioined vnto Christe spiritually by right faith, and sincere Charitie: But that wee haue no coniunction with him after the flesh, verely that wee denie vtterly, and saie, it is wide from the Scriptures. For prouse hereof, heare Paule (saith he) saying: that al we be one Bodie in Christe. For although wee be many, yet in him wee are one. For all wee take parte of one Breade. What troweth hee (hee meaneth the Arian Heretike) we knowe not the vertue of the Mystical

blessing

Mystical blessing? Which when it is in vs, doth it not cause, that Christe dwelleth in vs also corporally by the Communicating of Christes flesh? And there within a fewe wordes after, Our Sauiour also saith: he that eateth my flesh, & drinketh my bloud, dwelleth in me, and I in him. Wherof it is to be considered, that Christ is in vs not by inward or spirituall dispositiō only, but also by naturall participation. There he compareth the vnion and coniunction that is betwen Christe and vs through the communion, to the coniunction of sundry waxes molted together and so mingled into one. *Ioan.6.*

Of this vnitie and coniunction S. Hilary speaketh much in his eight booke de Trinitate. Where hauing said that Christe is in vs by truth of nature, because in our Lordes meate we receiue verely the worde made flesh: He concludeth thus. Si verè igitur carnem &c. Then if Christe tooke to him the flesh of our body verely, and if that man, which was borne of Mary, be Christe verely, and we receiue the flesh of his body vnder the Mysterie verely, and through this shalbe one thing, because the Father is in him, and he in vs: how is the vnitie of wil auouched (by the Ariās) where as the naturall proprietie through the Sacrament, is a Sacrament of perfite vnitie? There at large he proueth this vnitie and coniunction of vs with Christe, not to bee vnitie of will, or spiritual only: but in dede, perfite, & according to nature, through the Mystical Communion. That I may vse the more breuitie here, I referre the reader to that eight booke de Trinitate, where S. Hilarie speaketh more largely hereof. *Hilarius de Trinitate lib.8.*

As, that by faith and charitie weare incorporate and ioyned vnto Christe, I graunte and confesse: so that we be not also by an other meane incorporate and ioyned vnto him, and knitte together, as it were into one body: I denye. That other meane of this *The meane of our* natural and perfite vnitie with God, is ye worthy receiuing of Christes body into our bodies in the Cōmunion.

this vnion, which the Fathers in consideratiō of the further perfection it is of, cal natural and perfite: is the worthy receiuing into our bodies of the body of Christ in the mystical Communion. That Christe (saith Cyrillus) might vnite euery one of vs within our selues, and with God, although we are distant both in body & soule: yet he hath deuised a meane cōuenable to the father, and to his owne wisedom. And wilt thou knowe reader what this meane is? There he sheweth saying. Suo enim corpore credentes per Communionem mysticam benedicens, & secum, & inter nos vnum nos corpus efficit. For in that he blesseth them which beleue with his own body through the mystical Communion, he maketh vs one body both with him selfe, and also betwene oure selues. This meane whereby this vnitie that we speake of is wrought, is special: and is not vsed in that vnitie, coniunction, or incorporation, which is spiritual onely. In dede this presupposeth that. For except we be first spiritually vnited vnto Christe by faith and charitie, the receiuing of his body in ye mysticall Communion, shall further separate vs from Christ, frō God, and from the Church Christes mystical body, and be to our condemnation, as S. Paule saith.

In Ioan. lib. 11. cap. 26.

1. Cor. 11.

M. Iew. laboureth to disproue our natural vniting with Christ, by proufe of our spiritual vniting, & so to beare ouer one truth by another truth.

Seing then there is a double incorporation, vnion, and coniunction of vs with Christe, and of vs with our selues, the one spiritual onely, and the other natural, & according to the flesh, as I haue now declared: M. Iewel by the affirmation of the one going about to induce the denial of the other, doth vntruly, and guilefully, besyde reason, besyde learning, besyde ye doctrine of the Fathers, besyde the scriptures. The better to proue the spiritual vniting onely, and to denye the vniting according to the flesh, he cōfesseth the spiritual eating of Christes body, which we also confesse: and denieth the corporall and real eating, yea any eating at al with the seruice of the body. And therof saith thus,

Ievvel.

*Neither may vve thinke that Christes body must grossely and *bodily be receiued into our bodies.* The. 101. Untruth. We must beleue y Christes body is bodily receiued into our bodies as here it is proued.

Harding.

Syr you use craft to ioyne these two wordes grossely and bodily together. We receiue Christes body bodily, because we receiue it into our bodies, and that by the seruice of our mouth, and therfore bodily, for els how coulde we receiue it into our bodies? But grossely we receiue it not, as the Capharnaites imagined, that is tu say, so as we eate beefe or mutton by peecemeale from the shambles. First let vs see by what scripture, reason, or Fathers you proue, that we must not eate the body of Christe bodily, that is to say, by the seruice of the body. And then shal you heare, what I can allege for the affirmatiue parte. *Ioan. 6.*

Ievvel.

*S. Cyprian *saith,* It is meate not for the belly, but for the mynde. *And S. Augustine saith,* Crede & manducasti. Beleue in Christ, & thou hast eaten. *And Cyrillus that is here alleged, vvriteth thus against the obiections of Theodoritus.* We do not mainteine the eating of a man, vnreuerently drawing the myndes of the faithful vnto grosse and prophane imaginations: neither do we submitte these thinges vnto mans fantasie, that be receiued onely by pure & tryed faith. *Therfore saith Athanasius.* It is spiritual meate, and spiritually is digested in vs. *Thus is Christe set forth vnto vs in that most holy Supper, *not to be receiued vvith the mouth: for that as Cyrillus *saith, vvere a grosse and profane imagination: but to be imbraced vvith a pure and a single faith.* The. 103. Untruth. S. Cyprian saith not so. *Cyprian. de cœna Domini. De consec. Dist. 2. Vt quid.* The. 104. Untruth. That not is no true. The. 105. Untruth. Cyrillus speaketh not of the due Sacramental eating of Christes body with the mouth, but of the grosse eating of a man called in greke Anthropophagia.

Harding.

Here you pretend to allege S. Cyprian, S. Austine, Cyrill, & S. Athanasius. And what so euer they say, it proueth not at al your erroneous doctrine, which is, that we must not eate the body of Christe bodily, to witte with our mouth, for so your selfe do expounde it. First S. Cyprian is falsly recited. In his Sermon de cœna Domini, he hath not those wordes. And yet you haue alleged them vnder the name of S. Cyprian in ẏ Sermon more then once in your Replie, likewise they that patched together the Apologie, haue alleged it, as S. Cyprians. wherin what part you haue, you knowe. The more, the vntruer man you haue shewed your selfe to the worlde. Like it is, that touching this saying by you fathered vpon S. Cyprian, you gaue to much credite to your note booke.

M. Iew. doth attribute a saying to S. Cyprian, that is not S. Cyprians.

But if S. Cyprian had so said, as we cõfesse the sayinge to be true in a right sense: how could you therof conclude your purpose? If Christes body bee not receiued in the blessed Sacrament to thintent to fil the belly, but to feede the soule and body to immortalitie: wil you say therfore, it must not be receiued with our mouth, & with bodily seruice? By what Logique make you that argument good? Know you not that there be two wayes of eating the body of Christe, spiritual, and Sacramẽtal? As he is eaten spiritually without the seruice of the body, so can he be eaten Sacramentally otherwise thẽ by the seruice of the body? Of those the one excludeth not the other, as the spiritual vnion of vs with Christe, excludeth not the natural vnion, or that which is according to the flesh. This kinde of argument and reasoning is very simple, where the affirmation of one truth, is brought to proue the denyal of an other truth. As if one woulde say, M. Iewel is wel sene in colours of Rhetorique, ergo he is not profoundely sene in the sciẽce of Diuinitie: you would reply, it were fõdly reasoned, for you might be wel sene in both, as sundry auncient Fathers haue ben. And if I would so argue, I dare say, besyde reproue of the weake argument, you would shew your selfe angry

Two waies of eating the body of Christe, spirituall, and sacramentall.

M. Iew. auoideth one trueth by an other truth.

with

with the whole tale, were ech part of it neuer so true.

As for S. Augustine, where he saith, Crede, & manducasti, beleue, and thou hast eaten: it proueth that eating of the flesh of Christe which is by spirite onely, to be without the seruice of the body, which is not denyed. But that Christes flesh is not verely and really also eatē by the seruice of our body vnder the forme of bread, it proueth not. *De conse- crat. dist. 2. vt quid.*

Concerning Cyrillus, you haue alleged him vntruly, and farre otherwise then he wrote. So haue you falsified him to like euil purpose, you, or who so euer of your felowes was author of the Apologie. The whole place maketh most directly against your Sacramētarie doctrine, and against that which you would here so fayne proue. Because the opening of this whole point, and ful answere vnto it, requireth many wordes, and I haue already treated thereof sufficiently in my Confutation of the Apologie: I thinke it not good to repeat againe here, that I said there, but for answere to direct the reader to that place. By good and due consyderation wherof, he shall vnderstand Cyrillus to be wholly on our syde, and in that place specially most contrary to the Sacramentaries. If the reader being him selfe vnlearned, conferre with some learned man to atteine the better vnderstanding of that I haue said there touching this place of Cyrillus: it shal not repent him. For it geueth great light to the further vnderstanding of this secrete Mysterie. Now these premisses seruing you to so litle purpose, your *Therfore saith Athanasius* with which you conclude, must nedes seme to be weake and of smal force.

M. Iew. doth falsly allege Cyrillus, and corrupteth his sense.

In my Confutation, Fol, 108. a. &c.

It remaineth, that I allege somewhat for the affirmatiue part, that is to say, that the body of Christe is receiued of vs not onely by faith, but also bodily, by our mouth, and so by the seruice of our body. First, touching scripture, how say you syr, do we not eate the body of Christ, as the Apostles did eate it? You deny it not I am sure. Then how did they eate it at our Lordes supper? Did they not eate it, as Christe bad them eate it? who denyeth? Then wheras Christe said after he had taken bread, and geuen thankes, take ye, and eate ye, this is my body: Did they not take it in their mouth and eate it? If you make faith the onely meane, wherby our Lordes body is eaten, then was it not to be delyuered with our Lordes hand. That which they did eat, they receiued from our Lords hand, and that which he bad them eate, he gaue them with his hand. Now both our Lord hath professed (as S. Hilarie saith) and we beleue the same to be his flesh in dede: but that which is eaten by faith only, is spiritual, and what is spiritual, it is neither geuen nor receiued with handes, but with spirite: therfore the body of Christe was not eaten of the Apostles, with spirite or faith only, but also with their mouthes, and with the seruice of their bodies.

Then the body of Christ is eatē of vs bodily.

De trinit. lib. 8.

Testimonies of the Fathers, for the bodily eating of the body of Christe.

But let vs see whether the Fathers haue acknowleged Christes body to be eaten bodily, and with the seruice of our body, and not by faith only. S. Ireneus saith, Quomodo dicunt carnem in corruptionem deuenire, & non percipere vitam, quæ à corpore & sanguine domini alitur? How say they that the flesh commeth into corruption, and taketh not life, which is fed with the body and bloud of our Lorde? Againe in an other place, How do they deny (saith he) the flesh to be of capacitie to receiue the gift of God, that is life euerlasting, which is nourrished with the bloud and body of Christe?

Irenæus. lib. 4. cap. 34.

Lib. 5.

Tertullians wordes be plaine. Caro corpore & Sanguine Christi vescitur, vt anima de Deo saginetur. The flesh eateth the flesh & bloud of Christ, that the soule may be ful fed of God. Let

Tertullian. lib. de resurrectionē carnis.

M.

M. Jewel shew vs, how the flesh eateth without a mouth.

Here haue we plaine testimonies, ŷ the flesh of man is fed & nourished with the body and bloud of Christ, & that our flesh eateth the body and bloud of Christe. If these fathers had said, that man eateth the body or flesh of Christe, perhaps M. Jewel wold haue made an only spiritual eating of it: now that they say it of the flesh, it cannot be vnderstanded so as the bodily eating, or eating with the mouth, be vtterly excluded.

Our flesh eateth the flesh of Christe.

S. Cyprian speaking of certaine, who had in time of persecution denyed Christ, & had eaten of thinges that were offered to Idols, & yet presumed to come vnto our Lordes table: saith, plus modò in Dominũ manibus atq; ore delinquunt, q̃ cùm Dominũ negauerunt. They synne more now against our Lord wt hands & mouth, then when they denied our Lord. How could S. Cypriã seme truly to haue vttered this saying, except ŷ body of our Lord were in dede receiued with handes, and eaten with the mouth?

Histo. tripart. lib. 9. cap. 30. August. ad Ianuariũ epist. 118. Cyprian. Serm. 5. de lapsis.

S. Chrysostome maketh mention of taking Christes body with our handes, and with our mouth in sundry Homilies.

Homil. 82. & 83. in Mat. & 24. in. 1. ad Corinth. & 60. ad poopul.

How wilt thou receiue the holy body of our Lord with such handes, saith S. Ambrose to Theodosius the Emperour, Qua temeritate ore tuo poculum sanguinis pretiosi percipies? with what temeritie wilt thou receiue with thy mouth the cuppe of the pretious bloud? It hath pleased the holy Ghost (saith S. Augustin) that for the honor of so great a Sacramẽt our Lordes body should enter into the mouth of a Christen man, before common meates.

Leo de ieiunio. 7. mensis. Serm. 6.

Ye ought so to Communicate of the holy table, saith S. Leo, that ye be out of al doubte touching the truth of Christes body and bloud. Hoc enim ore sumitur, quod fide creditur. For that thing is receiued with the mouth, which is with faith beleued. Mo testimonies might easily be alleged out of the Fathers for prouse hereof, were not these sufficient in a mater so manifest & certain.

That thig is receiued with the mouth, which is beleued with faith

Thus it is proued, that our Lordes body is receiued and eaten with the mouth, and not by faith only, as M. Iewel auoucheth, making much therein for the blasphemous heresie of the Arians.

This much being sufficient for answer to the chiefe pointes of this Diuision, passing ouer the rest, which is but mater impertinent, forged argumentes attributed to me after his common custome, misconstruing of Doctours, thwarting, wrãgling, and drawing of the plaine and most true saying of Cyrillus to a pretensed proufe of Priuate Masse specially, which was by me alleged against the necessitie of condition of place: Let vs now come to his. 14. Diuision.

The. xiiij. Diuision.

Here M. Iewel, as commonly otherwheres, slinketh a syde quite from the mater, and sheweth him selfe offended with certaine wordes of myne, which I inserted into a sentence by way of a Parenthesis. In those wordes he is noted to haue made a peeuish argument of the vse of Excommunication, and with certaine other childish reasons of that sort, to haue scoffed at some Catholike writers.

Touching the reproch of scoffing, his answer is, that he vsed the pulpite, as a place forsooth of reuerence, and not of scoffing. But how truly his reuerence hath therof discharged him selfe, I report me to his owne vnreuerent Sermon extant in Print. Which to euery indifferent iudge shalbe a testimonie both of his vanitie in making that proude Chalenge, and of his scurrilitie in vttering such store of scoffes. His peeuish argument made of the vse of Excommunication, wherin he thought the high estimation of his learning to be touched, he defendeth thus.

Ievvel.

Ievvel.

*Further touching Excommunication, I said thus. If the priest that saith Masse in Louaine, may communicate vvith the priest that saith Masse in Cælicute, vvhich is M. Hardinges greatest grounde for his priuate Masse: then hath the Church so farre forth as toucheth the priestes, lost the vvhole vse of Excommunication. For the partie excommunicate being a priest, *might say, he vvould say Masse, and so receiue the Communion, euen vvith the bishop of vvhom he vvere Excommunicate, vvhether he vvould or no. This saying hath M. Harding condemned for peeuish, by his authoritie only, not by reason.*

The. 106 vntruth. That might he not say, because he might not lawfully say it, for so he might not lawfully do, being excõmunicate,

Harding.

Syr you haue somewhat altered the wordes to your aduantage, and yet is your argument as peeuish as before. The same may thus be truly framed. An Excommunicate priest may say, he wil say Masse, and so receiue the Communion euen with the bishop that Excommunicated him, whether he wil or no. Ergo, the Church so farre forth as concerneth priestes, hath lost the whole vse of Excommunication. I appeale to your owne Logique M. Iewel, whether this argument be not very peeuish: neither are the peeces of it whole, nor hang they one of an other. For what if the Priest may say, he wil say Masse, and so receiue the Communion with his bishop, whether he wil or no: shal it folow of that his saying, that the Church hath lost the vse of Excommunication? Can one priestes vndue saying, depriue the Church of that due auctoritie? Verely the Church of Christ were a fickle and fraile thing, if with so light a blast of winde, her power so great and so weighty, were dissolued and broken.

Besides this, your antecedent is false. For the Priest which is duly Excommunicate, may not say, that he wil say Masse, and so receiue the Communion with the bishop, whether he wil or no. For that may he say only, which he may iustly say. And iustly he can not say it, For a priest Excommunicate is forbidden to say Masse: therfore he may not so say at al.

If you cauil and wrangle, replying, that he may so say, and also say Masse, because he is not excluded from it by case of impossibilitie: I answere, he is vtterly and simply excluded from habilitie or possibilitie lawfully and duly to say Masse, the band of Excommunication not being loosed: Otherwise he may say Masse so, as a man may steale, kil, and commit aduoutrie, who of God so to do is suffered. But then he saith it to his further damnation.

M. Iew. falsifieth the whole state of the mater by changing communicating into receiuing.

But Syr how conueigh you in this much, *and so (he might) receiue the Communion vvith the bishop?* I spake of communicating, and you falsifie the whole state of our mater, by turning communicating, into receiuing the Communion, I said of the Priest saying Masse alone, and at his Masse worthily receiuing the Sacrament alone, that he doth not communicate alone, but with other Christen folke worthily receiuing in other places. You pretend, as though I said, that receiuing the Sacramẽt alone, he receiued the Cõmunion with others, which word of receiuing tõ others, importeth the act done in one place. which I say not. For that were absurd: because ẏ receiuing of the Cõmunion together of many, requireth the being together of many in one place. But that many Communicate together, it is not of absolute necessitie, that they be together in one place.

A diuersitie betwen receiuing together, and communicatĩg together.

For the better vnderstanding of this point, this is that I meane. It is not one thing to receiue the Communion together, and to communicate together. For receiuing together doth determinate the identitie of the receiuers time and place. Communicating together, doth determinate the identitie of the thing, by diuerse receiued, and also of the receiuers. The first is called of S. Chrysostome commonly Μετοχὴ or μετάληψις, the second κοινωνία. Now as the outward acte of receiuing together is not done, but by them that be in time and place together, so the thing re-

receiued being one and the selfe same in sundry places, may be of many and diuers, enioyed together, though they be in distinct times and places. when mention is made of receiuing together, then this worde *together* determineth the outward act of receiuing, but when mention is made of Communicating together, the worde *together* hath respect to the thing receiued, to wit, the body of Christe: which being one, and the selfe same, in al that receiue it, maketh al the worthy receiuers to be one with it selfe, and within them selues.

Thus thē ther is ods betwen these two, to receiue ỹ cōmunion being ment therby the body of Christ, & to cōmunicate. The good & worthy only do cōmunicate in this sense, ỹ we vnderstād therby the receiuers to be made one wt Christe, the euil may receiue, though so they cōmunicate not. As Iudas receiued the cōmuniō with ỹ Apostles, but he did not (in this sense) cōmunicate, that is to say he was not incorporate & vnited to Christ, he did not enter into the common grace & benefite purchased by ỹ death of ỹ body of Christ wt the rest of ỹ Apostles. Euē so may your excōmunicate priest say Masse, & receiue the cōmunion, ỹ is, the body of Christ, (though not wt the bishop of whō he is excōmunicat, as you say, for what bishop wil suffer an excōmunicate person to receiue wt him) but thē vnworthily & wickedly he saith & receiueth against al order, & without ỹ feare of God, & to his condemnation. It is not inough for him ỹ is excōmunicate to say, ỹ he wil say Masse, & cōmunicate with any whether he wil or no: he must first be absolued, and then being disposed & duly proued, he may say Masse, receiue the Sacrament and communicate: els not. For els the true flesh and bloud of Christe may be receiued of him, and be in him, but how: as S. Gregorie saith, *essentia, non salubri efficientia*, in substance, not with holesom working. *Dialog. lib. 4.*

Thus the excōmunicate priest though he say Masse neuer so much, wel may he receiue the very body of Christe in substance, the helthful grace thereof wherby he might Communicate with Christe, and with the Church, so as he be made a member of that mystical body, and one with Christe: he receiueth not. And notwithstanding that his priuate presumption, if he be so desperate as to say Masse, and receiue the blessed Sacrament: yet is not the Church in danger to lose the whole vse of Excommunication, which M. Iewels peeuish argument falsly concludeth. And so for al his logique, rhetorique, or diuinitie, he hath not yet proued the contrary, but that a Priest which saith Masse at Louaine, or Sarisburie, doth Communicate with a nother catholike priest that saith Masse in Calicute.

How wel M. Iewel stode in his owne conceit for the deuise of this argument, it appeareth by that he singeth the same song agayne, where he saith at his conclusion thus.

Ievvel.

The. 107. vntruth. It is not my principle. I say not he mai receiue the Communion with others.

*Novv if M. Hardinges * principle stand for good, that the priest saying his priuate Masse, may receiue the Communion vvith al others in other places, that do the like: then can no priest be excommunicate. For not vvithstanding neither any other priest, nor any of the people vvil receiue vvith him, yet may he say a Priuate Masse, and by M. Hardinges nevv deuise straight vvay communicate vvith them al.*

Harding.

M. Iew. falsifieth my wordes

What nedeth this an answer being answered already? Yet this much may I say. It is an euident signe, that you are ouercome by force of truth, and yet wil not geue ouer for worldly shame. For not hauing what to say against that I say in dede, you fayne me to say that I say not, that you may seme to gainesay me. I tel you once againe, it is not my Principle, neither wil I haue it stand for good, that the priest saying his priuate Masse as you terme it, may receiue the Communion with al others in other places, that do the like. Read my wordes againe, though it be greuous vnto you so to be founde a falsifier. I speake nei-

ther

ther of priuate Masse, as who in dede acknowledge no Masse to be Priuate, nor of receiuing the Communion with al others in other places. Which implieth an absurditie, and impossibilitie. For can the Priest or any person receiue the Communion with al others in other places? Doth not the receiuing of one with others presuppose their being together in a place? For els how doth one receiue with an other? Now as al others besides some one person can not be together in one place, so neither is it possible, nor reasonably said, that one man may receiue the Communion with al others of other places, that do the like. For as receiuing signifieth the outward act of Participation, and requireth a being together of the receiuers in one place, so can al others neuer receiue together with the Priest. So many as be baptised do Communicate together in Baptisme, yet do they not receiue Baptisme together. So al Communicate together of our Lordes Body, but actually and outwardly they receiue not together.

The xv. Diuision.

Hauing saide before, that one may Communicate with an other, though they be in distinct places, and that it was thought lauful, and so vsed in ye Primitiue Church, in this.xv. Diuision I beginne to rehearse auncient testimonies for the same. First I recite S. Ireneus alleged by Eusebius, who writing to S. Victor Byshop of Rome, sheweth how the Bishops of that See vsed to sende the Sacrament to Bishops that came from forreine partes to Rome. Thintent thereof Ecclesiast. hist. lib. 5. cap. 26.

was, that by receiuing the Cōmunion their agreeing, consent together, and vnitie might be protested and signified. S. Ireneus wordes be there alleged. For view of which, & for the whole processe, I send the diligent Reader to the place of my booke. By which wordes it appeareth, that bishops comming from Asia to Rome, and the Bishops of that See, did communicate together before their persons met together in one place.

Fol. 16.b

If this be graunted, as by good witnesse it appeareth to be to be graunted: therof it foloweth ẏ the Masse is not vnlauful, wherat ẏ Priest receiueth ẏ Cōmuniō alōe, for which these Gospellers do condemne the Masse: sith notwithstanding he doth cōmunicate with others, that receiue in other places.

M. Iewel hauing litle to say hereto, before he come to the mater, fetcheth as it were a great floorish, as Maisters of Fence be woont to doo, before they playe in good earnest. In this floorish, hee letteth flee at holy and Blessed Martyrs freely. *Of the East and VVest Churches diuersitie in keeping Easter daye grevv contention* (saith he) *and the mater brake out into cruel heates. Victor vvas on the one side, and Polycarpus on the other side.* I thinke hee would haue said, if his memorie hadde not failed, *Anicetus* and *Polycarpus*: for the other twoo liued in sundrye ages. *S. Victor* by him *vvas a man* (forsooth) *of a fierie nature. S. Irenæus vvrote vnto him a sharpe letter, and handled him very roughly, and vsed not his stile of Superioritie, but called him and other bishops of Rome before him, by the name of Priestes.* At length after a sorte of blowes thus driuē at the most blessed Martyrs wherby to hurte their estimation in the conceit of ignorant Readers: he commeth to the mater, where he is as cold in answering the point, as he was in his extrauagantes hote to set Saintes at debate and strife. There he saith thus.

M. Iewels florish before he come to playe in ernest.

Ievvel.

But to the mater, These Bishops (*saith M. Harding*) *communicated together.*

together before they mette. If he meane in faith and Religion, it is not denyed. If in the vse of the Sacramentes, it is not proued.

Harding.

Syr my meaning is, not only that they agreed in one faith and Religion, but that they communicated together in the ecclesiastical and Sacramental Communion, the one by sending, the other by receiuing the Sacrament, in which was the Body of Christ vnder the forme of Bread. I meane the holy Eucharist, for so Ireneus calleth it. I speake plaine, what craft you meane by the vse of the Sacramentes, as you terme it, I know not. Eucharistia.

But you say it is not proued. To a contentious man it is hard to proue any thing, be it neuer so true and plaine, when he is desposed to wrangle. S. Ireneus saith, the Bishops of Rome sent the Eucharist or Sacrament to the Bishoppes that came from the Churches of Asia. To what purpose, but that it should be receiued? And by that receiuing the party that came from Asia communicated with the Pope, and signified him selfe thereby to agree with him in faith and Religion. For so to Communicate together, it was not of necessitie, that the one should come, and be at the others elbow.

Ievvel.

In my iudgement this vvorde Euchariſtia, *in this place of Ireneus, signifieth not the Sacrament already consecrate, but rather other common bread, vvherevvith one* Bishop *vsed then to present an other, as vvith a special token of consent in Religion, and Christian concorde: vvhich bread the receiuer aftervvard if he thought it good, might vse at the holy ministration. In that sense it semeth Paulinus vvrote vnto S. Augustine,* Panem vnum, &c. *Paulinus ad Aug. Epist. 35.*

Harding.

He that beleueth not the wordes of our Sauiour, Hoc est

M. Iewels vaine Gheasse. corpus meum, wil not beleue that the worde Eucharist, signifieth the Sacrament. Nay M. Iewel your priuate iudgement, or more properly to speake, your fansy is to light, & your gheasse to vaine, thus to make of the blessed Sacrament in S. Ireneus, none other but common bread sent for a present. Such presentes were in olde time called Eulogiæ, and Benedictiones, but that they were euer called by the name of Eucharistia, which is the special name of the blessed Sacrament, you shal neuer be able to proue. Neither were they sent, to thintent they should be consecrated, as your cōiecture is, for the loaues ȳ S. Paulinus sent to Licentius a yong man not yet Priest, shal sone control ȳ iudgement. Neither were such blessings, giftes, or presents, made of bread only, wherof mentiō is in certain epistles of S. Paulinus, one to Alipius, an other to Romanianus, which you or he ȳ gathered your notes for you report to haue ben writtē to S. Augustine: but also of other things, though specially of such whereby mā is fed: As it appeareth by ȳ we read in Gratian, where it is reported by Leo quartus, ȳ the Fathers had determined nothing cōcerning blessings or presēts to be brought vnto synodes: least the same might be an occasiō to Priests to withdraw them selues from cōming vnto them, ȳ they might not be put to charge. And S. Paulinus sent to Seuerus, not only Panem Campanū, Bread of Campania, where he was Bishop, but also a dish of Boxe.

Paulinus epist. 36. ad Roman. inter epist. August.

Epist. 35. & 36.

Dist. 18. c. de eulogijs

Paulinus epist. 31.

Verely S. Ireneus directeth his words to this end, to shew ȳ the Bishops of Rome who were before S. Victor, ioined them selues in ecclesiastical & Sacramētal Cōmuniō wᵗ the bishops of Asia, notwithstādinge thei held an other opiniō cōcerning the keping of Easter, then ȳ Church of Rome had. Now the ecclesiastical Communion is not made, nor is thought it can be made by any kinde of curtesie or humanitie, but by the Participation of the Body of Christe. For it may bee, that Presentes of

Paulinus epist. 1. ad Seuerū inter epist. Paulini.

common

common bread be sent from one to an other in tokē of frendship by such, as be not of one Communion. And as now the manner is to signifie loue and good wil by presenting wine, whē it happeth frēdes to be neare: so in olde time the Fathers vsed to send presentes of bread made in cakes or loaues one to an other, whē they where farre asunder, as it appeareth by the example of S. Paulinus and S. Augustine, who lyued the one at Nola in Italie, the other at Hippo in Afrike. And in very dede bread of his nature is such a thing, as conteineth in it a certaine resemblāce, signe, and token of vnitie, not only of ecclesiastical vnitie, which can not be but only betwen the membres of the Churche, but also of a certaine humaine and ciuile coniunctiō, which is wont to be common both to good and euil.

Againe this maketh specially against M. Iewels gheasse of common bread, that this name *Eucharistia*, which S. Ireneus here expresseth, is neuer wōt in the Fathers to be attributed vnto any bread, but only vnto the bread that is consecrated into the body of our Lorde. As for other breads how so euer they were halowed (as that bread which in olde time was distributed vnto the Cathechumens, and among the faithful people when they receiued not the Communion, wherof S. Augustine speaketh) how so euer they were holy and consecrated, yet they neuer obteyned the name of the holy Eucharist. To conclude, we can not admitte this light gleasse of M. Iewel, onlesse we wil also admitte the collection and reason which S. Ireneus vsed to persuade S. Victor to vnitie, to be not only vaine, but also ridiculous.

August. lib.2.cap. 26. de pec. merit. & remiss.

After many gheasses vttered to this ende, that *Eucharistia* in the place of S. Ireneus might not bee taken for the Sacrament, he commeth to his accustomed ieasting and scoffing. And yͤ same to performe the better, he fayneth as his manner is, an argument of his owne, & maketh gay sport at it, as if it were mine.

Ievvel.

This thing being graunted, that Eucharistia in this place of Irenæus be taken for the Sacrament, let vs novv see M. Hardinges reasons.

The Bishop of Rome saith he, sent the Sacrament vnto them, that came out of Asia: Ergo there vvas priuate Masse.

This conclusion is farre fette, and hangeth loosely. For I might demaūd, vvhich then of the three said Masse? He that sent the Sacrament, or he that receiued it, or els the Messenger that brought it? It vvere a straunge mater to see a Masse, and yet no man to say Masse.

Harding.

I allege S. Ireneus for proufe of Commu=nion amōg them that were in distinct places: & M. Iew. for answer scoffeth at the Masse

Wel scoffed. Make as good sport as it liketh your mery head, you scoffe at your owne selfe, not at me. For the argument is yours, it is not myne. That place is not alleged for priuate Masse, as you know well ynough, but for Communion among them that be in distinct places. Why scoffe you beside the purpose? Your pastime loseth his grace, for that it lighteth vpon no person. For no man hath so reasoned. You shewe your selfe to haue a prety grace in playing a mery vises parte, but pitie it is, the mater is not fitte for your sporting head.

Ievvel.

Verely Irenæus hath not one vvoorde neither of the communion, nor of the Masse: onlesse M. Harding vvil say, that mittere, *is Latine to cōmunicate, or* mittere Eucharistiam, *is Latine to say Masse.*

Harding.

The worde of S. Ireneus is, ἔπεμπον εὐχαριστίαν, mittebant Eucharistiam, they sent the Sacrament. To what intent but to be receiued? Ruffinus that turned Eusebius Ecclesiastical storye into Latine, who lyued in S. Hieromes time, and hath ben alwayes takē for a learned man, semeth to take the place for ẏ blessed Sacrament, in that he made translation of it thus, solenniter transmittebant, the Bishops of Rome sent them that came from Asia

Asia, the Sacrament solemnely, or with solemnitie. That a loafe of common bread should be sent with solemnitie, it hath no shew of reason. Now if it were not sent to be receiued, wherby a Cōmunion is proued, then shew vs to what other ende it was sent.

Ievvel.

If it vvere common bread, then vvas it but a present. If it vvere the Sacrament, then vvas it to be receiued, not streight vpon the vvay, or perhaps late in the night, or in the Inne at the common table emong other meates: but aftervvard at his pleasure in his Congregation.

Harding.

Is this the last shift you haue M. Iewel? How many holes wil you hide your selfe in like a foxe, rather then you wil be takē? Common bread is neuer in the auncient Fathers called Eucharistia. It was the Sacrament, how loth are you to confesse it? But it was not to be receiued say you, streight vppon the way, or late in the night, or in the Inne at the Common table among other meates. who saith, that so it was to be receiued? could you not appoint him, if it liked you, a more conuenient time and place, then late in the night, and the Common table among other meates? why might he not receiue it in a Churche, chapel, or in his chamber, kneeling on his knees, lifting vp pure handes vnto God, before he went to feede on Common meates, in presence of the priest or deacon that brought it, to thintent he might be a witnesse to the Pope of his receiuing?

M. Iew. starteth from place to place like a foxe, to finde hī a lurking hole.

And what meane you by his Congregation? Did euery Bishop in the primitiue Church, when ỷ Church had neither welth nor peace, bring his Congregatiō with him to Rome from Asia, that he might not receiue the Sacrament alone? You had rather (I see wel) make a fowle shifte, thē no shifte at al. But how litle al this serueth your turne, who perceiueth not that hath reason?

Ievvel.

But immediatly after folovveth a manifest mention, in vvhat order the Bishops vsed then to communicate together: vvhich thing M. Harding thought better to dissemble. Cum res ita haberent, communicabant inter se mutuò, & in Ecclesia Anicetus concessit Eucharistiã Polycarpo. *The matters betvven them standing thus, they communicated together: and* Anicetus *in the Church graunted the Sacrament, or the ministration of the Sacrament vnto Polycarpus.*

The.108. Untruth. S. Ireneus saith not so. read it again, & marke it better.

Here marke good Christian reader, then they communicated, saith Irenæus, vvhen they mette in the Churche, and not before they mette together, as M. Harding saith.* Anicetus, *as Irenæus* saith, receiued the Sacrament vvith Polycarpus in the Churche: and not as M. *Harding semeth to say, in his Inne or hosterie. Novv the truth of the mater stãding thus, vvhat hath M. Harding here founde for his priuate Masse?*

The. 109 Untruth. Neither ŷ saith he.

The.110. Untruth. I neither say it, nor seme to say it. For Anicetus cã not be thought to haue gone from his own house at Rome, vnto an Inne or Hosterie for that purpose.

Harding.

As M. Iewel here requireth thee good Christian reader to marke, so require I thee also to marke, and that with al diligẽce. For if thou do not, thou maist easily be deceiued. It is not altogether one thing (as I haue said before) a man to communicate with an other, and to receiue the Communiõ with an other, that is, outwardly to receiue the Sacrament in the same place with an other. A man may communicate with an other being distinct in place. They that receiue the Sacrament or Communion outwardly together, must be together in one place. M. Iewel by changing these wordes one in an others place, belyeth mee, and begyleth thee, and falsifieth the holy Fathers saying.

To cõmunicate & one, & to receiue ŷ communiõ is not al one thing.

This much is reported by S. Ireneus in the Epistle that he wrote to S. Victor, exhorting him by the example of holy forefathers, to deale mercifully with them of Asia, and not to excommunicate them for keping Easter vpõ an other day, then it was kept in the Church of Rome. Whẽ blessed Polycarpus (saith he) came to Rome in the time of Anicetus, they varied a litle about some

M. Iew. falsifieth S. Ireneus.

ſome other thinges, and alſo for this point of keping Eaſterday: yet they kept peace, and would not fal out one with the other in no wiſe. For neither could Anicetus perſwade Polycarpus to leaue that, which he had obſerued folowing S. Iohn, and other Apoſtles: neither could Polycarpus perſwade Anicetus to depart from the cuſtome of his forefathers biſhops of Rome.

Now folow the wordes in S. Ireneus, wherby it might appeare, that notwithſtanding this diuerſytie of myndes, they were at peace and vnitie one with an other. καὶ τούτων οὕτως ἐχόντων, ἐκοινώνησαν ἑαυτοῖς. That is to ſay, theſe maters ſtāding thus, they communicated the one with the other. Whether they receiued the Sacrament together in one place, or communicated before they mette together: by the Greke phraſe it can not without probable gaineſaying be determined. And here maketh the Greke a ful ſenſe, and endeth one parte of the ſentence. So here haue we a Communion betwen theſe two holy Biſhops.

Immediatly foloweth an other parte of the Periodus, as if it were a newe ſentence. It is this. καὶ ἐν τῇ ἐκκλησίᾳ παρεχώρησεν ὁ Ἀνίκητος τὴν εὐχαριστίαν τῷ πολυκάρπῳ κατ' ἐντροπὴν δηλονότι. Atq; in eccleſia conceſsit Anicetus Euchariſtiam Polycarpo honoris cauſa. As much to ſay in Engliſh. And in the Church, Anicetus yelded vnto Polycarpus for honors ſake, the Euchariſt, or the doing of the prieſtly office, for ſo it may rather ſignifie here, and ſo hath Ruffinus turned it, Sacerdotali miniſterio perfungi. And to do the Prieſtly office, what els was it, but to conſecrate, offer, receiue, and to deliuer the Communion, if others were diſpoſed to receiue, which is that we cal ẏ Maſſe: whether in the Churche S. Polycarpus miniſtred the Communion to S. Anicetus or no, I define nothing. Theſe wordes force it not. If M. Iewel were dryuen to proue it, as he boldly affirmeth it: for al his ſhiftes he ſhould leaue it vncertaine.

who so euer duly examineth this place, and considereth the order of the wordes, can not but iudge they communicated together, before they met at Church. Els how can he excuse S. Ireneus of vsing a preposterous order? For these wordes, καὶ ἐν τῇ ἐκκλησίᾳ, (that is to say, and in the Church) geue the reader to vnderstand an other thing donne before.

And though it were graũted, that S. Polycarpus ministred the Sacrament to ẏ blessed Pope S. Anicetus, yet whereof wil it appeare, that ther was a number of others to receiue besides? If none receiued but the two Bishops, how stãdeth it with M. Iewels doctrine to allow it for a lawful Communion, sith that the booke of common prayers to be vsed in the Congregations of England acknowledgeth none for a sufficient Communion, onlesse there be three to receiue with the Minister at least, be the parrish neuer so little? And the order of the Primitiue churche semeth to require, that al the people should receiue, or depart the Churche.

where you say then M. Iewel, and wil the reader to marke it, *then they communicated, saith Irenæus, vvhen they met in the Church*: there is one vntruth, for Ireneus saith not so, as I haue now declared. Againe. S. Ireneus speaketh those wordes of the special case of S. Polycarpe: And my words are spokẽ in general of the bishops of Asia that came to Rome. wherefore your Replie is not aptly applied to the purpose. And it appereth that S. Polycarpe was receiued of Pope Anicetus with a more special priuilege of honor for his singular worthinesse, then other Bishops of Asia of lesse estimation were of other Popes.

Furthermore where you say, *Anicetus, as Irenæus saith, receiued the Sacrament vvith Polycarpus in the Church: and not as M. Harding semeth to say, in his Inne or hosterie*: there be two vntruthes at once. For neither saith S. Ireneus the one, nor I ẏ other. And though

I might say, that S. Anicetus communicated with S. Polycarpus before they met together in one place, for asmuch as the one sent the Sacrament, and the other receiued it: yet that S. Anicetus receiued the Sacrament with S. Polycarpus, specially in an Inne or hosterie: I do not so much as seme to say it. Here you deceiue the reader by vsing the worde receiuing the Sacrament together, for communicating together.

Now the truth of the mater standing thus, what hath M. Iewel here founde against the Masse? whereas I on the other side prouing a Communion to be betwen men that be in distinct places, haue proued the Masse for ẏ cause is not to be condẽned for the Priestes sole receiuing. Because notwithstanding, he may at the same time Cõmunicate with others, that worthily receiue in other places.

The. xvi. Diuision.

HEre I continue to confirme that I went about to proue before, that many may cõmunicate together, who be not in one place together. For witnesse and proufe hereof as in the diuision, which M. Iewel maketh before this, I alleged S. Ireneus writing to S. Victor: so here I allege the knowen place of S. Iustine the Martyr in his second Apologie. Where he declareth, how in his time, after that the Seruice was done, and the people had ben houseled in the common place of prayer: the Deacons caried the Sacrament to them ẏ were absent, to the intent they should also be partakers and Communicate with the rest, as if they had not ben letted frõ being in the same selfe place with them, by sickenesse, busynesse, or by some other occasion.

In the primitiue Church, some were thought to communicate together that were not in one place together.

Who doubtelesse if they might not haue communicated with them, because they remained at home in their houses, and were absent from the companie of the rest gathered together in place of prayer: the Deacons had not ben commaunded to beare the Sacrament vnto them. For it should haue ben said, as M. Iewel now saith, it is no Communion, onlesse the partie that receiueth, haue a companie to receiue with him in the same place: Item, it is the Institution of Christe, that many Communicate together, and that none receiue alone. Hereof it foloweth, that in the Primitiue church they were thought to communicate together, who were in distinct places, and so to do was iudged to be no breach of Christes Institution. If there were a communion then betwen them notwithstanding the distinction of places, why may not the Priest now also be thought to Communicate with others that receiue in other places, when at his Masse they that be present, be not prepared to receiue with him? Thus it is euident, the priest at Masse doth not communicate alone, for which these great Gospellers storme so much at the Masse, and nedes wil cal it Priuate, whereas in dede the Masse it selfe in respect of the Sacrifice is not, ne can not be Priuate, though the receiuing of the Sacrament, be sole or priuate. So that it ought not to be called priuate Masse, but this act of receiuing may be called Priuate receiuing, for which the Masse is not made vnlawful.

Read who wil, the Replie of M. Iewel vnto this place of S. Iustine, And he shal fynde in effect nothing answered against the purpose, for which it was chiefly aleged: which was to proue, that some may communicate together, that be not in the same selfe place together. M. Iewel here pretendeth, as euery where els almost through this Article, that I haue brought this place for Priuate Masse. And if of euery thing by me alleged or said, the prouse of Priuate Masse (as he termeth it) can not immediatly be concluded in forme of a good argument, then he iesteth and

When M. Iewel is not able to auoid the force of my reasons or allegati and scoffeth out the mater, vseth tauntes for answeres, and silēce (concerning the force of the reason) for confutation.

Yet that thou haue iust occasion good Reader to consider, how faithfully he demeaneth him selfe in this place: two open and manifest vntruthes I shal disclose, that he is not ashamed to report as very truthes. The one is this. *The priest* (saith he) speaking of such order of Prayers as S. Iustine mentioneth,) *prayeth and geueth thankes in the *vulgare tonge.* which he shal neuer be able to iustifie, if by a vulgare tongue he meane any tong beside the learned tonges. This is his owne glose beside the text. The other is, that he reporteth me to say, *that euery Priuate Masse is common.* which I say no where: but that euery Masse is common.

After this I enter into an other mater, wherein by good euidence and witnesse I proue sole receiuing to haue ben vsed in the primitiue Church by sundry deuoute persons both men and wemen. And this much I professe to do, because M. Iewel (as there I say) is so vehement an ennemie to Masse calling it Priuate, for that the Priest receiueth alone. Al this he dissembleth, for any reasonable answer that he maketh to the contrary. And no maruel, for the mater being so certaine and so euident, how should not he be borne with al for saying so litle, where nothing was to be said? Yet somewhat he saith, least he should seme to say nothing, and so be required to yelde and subscribe.

ons, commonly he shifteth the mater of with saying: it proueth not Priuate masse

The. 111. Untruth. not in the vulgar tong of the countrie, where S. Iustine was born.

The. 112. Untruth. I say not so.

Fol. 17. a.

Ievvel.

M. Ievvel triumpheth, saith M. Harding, and maketh him selfe mery, as if he had vvoonne the feelde. No, no, M. Ievvel triumpheth not, but geueth al triumph, victorie and glorie vnto God, that vvil subdue al them that vvithstand his truth, and make his ennemies his foote stoole.

Harding.

O that God would subdue them quickely, that M. Iewel

 and

and the rest of his Companions may be staid from seducing the people, and from leading them to euerlasting damnation by their wicked doctrine. But syr, why altered you my wordes? If you would seme to answer them, reason would, you should haue reported them truly. But truth is the thing that least helpeth you. I say, you triumph as if you had woonne the feelde, making your selfe mery with these wordes, *vvhere then vvas the priuate Masse, vvhere then vvas the single Communion al this vvhile?* Why dissembled you these wordes? They be to be found in your sermon. Are you ashamed of them? And how could you not be ashamed of them, were you not shamelesse? But because you saw, what good number of testimonies I had brought for ye single Communion, as you cal it: you thought it best to let your boasting wordes be couered with silence, least by rehersal of thē, you should the rather haue vttered your owne ignorance, and vaine bragging. But what haue you to say to the witnesses of single Communion or sole receiuing, which you craked that no man was able to proue? You reproue the Masse because the priest receiueth the Communion without companie in the same place, that is to say for the single receiuing. But the single receiuing I haue proued to be lawful by good euidence: Then must you no more raile at the Masse for the single Communion or receiuing. Let vs heare what you answere to those witnesses.

M. Iew. changeth the sense bi altering my words as being loth his bragges should appear being thorowly confuted.

Ievvel.

*Excepting onely the fable of Amphilochius, and Iohn the Almonare, vvhich vvere not vvorth the reckening. I alleged * al the rest in mine ovvne Sermon. I knevv thē, and had vveighed them, and therfore I alleged them.*

The. 113. Untruth. He allegeth not al

Harding.

What is impudencie, if this be not impudencie? Because he wil nedes seme learned, and to be ignorant of nothing: he is not ashamed to say, that he alleged in his Sermon al the testimonies

M. Iewels impudencie in lying.

nies, which I bring in my booke for Sole receiuing, two only excepted? The booke of his Sermon is extant, any man may read it that wil. He allegeth not al the testimonies which I bring for proufe of Sole receiuing in the primitiue Churche. Onely he telleth that in the time of Tertullian, and of S. Cyprian, wemen commonly tooke the Sacrament home with them in their napkins, and laied it vp in their chestes, and receiued a portion of it in the morning before other meates, and this he telleth for an abuse of the Sacrament. Of al other so many testimonies, which in my booke I bring for prouse thereof, he toucheth not so much as one. Yet *I knevv them*, saith he, *and had vveighed them, and therfore I allegee them al in myne ovvne Sermon*. Now good Reader take the paines to peruse M. Iewels said Sermon, and if thou fynde not al these testimonies there alleged, as certainly they be not there to be found: then geue such credite vnto him, as an opē and manifest lyer deserueth. But let vs see what the force of those euident testimonies hath driuen him to graunt.

Ievvel.

That certaine godly persons both men and vvemen in time of persecution, or of sickenesse, or of other necessitie receiued the Sacrament in their houses, it is not denied, neither is it any parcel of this question.

Harding.

The sole receiuing of godly persons in their houses perteineth to this question. For wheras Priuate Masse as you cal it in that respect the receiuing is Priuate, is by your sect condemned onely for the priestes Sole receiuing, if it may be proued that deuoute persons of olde time receiued in their houses alone, and were not reprehended for it as breakers of Christes Institution, the breach wherof is not excused by any necessity ỳ may happē to mā if this may be proued, then is the Masse, whereat the Priest receiueth alone, for which Luther first of al men called it Priuate, not to be condemned. And so farre as this is proued, M. Iewel by his owne worde is bounde to yelde and subscribe. Hauing scoffed out the mater after his common mãner with a foolish argument or two of his owne forgerie, he maketh this reason, and layeth it for his chiefe grounde.

Ievvel.

The.114. vntruth. It was not abolished. The.115. vntruth. The Cōncel of Cesaraugusta was not general, but prouicial.

*This manner of priuate receiuing at home vvas not lavvful for the laie men, for it vvas *abolished by godly bishops in *General Councel: Ergo, it vvas not lavvful for the Priest to say priuate Masse.*

Harding.

What you meane by this manner of Priuate receiuing at home, I know not. Sure I am that godly folkes Priuate receiuing at home was both permitted in the Primitiue Church, and also wel alowed. And that sicke persōs should haue the Sacrament brought home to them, to receiue before they departed this life, it was ordeined by the Nicene Councel. The Councel of Cæsaraugusta, which you allege for General, was not General, but prouincial: it was kept but by twelue bishops of Spain. Neither was it there decreed, that no deuoute person should be honseled at home, or for any cause be permitted to receiue the blessed Sacrament priuately in his house: but that for auoiding certaine abuses, that then beganne to crepe in among the people, it should not be lawful for any person that had receiued the blessed Sacrament, to conueigh it away priuely, and not forthwith to consume it in the Church. Of Priuate receiuing at home, the Councel speaketh neuer a worde.

Nicen. Concil. ca.13.

The true meaning of the Canō by M. Iewel alleged.

The wordes of the Decree be these. Eucharistiæ gratiam si quis probatur acceptam non consumpsisse in ecclesia, anathema sit in perpetuum. If it be proued that any person haue receiued the

Concil. Cæsaraugust. Cap.3.

the

the grace of the Eucharist, and hath not cõsumed it in ẏ Church: be he a cursed for euer. Where by the grace of the Sacrament, doubtlesse those Fathers vnderstode the true body of Christe, which is the thing of the Sacrament. For neither could they cal bread by the name of grace, nor can a spiritual grace, what so euer the Sacramentaries wil make of it, be properly said to be consumed: but of the body of Christe, which in that Mysterie is eaten, in respect of the outward formes it may be said. Thus M. Iewels vntruth appeareth manifest, and by that prouincial Synode priuate houseling at home is not proued to haue ben abolished, as he saith it was.

The grace of the Eucharist.

Because M. Iewel pretendeth to haue great aduantage out of S. Iustinus Martyr against the Masse, let vs see whether it be so or no. *In Iustinus Martyr* (saith he) *is set forth the vvhole and plaine order of the holy Ministration vsed in the Church at that time.* Why then do ye not stand to that order, specially sith that he was so neare vnto the Apostles time, and so farre within the compasse of your first six hundred yeres? After that order the cuppe was mingled with wine and water. But, *neither Christe,* say you (in the .xij. Diuision) *nor any of his disciples gaue such commaundement. No man maketh any accompt thereof, the superstition onely excepted.* In your Communion this order is not obserued, neither thinke you it necessary. Yet you tell vs it was the plaine order of that Church, whereunto ye would now bring the whole worlde. The bread and wine mingled with water by that order were with the Mystical prayer blessed, and with the wordes of our Lorde, Christes body and bloud were consecrated.

Iustinus in Apolog. 2.

This is not obserued in your Communion. Water vse ye none. Bread and wine ye blesse not. The real presence of Christe ye beleue not. Consecratiõ ye intẽd not. In S. Iustinus time the blessed Sacrament was sent to them that were absent. *This manner of priuate receiuing at home vvas not lauful* (say you) *for the laie men. It vvas abolished in the Councell of Cœsaraugusta.ca.3.*

Thus you abbrige three partes of the whole, telling vs of an order, which was vsed in S. Iustinus time, that now in the time of your Gospel, and bragge of Reformatiō, ye vse not at al. How then do you cal vs backe againe to the order of the primitiue Church? For let vs compare S. Iustinus Masse (for so you cal it your selfe) with your new founde Communion. In S. Iustinus Masse the mater of the Sacrament was bread, wine, and water. In your Communion ye vse no water at al. In S. Iustinus Masse the body and bloud of Christe was consecrated. In your Communion there is no such Consecration. In S. Iustinus Masse was the oblation and Sacrifice. In your Cōmunion there is no such oblation and Sacrifice. In S. Iustinus Masse the faithful people receiued the body and bloud of Christe. In your Communion you teach them they receiue but bread and wine. In S. Iustinus Masse the blessed Sacrament was sent to sicke persons. In your Cōmunion it is not accōpted necessary, or any cruel iniurie at al: if ỳ sicke persons passe away, and departe this life without it. Al this being so, with what countenaunce can you allege ỳ authoritie of S. Iustinus Masse, to proue the antiquitie, and the right order of your Communiō, wherein ye haue thus forsaken the whole order of S. Iustinus Masse? Verely your new deuise whereof ye make so much, differeth from S. Iustinus Masse, nolesse then the shadowe from the bodie, then darkenesse from light, then prophane thinges from holy thinges.

S. Iustinus masse and M. Iewels Cōmuniō compared together.

The. 17. Diuision.

IN the. 17. Diuision I come to reherse testimonies for proufe of priuate receiuing, or single Communion, as M. Iewel calleth

leth it. I folowe the same in the.18.19. and.20. Diuisiõ. Thou wilt demaunde Reader perhaps, wherfore I haue so done. Understande I praye thee, that M. Iewel hath taken upon him to inueigh at the Masse specially because of the single receiuing, pretending it to be vtterly vnlauful and against the Institution of Christe. For this cause I thought good to fortifie this point with some good number of testimonies. Of the whole this much redoundeth. If M. Iewel haue no other special mater, for which he condemneth the Masse, but single or sole receiuing, who so euer can by testimonies of atiquitie proue sole receiuing to haue ben vsed, and not accompted vnlauful, he driueth M. Iewel either to recant, or to shew for what els he condemneth ye Masse. If ye shew ought els, he is promised to be answered, if it be worth the answering.

In this Diuision, as it hath pleased him to diuide my treatise, three testimonies for prouse of single receining be recited. The one is out of Tertullians second booke to his wife, the other out of S. Cyprians sermon de lapsis, the third out of the Ecclesiastical historie of Eusebius, reporting after what manner one Serapion was houseled before he departed this worlde. I referre the reader to my booke, that is desirous to vew & cõsider the places. To repeat againe here that I haue said there, were a nedelesse doubling of labour.

Testimonies for Single Cõmuniõ

Euseb. eccle. hist. lib.6.cap. 44.

Fol.17.b &c.

Ievvel.

M. Harding shooteth faire, but far from the marke. To proue priuate Masse in the primitiue Church, for lake of priestes he allegeth Tertullians vvife, certaine vvemen out of Cyprian, and Serapions boy: not the fittest people that might haue ben founde to say Masse.

A burthen of lyes.

Harding.

The praise of faire shooting, but far from the marke, I leaue to M. Iewel. I coneit not so much to shoote faire, as to shoote

t ij home

home, and strike the marke. Here ỷ marke that I shoot at, is single Communion, for which M. Iewel condemneth the Masse, and whereof with a vaine bragge he made his vaunt, *vvhere then vvas the single Communion al this vvhyle?* This marke whether I strike or no, I am content to be tryed by who so euer hath eyes to see, and reason to iudge.

In his sermon.

Yea M. Iewel him selfe semeth (though it be much against his wil) the same to acknowledge. For where as he seeth him selfe not able to auoide the plaine and most euident testimonies, he seeketh occasion to wrangle vpon my argument: As though when I proue priuate receiuing, forth with I concluded priuate Masse, in such a sense as he imagineth. And therfore he would bleare his readers eyes, and beare him in hand, that I bring all these places to inferre of ech of them ỷ proufe of priuate Masse. For which I bring them not specially, as priuate Masse is taken for the daily Sacrifice of the Church: but for priuate receiuing or single Communion. And though there be in the margent of my booke a note of proufes for priuate Masse, which may wel stand sith that he semeth to take priuate Masse for priuate Communiō: yet can no man be ignorant, who so euer readeth the place with that goeth a litle before, and that foloweth: but that al those testimonies be alleged specially to proue single Communion. Before, these be my wordes. I wil bring in good euidence and witnesse, that longe before S. Gregories time that he speaketh of, faithful persons both men and wemen receiued the Sacrament alone, and were neuer therfore reproued, as breakers of Christes Institution. There before I enter into my rehersal, I say thus. Wel, now to these places. After I haue rehersed the testimonies, I say thus. Here haue I brought much for proufe of priuate and single Communion, &c.

Fol. 17. a.

Fol. 17. b

Fol. 21. b.

Thus my booke it selfe is a cleare witnesse, that I alleged those

those testimonies not for priuate Masse principally, as it signifieth the Sacrifice, but for priuate Communion. Which as M. Iewel sawe wel inough, as it appeareth by his owne wordes: so, if he had not purposed to abandon al sinceritie & plaine dealing in this mater: he would not haue grated so much vpon a bare margent note, but would haue replied to that which the booke it selfe, and the argument of that place most expressely reporteth. But this is his accustomed policie through his whole Replie, where learning, truth, and reason faileth, there to supplie with scoffes. Which how so euer they delite lighte heades, can not satisfie a godly minde desirous to be taught the sound doctrine of truth.

M. Iewels cõmon policie to supplie wt scoffes, where good mater wãteth

Say not therefore M. Iewel, that for proufe of priuate Masse, for lacke of Priestes, I allege Tertullians wife, certaine wemen out of S. Cyprian, and Serapions boye, as though they were reported to say Masse: I alleged not Tertullian, S. Cyprian, and Eusebius, to that purpose, but to the proufe of Sole receiuing. What say you to these Allegations? Answere directly to the point. After a long superfluous processe, wherein you say againe, that I said before touching Tertullian, and after the discharge of choler wherof your stomake boyled against me, for that my boke calleth you and your felowes by your common name, Gospellers: at length thus you answere.

The. 116. vntruth. I say it not. Loke better on my words

Ievvel.

*M. Harding hath manifestly corrupted both the vvordes, and meaning of Tertullian. *He saith, the thing that vve receiue is no breade. But so Tertullian saith not. *His vvordes be these,* Thy husband wil thinke it (only) bread, and not that bread, that it is called.

The. 117. vntruth. These be not his wordes, this is a plaine corruptiõ,

Harding.

I haue not corrupted neither the wordes, nor the meaning of Tertullian. It is you rather that haue falsified and corrupted

ted both, specially the meaning, as to euery one it shal manifestly appeare, that listeth to conferre the place with your false handeling. For trial of your truth, euen at the first, you are taken with a lye. Where saye I, the thing that wee receiue, is no bread? Looke Reader in my booke, thou shalt finde, that I say not so, and therefore M. Iewel is founde an vntrue man.

Fol.18.a.

Among ẏ three points, which I note out of Tertulliā by occasiō of his wordes, the third is, that the thing reuerently and deuoutly before other meates receiued, is not bread, as the Infidels then, and the Sacramentaries now beleue, but the Body of Christ. Marke M. Iewel, I say, it is not bread, I say not, it is no bread. There is great difference between saying, not bread, and no bread.

Ioan.6.

If I had said, it is no bread, I had said vntruely, for it is the bread of life, it is the bread that came doune from heauen, it is the bread, of which who so euer eateth worthily, shal liue for euer. But that it is not bread, I might wel and truely say, for so is the faith of the Church, specially after Consecration, not bread, as the heathens beleued. If you beleue it to be bread stil after Consecration, then is your beleefe touching that point, no better then the Painimes. Then when you see vs, if euer your faithlesse hearte wil serue you to be present, receiue the Body of Christ vnder the forme of Bread, you wil thinke, as the heathens of whom Tertullian speaketh, thought, it to be bread, not him, who it is called, or that bread, which it is called, which is al one in a right sense.

Tertul.lib. 2.ad vxorem.

But let vs examine the place. Tertullians woordes to his wife, aduertising her not to match in mariage with an Infidel after his death, be these, thus truely pointed, as the later edition of Basile, and that also of Paris hath. Non sciet maritus, quid secreto ante omnem cibum gustes? Et si sciuerit, panem,

non

non illum credet esse, qui dicitur. Which woordes be so put in my booke, and thus englished. Wil not thy husbande know, what thou eatest secretly before al other meate? And if hee doo knowe, hee wil beleeue it to bee breade, and not him, who it is called. What Christen man is there, that beleuing, as the Catholique Church teacheth, wil finde fault with this translation?

M. Iewel not beleuing concerning ỹ presēce of Christes body in the blessed Sacramēt, as the Catholique Church doth, but as Caluine, Peter Martyr, Hooper, Bale, and the rest of the Sacramentaries do: bitterly reproueth me, for that I haue not so englished the wordes, as I might seeme to make of that high Mysterie no better then Bakers bread. Let vs consider then how he hath corrected my translation. Reason were, that so impacient and hasty a reprouer, should him selfe do nothing reprouable. *Tertullians vvordes be these,* saith M. Iewel. *Thy husband vvil thinke it (onely) breade, and not that bread that it is called.*

Yea M. Iewel: Is that the true english of these Latine woordes, Panem, non illum credet esse, qui dicitur? Why put you in by your Parenthesis, this worde onely, in the first parte of the sentence? Againe who taught you to be so bolde, as to adde an other worde, bread, to the second parte? And who gaue you aucthoritie to alter the order of the woordes? Who more openly worketh corruption, you, that adde of your owne, and make such a change of the order: or I that turne it truely, as I finde the place, worde for worde? Yet what a doo make you about it, and haue neuer done? Wherein you shewe more spite then witte, more rancour then learning.

M. Iew. corrupteth Tertullian, to draw him to serue his Sacramentarie heresie

In the. xij. Article of your booke. xi. Diuision, you enter into it againe, where you spitte forth more of your malice vpon me, then you bestowe proufe vpon the mater. Yea you seme to mistrust your holde, and for your credites sake, you are faine to alter the sentence, and to patch on wordes of your owne, therein confessing openly, that without the craft of a corrupter, and falsifier, you were not hable to make that good, for which you haue so laden me with cartloades of spiteful reprochés. In that place you falsifie both Latine and English. For you make Tertullian to speake thus, Si scierit maritus tuus, panem esse credet, non illum (Panem) qui dicitur. If thy husband know it, (being an Infidel) he wil beleue it to be (bare) bread, but not that (bread) that it is called. Where as Tertullian saith thus, Panem, non illum credet esse, qui dicitur: This corrupter hath quite changed the order of the wordes, and maketh Tertullian to speake not like Tertullian, that if he were aliue at this day, he could not wel knowe the sentence to be his. Into one litle sentence of seuen wordes, he hath put three Parentheses, to bodge vp a sense after his owne liking. And al to thintent the Reader should beleue, that bread that it is called, to bee the only Sacrament, Mysterie, or signe of our Lordes Body, not the very Body in dede.

For he meant by illum qui dicitur, Christes very true flesh in
Ioan. 6. dede, of which it is said, My flesh is verely meate: I would ẏ better holde with his translation, though it seme more violent, ẏ order and pointing of the wordes duely considered. And what a busines maketh hee about illum panem, as though Tertullian had ioyned panem to illum? which because hee hath not so done, who so euer englisheth illum, him, meaning Christe, who is the bread of euerlasting life, englisheth it as truely and according to the faith of the Church, as he that turneth it, that breade. If M. Iewel beleued this bread to be ẏ flesh of Christ, vnder ẏ forme of bread, my traslation should seme to him right and good.

But

But he fyndeth fault with me for Englishing illum, him, because it soundeth in his conceite, as if it were the person of a man. For so he reproueth that my translation both here, and also in the. 12. article. 11. Diuision. And that his reprouse might haue some colour, he imagineth me to haue a very false and absurd meaning: which is as *he falsly reporteth, that it was the very *person of a man,* which the woman had in her hande, and did eate before other meate. Then commeth me he in with the saying of Cyrillus which he allegeth oftentimes, and yet it maketh most clerely against him, as I haue declared in the second part of my Confutation of the Apologie. The saying of Cyrillus is this, as he pretendeth, though in dede it be otherwise by that Father vttered: non asseueramus anthropophagia: *VVe teach not our people to eate the person of man.*

The defēce of my translatiō of Tertullians wordes.

The. 118. Untruth. It is the body of Christe, or Christ him selfe God and man.

Fol. 108. a.

By Anthropophagia, Cyrillus vnderstandeth the beastly and vnkindly eating of the body of a mere common man. And because Nestorius the heretike diuided Christe, and dissolued the whole Mysterie of his Incarnation, teaching the worde to be the Sonne of God, not of Mary, and Christe man the sonne of Mary, not of God: wherby he destroyed the meane of the vnion of both natures in Christe, to thintent the body of Christe might be estemed but for a common body as men haue, and not the wordes proper body, which hath power to viuificate and quicken al thinges: Cyrillus to shew the absurditie of this heresie, dryueth him to the consideration of the blessed Sacrament, and demaundeth of him, who by his doctrine made of Christe two Sonnes, and so two Persons, diuiding God the worde, from Christe the man, whether in these mysteries he thought, that we eate a man. What (saith he to Nestorius) doest thou pronoūce this our Sacrament to be the eating of a man? and driuest vnreuerently the mindes of them which haue beleued vnto grosse imaginati-

Cyril. in respōsione ad vndecimū anathematisinū Theodoriti.

nations, and attemptest with humaine imaginations to treate of those thinges, which are atteined vnto by an only, pure, and exquisite faith? Of this whole point I haue more fully treated in

Fol.108. my Confutation of the Apologie. There I aduise the reader to see further.

Now to answere you M. Jewel, I tel you, as Cyrillus told Nestorius, that forasmuch as we eate not in these Mysteries a common body of a man, but the body of Christe the Sonne of God, that is to say, that body which is proprium verbi, the proper body of the word, which quickeneth al thinges, and by receiuing the same, we receiue whole Christe God and man: in translating the forementioned wordes of Tertullian spoken of the blessed Sacrament, hauing in mynde the body of Christe after Consecration to be really present vnder the forme of bread: I may iustly English those wordes illum qui dicitur, thus, him, who it is called. And therein I can not seme to any christen man to meane, as M. Jewel sclaundereth, that it was the very person of a man which the woman is reported to haue had in her hand to eate before other meates. For my faith which is the faith of the Catholike church presupposed, it is manifest, that by illum, him, I meane not the person of a common man, which M. Jewels obiection vnderstandeth, but the only and singuler person of Christe, who is both God and man. Let vs see, what he saith to other testimonies.

The, 119. Untruth. God was not offended with the kepig, but with the presumption of the woman, who opened the chest with vnworthy handes.

Ievvel.

*The storie that S. Cyprian reporteth, as it shevveth the manner of keping the Sacrament, *so it seemeth also to shevv, that God vvas offended vvith the same.*

Harding.

No syr, that is your Priuate collection. S. Cyprian in that storie vttereth not so much as one worde, wherby he may seme to shew, that God was offended either with keping the blessed Sacrament at home, or with Priuate receiuing of it. God was offended not with the keping, but with the woman, who presumed to open the chest wherein the holy thing of our Lord was laid, indignis manibus, with vnworthy handes. And it appeareth by the circumstance of the place, that in time of persecution, for feare she had denyed Christe, and done Sacrifice to Idols. For which she was vnworthy to receiue it. And when notwithstanding her haynous offence, she attempted to touch it, fyre rose out of the chest, and frayed her awaye. This storie witnesseth vnto vs the accustomed mãner of the reuerẽt keping of the Sacramẽt at that time. And if this woman had not cõmitted that greuous crime, but had kept her selfe like a true and good Christen womã: God had not only not shewed him selfe offended with the keping and Sole receiuing of the Sacrament, but also for the same had geuen her increase of grace.

Cyprian. serm.5. de lapsis.

S. Cyprians place opened.

Concerning the storie of Serapion, when M. Iewel hath scoffed his fil at the most holy Masse, and said al that his scornful witte could deuise: he can say nothing wherby to auoid Priuate receiuing, for proufe whereof, & not for proufe of Priuate Masse directly, as he would fain men should beleue, I alleged the same. This is the Priuate, single, or Sole receiuing, for which chiefly the Masse is reproued, by three good and sufficient testimonies approued.

Serapion.

Now for answer to certaine the chiefe points of his scoffing Replie in this.17. Diuision briefly set together:

Ievvel.

To proue Priuate Masse, for lacke of priestes he allegeth Tertullians vvife, vvemen out of Cyprian, Serapions boye, and geueth a special note in the margent of his Booke, Proufes for priuate Masse. &c.

y ij Harding.

Harding.

Proufes for Sole receiuing.

The aduertisement of Tertullian to his wife, the presumptuous putting of vnworthy handes to the Sacrament of the woman out of S. Cyprian, the sending of Serapions boye with the Sacrament, make proufe, that in those daies, and in those churches, there was sole receiuing, the mater pertinent, the authours auncient, the truth euident, and yet herevpon M. Jewel forceth arguments like visardes and Antikes, to moue laughter, telling vs that Tertullians wife, the woman out of S. Cyprian, the boye of Serapion be brought in to proue priuate Masse, and ỳ they be no fitte persons to say Masse. whether he missetell not the tale, and scoffingly conclude, what was not meant: let him iudge, that hath eyes to see, let him vnderstande that hath eares to heare. And this was one point, for proufe whereof he cried so importunatly in his Chalenge, *Vvhere vvas then* (quod he) *the priuate Masse? Vvhere vvas then the single Communion?*

The crye that M. Jewel made in proclaiming his Chalēge, is by these and sūdry mo examples answered.

And because the Sole receiuing or single Communion was then vsed, as wel by the people as by the Priest, which thing he said could not be proued: proufe was first entred for single Communion, and a note in the Margent added (Proufes for Priuate Masse) by principal consequent intended. whereat M. Jewel scoffingly solaceth him selfe, as though some cracke had ben made, or through placing of a margent Note substance of Doctrine could be diminished. By such hasty noting a man might note to him, that his note in the frounte of his first Article is not to the purpose, sith his principal point is (if he mynde to proue aught) to prone his Communion.

Tertull. lib. 4. contra Marcionem.

To mainteine his Sacramentarie heresie, he doth great wrong vnto Tertullian, whom by false translation he would make a Sacramentarie, whose doctrine in that Article is catholike. Acceptum panem & distributum discipulis corpus suum il-

lum

lum fecit. The bread (saith he) which he tooke and distributed vnto his Disciples, the same he made his body. In respect of his doctrine and common faith, he may not otherwise turne Tertullian, then I turned the place, except he turne al to bread, as he doth in his bakerly Communion. Al his shiftes and forgeries are to prophane the holy and blessed Sacrament, and therfore he calleth it very bread. For saith he:

Ievvel.

The thing vvhich our bodily mouth receiueth, is very bread. Both the scriptures and also the olde catholike Fathers put it out of doubt, S. Paule fiue times in one chapter nameth it bread.

The .120. Untruth. Both the scriptures & Fathers report it to be the true body of Christe.

Harding.

You offend syr by your leaue in bearing false witnesse against the Scriptures, the Fathers, against S. Paule, against Christe. Christe said, this is my body. S. Paule saith not that Christes body is very bread, as ye take bread. The Fathers witnesse that our mouth and flesh, touch and eate his flesh. He hath permitted vs to fasten our teeth in his flesh, saith S. Chrysostome. Where the wordes of Christe haue wrought, there is the bloud made, that redemed the people, saith S. Ambrose. Againe saith he, The priest speaketh Corpus Christi, the body of Christe: and thou saist, Amen, that is, true it is. What the tongue confesseth, let thy harte holde. The flesh eateth the body and bloud of Christe, to thende the soule haue his fil of God, saith Tertullian. That Christes body is very bread, neither scripture, nor Father reporteth.

Mat. 26. *Chrysosto. hom. 45. in Ioan. Ambrosius de sacram. lib. 4. ca. 5. Ibidem. Tertullian lib. 1. de Resurrecti one Carnis* I. Cor. II.

But S. Paule say you nameth it bread in one Chapter fiue times. This is not denied, but we answer you according vnto your owne sense, bringing vnto your remembrāce, what you a-nouched before in the .15. Diuision: that Eucharistia in S. Ireneus might signifie bread, that was prepared for the Sacrament.

May it please you then to vnderstand, that S. Paule likewise, and the catholike Fathers meane euen so, when they cal the Sacrament bread.

Foure kindes of bread. The Gospel mentioneth vnto vs. iiij. kindes of bread. First that bread, wherwith Christ fed. v. M. persons in wildernesse.
Mat.14. Luc.9. Secondly, that bread which was called Manna. Thirdly, that
Ioan.6. bread, which is Christ the Sonne of God. Fourthly that bread,
Ibidem. which Christe promised to geue, to witte, his flesh. The name
Ibidem. maketh smal prouse. Manna is called bread, and so is Christ, yet neither of them is bread in nature.

this bread that bread S. Paule calleth it panem hunc, this bread, and panem illum that bread, which is a note material, because it is so named with demonstration, & hath relation vnto the body whereof S. Paule
1. Cor. 10 speaketh, no lesse then of the bread. The bread which we breake, saith he, is it not the communicating of the body of Christe? Lo there is the body. And reporting the wordes of Christe, This is
1. Cor. 11. my body. Againe, reus erit corporis, he shalbe gilty of the body. Item where he saith, nondijudicans corpus domini, putting no difference betwen the body. &c. Neither could S. Paule meane otherwise, then Christe and his Gospel had taught him.

A peculiar phrase of the Scriptures. Adde you hereunto, which you are not ignorāt of, the proper and peculiar phrase of the scripture, which is to retain names of thinges once chāged: As Man is called earth, the Serpēt is called a rod, wine is called water, for that Man was made of earth,
Gen. 2. 3. the Serpent was before a rodde, the wine was once water. Euē
Exod. 7. so the body of Christ beareth ye name of bread, because bread that
Ioan. 2. was prepared for the Sacramēt, through the almightie power of the word in consecration is cōuerted into the body of Christ, and is then made such a bread as Ignatius meant, where he said, Panē Dei volo, panem cœlestem, panē vitæ, qui est caro Iesu Christi filij Dei viui. I desire the bread of God, the heauēly bread, ye bread of life, which is the flesh of Iesus Christ ye sonne of ye liuing god.

Ignatius epist. ad Romanos.

The

The places of Gelasius and Theodoritus are answered in my Confutation of the Apologie. S. Chrysostome, Origen, S. Iustinus Martyr, S. Ireneus, S. Clement, and your pretensed others, shalbe answered, when we heare them speake. In this place they are brought in like Mummers in a Mummerie for a shewe, and say nothing. Neither when they speake, do they say as you report, which is this great vntruth.

In the Confutation. Fol. 98. a.

Ievvel.

They al together vvith one consent haue confessed, that in the Sacrament there remaineth the nature and substance of bread.

The. 121. Untruth. They cōfesse vtterly the contrary.

Harding.

For disprouse of your false witnesse, take you here some of their sayinges. S. Chrysostome, how farre he is from that you father vpon him, signifieth by these wordes.

Num vides panē? num vinum? &c. what, seest thou bread? seest thou wine? Go they (trowest thou) into the draft? God forbid. Thinke not so. For euen as waxe, if it be put vnto the fire, is made like vnto it, nothing of his substance remaineth, nothing abideth of it: so thinke here, that the Mysteries are consumed away by the substance of the body (of Christ). What saith this learned father els, but ŷ the substance of the elemēts in these mysteries are quite done away, and consumed by the substance of our Lordes body, which is the Transubstantiation that the Catholike Church by the vse of a fitte terme teacheth? Here doth not S. Chrysostome confesse the remaining of the substance of bread, as you haue falsly reported of him, but the quite contrary.

Chrysosto. hom. de Eucharistia in Encaniys.

Transubstātiation.

S. Ireneus saith, Quomodo cōstabit eis, panem in quo gratiæ actæ sint, corpus esse Domini sui, & calicem sanguinis eius, si non ipsum fabricatoris mundi filiū dicant? How shal it be certain vnto them, that the bread, vpon which the thankes are geuen, (whereby he meaneth Consecration) is the body of their Lorde, and that the cuppe is of his bloud, if they say, he is not the sonne of the maker of the worlde?

Irenæus lib. 4. cap. 34.

Origenes contra Celsum. lib.8. We eate (saith Origen) the offred breads which through Consecration and prayers are made into a certaine holyer body, in sanctius quoddam corpus constantur, which wordes importe a chaunge of substance.

The final reuerence that M. Jewel beareth to the Sacrament. Also here M. Jewel semeth to geue no more reuerence & worship to the body of Christe in the Sacrament, then to the water of Baptisme, to the booke of the Gospel, no more thē the Jewes gaue to their Manna. For a shift at a pintch he cōpareth the one Sacrament with the other, the Eucharist with Baptisme, which two agree in cōmon nature of Sacrament, but otherwise differ wholly. The presence of Christe in Baptisme, and in the Eucharist is declared to be diuerse in the Confutation of the Apologie. fol.106.a: The one is a Sacrament onely in fieri, as the Scholemen speake in vse and action, not hauing after the Sacramental words pronounced any such being. The other remaineth afterward. Christes wordes assure vs of his being present, no worde teacheth vs of his departing. The Eucharist is perfited by Consecration, Baptisme in application. In the Eucharist there is Transubstātiation of creatures, in Baptisme there is nōne. The priest in the administratiō of Baptisme speaketh in his own persō, Ego baptizo te, I baptise thee. &c. In ỷ Cōsecration of ỷ Eucharist, he speketh in the persō of Christ, hoc est corpus meū. This is my body.

Neuer was it taught, nor Christen people euer beleued, that in Baptisme Christe was present in forme of water, but Christe taught, and his Churche beleueth, that in the Eucharist through Consecration he is present in forme of bread. And therfore is that Sacrament reuerenced in an other degree, then Baptisme.

Augusti. in Psal. 98. Because Christe walked here in flesh, saith S. Augustin, and the very same flesh he gaue vs to eate to our Saluation, and no man eateth that flesh, except he adore it: it is founde out how such a footestoole of our Lorde may be adored.

In

In the place by M. Iewel alleged out of S. Augustine touching like diligence to be imployed for the keping of the word of God, ye it fal not out of our hart being once receiued, as we take heede that nothing of the body of Christe fal downe on the groũd, when it is ministred vnto vs: in that place S. Augustine rebuketh the people of negligence, and inuiteth them to more readinesse in hearing and bearing away the worde of God. He doth not say wherby we should conceiue, ye it is as great offence to receiue the worde of Christe negligently, as the body of Christ vnworthily. That were a dredful saying, and a heauy meaning. A negligent eare, a slothful hart may sometimes happen without gilt of Christes death, which they incurre, who receiue his body vnwortily.

2.q.1. Interrogo vos. Inter homilias quinquaginta hom. 26.

This much is here to be noted by the way, that in this homilie S. Augustine speaking of the reuerence that people thẽ did beare to the blessed Sacrament, saith they tooke great heede, that nothing of the body of Christ might fal out of their hãdes downe vpon the ground. By which wordes the real presence is plainly auouched.

What reuerence is to be geuen to the Gospel booke, may be iudged by that we read in the fourth Councel of Cõstantinople, We decree, (say the Fathers there) that the holy Image of our Lorde Iesus Christe Sauiour of al be worshipped with equal honour with the booke of the holy Gospels.

Synodi generalis. 8. can. 3.

And what honour we ought to do vnto the wordes of Christe pronounced, we may learne of ye auncient Father Pope Anastasius, whose decree is, that priestes & al others that be preſẽt at the Gospel, sit not, but stand stooping downe reuerently, and attently heare the wordes of our Lord, and worship them faithfully.

Anastasius 1. epist. ad Episcopos German. & Burgũdiæ. cap. 1. Fideliter adorent.

But now let vs consider what answer is made to auoid other witnesses, which I alleged to proue sole receiuing.

The. 18. Diuision.

For priuate Communion or sole receiuing I allege S. Basil ad Cæsariam. Who writeth that holy Eremites lyuing in wildernesse solitarily, and aparte from al companie, hauing no Priest nor Deacon among them, receiue the Communion euery one by him selfe, which for that purpose they kepe in their celles. He reporteth also that in Alexandria and in Egypt euery one of the people, hath for the more part the Communion in
Fol.19.a. his house, to receiue as deuotion serueth. Who desyreth to reade the place set forth more largely, him I referre to my booke. By testimonie of this place reseruation and sole receiuing of the Communion is plainly proued.

M. Iewel in his Replie pretendeth this place of S. Basil to be impertinent, because it maketh not mention of the Masse. Yet seeing it hath pleased me to colour and to embosse out this auncient Father, as he sayth, as if he spake plainely of my syde, whereas in dede he uttereth manifest recorde against priuate Masse: he wil not vtterly leaue him in silence.

M. Iew. misreporteth S. Basils epistle ad Cæsariã Patritiã.

First he misreporteth the point which S. Basil treateth, sayning that the noble woman Cæsaria doubted, whether one might touch and receiue the blessed Sacrament with his owne handes, and therfore demaunded S. Basiles resolution. This he calleth *a very nice question, and meete for a Gentle vvoman as* Cæsaria *vvas, to demaunde.* Upon this he entreth into a cõmõ place, and with many wordes proueth, that the practise of the Church for a long time was, deuout persons to receiue the Sacramẽt in their handes,

des, which noman denyeth, and therfore the whole processe is nedelesse and inpertinent.

The point wherof this deuout noble woman Cæsaria stode in doubte, was not whether one might touch & receiue the Sacrament with his owne handes: but, as it appeareth by S. Basil, whether in time of persecution, when there is neither Priest nor Deacon present, one might without offence minister the Sacrament vnto him selfe with his owne handes. This doubte rose of reuerence and deuotiō, and of feare to offend by presumption, not of a foolish nicenesse, as M. Iewel saith. For answere and resolution of this doubte, S. Basil reporteth vnto her, the custome and manner of holy men that liued alone in wildernesse, and of the faithful people of Alexandria and Egypte, mouing her by their example, thereof to make no conscience. M. Iewel after that he hath shewed his copie for proufe of a matter, that no wise man doubted of, and hath reported againe the whole saying of S. Basil, which I laid forth plainely in my booke: at length for answer to me saith thus.

The special point treated by S. Basil ad Cæsariam.

Ievvel.

But much I maruel, hovv M. Harding can geather hereof his priuate Masse. Touching his fiue special notes, if vve graunt them throughly euery one, yet is he nothing the nearer his purpose. For his masse is none of them.

Harding.

I maruel much M. Iewel, with what face you require me of these testimonies to cōclude priuate Masse, as it is the Sacrifice of the Church. You know wel ynough, where about I go in this place, not to proue priuate Masse directly, but priuate receiuing of ẏ Cōmunion, & consequently priuate Masse. For ẏ is it, for which you condēne ẏ Masse. My booke reporteth it plainly, what blīde answer make you? why do you so vnhonestly abuse your reader? At the building of the tower of Babylon, they say, through confusion of language, when one called for mortar, an other brought a hammer, and what so euer was demaunded, a cōtrary thing was answered. Do not you the like M. Iewel? Yea do you not worse, how much worse it is to do a misse wittigly, thē ignorantly? I bring proufes for priuate receiuing of the Communion: you replie ouerthwartly and beside the purpose, saying the testimonies which I bring proue not priuate Masse. So in the beginning of this Article, I alleged sundry places for the vnbloudy Sacrifice, and you replie to euery one, that they proue not priuate Masse. Both there and here my allegations be directed to proue that which is denyed presently, not to proue that which so is not denyed.

M. Iew. doth like vnto the builders of ẏ tower of Babylō

Ievvel.

The Eremites sole receiuing, as it nothing hindereth vs, that denie not the fact, so it nothing furthereth him, onlesse he vvil haue lay mē, and vvemen to do so stil.

Harding.

Examples of sole receiuing be not alleged to the ende ẏ lay men and wemen should do so stil. But forasmuch as you grāt the fact of sole receiuing, I demaunde of you, whether it were lauful, or vnlauful. If it were lauful in Eremites, in euery of ẏ people of Alexandria, and of Egypte, in Tertullians wife, in Serapion, and in other lay men and wemen: why is not the same lauful in a priest? Shew vs some good reason, scripture, Councel, or auncient Father, wherby it may clerely and sufficiently be proued, that though it be lauful in lay folke, yet it is not lauful in a priest. If you say, it was alwayes, & in al persons vtterly vnlauful to receiue alone without cōpanie: what if hauig so good witnesse of it we beleue you not? How are you able to proue it?

If

If you proue it not, these manifest testimonies & examples must eme vnto vs proufe sufficient that it was not vnlawful for the time it was so vsed. And thus sole receiuing proued lawful furthereth our purpose.

Ievvel.

The reason that S. Basile maketh of custome and continuance, being vvel considered, is very vveake, both for many other good and iust causes, and also for that the same custome, as it vvas neuer vniuersally receiued, so vpon better aduise by order of the Church it vvas cleane abolished.

Harding.

If you reproue S. Basile that light of the worlde, for making very weake reasons, it is no maruel, if I finde so litle fauour and equitie at your handes. Sith that you presumed so farre vpon that most excellent Father, it was reason you should haue shewed som of your other good & iust causes, specially seing the cause which here you pretend, is no cause at al. For you must shew vs, where this custome was reiected, and when, in what Prouince, by whom, & by auctoritie of what general Councel ŷ Church tooke order for the vtter abolishing of the custome that we speake of, that is to say, where it was decreed, that no faithful person in time of persecution should haue the Sacrament at home, and receiue it priuately. It is not inough for you to say it. We haue litle cause to beleeue your bare woorde. If you haue no better place to allege, then the Decree made by twelue Spainish Bishops assembled at the Synode of Cæsaraugusta, then are you destitute of proufe, for that Decree perteineth not to this case, as I haue declared here before. For those Fathers forbad not the godly vse of Sole receiuing at home in time of persecution, but the abuse of not consuming the Sacrament receiued in the Church, but secretly reserued vneaten to euil purposes, in time of peace and quiet.

M. Iew. reproueth S. Basile for making a weake reason which is contrary to his purpose.

Concil. Cæsaraugust. cap. 3.

Ievvel.

Vvise mē in Gods causes haue euermore mistrusted the auctoritie of custōe.

Harding.

Customs contrary to truth, & customes agreable to truth. *Cyprian ad Pomp. contra Epist. Stephani.*

Customes be of two sortes, contrary to truth, or agreable to truth. Such customes as be contrary to truth, the auncient Fathers haue not onely mistrusted, but also haue abrogated, and purged the Church of them. Custome without truth, is an olde maintenance of Errour, saith S. Cyprian. But to such customes as be agreable to truth, the wisest of the Fathers haue alwayes geuen reuerence, credite, and aucthoritie.

M. Jewel seeing him selfe driuen to shiftes, cauilleth and wrangleth vpon wordes, & geueth out a surmise ỷ the Eremites which S. Basile speaketh of, came togeather as it were to the celebration of a solemne Communion, in which one tooke vpon him the Priestes and Deacons office, and ministred to the rest. But this is a mere gheasse of M. Jewels owne head. For neither is it likely, that any Eremite professing so great humilitie as they did, would take such preeminence vpon him, specially without al example of the Church: and the wordes of S. Basile seme plainly to reporte the contrary. For the question being moued, whether any man through compulsion of necessitie in times of persecution, no Priest nor Deacon being present, might with his owne hand take the Cōmunion & minister to him selfe: how had he satisfied the question, by making answere, ỷ it was found lauful by long custome & practise of the Eremites, among whom one was wont to take vpon him the office of a Priest and Deacon, and ministred vnto the rest? The question was not of touching the Sacrament with the hande, for the custome of the Church had put ỷ mater out of doubt long before: but whether one might priuately minister vnto him selfe alone without Priest or Deacon, Propria manu, with his owne hand. Againe if they

resorted

resorted together, and assembled them selues into cõgregations, how may thei be said in that respect to haue liued a solitary life in wildernesse, which S. Basile reporteth of them? So their life had ben sociable & cõpanable, not solitary. Besides this S. Basils wordes must be referred specially to ỹ single receiuing of one person. For he saith expressely, It is no hainous mater in absence of Priest and Deacon, quempiam propria manu Cõmunionem sumere, for one to receiue the Communion with his owne hande.

Furthermore M. Jewels ghesse is quite dasshed, except he were able to proue, ỹ euery one of ỹ people in Alexandria, & ouer Egipt, had a wife, children, or familie, among whom he might play the Minister. For I wene hee shal hardely persuade any wise man the contrary, but that among so many thousands some were without wife or familie to minister vnto. which if it were true, thei then by S. Basils report ministred to thẽ selues alone. For that they went to their neighbours houses to receiue with companie, as the Jewes did in old time to eat the paschal lambe, so much can not be wroong out of S. Basiles saying. *Exod. 12.*

As for the storie that M. Jewel telleth vs of Hippolytus Martyr, who as he saith, being a lay mã, ministred the Cõmunion to his wife, his children, and his seruaunts: though it proue nothing against vs, yet we haue M. Jewel in so good credit, that we wil recken it for no better then for a tale of his owne deuise, vntil he shew vs by what approued Author it is recorded.

Let M. Jewel shew him selfe not to haue forged this tale of his own head.

Al this duely considered, it was lauful for me to turne S. Basiles wordes as I did: ἀφ' ἑαυτῶν μεταλαμβάνουσι, they do Communicate with them selues alone: wherin I rendred sense for sense truely, though not worde for worde curiously. With which libertie, yea where the sense is somedeale changed, if I should charge M. Jewel so oftentimes as he hath abused the same, of that very thing I should fil a booke.

Ievvel.

This long Allegation of S. Basiles vvordes, vvith al furniture therof, may shortly be gathered into this reason. These Eremites being no Priestes receiued alone: Ergo these Eremites being no Priestes, said priuate Masse.

Harding.

By M. Jewels scoffing Logique it may perhaps be gathethered into such a foolish conclusion: but by good reason it can not, and in sooth it is not: as neither a number of the like Arguments made in his vaine forgerie, set forth through his whole booke, rather to shew of his light scoffing witte, then to the discredite of the Catholique doctrine. For answere to the point, if by priuate Masse you understande none other thing, but the Priestes sole receiuing: so farre may the example of these Eremites be alleged for proufe of Priuate Masse. But if by priuate Masse you understand the Sacrifice of the Masse, as it is celebrated in the Church, in remembrance of Christes death, and is not in dede priuate: so it ought not specially and immediately for proufe thereof to be alleged.

Ievvel.

The. 122, untruth, Sole receiuing was not in the time of persecutiõ taken for an abuse, neither was it abolished by the Church.

*This sole receiuing vvas an abuse, and therefore * vvas abolished by the Church notvvithstanding custome: Ergo, Priuate Masse likevvise is an abuse, and ought to be abolished notvvithstanding custome.*

Harding.

Before I examine the goodnes of your Argument, I deny your Antecedent. How are you able to proue, that this Sole receiuing whereof S. Basile speaketh, was an abuse? And for what consideration was it abolished by the Church? In what General Councel was there any decree made for the abolishing of it? What Bishops were assembled for that purpose? By whom were they called? Who was the President? Why recite you not the wordes of the Canon? Must we nedes beleue

it,

it,because M.Iewel saith so? Nay rather wil not men mistrust him euen when he telleth trouth, because he is so cōmonly found a lyer? This apperteineth very much to your purpose M.Iewel substantially to proue. And when you haue proued that his sole receiuing was an abuse, which you shal neuer be able to do, for your place of the Synode of Cæsaraugusta can not serue your tourne: then shal it behoue you also to proue, that sole receiuing in general was an abuse, or els your conclusion ẏ priuate Masse is likewise an abuse (that being meant by priuate Masse which we cal the Masse) wilbe espied halting. So long as by al the wicked learning of the founders of your Gospel Luther, and Zuinglius, by the crafty conueiance of Peter Martyr, Caluine, and Cranmare, by the suttiltie of Sathan him selfe, you shal not be able to proue sole receiuing to be an abuse, and contrary to Christes Institution: the Masse shal remaine vnshaken. Can.3.

Ievvel.

Novv let vs see, vvhether these very selfe vvordes of S. Basil here alleged by M Harding, make any thing for the holy Communion. And vvhat authoritie can be against vs, if M.Hardinges ovvne authorities be founde vvith vs?

Harding.

What meaneth this preface of so great confidence? You seme to promise much. If you performe litle, how shal not your own fauourers thinke you to haue more ostentation in wordes, then substance in mater? Marke wel, what you promise to performe. See that you steppe not a syde from your owne offer. Go not from these very selfe wordes by me here alleged. As touching the Communion, for the single and priuate receiuing of it, the place by me was brought, it shalbe nedelesse to proue that, which no man denyeth.

Ievvel.

S. Basil in the same place saith thus. We do Communicate foure times in the weeke: vpon the Sunday, Wensday, Fryday, and Saturday. *If vve may founde any thinge vpon vvordes, he saith,* We Communicate: *He saith not,* We say Masse. *And thus saith S. Basil, vve do foure times in the vveeke.*

Harding.

But where be the very selfe wordes of S. Basil here alleged by M. Harding, that you pretended to make for you? haue you so soone forgoten, what you promysed? I looked for the very selfe wordes, els why craked you so much of them? These were not by me alleged pardy. Yet what make they against vs? what make they for you? S. Basil saith in that epistle, we communicate foure times in the weeke. what then? He speaketh it of himselfe, and of his priuate custome: neither saith he that he cōmunicated only foure times in the weeke, but also vpō other dayes, if ye memorie of any Sainct were kept. which you dissembled, least you should allege ought, yt might sounde to thestimation of Saintes.

And what if we say, S. Basil meant by those wordes, that he consecrated and offred the body and bloud of Christe foure dayes in the weeke, and at euery time communicated, that is to say, receiued, as of right the Sacrifice offred ought to be receiued? To yt perteineth the prayer, which he was wont to say at his Masse, whereof he wrote a forme. In which he praid thus. Make me O Lord meete by the vertue of thy holy spirite, that being indued with the grace of priesthode, I may stand at this holy table, & cōsecrate thy holy and pure body, and thy pretious bloud. For thou art he that offerest, and art offered, he that takest, and doest geue, Christe our God. Now if we graunt you, that S. Basil consecrated, offred and receiued the Communion which he had consecrated, that is to say, celebrated or said Masse (as now we speake) foure times euery weeke, and when so euer a Saintes day, or a

Basil. in liturgia.

com-

commemoration of some Saint came besydes: what thereto haue you to replie?

But say you, S. Basil saith, We Communicate, he saith not, We say Masse. what then? what conclude you? Of two thinges that be not cōtrary, he ẏ affirmeth the one, denieth not the other. we say he did both. For if of the affirmation of the one, you conclude the denial of the other, by making this argument, he communicated, ergo, he said not Masse: you reason foolishly, besides al arte of logike, & too ministerlike. Yet nothing is so common in your whole booke, as that māner of reasoning, wherein you exclude one truth by an other truth. As if one should reason thus. M. Iewel preached to day, ergo, he said not his Seruice to daye. Though perhaps the conclusion be true, yet is the argument naught. For he might do both, and were he as he should be, he would do both, if his religion had any good Seruice at al.

M. Iewels customable reasoning is, to put away one truth by ẏ affirmatiō of an other truth.

Thus then we say: S. Basile celebrated, or said Masse foure times in the weeke, and at euery time receiued the Communiō. Many priestes do likewise at this day, and no smal number is of them, who say Masse, & at the same do Communicate euery day. Whether S. Basile so oftentimes receiued the Communiō with the people al together, and whether, if the people were not at al times so disposed, he forebare to consecrate, offre, and communicate, which is dōne in ẏ Masse: this remaineth for you to proue, before you can iustly allege the example of S. Basil against the Masse, & against the order through out al Christes Churche now vsed, and these many hundred yeres practised.

Ievvel.

S. Basil saith, We do communicate foure times in the weeke. *Then had they not the daily Sacrifice, vvereupō priuate Masse is grounded. He much missereckeneth him selfe, that saith, that thing is daily donne, vvhich is done but foure times in seuen dayes.*

Y ij *Harding.*

Harding.

Remember you wel, what you say, and how you reasō? you are welcome home, that thus shew your selfe to acknowlege the Sacrifice. Holde you there, and go not from it againe. Truth it is, foure times in the weke, beside Saintes dayes, S. Basil did Sacrifice and communicate. This much touching the Sacrifice you confesse, els how vaine is your obiection against the daily being of the Sacrifice? And now syr for that point, what if S. Basil did Sacrifice and cōmunicate foure times in the weeke: might not therfore other priestes do so at other times, and vpon other dayes of the weeke? Shal it not be called the daily sacrifice except it be offred daily of S. Basil, and so likewise of euery particular priest? Shal we not say, the bread whereof at Gods boūtiful hād we are daily fed, is our daily bread: if perhaps some persons through sickenesse, deuoute abstinence, or other causes, at certaine dayes abstaine from eating? Verely such weake reasons bewray the weakenesse of your cause.

M. Jewels weake reason. S. Basil Sacrificed foure times euery weeke: ergo the Church hath not ȳ daily Sacrifice.

Ievvel.

More ouer S. Basil saith. After the priest hath once consecrate, & diuided the Sacrifice, we must thinke that we ought to receiue, and to be partakers of it accordingly. For in the Church the priest geueth parte, and the Communicant receiueth it with al freedome of conscience, and with his owne hande putteth it to his mouth. Therfore is the vertue al one, whether it be one portion onely that he receiueth of the priest, or moe togeather. *Here marke good reader, hovv many vvayes S Basil ouerthrovveth M. Hardinges Masse.*

Harding.

Remember then I pray you, that S. Basile acknowlegeth the Sacrifice, which you denye. And for my part I pray thee also, marke wel good reader, what substantial stuffe M. Jewel

bringeth

bringeth out of S. Basil against the Masse, as in these dayes, we haue it in the Church, which it pleaseth him to cal M. Hardings Masse.

As for this place taken out of S. Basiles epistle to Cesaria, it is directed to the state of the questiō then treated, so as al scruple and doubt of conscience touching the receiuing of the blessed Sacrament when neither Priest nor Deacon is present, in time of persecution, might be taken from her mynde being fearful & loth to offende. Wherfore we must thinke, that S. Basil in that epistle did not so much declare vnto her, what ought alwayes to be don, as in those times of persecution what was to be donne, & what might safely be donne. Neither perteineth al that he saith to the priest, but also and rather to the people.

After that the priest hath once consecrated and diuided the Sacrifice, we must thinke, that we ought to receiue & to be partakers of it, saith S. Basil. Thus he saith concerning the receiuing of the Sacrifice. It must be receiued, and to that end it is consecrated. If it be distributed vnto the people, they may not kepe it to any other vse, but onely to receiue and consume it, and to be partakers of it. So neither at this day is ẏ Sacrifice at any time consecrated but to be receiued, and it is receiued of the priest at euery Masse, and somtimes of the people in great number, and at al times, when so euer any of them be disposed and require it.

As thouching the receiuing with the hand, it was the maner of ẏ time. Sithens it hath ben thought conuenient, the people to receiue it with their mouthes at the priestes hande, and that for the more reuerence of the Sacrament. This is a thing so indifferent, that we thinke it not to be striued for.

Concerning the Sacrifice it selfe, whether it be (saith he) one portion only that is receiued of the Priest, or moe portions together: the vertue of it is al one. The Sacrifice is one, though it be receiued in diuers portions, and the portions carried home in time of persecution to be receiued of deuoute persons at their conuenient time, were of like vertue, as if the whole were receiued at once in the Church. We at this time haue the like faith touching these Mysteries, though we haue not cause of the like practise. But let vs see how many wayes S. Basile by M. Jewel, ouerthroweth M. Hardings Masse.

Ievvel.

The best reasō that M. Jew. can finde in S. Basil against ỹ Masse.

S. Basile saith, We do Communicate: *M. Harding in his Masse doth not Communicate.*

Harding.

With you M. Jewel, and with your sect I do not communicate. With others that be Catholique, and likewise receiue the Communion I do communicate, though we be not together the one at the others elbow.

Ievvel.

S. Basile diuideth and distributeth. M. Harding diuideth in dede, but distributeth nothing.

Harding.

Being lauful for me to take vpon me the person of a Catholique Priest making answere for al, thus I say. If others
1. Cor. 11. that be proued and examined, as S. Paul requireth in this case, be ready and willing to receiue: I distribute vnto them. If there be none, yet ought I to receiue that which I haue consecrated and offered. Wherein I Communicate with those that receiue otherwhere. If others wil refraine, the fault (if any be) is not mine. In that case it is no reason, that I be kept from that heauenly food, which I hunger and thirst after, and in the celebration whereof according to the commaundement of Christ I render thankes to my Redemer, and celebrate the memorie

of his death and passion.

Ievvel.

In S. Basiles Masse the people receiueth: in M. Hardings Masse the people receiueth not.

Harding.

Sometime the people receiueth, sometime they receiue not. As when their deuotion is feruent, God is to be praised, who geueth that grace: So when it slaketh, for doing Priestly dutie at Masse, I am not to bee blamed. If the people growe to negligence and vndeuotion, through lacke of preaching and good exhortations: then am I faulty, my Masse is faultlesse, then am I to bee punished, the Masse is not to bee abandoned. Except you can proue, that Christes Institution is broken, for that the people at euery Masse receiueth not the Sacrament with mee, which you haue attempted, and can not performe: barke no more at the Masse, seeke meanes how to amende the people.

Ievvel.

In S. Basiles Masse eche man receiueth vvith his ovvne hande. In M. Hardinges Masse no man receiueth, no not vvith the Priestes hande.

Harding.

If you sing not one song, I knowe not what you meane, nor your selfe I suppose. If the hande were al that made you at variance with vs, I woulde ye had the free vse of your handes, so that due reuerence were kept. How men may receiue with the Priestes hande, I doo not wel vnderstande. That of the Priestes hand they would oftener receiue, it were much to be wished. But though the peoples deuotion now be wexen colde, in comparison of their heate, that liued daily in feare of life among the persecutions of the Primitiue Churche: yet that it is no sufficient cause, why the daily Sacrifice of the Church shoald be abolished. Let vs not preuent Antichristes iniquitie.

Ievvel.

In S. Basiles Masse, the people besides that they receiued presently there, had portions also deliuered them to receiue at home. In M. Hardings Masse there is no portion deliuered vnto the people, no not so much as presently to be receiued in the Church.

Harding.

If the faithful people liued in like feare of their life now, as they did then, when they prepared them selues euery day, & loked to be done to death or were like otherwise to bee persecuted for their faith, & therfore would now also be desirous to receiue in the Church, and to haue hostes consecrated home with them, that how soddainly so euer they were taken, they should not departe without that diuine viage prouision: In this case, specially order thereof being taken by publike aucthoritie, such holy portiōs should be prouided and deliuered vnto them also to carry home with them. But nowe an other state of times, requireth an other condition of manners. If they receiue not in the Church so often as they should, lay the fault where it is: Amende your owne selfe, you shal finde lesse fault with vs.

Ievvel.

The 123. vntruth. the whole people eateth not by the mouth of the Priest as M. Jewel meaneth.

*In S. Basiles Masse ech man receiueth and eateth for him selfe. In M. Hardings Masse the vvhole people *eateth by the mouth of the Priest.*

Harding.

What is that eche man receiueth and eateth in S. Basiles Masse? Why vtter you not that is in your harte plainly? Coffe vp the crummes of your Sacramentarie heresie. Is it any other by your new Gospel then Bread? If it be not bread, but the

the very body of Christ, into the which the bread by the almighty power of the worde is conuerted: say so, that we may know what you meane.

If it be bread, as the deuisers of your Gospel teach, tel vs, who euer among the Catholikes said, the whole people eateth bread in the Masse by the mouth of the Priest? You can neuer shew it, I am wel assured. what you haue brought in your .xviij. Article touching this mater, I haue wel considered. Neither Biel, nor Vincentius de Valentia, nor Eckius, whom therby you would faine discredite, being rightly vnderstanded, can seme to any learned man to say, that the whole people eateth the bread, or as you perhaps had here rather to terme it, the Sacramental bread, or that they eate at al Sacramentally, by the mouth of the Priest. And yet that it might so seme, you haue stretched, racked, and falsified their wordes to an other sense, then euer they ment, specially in that you would the worde of Communicating, to signifie none other thing, but the outward receiuing of the Sacrament. These two schoolemen, and Eckius, were not so simple of witte, howsoeuer ye gospellers contemne their plaine mãner of vtterance in comparison of your owne painted sheath, and affected finenesse, as to speake so farre wide of reason.

M. Iew. falsifieth Biel, Vincentius, and Eckius in the.18. Diuision.

And as concerning Eckius, you haue most impudently belyed him, where you say of him thus. *Likevvise Doctour Eckius saith,* Populus bibit spiritualiter per os sacerdotis. The people drinketh spitituall y by the mouth of the priest. And then for Cõfirmation of the matter, you adde these wordes of credite. *These vvordes* (say you) *be plaine, and truly reported.* And al is starke false. For Eckius in his common places, where he treateth De vtraq: Specie, as you haue noted in the margent of yout booke, hath no such wordes at al. If thou desire to know Reader, what be Eckius wordes, they be these. In sacerdotis persona totus po-

Pag. 588

pulus quadam spirituali sumptione sanguinē Christi bibere gaudenter debet credere. The whole people (saith he) ought gladly to beleue, that they drincke the bloud of Christe by a certaine spiritual receiuing in the person of the Priest. Of the Priestes mouth he speaketh not. Yet these wordes be truly reported saith M. Iewel.

O what meane you M. Iewel, thus to play the falsary, and shamelesly to lye? Thinke you to grow in credite with ẏ world by such open lying? Is not the truth of our cause to wise mens iudgement much commended, and your whole doctrine brought into suspition, when they see you conuicte of so many, and so manifest lyes?

Touching the thing it selfe. If it be the bodye and bloud of Christe, which the Priest receiueth at Masse, as
Mat.26. Luc.22. thereof we are assured by Christes owne profession: so many of the people as be in the vnitie of the Church, do communicate with him Spiritually, and wyth some effecte of grace, when so euer he receiueth. That is to say, forasmuch as he and they are members of one body knitte and ioyned together by Faith and Charitie, euen as in a natural body, when one member is fully nourrished, the rest also take parte of their sustenance: so when the Priest receiueth the body and bloud of Christe at Masse, some portion of the grace, vertue, and effect thereof redoundeth vnto the Deuoute people being Members of the same bodye with the Priest, specially vnto such as be present at the Celebration of the Sacrifice, who by vow do also Offer the same. For among the faithful there is a felowship and Communion of al good thinges, as the Prophete Dauid saith, Particeps ego sum omnium timentium te: I am partaker of al that feare thee.

The faithful people do spiritually communicate with the Priest, which receiueth the sacramēt at Masse.

In

In this ſenſe it might wel and rightly be ſaid of thoſe Diuines, whom M.Iewel ignorantly and preſumptuouſlye condemneth, that the people doe ſpiritually Communicate with the Prieſt, as receiuing ſome effecte of grace by his worthy receiuing of the Myſteries. But that they eate, that is to ſay, that they receiue the Sacrament, or Communicate Sacramentally by the mouth of the Prieſt, as M.Iewel reporteth: neither Gabriel Biel, nor Vincentius de Valentia, nor Eckius, whom M.Iewel allegeth, nor any other learned man, Scholeman or other, euer ſpake or wrote ſuch abſurditie.

M. Iew. charged with a fowle vntruth.

But if it be lawful to proue one thing, by an other like thing, one reaſon ſeruing to both, I demaunde of you M.Iewel, whether by S.Auguſtines doctrine we may not boldly ſay, that the faithful people doth receiue the Communion, in ſome reaſonable and true ſenſe, that is, ſpiritually and effectually, not Sacramētally, by the mouth of prieſtes, or rather in prieſtes, ſpecially vnder the name of the Churche the people being compriſed. For as S.Auguſtine ſaith of a man that hath receiued the holy ghoſt, whoſoeuer he be, that he ſpeaketh with the tōges of al nations, becauſe he is one of Chriſtes body the Churche which ſo ſpeaketh: So what reaſon is there, why a man may not ſay the like of the faithful people, touching the Communion? S.Auguſtines wordes be theſe. Si quiſq̃ dixerit alicui noſtrũ. &c If any ſay to one of vs, Thou haſt receiued the holy ghoſt, why ſpeakeſt thou not with al tonges? He ought to anſwere, I ſpeake with al tonges, becauſe I am in that body of Chriſt, in the church, which ſpeaketh with al tōges. Tel me M.Iewel, why I may not as wel ſay of the faithful people, that they do receiue the Communion ſpiritually and effectually, yea though ech ſingular perſon receiue it not ſometimes in his owne perſon Sacramētally,

How the faithful people receiue the Communion by that the prieſtes do worthily receiue.

Auguſtin. De tēpore ſerm.188.

for as much as they be in that body of Christ, to wit, the Church, which doth receiue? But in whom doth the Church receiue? In vertuous and holy priestes. For as S. Augustine saith. In some Sainctes the Church worketh miracles, in other Sainctes it speaketh the truth, in other Sainctes it kepeth virginitie, in other Sainctes it kepeth the chastitie of wedlocke, in others this, in others that: so why might he not haue said, in some Saintes, that is to say in holy priestes, the Churche doth receiue the Communion, that is to say, the vertue and effect of the Communion?

Augustin. de tempore Sermo. 186.

Certaine vertues though al persons haue not, (saith a holy Father, whose words M. Jewel hath in this Article alleged vnder the name of S. Bernard) yet let them loue him, who hath that which they finde not in them selues: and then haue they in him, that which in them selues they see not. As Peter in Iohn hath the merite of virginitie, so Iohn in Peter hath the reward of Martyrdome. Thus it may be truly said, that the godly and wel disposed people do receiue the effect, vertue, and grace of the holy Communion in their priest, by whom as by their Publike minister they also offer vp the Sacrifice: but in what measure, that we leaue to Gods determination, who geueth his grace, as it pleaseth him: verely we say not in like measure, as if they receiued the Sacrifice worthily ech one in his owne person.

Guerricus Abbas Igniacensis Sermone in die Purificationis.

The. xix. Diuision.

AMong other testimonies for single or Sole receiuing, I bring the place out of S. Hierome, in Apologia aduersus Iouinianum. where he speaketh of a custome that was at Rome, that many faithful persons receiued the body of Christe euery day. which thing he neither reproueth, nor commendeth. This thing yet he thought was to be reproued, that, whereas S. Paule would maried folke for cause of prayer to forbear their carnal imbracinges for a time, they of Rome refrayned not from comming to that holy table daily, notwithstãding they had done the carnal acte. And yet feeling some remorse of conscience by reason thereof, they receiued at home, and durst not go to Churches, specially where the Martyrs toumbes were, there to receiue. Wherfore he apposeth their consciences that so did, whether they did wel or no. And concludeth as it were vpon confession they semed to make by their owne facte, that they did euil. For where as they had done that, for which they durst not communicate openly in Churches, they did euil to be so bolde, as to communicate at home. For (saith he) vvhat is not lavvful in the Church, neither at home is it lavful. The whole place is to be sene in my booke set forth at large and plainely. Certaine it is, that it conteineth a witnesse of priuate Communion and of Sole receiuing of Christes body, for proufe whereof it was alleged.

1. Cor. 7.

Fol. 20.

M. Iewel in his Replie kepeth him self a looffe of from making directe answer to the point, and discourseth at pleasure vpon other maters, the discussion whereof as it requireth large treatises, and yet they be sufficiently determined by the Church, so it perteineth not to the mater presently handled. He calleth now the Priuate receiuing of our Lordes body at home, a superstition. He reproueth S. Hierome for writing and speaking vnsemely of the state of Mariage, for which, as he saith, he was driuen to make his answere by way of purgation vnto Pammachius. He taketh vpon him to reproue also Tertullian, and Origen for hainous errour touching Matrimonie. And as for Origen, he belieth him fowly, and falsifieth his wordes, making him to speake otherwise then euer he wrote, or meant.

M. Iew. reproueth S. Hierome to lessen his authority.

Origen belied and falsified by M. Iew.

M. Iew, is ennemie to the Saintes reliques and Miracles. He speaketh against the shryning of Martyrs bones, and misseliketh both the reliques and also miracles of Sainctes. Then he allegeth sayinges out of S. Paule, and S. Chrysostome in commendation of Matrimonie, which no wise man dispraised. By doing whereof he semeth to pike a thanke of his fellow Gospellers, who being Monkes, Frieres, and Priestes, bounde by deliberate and solemne vowe to liue chast in single life, haue notwithstanding in pretensed wedlocke taken to them selues their yokefelowes for better oportunitie to studie, preach, and pray, which ought to be the exercises of that vocation.

After this he commeth to Erasmus, and when he hath said al that he could for him, he maketh him but a double man, saying vpon S. Paules wordes, haue ye not houses to eate in, one thing in his Annotations vpon S. Hierome, an other in his Paraphrase vpon S. Paul. Yet the plaine testimonie of Erasmus for Sole receiuing, by no shifte he could auoide. His wordes be these. Of this place (saith he) we gather, that in the olde time euery one was wont to receiue the body of Christe at home in his house, that woulde.

1. Cor. 11.

Erasmus in scholijs in Hierony. Apologiā aduersus Iouinian.

Thus is Erasmus founde to agree with me in the vnderstanding of the forementioned place of S. Hierome. His chiefe Replye to the place is this.

Ievvel.

This is not a necessary forme of reason, men receiued the Sacrament in their houses: Ergo, they receiued the Sacrament alone. For they might receiue in their seueral houses vvith their vviues and families altogeather, as it is already proued by the example of Hippolytus Martyr. And S. Hierome saith, the Sacrament vvas sent hame to the man and vvife.

Harding.

Harding.

I claime not Sole receiuing by a necessary forme of argumēt out of this place. I haue proued that already by a necessary forme of reason, in the example of Serapion and others. This place also of S. Hierome geueth vs a clere witnesse thereof, except one would cauil, as you do, and say, that the wife and familie at al times, receiued with the husband. For as ẏ is spoken only by gheasse, and can not be proued: so is it more then probable, that if the wife and familie had at al times receiued with the good man of euery house, S. Hierome would haue disposed his saying otherwise, then we find it written, and would haue said some what touching the seueral companies, specially if he had ben of M. Iewels opinion, that the Sacrament may not be receiued, but of a Congregation assembled together in one place. Verely whereas he saith in this place by me alleged, Probet se vnusquisq;, & sic ad corpus Christi accedat, let ech man trye him selfe, and so come to the body of Christe: He semeth not to thinke, nor to teach that a man, who hath sufficiently and duly tryed and examined him selfe, and is desyrous to receiue that heauenly foode to his comfort, should not be admitted at any time to receiue, except his wife and familie be ready to come to the same place, and receiue with him. And because it standeth not with reason, that one be restrained from the fruite of his deuotion, by the case, happe, or fortune of an other: S. Hierome may iustly be thought to meane, that, if any man haue duly proued and examined him selfe, he may in Gods name go and receiue the body of Christe, whether his wife and familie be likewise disposed or no.

Sole receiuing proued.

Hieron. in Apologia aduersus Iouinian.

Let ech man proue him selfe, saith he, and so go vnto the body of Christe. What meaneth he by this worde Sic, so? Meaneth he any more, then that a man be wel tryed?

This worde Sic, so, to be noted in S. Hierome.

And so, that is to say, being duly examined, let him go vnto the body of Christe. He is not required to tarry, vntil he gete his wife and familie also vnto him, but sic accedat, so, that is, when so euer he is wel tried and examined, let him come to receiue, saith he.

And as concerning ech mans familie, which M. Iewel by his gheasse surmiseth to be a parte, to make vp his number for a Communion: the surmise is very foolish. For whereas S. Hierome speaketh onely of them, that Communicated the same day in which they had done the wedlocke seruice of the fleshe: how is not the familie excluded out of that number, onlesse M. Iewel imagine the wife to be naught with the seruauntes, or them also to haue wemen otherwise? Certainly he speaketh in that place of none other, but of such, as receiued the Communion after they had done the carnal worke of wedlocke. And although M. Iewel suppose, the man neuer receiued, but when the wife receiued with him, which is a very vncertaine gheasse: yet in his iudgement is that no Communion, because there lacketh a third. For as three make a College, so by these mennes new founde gospel it is no Communion, except there be three at least in one place together to receiue.

That S. Hierome meaneth Sole receiuing.

without three receiue together, it is no Cōmunion by the new Gospel.

As for the example of Hippolytus Martyr, by which you say, you haue proued the custome of the householders ministring of the Sacrament vnto his wife, children, and familie: First, we doubt of the storie. You allege no author for it. Your truth is so wel knowen, that we can not trust you farther then you shew good euidence. Perhaps we may say, it is taken out of your owne Legenda aurea. So wil we beleue, vntil you shew vs your sufficient warrant, you that be so ambitious in your blasing Cotations, should not haue left this pore example vncoted. And though it were so, yet as one swallow maketh not ẏ spring-

The example of Hippolytus fained, as it appeareth.

tide,

kinde, as Aristotle saith, so neither can one singular exāple be alleged to proue a custome. And though Hippolytus did so in the Greke Church, what proofe is ẏ of a common custome in Rome?

Neither is ẏ to be foūd expresly in Apologia aduersus Iouinianum, of the Sacrament sent home to the man and his wife, as you report it of S. Hierome. In dede this much I finde there, which liketh not you, nor your companions, I belieue. Ecce perspicuè nuptias &c. Loe we haue said plainely, that Mariage is accompted lauful in the Gospel: yet the same, though it continewe in his due office, can not receiue the rewardes of chastitie. Which thing if maried men take greuously, let them not be angry with me, but with the scriptures: yea with Bishops, with Priestes, with Deacons, and with the whole order of Priestes and Leuites: who knowe, that they can not offer Sacrifices, if they attend vpon the wedlocke worke.

More attributed to S. Hierome, then S. Hierome saith.

In Apologia contra Iouinian.

They that attēd vpō wedlocke worke, cā not offer Sacrifices.

Which saying of S. Hierome I would the reader to compare with that you haue brought out of S. Chrysostome, vnto which you haue geuen a dangerous sense by your partial translation. Vse thy Mariage with sobrietie, and thou shalt be the chiefe in the kingdom of Heauen. If he shalbe chiefe in the kingdom of heauen, how is that true which S. Hierome saith, that he can not receiue the rewardes of chastitie? If the rewardes of chastitie be so great, that the state of mariage can not attaine them, how shal the maried man, though he vse his mariage with sobrietie, be the chiefe in the kingdom of heauen? The virgin shal haue such reward, as he can not be admitted vnto, how then shal not the virgin be preferred before him?

Chrysost. ad Heb. hom. 7.

The differēt sayinges of S. Hierom & S. Chrysostom by right interpretatiō accorded.

S. Chrysostom saith thus to a Christen maried man. Vse thy mariage with moderation, and thou shalt be first, (or rather if our tongue would beare it) a first or a foreman in the kingdome:

that is to say, one among them, that shalbe first in the kingdom of heauen. For in that place S. Chrysostome doth allude
Mat. 20. to ý saying of ý Gospel, erūt nouissimi primi, the last shalbe first. What he meaneth by the moderate vse of mariage, there he sheweth.
Ad Heb. homil. 7. It is possible saith he, yea very possible for vs that haue wiues, to become vertuous, if we wil. How? If hauing wiues, we
1. Cor. 7. be as though we had none. If we take not ioye in the thīges which we possesse. If we vse the worlde, as though we vsed it not.

A brief lesson for maried mē to becōme vertuous.

A maried man doing thus, and vsing such a moderation, may be a first or a foreman in the kingdom of heauen. Yet state with state compared, after the saying of S. Hierome, the rewarde of chastitie is of higher preferment, then mariage. But let vs see how M. Iewel replieth against that I allege out of S. Hierom.

Ievvel.

If the people did vvel, vvhy doth S. Hierome thus reproue them? If they did il, vvhy doth M. Harding thus allovv them?

Harding.

What is ý S. Hierome reproueth in ý Romains receiuing priuatly at home.

S. Hierome reproueth them not for receiuing the body of Christe at home priuatly: but for that they receiued after they had done the Carnal worke of wedlocke, for which they durst not receiue in Churches, as though Christe saw not the secretes of their consciēce as wel in their priuate houses, as in the Churches: and as though that which was not lauful to be donne in Churches, yet might laufully be donne at home. This wrong conscience of theirs S. Hierome reproueth, their dayly communicating he neither reproueth, nor commendeth. But that they receiued the body of Christe priuatly, he semeth in no wise to mislike. The commendation or reprouse dependeth of their worthy, or vnworthy receiuing, not of priuate or publike receiuing.

Ievvel.

Here M. Harding interlaceth other mater of the office of vvedlocke, the vvordes of Persius the pagane poete, and the superstitious ceremonie of the heathens, as I take it, litle perteining vnto his Masse.*

The. 114. Untruth. It is not I that interlace this mater It is S. Hierome.

Harding.

This is vtterly false. For these be not my interlacinges, but S. Hieromes, as euery man may see. whose wordes I thought necessary to set forth wholy and truly together, as he writeth, least I should falsifie him by clipping the sentence, which is the practise, of you M. Jewel now, as euer it hath ben of heretikes heretofore. If you blame him that mentioned Persius the pagan poete, and the superstitious ceremonie, which you mislike: quarel with S. Hierome, whose fault that is, if it be a fault: & shew not your selfe so malicious towardes me, as to reproue me for that which is not myne, but S. Hieromes. If you could espie faultes in me, I perceiue of your courtesie you would not let to tel me of them, and al the worlde besides.

For asmuch as I see you so offended with me for translating this saying of S. Hierome, I thinke verely you would haue ben much more offended, if I had translated certaine other sayinges of his in that very booke quite contrary both to your doctrine, and procedinges. Of which this is one for example. The Apostles (saith he) either were virgins, or after mariage they liued in continencie: Bishopes, Priestes, Deacons, they be chosen either virgins, or widowers, or verely after priesthod they be chast for euer. What Bishops, Priestes, Deacōs your sect choseth, & how chaste a life they lead after they be chosen: the worlde seeth, and cryeth out, fy vpon them. Thus then what is in this Diuision specially intended, is not by this Replier answered. Cuckow-like alwayes he singeth one song, This is not priuate Masse. Upon very smal occasion he pyketh a quarel to S. Hierome, as

In eadem Apologia aduersus Iouinian.

as though he had vnsemely spoken against priestes mariage, and letting passe the principal mater, after a ministerly fashion he ministreth much impertinent talke in contempt of reliques ad miracles, by alleging S. Augustine, where he complaineth of certaine abuses committed by some about dead mennes graues. After this to requitte S. Hierome, he bringeth in a sober saying of S. Chrysostome, that maried men vse their mariage soberly so to please his maried companions, and to prepare away to saue his own estimation, if perhaps hereafter ẏ sprite shal moue him to yoke him selfe to a sister, which hath moued his good brethren. And so he maketh vp the mater with Erasmus a good honest mā pardie in his iudgement, for he spake not one word of the Masse. For where he saith these wordes,

Ievvel.

The. 125. Untruth. I say not so. *Thus saith M. Harding, Erasmus gathereth the priuate Masse out of the Scriptures, M. Harding is euer quicke in his conclusions, &c.*

Harding.

Hereto I answer quickly, how quicke so euer I be in my Cōclusions: M, Jewel is ouer quicke in his lyes. For soothly I say not so of Erasmus. One of vs two is here founde a lyer, whether of vs it is, let the booke be trial.

The. 20. Diuision.

Hauing before alleged many testimonies for sole receiuing, for which chiefly M. Jewel cōdēneth ẏ Masse: to ẏ rest in ẏ ende I adde a place out of Damasus, who writeth ẏ S. Milciades Pope & Martyr ordeined, ẏ ẏ Sacramēt in sūdry portiōs consecrated by a Bishop, should be sēt abrode per Ecclesias,

that

that is, among the Churches. And because Ado a learned Father by putting these two wordes, Propter Hæreticos, For cause of Heretiques, vnto that Decree, semeth thereby to declare, what was ẏ purpose and intent of that holy Martyr therin: I thought I should not speake beside reason, if I said such holy portions to haue been directed abroad, to the intent the wel disposed Catholike people might receiue the Communion after the Catholike vsage, and not communicate with Heretikes. For better vnderstanding of that decree, I said further, the worde Churches, not to signifie the material Churches, vnto which faithful folke are wont to resort to serue God, but the people of the Parrishes, so as the Greeke worde παροικίαι oftentimes signifieth. Now this much being supposed, that this was done for cause of Heretikes, as Ado expoundeth the place: what may we conceiue thereof, but that Heretiques in those places, where this was done, bare the sway so, as the Catholique Priestes were not suffered to do their dutie, but rather were driuen away, or otherwise restrained from consecrating after the Catholique vsage? For els if Priestes might without any lette or trouble so haue done, what nede had it ben for Milciades to make such prouision, in sending abroade those holy portions sanctified by the Consecration of a Bishop? This place the Reader may see more clerely in my booke. The pith of M. Iewels Replie to this, standeth in his accustomed scoffing and surmising, that al this is but a gheasse. He saith thus.

Churches.

παροικίαι

Fol. 21. a.

Iewel.

This gheasse is one of the weakest of al the rest, and therefore M. Harding hath staid it vp on euery side with other gheasses, that one gheasse might helpe an other.

Harding.

First the thing it selfe is no gheasse. For it was done by

S. Milciades that blessed Martyr and Pope aboue twelue hundred yeares past. If you wil demaunde my prouse, heare the wordes of Damasus in Pontificali. Milciades fecit, vt oblationes consecratæ per ecclesias ex consecratu Episcopi (propter hæreticos) dirigerentur. Milciades caused, that Hostes consecrated by the Consecration of a Bishop, should be sent abroad among Churches, for cause of Heretiques. Which two wordes Propter Hæreticos, are added by Ado, for better declaration of the Decree. If the addition of those two wordes Propter Hæreticos, be but a gheasse, wherby Damasus meaning is declared, as you surmise in the note of ẏ manifold gheasses which you haue forged: it is not mine, it is the Authors whom I allege. Neither is there cause why you should make so light of Ado, whom in ieast you cal Doctor Ado, and say he was a late writer. He liued aboue fiue hundred yeares past, and was Archebishop of Treueris, of so good aucthoritie and estimation in his time, that he was thought a meete man to trauaile betwene the two great Princes, Henricus and Radulphus, for peace and concorde to be made betweene them, who then striued for the Empire of Rome.

Damasus in Milciade.

Ado a mā in his time of great aucthoritie & fame.

Ievvel.

*Furthermore to increasse absurdities he saith, by these vvoordes, Per Ecclesias, is meant, not the material Churche, but the people of the Churche, * that is to say in plainer termes, Ecclesia, is not a Church, but a priuate house.*

This that is to say, is an vntruth. For it signifieth not so.

Harding.

When you tel an absurde and foolish tale for mee, it is easy for you to replie what you list, and you wil be sure, vsing the libertie you do, to make me speake so, that you nede not to study long for an Answere. The order of Learned men is, not to attribute to their Aduersaries such vaine vntruthes, and weake reasons,

M. Iew. reporteth my wordes vntruly to be the better able to make his Replie.

reasons, as your manner is, but to set forth their sayinges, as they be, with al truth. Els what praise is it, to fight with the shadowe of a man, and afterwarde to crake of victorie? Falsifie not my wordes, and say your pleasure. You make me so simple, as though I knew not what Ecclesia signifieth. And after that you haue vntruely said of mee: that I make the woorde Ecclesia, to signifie not a Churche, but a priuate house: then you besturre you, as though you hadde great aduantage at mee, and make your ignorant Reader beleue, what you list. Ecclesia.

But if the Reader, be he neuer so much addict to your side, wil reade what I saye in my booke my selfe, and not what you belie me to say in your Replie: he shal find mee true, and you a forger, a falsifier, and an vntrue reporter. Who saith this woorde Ecclesia, is not a Churche, but a priuate house? My woordes bee plaine. Which woorde Churches (saye I) here signifieth, as the Greeke woorde παροικίαι dooth, so as it is not necessarie to vnderstand, that the Sacrament was directed onely to the material Churches, but to the people of the Parishes. Loe M. Jewel, I make the woorde Churches to signifie the people, not a priuate house. Why say you so of me then? And why haue you noted your booke in the Margent, thus, *A Church by M. Hardinges iudgement signifieth a priuate house?* For shame either write not so many lyes, or geue ouer writing altogether. These be my words Fol. 21, a. M. Iewels lying note in the Margent. *Pag. 53.*

For the rest, what a doo make you about the worde παροικία, to no purpose, but to ostentation of Learning, and of knowledge in the Greke tongue, as though it were not openly knowen, by whom of Oxford you were holpen therein? And I pray you who moued any question touching the woorde παροικία, what it signifieth? And now that you haue shewed παροικία, your owne, and your frendes high knowlege therin, what haue ye wonne by it.

Ievvel.

Certainely I thinke, he him selfe vvil say, that sithence the Church vvas once in peace, neither this vvorde Ecclesia, *nor this vvoorde* Parochia, *euer signified a priuate house, in any kinde of Vvriter, or in any time.*

Harding.

Haue you not yet done with your Grammer pointes? You thinke truely of me. I say so. I confesse it, I deny not. And who euer said otherwise? Certainly I thinke you be very sorry, that I haue ministred vnto you no better mater to replie, seeing that you make so much a doo in auouching that, which neither I, nor any man els euer denyed. But Sir what

Parochia

meane you to speake of Parochia? Who made mention of it? Why make you that a peece of your quarrel? Who euer saide, that Parochia signified a priuate house? Consult againe with your Greke frend of Oxford. If no man spake of it, why do you so bitterly obiect it? The eager desire you had to reproue mee, carried you quite away from seeing what you wrote. Though Parochus be founde in Cicero and Horace, good Authors of the Latine speach, yet your worde Parochia, I suppose you finde not in them nor in any other auncient and approued Greeke writer. That the ecclesiastical writers of the Latine Church haue vsed it in place of the Greeke woorde παροικία, I denie not.

The effect of that I say in my Answere touching this place of Damasus.

Whereas yet you wil not in any wise the worde Church to signifie a priuate house, as no man would it so to signifie: This is that I saye in my booke. If the Hostes consecrated by a Bishop were sent abroade among certaine Churches by order of S. Milciades, and might not be openly consecrated and ministred to the people by Catholike Priestes, as it appeareth by the

wordes

wordes of Damasus, specially so opened by the addition of the two wordes put in by Ado: the same being sent onely to the intent they should be receiued: where (may we iudge) were they receiued, (heretikes in those partes bearing rule) but in mennes houses, which in respect of Churches, may wel be called Priuate houses? Now that in those Priuate houses some deuoute person sometime receiued alone, not tarying vntil others were ready to receiue with him, the coniecture is not vnreasonable. Albeit if this confirme not our mater of Sole receiuing sufficiently, in the iudgement of a wrangling aduersarie: it skilleth not, there is ynough besydes.

Ievvel.

This manner of sending abroade the Sacrament, vvas aftervvard abolished by the Councel holden at Laodicea.

Harding.

It is not euident that the Councel of Laodicea speaketh of this manner of sending abroade the Sacrament, neither that it speaketh of the blessed Sacrament at al. It forbiddeth the Oblations that were brought to the Church, which were of diuerse kyndes, to be sent to other Churches for giftes and presentes, for so doth the worde Eulogiæ signifie, wherof I haue spoken before.

Concil. Laodien. cap. 14.

The. xxi. and. xxij. Diuision.

WHat I haue ioyned together for a briefe conclusion of the thing which I promised to proue, that hath M. Iewel here set a sunder, and for his pleasure hath

 parted

parted it into two Diuisions. The effect of al is this, that I haue now brought much for single Communion, and yet more could bring for proufe of the same, but that I iudged this to be ynough. To this M. Jewel, who at the begynning purposed to reprehend what so euer I said, were it neuer so reasonable, and neuer so true: so replieth, as he may seme rather to wreake his malice vpon my person, and vpon the Churche of Rome, then to weaken the cause, which he would so faine to be ouerthrowen. He findeth fault with my Logike, and saith:

Ievvel.

The. 126. Untruth: I pretended not here to proue priuate masse principally, but single Communion.

M. Harding vseth a straunge kinde of Logike. * *He pretendeth Priuate Masse, and concludeth single Communion. And vvhy might he not aswel plainely and vvithout colour conclude his priuate Masse?*

Harding.

M. Jewel vseth a straunge kinde of quarreling, reprouing my Logike, where I make no argument. What Logike vse I in this place? do I other then plainely report, what I haue said? What I pretended to do, that haue I done. I pretended by good and sufficient testimonies to proue single Communion, and that haue I now performed. Read the discourse who wil, he can not denye, but that I pretended to proue single Communion. Your selfe do acknowledge and confesse no lesse, toward the ende of the next side of your leafe. Where you say, I haue *taken paines to proue that thing,* to witte, *Sole receiuing, and single Communion, that vvas neuer denyed.* And yet is your Sermon a witnesse against you, in which you denied it. Or heere or there you must confesse, you said vntruth. Thus you say, and vnsay, know, and pretend ignorance, colour and dissemble, slip from one thing to an other, and shew your selfe plaine and stedfast in nothing, but in wrangling against the truth.

Thus saith M. Jewel, pag 57. 10 lines from the ende. M. Jew. in his Replie, is contrary to M. Jew. in his Chalenge

That

That I haue so largely proued single Communion, it was to good purpose. For whereas you condemned the Masse for it, and made the priestes Sole receiuing a breach of Christes Institution: now that the same is so sufficiently proued, what remaineth, but that you recant, and allow the Masse, onlesse you can shew good reason, why Sole receiuing may be good in other faithful persons, and il in a Priest?

Touching the Church of Rome, against which the heretikes of al ages haue euer barked, of whose Bishops, Cardinals, and Priestes you say as besemeth your railing sprite, that they do neither teach, nor exhorte, nor comforte, nor any other parte of their duties, and that the people is carelesse and voide of deuotion: to answer al these sclaunders, it were besides our purpose, and the same I haue already answered in my cōfutation of your Apologie. Sainct Bernard, whom you allege much both here, and other where against the Prelates of that Church, reprehendeth their euil life, he condemneth not their doctrine. As for your Doctrine, he hath thoroughbly condemned in your predecessours, Berengarius, Abailardus, Arnaldus de Brixia, the Henricians, the Apostolikes, the Peterbrusians, and other murreins of that age.

M. Iew: raileth at the prelates of the church of Rome.

The predecessors of the Caluinistes.

The.xxiij.Diuision.

After that I haue proued single Communion, for which M. Iewel condemneth the Masse: I prouoke him to answer my demaunde,

How say you syr, say I, do you reproue the Masse, or do you reproue the Priuate Masse? The rest is to be seene in my booke. Page.22.a
To this he answereth not directly. But vseth his wõted shiftes.

Ievvel.

Hitherto M. Harding hath brought Doctours vvithout reason: novv he bringeth reason vvithout Doctours. &c.

Harding.

The Doctours I bring, had good reason. They are auncient and learned. who tryeth out a doubteful mater by testimonies of such Doctours, he doth that which learning requireth. The reason that now I bring, is concluded out of the Doctours, and therfore I bring it not al together without Doctours. But this taunte answereth not my question. I would your answer were plaine, then should you soone perceiue, what I would conclude.

Ievvel.

Marke vvel, good Christian Reader, and thou shalt see, hovv handsomely M. Harding conueigheth and shifteth his handes to deceiue thy sight. First he hath hitherto foreborne both the name, and also the prouse of Priuate Masse, and only hath vsed the vvordes of Sole receiuing, and Single Communion. &c.

Marke reader, I haue forborne hitherto (saith he) the proufe of priuate Masse, before he twiteth me with it.

Harding.

I haue before proued Sole receiuing or Single Communion out of the Doctours, not to deceiue the sight of the Reader, but to proue in dede thereby consequently Priuate Masse, (not as it is commonly said, but) so fare as it is a Sole receiuing on the Priestes parte. Now it remaineth for you to shew, as I haue before expressely required you, why it may not aswel be lawful for a Priest to receiue alone, hauing none disposed to receiue with him, as it was and is for lay persons to receiue alone in time of sickenesse or otherwise, hauing none also disposed to receiue with them.

Marke

Marke good Reader how M. Jewel contrarieth him selfe. Here he saith, I haue *hitherto forborne the name, and also the prouse of priuate Masse.* And what hath he borne thee in hand thorough out his. 17. 18. and. 19. Diuision, but that I went about to proue Priuate Masse? wherfore hath he so scoffed at me al this while, but for that he would me to seme to proue Priuate Masse? whose wordes be those in the. 17. Diuision? *To proue priuate Masse in the primitiue Church, for lacke of priestes he allegeth Tertullians vvife, certain vvemen out of Cyprian, and Serapions boy. &c.* Yet now he saith I haue forborne to proue Priuate Masse. How squareth this together? It is you M. Jewel, whom the Reader hath good cause to mistrust, least by vsing such craft, and shiftes, such doublenesse, such contradiction, and skipping from one thing to an other, you deceiue his sight.

M. Jew. contrary to himself. A manifest contradiction.

M. Jewels wordes.

Ievvel.

Vvhat meaneth this, that priuate Masse, and Sole receiuing be so sodainely grovven in one? Surely M. Harding vvel knovveth, that the nature of these vvordes is not one. Neither vvho so euer receiueth alone, doth therfore of necessitie say priuate Masse. This so sodaine altering of termes may breede suspition.

Harding.

As for the Catholikes, they acknowledge in dede no Priuate Masse at al, as Luther and the Protestantes of our time vnderstand Priuate. In which sense being taken I refuse the terme vtterly, and retourne it backe to Luthers skoole, and to you in that point his scholer. But if you meane by Priuate Masse nothing els, but the priestes Sole receiuing, as somtimes you seme to meane: then may you wel iudge, that by how many testimonies I haue proued Sole receiuing, by so many I haue proued that you cal Priuate Masse to be lawful. For if it be lawful in an other, why is it not lawful in a Priest?

If you wil dispute orderly hereof, it behoueth first you agre with vs vpon the terme. That which you cal priuate Masse, you may better cal it Priuate or Sole receiuing. As for the blessed Masse, we know what it is, though ye blaspheme it neuer so wickedly. The Masse and Priuate touching the Sacrifice can not grow into one. As that which is common and publike can not be Priuate.

Ievvel.

To the Sacrifice of the Crosse, the Sacrifice that is imagined in the Masse is mere iniurious.

Harding.

Thus saith M. Jewel, but he proueth it not. It is easy for such a sprite to blaspheme. And yet doubtelesse he beareth witnesse against his owne conscience. For whether the Sacrifice of the Masse be iniurious to the Sacrifice of the Crosse, him selfe could haue called S. Augustine to recorde, who hereof among other many the like sayinges saith thus. Nonne semel immolatus est Christus in seipso, & tamen in Sacramento non solum per omnes paschæ solennitates, sed omni die populis immolatur. Was not Christe once sacrificed in him selfe? And yet notwithstanding he is sacrificed in a Sacrament for the people, not only through al the feastes of Easter, but also euery day. Againe in an other place he saith. Cuius rei Sacramentum quotidianum esse voluit Ecclesiæ Sacrificium. Christe would the daily Sacrifice of the Church (wherby he meaneth the Sacrifice of the Masse) to be a Sacrament of his Sacrifice vpon the Crosse. And in an other place speaking of the Masse plainely. Israel secundum carnem seruiebat in vmbris Sacrificiorum, quibus significabatur singulare Sacrificium, quod nunc offert Israel secundũ Spiritum. Israel that was after the flesh serued in shadowes of Sacrifices, by which the singular Sacrifice was signified,

Augustin. epist. 23.

De ciuit. lib. 10. cap. 20.

Aug. contra aduersarium legis & prophet. lib. 1. cap. 20.

which now Israel that is after the spirite offereth. This singular Sacrifice now offered vp by the Church the spiritual Israel, can be vnderstanded to be no other Sacrifice, then that of Christes body, which (as S. Augustine there a litle before saith) he gaue vpon the Crosse for al the olde Sacrifices, & now the church offereth in the Masse through al the worlde.

This is the faith of the Church, this is the doctrine of the Fathers, by this Sacrifice christen people be put in mynde of their redemption. Of this Sacrifice is the expresse commaundement of Christe. From Christe to the Apostles, from the Apostles to their scholers, from succession to succession this Sacrifice hath spred, and shal remaine in the Church for euer. Cease M. Iewel to cal the Sacrifice of the Masse iniurious to the Sacrifice of the Crosse. One and the same can not be iniurious to it selfe. If you contemne the Church, yet thinke I it good, to aduertise the Christen reader of the state you stād in, as al others of your wicked opinion, by this sentence of the Tridentine Councel. If any say, that blasphemie is done vnto the most holy Sacrifice of Christ donne vpon the Crosse by the Sacrifice of the Masse: or that this is derogatorie to that: be he accursed.

Mat. 26. Luc. 22. 1. Cor. 11.

Concil. Tridentini Session. 22. can. 4.

Your other talke in this Diuision toucheth me, and not the mater, and therfore I omit it.

The. xxiiij. Diuision.

AS in the Diuision before this M. Iewel founde shiftes, by saying thinges impertinent, and would not directly answer my demaunde: so neither here can he be induced to answer the argument which I make.

To thintent the Reader may the better consider it, I shal not let here to reherse it againe.

If the priuate Masse in respect onely that it is priuate after Luthers meaning, be reproueable, it is for single Communion, that is to say, for that the Priest receiueth the Sacrament alone. But the single Communion is lawful, yea good and godly: Ergo, the priuate Masse in this respect that it is priuate, is not reproueable. If the first proposition or Maior seme to be of you to be denyed, then must you shew, for what els you reproue priuate Masse in respect onely that it is priuate, then for single Cōmunion. If you shew ought els, then do you digresse from our purpose, declaring your selfe to reproue the Masse in general. The minor, or second proposition you can not denye, forasmuch as I haue before so sufficiently proued it. And so the Masse in that respect onely it is priuate, is to be holden for good and godly. Now let M. Jewels answer hereto be vewed and considered.

Ievvel.

Out of al these former authorities of Tertullians vvife, Monkes in the Vvildernesse, laye men, vvemen, and boyes, M. Harding gathereth this conclusion, vvhich as he vvould haue folke thinke, standeth so soundly on euery side, that it can not possibly be auoided.*

The. 127. Untruth. I gather not this fond conclusion, it is M. Jewels forberie.

The Priuate Masse is single Communion:

Single Communion is lavvful:

Ergo, Priuate Masse is lavvful.

This Syllogismus vnto the vnskilful may seme somevvhat terrible, as a visard vnto a childe, that can not iudge vvhat is vvithin it. But M. Harding, that made it, knovveth it is vaine, and vvorth nothing.

Harding.

M. Jewel requireth simple, plaine, and sincere handeling.

The

The Syllogismus (for so you cal it) ẏ here you haue made, how terrible it is to fooles, I know not: certaine I am to wise men it shal appeare but a counterfeit visard. Myne it is not, as you know: therfore may you take it vnto you againe, and make the best of it you can. What, thought you that noman would vewe my sayinges, and vnderstand, whether I made such a reason or no? If you thought so, you were very simple. If you thought otherwise, in doing as you haue donne, you were very impudēt. Is it maruel, that you falsifie the Doctours that lyued so lōg sythens, seing you falsifie the sayinges of your lyuing aduersaries? M. Iew. forgeth peeuish arguments of his own & attributeth thē to his aduersarie.

Now syr my argument was farre otherwise, and not as you frame it. Both my booke, and your owne booke, into which for some colour of a confutation you haue put my wordes, is a witnesse against you, and to al that read it, declareth your impudent falsifying. Answer it, if you can. By chaunging my reasons, and by setting forth such false visardes, what do you els, but tel the world, your cause is desperate, and that you haue not what to answere? Now that you haue taked this libertie vpō you to deuyse argumentes of your owne, and say, they be myne: what maruel is it, if to the simple you seme to haue the better syde: specially if any be so simple, or so farre addict vnto you, as wil beleue, what so euer you say? For you wil be sure to frame your forged reasons so, as you may be wel able to confute them. I haue told you hereof els where, but I see no amendmēt.

I nede not to reherse my argument again. Peruse it, consyder it wel, and answer it. What nede you to couer the light of the mater with so many vaine argumentes of your owne forgery, and with making so much a doo with Medius terminus, subiectum, and prędicatum, points vnknowen to the common readers? whiles you geue others warning to be ware of deceit, you vse al deceit your selfe. The whole demeanour of your shiftes sheweth, how litle able you are to auoid my reason. Yet let vs heare your most serious and chiefe answer.

Ievvel.

Novv touching M. Hardinges Syllogisme, thou maist see, that the Minor or secōd propositiō is not true, as they term it Simpliciter, and vvithout exception. For the single Communion vvas neuer so taken for lauful, but only in cōsideration of circumstances, and cases of necessitie. VVhich casesbeing either remoued, or better examined, the same kinde of single Communion is no longer thought lauful.

Harding.

The second proposition of my argument is this. Single Communion as you terme it, or rather sole receiuing, is lauful. This proposition say you, is not true simpliciter, and without exception. It is true say I simpliciter, and without exception, for sole receiuing is lauful simpliciter and absolutly, ergo the second proposition is true simply and without exceptiō. Thus I proue it. It is simpliciter good, ergo it is simpliciter lauful. For to what thing so euer no parte of his substance wanteth, the same is simply good in his kind. But to sole receiuing of the Cōmunion nothing wanteth on the behalfe of the thing it selfe, therfore it is in it selfe good and perfite: & so lauful simply, & without exceptiō & al relation to your circūstances & cases of necessitie. And thus is the priests sole receiuing proued, which you denie: but of your owne auctoritie, without scripture, Doctor, Councel or reason, & contrary to the custome and auctoritie of the Church, & contrary to the determination of the Tridentine Councel, you denie it.

Cōcil. Tridēt. Sess. 13 can. 10. & Sess. 22. can. 8.

And if sole receiuing were lauful only in consideratiō of circūstances, & in cases of necessitie whereof you dreame: your part had ben to haue proued, that these circumstances and cases, were of the substance of the thing. which because you were not able to doo, you did politikely to passe it ouer in silence. If it were lau-

ful

ful in consideration of circumstances and cases of necessitie, then was it not cōtrary to gods lawe. For what so euer is absolutely contrary to gods law can be made lauful by no circūstances, nor cases of necessitie to be appointed by man. As for example, fornication is contrary to Gods lawe. were it so that a man might be in case to dye through some kind of disease, except he haue carnal doing with a woman: In this case life is a thousād tymes to be lost, rather thē fornication is to be donne, because it is cōtrary to Gods law. Again, by Gods law no man can baptise him self. Therfore no circumstance nor case of necessitie can be deuised, in which a man may minister baptisme to him selfe. Forasmuch thē as you confesse that sole receiuing was lauful in consideratiō of circūstances & cases of necessitie: you acknowledge & graunt it not to be absolutly contrary to Gods lawe. If it be not absolutly contrary to Gods lawe, then the Church assisted with the spirite of God, may take order therein, as it is sene most behooful for Gods honour. And so it hath taken order, that a priest, if the people be not disposed to receiue the Sacrament with him, may notwithstanding say Masse, and receiue alone.

What is vtterly cōtrary to Gods law cā be made lauful by no circumstance or case of necessitie.

And notwithstanding the Church suffereth a womā (whereof you speake) in cases of necessitie to baptise, because baptisme is a Sacrament necessarie to salutation, whereas there is no such necessitie of the Communion but that a man may be saued without it, hauing no contentempt of it: better it is neuer to receiue the Communiō, then to receiue it in any such case, wherein it should not be simply and without exception good and lauful.

This then is that I say. One to receiue the Sacrament alone, it is simply and absolutly lauful in it selfe. If any person offēd in receiuing alone, it is not because he receiueth alone, but because otherwise he receiueth vnworthely. Consider in what cases of necessitie a woman or a lay man may baptise

To receiue alone is absolutely lauful.

at home, in the like cases of necessitie they may baptise also in the Church. In like manner if sole receiuing be lauful at home, as you confesse, in cases of necessitie: it is lauful also in the like cases of necessitie to be donne by the priest in open Church. The thing it selfe which ẏ lay persõs do in baptizing is not vnlauful in it selfe, for if it were, they myght nowhere baptise.

Right so to receiue the Sacrament, it is absolutely and simply lawful in it selfe, and without exception: for els it were vtterly vnlauful. Wherein soeuer a man offendeth when he receiueth, that concerneth circumstance of some order appointed by the Church. But there is no order taken by the Churche, that forbiddeth a man to receiue alone: yea rather order requireth ẏ in some cases a mã ought to receiue alone. by which order ẏ priest at Masse is boũd to receiue alone, if none els be disposed to receiue with him. Therfore Single Communion is absolutely and simply lauful.

Ievvel.

The 128. Untruth. I brought not those examples to proue ẏ Masse by thẽ directly, but sole receiuing.

*Therfore thou maist thus say to M. Harding hovv say you syr? Do you allovve the examples that you haue brought *to proue your Masse by, or do you not allovv them? If you allovve them, vvhy then suffer ye not vvemẽ to carie home the Sacramẽt, and to kepe it in cheastes, and napkins as they did of olde? If you allovve them not, because they vvere abuses, vvhy then seeke you to proue your Masse by the same, and so to establish one abuse by an other?*

Harding.

M. Iew. susteining the parte of ẏ answerer, opposeth, which is cõtrary to al good order of schooles.

Although it be besides the course of an orderly disputatiõ, & contrary to the mãner of schooles, for the respõdent whose parte you susteine, specially when he is vrged with an argument him selfe, to oppose the opponent, and to put him to the office of a respondent: yet least your question should seme to the vnlearned to haue more pith and substance, then it hath in dede: thus I answer, The examples which I brought not to proue the Masse by

as

as you say, but to proue the Sole receiuing of the Priest, which you cal priuate Masse: I allowe as good and laudable for that time. The cause why we suffer not wemen to carry home the Sacrament, and to kepe it, as they of olde time kepte it, is, for that the Church now hath no such custome, but contrary wise commaūdeth the holy hoste receiued in the Church, forthwith to be consumed, and not to be caryed home. Of that order it hath good reason and consideration. For whereas of olde time it was carried home to be receiued at times when they might not safely assemble them selues together for feare of the Infidels, vnder whom they stode in feare daily of persecution to death: now that feare ceassing, the custome of carrying it home is restrained. That custome being a thing indifferent, the Churche hath aucthoritie for diuersitie of times and manners to alter, as in other things of them selfe indifferent, it hath the like aucthoritie to dispose so or so, as occasion semeth good. For this cause and also for the auoiding of certain abuses therin committed in old time, the Church doth not now allow ẏ custome of carrying home the blessed Sacrament, not because it was an abuse, as you woulde vs to graunt: for at that time so to doo, it was a godly vse, and no abuse. And it may so be done now also of faithful persons, where Antichriste or any of his do stirre the like persecution.

Why the Sacrament is not carryed home from the Churche now, as in olde time.

Ievvel.

*That it might seme lavvful for a Priest to say priuate Masse, he hath brought in examples of Laie men, Vvemen, Sicke folke, and Boyes. Alas doth M. Harding thinke, it vvas the manner in olde times, that laye people should saye Masse? Or vvas there no Priest al this vvhile in the vvorld for the space of sixe hundred yeares, that vvemen and children must come forth to proue these maters? Or vvas there no difference then betvven Sole receiuing, and Priuate Masse? Or shal vve thinke that vvemen and boyes did then consecrate the holy Mysteries, or offer vp Christes Body: or make Sacrifice for quicke and dead: or applie Christes death

The. 129. vntruth. It is not so, I brought those examples in for proufe of single receiuing.

vnto others? Vvhere is M. Hardings Logique becomme? Vvhere is the sharpeness of his vvite?

Harding.

What do you M. Jewel but deceiue the vnlearned Reader with confusion of termes? You seeke not truth, but only to seme to geue your Aduersarie a foile. You triumph wantonly without cause. You make awise, as though I had quite forgotten my Logique, & lost my witte. Al these busy bragges, be but winde. To answere ẏ mater, if a due distinctiō of Masse, priuate Masse, and Single Communion or sole receiuing, be considered, these puffes of vaine wordes wil sone be laid. I haue not brought in examples of laie men, wemen, sicke folke and boyes (wherwith your shamelesse vanitie hath neuer done, for I bring no exāples of any boyes sole receiuing at al) that it might seme lawful for a Priest to say priuate Masse. Neither acknowledge I (as the Masse importeth the Sacrifice of the Church) any priuate Masse at al, such as may be said by a Priest. If you wil nedes haue the Priestes sole receiuing to be termed a priuate Masse, who can let you? Verely ẏ same is not that which is said, but a thing which is done. And that this thing might seme lauful in a Priest, the forsaid examples may wel be alleged for proufe.

That which is said by the Priest is not priuat Masse.

Shew vs what you meane by priuate Masse, and what difference you make betwene priuate Masse and sole receiuing, and then may you talke more directly and more plainely. For lacke of a due distinction of it from al that is not it, and of a clere definition of the terme, you skip in and out vncertainely, and with your confuse Sophistrie deceiue the simple. Crye out no more Alas, so foolishly. Scoffe no more, as though I made lay men wemen, boyes, and sicke folke to say Masse. How so euer you perswade your Prentises, wise men wil not beleue it of me. Be

not

not so lusty in making your triumph before the victorie. By this you do much discredite your selfe and your cause. Let vs haue lesse of your boyish mockeries, and more substance of good and learned reasons. If you haue no better stuffe then this, remember who hath chalenged you for his Prisoner. I trow the chiefe comfort you haue is this: Though you be found reasonlesse and witlesse, yet you wil not be founde tonglesse and speachelesse.

The. xxv. Diuision.

AMong other things that I speake of in the .xxv. Diuission, hauing shewed the Masse not to be reprouable, for that the Priest receiueth alone: I adde therunto an expresse cõfession, wherby I commend the peoples deuoute and worthy receiuing with the Priest. My wordes be these. I denie not, but that it were more commendable, and more godly on the Churches parte, if many wel disposed and examined, would be partakers of the blessed Sacrament with the Priest.

I reporte mee to thy conscience Christian Reader, as before God, whether these woordes can iustly seeme to conteine in any respect an euil meaning. weigh them, wel, and iudge wherein I am to be reproued for so saying. If no euil can be piked out of them, consider with thy selfe, whether M. Iewel, who maketh so much a do with me for them, ought not to be taken for such a one, as desyreth rather to depraue me maliciously, then to set forth the truth plainely. what I said, euen now I say againe, and vpholde it to be wel said. Because I confesse, it were more commendable on the peoples behalf, that thei would dispose them selfe worthilye to bee partetakers of the Blessed

Sacrament with the Priest: he compareth me with the picture of Medea, in whose face a Painter by his skil of painting made two contrary affections to appeare, cruel furie stirring her to kil her childe, and motherly pitie mouing her to spare her childe.

Ievvel.

The.130. vntruth. I deface not the Cōmuniō but make it a necessary parte of ẏ masse. But I meane not the new Geneuian Communion.

Such tvvo contrary affections (saith he) *vve may here see in M. Harding, both painted and sette out in one face. For notvvithstanding for his credites sake he aduaunce his Masse, and* * *deface the holy Communion vvith al that he is able: yet here againe for conscience sake of the other side he confesseth, that the Communion is the better: and so rippeth vp al, that he hath sevved before. Goddes name be blessed, that is thus able to force out his truth, euen by the mouthes of them, that openly vvithstand his truth.*

Harding.

Seing M. Jewel seeketh nothing els, but to carpe, and reproue, what so euer I say: consider I pray thee good Reader, whether it may be gathered out of my wordes, that I make the holy Communion, which M. Jewel speaketh of, better then the Masse. Verely I make no comparison betweene them. I knowe that Consecration serueth to the Communion. And the Sacrifice that is Consecrated, is to this ende Consecrated, that the Oblation done, it be receiued. Which whether it be receiued of many atonce in one place together, or of the Priest alone: it is truely named Communion, because thereby the person that receiueth, is ioyned to God, and made one body with Christe, and one with al others, that be likewise partakers of the same Sacrifice. For that host or Sacrifice is one, as S. Chrysostome and other aūcient Fathers teach, not diuers Sacrifices, in how many places, and of how many persons so euer it be receiued. The vnitie of that Sacrifice which is the Body of Christe, maketh al that worthily receiue it, one with Christe, so

The hoste or Sacrifice is one euery where. *Chrysost. in Epist. ad Heb. homil. 17.*

as

as he and they be one, which the word Communio reporteth. This Communion is a parte of that which we cal the Masse. And there is no Masse without Communion, because it is required to the perfection of a Sacrifice, that it be consumed: and therfore the Priest that consecrateth and offereth, is bounde to receiue the Oblation. Therfore if I say, that the Communion is better then the Masse, I should vndiscretely say, that parte were better then the whole.

Now I speake not of the goodnesse of the one, nor of the other, much lesse by a foolish comparison make I the one better then the other. The comparison that I make, is betwen the worthy receiuing of many with the Priest, and not receiuing. whether many receiue with the Priest in the same place, or none receiue with him: yet in that he receiueth, there is a Communion. In deede I confesse, ỷ it were more commendable & more godly on the peoples parte, if many wel disposed and examined would receiue the blessed Sacrament with the Priest. That is to say, it were more commendable and more godly for many to be wel disposed, and to enioy that inestimable benefite: then through vnworthynesse & vndeuotion to lacke it. How be it they do not altogether lacke it, that do spiritually Communicate. In effect the sense of my saying is this. It is a more commendable and godly thing on the peoples behalfe, worthily to receiue the Communion with the Priest, then the Priest to receiue alone.

Marke my wordes, on the Peoples behalfe, on the Churches parte. By which I exclude al comparison betwen Communion, and Communion. The Communion of the Priest lacking a number to receiue with him in the same place, is as wel a Communion, and as good a Communion in it selfe, as if a great number receiued with him. It is not number more or lesse, that increaseth, or diminisheth the goodnesse of the Communion in it selfe. Say not therfore M. Iewel, that I confesse, the Communion to be better then the Masse, that is to say, parte better then the whole, or that one Communion is better then an other Communion.

If M. Iewel meane by this terme, *the holy Communion*, that new deuised toy, which hath ben inuented by our English Gospellers of the Sacramentarie secte of late yeres, and with terrour of the sword commaunded to be practised, which is both Schismatical and Heretical, and tendeth directly to the condemnation of the Catholike Churche: be he wel assured, that I beare not that affection to it, which he would his vnlearned fauourers to thinke me to beare, neither confesse I at al for conscience sake, as he vntruly reporteth of me, that it is better then the Masse. But contrarywise I confesse that it is vtterly to be detested as wicked in the sight of God, and damnable: and that if any man suffer death for not subscribing, comming, or yelding vnto it, he dieth a Martyr, and shal enioy therfore the crowne of Martyrdome. Say no more therfore M. Iewel, that I haue ripped vp al that I haue sewed before. My seame contineweth whole, as before. So may you recant and crosse out the note you haue put in your bookes margent. *M. Harding confesseth, that the Communion is better then his Masse.* which note is false, sclaunderous and absurd, as I haue now declared.

And syr if occasion were offred me to speake honorably of the holy Communion, in case I should much commend it, and praise it, as it is worthy of al praise: would you beare the simple people in hande, that for conscience sake I said much good of your English Communion? No syr, if I speake ought in praise of the Communion, perswade your selfe, that I meane not your new deuise, about the which ye were neuer yet wel agreed

with-

within yyur selues, but of the Communion of Christes Catholike Church, which is farre different from your new framed fansy.

Our Communion hath the Real body of Christe, your Cōmunion after your owne Doctrine hath but bakers bread, and is not made a holy thing in it selfe, but the signe only of a holy thing. we take bread and wine mingled with water after the example of Christe, and pronounce the wordes of our Lord ouer them, with intention to do that which the Church doth, by which wordes spoken by the Priest in the person of Christe, his body and bloud are Consecrated. Ye take not the bread, but let it lye on the table, whiles the Minister is talking in the pulpite, or other where, wherein ye folow not thexample of Christe, nor put ye water to the wine as Christe did, nor haue that intention which the Church hath, and therfore pronounce not the wordes to such purpose as the Church teacheth, but only reade them, as one would tel a tale, not directing your mynde and intention to the Consecration. we adore that is Consecrated, as being the very body and bloud of Christe: ye adore not, beleuing al to be but worldly creatures of bread and wine. That which we receiue at our Communiō, is before offred, as we haue ben taught of our Lorde, who as S. Irenëus saith, taught vs the new Oblation of the New Testament. Ye make no such Oblation, neither beleue ye any such Oblation to be made at al.

The difference betwen the Communion that is in the Masse, & the new ministring Communion.

Cyprā. ad Cæcilium.

Irenæus. lib. 4. cap. 32.

To conclude by our Communion worthily receiued, we are ioyned to God, and made one with Christe, and within our selues by a natural vnion, as out of S. Hilarius and Cyrillus I haue before declared. Ye by your Communion are the more separated from God, sundred from the mystical body of Christe the Churche, and the nearer ioyned to Sathan the ennemie of God, author of Diuision.

DD ij. This

This considered, you see M. Jewel, how litle cause you haue to say, that I confesse your Cōmunion to be better then the Masse, whereat we haue the true Communion, though the number of receiuers together in one place be not sometimes equal to the numbers of your Congregations.

The masse is impugned, not bicause of ÿ Priestes Sole receiuing chiefli, but for the Sacrifices sake, whiche Satan most of al hateth.

And where as ye professe such hatred and hostilitie against the Masse, & without al example of antiquitie cal it by a strange name Priuate, for that the Priest, though neuer so much without any his default receiueth the blessed Sacrament alone: what if it may be brought to passe, that some shal alwaies receiue it with the Priest? wil ye then alow the Masse? As for example, at Easter, and at certaine other feastes, the people were wont to receiue their rightes in England, in these countries here, and in other places, they receiue oftentimes. In this case what say you of the Masse? If this be obserued, wil the Masse then like you? If neither then ye wil alow the Masse, as doubtlesse ye wil not: then cloke the mater no more with the name of Priuate Masse, but openly professe your selues ennemies to the Masse, in your railing bookes and Sermons spitte out your malice, at the Masse, at the mystical Oblation of the body and bloud of Christ, at the daily Sacrifice of the Churche. For most certaine it is, how many so euer of the deuoute people receiue their rightes with the Priest, neither ye, nor Sathan for al that wil alow the Masse.

Where I say in this Diuision, As touching the substance of the Masse it selfe, by the Single Communion of the Priest in case of the peoples coldnesse and negligence, it is nothing impaired: M. Jewel findeth fault with the manner of my vtterance, and liketh not these new founde termes (as he termeth them) of Substance and Accidentes in the Institution of Christ. So he calleth it, for he hath a Conscience to cal it by the name of

Masse,

Masse, but when he either scoffeth or raileth at it. Now I cal so much of the Masse by the name of Substance, as is necessary by Christes Institution, and expresse commaundement. As for the terme of Accidentes, I vse it not. If I did, I might seme to do it not without reason, vnderstanding thereby that, which we haue of the institution of holy Fathers, and is commaunded by the Churche to be donne for the more reuerence of the blessed Sacramēt, for encrease of deuotion, for the better and more truely setting forth of Christes Passion. &c. M. Jewel hereto replieth thus.

Ievvel.

This difference in termes of Subst ance, and Accidentes in Christes Institution, is nevvly founde out, and hath no vvarrant neither of the scriptures, nor of the olde Fathers.

Harding.

Why sticke you so much at the difference in termes, seing that ye haue a difference in thinges? Did not Christ at his supper certaine thinges, that must be done of vs necessarily? Did he not certaine other thinges, which we are not bounde necessarily to folow? what if we say then these be of the substance of Christes Institution, these be but accidentary: shal we be reproued of gay Rhetoricians for vsing that difference in termes? Concerning the Sacrament of Baptisme, that the body be baptized or touched with water, that the partie which baptizeth say, I baptise thee in the name of the Father, and of the Sonne, and of the holy Ghoste: be not these necessary, and of the substance of Baptisme? Other Ceremonies from the Apostles time to this day vsed generally in the Church, vntil that ye with manifest contempt of the Church abolished them: be they not in comparison of the essentials, accidentarie?

Differēce of thinges is to be vttered with difference of termes.

Thus in al Sacramentes there is a difference in thinges, and therfore to expresse the same, we may lawfully vse the difference in termes.

Ievvel.

*Christes example in doing, and commaundement to do the same, may not be taken for a shevve or Accident, but for the effecte and *substāce of his supper. Do this saith Christe, the same that you haue sene me doo: Take, blisse, breake, Diuide, in my remembrance. &c. This is no Accident or light fantasie, that may be leafte at our pleasure, but the very substantial point of the Sacrament, vvhich vve are specially commaunded to continue vntil he come. &c.*

The. 131. Untruth, Christes whole exāple, is not of the substance of the Sacrament.

Harding.

Mat. 26.

Yea M. Iewel? How handle you the Scriptures? How abuse you that most holy Mysterie? Haue we nothing els to do, but to take, to blesse, to breake, and to diuide in remembrance of Christe? why expresse you not, what we must take? what ment you by hudling these wordes together? If you sought the truth, you would not haue vsed such confusion. This thing would haue ben more plainely & more distinctly handled. That which is of most substāce of al, you thought best to leaue out, least your falshed should be espied. where is the special Consecration? why vttered you not the wordes, by which our Lorde consecrated his body and bloud, this is my body, this is my bloud? Be you loth to heare them? Be you afrayd, they shal confoūd your Sacramentarie heresie at length, as those wordes of Christ, Ego & pater vnum sumus, confounded the heresie of the Arians?

M. Iew. mangleth and much abuseth ẏ scriptures

Speakīg of the institution of ẏ sacramēt, he leaueth out the cōsecration.

John. 10.

It is like, you are of the opinion that your companions were of at Geneua in Quene Maries time. who in the Communion of their English congregation there, least out the wordes of Consecration, as their printed booke is a witnesse thereof, least the people by rehersal of the wordes should be moued to thinke, that there is alteration made in the bread & wine.

The Cōmunion of the English Congregation at Geneua had not the words of Conse-

Syr before you talke so confidently of this great mysterie,

you

you should do wel to learne, how much, and what Christe commaunded to be done, in that he said, Do ye this in my remembrance. And where should you learne it, but of the Churche the spouse of Christe, to whom he promised the holy ghost the spirite of truth? The Church teacheth you, that Christe by that he did and spake at his Supper, the due mater and minister presupposed, ordeined the Consecration, Oblation, and Communion of his body: and that certaine other thinges be but Ceremonies, whiche Christ obserued and did: and be not of necessitie either of the Sacrament, or Sacrifice, but lefte to the disposition of the Church, as number, time, place, &c. So that Christes example is of necessitie to be folowed but in parte, not for euery circūstance: For els the blessed Sacrament were not to be geuen to fewer thē to twelue, and that after supper, with other circumstances conteined in his example. His commaundement is thoroughly to be donne without any exception. Thus you may see, a difference betwen that which is absolutely necessary by Christes cōmaūdement, & that which is not in such wise necessary, as depēding of his example: And though the same be in dede an Accident in respect of ỹ substāce of the Sacrament, yet is it not a light fantasie, as it liketh you to terme it, ỹ may now be left at our pleasure. Neither at al be the thinges at our pleasure, wherein the Church hath by authentical decrees taken determinat order. Hereof I thinke it not nedeful to speake much in this place, seing that I haue spoken of it before, and hereafter occasion shalbe geuen to speake againe.

cration for feare of Transubstantiatiō. Mat. 26.

How is Christes example to be folowed touching the holy mysteries.

Christes commaundement is to be done without al exception.

You allege Alexander de Ales, and one Humbertus, *tvvo* (as you say) *of M. Hardinges ovvne Scholastical Doctours*, and yet I trow Hūbertus was no Scholastical Doctour. Alexāder de Ales saith nothing, as you allege him, ỹ maketh ought either for you, or agaist me. As for Hūbertus cited by Cassāder, who bēdeth his whole force against the Masse whereat the people doth not Sa-

Hūbertus. Cassander

cramentally communicate with the Priest: for Cassanders sake, we may iustly suspect him. But what saith he, according to the reporte of Cassander our Aduersarie? *Of these three* (saith he) *Consecration, Breaking, and Distributiō, vvhich one of them so euer is done vvithout the* (two) *other, it representeth not the memorie of Christe.* Truth it is. The Priest celebrating Masse, doth celebrate and represent the memorie of Christ. These three to that ende must go together. The Body which is consecrated, ought in the forme of bread to be broken, and then receiued, for that is meant by distribution. And so Humbertus calleth it, for that it is to be geuen to as many as be proued and require it. If none be ready to receiue, the Priest may and ought to receiue alone. It is inough if he haue a wil to distribute to the people, if it be worthily demaūded. For onlesse it be receiued, Christes memorie is not represented. If by distribution he meane, that a number be alwayes together in one place, to whom the Sacramente may be deliuered: and that except it be geuen to many to receiue and consume it together, the memorie of Christ is not represented: if this be his meaning, as I thinke verely it is not: forasmuch as it is contrary to the practise of the Church, and alleged by Cassander in this point the Aduersarie of the Church, and he otherwise an obscure man: I make smal accompt what he saith.

Further more I say in this Diuision, that if the publike Sacrifice of the Church, might not be done without a nūber of communicantes receiuing wͭ the Priest in one place, forasmuch as ẏ Fathers complaine oftentimes of ẏ slackenes of ẏ people for not resorting to the receiuing wͭ the Priestes: they would haue complained somwhere in their writings of the ceasing of that, which euery where they cal Quotidianum & iuge Sacrificium, the Daily and continual Sacrifice. But they complaine of ẏ peoples not comming to receiue, and not of the ceasing of the daily Sacrifice:

Therefore

Therfore an argument thereof may be gathered, that the publike Sacrifice of the Church, which we cal the Masse, was at sundrie times celebrated, when such numbers of the people to receiue with the Priestes wanted. To this M. Jewel saith.

Ievvel.

The olde Fathers neuer complained of ceasing thereof, because they knevv it could neuer cease. For the strength and vertue of Christes Sacrifice resteth in it selfe, and not in any diligence, or doing of ours.

Harding.

You answere not directly. I speake of the publike external and visible Sacrifice of the Church, wherby I vnderstand the Masse, as you may perceiue: and you speake of the strength and vertue of Christes Sacrifice, which, as you say, resteth in it selfe, and not in the diligence or doing of man. That the vertue of Christes Sacrifice should rest in mans diligence or doing, it is to absurd for any man to say. Therfore your denial of it, is more odious thē necessary, as though it had euer ben affirmed. And although the strength and vertue of Christes Sacrifice, rest not in the diligence or doing of man: yet is it by the ministerie of man applied to man. As for example, the vertue of Christes Sacrifice and passion, wherby ve are redemed, is imparted vnto vs in Baptisme, and in Baptisme we put on Christ: And Baptisme is ministred by man.

But concerning the ceasing of the Sacrifice which I spake of, what though the strength and vertue of Christes Sacrifice on the Crosse rest in it selfe, might not the old Fathers neuerthelesse complaine of the Churches publike Sacrifices ceasing? How hangeth your reason together? Thinke you perhaps there is no such publike Sacrifice, that may cease? How say you to the Prophecie of Daniel? Saith he not speaking of the comming Dan. 12
of Antichrist, that when he shal come, the continual Sacrifice

shal by him be taken away, Per tempus, tempora, & dimidium temporis, that is, by the space of thre yeares and a halfe, as many understand it?

What is the continual Sacrifice, which according to the saying of Daniel shalbe taken away for a time.

Of what Sacrifice can this be taken, but of the publike Sacrifice of the Churche commonly called the Masse? First as touching the Sacrifice of Christe upon the Crosse, whiche was made but once, and shal never be iterated nor made voide: certaine it is that al the power of Antichrist can not take away that Sacrifice. Neither the inwarde spiritual Sacrifice of mans hart can he take away. For the more vehement is the persecution, the more fervent and earnest is the devotion of the Elect to offer the inwarde spiritual Sacrifices in their hartes. Seing then the publike Sacrifice of the Church is such as may be taken away, as now it is taken away from Christian people in England, if it be not that of the Masse, which Antichrist shal take awaye at his comming: it remaineth, you tel us M. Jewel, what other Sacrifice beside that of the Masse, you can appoint.

Ievvel.

Ths. 132. Untruth. It is not so called, as you meane.

*This Sacrifice of Christe on his Crosse, *is called the daily Sacrifice, not for that it must be renevved euery day, but for that being once done, it standeth good for al dayes and for euer.*

Harding.

The daily Sacrifice of the Churche.

This have you said more then once before, but yet you never proved it. Neither speake I of the Sacrifice which was once offered by Christe on the Crosse in his owne person with shedding of his blood, but of the Sacrifice of the Church, which is celebrated in memorie of that, and is unbloudy. Which is called Daily, because it is daily repeted and iterated, wherein the Sacrifice of the Crosse is represented, and the memorie

morie thereof by daily recourse of this being a Sacrament of that, is renewed. And that other Sacrifice of the Crosse, forasmuch as it hath no daily recourse, can not properly be called daily, though it stand good for al daies, and for euer: no more then his worde or the Gospel may be properly called the daily worde, or Daily Gospel, and yet it remaineth for euer, and it standeth good for al dayes, and euerlastingly. To this I haue answered before in the.ix.Diuision.

Ievvel.

It may be ansvvered in one vvorde. They had the holy Communion euery day, and therfore they complained not. Hovv be it neither is the holy Communion that daily Sacrifice it selfe, but a memorie of the same: neither vvas the Communion then ministred euery daye.

Harding.

No syr, your one word wil not serue for a sufficient answer, because the Communion which you speake of is one thing, and the daily Sacrifice whereof I speake, is an other. But me thinketh your one worde is little worth, because you wil not abide by it. For as now you say it, so within two lines after you slite from it. For how standeth this together, *They had the Communion euery daie*, and, *neither vvas the Communiō ministred euery day?* Had they, and had they it not euery daye? Or had they it, when it was not ministred vnto them, or was it ministred, when they had it not? If they had it euery Day, how was it not ministred euery day? If it were ministred euery daye, how had they it not euery daie? It is no maruel, if M.Iewel agreeth no better with others, that so farre disagreeth with him selfe. He saith, and vnsaith for aduantage, what him listeth.

M. Iew. is contrary to him selfe.

The. xxvi. Diuision.

IN these three Diuisions folowing. xxvi. xxvij. xxviij. prosecuting the Argument before touched, which concludeth the Sacrifice to haue ben celebrated, though ỹ people forbare to receiue: I allege first S. Ambrose, and S. Augustine witnessing, that they of the East were wonte to be houseled but once in the yeare, or very seldome. Then in the. xxvij. Diuision, I bring in a place of S. Chrysostome affirming the same. What meaneth this? saith he, The most parte of you be partakers of this Sacrifice but once in the yeare, some twise, some oftener. And this proueth the seldome receiuing of the people. Then after in the. xxviij. Diuision, I proue by witnesse of S. Chrysostome, that the Sacrifice was daily offered (whereby the Masse is proued) notwithstanding that the people forbare to receiue, with them that offered. His wordes be plaine. Quid ergo nos? Nonne per singulos dies offerimus? Offerimus quidem. Then what do we? Do we not offer euery day? Yeas verely we do so.

In. 10. cap. ad Heb. Homil. 17.

Ad Heb. Homil. 17.

Now out of al this, we may gather this Argument. In the East Church the Sacrifice was euery day offered, but the people did not euery day receiue with them that offred: Ergo the Sacrifice was offered sometimes without such a Communion, as M. Jewel speaketh of. The first Proposition is proued by S. Chrysostome, the second by S. Ambrose, and S. Augustine. Therefore the conclusion is good. If M. Jewel replie, and say, that some Deacons or Priestes receiued with the Priestes, when they said Masse and offered: wee tel him that this is but a slender gheasse of his owne heade, and that if it had alwayes ben so, when the people forbare to receiue: it should haue ben mentioned in one place or other. And he ought to shew vs

where

where the Priestes and Deacons were commaunded alwaies to be in a readines to supplie the peoples forbearing. If there can no mention thereof be founde, sith it is otherwise now, and that not contrary to the Scriptures, constitution of any General or prouincial Councel, nor to the saying of any auncient Father: he ought to beare with vs, if wee vtterly reiect and contemne his light gheasse. Al that M. Iewel replieth in any of these three Diuisions, is not of any great weight. In this. xxvi. Diuision he saith thus.

Iewel.

S. Augustine saith touching Priuate Masse. Panis quotidianus potest accipi pro sacramēto Corporis Christi, quod quotidie accipimus. *The daily bread may be taken for the Sacrament of Christes Body, vvhich vve receiue euery day * S. Augustine saith, the people then receiued the Sacrament euery day: vvhereof it folovveth necessarily, that the priuate Masse vvas then said neuer a day.*

In. 2. lib. de sermone dom, in monte. cap. 12.

The 133. Untruth. S. Augustine saith not so.

Harding.

By priuate Masse you vnderstand (as I suppose) either the Masse, and ỳ Priestes sole receiuing: or onely the Priestes sole receiuing. If you meane the Priestes sole receiuing only, and can also proue out of S. Augustine, that the people receiued the Communion together with the Priestes euerye daye: then proue you that euery such Masse was not priuate by the aucthoritie of S. Augustine. But if you meane by your newe founde terme priuate Masse, the blessed Masse it selfe, in which the Body and Bloud of Christe are of the Priest consecrated, and offred vp to God the Father vnbloudily, and forthwith receiued of the Priest, hauing no others to receiue with him in the same place: of the words which you reherse out of S. Augustine, it foloweth not necessarily, that the priuate Masse was then said neuer a day. For although some Priestes receiued with the people, yet some others might haue said Masse, and receiued alone.

S. Augustine misreported by M. Iewel.

But saye you, S. Augustine saith, the people then receiued the Sacrament euery day. You say so, S. Augustine saith not so. The Dailye breade may be taken for the Sacrament of Christes Body, which wee receiue euerye daye, saith he. What then? Yet wil it not follow, that the people receiued euery daye. For S. Augustine might meane that either of him selfe, and other Priestes as he was, or, which is more likely, he spake and meant indefinitely of al beleuers, among whom some receiued the Body of Christe euery day. Which may be vnderstanded of the Priestes them selues, among whom some said Masse and receiued euery day. Thus it is euident, that S. Augustine in that place doth not ouerthrowe the Masse, which you terme Priuate, and is Common and Publike, notwithstanding any thing that you haue said to the contrary.

Ievvel.

But the Grecians custome vvas to receiue once onely in the yeare: Ergo the Priest at other times receiued alone.

Harding.

You neuer reporte my Argument truely. This it is.

Lib. 5. De Sacramēt. cap. 4. *Homil. 17. ad Heb.*

The Greekes in the East were wont to receiue but once in the yeare as S. Ambrose saith: But the Sacrifice was offered euery day, as S. Chrysostome saith: Ergo, the Priestes oftentimes receiued without the People.

Ievvel.

No saith S. Augustine, this custome, or negligence, vvas not vniuersal among al the people of Grecia, but among a certaine of them onely.

Harding.

Were it that I denye not the thing it selfe, yet S. Augustine saith

saith not as you report. O that once you would vse truth.

Ievvel.

For thus he saith. Plurimi in Orientalibus partibus non quotidie communicant. *Many in the East partes do not daily communicate. Vvherein may be vvel implied, that some daily did Communicate. Othervvise the exception of many had ben in vaine.*

August. De serm. Dom. in monte. lib. 2. cap. 12.

Harding.

Although S. Augustine say so in that place, meaninge of the more parte, yet S. Ambrose Lib. 5. De Sacramentis. Cap. 4. And S. Augustine him selfe De Verbis Domini secundum Lucam, Hom. 28. speake of the Greekes in the East without exception. Of the thing I contend not. But how holdeth your Argument M. Jewel, Many in the East partes did not daily Communicate. Ergo, some daily did Communicate? This conclusion say you, may wel be implied. For els the exception of many had been in vaine. Sith that you wil haue this Argument to be so good here for your purpose, I pray you why may not the same Argument be as good for an other purpose, that you like not? By your owne Logique you must nedes allow this Argument for good. Many in the East Churche, where the Greeke seruice was vsed, spake not naturally the barbarous Tongues onely: Ergo, some spake naturally the barbarous Tongues onely. Of this Conclusion I inferre an other, Ergo, they had their Churche Seruice in a straunge tongue whiche they knewe not. which if you graunt, you must recant your thirde Article.

But Syr, though the Grekes in the East, as S. Ambrose and S. Augustine do say, did communicate but once in the yere: yet might the Priestes among them offer the Sacrifice daily, or very often notwithstanding. which being true, as it is true by S. Chrysostomes testimonie: then was the Sacrifice offered, and Masse celebrated, without and beside the which, the vnbloudy Sacrifice is not offered, whē ȳ people forbare to cōmunicate. And so farre is the Masse proued without the peoples receiuing, which you impugne and condemne.

Ievvel.

And that in such places, vvhereas the Sacrament vvas not daily receiued of the people, it vvas not receiued priuately and daily of the Priest for continuance of the daily Sacrifice, as M. Harding surmiseth, it appeareth vvel by sundry good recordes. S. Augustine saith, Huius rei sacramentū alicubi quotitie, alicubi certis interuallis dierum, in Dominico præparatur, & de mensa Dominica sumitur. *The Sacrament of this thing is prepared, or consecrate in the Churche, and receiued of the Lordes table, in some places euery day, in some places vpon certaine daies.*

August. in Ioā. tract. 26.

Harding.

By three places you would proue, that, whereas the Sacrament was not daily receiued of the people, there was not offered daily the Dailye Sacrifice, which you had rather cal the Priestes priuate and daily receiuing. For that the Priestes did daily offer vp the vnbloudy Sacrifice, you can not abide so much as to name it. Satan hateth the thing, you hate both the thing and the name. And by this you shewe your selfe to meane by priuate Masse, nothing els but the Priestes priuate receiuing of the Sacrament. For which priuate and sole receiuing of the Priest, there is no reason why the Masse should be called Priuate.

But how proue you your purpose by this place of S. Augustine? The Sacrament, saith he, is somewhere euerye daye, somewhere vpon certaine dayes prepared in our Lordes table, and from our Lordes table is receiued. For so is the sentence truly to be translated . why you haue falsified S. Augustines wordes putting in Dominico in the churche, for, in Dominica mensa, in our lordes table: I know not, onlesse it were, for that you feared least an aulter should be thought necessary by S. Augustine to consecrate and offer that sacrifice vpon. The Sacrament in some places is euery day prepared and consecrated by priestes in our lordes table, and from thence by the same priestes is daily receiued. In some places this is donne now and then certaine dayes comming betwen. Wil you of this conclude, that where the people receiued not daily, the priestes offered not vp the Daily Sacrifice? How holdeth your argument? Verely you can neuer of S. Augustines wordes conclude that negatiue. Let vs then see, whether you gather it better of your other places.

M. Iew. corrupteth S. Augustine by putting in one worde for an other.

Ievvel.

*Likevvise also * saith S. Ambrose, Euery vveeke vve must celebrate the Oblation, although not euery day vnto strangers, yet vnto the inhabitantes at least tvvise in the vveeke. S. Augustine saith, the Sacrament vvas ministred at certaine daies, S. Ambrose saith, sometimes tvvise in the vveeke, and not euery day.*

The. 134. vntruth. S. Ambrose saith otherwise, the place is altogether falsified.

Harding.

You report S. Ambroses wordes otherwise then he spake or meant. He spake not of ministring the oblation, as you falsifie his saying, wherby you meane your owne ministration of the Communion: he spake plainely of the Oblation and Sacrifice of the Church, which is the body and bloud of Christe, that is consecrated on the aulter, which S. Augustine, as is before rehersed, calleth the table of our lorde. S. Ambrose wordes be these in that place where he saith, Priestes and Deacons must forbeare the companie of a woman, because it is necessary they be present in the church daily, Omni enim hebdomada offerēdum est, etiam si non

M. Iew. corrupteth S. Ambrose.

Ambros. in 1. Tim. c. 3.

si non quotidie peregrinis, incolis tamen vel bis in hebdomada. That is to say. For euery vveeke the oblation is to be made, or Sacrifice is to be offred, although not euery day for strangers, yet for the inhabitantes at least tvvise in the vveeke.

For stran gers.

Maruel you not that I English peregrinis, and incolis, *for strangers, and for the inhabitãtes*, for so it ought to be Englished, not *vnto strangers, and vnto the inhabitantes*, as you haue corrupted the place. For the oblation which S. Ambrose speaketh of, is to be offred vp vnto God in the Masse, and not vnto strangers or inhabitantes. neither is it at al lauful to offer Sacrifice vnto men, as you know pardy. And that holy Father here speaketh of the Sacrifice, not of your new founde Ministration, for offerre, is to offer or to Sacrifice, it is not to Minister, onlesse the worde of Ministring implie oblation, as a worde more cōmō and general implieth the signification of the particular or special, which to thinke in this place is beside iudgement and reason. albe it by you it signifieth to Minister the Sacrament.

offerre

If you presse me with the two datiue cases peregrinis and incolis, & reproue my translation for strangers and for the inhabitãtes: remember your Grammer rule M. Iewel: Verbes put acquisitiuely, that is to say, with the token for, require after them the Datiue case: as habeo huic, non habeo illi. I haue for this man, I haue not for him. So by S. Ambrose, offerendum est peregrinis, we must offer, or oblation must by made although not euery day for strangers, yet for the inhabitantes tvvise in the weeke. This place is clere for the Sacrifice which is offered vp in the Masse, and so maketh for the Masse, it maketh not against the Masse, nor against the Daily Sacrifice of the Church. For although in the Church where S. Ambrose lyued, the Sacrifice was offred but twise in the weeke, yet might it haue ben oftener, yea daily offred in other places. For S. Augustine writing to Ianuarius

A manifest testimonie for the Masse

nuarius, saith, alibi nullus dies intermittitur quo non offeratur. In some places no day is let passe in vvhich the Sacrifice is not offred. Speaking of that blessed woman Monica his mother, he saith that before she died, she gaue no commaundement touching any sumptuous and honorable burial, but only desyred her Memorie to be made at the aulter, which aulter she serued (doubtelesse by offering the Sacrifice with Vowe which the Priest offered in ministerie) without intermission of any day, from whence she knewe the holy Sacrifice to be dispensed, whereby the handvvriting that vvas contary vnto vs, is quite blotted out. Of this place it is clere that S. Augustines Mother had Masse euery day. and that in the same was a propitiatorie Sacrifice of Christes body really present offered vp. Neither is the Sacrifice of the Church called the daily Sacrifice for that it is offred by Priestes euery day precisely in euery place: but for that it is very often offred, and for that there is no day excepted, in which it is not, or may not be offred.

August. ad Ianua. epist. 118.

Aug. lib. 9. Conf. c. 13.

S. Augustins Mother had Masse euery day.

Colos. 2.

Your epiphonema, by which you auouch both S. Augustine, and S. Ambrose to speake on your side, is no lesse false, thē your translation of their wordes was corrupte, and the whole handeling of them was besides their meaning. For where as you say thus, *S. Augustine saith, the Sacrament vvas Ministred at certaine daies, S. Ambrose saith, sometimes tvvise in the vveeke, and not euery day:* Al this runneth on false grounde. For neither S. Augustine speaketh of the Sacrament as it was ministred, but as it was prepared vpon our Lordes table, and frō thence receiued, which may wel be vnderstanded of the Priest: Neither speaketh S. Ambrose of it as it was ministred and vsed for a Communion, but as it was offred in Sacrifice to almighty God. Seing then these two places make nothing for you, of like your thirde shal be of better force, and recompense the weakenes of the other.

Verely the good face that you put on it in the entrie, promiseth nolesse, where you say thus.

Ievvel.

But vvhat recorde hereof can be plainer, then the Councel of Toledo? The vvordes in English be these: There be sundrie Priestes in Spaine, that touching the prayer that the Lorde taught, and commaunded Daily to be said, say the same onely vpon the Sonneday, and vpon no day els. *Hereof vve may very vvel geather, that if the Priestes in Spaine said the Lordes prayer onely vpon the Sonneday, forsomuch as the Communion is neuer ministred vvithout the Lordes prayer, therfore the Priestes in Spaine ministred not the Communion, but onely vpon the Sonneday.*

Conci. Tolet. 4. ca. 9.

Harding.

What is that M. Iewel hath take in hande to Proue.

This place serueth M. Iewels turne no better, then the two former. Forgete not Reader, what he hath taken in hande to proue. It is this, that in such places, where as the Sacrament was not daily receiued of the people, it was not receiued Priuately and daily of the Priest, when he celebrated the daily sacrifice, as much to say as this: where the people receiued not, there the Priestes did not say Masse. This negatiue proposition onlesse he proue to be true vniuersally, he proueth nothing. For we may alwaies obiecte, that although it were not so in places by him alleged: yet it might haue ben in other places. And if it be proued of any one place, then is the priuate Masse proued.

This testimonie out of the fourth Councel of Toledo, were it without corruption alleged, as it is not: yet it speaketh onely but of the Priestes of Spaine. What if we graunted, that the Priestes of Spaine ministred not the Communion, but onely vpon the Sonneday? yet wil it not folow thereof, but that some otherwhere priestes might say masse and offer daily.

Albeit the question is not of the ministring of the Commu-

nion,

nion, but of the sacrifice, which the Priestes oftentimes offred, whē the people had not the Cōmunion distributed vnto thē. M. Iewel because he can not away with the Sacrifice, neither with the terme of sacrifice: turneth alwaies his tale, that should expresse the Priestes sacrifice or oblatiō, into the Ministratiō of the Communion, as though it were one thing, to offer vp the Sacrifice which is the body and bloud of our Lorde, and to minister the Communion, wherby he meaneth his Geneuian Ministration. Now the Communion is ministred vnto the people after that the Sacrifice is offred, and as we may say, when Masse is donne. For when the Priest hath once receiued the holy oblation him selfe, al is donne that is required to this Sacrifice. And though the people receiue not, yet is al donne that is necessary to the condition of the Sacrifice.

M. Iew. turneth the worde Sacrifice or oblatiō, into Ministration of the Communion.

And where as he saith, the Communion is neuer ministred without our Lordes Prayer, he deceiueth the vnlearned with amphibologie of the worde. If he meane by his worde of Ministration, the Consecration, and al that is necessary by Institution of Christe, and is obserued religiously of the Churche: so we graunt, the Communion is neuer ministred, that is to say, the hoste or oblation is neuer prepared, as S. Augustine termeth it, and consecrated, without our lordes prayer, and yet therewith as with the essential wordes of the Sacrament, it is not consecrated, but with the special wordes of our Lorde with which he consecrated at his supper, as is before said. But if he meane by the Ministration, the delyuery, geuing, reaching forth, or imparting of the Sacrament, which is the Priestes office, and also the Deacons in some cases: this is alwaies done without our Lordes prayer. By this it is euident, that this place proueth not his purpose, though it had ben truly alleged. But now may it please thee Reader to consider, how truly and syncerely M.

In Iohan. tracta. 26.

M. Iew. corrupteth the Coũcel of Toledo. Iewel hath handled this Coũcel of Toledo. As thou findest him in this, and sundry other places, so credite him. First shamelesly he corrupteth and falsifieth the wordes of the Coũcel. For wheras it speaketh but of certaine of the Priestes of Spaine, by his false translation, and glosing vpon it, of some or certaine, first he maketh sundry, then proceding forth, he calleth them Priestes indefinitely, and at length concludeth with the Priestes of Spaine in general, as though the Coũcel had meant of al. The wordes of ÿ Coũcel be these. Nonnulli Sacerdotũ in Hispanijs reperiũtur, qui Dominicã orationem, quam Saluator noster docuit & pręcepit, nõ quotidie, sed tantũ die Dominica dicant. In English thus. There be certaine of the Priestes in Spaine found out, that say not our Lordes prayer daily, which our Sauiour taught and gaue in cõmaundement to be said, but onely vpon the Sonday.

Concil. Toletan. 4. cap. 9.

Of this wheras M. Iewel cõcludeth, ÿ Priestes in Spaine said our Lords praier only vpon ÿ Sonday, & therfore ÿ priestes in Spaine ministred not ÿ Cõmunion but only vpon the Sõday he ÿ readeth these wordes, & doth not cõferre them with ÿ Coũcel, what is he by them moued to beleue, but ÿ it was the general custome of Priests in Spaine neuer to say the Pater noster, but vpon the Sonday? This worde Nõnulli, which signifieth certaine or some of the whole multitude, specially depẽding of a genitiue case, as here, nonnulli Sacerdotũ, is a worde restrained & limited to signifie som part of ÿ multitud signified by ÿ genitiue case, and if the worde of the genitiue case be put indefinitely, it signifieth ÿ general multitude without limitation. So that there is a great difference implied betwen these two, nonnuli Sacerdotum, some of the Priestes, and, Sacerdotes, the Priestes. The like difference is in our English tong. So greate oddes there is, whether whẽ a mã speaketh of any multitude, he say some, or the. Doth a Bẽtle that loueth his game wel, heare these two reportes with one af-

The maister of a flocke of sheep conceueth not one sense of these

fection

fection of minde, Syr, some of your deere be hunted out of your parke, and, ỹ deere of your parke be hunted out of your ground?

No lesse difference is to be vnderstãded in ỹ place of this Coũcel, which M. Iewel fowly corrupteth by reporting ỹ of the priestes in Spaine, which was to be reported only of some or certain of ỹ Priestes in Spaine. I wil not deuise a fond argument, & say it is his, which is his wont towardes mee, albeit I can not here deuise a fonder, then he maketh him selfe: but if he would frame his reasõ as the place leadeth him, and ministreth mater, thus he might say: Certaine of ỹ Priestes in Spaine said not our Lordes prayer euery day, but vpõ the Sonday only: The daily Sacrifice is neuer offered wout our Lordes prayer: Ergo, certaine of the Priestes in Spaine offered not euery day, but only vpon ỹ Sonday. This Argument may be graunted without preiudice of any thing that I said, and the conclusion may be admitted for true, so farre as the Minor is true.

two tales: the sheepe be in your corne, and, some of your shepe be in your corne. By the sheepe he vnderstandeth ỹ flocke, by some, hee vnderstãdeth a smaller number. Oddes betweene Some, & The.

Of this saying of the Councel it may wel be inferred, that other Priestes in Spaine did say our Lords prayer euery day: otherwise the exception of some had ben void by M. Iewels owne logike, as is before noted. And there is nothing here to ỹ cõtrary, but ỹ they might also haue offred euery day ỹ daily Sacrifice.

I maruel that M. Iewel would bring this testimonie to proue his mater by, seing that the Priestes whose il doing he taketh for his defence, were condemned by that Councel for so doing, and by the storie of the time it may be gathered, they forbare to say the prayer of our Lorde daily, because being proude in their owne conceit, they thought them selues so pure of life, as they needed not to saye that necessary prayer euery day. For redresse whereof, the Fathers assembled there, decreed thus. Who so euer of the Priestes or inferiour Clerkes doo omitte to saye this our Lordes prayer euerye daye, eyther in Publike or Priuate Seruice: Let him bee depriued of the honour

Concil. Toletan. 4. cap. 9. in fine.

 of

of his order, as condemned for his pride.

By this condemned pride and euil demeanour of a fewe Priestes in Spaine, M. Jewel would proue, that there was no Sacrifice celebrated in other times, when as the people receiued not the Sacrament, and that the Communion was ministred onely vpon the Sonnedayes. which if it be true, I meane if the Communion were not ministred in Spaine but vpon the Sonnedayes, then certaine it is, that there was Masse said, and the Sacrifice offred at certaine times when the Cõmunion was not ministred. For the Fathers of that Toletane Councel finding fault with certaine Priestes, that would not sing the song of the three children, wherein the Uniuersal creature of heauen and earth praiseth God, in Missa Dominicorum dierum, & in solennitatibus Martyrum, in their Masse of the Sõnedaies, and in the solemne feastes of Martyrs: ordeined, that it should be song through al the Churches of Spaine and Galicia, in omnium Missarum solennitate, at the solemnitie of al Masses. Forasmuch as they refused to sing that song of the three children in their Sonneday Masses, and in those which they celebrated in high feastes of Martyrs, and thereupon a Decree was made, that it should be song in al Masses: it is cleare, that they vsed to sing or say that song at other Masses, neither would the Fathers haue made a Decree for it to be song in al Masses, had not there Masses ben said in other times beside Sonnedaies, and Martyrs feastes.

Ca. 13.

Againe if the Communion were ministred in Spaine vpon the Sonneday onely, then was there no such Communion of a multitude ministred at the Masses in the Martyrs feastes and at other times. And so by that Councel Masse wil easily be proued to haue ben celebrated in Spaine without the Communion of a number, which M. Jewel calleth the priuate Masse. For it foloweth necessarily, The Communion was ministred onely

An argument for profe of Priuate Masse.

onely vpon the Sonneday, Masse was said in other times and feastes, Ergo, there was Masse without the ministration of the Communion. Here must he either recant what he said before, or yelde to priuate Masse.

Finally, sith that M. Iewel aloweth so wel the auctoritie of the fourth Councel of Toledo, we require him by auctoritie of the same Councel, to confesse and acknowledge the Masse, which is so much mentioned and alowed of the same, for proufe wherof I referre him to sundry places thereof, namely to the. 12. 13. and 16. Canon. If he and his felowes would be induced to admit the Masse, wherof there is no doubt by that Councel, there should not so much a doo be made touching priuate Masse, as they cal it. For if the Masse be good and holy (as it is) of it selfe, the peoples receiuing or forebearing from receiuing with the Priest for a time, maketh it nor better nor worse. Neither can he now iustly reiect that Councel, whose witnesse he vseth. For by the ciuil Lawe, if a man vse any witnesses in one cause, and the same witnesses be brought forth against him in an other cause: it shal not be lawful for him to make exception against their persons. *L. si quis. C. d. test.*

The. xxviij. Diuision.

IN this Diuision I allege these wordes of S. Chrysostome, to proue that the Sacrifice was Daily offred. Quid ergo nos? Nonne. &c. Then what is that we doo? Doo we not Offer euery day? Yeas verely. But we doo it for the recording of his death. And it is one hoste, not many. Because this is a mani- *Chrysost. in. 10. cap. ad Heb.*

fest place for witnesse of the Daily Sacrifice, and in dede such as can not be auoided, specially the circumstance of the mater treated in the homilie of S. Chrysostome from whence those wordes be taken, duly weighed and considered: M. Iewel being ennemie to the blessed Sacrifice, thought best so to order the talke of his Replie, as he might bring the whole processe to an vncertaintie and darkenesse, and the reader to a confusion. First he coueteth to discredite me, thinking therby to diminish the auctoritie of the Doctors saying.

Ievvel.

The.135. Vntruth, Those wordes be to ẏ mater.

*Here M. Harding (saith he) notably betrayeth himselfe, laying forth for a countenance a fevve of Chrysostomes vvordes, *and the same nothing to the mater, *hevving and mangling them, as him listeth best.*

The.136. Vntruth. I allege thẽ truly without hewing or mangling, as it shal be tried by conference of ẏ place.

Harding.

Here M. Iewel not able to answere S. Chrysostome, saith his pleasure of me that alleged him. What cause he had to say, that I doo notably betray my selfe, he sheweth not. That the words of the Doctour perteine to the mater, it can not be denied, yet because he is so impudent, as to deny it, it shal be proued. That I hewe them and mangle them, it is not so vncourteously, as slaunderously spoken. That false practise I leaue to him self, who vseth it more, then any of his false Brethren, of what secte so euer they be. And in this very place he vseth it.

Ievvel.

These vvordes of S. Chrysostome, as they make nothing for Priuate Masse, so do they very vvel declare, vvhat the olde Fathers meant by these vvordes, Oblation, and Sacrifice in the holy Ministration. Chrysostome compareth the Sacrifices of the Ievves in the lavve, vvith the Sacrifice of Christe in the Gospel. He saith, the Sacrifices of the Lavve vvere many, and vnperfect, and therefore daily renevved. This of the Gospel, is one, and persite, and therefore euerlasting.

Harding.

Harding.

These wordes of S. Chrysostome I alleged not for the priuate Masse, as it is priuate in your sense, but for the daily Sacrifice, yea, if you wil so take it, for the Masse. For besides the Masse & without the Masse, the Sacrifice of the Churche is not offered, and to proufe of that mater they perteine. Neither do his wordes so much declare, what the Fathers meant by these wordes oblatiō, & Sacrifice, in ẏ holy Ministratiō, which you say, as thei witnesse, that they offered daily for ẏ recording of Christes death.

Truth it is also, that he compareth the Sacrifices of the olde Lawe, and the Sacrifice of the Gospel together, saying, they were sundrye and vnperfite, and therefore daily renewed: This, one, perfite, and euerlasting. He resembleth also the olde Sacrifices to salues, of litle strength, which be daily laid to the wounde, and heale it not. This Sacrifice he likeneth to a soueraine salue, that being once laid on the wounde, maketh it perfitely hole, so as it neede no more to be renewed and laid on againe.

Al this is true, I confesse. You needed not to haue bestowed so many woordes in a mater not doubtful. Wee varie not (you knowe) about the Sacrifice of the Crosse. That was once offered with shedding of Bloud for redemption of the worlde, and is not so to be offred any more. But what say you to the external and publike Sacrifice of the Church? we would gladly heare you tel vs a plaine tale thereof, whereby we might vnderstand your faith to agree with the faith of the Churche therein. Corrupt not the meaning of S. Chrysostome in that Homilie which I allege, and yeelde vnto it: and wee shal in that great point agree wel ynough. Hereto you say thus.

The Sacrifice of the crosse. The external Sacrifice of the Churche.

Ievvel.

He saith further, that vvee of the Gospel haue a Sacrifice also, and that daily, but in remembrance of that Sacrifice once made vpon the Crosse. And although vve Sacrifice in sundry places, yet saith he, the Sacrifice is but one, because it hath*relation vnto that one Sacrifice of Christ. And therfore he addeth, Quomodo vna est hostia, & non multæ? &c. Hovv is it one Oblation, and not many? Because it vvas once offred, it vvas offred into the holy place: *But this Sacrifice (meaning the ministration of the Sacrament) is an example of that. And vvhat he meaneth by this vvorde exemplar, he shevveth a fevve lines before. Quæ formam tantum alicuius habent, exemplar ostendũt, non autem virtutem. The thinges that beare onely a likenesse, shevv the samplar of some other thing, but not the povver of the same: as an Image shevveth the paterne of a man, but not the povver of a man. Hereof S. Chrysostome concludeth thus: The thing that vve doo, is donne in remembrance of that thing that vvas donne before. For Christe said, Do this in my remembrance. Hereby it appeareth in vvhat sense the olde Fathers vsed these vvordes Oblation, and Sacrifice.

The. 137. Untruth. S. Chrysostome rendreth no such cause.

The. 138. Untruth. S. Chrysostome saith not so. this place is fowly corrupted & falsified.

Harding.

Such hewing and mangling of S. Chrysostomes wordes, bewrayeth your mater M. Jewel, and causeth it worthily to be suspected. If you had meant good faith, you would haue laid them forth plainely and truly: now that you bring them in so by peecemeale, taking what semeth to make for your purpose, and leauing out the chiefe substance, which you impugne, alter the order of them, and wrest the whole to a contrary sense of the Sacramentaries; as you deceiue the ignorant, so among the learned you procure discredite to your whole doinges, and by this make them witnesses of your false dealing.

M. Jew: heweth & mangleth S. Chrysostomes wordes, & racketh thẽ to his Sacramẽtary heresie.

Your intent is to perswade the external and publike Sacrifice of the Churche not to be the true Sacrifice in deede, but a figure, signe, token, samplar, or paterne of the true Sacrifice. A Sacrifice we haue, you say, and that daily, but in remembrance of the Sacrifice once made vpon the Crosse. Truth it is, the daily

M. Jewels euil intent touching the Sacrifice.

ly Sacrifice of the Church is a Sacrifice commemoratiue, and that we do, is donne in remembrance of that which was donne vpon the Crosse. Yet is it the true Sacrifice, because the thing that is Offred now, and that was Offred vpon the Crosse, is one thing. It is one, say you, because it hath relation vnto that one Sacrifice of Christe. And you report it as out of S. Chrysostomes mouth, where as he neuer said it, and what you meane by your relation, I referre it to your selfe. Sure I am, that learned Father neuer spake so. He affirmeth it to be one Sacrifice, that is offred of many and in many places, as Christe is one, and not many Christes, one body, and not many bodies.

But this Sacrifice say you, is an example of that. It is exemplar, a samplar, or paterne of that, I graunte, and so saith S. Chrysostome. Knowe you not that a thing may be a samplar, and the truth or thing it selfe? Saith he not there, Veritas & exemplar communicant inuicem? It is a sampler in respect of the way or meane of Offering. The truth, in respect of the substance it selfe of the thing Offred. It is not Offred in the Church, as it was Offred vpon the Crosse, and therfore this is a samplar of that. Yet that which is Offred in the Church daily, is the same body of Christ, that was once Offred vpon the Crosse, and so it is the truth, so it is the true Sacrifice, so it is the same. Therfore after that S. Chrysostome, had called this Sacrifice a samplar of that, as though he had forsene the Obiection that the Sacramentaries at this day make against the veritie of this Sacrifice: he addeth immediatly in the same sentence, id ipsum semper offerimus, we Offer vp alwaies the selfe same thing. which part of the sentence M. Iewel could craftily nippe away from the rest, least it should betray his whole mater.

M. Iewel nippeth & clippeth from S. Chrysostom ŷ maketh against his vntru doctrine.

And as here he nippeth and clippeth away wordes, so in the same sentence, he altereth the sense by putting in wordes of his owne with a Parêthesis. For wheras S. Chrysostome saith, hoc autem sacrificium exemplar est illius, id ipsum semper offerimus, This Sacrifice is a samplar of that, we Offer euermore one selfe thing: he by cutting of the ende of the sentence, and by putting into the rest a patch of his owne, maketh him to say thus. But this Sacrifice (meaning the ministration of the Sacramêt) is an example of that. I tel not here what he intended, in that he corrupteth and altereth S. Chrysostomes wordes, whom whereas he said, quæ formam habent alicuius, tantum exemplar ostendunt, non autem virtutem: he maketh to speake thus, quæ formam tantum alicuius habent, exemplar ostendunt. &c. Thou wouldest iudge it a thing intollerable good Reader, if thou sawest, how he skippeth to and fro, how he wresteth and wringeth, how he parteth and setteth together, how he hackleth and mangleth this Doctours sayinges in this very Diuision. Yet is he not ashamed in this place it selfe to put in the Margent of his booke this Note of such vntrue dealing against me, *M. Harding nippeth Chrysostomes vvordes*: for that I alleged not certaine long sentences by him brought in, which perteined nothing to my purpose. wherein he semeth to folow the counsel that a gyrle once gaue her mother, as she began to chide wͭ an other woman. Mother, (quod she) cal her hoore first, for she wil cal you so els by and by. So M. Iewel knowing in his owne conscience I should haue cause to reproue him of hewing, mangling, and nipping S. Chrysostomes wordes, thought best to preuent me, by imputing vnto me the same fault first.

Because M. Iewel bendeth his whole force against the Sacrifice of the Church, & would men to beleue that we haue not ỹ true Sacrifice in dede, but only a figure and samplar of it, & hath much abused the Reader wͭ the autoritie of S. Chrysostome: ỹ it may be sene what he thought here of, I thinke it good, truly to

lay

lay forth his wordes touching this mater. After that he hath declared the weakenesse and imperfection of the Sacrifices of the olde lawe, which were continually renewed day by day, and like a bad salue were stil laid vnto the wound, and wrought no perfite health: he commeth to speake of the external and publike Sacrifice of the Church, and saith. Quid ergo nos? Nonne per singulos dies offerimus? &c.

Then what is that which we doo? Doo we not offer day by day? Yeas verely we doo so, but we doo it for remembrance of his death. And this hoste or Sacrifice is one, not many. How one, and not many? Because it was once offred, it was offered into the holy place. And this Sacrifice is a samplar of that, wee offer alwaies the selfe same thing. Neither doo we offer one Lambe to day, an other to morow, but alwaies we offer the selfe same. Therfore in this respect this Sacrifice is one. Els forasmuch as it is offred in many places, what shal we say, there be many Christes? Not so, there is but one Christe in euery place, being here ful and whole, and there ful and whole, one body. For as he which is offred euery where, is one body, and not many bodies: so also it is one Sacrifice. And he is our high bishop, that hath offred vp the Oblation that purgeth vs: the same offer we also now, which hauing then ben offred, can not be spent. And that which we doo, is donne in remēbrance of that which is already donne. For doo ye this, saith he, in my remembrance. It is not an other Sacrifice that we doo, as the high Priest did, but alwaies we do the selfe same: yea rather we worke a remembrance of the Sacrifice. Thus farre S. Chrysostome.

Chrysosto. hom.17. in Epist. ad Heb.

Luc.22.

Here is to be noted, first, that we, that is to say, the Church, or rather priestes of the new testament the publike ministers of the Churche in this behalfe, doo offer vp the Sacrifice euery day.

The declaratiō of S. Chrysostomes saying.

Secondly, that it is one Sacrifice, and not many, how often, and in how many places so euer it be offred. Thirdly, how is it one Sacrifice? because we offer alwaies one selfe same thing. Fourthly, what is that one selfe same thing? It is the body of Christe, it is the Lambe, it is the Sacrifice that cleanseth vs, which Iesus our high Bishop offered. Fiftly, this body though it be offred so many times, and in so many places: yet it can not be consumed, as the Sacrifices of the olde lawe were.

A samplar and the thing it selfe.

Yet this notwithstanding, saith M. Iewel, it is a samplar, and it is done in remembrance. True it is, but it is not onely a samplar, that is to say, the truth is not shut out. And it may be donne in remembrance of the death of Christe, though the thing now offred in Mysterie and in a Sacrament, be the same that was then offred openly to eyes and other senses of flesh in manifestation of flesh.

And as touching that it is a samplar, where S. Chrysostom so calleth it, there he calleth it also the thing it selfe, Id ipsum semper offerimus, we offer alwaies the selfe same thing, saith he, not one Lambe to day, and an other Lambe to morow, we offer alwaies one Lambe. It is a samplar concerning the manner of offering, which is vnbloudy, or without bloud sheding, but concerning the substance of the thing that is offred, it is the very thing it selfe, that was geuen and Sacrificed for the redemption of the worlde. The vnitie, or if it be lawful so to speake, the onenesse of the thing offred, maketh that of the Crosse, and this of the Church, to be one Sacrifice.

The end of both oblations is diuerse.

And as the manner of offering is diuerse, so is the ende of both offeringes also diuerse. That vpon the Crosse was done to purchase saluation to mankinde. And the same by that Oblation was sufficiently, as touching Christes behalfe, to al beleuers procured.

Now

Now we offer the same Lambe, the same Hoste, the same Sacrifice after an vnbloudy and impassible maner, not to thintent we may now first of al worke any new redemptiō therby: But ꝧ celebrating the Memorie of our Lordes Passion, wee may geue God thankes for our saluatiō already obteined vpon ꝧ Crosse, & that God vouchsafe through our faith and deuotion, and the presence of his Sonnes blessed Body vpon the Aulter to applie the merite of the same Death and Passion vnto vs.

This notable place of S. Chrysostome geueth vs to vnderstand, what was the Fathers faith touching the daily Sacrifice in the Greke Church. It shalbe to good purpose, to declare by witnesse of some of the Latine Fathers, that the same doctrine was likewise taught in the Latine Church. That may we learne of him, which among al is esteemed for a most excellent learned man: S. Augustine I meane. Who writing vpon the. xxxix. Psalme, after that he hath declared, that the Sacrifices of the old Lawe were figures of the Sacrifice to come, and as promising wordes that were then spoken, when the thing promised was not yet perfourmed: and afterwarde when the thing promised was performed, were to be spoken no more, but to be taken away, because that which they promised was fulfilled: saith by way of question, the rather to commend it vnto memorie: Quid est quod datum est completiuum? What is that which is geuen for the accomplishment, that is to saye, for perfourmance of the olde Figures that continually spake as it were, and wrought not, promised a true Sacrifice, and perfourmed not? To this question thus he answereth. Corpus quod nostis, quod non omnes nostis, quod vtinam qui nostis omnes, non ad iudiciū noueritis. It is the Body which ye knowe, which al ye knowe not, which al ye that doo knowe, I pray God ye know it not to your damnation.

The faith of the Latin church touching the Sacrifice.

Aug. in Psal. 39.

Againe to make the mater more clere, he saith further, Exhibita est veritas promissa. The truth which was promised is presently deliuered. We are in this body, of this body we are partakers, we know what we receiue, and ye that know not, know it, and whẽ ye shal haue learned it, I pray God ye take it not to your
1.Cor.11. damnation. For he that eateth and drinketh vnworthily, eateth and drinketh damnation to him selfe. Here S. Augustine most euidently calleth the Body which Christen men receiue in the Sacrament, the very truth exhibited, which fulfilleth and performeth that the olde Figures promised. This body by his teaching is the accomplishing Sacrifice. Wherby it is euident, the body that we receiue, to be the same that suffered. In this body we are, because through Gods grace we are in the vnitie of the Church, and being so we worthily receiuing it, receiue it to our great benefite. As for you M. Iewel and your companions, ye be not in this body, because ye be not in the vnitie of the Church, neither beleue ye any real presence of this body in your congregations, and though ye haue any, yet ye haue it not but to your further condemnation. Thus is the faith of the auncient Greke and Latine Church cõcerning ẏ Sacrifice of the Churche, sufficiently witnessed by these two most learned Fathers. In comparison of whom in the iudgement of al such as bee not carried away with euery winde of doctrine, the wanton Chalenge of M. Iewel ought to haue litle credite.

After that I haue sufficiently proued by the testimonie of S. Chrysostome, that the Sacrifice was daily offered in the Church, notwithstanding the complaint hee maketh for that the People came not daily to receiue with the Priest: I saye, that although M. Iewel graunt the daily Sacrifice, yet he wil stand stil in his
Fol. 24.b. negatiue, that is to say, he wil denie, there was euer any such

Sacri-

Sacrifice celebrated without a company receiuing together with the Priest. For proufe of this (I say there) these be such places as I am persuaded withal. The better Learned men that be of more reading then I am, haue other, I doubt not. To this M. Iewel replieth as foloweth.

Ievvel.

By this colde conclusion he cutteth of credite from al that he hath hitherto said, as not making shevv sufficient to vvinne his purpose, and so cōdemneth his note made in the Margent, vvhich vvas, Proufes for Priuate Masse: and layeth al the burthen of his groundes, vpon these other gheasses that hereafter folovv.

Harding.

Conclusion properly to speake, in that place I make none, colde nor hote. Onely I do soberly reporte, what you wil denye, and wherewith I for my parte am persuaded in a point not very necessarie. For whether I can shewe, that a Masse was said without companie present to receiue with the Priest that said it, or no: what skilleth it? It might haue so ben, though it were neuer writtē. And what a vaine thing had it ben, any man to write, that such a day in such a place, such a Priest or such a Byshop, celebrated the Sacrifice, and no man receiued the Sacrament with him? And if no man euer wrote it, how should I proue it? Such particularities and specialties of a facte in maters of smal weight, were very seldome recorded by the writers of the First six hundred yeares. What reason is it, wee should be driuen to proue it of the time so long agon, sith that it can not be proued of the time of our owne age? For how am I able to proue, that no companie of Communicantes receiued with the Priestes in Spaine this last yere, whē they said Masse? And yet there is no doubt, but many Masses were there said, whereat none receiued with the Priestes.

the proufe of a circūstance of a factial act can not reasonably be required.

That Priestes within the first sixe hundred yeares did consecrate the body and bloud of Christ, vnder ye formes of bread & wine, that they offered, and receiued the same, wherein consisteth the Masse, which things done we vnderstand, when we speake of the external and publike Sacrifice of the Church: this haue I now proued, and hereafter it shal be more largely proued. But forasmuch as the Sacrifice is not impaired nor loseth his vertue by the lacke of companie receiuing it with the Priest, to what purpose is it to proue, that some times within the first six hũdred yeares some Priestes at some times had no companie to receiue with them?

If companie of receiuers together with the Priest be not of the necessitie of the Sacrifice, why maketh M. Iewel so much a doo about it, which being procured and obserued, yet would not he allow the custome of the Church? That company of receiuers together is of necessitie, we deny it. If he wil needes haue the world so to beleue, it is his parte to proue it: which as hee hath gone about to do, and performed it not: so when so euer he shal attempt it hereafter, he shal eftsones shew his vnablenesse.

How the proufes of sole receiuing serue for proufs of priuate Masse.

As touching the note of my bokes margẽt, which is, Proufes for Priuate Masse, though in that place I proue specially the sole receiuing: the aucthorities of the same sole receiuing, serue very wel for proufe of priuate Masse, which after your meaning is nothing els, but the Priestes sole receiuing. For if the sole receiuing be proued lawful in other faithful persons, as by sundry examples I haue proued: then what reason can be alleged, why it should not be good and lawful also in a Priest? So in this respect, and for this cause, my note may be vpholden, as good and reasonable, and to the purpose. For by what right sole receiuing is good, by the same is Priuate Masse, as you terme it, also proued good.

Neither

Neither resteth the weight of our groundes touching the unbloudy Sacrifice in the examples onely that here in my booke do folowe, which examples it liketh you to cal gheasses. By priuate Masse which terme we admit not, as neither do we admit that the Masse in respect of the Sacrifice is priuate: we may understād two thinges by you to be meant, the Sacrifice of the Masse, and sole receiuing of the Priest. The groundes we haue for the one, and for the other being sufficient, and so both being proued, we care the lesse, how you take your pleasure at the newe terme Priuate Masse, deuised in that sense which you attribute unto it, by Martin Luther the founder of your pleasant Gospel.

By priuate Masse two thinges be understāded, the Sacrifice, and the Priestes sole receiuing of the Communion.

The. xxix. Diuision.

Of the Decree which the auncient Martyr and Pope S. Soter made, that onlesse two were present, a Priest should not celebrate Masse, to thintent they might aptly make answer unto his salutation uttered in the plural number: I take occasion so to reason, as it might at that time seme lauful a Priest to say Masse, without companie receiuing the Sacrament with him. My wordes there be these. Whereas the receiuing of Christes body is a farre greater thing, then to answere the Priest at Masse, if that holy Bishop and Martyr had thought it so necessary, as that the Masse might not be donne without it: doubtelesse of very reason and cōuenience, he would, and should haue specially spoken of that, rather then of the other. But for that he thoght other wise, he required onely of necessitie, the presence of two for answer conueniently to be made.

De consec. dist. 1. can. hoc quoque statutum.

Fol. 25. a.

This M. Jewel in his Replie answereth very sclenderly, as euery man may see, and here it shal appeare. But before he cometh to make his answere, he vttereth many wordes to an other purpose. First, he goeth to discredite al the Popes Decretal Epistles. Then he trauaileth to disproue this Decree of S. Soter. After this he wandereth abroad in other talke both vaine & vntrue, not worthy to be aswered. Touching the Disprouse of the Epistles Decretal, thus he saith.

Ievvel.

The. 139. vntruth. Gratian doth not shew so much, as it shal appeare.

Gratian shevveth that the Decretal Epistles haue ben doubted of among the learned. And Doctor Smith although his auctoritie be not great, declared openly at Paules Crosse, that they can not possibly be theirs vvhose names they beare.

Harding.

Gratian is quite contrary to that M. Jewel reporteth of him.

The lerned schoolemen are not to be thought to doubt of al those thinges, whereof they moue question by this word quæritur.

If a man were in doubte before of the Decretal Epistles, by reading the argumentes which you bring to disproue them, he might iustly doubt of them lesse. Had you no better reasons then these, you should not haue aduentured to disproue them. That you say of Gratian, is false. He sheweth no such thing, as you reporte. The contrarie rather he sheweth. Onely he saith, it is demaũded whether they haue force of auctoritie, forasmuch as they be not founde in the body of the canons. His worde is quæritur, not dubitatur. And thereof he taketh occasion to allege good and substantial witnesse for their autoritie. If we should say that learned men doubted of al thinges, whereof they moue question in their bookes: then should we beare the world in hande, they douted of God himselfe, of ye Articles of our Crede, & of ye pointes of our faith that be must certaine, and most out of doubte. Of al which they moue questions by this worde quæritur, not because they thẽ selues doubte, but because by trial of argumẽtes & learning, they would remoue al others from occasion of doubte.

That

That the Bishops of Rome wrote decretal Epistles, and that they ought to be in Auctoritie, it is witnessed by the two great learned Fathers S. Leo. and Gelasius. We do so commaund by our declaration (saith S. Leo) al the Decretal constitutions as wel of Innocentius (of good memorie) as of al our predecessours, which haue ben openly set forth for orders and rules of the Churche: that if any presumptuously committe offenses against them, he shal not obteine forgeuenes hereafter.

Of the auctoritie of the Decrees and Decretal Epistles. Dist. xix. ca. Si Romanorū.

Of those Epistles Decretal thus writeth Gelasius. Decretales epistolas, quas beatissimi Papæ diuersis temporibus ab vrbe Romana pro diuersorum Patrum consolatione dederunt, venerabiliter recipiendas. We ordeine, that the Decretal Epistles, which the most blessed Popes at diuerse times for the comforte of diuerse Fathers haue geuen forth from the Citie of Rome, to be reuerently receiued.

Decretum Gelasij in Conci. 70. episcoporū

The graue auctoritie of these two learned and auncient Fathers commending vnto vs those Epistles, ought to be of more weight, then that the light gheasses and surmises of M. Iewel should ouerweigh them, and bring them to discredite. As for my selfe, I define nothing. Yet I fynde no cause, for ought that he saith in disprouse of them, why I should contemne them.

As for D. Smith, whether he said so at Paules Crosse as you reporte, or no, I knowe not. The mater can not be decided by autoritie of his worde, specially spoken at that time, which you note, in the second yere of king Edwarde. As in that place about that time he spake the truth, when he spake according to his conscience: so at an other time sone after he vttered certaine vntruthes for feare of persecution against his conscience, whereof as I can not excuse him, so if you accuse him, remember, that your selfe did the like in Queene Maries time, when in a solemne assemblie at Oxforde you were

Doctour Smith.

as ready as any other man there, to subscribe to the Masse, and other pointes of the Catholike faith, against which now you professe such spite and hatred. But let vs heare the reasons, which you promise to vtter for prouse, that the decretal Epistles be not theirs whose names they beare.

Answer to M. Iewels reasons against the Decrees and Decretal Epistles.

The. 140 vntruth. A burthen of lyes layd together.

Ievvel.

* *These decretal Epistles manifestly depraue, and abuse the Scriptures, they mainteine nothing somuch as the state and kingdome of the Pope. They publish a multitude of vaine and superstitious ceremonies, and other like fantasies, they proclaime such thinges as M. Harding knovveth to be open and kovven lies.*

Harding.

Railing is no prouse. This pelse may serue for your pulpite, when you lacke better stuffe. Thus to disproue the Decretal Epistles, it is too Ministerlike.

The. 141. vntruth. Anacletus commaunded no such thing concerning S. Peters Churche.

Ievvel.

* *Anacletus, that vvas next after Peter, vvilleth and straitly commaundeth, that al Bishops once in the yere, doo visite the entrie of S. Peters Churche in Rome, vvhich they cal* limina Petri. *Yet vvas there then no church built there in the name of Peter. For Pope Cornelius saith (as he is alleged) that he first tooke vp S. Peters bodie, and buried the same in Apolloes Church in Rome, at the least one hundred and forty yeres after that Anacletus vvas dead.*

Harding.

That Anacletus was next after S. Peter, it is not throughly agreed vpon among the best learned writers. And what maketh this against the Decretal Epistles, which is writtẽ in none of them? A Decree in dede is extant vnder the name of Anacletus, not that al Bishops should once in the yere visite the entrie of S. Peters Church in Rome, but that al Bishops which were imme diatly subiect vnto that See Apostolike, and were nigh

Distin. 97. iuxta Sanctorũ.

vnto

vnto the Citie, should either yerely present them selues there in person, or appeare by their proxie. Of any Churche there is no mention made at al. If you thinke, we must graunt a church, because the Decree speaketh of limina Petri & Pauli, you are much deceiued. Limina be the thresholde and haunce of a dore, through which one goeth into a house, and therfore the worde signifieth an entrie into a house.

By limina Petri & Pauli, which be the wordes of the Decree, is nothing els signified, but the place where the blessed bodyes of those two holy Apostles were laid. And because at the first comming to the faith there was nothing in Rome, neither els where al the worlde ouer in the opinion of the deuoute faithful people so reuerent, so honourable, and of so much estimation, as the bodies of those most blessed Apostles: thereof the place where they rested became to be famous among the Christians. And because it was vnder the grounde within a long vault or denne, and had but one entrie into it, not diuerse gates and dores, as Temples, and Palaices haue, as it was most conuenient in that time of cruel persecutions, being but an entrance as it were into a house, and no house in dede: they called it by the name of limina Apostolorum, which name continewing to this day, though it signifie now the famous Church, where their bodies be kept, yet is it not necessary to say that then also it signified a Churche. wherefore this obiection of M. Iewel against the Decretal Epistles is of smal accompte.

What is signified by limina Petri & Pauli.

That S. Cornelius the Pope tooke vp the bodies of S. Peter and S. Paul, out of Catacumbe (so is the place called where first they were layd) at the desire of the holy Matrone Lucina secretly by night for feare of the infidels: this is recorded both by S. Cornelius himself in his Epistle decretal, & also by Damasus. S. Paules body was laid by Lucina in via Ostiensi, nigh to the

The place where S. Peters & S. Paules bodies first lay, was called Catacumbæ.

Damasus in Pontificali.

place where he was headded, and S. Cornelius laid S. Peters body in Vaticano among the bodies of holy Bishops, near vnto the place, where he was crucified, saith Damasus. As for the teple of Apollo, you might rather haue called it Apolloes temple, then Apolloes Churche. But it semeth you esteme the one as much as the other, els what meant you to cal an Idols prophane temple, by the name of a Churche? Idols had neuer no Churches, neither euer spake any before so prophanely, that was of the Churche.

M. Iew. prophanely calleth an Idols temple by the name, of a Churche.

Ievvel.

Pope Antherus maketh mention of Eusebius Alexandrinus, *and* Felix, *vvhich lyued a long time after him, and therfore vvas it not posible for him to knovv them.*

Harding.

In epistola Antheri.

Pope Antherus being consulted of certaine Bishops of Spaine, whether a Bishop might change his Bishoprike and take an other: answereth them, that in case of common vtilitie & necessitie it may be, not for the pleasure or ambition of any man. And for example he allegeth S. Peter, who was translated from Antiochia to Rome. Likewise Eusebius, who was taken from a litle towne, and made Bishop of Alexandria: And Felix, who for his learning and vertue was translated from the place where he was first elect, to Ephesus. That these two lyued a long time after Antherus, you say it, but you proue it not. Verely I can not fynde it. You speake it of your owne head boldly, as you do many other thinges. were it so that you had any good witnesse of it, it should haue ben put in among other your ambitious Paintinges of your margent, whereby you thinke to winne opinion of great learning among the vnlearned.

Iewel.

Fabianus vvriteth of the coming of Nouatus into Italie. And it is cleare by S. Cyprian, and by Eusebius, that Nouatus came first into Italy in the time of Cornelius, vvhich vvas next after him.*

The 142. vntruth. It is not cleare.

Cyprian. lib. 1 epi. 3. Euse. lib. 6. cap. 43.

Harding.

It is not cleare neither by S. Cyprian, nor by Eusebius in the places by you alleged, that Nouatus came first into Italy in the time of Cornelius. Marianus Scotus who lyued about seuen hundred yeres past, and is wel estemed of the learned for his diligence in computation of times, mentioneth and alloweth the first Epistle Decretal of S. Fabianus, in which he speaketh of Nouatus comming into Italie. which argueth that it was taken for the Epistle of Fabianus before his time.

Marianus Scotus.

Platina in the life of this blessed Martyr concerning this mater writeth thus. Huius tempore exorta est Nouatiana hæresis. In the time of Fabianus rose the heresie of the Nouatians.

That Nouatus came to Rome in the time of Fabianus

That Nouatus came to Rome before the time of Cornelius, who succeded Fabianus, thus it may be proued. Nouatus peruerted Nouatianus a Priest of Rome, as it is reported by Platina and others. Nouatianus being as some write, separated from the Church, as some reporte, ordred or made Bishop out of the Church by Nouatus that came to Rome from Aphrica, for that he was very desyrous of a Bishoprike, made a great stirre against Cornelius, and did what he could, that he might not be made Pope. Now Nouatianus could not worke troubles agaist Cornelius, that he might not be chosen Pope, vnlesse he had ben at Rome before ye election: Againe he was not knowen for such an euil man, but after that he had ben separate from the Church, and seduced by the conference yt he had with Nouatus: wherefore it semeth plaine Nouatus was at Rome in the time of Fabianus. For after the Martyrdome of Fabianus the See was

Platina in vita Fabiani, & Cornelij.

Hieron. li. de scriptorib. Ecclesiast.

Damasus in Pontificali.

vacant but six dayes, as Damasus writeth. So there is no inconuenience, but that Fabianus might write of Nouatus coming into Italie, and geue the Bishops to whom he wrote, warning to beware of the infection of that heresie. And thus you haue said nothing hitherto that proueth the Decretal Epistles not to be theirs, whose names they beare.

Ievvel.

The. 143. vntruth. Damasus maketh expresse mention of such Decrees. Let his boke be trial.

*Neither S. Hierome, nor Gennadius, nor * Damasus euer made any mention, either of such epistles, or of any such Decrees: vvhich they vvould not haue dissembled, if there had ben any such extant or knovven in their time. Thus haue I briefly geuen a taste of these Decretal authorities, that the reader may the better vnderstande, of vvhat credite they ought to be.*

Harding.

You know the weakenes of this argument, I doubt not M. Jewel. Your selfe say of it, that in scholes it is called argumentum ab auctoritate negatiuè, and that it concludeth not necessarily. And syr if we should condemne what so euer is not mentioned of S. Hierome, Gennadius, and Damasus, to haue ben written by the auncient Fathers before their time, how many thinges should we reiect, that be acknowleged to be authentical by witnesse of other good writers? were there not certaine Epistles of Julius the first spoken of by Athanasius, Sozomenus, and others, and be yet extant partly in Greke, partly in Latine, of which neither S. Hierome, nor Gennadius, nor Damasus euer made any mention? Many other thinges of good auctoritie might here easily be rehersed, of which S. Hierome, and the two other neuer spake worde.

Athanasius in Apologia. 2. tripart. histor. lib. 4.

The cause why S. Hierome and Gennadius made no mention

That S. Hierome and Gennadius made no mention hereof, it is no maruel. For their profession is in the booke whiche you meane, to write de Scriptoribus Ecclesiasticis, among

among whom they thought not good to recorde them, that wrote nothing but Epistles, and briefe Decrees. Had these Decretal Epistles beene iust volumes, or such as might haue deserued the name of workes and bookes, they had ben mentioned.

of the decrees and decretal Epistles.

But I marueil what you meant in saying that Damasus made no mention of any such Decretal epistles or Decrees. Eyther you haue read Damasus, or you haue not. If you euer read him, what impudencie was it to denie that is so manifest, and that you could not be ignorant of? If you neuer read him, who may trust you, that so boldely pronounce of a thing you knew not? If you folowed your noteboke, or ye aduertisemēt which some of your brethren gaue you toward the filling of your booke: Let your Reader vnderstand, that so you may deceiue him in many other pointes, as you haue deceiued him in this.

M. Jew. by this is proued either impudent in lying, or rash in affirming that he knew not, and might sone haue knowen.

For truth it is, Damasus writing briefly the liues of the Popes that were before his time, mentioneth almost throughout his whole boke their Decrees, which in their Decretal Epistles they propounde to be kept and obserued.

Damasus mencioneth sundry popes decrees & decretals.

Concerning S. Clement, he speaketh of two Epistles that he wrote, named Canonical, and expressely of the Epistle which he wrote to S. James. In the life of the blessed Martyr Pope Alexander, he maketh mention of his Decree touching the vse of Holy water, which is expressed in his Epistle Decretal. So he mentioneth the Decrees of Sixtus, of Telesphorus, of Pius, of Anicetus, of Soter, of Eleutherius, of Victor, of Zephyrinus, of Calixtus, and likewise of other Popes, which Decrees he toucheth in manner with the very same woordes, with which they be vttered in ech Popes Decretal Epistle.

Damasus in Pontif. In vita Clement.

S. Clementes Epistle to S. James.

Holy water.

For the Decretal Epistle of Innocentius the first, which he

August. epist. 106.

witnesse for certain the popes Decretal epistles. *In prima epist. Cælestini ad Episcopos Galliæ. Ibidem in fine operū Prosperi.*

hee wrote to the Councel assembled at Carthage, teaching free wil and grace, beside S. Augustine, wee haue the expresse witnesse of the learned Pope Cælestinus. Likewise wee haue his testimonie for the Decretal Epistle of Pope Zosimus concerning Grace, written to the Bishops of al the worlde.

The Fathers of the Councel of Triburia confirmed many of their Decrees by aucthoritie of sundrie Popes Decretal Epistles. which they woulde not haue donne, had they ben of M. Jewels opinion. By expresse name they mention the Epistles of these Byshops of Rome, of S. Clement, Anacletus, Euaristus, Alexander, Zepherinus, Calistus, Urbanus, Syricius, Innocentius, Leo, Gelasius, Gregorius. Againe Burchardus who liued aboue fiue hundred yeres past, mentioneth the first epistle of S. Alexander the first. Hauing ye witnesse & aucthoritie of so many, so auncient & so learned Fathers for the Decrees and decretal Epistles, beside the credite of Isidorus, who gathered them together into one volume: M. Jewel of reason must beare with vs, if for verdite of this mater, we bid him stand backe, and geue place to his betters. More I could say for the Decrees and Decretal Epistles, but this may suffice for this time.

The. 144 vntruth. the decree speaketh not of cōpanie present, but of twoo to make answere.

The. 145 vntruth. Neither speaketh S. Augustine of the people of Rome, nor both they of the peoples receiuig euery day together.

Ievvel.

*Novv tovvching the mater, that by this Decree of Soter, it should then be lauful for the Priest there to say Masse, hauing onely tvvo ohers in his * companie, the state and storie of the time considered, it semeth very vnlikely. For both S. Augustine, and S. Hierome, haue recorded that the people of Rome, euen in their time v'ed to receiue the Communion * togeather euery daie. Vvhich practise can hardly stand vvith that is here imagined.*

Ievvel.

Harding.

What if the people of Rome were of so good deuotion, as to receiue the Cōmunion together euery day, in case you said truth? Might it not be lawful for al that a Priest to say Masse hauing two others present to answere him? Whether hee haue moe or no, of that the Decree speaketh not, as neither of Rome specially, but generally of what so euer place. And therefore you falsifie it, as you reporte it. The Decree requireth two to be present, for the conuenience of the answere, that is to be made to the Priestes salutation. It presupposeth not that others be absent.

Soters Decree falsly reported by M. Iew.

S. Augustine and S. Hierome in the places by your quotation noted, maketh nothing against Soters Decree. S. Augustine saith, that in some places the Sacrament was receiued euery day, in some other places, vpon certaine daies. Neither speaketh he of Rome at al. Likewise in his Epistle to Ianuarius, he saith, Some do receiue the Body and Bloude of Christe daily, some vpon certaine dayes. Neither meaneth he of Rome, as you say. S. Hierome in dede telleth, that it was a custome at Rome to receiue the Body of Christe euery daie. But there he declareth that many receiued secretely in their owne houses, and woulde not receiue in Churches. In these three places is mention onely of daily receiuing, but that the people of Rome receiued the Communion euery day together, that is to say in one place, that is not auouched. And therfore the Decree of S. Soter may wel stand with the state and storie of the time, notwithstanding any thing that out of S. Augustine, or S. Hierome is here alleged.

August. In Ioan. tract. 26.
Ad Ianuarium. Epist. 118.
In Apologia aduersus Iouinian.

Ievvel.

The vvoordes also them selse implie a manifest contrarietie.

The.146 vntruth. the worde Solēnia, doth not so import.

For this vvorde Solennia, vvhich here is vsed, semeth to importe * a solemne companie or resorte of the people. And yet this Soter requiring to this action * onely the companie of three persons, neuerthelesse calleth it Missarum solennia.

The.147. vntruth. Soter requireth not onely the companie of three to this actiō, but that two at the least bee present to answer ẏ Priest.

Solēnia, what is signified by the word, and whereof it is so called.

Harding.

This worde Solennia, hath not his name in consideration of a companie or resorte of people, but in respect of a common custome, be it yearely, daily, or at certaine prescript times. It is deriued of Solus, and Annus. Cicero vseth solenne, for wont or custome: as Ad Atticum. lib. 7. Nostrum illud solenne seruemus, vt ne quem istuc euntem sine literis dimittamus. Let vs kepe our olde wonte, that we let no man that goeth thither, to go without our Letters. The woorde Solennia signifieth in Ecclesiastical writers, either holy feastes, or any whatsoeuer celebritie and religious obseruance to be donne at holy actes after a prescript manner and custome. And it is commonly put with woordes signifying Sacramentes, or other things wherat faithful people shewe them selues reuerent. As Missarum Solennia, Baptismi solennia, Ordinationis solennia, nuptiarum, funeris, exequiarum solennia. Wherefore that the worde should importe a solemne companie, or resorte of the people, it is but your gheasse of a thing that to you onely seemeth, and is not.

Soters Decree misreported by M. Iewel.

And wheras you say of Soter, as though he required to this holy action only the companie of three persons: therein you folow your common custome of falsifying, and misreporting. He is so farre from requiring the onely companie of three persons thereto, that by the Decree there is no let, why there may not bee presente at euery Masse, not onely the companie of three persones, but also of three score, three hundred, three thousand,

Ievvel.

*It may vvel be doubted, vvhether Dominus vobiscum, or Orate pro me fratres, vvere any parte of the Liturgie of Rome in Soters time. For Damasus vvhich vvas Bishop of Rome tvvo hundred and fiftie yeres after that, vvriteth vnto S. Hierome, that thinges vvere donne vvith such simplicitie in the church of Rome in his time, that vpon the Sonneday there vvas nothing els but some Epistle of the Apostle, or some chapter of the Gospel read openly vnto the people: vvhich vvhether he meant of the holy ministration or no, I leaue further to be considered.

The. 148. Untruth. This can not wel & reasonably be doubted of by him that readeth Damasus boke of the Popes lyues and decrees.

Harding.

The simplicitie whereof Damasus complained in his Epistle to S. Hierome, was concerning the manner and order of singing, which in the Churche of Rome at his time was very simple in comparison of the Grekes. Therfore he wrote to S. Hierome then lyuing in the East, to sende him the manner of singing of the Grekes, that in the Church of Rome they might haue Psalmes and Hymnes sõg by day and night, as they were song in the East churches. Though Damasus there make mention but of an Epistle, and of a chapter of the Gospel, (for he speaketh of both together, and not of either disiunctiuely, as you vntruly reporte his wordes) saying, they only vpon the Sonneday were rehersed, that is, as he semeth there to meane, were songe, or pronounced with open voice song like: yet by those wordes he must not be thought to haue excluded ye Masse, which you had rather cal the Liturgie of Rome, and the holy Ministration, which worde for a shifte may serue you as wel to signifie your owne new deuised Communion, as the Masse of the Catholike churche. For it must nedes be graunted, that they of Rome receiued the Communion very often, and therfore had they the Masse necessary for the Consecration.

Damasus vntruly reported bi M. Iew.

Ministratiõ, a worde guilfully vsed by M. Iew. to diuerse intentes like a shipmans hose that may serue any legge.

Neither haue we cause to thinke, that the Masse was no at Rome in Damasus time, seing by his reporte we vnderstand, it

Prouves that masse was in Rome in, and before Damasus time.

Damasus in Pontificali.

The Passion added to the Masse by S. Alexander.

it was there vsed long before his time. For in the life of the blessed Martyr Pope Alexander, who was fifth after S. Peter, he writeth of the Masse by name, as of a thing before vsed. Hic (saith he) pasionem Domini miscuit in precatione sacerdotum, quando Missæ celebrantur. Alexander mingled our Lordes passion with the prayer of the priestes, when Masses are celebrated. Yet is M. Iewel afraid of the name of Masse, and therfore in stede of it, nameth the Liturgie of Rome.

Sanctus, Sanctus, Sanctus by S. Sixtus.

Of the holy Martyr Pope Sixtus, he saith, that he ordeined, that when the priest commeth to the action of the Masse (meaning that parte of the Masse wher'vnto the perfite Christians resorted, that which goeth before it, being that parte of the Masse whereunto the learners of the Faith called Cathecumeni were admitted) the people should sing the song, Holy, Holy, Holy, our Lorde God of hostes.

Gloria in excelsis by S. Telesphorus.

Of Telesphorus he saith, that he instituted the Angels song, Gloria in excelsis, to be said before the Sacrifice. Likewise in the life of Zephyrinus, and otherwhere he maketh expresse mentiõ of the Masse, and how it was to be celebrated. So that wheras Damasus describeth sundry thinges touching the Masse ordeined by the first Popes, and vsed before his time: there is no doubte but he mainteined it and kept it in his owne time. wherfore that which is here alleged out of his Epistle to S. Hierome, maketh no argument against the auncient order of the Masse, by which the priest saith, Dominus vobiscũ, and orate ꝑ me fratres.

Ievvel.

The. 149. Untruth. S. Soter requireth it not, it is vtterly false.

*Further this same Soter requireth, that both these tvvo, *and as many others as be present, make ansvvere vnto the priest : vvherin is included both nearenesse of place for the people to stand in, and to heare, and also a common knovven tongue : vvhich both are contrary to M. Hardinges Masse.*

Harding.

Harding.

Wil you neuer report the truth M. Iewel? wil you alwaies be founde a falsifier? wil you stil thus bewray the weakenesse of your cause by making the world witnesse, that you haue nothing to helpe you, but shamelesse lying? Why say you, S *Soter requireth, that bothe these tvvo, and as many others as be present, make ansvvere vnto the priest?* Why haue you conueied in of your owne false stuffe those wordes, *and as many others as be present?* What shameful shifte is this? Can not you helpe your mater but with such foisting in of wordes of your owne, to make some appearance of an vntruth? Soters Decree falsified by M. Iew.

Now then when you proue your owne forgerie to be good and plaine truth, your wordes to be S. Soters wordes, then maye you saye what you liste of the neareneſſe of place for the people to stand in, and of the common knowen tongue. But by such false additions of your owne, you proue nothing against the Masse of the Catholike Churche, which it liketh your pleasant head to cal M. Hardinges Masse.

Touching that you bring here out of the Canonistes, Gerson, Innocentius, and Durandus, whom you allege oftentimes rather to gainesay me, then for any regard you haue them in: I accompt it not worthy to be answered. As for my reason made out of this Decree, you report it otherwise then I make it. But your manifest vntruth and belying of my wordes I can not dessemble. Where you say thus.

Ievvel.

*But vvhat if these tvvo vvil not come, neither to communicate, nor to be present at al? *Verely by M. Hardinges mynde the Priestes deuotion ought not to stay for vvant of cōpanie. For these be his very vvordes a litle before: VVel none cōmeth: This is not a sufficient cause, vvhy the faithful and* The. 150. Untruth. There can no such meaning be gathered out of my wordes

godly priest enflamed vvith the loue of God, feeling him selfe hungry and thirsty after that heauenly foode and drincke, should be kept from it.&c. This is a cause suffycient saith Soter : it is no suffycient cause saith M. Harding. The iudgement hereof I referre vnto the Reader.

Harding.

M. Iew: falsifieth my āswer, and corrupteth the sense of my wordes.

As euen now you falsified S. Soters decree by adding vnto it of your owne, so here you falsifie my saying, specially the meaning of it, by taking away that, whereby the truth appeareth. My mynde is not, that the Priest should say Masse, whē he hath no person at al present, not so much as one to answere him: but that, if none be disposed to receiue the Sacrament with him, in this case he might receiue that heauenly foode him selfe alone. The lacke of others to receiue with him, is not a sufficient cause to kepe him from it, say I. Looke reader what I say in that place, and thou shalt easily perceiue, that I speake not of the absence of al others, but of want of receiuers. which M. Jewel knewe wel ynough. And yet of very purpose he reporteth it falsly. whereas I say in dede, Wel, none commeth: I meane, to receiue with the Priest. For so be my wordes in the sentence before. That oftentimes the priest at Masse hath no compartners to receiue the Sacrament with him. &c. which wordes presuppose an assistence of one or moe to answer the Priest. wherefore there is no contradiction betwen my wordes and this Decree, as M. Jewel hath vntruly said.

In my answer to the chalenge. Fol. 12.

Ievvel.

But (saith M. Harding) Soter requireth onely the presence of tvvo, and these tvvo vvere not commaunded to communicate: Ergo, the priest did receiue alone: and so there vvas vndoubtedly priuate Masse.

Harding.

M. Iew. corrupteth, and falsifieth al that he taketh in hande.

I frame not my argument, as you report it. I must alwaies syng one song vnto you, and tel you stil, that you falsifie al that you meddle with. Sith that you force me to repete it againe,

gaine, thus I say in the place by you falsified. Whereas the receiuing of Christes body is a farre greater mater, then to answer the Priest at Masse, if that holy bishop and Martyr had thought it so necessary, as that the Masse might not be donne without it: Doubtlesse of very reason and conueniēce, he would and should haue specially spoken of that, rather then of the other. But for that he thought otherwise, he required onely of necessity, the presence of two, for the purpose aboue mentioned. Thus I say there. Now let vs see and consider your Replie. Fol.25

Ievvel.

But marke vvel a litle, good Reader. If these tvvo vvere bounde to Communicate vvith the priest, then not vvithstādinge this Decree, M. Harding hath not yet founde his priuate Masse. Then consider this Decree vvritten in the name of Pope Calixtus. Peracta consecratione, omnes Cōmunicent, qui noluerint ecclesiasticis carere liminibus. Sic enim & Apostoli statuerunt, & sancta Romana tenet ecclesia. *The consecration being done, let al Communicate, onlesse they vvil be remoued from the Churche. For so the Apostles appointed, and so holdeth the holy Church of Rome. By this Decree *these tvvo vvere bounde, either to Communicate vvith the priest, or to departe forth of the Church. If they did communicate, then hath M. Harding here no priuate Masse. If they departed forth, then could the priest say no Masse at al. For Soter at least requireth the presence of tvvo.*

De Consf. dist. 2. Peracta.

The. 151. Untruth. The Apostles Decre extendeth only vnto the clergie, & bindeth not al the laitie.

Harding.

I must now and then tel you by the way, that I seeke not for Priuate Masse, whiche to finde, your scoffing pretendeth me to be desyrous. I seeke not for that, which I acknowledge not. For as I haue before said, the Masse is publike and common, as Christes death is the publike and common benefite of the whole Church, the memorie whereof in the Masse is celebrated. That a Priest may receiue the Communion alone, in case none others be disposed to receiue with him, that is it that I proue, which you cal Priuate Masse.

If the Decree that here you allege, were, of Pope Calixtus, how could it bynde them of Soters time, that was made so long after? For there were almost forty yeres after the death of Soter, before Calixtus was chosen Pope. If you referre the mater to the constitution of the Apostles, understand you, that it speaketh onely of them that be, ex sacerdotali Catalogo, asmuch to say, Ecclesiastical persons. Of which vocation it is not necessary they be, which Soters Decree requireth to be present. Therfore Calixtus Decree is brought in to no purpose. And so these two might answer the Priest, though they receiued not with him. Neither could they be bounde to receiue by a lawe made so long after their time. For lawes bynde for time to come, not for time past.

Calixtus was after Soter, and therfore his decree can not be extended to Soters time.

Againe if I sayd, that these two, after they had serued the Priest, and answered him at Masse, might go forth of the Church when the Priest receiueth the Oblation, which is at the ende of Masse: M. Jewel were answered, and had no more directly to replie. For the lawe that forbiddeth them which do not communicate, to departe out of the Churche, is to be referred to the time of receiuing, not to the time of Consecration, Oblation, and other Prayers: so that they might answere the Priest at the Masse, though they taried not at the Communion: which Communion he might receiue without their presence. So although they departed forth in the ende, yet might the Priest haue vsed their necessary presence in saying Masse before. The presence of two was required at Masse, when answere was to be made, not at the receiuing of the body and bloud of our Lorde, when the office of answering was past, and had no place.

Albeit this answer might be made in consideration of

M.

M. Iewels person, yet for the Readers sake, I had rather not to abuse his ignorance to shew of aduantage, but to vse good faith, and plainely to vtter the truth. This much then is to be said.

It is not Calixtus, but Anacletus, that made this Decree peracta Consecratione. &c. M. Iewel, as others of his syde, is deceiued by the errour of Gratian. The same is oftentimes by them brought to the disprouse of the Priestes Sole receiuing, and to proue, that al the people should receiue with the Priest at euery Masse, or be dryuen out of the Churche. But the request of receiuing the Communion which in that Decree is conteined, perteineth not to the people, but only to the Priestes, Deacons, Subdeacons, and other Ministers in solemne feastes seruing the Bishop at Masse. who so euer wil reade the first Epistle of Anacletus, from whence the Decree is taken, shal euidently see it to be so. And that the Decree is to be restrained to the clergie onely, it is cleare by the Apostles constitution Canone. 9. Whereunto Anacletus maketh relation.

Anacletus in prima Epist. Decretali.

The Decree of Anacletus commaunding al that be present to receiue, perteineth only vnto ẏ clerkes that waited on the bishop.

Besides al this the wordes of the Decree geue vs so to vnderstand, as they be vttered in the Original, and in Burchardus, where we finde these very wordes in the ende of the Decree: & si hoc neglexerint, degradentur, ẏ is to say, If they wil not do this let them be degraded. Whereby it is made cleare, that it is meant onely of the clergie, who were present at the Consecration, and were admitted into Sancta Sanctorum, the holyest place of al, whither none came, but such as were in holy Orders, ἐκ τοῦ καταλόγου τοῦ ἱερατικοῦ, as the Canon of the Apostles termeth them.

Fol. 92.

Canonum Apost. Can. 9.

Hereof I haue treated sufficiently in my Confutation of the Apologie, to which place I referre the Reader.

Fol. 92.

Ievvel.

It may also stande vvith reason, and vvith the common practise of the Church at that time, that these tvvo, vvhose presence Soter requireth, vvere Priestes or Deacons, or othervvise of the clergie, and that ouer and beside the company of the people, as in dede *it is determined by the Glose. And so this Decree of Soter, * agreeth vvith an other Decree of Anacletus made to the like purpose, that is, that the Bishop at the Ministratiō haue about him a certaine number of Deacons, subdeacons, and other ministers, besides the common multitude of the lay people. And likevvise vvith an other decree of the same Soter, that is, That euery Priest making the Sacrifice, haue by him an other Priest to assist him, and to make an ende of the Ministration if any quame or sickenes happen to fal vpon him. And this assistance of the Priest is required notvvithstanding the presence of others, either of the Clerkes or of the Laitie. Novv being Priestes or Clerks, and being present at the Ministration, the lavve specially constreined them to receiue the holy Communion vvith the Minister, as it appeareth by this Decree vvritten in the Canons of the Apostles.

M. Iew. simple gheasse.

The. 152. Untruth. It is not assuredly determined by the Glose.

The. 153. Untruth. It agreeth not, as here it shal appeare.

De Cons. dist. 1. vt illud. Can. 9.

If any Bishoppe or Priest, or Deacon, or any other of the Clerkes, after the Oblation is made, do not communicate, either let him shewe cause therof, that if it be founde reasonable, he may be excused: or if he shew no cause, let him be excommunicate.

Thus vvho so euer these tvvo vvere, vvhose presence Soter required, vvhether they vvere of the Laitie, or of the Clergie, the lavv constreined them to receiue together vvith the Priest. And therefore M. Harding hath hitherto found a Communion, and no maner token or inkling of his priuate Masse.

Harding.

How hangeth M. Iewels Diuinitie together? How agreeth he with him selfe? He proueth and disproueth, aloweth and condemneth, what him listeth. A litle before in this very Diuision he vtterly condemned the Decretal Epistles with their Decrees. Now as though he were not the same man, he taketh

Page. 67. M. Iew. doublenes

keth them to be good and of aucthoritie. And allegeth them for prouse of the practise of the Primitiue Churche. Now he thinketh it no shame to take helpe of Soter, of Anacletus epistle, of the Apostles Canons, yea of the very glose it self that is made vpon the Decree. Thou maist see Reader, he wil playe smal game, as they say, rather then sit out. Who so euer thus demeaneth him selfe in questions of religion, he sheweth him selfe to be but a shifter, and not a stedfast teacher of the truth. But sith that he alloweth these auncient Decrees, why doth he not recant, and yelde to the Catholike faith touching the doctrine of the Masse, and of the blessed Sacramēt in the same Decrees most plainely and vndoubtedly auouched and set forth?

Touching the present mater, to auoide my reason that proueth the Priestes priuate and Sole receiuing, you bring a very simple Gheasse, that the two, whose presence Soter requireth, were Priestes, Deacons, or otherwise of the Clergie: for where you say, that in dede it is determined by the Glose, in deede it is false. For al dependeth vpon Satis videtur, a seely coniecture: which semeth not so to others, how so euer it semeth to the glosemaker. Neither he semeth him selfe therein to be resolued, as appeareth by his obiection of the people answering Amen. Verely such a glosing determination is not of this matter a sufficient prouse. And in this point, onlesse you proue that, you faile of your purpose, and therefore ought you to yeelde to the Priestes sole receiuing, which you cal priuate Masse.

De cons. dist. 1. hoc quoque in Glosa.

Where you say, as though you had proued your former gheasse, *And so this Decree of Soter agreeth vvith an other Decree of Anacletus,* I must tel you that which I am ashamed to say so often, that you say false. For Soters Decree varieth from that of Anacletus in the point wherof we speake. That speaketh of a Priest at any time celebrating the Masse (of which woorde you be afraide, and therefore cal it the Ministration) this of a Bishop celebrating in a solemne feast.

Soters other Decree, wherof you would faine take a poore holde, required not an other Priest to be in a readinesse, when so euer Masse were said, at al times, and in euery place: but onely where it might easily be done through multitude of Priestes: for so be his wordes, Vbi temporis, vel loci, siue cleri copia suffragatur. Where there is good oportunitie so to do, by reason of time, or place, or number of Clergie.

De Cons. dist. 1. vt illud.

The ninth of the Apostles Canons speaketh onely of such as be of the Clergie. And because you are not able to proue, that the two, whom Soters decree requireth to be present at ŷ Masse, ought necessarily to be of that order and vocation: it is to no purpose by you alleged. And if it were graunted vnto you, that they ought to be of the Clergie, which I do not graunt: yet by the Apostles, their forbearing from the Communion with the Priest, is admitted in case of a reasonable cause. For so saith the Canon. Si causa rationabilis fuerit.

Cā. Apost. Cap. 9.

An Argument whereby the Priestes sole receiuing at Masse, which M. Jewel calleth priuat Masse, is proued.

Now hereof I gather this Argument, which M. Jewel by no shifte shal auoide. By Soters Decree the Priest may say Masse, if he haue onely two present to answere him: which two by M. Jewels ghesse must be of the Clergie. But those two in case of a reasonable cause be by the Apostles Decree, without punishment of excommunication permitted not to receiue the Sacrament with the Priest: Ergo where there is a case of such a reasonable cause, the Priest doth and may receiue alone. For if by any reasonable cause they that be presēt may be excused, what reason is there, why the Priest should be inexcusable, specially where there is no default of his behalfe, and that which he hath Consecrated must nedes be receiued? And so farre is the Priestes sole receiuing, which in your schoole is priuate Masse, proued, and found not contrary to Christes Institution.

And whereas Soters Decree requireth an other Priest to be present at euery Masse that is said, where the nūber of Priestes sufficeth, that if he that hath begonne Consecration faile by chaunce of infirmitie, the other may procede and ende the Sacrifice: if he had iudged that Christes Institution should be broken, except the Priest receiued the Sacrament with a number of others: he would haue made also a special Decree for prouision in that behalfe.

Your Epiphonema at the ende of this Diuision is not truly gathered of the premisses. For al dependeth of the two that answere the Priest. whom because you can not proue, that of necessitie they ought to be of ỹ Clergie, neither that being Laie they be bound alwaies to receiue: litle cause had you to crake, that hitherto I had not found any token or inkling of that you cal the Priuate Masse.

The. xxx. Diuision.

Here I allege the auncient Councel of Agatha, where an olde Decree of Fabianus and also of the Elibertine Councel was renewed: That al secular Christen folke should be houseled thrise euery yeare, at Easter, witsontide, and Christmasse. It was there also decreed, that they should heare the whole Masse euery Sonneday, and not depart before the Priest had geuen blessing. Seing then the people were bound to be present at Masse euery Sonday, and to receiue the Cōmunion but thrise in the yeare: herof a coniecture not without reason may be gathered, that in some Churches, specially where the number was smal, Masse was sometime celebrated, when a sufficient cōpanie, such as ỹ English Cōmunion requireth, receiued not the

De Cons. dist. 1. Ca. ad Celebrandas Missas.

Sacrament with the Priest. That in euery smal parrish, as by commaūdement of that Coūcel, they were bound to haue Masse euery Sonday, so also they receiued the Communion by lawful companies: I am sure that neither M. Iewel, nor any of his fellowes is able to proue. Unto this he replieth and saith.

Ievvel.

*M. Harding *knovveth vvel, that these Decrees vvhich he here allegeth, could neuer be found vvritten, neither in the Councel holden at Agatha, nor at the other Councel holden at Eliberis: but vvere set forth many hundred yeares after in the name of those Councels, by one Gratian, &c.*

The. 154 vntruth. I knowe it not.

Harding.

As though Gratian that liued three hundred yeares before Peter Crab, who hath laid together the Canons of ech Councel, as he found them in his olde copies, might not haue sene some other and truer copies of these two Councels, then came to the handes of the said Peter, when he committed them to print. And what moueth you to deny the Decree aboue mentioned euer to haue ben found in the Councel of Agatha? Wil you say it is not any part of that Councel because Gratian allegeth it? So may you deny many decrees, that be of most assured auctoritie. And find you it not in the booke among other decrees of that Councel? O say you perhaps, the booke it selfe telleth that the copie of Gemlake had in it, but. 46. Canons, wherof this is none. Why Syr haue you no more to say for you? Then if you refuse Gratian, because the booke of Gemlake hath it not, why may not I aswel refuse that booke, because Gratian hath it? Why should Gratian be found a lyer by that copie, rather then that copie be tried to lacke by Gratian? Uerely M. Iewel you vtter two greate vntruthes in one sentence. For neither knowe I, that this Decree was neuer written in the Councel of Agatha, neither is the same set forth in the name of that Councel by the forgerie of Gratian: whose iudgement in gathering you dispraise, because he hath gathered so many good testimonies of antiquitie together, whereby your heresies are confounded.

This is your maner as euer it hath ben ẏ maner of heretikes, when you be not able to iustifie your false doctrine against ẏ sayinges of ẏ Fathers, then either to deny ẏ Fathers, or to cal their workes into doubte & question. Whereby you thinke to winne, whiles you draw vs frō proufe of their doctrine, to shew proufe of their bookes. Whither tendeth this inpudēt policie of yours, but that we should geue ouer writing against you, and wander abroad to serch libraries for proufe of bookes by you denied? Which when we haue founde, yet wil you denie the same with no lesse impudencie, then now you denie the Councel of Agatha alleged by Gratian. But let vs see whether you haue any better stuffe then this.

The maner of heretikes hath euer ben to denie the Fathers, or to cal their bookes in question.

Ievvel.

These Decrees vvil stand M. Harding in smal stede, for thus they conclude. Qui in natali Domini, Paschate, & Pentecoste non communicant, Catholici non credantur, nec inter Catholicos habeantur. *They that receiue not the Communion at Christmasse, Easter, and VVitsontide, let them not be taken, nor reckened for catholike people.* *. *It appeareth by these general councels, that in the vvhole churche of Rome, sauing onely a fevve Massing Priestes, there is not one man vvorthy to be accompted catholike.*

De cons. dist. 2. Seculares.

The. 155. vntruth. This is a sclaunderous lye. For the contrarie is knowē and sene.

Harding.

This impudent tale and false sclaunder hangeth of a peeuish gheasse, that in the whole Catholike Church there is not so much as one man, that receiueth the Communion at these three solēne feastes: which impudent surmise sheweth this man not to care what he say, so he say ẏ best besemeth ẏ Mouthe of him, who is ẏ Father of lying. True it is God be thanked for his grace, it

Iohan.8. is wel knowen that infinite numbers of godly persons men & women, both at these three and sundry other feastes, do ordinarily receiue the Communion in the countries that remaine Catholike, which M. Iewel might him selfe haue sene and knowen when he was out of the realme in Quene Maries time, had not Satan possessed him, and kept him from the companies of true beleuing people. If it shal please him to send hither any of his frendes for trial hereof, we can direct him to a citie not far from this Uniuersitie, where he may see two or three hundred godly and deuoute persons communicate euery Sonneday, and at certaine high feastes aboue a thousand in one Church.

This last yere, which was the yere of our lorde. 1565. there were spent in Saint Gertrudes Parish here in Louaine among the Communicantes, thirty thousand three hundred hostes. Neither is the same the greatest parish in the towne. The number of houseling people therof is about two thousand. This much haue I learned by the Pastor of that Churche, who is a learned, godly, and graue man. Much the like rate of number of Communicantes should I fynde in other parishes here, I doubte not, if I were disposed to examine the matter. Of this it appeareth how rashly and wickedly M. Iewel sclaundereth the people of God. If the Communion be so frequented in this parte of Brabant, the discrete Reader may iudge, what accompt is to be made of al Christendome. But this man would faine aduaunce his owne Synagog by discommendation of the Church. Were it so that I fauoured his syde, I should say, pitie it is this swete Doctrine is set forth with so many and so manifest vntruthes.

The 156. vntruth. This is not proued by either of them. S. Augustine doth not so much as name Rome in that place.

The 157. vntruth. It is not included. For the people might bring their offe-

Ievvel.

These Decrees can not stande vvith the very forme and order of the Churche of those dayes. For besides that I haue already proued by the autoritie of S. Hierome and S. Augustine, that the holy Communion vvas then ministred*

stred vnto the people in Rome euery day,

Fabianus also Bisshop of Rome, hath plainely decreed, that the people shold receiue the Communiō euery Sonneday. His vvordes be plaine. Decernimus, vt in omnibus Dominicis diebus altaris oblatio ab omnibus Viris & mulieribus fiat, tam panis, quàm vini. *VVe Decree, that euery Sonneday the oblation of the aulter be made of al men and vvemen, both of bread and of vvine.*

*Here besides that in these vvordes * is included the receiuing of the cōmunion euery Sonneday, may be noted also by the vvay, that by this autoritie of Fabian, men and vvemen* made the Sacrifice of the aulter, and that of breade and vvine, and therfore after the order of Melchisedech,*

Therfore S. Bernard saith.* Non solus Sacerdos sacrificat, sed totus conuentus fidelium. *Not onely the Priest sacrificeth, but also the vvhole companie of the faithful. These thinges vvel considered, the sense that M. Harding vvould so faine vvring out of these Decrees, vvil seme vnlikely.*

Harding.

This Paragraph conteineth good store of vntruthes. First, it is not proued by S. Augustine, that the Communion was then ministred vnto ẏ people in Rome euery day. For as I haue before declared, in the places to that purpose alleged, he speaketh not of Rome at al, neither speaketh he expressely of the people. That he saith of daily receiuing of the Communion in certaine places, may be aswel referred to the Priestes, who daily in their Masses offered, as to the people.

But what meane you to allege Fabianus? Haue you not already condemned the Popes Decrees and Decretal Epistles? If you admitte them here, you must recant al that you spake against them before. If you wil that iudgement to stande, whereby you condemned them: then renoke that you

[Margin notes:] ringes to Churche, though they receiued not ẏ sacramēt. The 158. vntruth. Fabian doth not attribut to the people the making of the Sacrifice of the aulter. *Bernar. in serm in die Purificat.* The. 159 vntruth. Bernard saith it not, it is one Guerricus that saith it, but not in your sense *tracta 26. in Ioā. & epist. 118. ad Ianua.* M. Iewel alloweth and condēneth ẏ Decretal Epistles, so we know not where to haue hi. page. 66.

you say here acknowleging them to be of good auctoritie. If you reiect them in one place, and allow them in a nother place, it is a signe, you seeke not the truth, but ÿ defence of your owne vntruthes. And in dede that is the marke you shoote at, how to defend your false, and insolent Chalenge. which to do, you care litle what you say, so you gainesay me, and seme to impugne my Answer. wherefore from henceforth let vs vnderstand, where to haue you. Leane not to the authoritie of those, whom you condemne: Condemne not those, to whose authoritie you leane. Els shal you be taken for a shifter, and not for a plaine dealer. Of this I warned you before, because your doublenesse so deserued. I trust you wil not geue me occasion eftsones to warne you of the same.

The marke that M. Iew. shooteth at.

But touching this Decree of Fabianus, you vtter two fowle vntruthes atonce. *In these vvordes* (say you) *is included the receiuing of the Communion euery Sonneday.* How so I pray you Syr? which be those wordes? wil you them to be rehersed againe? Decernimus, &c. *VVe Decree that vpon al the Sonnedayes the oblation of the aulter be made of al men and vvemē, as vvel of bread as of vvine.* Here haue we mention of the Oblation, but of the Communion to be receiued, haue we none. It is included say you. Then tel vs where it is included, for we vnderstand it not. Is it included in the bread, or in the wine? in the men, or in the wemen? in the aulter? or in the Oblation? or in the Sonnedaies? In any of these seueraly, or in altogether iointly? If you can not shew vs in which of these it is included, then cal backe your worde, and you shal haue leaue to tel your tale againe as the Normans (in regard of their credite) haue in Fraunce.

Inter decreta Fabiani, decr. 3.

But you wil say perhaps, it is included in the Oblation. I deny it vtterly. For the act of the Oblation is diuerse from the act of receiuing the Communion. In dede I confesse, that where the Sacrifice is cōsecrated & offered, there it must also be receiued: but of the Priest necessarily, who by his special Ministerie doth Consecrate and offer the same. The people of whose receiuing you meane, and doth not, ne hath not the aucthoritie to Consecrate those holy Mysteries: is not so bound as often times as the Mystical Oblation is made.

Your other vntruth reported of Fabianus Decree, is, which (you say) may be noted by the way, that men and wemen made the Sacrifice of the Aulter, and that of bread and wine, and therfore after the order of Melchisedech. And to make your mater good, you auouch al this, by this aucthoritie of Fabian.

But let vs see better to your fingers. Where finde you good Syr, by this aucthoritie of Fabian (for so you say) that Men and wemen made the Sacrifice of the Aulter? what? make you al Laie men and wemen Priestes by this place of Fabian, and that after the order of Melchisedech? Marke say you, Fabian decreeth that euery Sonday (Altaris Oblatio ab omnibus viris & mulieribus fiat) the Oblation of the Aulter be made of al men and wemen. Al this I graunt, yet he saith not that men and wemen made the Sacrifice of the Aulter.

M. Iew. maketh al mē & wemē Priestes after the order of Melchisedech.

For the right vnderstanding aswel of this Decree, as of sundry sayings both of Scripture and Doctours, this much is to be considered: that there is a great difference, if we wil speake properly and exactly, betwen Oblation, and Sacrifice. It is properly called a Sacrifice when the thinge which is offered vnto God, is of the Priest altered by somewhat done in it, or vnto it, for religion sake. As for example, If he shed the bloud of a beast, if he caused the incense to burne, if he brake corne, if he sprinkled oile vpon meale, and fried it in a Frying panne: then he made a

Great difference to be noted between Oblation and Sacrifice.

Sacrifice what is it properly.

Leuit.2. & 6. Num.5. 2. Paralip 28.

Sacrifice. For that of al these thinges there were Sacrifices made, the Scriptures in sundry places do witnesse.

Oblation, what it is properly. Marc.12. Luc.21.

Oblation properly and directly is said, when any thing is offered vnto God, though nothing be done vnto it, or in it. As coines of money, the two mites that the poore widow did cast into the tresorie, loues of bread on the Aulter, &c. about which thinges nothing is donne, and so they remaine vnaltered.

Euery Sacrifice is an Oblation, but not cōtrariwise.

So that euery Sacrifice is an Oblation, but euery Oblation is not a Sacrifice.

First fruites. Deut.26

The first fruites were an Oblation, because they were offered vp vnto God, as wee read in the Scripture: but they were not Sacrifices, because there was no holy thing donne about them.

Tenthes.

The tenthes were no Oblations properly to speake, because they were not offered vp to God immediatly, but were geuen to the Priestes the Ministers of Gods Seruice for their maintenance.

Oblation and gifte taken for one thing. *Theophylactus In Epist. ad Heb.c.8.*

This difference between Oblation otherwise called a gift, and Sacrifice, is very wel noted of Theophylacte. If we interprete the difference between a Gift and a Sacrifice exactly, saith he, this oddes is between them, that a Sacrifice is offered by bloud and flesh: and Giftes consist of fruites, and such other thinges as be vnbloudie or without bloud.

Sacrifices are offred by bloud or fyre. Heb.5. & 8.

Neither are those thinges onely Sacrifices which are offered by bloud, but also such as are sacrificed by fyre. S. Paule hath obserued this difference in his Epistle to the Hebrewes. Euery Bishop, saith he, is ordeined to offer vp giftes and Sacrifices.

In epist. ad heb. ho. 18. Psal.39.

And S. Chrysostome expounding those wordes of the Psalme, thou wouldest not haue Sacrifice and Oblation, hath noted diligently this difference betwen Oblation and Sacrifice.

the worde Sacrifice is some times taken Me-

If it be replied by any man, that these termes be some times confounded, and indifferently vsed in the Scriptures, and

and that the name of Sacrifice is attributed to thinges, of which is no such alteration made by shedding of bloud, by burning with fyre, or otherwise: To him this much be said for answer, that in such places, which in the Scriptures and Fathers be founde not seldome, the worde Sacrifice is taken Metaphorically, not properly. As when S. Paule saith, I besech you, that you geue vp your bodies a liuely Sacrifice. Likewise the Prophete Dauid, A troubled spirite is a Sacrifice to God.

taphorically.

Rom. 12.
Psal. 50.
Gen. 4.
Heb. 11.

For proufe also that these termes be some times confounded and indifferently vsed, the place of Genesis is alleged. Respexit Deus ad Abel, & ad munera eius. God looked vpon Abel, and vpon his giftes. But vpon Caine, and his giftes he looked not. Whereas for al that it is certaine, saith Theophylacte, that Abel offered of the first begotten of his sheepe, and Caine gaue of the fruites of the earth. Though the one made a true Sacrifice, the other gaue but giftes onely without bloud or fyre: yet both indifferently are called Munera, Giftes. Forgete not (saith S. Paule) to do good and to bestowe parte of your goodes, for with suche Sacrifice God is pleased. Where he calleth giftes for Gods sake geuen to men by the name of Sacrifices. But such Tropical speaches vsed in some few places, exclude not the exact and proper signification of these wordes, Oblation or gifte, and Sacrifice, most commonly vsed.

Sacrifice and gifte, somtimes are confounded, & vsed indifferently, one for an other.

In Epist. ad heb. cap. 8.

Giftes called Sacrifices.

Heb. 13.

Now touching S. Fabians decree, requiring the Oblation of the aulter to be made euery Sonday of al men and wemen, as wel of bread as of wine: it meaneth, þͭ euery Sonday al faithful folke should bring their giftes and Oblations of Bread and wine to the Churche. For as the Iewes, when they repaired three times in the yeare vnto the place where God would specially be honoured, might not appeare before him wͭ empty hands:

The true declaratiō of S. Fabians decree.

Deut. 16.

The custome of offering vpon euery Sondaie.

so likewise the Christian people in the Primitiue Churche were accustomed vpon the Sondayes to bring their Oblations to the common place of prayer, that is to say, portions of those thinges, with store whereof God had blessed them. wherby they confessed and acknowleged God to be the geuer of al that they had, and by rendring vnto him part of his owne, they would shewe them selfe thankeful. It behoueth vs (saith S. Ireneus) to make offering vp vnto God, and in al thinges to shew our selues thankful to God the Creator. There is a special prayer in the Masses of S. James, S. Basil, and S. Chrysostome for them that brought such Oblations vnto the Churche, which because they offered them vnto God, they laid vpon the Aulter, and therfore were called the Oblations of the Aulter. S. James prayeth thus. Præterea meminisse digneris Domine, eorum, qui has Oblationes obtulerunt hodierno die ad sanctum altare tuum, & pro quibus vnusquisq; obtulit, vel in mente habet. &c. Furthermore vouchesaue to remember O Lorde them that haue offered these Oblations at thy holy Aulter this present day, and them for whom ech one hath offered, or thinketh of in his minde. Likewise S. Basil in his Masse. Memento Domine eorum, qui munera ista tibi obtulerunt, & per quos, & pro quibus obtulerunt. Remember O Lorde them, who haue offered these giftes vnto thee, and them by whom & for whom they haue offered. S. Chrysostome in his Masse praieth in much like manner.

Irenæus lib. 4. c. 34

In Missa Iacobi.

In Missa Basilij.

What thinges in olde time were commonly offered.

Ca͞. Apost. Can. 3.

Bread & wine offered, and to what vse.

What thinges were then commonly offered, it appeareth by sundry olde Decrees. Among the Canons of the Apostles, one Canon maketh mention of honnie, milke, wine, birdes, beastes, puls, newe eares of corne, clusters of ripe grapes, oile, incense. Of al other thinges breade and wine was most co͞monly offered. Thereof parte serued for the Comunion, parte for the Priestes, Deacons, and other Ministers, parte for the poore.

And

And part of the bread was cut into peeces, blessed, and after Masse distributed vnto such of the people, as were not dispo- sed and prepared to receiue the Communiō, as it is expressed in a Decree of Pope Pius the first. Those portions of bread so blessed, and to be distributed, were some times called Eulogiæ. This is that we cal holy bread.

Holy bre- ad, and the vse of it.

Inter decreta Pij, Decreto.9.

Now because the people that brought bread and wine with them, laid the same, as the manner was, vpon the aulter: therof it is, that in S. Fabians Decree, such offering is called Oblatio altaris, the Oblation of the aulter, and not for that the men and wemen, who offered it at the aulter, made of it the Sacrifice of the aulter, for that ministerie belongeth onely vnto Priestes. Part of it might serue to that purpose, it is not denied. But in that M. Jewel skippeth from a common Oblation of bread and wine, to the Sacrifice of the aulter, and auoucheth it to be made of lay men and wemen, and that after the order of Melchisedech: he sheweth him selfe either blindly ignorant, or maliciously despising the most blessed Sacrifice.

Oblation of the aulter, wher- of it is so called before con secration.

M. Jew. sheweth him selfe a prophane despiser of the blessed Sacrifice.

And whereas to bolster vp that wicked and prophane Do- ctrine, he allegeth S. Bernard as saying thus in sermone in die Purificationis, Non solus Sacerdos sacrificat, sed totus conuentus fidelium: Not onely the Priest Sacrificeth, but also the whole companie of the faithful: the mater is sone answered. First S. Bernard saith it not. They be the wordes of one Guerricus Abbas Igniacensis in a Sermon made in die purificationis. Nexte I confesse, that in a right sense, as this Sacrifice is called the Sacrifice of the Churche, so the faithful people may be said to offer it and to Sacrifice, but farre otherwise, then the Priest. For that which is specially and in outward act offered by the ministerie of the Priest, is donne vniuersally by the vowe of the faithful people. And so doth not onely the Priest offer or sacrifice, but also al

Ad finem operum Diui Bernardi.

the faithful. Therfore it is said in the Masse, Memento Domine, pro quibus tibi offerimus, vel qui tibi offerunt. Remember them O Lorde, for whom we offer, or who do offer vnto the, et c. So S. Augustine, tam ipsa per ipsum, quàm ipse per ipsam suetus offerri: Aswel is the Church (saith he) woont to be offred vp vnto God through Christe, as Christe through the Churche. But that euery one of the people both men and wemen in their owne person do outwardly and ministerially consecrate the body and bloud of Christe, and so offer and make the Sacrifice of the aulter after the order of Melchisedech: Neither is it signified by the Decree of the blessed Martyr S. Fabian, neither was it euer before M. Jewels Replie came forth, with such impudencie reported.

Aug de ciuit. Dei lib. 10. cap. 20.

Ievvel.

More ouer vvhen did S. Augustine, S. Hierome, S. Chrysostome, or any other learned Father or Doctour of that age euer vse this manner of speache, audire Missas, to heare Masse?

Harding.

M. Jew. wost commonly maketh his argumentes ab authoritate negatiue.

It is a shame for one that desyreth so much the fame of a learned man, so commonly to deduce his argumentes, ab authoritate negatiue, which maner of arguing is of litle force. what if they vse not so to speake, shal we therfore abolish the thing? None of them al euer said, that M. Jewel is a true man: what then? shal we thereof conclude, that M. Jewel is a false lyer? Be the argument neuer so good in mater, yet in forme it is naught. And yet is it as good as that M. Jewel maketh here.

M. Jew. for lake of better mater pyketh a quarel to this phrase audire Missas, to heare Masse.

Ievvel.

Certainely this phrase vvas so farre vnacquainted, and vnknovven in that vvorlde, that the very Originals of these Decrees haue it not, but onely haue these vvordes, tenere Missas, to holde Masse: *as may be sene in the booke of Councels noted purposely in the margent.*

Harding.

Harding.

what the very Originals haue, you gheasse rather then knowe. For if the true Originals had had tenere, and not audire, then would Peter Crab haue caused the booke so to be printed: els you make him a falsifier. with which crime I trow, you of al men wil not charge him. Very euil should it becomme you being so notorious a falsifier your selfe. And why beleue you rather ẏ note of the margent, then the text it selfe? yea why condẽne you al the bookes of Gratian, that so haue it? May we not beleue Gratian, aswel as the note made, we know not by whom?

De cons. dist. 1. Missas die Dominico.

Ievvel.

The Italians this day seme to speake farre better. For of them that heare Masse, and vnderstand not vvhat they heare, they say, Videre Missas, *that is, not to heare, but to see Masse.*

Harding.

Lo, as euil as you can away with the phrase, yet here you vse it your selfe. so haue you vsed it in sundry places of your Replie both before this place gaue occasiõ, as pag. 37. 39. and after, pag. 74. 85. 92. 479. And yet do not you reporte truly of Italians, as good an Italian as you are. For they say not videre Missas, to see Masses, in the plural number, but *veder la Messa*, to see the Masse, in the singular number, vnderstanding therby the Diuine Oblation, which they haue learned (as Villagagnon writeth) in the Syrian tongue to be called by the name of Masse. And so say they of them that vnderstãd what they heare, as wel as of them, that vnderstand not.

In libello gallico des choses contentieuses contre Caluine. ca. 31.

The Masse, as it is taken not only for the Sacrifice it selfe, but also for the whole seruice, so it consisteth in action, and in wordes. In respect of the one it may wel be said, that it is sene, in respect of the other, that it is heard, and so certaine aũcient Fathers haue spoken, whom I shal allege hereafter. So where the Italians say, they haue sene Masse, the English, Frenche

Both phrases to see, and to heare Masse, may wel be vsed in diuerse respect.

and Doutch, they haue heard Masse: in diuerse respect al say wel, neither is there any iust cause, why you should fynde fault with the maner of speach. But what shal I multiplie wordes about these two phrases, whether is better, to say, I haue sene Masse, or, I haue heard Masse, wt you, who cã not abide neither doing, nor saying, neither seing, nor hearing the Masse, nor any other part of Diuine Seruice, as it is donne in the Catholike Church? Yet remember, al this quarreling that you make for hearing Masse, toucheth not me, but Gratian, and the auncient Fathers assembled in Councel at Agatha, whose speach it is, and were neuer hitherto blamed for it.

In epi. Felicis. 4. De cons. dist. 1. Sicut non alij.

Neither is the phrase audire Missam, to heare Masse, so strãge as you beare the worlde in hande. Felix vseth it in his Epistle to the Bishops of diuerse prouinces. whose wordes these be. Satius ergo est, Missam non cantare, aut non audire, quàm in locis illis vbi fieri non oportet, nisi pro summa contingat necessitate, quoniam necessitas non habet legem. It is better therfore not to sing Masse, or not to heare it at al, then in those places, where it ought not to be donne, onlesse it happen for very great necessitie, for necessitie hath no lawe. Againe the learned Father S.

Germanus in consid. rerum ecclesiasticarum.

Germanus a Greke Doctor writing vpon S. James Masse, vseth this phrase in these wordes. Mentes nostras firmas habentes audiamus mysticum & viuificum Sacrificium. Hauing our myndes stedfast, let vs heare the mystical and lifegeuing Sacrifice, so he calleth ỳ Sacrifice of the Masse. S. Chrysostome speaking of those ỳ were vnworthy to receiue ỳ blessed Sacrament, saith, indigni sunt oculi istiusmodi spectaculis, indignæ aures. The eyes be vnworthy of these sightes, vnworthy be the eares. By which wordes he sheweth hĩ selfe to like the phrase of hearing these holy mysteries, or hearing the Masse. For whereof be the eares that he speaketh of vnworthy, but of hearing the Masse?

Chry. in epist. ad Eph. hom. 3 et ad po. Antioch. Hom. 16.

In the Councel of Cabilonum, which M. Jewel allegeth in the last Diuision of this Article, we haue ẏ phrase of hearing Masse. Audiunt Missas, that is to say, they heare Masse, is twise founde in the. 19. chapter of that Councel.

Now you enter into a commõ place not necessary, to proue that hearing without vnderstanding auaileth nothing. And here, you thinke to shew great learning by shuffling together Scripture and humanitie, Christe, and Cicero, Apostles, and Aristotle, the olde Testament, and the Ciuile Lawe. Out of which is brought in one Titius like the man in the Moone, or John at Nokes. Then commeth forth Alciate the Lawyer that dyed of late, to strike the stroke. Last of al one Epicharmus a Philosopher closeth vp the mater, and endeth the tedious bibble bable made of the sense of hearing, that a man would be loth to heare.

That hearing without vnderstãding auaileth nothing, an vnnecessary commõ place handled by M. Jewel.

In al that large processe your purpose is to perswade, that Christen people by being present in the Church, when the Masse is celebrate, are neuer the better, because they vnderstand not what is donne and said, for that they know not the tongue wherein the Masse is said. But herein you deceiue them that beleue you M. Jewel. For though the common Prayer of the Church vttered by the mouth of the Priest be not perfitely vnderstãded of the people, yet may it be profitable vnto thẽ, specially if they haue a general knowledge of the thing that is asked, of him of whom it is asked, and through whom it is asked. Neither is it necessary they vnderstand what so euer the Priest saith. For they may be partakers of his Prayers, though they perceiue not ne heare not distinctly al that he saith.

The faithful people receiueth benefite by the praiers of the Church, though they vnderstand not the tongue they be made in.

It was straitly commaunded by our Lorde, that no man should be in the Tabernacle, when the high Bishop entred into the holy place, to pray for him selfe, for his house, and for the Leui. 16.

 whole

whole companie of Israel. Now although the people neither heard nor sawe, what the Bishop said or did in the holy place, yet they knew in a generalitie, that he prayed for them, and thought them selfe partakers of his publike Prayer and Sacrifice. In the day of the Purification, the high Bishop Sacrificed in the holy place for the synnes of the people, at what time
Luc.1. they stode al without, during the time of the incense, as S. Luke declareth speaking of Zacharie.

David ordeined that God should be praised with certaine
2. Parali. 16. &.25. musical Instrumentes, and appointed certaine Leuites to serue in that Office, commaunding them to sing and play on their instruments in the morning and at euening euery day, and at al solemne feastes, according to the rite and custome of euery feast. Who dareth say, the people were not partakers of these praises of God, and prayers? Yet the people vnderstode not in particular euery Obseruation of the Sanctuarie or holy place, nor al the Psalmes that so were Daily song. But you presse vs with the wordes of S. Chrysostome, and of S. Paule, where you say thus.

Chrysost. in.1.Cor. hom.35.

Ievvel.

Chrysostome speaking of him that heareth the prayers in a strange vnknovven tongue, saith thus. Tu recte oras, Spiritu scilicet concitatus sonas: sed ille nec audiens, nec intelligens ea quæ dicis, paruam ex ea re vtilitatem capit. *Thou prayest vvel, for thou soundest vvordes being moued by the spirite: but the vnlearned neither hearing nor vnderstanding, vvhat thou saist, hath thereby smal profite. Likevvise saith S. Paule,* Qui loquitur lingua, non hominibus loquitur, sed Deo: Nullus enim audit. *He that speaketh vvith tongue, speaketh not vnto men, but vnto God, for no man heareth him.*

That

That S. Paule in the. 14. Chapter of the first to the Corinthians speaketh not against hauing the Seruice of the Church in a learned tongue.

Harding.

They that in this age haue cut them selues from the Church, proceding out of Martine Luthers Schoole, haue neuer donne with this place of S. Paule to the Corinthians, thinking to haue a greate aduantage against the Catholikes, for that they haue the Masse and their other diuine Seruice in the Latine tongue. which they affirme to be quite contrarye to the Doctrine of S. Paule. wherefore it shal be to good purpose here to declare, that of the wordes which the blessed Apostle there vttereth, nothing can be gathered, wherby the auncient custome of the Catholike Church making Sacrifice, Prayers, and praise to God in the Latine tongue, may seme to be reproued. For better declaration hereof I wyl not be ashamed to vse some parte of that a graue and a learned man one of the Readers of this Uniuersitie hath noted touching this point. Uerely the onely thing which S. Paule forbiddeth, is this, that in the common assemblie of the Church, no man speake with a tongue vtterly vnknowen, and such as no other Person vnderstandeth, except there be an interpreter, who may expounde what is said, to them that vnderstand not. For this is to be considered, that among the Corinthians for the gifte of Tongues one swelled againste an other, and preferred (very vnskilfully) this gifte before other more profitable and more excellent giftes, as though by the same they had ben like vnto the Apostles, who vpon the fiftith day after our Lordes Resurrection receiued the gyfte of tongues, as S. Chrysostome noteth.

What is that S. Paul forbiddeth. 1. Cor. 14

In 1. Cor. 12 & 14.

In comment. in 1. Cor. 14

S. Ambrose also (or who so euer he was that wrote the Cōmentaries which beare his name) saith further, ỹ there were certain Hebrewes at Corinth, who sōetimes in their treatises or Oblations used the Syrian tongue, and most commonly the Hebrew tongue, therby to winne commendation. For they estemed not a litle to be called Hebrewes, for the merites sake of Abraham. As if now one, to shew that he could do a woonder, would at the diuine Seruice openly pronounce a Psalme in Hebrewe, or say Masse in Greeke.

Now for this cause S. Paul would not that any mā spake with an unknowen tongue at the meeting of the faithful together, except there were one to interpret it forthwith, because his wordes could not so be borne in memorie, as their interpretation might be differred until a conuenient time to be expounded by a sermon, and it was uncertaine what euery one spake with the

1. Cor. 14

unknowen tongue. Therfore in the same place he commaūdeth, that when the Prophetes, that is to say the expositours, haue declared it, the others do iudge of it, meaning such as haue the gift to discerne spirites, that if they saw that which was spoken with the unknowen tongue, was to be reiected, they should reiect it, if they saw, it was to be approued, they should approue it.

It is to be noted, that where S. Paule commendeth prophesying, that is, expounding of the scriptures, he saith, the Church is edified by prophesying: And where he describeth the gifte of tongues the gifte of interpretation secluded, there he saith, that no man understandeth the tongue. He that speaketh with tongue

1. Cor. 14

(saith he) speaketh not vnto men, but vnto God. For no man heareth, that is to say, no man understandeth. And againe. If thou blesse with the Spirite, how shal he that supplieth the roome of the idiote (by which worde S. Paule meaneth not a foole, as commonly we meane: but such a one as knoweth no language

Idiote is he that knoweth no tongue but his owne vulgar tōgue.

guage

gnage,but only his owne vulgare language,) say Amen at thy blessing, seing he vnderstandeth not what thou sayest? Loe,he speaketh of a tongue vtterly vnknowen , which no man in the Church vnderstandeth, no not he who being better learned then the rest,is wonte to answer Amen for the Idiotes.

And here it is specially to be marked , that the Apostle saith not,the idiote or vnlearned person vnderstandeth not thy blessing,but,he that supplieth the roome (saith he) of the idiote or 1.Cor.14
vnlearned person. which is an other manner a thing, then to say, Idiota, the Idiote or vnlearned person, as it hath ben diligently noted by certaine Doctours, specially Primasius, Haimo,and Petrus Lombardus. For in these wordes S.Paule putteth before his eyes as it were the manner of the Iewes, and doth allude to the fashion of their Ceremonies. For in the begynning of the Synagogue, before the people were increased, the whole people was wont to answer Amen, and what so euer els was to be answered by the people at the holy Ceremonies. But after that Dauid had appointed synging men, then began they peculiarly to answer at the rites of the Sacrifices. Yea the inferiour Priestes answered the high Priest, as thereof we read in the booke of the Machabees. Orationẽ faciebant omnes sacer- 2.Mach.1.
dotes,dum consummaretur sacrificium, Ionatha inchoante, cæteris autem respondentibus. Al the priestes made prayer, whiles the Sacrifice was a doing, Ionathas began,& the rest answered.

And because it was commaunded by Moyses lawe,that the Deut.26.
Iewes, as they made their Oblations, should speake certaine wordes before the Priest, and no other tongue was vsed at Sacrifice but the Hebrewe,and many both Iewes dispersed abroad among the Gentiles, and specially Proselytes, who came from Gentilitie to the religion of the Iewes,knewe not the Hebrewe tongue,and yet came oftentimes to offer in the Temple : some

were founde to supplie the roome of these vnlearned persons called in Greke by S. Paule, Idiotes and to speake Hebrewe for them, and to answer Amen. As in smal Parrishes the Deacon, Clerke or Sextin maketh answer in al the Seruice in the name of the whole people: so whereas long before at the begynning of the Church, the whole people was wont to syng, afterward in a Councel holden at Laodicea about the yere of our Lorde. 370. it was ordeined, that none should sing præter canonicos Psaltes, but Canonical syngers, that is to say, such as by rule and common order were appointed to be the synging men in Churches. These appointed by rule to sing, be they, who by S. Paule doe supplie the roome of the vnlearned people. whom for that they speake but with one Priuate and special tongue, and know not the Common tongue, as Greke or Latine, and for the most parte be vnlearned, S. Paules language calleth Idiotes, which is no odious name nor terme of cōtempt, howsoeuer it sound otherwise in our common English speache.

Concil. laodicen. ca. 15.

Now then as S. Paule saith in the begynning, that no man vnderstandeth him that speaketh with tongue, so here he saith, that neither he which supplieth the roome of the Idiote or vnlearned person, can answer Amen ouer the blessing of him that speaketh with an vnknowen tongue, because he knoweth not what he saith, whether it be true or false, good or euil, for asmuch as he him selfe who is of more cunning and knowledge then the Idiotes or vnlearned persons, vnderstandeth not the tongue wherein the prayer is made.

A comparison betwen the state of the Corinthians, and the church now, wherin great difference may appeare.

Thus then there appeareth a great and manifold difference betwen that which the Apostle forbad to be donne among the Corinthians, & that which of custome is commonly donne in the Church. There saith he, no man heareth, and he that supplieth the roome of the Idiote, knoweth not what thou sayest. Here al that

be

be of the Clergy vnderstand the latin tongue, and they that answer in stede of the lay people, vnderstand wel ynough what the Priest prayeth, yea many of the lay folke them self be not vtterly ignorant of the Latine tongue. There through the vnknowen tongue no man was furthered to pietie, & as S. Paule speaketh, an other is not edified. But here both the clergy is edified, and is taught what they ought to deliuer vnto the people. There, were spoken in an vnknowen tongue, thinges vncertaine, and such as were yet to be discerned: Here nothing is read or song, which before hath not ben assuredly approued, and taken either out of the holy scriptures, or authentical Doctours. There the interpretation could not be differred, because the wordes passed away, and could not be kept in memorie: Here al thinges be rehersed out of writing, and the interpretation is differred vntil a cōuenient time, that when the people assemble thē selfe together, what so euer concerneth them, may be expounded vnto them. There vaine praise was sought for childishly by a strange & vnknowen tongue: Here in a most common and knowen tongue God is deuoutely praised and prayd vnto.

To conclude, among the Corinthians thinges were donne with confusion, and by occasion of the tongues the necessarie instruction of the people was let and hindered, insomuch that if, as al were speaking with vnknowen tongues, Infidels or Idiotes had come into the assemblies, they would haue thought thē to be madde and out of their wittes. But now as the state of the Church is ordred, al thinges be donne orderly, & the diuine Seruice is with such wisedome disposed, that the preaching of Sermons therby susteineth no hinderance: And if Infidels or Idiotes (whom S. Paule so calleth) come into our Churches, they be offended rather that the Clerkes sing negligently and loosely, then that they sing in Latine.

These thinges being wel considered, it shal appeare plaine I doubt not, that, what so euer S. Paule writeth against speaking with Tongue amonge the Corinthians, or S. Chrysostome in his Cōmentaries vpon that place: it maketh nothing for disprouf of the Latine tongue vsed in the Sacrifice and other Diuine Seruice of the Latine Church. This much for answer to your long vnnecessarie processe against the terme of hearing Masse.

Ievvel.

Novv let vs see, vvhat M. Harding gathereth out of these tvvo Councels. Then of like (saith he) *specially in smal tovvnes and villages, they had Masse vvithout the Communion of many together.* Of like *vvas neuer good Argument in any Schooles.*

Harding.

Yeas Syr, Aristotle the chiefe Maister that euer Shooles had, teacheth, that Argumentes be many times made of coniectures and likelihodes. Such of him be called τεκμήρια. Read his second Booke De arte dicendi, and there shal you finde this manner of reasoning handeled. Looke where he treateth, De Argumentis factum coniectura ostendentibus. If the coniecture be probable, the Argument is probable. And for proufe of a fact, which to proue is harde, it is sufficient to bring a probabilitie. Now forasmuch as whether any Priest said Masse without cōpanie of Communicantes within the first six hundred yeares, that you make so much a do for, is quæstio facti, as they say, and not iuris: If I can shewe it by any probable Argument, I do that belongeth to duetie in this case. The Coniecture is this.

De Arte dicēdi. lib. 2. cap. 35.

Because the people withdrew them selfe much from receiuing the Communion, it was decreed by the Councel of Agatha, as it was long before by S. Fabian the Pope, and also by the

Concil. Agathen. cap. 18.

the Councel Elibertine as Gratian recordeth, that so many as would not receiue at the three solemne feastes, Christmasse, Easter, and witsontide, should not be accompted for Catholike. yet was it by the same councel commaunded, that the people should holde, heare, or see Masses (let M. Jewel choose of thes three termes which he lyketh best) euery Sonneday, & not depart before blessing were geuen.

De cons. dist. 2. Seculares. De cons. dist. 2. Omnis homo. Conc. Agathen. cap. 47.

This compulsion of the people to receiue at the three feastes of the yere, argueth a negligence and a drawing backe from the vse of the Cōmuniō at other times. If this be presupposed, wheras they were excused in case they receiued at the said three feastes onely, and yet were bounde to be at Masse euery Sōneday: I report me to any mā that is not contentious, whether hereof a probable coniecture may not be gathered, that at the Masse of some Sonnedayes the Priest had smal, yea rather no companie to receiue the Cōmunion with him, specially in such places wher the Churches had but fewe people. For if the people had ben disposed to receiue by conuenient numbers euery Sonneday, then should the Fathers of that Councel haue had no cause at al to make that straight Decree. But seing you make light of what so euer is not proued by a strong demonstration, this argument here I propounde vnto you, which is as good as a coniectural mater permitteth to make.

An argument to proue priuate Masse in mater coniectural.

what so euer ẏ people be loth to do, & do not but by cōpulsion of lawe: ẏ doing therof they may reasonably be thought to omit, at least sometime, when the lawe setteth thē at libertie. But to receiue ẏ Communion euery Sonneday they were loth (for els the lawe cōpelling them to receiue thrise in ẏ yere had ben nedelesse) & had libertie to forbeare, so ẏ they receiued at the said three solēne feastes: Ergo, it is not besides reason to thinke of thē, that they forbare to receiue at least some Sonnedaies in ẏ yere. Vpō graunt of this, I procede further, & say, They forbare to receiue some Sonnedaies, but they had Masse every Sonneday: ergo, they had Masse, when they receiued not with the Priest. And so farre is that proued, which you cal Priuate Masse.

An other argument for the same.

Againe, If the Masse may not be donne, except a cōpanie receiue the Sacrament with ẏ Priest: then it appeareth, ẏ the Fathers of Agatha Councel were vnwise and vnprouidēt men. But ẏ is not to be thought of so graue, so learned, so godly, & so wise Fathers: Ergo, the Masse may be dōne without companie receiuing with the Priest. If any of the premisses be to be doubted of, it is the maior or first proposition. But the same, thus I proue.

Who so euer maketh a law for a thing to be donne, and omitteth to prouide for the meanes without which the thing can not be donne: he is an vnwise & an vnprouidēt lawemaker. But the Fathers of Agatha Councel, as also they of the Councel Elibertine, and S. Fabian, made a law and Decree, ẏ the Masse should be dōne euery Sonneday in the yere, and tooke no order for the people, or conuenient cōpanies of the people, to receiue ẏ Sacrament at euery Masse with the Priest, without the which ẏ Masse can not be donne after your doctrine, but leafte them to their libertie: Ergo, those Fathers were vnwise & vnprouidēt men. But you may not condēne those graue, wise, holy, & learned Fathers, neither reiect the auctoritie of that aūcient Councel: For by your owne Chalēge you haue bound your self to stand vnto it, & to allow it, because it was holdē within ẏ first six hūdred yeres after Christe: what remaineth then, but that you graunt, which must nedes be graunted, that Masse might be donne without a companie receiuing the Sacrament together with the Priest?

Certainely if those Fathers had ben of your opinion, and had ben persuaded, the Masse might not be donne without a number receiuing with ẏ Priest, whereas they decreed Masse to be donne euery Sonday: they would & should also haue made a special ordinance for such numbers and companies of Communicantes

alwaies

alwaies to be in a readinesse. Which forasmuch as they did not, therof it is euident, that Masse may be celebrate, though there be none disposed to receiue the Communion with the Priest. And thus is that you terme priuate Masse, proued.

The. 160 vntruth. These be not the wordes of the Councel.

Ievvel.

*But vvhat if the very vvordes of these Councels, vvhere vpon M. Harding hath founded his Masse, make manifest proufe against his Masse? *The vvordes be these:* Al Secular Christian folke, be bounde to receiue the Communion at the least thrise in the yere.

The. 161. vntruth. It is neither Relaxation nor priuilege. It is a paine annexed in case of contempte.

**This Relaxation or priuilege is graunted onely vnto the Secular Christians. vvhereof it folovveth necessarily, that al Ecclesiastical persons, as Priestes, Deacons, Clerkes, and others vvhat so euer of that sorte vvere not excepted, but stoode stil bounde to receiue orderly, as they had donne before: *and that vvas at al times vvhen so euer there vvas any ministratiō.*

The. 162. vntruth. Ecclesiastical persons were not at al times bounde to receiue when the Sacrifice was offered, as it appeareth by the canōs of the Apostles. can. 9. and otherwhere.

And so by the plaine vvordes of these Councels the Priest receiued not alone: neither hath M. Harding yet founde out his priuate Masse.

Harding.

There is neither truth in your wordes, nor reason in your argumentes. The wordes of the Decree be not as you report them, but somewhat otherwise. The Seculars (saith that Councel) that wil not Communicate at Christmasse, Easter, and VVitsontide: let them not be beleued to be Catholike, neither let them be accompted among the Catholikes. These wordes, as euery man may see, import not a Relaxation or priuilege graunted onely vnto the Secular Christians as you say, but a punishment binding them to do that of necessitie at certaine times, which was at al times left before to their deuotiō. so that it is a bond of it self, & confirmatiō, not a relaxatiō or release of a bonde or dutie, which you presuppose. Being therfore a Decree made ad augmentū as ỷ lawyers say, it can not import diminutiō or relaxatiō. For ỷ one cause cā neuer bring forth contrary effectes. This Decree therfore bindeth ỷ seculars to more then by necessitie of positiue

Conc. Agathen. c. 47 De cons. dist. 2. Seculares.

 lawe

Relaxatiō or priuilege. lawe they were bounde vnto before, and for the straiter obseruation of the same thereto a paine is annexed in case of contempte or transgression, which is not ye nature of a relaxation or priuilege. For a relaxation or priuilege is euer graunted to release the rigour of the lawe, or any bonde or burthen, for the fauour, ease, and benefite of the partie to whom it is graunted.

And whereas by a priuilege there is an exemption graunted out of the common lawe: it behoueth you to shewe vs, yt by the common lawe al were bounde to receiue the communion euery day, or euery Sonneday. If al had ben bounde to receiue euery day, or euery Sonneday, or so often as ye Masse was celebrated: what meane the Fathers, namely S. Chrysostome, S. Ambrose, and S. Augustine, where they speake of the Sacramēt either but once in ye yere receiued, or but once in two yeres, or very seldome receiued: to speake so coldely of it, and not sharply to rebuke the offenders for breaking a thing commaunded by a cōmon lawe? Most certaine it is, if it had ben a law, they would neuer haue so wincked at it, their pulpites in that age should haue rong of it, & their bokes at this day should haue spokē of it. Yea wher they receiued not daily, but seldome, S. Augustine saith, they caused thereby none offence to be taken, neither were they by ye gouernours of the Church commaunded to do otherwise, and whē they obeyed not their request therein, yet for the same they were not condemned.

Chrys ad heb. ho 17. Ambr li. 5. de Sacra. cap. 4. August. de verb. Domi. secūd. Luc. hom. 28.

Seing then there was no such common lawe, commaūding al persons to receiue euery day, or euery Sonneday, or when so euer the Masse was celebrated: it is besydes al truth and reason, that this Decree of Agatha Councel requiring and compelling vnder a great penaltie the seculars to receiue the Sacrament at the forsaid three feastes at least, should be taken for relaxation or priuilege.

De Sermone Domini in monte. lib. 2. cap. 12.

Your

Your grownd then thus proued false, that you say foloweth therof necessarily, foloweth not at al: that is to say, it foloweth not of your false pretensed priuiledge, that al Ecclesiastical persons receiue with the Priest, when so euer there is Masse celebrated: which Masse you refuse to name, though it be often in auncient Councels, euen in those also which your selfe do allege and cal it by your common ministring worde of Ministration.

But what meane you, where you mention Ecclesiastical persons, to adde by way of exposition, as *Priestes, Deacons, Clerkes and others, what so euer of that sorte?* Acknowledge you any Ecclesiastical persons besides Priestes and Deacons? If you do, why haue ye not thē in your Cōgregations? what make you of Clerkes, a distinct order? If they be not distinct from Ecclesiastical persons, why recken you them as though they were a kinde of holy order by them selfe, as Priestes and Deacons are? Againe why put you into your reckening and diuision of Ecclesiastical persons, that other general worde *others?* If you acknowlege the primitiue Churche to haue had the other holy orders, which the Church now hath, to witte, Subdeacons, Acolytes, &c: Why cal you not them by their names? Be you so fine in your new Gospel, that you be ashamed to vtter the names, whereas you acknowledge the thinges by the names signified? But it appeareth manifestly, that you care litle what you say, so you seme to gainesay me, and to haue some mater of apparent aduātage against the pointes of my Answere to your Chalenge. Clerkes.

These Ecclesiastical persons say you, were bound to receiue with the Priest, and did alwaies receiue with him, when so euer Masse was celebrated: hereof you conclude, *the Priestes neuer receiued alone,* and *M. Harding hath not yet founde out his priuate Masse.* But Syr, a woorde with you. First, you haue not yet proued, that al Ecclesiastical persons were bounde to receiue,

Mini- stration. when so euer there was any Ministration, for in that worde you haue great delite, when you speake of the Masse. And although it were graunted you, yet how wil you proue, that there were Ecclesiastical persons in euery parrish, in euery Churche and Chappel, were it neuer so smal? was there no Church or chappel, where it was lawful to haue the Masse, but in the same also were either other Priestes, or Deacons (for other Ecclesiastical persons besides these your Gospel acknowlegeth not) and they of such number as might make vp a lawful Communion? Do you not require three at least besides the Priest to receiue with him, be the parrish neuer so smal?

In the new English Cōmunion booke,

How say you then, can you proue, that there were three Priestes or Deacons at the least in euery Church and Chappel, where the Masse was celebrated, beside the Priest that offered the Sacrifice? Can you proue there was so great multitude euerywhere of such Ecclesiastical persons, before the time of the Coūcel of Agatha? If euery Churche were not furnished with such a companie, as doubtelesse it was not, whereas the Masse was of necessitie notwitstanding to be celebrated euery Sonday, for thereto they were bounde by a straight lawe: what can you answere M. Jewel for a reasonable escape, that the Masse was not there done vpon sundry Sonnedaies without companie receiuing the Communion with the Priest?

That the Seculars receiued not, it is before proued, and by M. Jewel graūted, for els the Decree binding them to receiue at the three feastes had been void and needlesse: that there was Masse euery Sonneday among them, it is not denied, and the Decree of this Councel inferreth it. But that in euery Church where Masse was donne, there were at al times three other Priestes or Deacons at the least, besides the Priest that celebrated, to receiue the Communion with him, there is no probable reason

reason, nor so much as a coniecture leading vs so to beleue. What foloweth then of this, but that in Churches which lacked such number of Priestes and Deacons, they had Masse very often without a companie receiuing the Communion with the Priest, which M. Iewel calleth priuate Masse?

Ievvel.

*But that the vvhole mater may the better appeare, not by gheasse or ayme; but by the very Ecclesiastical order of that age, vve must vnderstand, that these and such other like Decrees vvere made, not for the greatest parte of the people, * that in those daies vsed to Communicate in al their assemblies, but for a fevve that vvere negligent, and haled backe. For othervvise the general order doth vvel appeare, by * al the Ecclesiastical recordes of that time.*

The.163. vntruth. The greatest parte of the people at that time vsed not to cōmunicate in al their assemblies as it is here proued.

Harding.

Now taketh M. Iewel the whole mater into his owne handes, and promiseth to put al out of doubt. And wil you know how? Forsooth not by gheasse or aime, but by a manifest lye. *Vve must vnderstand,* saith he. Now that he hath none other shift to auoid the proufe of priuate Masse, he seeketh how to escape by a new deuised vnderstanding, and telleth his Reader, he must vnderstand a false point or two. Which if he vnderstand & beleue for certaintie, it shal appeare vnto him, that then there was no priuate Masse. Wel then, what is that we must vnderstand? *That the greatest parte of the people in those daies vsed to Communicate in al their assemblies. That therefore these and such other like Decrees vvere not made for them, but for a fevve negligent felovves that haled backe.* But how is this proued? *For so it doth very vvel appeare by al the Ecclesiastical recordes of that time.*

The.164. vntruth. By sūdry Ecclesiastical recordes the contrary appeareth as here it is shewed.

So then the trial of this mater dependeth of ye records. *It doth vvel appeare by the recordes of that time,* saith M. Iewel, *that the greatest part of the people vsed in those daies to cōmunicate in al their assemblies.*

Marke wel what he saith Reader. vpon ỹ graũt I reason thus. If the greatest part of ỹ people vsed thẽ to cõmunicate in al their assemblies, forasmuch as they were straitly boũd to be at Masse euery Sonday, as ỹ decree made to ỹ end aboue mẽtioned commaũded: then it foloweth, ỹ they receiued the Communion euery Sonday. And then further. If they receiued the Communion euery Sonday, how was not the Decree superfluous, that commaunded them to receiue at least thrise in the yere? For what is commaunded by a new lawe to be done, is presupposed not to haue ben done before.

M. Jewel should haue done wel, if he had alleged those recordes for his credite sake, which is not growen so greate yet, that we may beleue him vpon his bare worde. Certaine it is, the recordes of that age be quite contrary. S. Chrysostome in whose age this Councel of Agatha was kept as some thinke, oftentimes complaineth of the peoples slacknesse in comming to the Communion. He rebuketh them sharply for that they could not be brought to Communicate oftener, but looked for some holy tide, as for Aduente, the Epiphanie, or Lente. In one place he saith thus. In alijs quidem temporibus cum puri frequenter sitis, non acceditis, in Pascha vero, licet sit aliquid à vobis patratum, acceditis. At other times when as ye are for the more parte pure and cleane, ye come not to Communicate, but at Easter, yea, though ye haue done somewhat amisse, yet ye come. At length he cryeth out, Sacrificium frustra quotidianũ. In cassum assistimus altari, nullus qui Communicetur. Ye haue daily Sacrifice to no profit, we stand at the aulter in vaine, there is none to be houseled, or to be Communicated.

That the more part of ỹ people receiued ỹ sacrament seldome in the age of ỹ Coũcel of Agatha

Chrysost. ad Pop. Antiochẽ. Hom. 61.

Againe in an other place he vttereth a manifest recorde of the greatest parte of the peoples forbearing the Communion, with these wordes. Plurimi ex Sacrificio semel accipiunt in toto anno,

In epist. ad heb. hom. 17.

anno, alij bis, alij Sœpius. The greatest parte of the people receiueth this Sacrifice, but once in the whole yere, some twise, some oftener.

S. Ambrose doth both witnesse that they of the East church, vsed to Communicate but once in the yere, and blameth them of the west Church, that folowed them. Si quotidianus est cibus, cur post annum illum sumis, quemadmodum Græci in Oriente facere consueuerunt? If it be our daily foode (saith he) speaking of the body of Christe really present in the Sacrament) why receiuest it but once in the yere, as the Grekes vse to doe in the East? S. Augustine recordeth the same in two sundry places.

Ambros. lib.5. de Sacramēt. cap.4.

De verbis dom. secūdum Luc. hom.28. & lib. 2. de Serm. do. in monte. cap.12.

Now what remaineth good Reader, but that thou lay these witnesses in a balance? M. Jewel saith, the greatest parte of the people in those dayes vsed to Communicate in al their assemblies. S. Chrysostome saith, the greatest parte of the people receiued this Sacrifice but once in the whole yere. With S. Chrysostome is S. Ambrose, and also S. Augustin, who say likewise, that they of the East vsed to receiue the body of Christe but once in the yere. These graue and holy fathers lyued in that age of Agatha Councel, and say quite contrary to M. Jewel. They bare no affection at that time to proue any thing they had affirmed by any stout Chalenge made to al the worlde, in so saying they went not about to defend their honour & estimation, when they wrote this, they contended with no man as it were for the garland, but spake soothly as they knewe: M. Jewel on the other side, it is wel knowen, what an enterprise he hath taken in hande, how much it standeth him vpon & the mainteiners of his cause, to vphold his Chalenge. How saist thou Reader, whose witnesse wayeth more, M. Jewels, or these holy Fathers?

Wherefore that being false, which he said we must vnderstande, and the recordes of that age touching the vse of the Communion, founde to be otherwise, then he beareth vs in hande: the seldom receiuing of the Sacrifice on the peoples parte, and the hauing of the Masse euery Sonneday considered, the Masse which he calleth Priuate is founde and proued.

Ievvel.

Concil. Gerundē. Ca 1.

The. 165. Untruth. The Councel of Gerunda speketh neuer a worde in that canon of the communion.

The. 166. Untruth. I neuer made any such graũt

*And vvhereas M. Harding hath taken exception of smal tovvnes and villages, vvhich he gheasseth had then the priuate Masse, it vvas decreed and straitly ordred in a Councel holden at Gerunda in Spaine, that al litle Churches in the countrie should conformе them selues vnto the great Cathedral Churches that vvere in Cities and Tovvnes, * as vvel for order of the Communion, as also for singing, and other Ministration. But by M. Hardinges ovvne * graunt there vvas no priuate Masse then in Cathedral Churches: It folovveth therefore necessarily (this Councel of Gerunda standing in force) that there vvas no priuate Masse then in tovvnes or villages.*

Harding.

Ca. 1.

M. Jew. corrupteth the Councel of Gerunda.

The councel of Gerunda alloweth the Masse.

The parcialitý and vntruth of M. Jew.

The Councel of Gerunda is vntruly reported. It speaketh neuer a worde there of the Communion, but requireth an vniformitie of Masses, that wheras diuerse Masses were then written and set forth, one vniforme order of Masse for singing and doing the Ceremonies, should be kept through the prouince of Tarracon in Spaine, according to the custome obserued in the Metropolitane Church. If M. Jewel stand to ẏ Councel, he must nedes subscribe to the Masse specially mentioned in the same, by the expresse name Missa. which he can not finde in his hart once to name, though it be expressed in the very place, which he allegeth. wherein he sheweth how parcial he is, and with what vntruth he defendeth his cause, pretending the weapon to serue in his defence, wherwith he is striken downe.

And

And as he falsifieth the Councel of Gerunda, so he belyeth me, saying, that I graunt, the priuate Masse was not then in cathedral Churches, which I neuer graunted, albeit I acknowledge not the terme Priuate in respect of the Sacrifice to apperteine vnto the Masse. in alleging the Councel of Gerunda.

And though the Councel of Gerunda conteined that he reporteth of it (which it doth not) yet could it not be drawen to helpe his cause, forasmuch as it was holden in a time much distant from the time of the councel of Agatha, for to that age M. Iewel referreth al. And what if contrary order were in Spaine? Yet might it haue ben otherwise in Fraunce, whereof Agatha was a Citie. For how so euer it were in Spaine, if I proue Masse to haue ben donne without companie receiuing the Sacrament with the priest, in the Dioceses of the bishops that were assembled in Councel at Agatha, I proue my purpose. The Coũcel of Gerũda, was long after the Councel of Agatha.

Ievvel.

And that the people did then commonly receiue the Sacrament euery Sonneday, it appeareth by most certaine and vndoubted proufes. The Councel holden at Matiscona in Italie hath this Canon:* Decreuimus vt omnibus dominicis diebus altaris oblatio ab omnibus viris & mulieribus offeratur. *VVe haue decreed that euery Sonday the oblation of the aulter be offred of al both men and vvemen. Likevvise the Councel holden at Antisiodorum.* Decernimus, vt vnaquæq; mulier, quando communicat, Dominicalem suum habeat. Quod si non habuerit, vsq; in alium diem Dominicum, non communicet. *VVe decree that euery vvoman, vvhen she doth communicate, haue her Dominical. If she haue it not let her not communicate vntil the next Sonday. Likevvise Carolus Magnus a long vvhile after, emong other his Ecclesiastical lavves vvriteth thus:* Vt populi oblationes Sacerdotibus in ecclesia offerant, & in die Dominico communicent. *That the people offer their*

The. 167. Untruth. This appeareth not by ought that here is brought to proue it.

Concil. Matiscone. 2. ca. 4.

Concil. *Antisiodoren. ca. 42.*

Lib. 6. cap. 162. ex Cassandro.

Oblations vnto the priestes in the Churche, and receiue the Communion vpon the Sonneday. By these Councels and Decrees, it appeareth plainely vvithout gheasse or Glose, that the people vsed commonly in al that time, and long after, to Communicate the holy mysteries euery Sonneday. Therfore M. Harding must yet seeke further for his priuate Masse.

Harding.

M. Iew. proueth a thing done in old time by a thing donne of later yeres. *Then.*

Remember what you promise, and what you haue to do M. Iewel. You take in hande to proue, that the people did *then* commonly receiue the Sacrament euery Sonneday. *Then* say you. when was that then? In the time of the Councel of Agatha: which was, farre within fyue hundred yeres after Christe, for of that time speake we. Now you would proue it by the second Councel of Matiscona, by the Councel of Antisiodorum, and by wordes fathered vpon Carolus Magnus, which were long after the Councel of Agatha. But you know. if a thing be donne now, it can make no proufe it was so donne a hundred yeres past, no more then it foloweth that it rayned yesterday, because it raineth to day. What a foolish reason is this? The Seruice of the Church in England was in English in the time of king Edward the sixth, Ergo, it was so in king Edwardes time the fourth? By no better nor wiser argument proue you, that the people *then*, that is to say in the time of Agatha Councel, commonly receiued the Sacrament euery Sonneday.

Oblation of the aulter, made by laye folk what it was.

But let vs examine your proufes. First the Decree of the Councel at Matiscona maketh no mention of the Communion, but only of an Oblation, which al men and wemen were commaunded to make of bread and wine euery Sonneday. And because they brought their Offering to Churche and laid it vpon the aulter as the manner was, thereof it was called Oblation of the

the aulter. Of such Oblations speaketh S. Gregorie, where he saith thus. Omnis Christianus procuret. &c. Let euery Christian man prouide to offer vp vnto God somewhat at the Masse, and to bring vnto his remembrance, that God said by Moyses, thou shalt not appeare with empty handes in my sight: It appeareth plainly in the Collectes of the holy Fathers, that al Christian folke ought to offer vp vnto God somewhat after the custome of the holy Fathers. That this was such a temporal Oblation it may be gathered by the circumstance of the woordes folowing in the Councel of Matiscona. Vt per has immolationes & peccatorum suorum fascibus careant, & cum Abel, vel cæteris iustè offerentibus promereantur esse consortes. That by these Oblations, they may both lacke the bandes of their synnes, and obteine to be in felowship with Abel, or with the others that righteously offred. But hereof I haue sayd inough before in this very Diuision, where the same very wordes be alleged, as out of a Decree of S. Fabian.

De Cons. dist. 1. Omnis Christianus. Exod. 23

Concil. Matisco. 2 cap. 4.

Matiscona, (to say this much by the way to deliuer the reader from errour) is not in Italie, as you write, but it is a City in Fraunce (as you might haue learned of the bishops subscriptions) set vpon the ryuer of Sone, one daies iourney from Lions, in French commonly called Mascon.

Matiscona a citie of Fraunce, not of Italie.

The Decree of the Councel of Antisiodorum proueth nothing at al, that the people receiued the Sacrament euery Sonneday. I maruel what you meant to allege it. Before you make an Argument against the Masse out of that Decree, it behoueth you to serch diligently the Antiquities of the Ecclesiastical wryters: and when you haue learned what is meant by Dominicalis, yet shal you not therby proue your purpose.

Those wordes, quando communicat, when she doth Communicate, do presuppose that she communicated not euery Sonneday. And forasmuch as if she had not her Dominical, she was kept from the Communion vntil an other Sonneday, it is an argument, that it was not so rife, as you pretend it was. For sith it was lawful for euery woman to forbeare in this case, why may we not iudge the like of others?

If I would folow you, here could I reporte your sclender argument, which a learned man would be ashamed of. And yet is it your owne, it is not forged. For thus you reason. By the Councel o Antisiodorum, if a woman had not her Dominical, she might not Communicate vntil an other Sonday: Ergo, the people did Communicate with the Priest euerye Sonneday. Neither is vsque in alium diem Dominicum, to be Englished, vntil the nexr Sonneday, but vntil an other Sonneday, so that there might three or foure Sonnedaies come betwen without her Communicating the Decree notwithstanding.

False trãslation.

As for the place of Carolus Magnus, as it is pretensed, it is of litle force: both for that your author, out of whom you allege it, (Cassander I meane) is a man in this point of smal credite, as your selfe are being ennemye to the cause: and also for that being so mangled and cut from the body of his whole discourse, it is hard to iudge without conference of the booke, what therby is meant. It may be thus construed, that, whereas the people was wont to bring their Offeringes to the priestes home to their houses, or to other places: that from that time forward they should bring them vnto them in the Church. And that whereas they Communicated vpon other daies, and not vpon the Sonneday, he commaunded them to Communicate vpon the Sonneday.

Thus

Thus it is cleare, that M. Iewel hath no substantial matter against the Masse as he understandeth it to be Priuate, but onely gheasses and aymes. Therfore he must yet yelde and subscribe, if he be not lesse ashamed to breake his promise, then to stand to his promise.

The. xxxi. Diuision.

Furthermore I allege a Decree made in this Councel of Agatha, that permitted the Masse to be celebrated in Priuate Oratories or Chapels at al times when there fel not a high feast, as that of Christes birth, the Epiphanie, Easter, Ascension, &c. At which Feastes al were bounde to come to their parrish Churches. Of this I gather, forasmuch as the people did then vse to be houseled not commonly, but vpon the solemne Feastes, specially at the three highest Feastes, as by that Councel it appeareth: that at other times in such places Masses were said sometimes, when no companye receyued with the Priest. Verely where the peoples slaknesse and vndeuotion was so great, that those Fathers thoughte it necessary to binde them to Cōmunicate thrise in the yere at least, as though els they would not haue done it at al, & to haue Masse euery Sonneday notwithstanding: how wil it appeare likely to any wise man, that in such Priuate Chapels, to ech of which one onely familie resorted, the Priest had vpon euery Sonneday a sufficient companie to receiue with him at his Masse? If he

Concil. Agathen. ca. 21.

Can. 18. & can. 43.

Can. 47.

had not, then he proceded without them, and so farre is priuate Masse (as the Gospellers cal it) proued.

How many waies *Missa* may be taken after M. Iewels shifting deuise that it be not taken for that in dede it signifieth.

M. Iewel in his Replie to this, goeth not to the point directly, but as one driuen to shiftes, staieth vppon the woorde Missa. This worde he would faine haue to signifie, what so euer it were, so that it were not the Masse. At one time he handeleth the mater so, that Missa must signifie a Communion: at an other time, an assemblie of the people: at an other time, al mãner of common prayers, or ordinary prayers: at an other time, *Missa is neuer taken for the priuate Masse*, saith he: at an other time, *But let the vvorde Missa* (saith he) *be taken for the Masse* (but this graunt is not worth God a mercy, for by and by he addeth) *that is to say, for the Ministration of the Sacramentes*. Such shiftes must he vse, that defendeth a manifest vntruth. So that now he is come to this point, that he accompteth it lesse shame, to seeme impudent in lying, then hũble in yelding. Now let vs see what pith, and what truth is in his Replie. Loth I am thus to spende my time, and so long to trifle with a trifler. Yet because he is taken of many a one that litle can iudge, for a greate Clerke: Let vs trie what substantial learning he bringeth for his purpose.

Ievvel.

This vvorde Missa, in the olde vvriters sometime signifieth no Masse at al, neither Priuate *nor* Common: *but onely a resorte and meeting of the people together in place and time of prayer, as it may sundry vvaies appeare, and namely by Olde translations out of the Greeke into Latine touching the same. For that the Greeke vvriter vttereth by the vvorde that signifieth an assemblie or meeting of the people, the same doth the Latine Interpreter oftentimes translate by this vvorde Missa.*

For

For example. Sozomenus in Greeke vvriteth thus: ἐκκλησιάζοντος τοῦ λαοῦ, *that is, vvhen the people came togeather: that doth Epiphanius translate into Latine thus:* Cum populus congregaretur ad Missas, *Vvhen the people came to Masse.* *Zozom. lib. 7. c. 5. Epiphan. in tripart. histor. lib. 9. cap. 9.*

Harding.

Syr wil you nil you, Missa signifieth the Masse: And more I require not. I say not it signifieth the priuate Masse, nor the cõmon Masse, but ẏ Masse, what a doo make you about nought? Yet is euery Masse Common in respect of the Sacrifice in the same consecrated and offered, as I said in the beginning. But you say, the Masse is taken for an assemblie of the people. And that would you proue if you could. To this purpose is one Epiphanius Scholasticus alleged, a man of simple autoritie God knoweth touching any doubt to be discussed with skil of ẏ Greke and Latine tongue. He is to be commended for doing so wel as he could, rather then to be folowed in translating Greke into Latine. Yet what hath he, whereby we should thinke, that Missa, signifieth an assemblie of the people, and not the Masse? He hath turned ἐκκλησιάζοντος τοῦ λαοῦ, thus in Latine: Cum populus congregaretur ad Missas: that is, as the people were togeather at Masse. For as you haue turned it, when the people came to Masse, it is neither the true translation of the Greke, nor of the Latine.

Missa signifieth the Masse.

Epiphanius Scholasticus a trãslator of Zozomenus of very meane skil

Ex Sozomeno. lib. 7. cap. 5. hist. trip. lib. 9. c. 9.

False translatiõ.

Now because that Greke worde signifieth a comming together of the people to some solemne and publike businesse, and nothing is done in Churches more solẽne then the diuine Seruice, and of al the Seruice the Masse is the chiefe: speaking of a great miracle wrought by God in ẏ Church named *Anastasia* at ẏ prayer of the people, to expresse so much as was in the Greke, he thought good to turne the place as he did, Cum populus congregaretur ad Missas, As the people were assembled together in

 the

the Churche at Masse. which wordes at Masse are added for more plainesse, and for the better signification of so much as the Greeke worde implieth. So that if you thinke Epiphanius herein to be folowed, τὸν λαὸν ἐκκλησιάζειν, shal signifie the peoples comming together at Masse or other Seruice, rather then Missa shal be taken simply for assemblie of the people. And thus that place maketh for the antiquitie of the woorde Missæ, so farre as that Epiphanius is to be estemed.

Ievvel.

Socrat.lib. 5.cap.15. Epiphan. in Tripart. lib.7.c.31. *Likevvise Socrates vvriteth thus in the grek,* *καθ᾽ ἑαυτοὺς ἐκκλησιάζειν, *that is to say, to haue a congregation, or assemblie by them selues: That doth Epiphanius translate into Latine thus:* Apud se ipsos Missarum celebrare solennia, *that is, Emong them selues to celebrate the solemnities of the Masse.*

The.168. vntruth. This is forged. There is no such thing in that place of Socrates.

Harding.

Though al this were true, yet maketh this place no more for your purpose, then the other before. But Socrates in the booke and chapter by you quoted, hath no such words, nor speaketh of any such matter at al. And the place of Epiphanius translation onely geueth vs an other testimonie for the Masse. As false reckening (they say) is no payment, so false allegation maketh no proufe of what so euer is in question. How be it I confesse ŷ ἐκκλησιάζειν, & συνάξεις ποιεῖσθαι, are found oftentimes in the Ecclesiastical historiographers. which wordes how so euer they be turned into Latine, yet shal Missa kepe his olde signification, and be taken stil for the Masse. Neither by that Greeke worde do we vnderstande what Missa signifieth, but rather by Epiphanius translation we are taught, what is meant by that Greke worde.

Ievvel.

But let this vvorde Missa, in these Decrees be taken for the Masse,

that

*that is to say, * for the Ministration of the Sacramentes. Yet is not M. Harding much therefore the neare to proue his purpose.*

The.169. vntruth. Masse signifieth not ỹ Ministration of the Sacraments.

Harding.

This man is very free in his graunt. *Let Missa* (saith he) *be taken for the Masse.* but how? with a *that is to say, for the Ministration of the Sacramentes.* But Sir, the ministration of the Sacramẽtes being an other thing besides the Masse, as it is euident: what is your graunt, but this, Let Missa be taken for the Masse, that is to say, not for the Masse? And so by you, Missa, shalbe the Masse, & not the Masse, and consequently the Masse shal not be the Masse. Then because euery propositiõ that is true for the time to come, shal once be true for the time present, there shal a time be, when this proposition shal be true, the Masse is not the Masse, which is absurde, foolish and impossible. From this foolishnesse, you fal into crying out, *Alas,* vpon foolish argumentes of your owne forging, which you attribute vnto me, which you take to be a very fine Deuise, for els you would not vse it so often as you doo. From that gay sporte, you fal vnto manifest lying, where you say thus.

the Masse is not the Masse by M. Iew.

The.170. vntruth. There was no prouision made by ỹ Decree for a lawful & ordinary company to be assembled in chapels abroad.

Ievvel.

*Vvhat vvas there no companie at al in the Chappel to Communicate vvith the Priest? * Verely it is prouided by the Decre it self, that there should be a lavvful, and an ordinarie companie.*

Harding.

At the Masse in such priuate Oratories or Chappels there was the familie of the house, which was licensed to haue the seruice there done. But that there was a sufficient companie ready to make vp a iust Cõmuniõ after the new deuise of our English Gospellers in ech one familie, and that euery Sonday, which deuotion the Decree that bound the seculars to receiue thrise in the yeare at least, presupposeth to haue wanted in the people in general; this much you shal hardly persuade any wise man.

The new Cõmuniõ booke requireth three besides the Priest at the least.

But where you say and auouch it with your oth *Verely*, that it was prouided by the Decree it selfe, that there should be a lauful and an ordinary companie: I say vnto you verely verely, that concerning priuate Oratories and Chappels, wherof we speake, it is a very false lye. Read the Decree who wil, so he shal finde it. I denie not but it maketh mention of Legitimus ordinariusque conuentus, lauful and ordinarie assemblie together: but the Decree meaneth it of the parrish Churches. For thither did the people resorte and assemble them selfe legitime and ordinarie, as lawe and common order required. That the Maister of a house had the Masse in his priuate Chappel at home, it was a special priuilege besides the common lawe and order, propter fatigationem familiæ, that is, in consideration of the families wearinesse, if they should alwaies be compelled to go farre to their parrish Churches. The words of ẏ Decree (least any man should thinke M. Jewel doth not deale so vntruely) be these. Si quis etiam extra Parochias, in quibus legitimus est ordinariusque conuentus, Oratorium in agro habere voluerit, &c. Also if any man wil haue an Oratorie or chappel abroad in the countrie besides ẏ parrish Churches, in which the lawful and ordinarie cōming together (of the people to their diuine Seruice) is, &c. To what other worde here can in quibus, in which, be referred, but onely to Parochias? Therefore the Note put in the Margent of his booke, In quibus est ligitimus ordinariusque conuentus, is but a doubling of his vntruth. what may not a man defende, if such manifest lyes may go for mater of good sooth?

Concil. *Agathen. can.* 21.

M. Jew. falsifieth the Coūcel of Agatha.

Replie. Pag. 73.

Iewel.

And that in such companies, yea and in mens seueral houses they had the Cōmunion ministred, it is euidēt by the preface of the Coūcel of Gangra, *against the heretike Eustachius. These be the vvordes.* In domibus coniugatorū ne orationes quidem debere celebrari persuaserūt, in tantum tū, vt eas fieri vetēt: & oblationibus quæ in domibus factæ fuerint, minime communicandum essē decernant. *They haue persuaded the people, that prayers may not be made in maried mens houses: and that so farre forth, that they forbid any such prayers to be made, and determine, that noman may communicate of the oblations made in houses. Here vve haue not onely the Communion, but also the ordinarie vse of the Communion in priuate houses.*

Harding.

By this place if the translation be admitted two thinges seme to be proued, which I graunt both, M. Iewel denyeth one. That the Communion, that is to say the body of Christe, was geuen and receiued in priuate houses, I denie not. But that the body and bloud of Christe was also offred vp vnto God, in priuate houses, or rather in the oratories of priuate houses, which in that Councels preface semeth to be signified by the worde Oblations, wherby the Sacrifice of the Masse, and so the Masse it selfe is meant: This M. Iewel can not a way with, and therfore dissembleth, and speaketh of the Communion, which noman denied. But it had ben his parte to proue, that in priuat houses the Communion was alwaies receiued of a companie together with the Priest, and neuer of one alone. For the worde Communion helpeth not his opinion, because it is called a Communion, though it be receiued of one alone without other companie in the same place, as I haue before declared.

How be it I thinke, the Fathers assembled at the Councel of Gangra meant not by these wordes the Communion, for proufe whereof they are here alleged by M. Iewel, but rather the sober and moderate feastes, which at those daies Christian people kept, one bidding an other for brotherly loue and charitie, which of them were called ἀγάπαι, agapæ, which feastes as Tertullian recor-

Of the holy feastes called agapæ.

recordeth, they began and ended with prayers, and at them they offred and gaue giftes, partly to be spent forthwith at the feastes, partly to be distributed for reliefe of the poore brethren. This proceded of a custome in the begynning of the Churche. For the disciples vsed to assemble the faithful brethrē together into priuate mens houses, teaching and preaching Christe frō house to house. There their manner was, to breake bread, and eate together, as thereof mention is made in the actes of the Apostles. In which places S. Chrysostome doth expounde panem frangere, to breake bread, to be as much as alimentum cum ieiunio & austeritate sumere, to take nourishment with abstinence and austeritie. And so we read in Oecumenius. Hoc autem, frangentes panem, dicit, vt frugalem & inelaboratum ostenderet ipsorum victum. Frangentes vero panem, sumebant alimoniam, non autem delitias. S. Luke (saith he) vttereth this worde, breaking bread, to shewe, with how smal and homely meat they liued. as they brake bread, they tooke but their foode, and not delicate disshes. This custome of comming together and of breaking bread, that is to say, of making cheere with reioising and simplicitie of harte, continewed many yeres in the primitiue Church, as by the report of this Councel & of many Ecclesiastical stories it appeareth. After what sorte these holy feastes were kept, Tertulliā in most goodly wise descrybeth.

Tertulli. in Apologetico. cap. 39. The manner and custome of breaking bread at the begynning. Act. 2. & 5.

The name (saith he) of our feasting sheweth, what it is. It is called Agape, asmuch to say among the Grekes, as loue. How much so euer it coste, it is accompted gaine, to be at coste for godlinesse sake. For by this refresshing we helpe al that be poore. No vilenesse, no sawcinesse is committed, They sit not downe, before prayer vnto God be foretasted. They eate so much as hunger desyreth. They drinke so much as is good for chaste persons. They fil their bellies so as they that remēber, they must pray vnto God also in the night, They talke so, as they that knowe, God hea-

Tertulli. in Apologet. cap. 39. How the holy feastes were kepte in the primitiue Churche. *Agape.*

reth

reth thẽ. After that water for their handes, and lighte is brought in, echone is prouoked to sing somewhat vnto God among thẽ, as he can out of the Scriptures, or of his owne head. Thereby it is tryed, how he dranke. Likewise prayer endeth the feast. Thence they departe, as they who haue made a feast not so much of meate, as of discipline. Thus, and much more there, saith Tertullian.

S. Augustine speaking hereof saith thus. Agapæ nostræ pascunt pauperes, siue frugibus, siue carnibus. Our Churchfeastes do feede the poore, either with corne, or with flesh. He answereth Faustus the heretike of the Manichees secte, who condemned the eating of flesh, and obiected to the Christians, as though they had changed certaine Sacrifices of the Paynimes, in which they made a publike feast, into their Churchfeastes. *Contra Faustum Manichæũ li.20.c.20.*

These holy feastes, whereat Christian folke brought and offered their portions according to their deuotion, partly to chere them selues after a most louing sort, and partly to refresh ẏ poore and needy, which portions in this councel are called προσφοραί that is, oblations, and the whole maner of the same, Eustathius the heretike taught his folowers to contemne and despise, if they were made in maried mens houses, because he condemned mariage it selfe. And these fewe wordes here alleged out of the Bishops epistle set before the Decrees of their Councel, be as it were the argument of theleuenth Canon of the same Councel. Which. 11. Canon hath thus according to the Greke. Si quis illos despicit, qui Agapas in fide faciunt, & fratres inuitant in honorem Domini: neque velit his inuitationibus communicare, propterea quôd vilipendat id quod agitur, Anathema esto. If any man despise those that make Churchefeastes as the faith requireth, and bid the brethrẽ thereto in the honour of our lorde, and wil not be partaker of such biddinges, for that he despiseth the thing that is donne, let him be accursed.

Oblatiõs. The argument of theleuẽth canon of the Councel of Gangra.

ἐκ πίστεως ἀγάπας.

Thus right wel may this place of those Fathers epistle be vnderstanded, so as it may seme to speake nothing at al of the Communion pretended to be in priuate mens houses. And so it maketh nothing for ye purpose, for which it is alleged. which wil better appeare to him that examineth the wordes, as they are vttered in the Greke Original: from which the translation that M. Iewel vseth here, varieth not a litle.

One of the heresies which Eustathius helde. *In præfatione Concilij Gangren.*

The whole wil be the better perceiued, if it be considered, that Eustathius, against whom the Councel of Gangra was holden, among other his heresies, helde, that the vse of flesh was il, and that wedlocke was vnlawful. The Greke Original hath thus. Καίτινες αὐτῶν (εὑρίσκοντο) μεταλήψεις κρεῶν βδελυττώμενοι. καὶ ἐν οἴκοις γεγαμηκότων εὐχὰς ποιεῖσθαι μὴ βουλόμενοι, καὶ γινομένων εὐχῶν καταφρονοῦντες. καὶ πολλάκις προσφορῶν ἐν αὐταῖς ταῖς οἰκίαις τῶν γεγαμηκότων ὑπερφρονοῦντες. Atque ex istis nōnulli (cōperiebantur) qui sumere carnes eisq; vesci detestantur. Et qui nolunt in ædibus coniugatorū facere preces, factasque despiciunt: ac sæpe oblationes in illis coniugatorum domibus aspernantur. And of these certaine were founde out, who abhorre to be partakers of flesh. And wil not make prayers in the houses of maried persons, and despise such as be there made. And oftentimes set naught by the offeringes in maried folkes houses.

Thus is the place truly laid out before thee good reader, which how litle it maketh either for the ordinarie vse of the Cōmuniō (for proufe wherof M. Iewel allegeth it) or for the Communion at al in priuate houses, thou mayst soone perceiue. For these offeringes here mentioned were not the body and bloud of Christe vnder the formes of bread and wine cōsecrated and offered vp vnto God by a Priest, of which bread and wine M. Iew.

sur

surmiseth and gheasseth the Communion that he speaketh of to haue ben made : but other thinges by the Deuotion of the faithful people geuen, to those charitable feastes, to the refreshing of the poore, and to other godly vses by Tertullian expressed, to be employed. *Tertullian. in Apologet. cap. 39*

Concerning the rest that M. Jewel saith in this Diuision, wherin he goth about to proue that the people receiued the communion with the priestes, forasmuch as it is not denied: answere is nedelesse. If he wil take vpon him to disproue the Masse, whereat the people is not disposed to receiue with the Priest, which he calleth priuate Masse: then his parte is to proue, that within the first vj. C. yeres there was neuer Masse celebrated, wherat the people did not receiue, or at least some other sufficient nuber meete for a communion, which he himself alloweth for sufficient. which I am wel assured he shal neuer be hable to performe. And yet the examples & auctorities which here he bringeth out of the councel of Agatha, Can 60. and out of Siricius Decretal Epistle, Cap. 5. serue to proue, not ẏ three or foure were alwaies ready to receiue with the priest, which new deuise serueth him oftentimes for a shifte: but that al the Christian people besides those that did open penaunce receiued with the Priest. which condēneth the order of his owne new Communion. For in this our new primitiue Church of England, where the gospel is hotest, & the blessed Sacrifice of the Masse most despised, it is wel knowen, that al their faithful brethren and systers do not receiue as often as their Communion is ministred. *what hath M. Jew. to do, if he take vpon him to disproue priuate masse*

And here is to be noted by the way, that wheras before M. Jewel refused the authoritie of such Canons, as be put in by Gratian, & by him added vnto those. 46. Canōs, that Peter Cras found in his old writtē copie: now he can be content to vse their autoritie himself, because he imagineth the same to help his cause. *M. Jew. allegeth now that before he cōdemned.*

Likewise here he allegeth the Decretal epistle of Pope Syricius, whereas before he condemned al the Decretal Epistles in general. Thus in one place he condemneth for his pleasure what maketh against him, and in an other place, if it sounde any thing to his purpose through some false construction or colour cast vpon it, the same, as being of good autoritie, he alloweth and boldly allegeth. So now for a shifte he appealeth to the.60. Canon of the Councel of Agatha, and to the Epistle Decretal of Syricius, which not farre before he condemned.

The.xxxij. Diuision.

IN this Diuision for proufe of Masse said without a companie receiuing the Communion with the Priest, I allege a story out of the life of the holy Patriarke of Alexandria Iohannes Eleemosynarius, John the Almosegeuer, writtē in greke by Leontius bishop of Neapolis, a Citie in Cyprus. The story reporteth, that this Patriarke said Masse in his priuate Oratorie, hauing no other person with him that might receiue the Sacrament, but onely one of his seruauntes, whereby priuate Masse is

Fol. 62. a proued. For the circumstance of the story, I referre the reader to my booke.

Eleuen shiftes vsed by M. Iewel to auoide the testimonie of Leontius touching priuate masse

Because this mater is clear, and can not be auoided, it is a worlde to see, how M. Iewel starteth from one place to an other, and seeketh where to escape. First, he denyeth the autoritie of Leontius that wrote the storie. Secondly, he pretendeth this Masse to haue ben said a fewe yeres without the compasse of his first six hundred yeres, and to diminish the estimation of it, he falsifieth

sifieth Vincentius Bellanocensis, and maketh him to say, that the Masse was of the very age of Mahomet. Thirdly, he falsifieth certaine Decrees of Popes and Councels, saying them to forbid any man to say Masse in Chappel or priuate Oratorie. Fourthly, that this was no Masse, for ỹ there is no mētion made of bread, and wine, Consecration, eleuation, aulter, vestimēts. &c. Fifthly, with a scoffe he would make it doubteful, which of the three said this Masse, the bishop, the seruaunt, or the noble man. Sixthly, he fyndeth fault with my translation. Seuenthly, he thinketh to escape, for that the Greke hath not the worde Missa, and because the interpreter was not a good Latine man. Eightly, he saith, Missa is not that, which we cal the Masse. Nynthly, he maketh it a strange case that I ronne to Alexandria to seeke the priuate Masse. Tenthly, he pretendeth nowe, as though he demaunded it to be proued by S. Hierome, or S. Augustine, or by some other catholike Doctour. Last of al, as though none of al these shiftes would sufficiētly serue the turne, he beareth vs in hand, that he demaunded proufe for the Masse said in open Churche, in the face and sight of the people.

M. Iew. falsifieth *Vincentius in Speculo.* He falsifieth certain Decrees of Popes and Coūcels.

Now if I shewe al these to be but vaine escapes, and shiftes besides the truth, I trust they that be of God, and haue care of their soules, wil notwithstanding any thing in his Replie conteined, esteme the Masse as it ought to be estemed, and beleue him as he deserueth. The chiefe places I wil lay forth, as he him selfe uttereth them, and the same confute, so briefly as I can.

Ievvel.

VVhat is this Leontius that vvrote this storie? Or vvho euer hearde of his name before? I trovve he hath raised vp one of the seuen Sleapers to helpe him to Masse. He should haue shevved vs as his manner is, vvhat this straunge Doctour vvas, vvhat bookes he vvrote: vvhere, vvhen, in vvhat age, and in vvhat credite he liued. If he had said, this

Iohn the Almonar liued aboue sixe hundred yeres after Christ, and this Leontius that vvrote his life, a great vvhile after that, this one circumstance vvould haue ansvvered the mater vvholy. &c.

Harding.

What if al this be shewed vnto you, and proued by good autoritie? Yet shal that do you no good. For you are at a point not to subscribe and yelde, what so euer you promised: though our proufes be neuer so euident. Not for your sake then, of whom I haue litle hope, but for their sakes, whom you and your companions with innumerable lyes haue dangerously seduced, I wil here satisfie your demaundes.

M. Iew. demaūdes cōcerning Leontius be answered.

This Leontius was bishop of Neapolis a Citie in Cypres, a holy and a learned man. He wrote diuerse workes, and among them one notable worke intituled, An Apologie for the Christiās against the Iewes. which was brought by Pope Adrians legates to the seuenth general Councel holden at Nice in Bithynia. And out of the fifth booke of the same Apologie, was read and openly pronounced by Stephanus Deacon and Notarie of that Coūcel, a very learned discourse against the Iewes touching Images. which after it was reade and heard, Constantinus bishop of Constantia a Citie in Cypres, stode vp and said in audience of the Councel, as foloweth.

Of Leontius the author of this story, and of his workes. *Concil. Nicen. 2. Actione. 4*

Pater hic, qui lectus est, in vna ex Ciuitatibus Cypri decenter & sanctè conuersatus est, multaq; encomia & panegyricas illius orationes etiam habemus. Inter quas extat oratio in trāsfigurationem domini. Scripsit & Sancti Iohannis Misericordis appellati, Episcopi Alexandrini vitā. Præterea beati Simeonis, turbationesq; propter Christum circa ea tempora in ecclesia factas. Scripsit & alia quædam, in quibus omnibus orthodoxus cognoscitur. Floruit circà tempora Mauricij Imperatoris. This father, which was now read, liued semely and holily in one of the Cities of Cypres.

And

And we haue many of his bookes and Orations made in praise of godly men or good thinges. Among which is extant his Oration, that he made vpon our Lordes Transfiguration. He wrote also the life of S. Iohn, named the Merciful, bishop of Alexandria. Furthermore the life of S. Simeones, and a Storie of the troubles, that happened in the Church about that time. He wrote also certaine other thinges, and in them al he is knowen to be of the right beleefe. He lyued about the time of Morice the Emperour.

After this it foloweth in the .4. action of that Councel, Iohn the most deuout priest of God, Vicar of the See Apostolike of the East, said: Clarum est. &c. It is cleare, that al thinges be true which haue here ben said in praise of the foresaid father. And more ouer the Legates of the most holy Pope haue exhibited this booke vnto the Councel. &c.

Thus be your Demaundes answered touching the auctoritie of Leontius. Mention is made of this Father also by Iacobus Philippus Bergomensis in supplemento. Who saith of this blessed man Iohn the Almosegeuer, that with his Sermons and learned Epistles he reuoked from heresie the whole Church of the East. And wheras it is here reported, that Leontius liued about the time of Morice the Emperour, in whose time S. Gregorie was Pope: therof it appeareth ỷ this bishop S. Iohn ỷ merciful or Almosegeuer, said Masse either before your sixe hūdreth yere was expired, or very soone after. And though it were a yere or two after, the mater is of as good credite, as if it could be proued to haue ben done a yere or two before. Onlesse you can shew vs credibly, that Christe forsooke his Church, and brake promise concerning his continual remaining with her vntil the worldes ende, suddainely, and iumpe at the very last houre and momēt of the forsaid yere, which to think as it is most blasphemous, so na- lesse absurde.

The time and age of Leontius.

Your selfe pardy do graunt, as it appeareth by your note in the margent, that this holy bishop John began to be in estimation in the yere of our Lorde. 610. Then it standeth with good reason, that he exercised a vertuous life, and vsed to doo notable dedes before that time. For so notable a fame as he was growne vnto, is not acheued in short space, but with long continuance. And so it is not to be doubted, but he might in like sort haue said Masse without any others receiuing the Sacrament with him, before the last day of the six hundredth yere was past. O M. Jewel, that you are not ashamed thus to claime aduantage of so smal a time. Doth not this bewray the vntruth of your cause? If it were vnlawful to celebrate the Masse without a companie of Communicantes in the same place ten yeres before the six hundredth yere, could it be lawful ten yeres after? If it were vnlawful, and contrary to the Institution of Christ, as you say, and proue it not: shal we thinke so holy and so learned a bishop would haue donne it? and that so graue and so learned a man as Leontius was, would to his praise haue made mention of it?

Vincentius in specul. li. 23. ca 17

Ievvel.

Vincentius in his booke that he calleth Speculum, *vvryteth thus.* After Gregorie was dead, Bonifacius ruled the Church of Rome. This Bonifacius obteined of the Emperour Phocas, that the Churche of Rome should be the head of al Churches, *and that because the Church of Constantinople vvrote it selfe by that title. The next yere after that, Augustine that vvas called the English mens Bishop, died. The yere folovving Iohn the Almonar vvas in great fame, at vvhich time also *Mahomet first spred his religion in Arabia.*

The. 171. Untruth. Vincentius doth not so write, and Mahomet first spred his religion afterward in the later time of Heraclius the Emperour.

Harding.

Now is Vincentius a good Doctour with you, and a man worthy to be brought in for witnesse, In your very next Diuision

uision he is but a fabler and a man of no reputation. M. Doctour Cole alleged men of a farre more excellencie as touching learning, then euer this Vicentius was, yet because they pleased not your humour, it liked you to cal them the blacke garde. And thus somtimes al is fish that commeth to the net with you, sometimes you cast away that is right good.

Vincentius liked & misliked of M. Iew: as he maketh with him, or against him. M. Iew. in his Replie to D. Cole.

Touching that you haue here alleged, out of Speculum Historiale Vincentij, I knowe not what I should note, but your great and notorious falsifyinges. As for your false quotation, I could sone beare with you, so it be not affected of euil purpose. The place is not In Speculo, lib. 23. cap. 17. as your booke hath, but, lib. 22. cap. 107. Concerning the mater, After S. Gregorie was dead, Vincentius telleth you, that Sabinianus was next made Pope: And after him Bonifatius. And speaking of S. Augustine the Apostle of our nation, whom you haue rashly and wickedly condemned for a proud and otherwise an euil man, he saith not, Augustine, that was called the English mens Bishop, as you haue falsified his wordes: but, Augustinus primus Anglorum Episcopus, Augustine the first Bishop of the English. Because you can not brooke ẏ faith which that blessed man planted first in our countrie, which is contrary to your new deuised Gospel, therefore you would rather play a false parte in chaunging your Doctours wordes, then seme to your owne brethren, before whome you haue so much railed at him, to laye forth plainely what is said to his commendation.

Vincentius falsified by M. Iewel.

Article. 3. Pag. 185. Augustin the first bishop of the English.

These false partes of yours be very bad, and vnsemely for one that taketh vpō him the roome of a Superintendent, and of a preacher of Gods worde: but that which foloweth is much worse. For whereas Vincentius saith in praise of the holy man S. Iohn the bishop of Alexandria thus, qui ob eximiam in Christum liberalitatē nomē Eleemosynarij habere meruit, ỳ is to say, who for his exceding great liberalitie towards Christ deserued or was accompted worthi to haue the name of merciful, or almosegeuer: you suppresse those words of his praise, & in stede of thē placed these in your falsified translatiō, *at vvhich time Mahomet first spred his Religion in Arabia.* which wordes you haue caused to be printed with the distinct letter of your Doctours allegatiōs, that they might so seme to be the wordes of Vincentius. It semeth you were loth to vtter any such good wordes in cōmendation of that holy Father, least by the same the more auctoritie & estimation might grow to the Masse, which he said in his oratorie without a company receiuing the Communion with him.

An intollerable falshed of M. Iewels.

And wheras you say by the way, that this story, which you cal a tale, proueth the Masse to be of the very age of Mahomet: you might better so haue said, if you had ben a Mahometane. Touching the Antiquitie of the Masse, it is so auncient, as the last Supper of our Lord is. For touching the essential partes of it, it was instituted by Christe, and commaunded to be continued in remembrance of his death vntil he come.

The antiquitie of the masse. Luc. 22.

The 172. Untruth, Damasus saith not so, as here thou maist see.

Ievvel.

*But to leaue both thaduantage of the time, and also the exception against the Author, let vs consider the likelihood of the doing: and if Iohn the Almonar said this priuate Masse in his chappel, hovv safely he might so doo by the order of the holy Canons, vvhich to breake *Damasus saith, is blasphemie against the holy goste. M. Hardinges Leontius saith, Iohn the Almonar said Masse in his Oratorie at home, being sure of no more companie but of one of his ovvne household seruauntes alone. But Pope Soter, as it is before alleged by M. Harding straitly commaundeth that no priest presume to celebrate the Sacrament vvithout the companie of tvvo together. And againe that *no priest dare to minister, vvithout the companie of some other priest.*

25. q. 1. Violatores.

The. 173. Untruth. Soters decree is not so general. It is limited.

The. 174. Untruth. That coūcel saith not so. It saith Domibus, and not at home.

And in the Councel holden at Orleance it is decreed thus. It is lawful for euery Christian man to haue a chappel in his house: but to haue Masse said there it is not lawful. *And in the Coūcel holden at Laodicea, it is not lavvful for Bishops or Priestes to minister the oblations *at home.*

Like-

Likevvise Pope Felix, It is not lavvful to minister the Communion at home, but vpō exceding great necessitie. *The same order vvas taken in the Councel of Acon, and in sundry other Councels. Vvhich Decrees being so many, and so straite, it is not likely that Iohn the Almonar being so holy a mā, vvil vvilfully breake them al vvithout cause.*

The.175. vntruth. Felix speaketh neither of ministring the Communion, nor of home.

Harding.

Here M. Iewel inmbleth together a meany of Councels and Popes Decrees for some shewe of learning, and him selfe esteemeth them no whit at al. Yet that it may appeare, how vntruly he allegeth them, and how he contineweth his common practise of falsifying his allegations, & how litle al this maketh for him: I require thee good Reader, if thou be learned, to do nomore but onely reade, what these Decrees do reporte. If thou be not learned, in case thou wilt beleue the truth, thus it is.

The.176. vntruth. This Councel speaketh not agaīst saying Masse at home, but forbiddeth it to be dō in vnconsecrated & prophane houses.

First, Damasus saith not simply that to breake the Canons, is blasphemie against the holy ghoste. But thus he saith. Blasphemare in Spiritum sanctū non incongruè videntur, qui contra Sacros Canones non necessitate compulsi, sed libenter aliquid aut proteruè aguut, aut loqui præsumunt. They, ẏ either doo ought, or presume to speake against the holy Canons, not compelled by necessitie, but gladly of their owne wil, and of a frowadnesse, not without reason seme to vtter blasphemie against the holy Ghost. Thus is the Decree of Damasus otherwise qualified, then M. Iewel reporteth. Neither is it spoken besides reason, that presupposed which Damasus in the same Decree layeth as it were for the grounde of the same. Which is, that the Canons were made and pronounced, by the instinct and gifte of the holy Ghoste.

Damas. falsified by M. Iewel.

25. q. 1. Violatores.

Touching the two Decrees of S. Soter the Pope, that no Priest presume to celebrate Masse without the presence of two, who might cōueniently make answere vnto his salutations: and

Cuius instinctu ac dono dicti sunt.

againe, that the Priest be assisted with an other Priest for to supplie his roome in case of soddaine infirmitie: hereto we say that, which in this case S. Gregorie said, as it is alleged by Gratian, Regulæ Sanctorum Patrum, pro tempore, loco, & persona, & negotio, instante necessitate, traditæ sunt. The Canons or rules of the holy Fathers haue ben geuen forth, according to ẏ time, place person, and businesse, when present necessitie so required. Therfore they bynde not in like sorte al persons, at al times, in euery place, neither perteineth their straite obseruation of necessitie in respect of euery circumstāce, to al cases. So the holy Patriarke John did not wilfully breake, as you say, that order, whereunto of necessitie he was not bounde. Besides this, in his age, those two Decrees of S. Soter were growen out of vse, as sithence that time many others haue.

De cons. dist. 1. hoc quóque. In argumento in Concilio Gangren.

A notable saying of S. Gregorie touching the Canons of the Fathers.

As for that you bring out of Gratian, as alleged out of a Councel holden at Orleance, what maketh it to your purpose? By that Councel it was lawful for euery man to haue an Oratorie in his house, and there to pray, but not to celebrate Masse, for so be the wordes, and not, to haue Masse said as you haue translated ẏ Decree. What concluded you of this? It was not lawful for euery man to celebrate Masse in an Oratorie at home, Ergo, was it not lawful for the Patriarke of Alexandria to say Masse in his Oratorie? what reason haue you in this? It is not lawful for euery mā to preach: shal we inferre thereof, Ergo, it is not lawful for M. Jewel to preach? where you founde this in Gratian, immediatly in the next line you found this, Clericos qui ministrant in oratorijs, quæ intra domos sunt, cum cōsensu Episcopi loci, hóc facere præcipimus. The clerkes which do minister in Oratories, that be within houses, we commaunde thē so to do with ẏ cōsent of ẏ Bishop of the place. Lo here you saw, ẏ with consent of ẏ Bishop, a Priest might say Masse in an Oratorie. Knowing this, you would not haue alleged ẏ other Decree of Orleāce to proue this

De cons. dist. 1. vnicuique.

De cons. dist. 1. Clericos ex sexta synodo.

holy

holy Patriarke a breaker of the holy Decrees and Canons, except you had bẽ disposed to set a side al sinceritie in your dealing. If it were lauful for any priuate Priest with leaue to say Masse in an Oratorie that is within a mans house, it is sone conceiued how farre that great Patriarke was from breach of lawe and order in that behalfe. Againe that Councel being Prouincial could not binde the Patriarke of Alexandria.

The Councel of Laodicea is here falsified. It hath, that Oblations ought not to be made by Bishops or Priestes in domibus, in houses. which Decree proueth no breach of order in this holy Father. For whereas this Councel by houses, meaneth Commõ and prophane houses, this Father offendeth not against it, as he that said Masse, not in such a house, but in his chappel or Oratorie appointed and cõsecrated to holy vses, and to Diuine Seruice. That this Decree is so to be vnderstãded, we are taught by the Epistle which Pope Felix the fourth wrote to al Bishops.

Conc. Laodicen. c.58

The Coũcel of Laodicea falsified by M. Iewels false translation of at home, for in *domibus* in houses.

As you haue falsified al the other Decrees mentioned before in this Diuisiõ, so now you falsifie the Decree of Pope Felix, which you make to say thus. It is not lauful to minister the Communiõ at home, but vpon exceding great necessitie. But the Decree speaketh not of ministring the Cõmunion, nor of home, but farre otherwise. The wordes be these, as they be laid together by Gratian, which be in the epistle of Felix, though some other wordes comming betwen. Sicut non alij, &c. As none others ought to celebrate Masse but Priestes that are consecrated vnto God, nor offer Sacrifices vpon the aulter: so neither is it lauful to sing Masse, or to offer Sacrifices in other places, then in those which be cõsecrated to our Lorde, that is to say, in tabernacles annointed by Bishops with holy prayers, except very great necessitie enforce otherwise. After these wordes it foloweth there immediatly: Satius est ergo Missam nõ cantare, aut non audire quàm in ijs locis vbi fieri non oportet, nisi pro summa necessitate cõtingat.

Cap.1. in fine tom. 2 Conciliorũ

The Decree of Felix falsified by M. Iewel.

In epistola Felicis quarti ad oẽs episco. cap.1.

De cons. dist.1. Sicut non alij.

It is better therefore not to sing Masse, or to heare Masse at al, then to haue it donne in such places, where it may not be donne, but vpon a very great necessitie, which place I allege the rather, that thou mayst vnderstand Reader, that to say, I wil heare Masse, is not a straunge and fond saying, as M. Iew. saith it is, and for which he hath made so much a doo: but such as hath of learned men ben vsed of olde time.

Mark reder, here hast thou the phrase audire Missas, to heare Masse, which M. Iew. saith to be fonde and straunge. Replie page. 70.

Concerning the Councel of Acon, what so euer was there decreed, it could not bynde this holy Patriarke of Alexandria, both for that it was Prouincial and not general, and also for that it was holden two hundred yeres after his death, in the time of Ludouicus the first, Emperour, in the yere of our lorde eight hūdred sixteen. And yet ỹ. 84. Canō of that Synode is the. 58. Canō of the Coūcel of Laodicea, which as I haue now declared out of the epistle of Pope Felix the fourth, forbiddeth Bishops and Priestes to offer vp the oblations in houses, that is to say, in prophane dwelling places not cōsecrated to gods Seruice by ỹ consecration of a Bishop. Thus be al your Decrees and Councels easily wiped away M. Iewel, which you haue here heaped together, to make your vnlearned reader thinke, that S. Iohn the Almosegeuer could not, ne ought not say Masse in his chappel or Oratorie. Now must you seeke better stuffe, for this is litle worth. Let vs see what substance is in that which foloweth in your Replie.

How litle the Councel of Acō maketh for M. Iewel. Concil. Aquisgranen. c. 84.

Ievvel.

Neither in dede if M. Harding vvil throughly beholde the mater, shal he finde here any Masse spoken of at al, neither bread, nor vvine, nor Consecration, nor Oblation, nor Eleuation, nor Aulter, nor vestiment, nor any other thing to the Masse belonging.

Harding.

In dede who so euer wil throughly beholde your Demea-

nour,

nour, shal see no truth in you, but altogether mocking and lying. What say you? Is not the Masse here spoken of at al? Did you not read the place, when you wrote this slender pece of your Replie? Haue you not these wordes Facit Missas in Oratorio suo, He saith Masse in his Oratorie? Can not we vnderstand there was a Masse, except Consecration, Oblation, and Perception, wherof chiefely it consisteth, and what so euer els perteineth to the Masse, as bread, wine, aulter, vestimentes, and other thinges be expressely mentioned?

Shal one that speaketh of M. Iohn Iewel by name, not be beleued, except he speake after this sorte, He that in Quene Maries time subscribed at Oxford in a solemne assemblie of learned men to the Masse, to the real presence, to the Sacrifice propitiatorie, and to other pointes of the Catholique doctrine, and now is a great impugner of the Church, and of the Catholique faith, an vsurper of the See of Sarisburie, he that made that insolent and foolish Chalenge to al Learned men in the world, and set it forth in Print, he ẏ is thought of his owne brethren therein to haue said more then he is able to iustifie, he ẏ now of late hath sent abroad a huge boke stuffed with mo lies then Paragraphes intituled A Replie, &c. Except, I say, he frame his tale after this sort, shal he not be thought to speake of M. Iewel? I thinke verely your selfe wil confesse, ẏ to require him to vtter so much, for credite sake in that behalfe were very absurde. Euen so may it be said here, what nede was it to speake of ẏ partes of the Masse, of Breade and wine, aulter and vestimentes, where the Masse it selfe is expressely named? Now what haue you next to say?

Ievvel.

And if vve agree there vvas Masse said there, yet may there grovve an other doubte, vvhich of these three said Masse, I meane the Bishop, or the Gentle man, or the Seruant.

Harding.

I perceiue our M. Iohn of Sarisburie would faine play Dicke Scorner, if he had a mery parte, for it semeth he hath on him a fooles cote already. But Syr I pray you, kepe your sporte in store vntil an other time, and perhaps if you play the Vise wel and varletlike, you may chaunce to make a good company laugh their bellies ful.

Ievvel.

The. 177. vntruth. My translation is true as here I proue it.

The. 178. vntruth. There be no such wordes in al this diuision.

The. 179. vntruth It is manifestly implied though not in precise wordes of Sacrament & Consecration expressed

The. 180. vntruth. This can not be said of mee in this place, but altogether of M. Iewel for he calleth thinges, ÿ be not here, as though they were here.

But he vvil replie, here is the very name of the Masse: & facit Missas. And to make the more appearance, M. Harding helpeth it forth vvith a preaty * false translation of his ovvne. For vvhereas it is vvritten in the Latine, Cum benedixisset sancta, he translateth it thus. Vvhen he had consecrated the Sacrament: * And likevvise these vvoordes, Post finem Orationum, he translateth thus, after he had done the praier of Consecration: not vvithstanding he knevv right vvel that in these vvordes there is no * mention at al, neither of any Sacrament, nor of any Consecration.

And thus * Vocat ea quæ non sunt, tanq̃ sint, He calleth thinges that be not, as though they vvere: and yet is not afraid of Lex Cornelia de falsis. But this I trovv he him self vvil confesse, is no sincere nor plaine dealing.

Harding.

Yea Syr here is the name of the Masse in dede, that you abhorre so much. how can you auoide it? what phrase haue you to colour the mater, that the Masse shal not signifie the Masse? And though Leontius wrote in Greke, and therfore vsed not the Latine worde Missa, yet the circumstance of the place geueth it to be the Masse. I helpe it forth say you, with a preaty false translatiõ of myne owne. why finde you fault with my translatiõ good Syr? Cum benedixisset sancta, I haue translated thus: When he had consecrated the Sacrament. In which worde finde you the

This is but pikīg of a quarel

faulte?

fault? In the translation of Benedicere, or of Sancta? If Benedicere be to Consecrate, and if the blessed Sacrament, or rather the thing of the Sacrament, which is the body and bloud of Christ, be called Sancta: then do you but pike a quarrel, and finde fault where none is.

Verely the auncient Fathers do commonly vse the word of benediction or blessing either for the Cõsecration or for the thing consecrated. S. Ambrose so taketh it, where he saith, Ipse clamat Dominus Iesus: hoc est corpus meum. Ante benedictioné verborum cœlestium, alia species nominatur, post Consecrationem Corpus Christi significatur. Our Lord Iesus him self cryeth, This is my Body. Before the blessing of the heauenly words, it is named an other kinde, after the Consecration it is signified to be the Body of Christe. Lo, what in the fore parte of his saying he calleth benediction or blessing, the same immediatly in the latter parte he calleth Consecration, wherby he sheweth by both words one self thig to be signified, which al do terme Cõsecratiõ.

That this worde Benedicere, is taken for Consecrare in the Fathers. *De ijs qui initiantur Mysterijs. cap. 9.* Mat. 26.

Cum benedictionem dico, Eucharistiam dico, when I say blessing, I meane the Eucharist, saith S. Chrysostome. who so euer is conuersant in the workes of Cyrillus, he can not be ignorant, how that learned Father in infinite places calleth this blessed Sacrament, benedictionem Mysticam, the Mystical blessing. So do the Fathers of the first Ephesine Councel. And some Doctours haue expounded the worde benedicere, by consecrare, where S. Paule saith, Calix benedictionis cui benedicimus, &c. Cui benedicimus, id est, quem nos Sacerdotes Consecramus: The cup which we blesse, that is, which we Priestes do consecrate, saith Haimo, and also S. Thomas. what the Latines signifie by consecrare, the same do the Greekes expresse by ευλογειν, which is to blesse.

Chrysost. in. 1. Cor. 10. hom. 24

S Thomas in. 1. Cor. 10. lect. 4.

Now if you denye the holy and dreadful Mysteries, to

witte, the body and and bloud of Christe, to be commonly called τὰ ἅγια, or τὰ ἡγιασμένα in greke, sancta, and sometimes sanctum Domini, in Latine, the holy thinges, or the holy thing of our Lorde: you shew your selfe either very cōtentious and froward in denying so manifest and knowen a truth, or very ignorant both of the auncient Coūcels, and also of the Fathers writings. What was meant but the blessed Sacrament, when the Deacons cryed out aloude in the Greeke Churches, ἅγια τοῖς ἁγίοις, Sancta sanctis, holy thinges for the holy?

The thig of the Sacrament is called τὰ ἅγια, Sancta. sanctum Domini. *Cyprian. In serm. de lapsis. In Liturgijs Græcorum. Nicol. Cabasila in expositione Liturgiæ. c. 30.*

But Syr what meant you to charge me in this Diuision, with translation of the other place which you note? *Likevvise* (say you) *these vvordes, Post finem orationum, he translateth thus, after he had done the prayer of Consecration.* Where so euer it is so translated, it may wel be allowed. But what? wil you burthen me here with ỹ translation? Doth ỹ helpe forth the mater here? Gentle Reader, I pray the cōsider, how falsly M. Iewel demeaneth him selfe. Read my wordes, either in myne owne booke, or as they be laid forth in his Replie. These wordes, Post finem orationum, thou findest not at al in al this. xxxij. Diuision. If they be not here, why reproueth he me for vsing *a preatie false translation?* This is not a preaty, but a very grosse and shamelesse kinde of falsehed, to charge me with that which here I say not. And yet O Lord, of what bitter gaul he voideth his stomake against me. This peece of Scripture, *he calleth thinges that be not, as though they vvere,* is miserably wrested against me: Lex Cornelia de falsis, is thundered out vpon me. And I my selfe must confesse, this is no sincere nor plaine dealing. The Margent also lacketh not a testimonie of his spite, where he hath caused this note to be put in sight. *M. Harding corrupteth and falsifieth his translation.*

Fol. 26. a. M. Iew. burthe‑neth me w that is not in this diuision to be founde. What wil he spare to say, when he findeth a fault, spetting such venime, whē none is cōmitted? Rom. 4.

God be thanked, I am not much troubled with the stinge of such waspes. It is an euident token that he lacketh good

mater,

mater, sith he forgeth so open lyes against me. But where this mater shal come to examination of mē that loue the truth, what shal he winne by such false and impudent dealing, but present discredite of his cause? Fight no more M. Iewel with your owne shadow. The poison of your stinge can not enter into me. Your blame is a false sclannder. The fault whereof you twite me, is not here by me committed. Your abused scripture I retourne ouer vnto you againe. Beware least the time come, when lex Cornelia de falsis, shalbe exercised vpon you.

A iustification of my Translation. Fol.28.a.

Touching the translation of these wordes, Post finem orationum, that is, After he had donne the prayers of Consecration: this being graunted and acknowleged, that in the place mention is made of the Masse: I affirme the translation to be good. For the author that so wryteth, vnderstandeth by Orationes, the praiers pronounced about the Consecration, or the very wordes of Consecration. For so the best learned & auncient Fathers haue spoken. For good proufe hereof I referre you to that learned Epistle, which S. Augustine wrote vnto Paulinus, who speaking expressely of the distinct kindes of prayers, there saith thus.

this word *Orationes* is taken for the wordes of Consecration.

Aug.ep.59.

Precationes accipimus dictas, quas facimus in celebratione sacramentorum, antequam illud quod est in Domini mensa, incipiat benedici: orationes, cum benedicitur & sanctificatur. &c. We take Precationes to be called those prayers, which we make in the celebration of the Sacraments, before that, which is on our lordes table, begin to be blessed: and Orationes (we take for the prayers that be said) when that (which is on our Lordes table) is blessed and sanctified, or consecrated. Marke you wel also those wordes folowing there, as perteining to this purpose. Excepto nomine generali orationis, ea proprie intelligēda est oratio, quam facimus ad votum, id est πρὸσ εὐχὴν. Vouentur autem omnia quæ offeruntur Deo, maximè sancti altaris Oblatio. &c.

As S. Augustine calleth the prayers of Consecration orationes, so S. Hierome calleth them Preces, meaning one selfe thing, whose wordes these be in his Epistle to Euagrius. Quid patitur mensarum minister, vt super eos se tumidus efferat, ad quorum preces Christi corpus sanguisq; conficitur? What aileth the minister of tables (wherby he meaneth a Deacon) to swel and aduaunce him selfe ouer them, at whose praiers the body and bloud of Christ is Consecrated? Lo he calleth the wordes of Consecration, prayers. S. Iustine the blessed martyr calleth the same so likewise, where he mentioneth, τὴν δὲ δι᾽ εὐχῆς λόγου τοῦ παρ᾽ αὐτοῦ εὐχαριστηθεῖσαν τροφὴν, the foode which is made the Eucharist through the prayer of the worde that we haue of him, that is to say of Christ.

Preces. Hieron ad Euagriũ.

Iustinus in 2. Apolog.

Forasmuch then as the wordes of Consecration, wherwith the body and bloud of Christe be Consecrated, are of these auncient Fathers called prayers, as also oftentimes of Nicolaus Cabasila, and Bessarion: my translation of the forementioned wordes, Post finem Orationum, after he had donne the prayers of Consecration, specially the Masse in the same place being spoken of, and the whole circumstance necessarily redring that sense, was not to be reprehended, but to be admitted for right & good. Neither should the same haue offended you, but that it made for the better proufe of the Masse.

In liturgię expositio. In lib. de sacramẽto Euchari- stia.

Iewel.

*Missa in this place importeth not the Masse. For *as I haue already proued by sundrie autorities, Missa is oftẽtimes vsed for any kinde of prayer. As it may further appeare by an epistle of Chromatius, and Heliodorus sent vnto S. Hierome touching Gregorie the bishop of Corduba, and by the vvordes of the *Councel of Cabilon. VVhich thing also very vvel agreeth vvith the custome and order of the Church of Alexandria at that time, vvhereof Nicephorus vvriteth thus.* Quarta hebdomadis die, & ea, quæ Parasceue dicitur, Alexandrini Scripturas legebant, Docto-

The. 181. Untruth. It is not yet proued as now it appereth.

The 182. Untruth. No such thing appeareth in the two Councels of Cabilon

ri-

ribus eas interpretantibus: omniaque quæ ad Synaxin pertinent, peragebant, præter diuinorum mysteriorum perceptionē. Atque eam illi antiquitus habuere consuetudinem. *At Alexandria they reade the Scriptures vpon VVenesdaies and Frydaies, and the Doctours or preachers expounde the same. And they doo al thinges, that perteine vnto the Communion, sauing only the receiuing of the holy Mysteries. And this custome they haue had of olde.*

num, the contrary appeareth *De Cons. dist. 1. Solet plures.* *Nicepho. li. 12. c. 34.*

Harding.

Before you did, what you could, to proue, that Missa signifieth an assemblie of the people. Here you would haue it to be taken for any kinde of prayer, as for Matens, Euensong, Complein, the Pater noster, Laudes, Prime, or Houres. I see wel you care not what it be taken for, so it be not taken for the Masse. As your proufes before were weake, so be these here not very stronge. If you haue no better meane to vpholde that strange opinion touching the signification of Missa, then an vnknowen or very litle estemed Epistle of one Chromacius and Heliodorus you may geue ouer this much, and begynne againe. But why allege you not their wordes? Be they dumme? Or haue they nothing to speake for you? Or be their wordes not worth the hearing? Thinke you their bare names can make proufe of a mater so strange? Consider, how your owne law rule may be verified of you, Qui mutum exhibet, nihil exhibet. Dumme persons you know, be not the fittest witnesses.

Pag. 72. Now to M. Jew. Missa signifieth any kinde of prayer.

As for the two Councels of Cabilonum, which is a Citie of base Burgundie commonly called Challon, there is not so much as one worde in them, that soundeth ought for you. Mary there fynde we much mater against you, and contrary to your whole Gospel. For there haue we the Masse set forth and comended vnto the Church in sundry Canons, Auricular Confession, Cap. 32. Masses, & prayers for ye rest of soules of Christē people departed. ca. 39. And this is there also proued by ye autoritie of S. Austine.

Concil. Cabilonē. 2. tēmpore Caroli Magni. Marke reader how much this Coūcel maketh for M. Jewel.

There haue we also, that Christen people do heare Masse, which phrase, M. Iewel condemneth vtterly. Audiunt Missas, they heare Masse, is twise founde. Cap. 19.

This phrase to heare Masse, is vsed of the councel of Challon.

Now ỹ you alleged the Councel of Challon for you, though to no purpose, we may reasonably require you to admit the auctoritie of it making against you, and that to good purpose. You that are so great a Lawier, or at least that vse the helpe of a lawyer so commonly, remember what the lawe saith, I doubt not. Si quis testibus vsus fuerit, ijdemque testes aduersus eum in alia lite producantur: non licebit ei personas eorum excipere. If a mã vse witnesses, and the witnesses be brought against him in an other cause: it shal not be lawful for him to take exception against their persons. When you shal proue by the Councel of Challon, that Missa is not taken for the Masse, but for any kinde of prayer, you shal fynde vs reasonable. In the meane time we require you, sith that you appeale to that Councel, to yelde and subscribe vnto the Masse, vnto Auricular or secret Confession, and vnto Masses and prayers to be donne and said for the faithful soules departed, vnto the terme and phrase of hearing Masse. For al these pointes of catholike Religion be in the Councel of Challon most manifestly auouched. And what if Missa were taken sometimes for any kinde of prayer, as you would haue it, wil it therfore folow, that it is so taken of Leontius?

L. Si quis. C. d. test.

But if I would admit the Chapter Solent plures, which you allege, to be a parte of the Councel of Challon, for Gratiãs sake, who reporteth it as out of that Councel, what conclude you therof? How proue you therby that Missa is taken for any kinde of prayer? Mary then say you, there haue we mention of Masse to be celebrated at the feastes of the foure times (which we cal Imber feastes) at the Euening, & in the holy saturday, which is Easter Eue, circa noctis initium, about the begynning of the night.

De cons. dist. 1. Solent plures.

why syr thinke you that Missa is taken for any kinde of prayer, because in that place it is required to be donne in the Euening, as though the Masse might not at any time be celebrated but only before noone? If you so thinke, you are deceiued.

For in old time it was not only lawful, but also commaunded, that Masse should be said at after noone vpon certain daies. That was, when the fast of the foure times was kept, and vpon Easter eue, which fastes were at that time much more straitlye kepte, then now they be. And this was donne because none then might take his refection and eate, vntil the Oblation was offred, and Masse donne. Now the time of refection vpon fasting dayes, was at the nynth houre, accompte made from the rysinge of the Sunne, as we reade in S. Augustine in his Epistle to Ianuarius. On Easter eue Masse was celebrated about the beginning of the night, that afterward the people might take their refection. which begynning of that night was accompted to apperteine to Easterday, as a parte of the same, for so we learne of Leo writing to Dioscorus.

The masse in the olde church was sometimes celebrated after noone.

Epiphani. in fine Pan. rij. Augustin. Epist. 118. ad Ianuarium ad finem. Dist. 75. quod a patribus.

And that Masse was celebrated both in the morning, or at least before Dynner, & also at the Euening vpon Maūdie thursday, we haue it clearly witnessed by S. Augustine in the said Epistle to Ianuarius. The forenoone Oblation (by which worde in that place the Masse is signified) was for them that being weake could not susteine both to faste, and, as the manner then was, to be washed. The Euening Oblation or Masse was for them, that were stronger and kept their faste. wherfore that Missa was celebrated at night, or in the Euening at certaine times, it maketh no argument at al, that it is taken in the Councel of Cabilon, or in the Canon Solent plures, (whose so euer it were) for al kinde of prayer.

If Missa be oftentimes vsed for any kinde of prayer, as you

say, why do you not shew vs some plain place, wher it signifieth either Matines, or Euensong, or Cōpleine? Or why allege you not at least one sentence of some Father, where it is vsed and taken for the prayers of the Third, Sixth, or Nynth houre, commonly named of the Fathers, Tertia, Sexta, Nona? If you haue no such place to shewe, cal backe your worde againe, and say nomore, that Missa is vsed oftentimes for any kinde of prayer.

Chrysost. hom. 59. ad popul. Antiochen.

Aug. serm. 55. de tempore.

In a Councel holden at Carthage, we haue a plaine distinction and difference expressed betwen Masse, and prayers in general. The wordes be these. Vt sacramenta altáris non nisi a ieiunis hominibus celebrētur, excepto vno die anniuersario, quo cœna Domini celebratur. Nam si aliquorum pomeridiano tempore defunctorum, siue episcoporum, siue cæterorum, commendatio facienda est, solis orationibus fiat, si illi qui faciunt, iam pransi inueniantur. We ordeine that the Sacramentes of the aulter be not celebrated but of men fasting, except one yerely day, in which our Lordes supper or Maundie is celebrated. For if commendation of any, either of bishops, or of the rest, be to be done at afternone, Let it be donne with prayers only, if they who do it, be found to haue dyned. Here it is ordeined that commendation of such as depart this life at afternoone, be donne forthwith with prayers, and not with Masse, in which the Sacramentes of the aulter are celebrated, in case the priestes that should say Masse, be not fasting. Which Decree argueth a plaine difference betwen Masse, and euery other kinde of prayers. For if the Masse then had signified any kinde of prayer, the Fathers of that Councel would not haue ordeined Commendation of the dead to be made Solis orationibus, with prayers only. For though Masse had ben said, yet the commendation had ben doone with only prayers, sith the Masse it selfe signified any kinde of prayer.

That the Masse is different & distinct frō other praiers.

Concil. Carthag. 3. Ca. 29.

Marke these wordes, with praiers only.

Of this Decree we may gather a probable coniecture, for that

that M. Iewel calleth priuate Masse. For wheras it is said here, that commendation of them that died in the afternoone, is to be made with prayers only, and not with Masse, if the priest haue broken his fast: & seing therof it appeareth, that if the priest were fasting, he might make the deads cōmendation also with Masse in the afternoone: then if a sufficient company of the people were not found fasting, and disposed to receiue the Cōmunion with the priest: certaine it is, that in this case saying Masse & celebrating the Sacraments of the aulter for the departed, he should say priuate Masse, that is to say, he should celebrate Masse without a company of others founde fasting and receiuing the Sacrament with him. And if the Fathers of that Councel had ben of the opinion that M. Iewel is of, that is, that Masse can not be done onlesse a number be ready to receiue the Sacrament with the priest: doutlesse they would aswel haue mentioned the faste of the necessary Communicants, as of the priest that should celebrate Masse. For els had their Decree lacked foresight in a thing of necessitie, which of so many wise, learned, and godly Fathers is not to be thought.

A very probable argument for proufe of priuate Masse.

To proue that Missa is oftentimes taken for any kinde of prayer, among other weake coniectures, you allege a place out of Nicephorus. which may wel seme to make against you, for you it maketh nothing at al. The place is this, as you translate it. *At Alexandria, they reade the scriptures vpon VVenesdaies, and Frydaies, and the Doctours or preachers expounde the same.* (These wordes folowing are specially to be considered.) Omniaque quæ ad Synaxin pertinent, peragebant, præterquam Diuinorum Mysteriorum perceptionem. And they do al thinges that apperteine vnto the Communion, sauing onely the receiuing of the holy Mysteries. And this custome there they haue had of olde.

Nicephor. lib. 12. cap. 34.

Verely I can not conceiue to what ende you haue brought

this place of Nicephorus, neither what dependence there is in your wordes. You pretend to proue, that Missa importeth not the Masse, in the place by me alleged out of Leontius. For say you, Missa is oftentimes vsed for any kinde of prayer. And for assurance therof you referre vs to your former proufes by sundry autorities, which be no proufes, as now I haue declared. Then you send vs further to an Epistle of Chromatius and Heliodorus, that (I trow) was neuer yet estemed nor alleged of any learned man. And where it is, God knoweth, very obscure it is and litle worth, for els you would haue shewed vs, where we might fynde it. If it be theirs so assuredly, as the wordes of the Councel of Cabilon, which you speake of, be the wordes of that Councel: then is it not their Epistle, for those wordes vnto which you direct vs by your quotation, be not to be found in al ẏ Councel. These be Mummers in dede, & speak nothing for them self, much lesse speake they ought for you. If they had ben worth ẏ hearing, you would not thus haue brought them in dumme. Neither can this strange mater so easily be proued by the names of dumme witnesses.

After this you procede forth and say thus. *Vvhich thing also very vvel agreeth vvith the custōe and order of the church of Aleāxdria at that time, vvherof Nicephorus vvriteth thus.* Quarta hebdomadis die, &c. But what thing is ẏ agreeth very wel ẇ the custome of Alexandria? Remēber you wherof your spake? How hangeth this to that goeth before? At Alexandria the Doctours expounded the scriptures vpon wenesdaies and Frydaies, And they had al thinges donne that appertein to the Synaxis, sauing the receiuing of the holy mysteries. What then? Conclude here of, Ergo Missa is oftentimes taken for any kinde of prayer? For this is ẏ you conclude, els you conclude nothing. If you conclude nothing, why did you allege it? If this be your conclusion, proue it not to be

M. Iew. maketh a foolish Conclusiō

a foolish conclusion. How holdeth the Argument? By what rules of Logique can you make it good? He that neuer learned Logique, may sone see the peeuishnesse of it.

As your Argument deduced out of this place of Nicephorus, is naught worth, so is your translation false, touching this worde Synaxis, wherupon ẏ whole mater dependeth. Synaxis signifieth in this place not ẏ Cōmunion of the body and bloud of Christ, but an assēblie & cōming together of ẏ people to ẏ church, or to some other holy place, to pray, to render thankes and praise vnto God. These comminges together to pray and worship God, were appointed by the Apostles to be kept vpon ẏ wenesdaies, Frydaies, and Sondaies, as Epiphanius writeth. The worde is much vsed of the Greke Fathers, and specially of them of the Councel of Gangra. In Latine of the best learned it is called Collecta. And wheras the Common translation of the Councel of Gangra, hath for σιωάξεις μαρ̣ύρων, Conuentus, qui per loca, & basilicas Sanctorum Martyrum fiunt: it is thought ynough for those two Greke wordes, to lay downe these two latine wordes, Collectas Martyrum. Where your worde Communiones Martyrum, wil not serue. And therfore is not the trāslation of Ianus Cornarius of Germinie to be liked, where he translateth out of Epiphanius the place aboue mētioned, σιωάξεις, into Communiones.

Synaxis, what it signifieth in Nicephorus & in many other places.

Epiphanius in fine Panarij.

Concilio Gangren. Cap. 20.

Collectas Martyrū

In the Primitiue Churche they signified this holy comming together by the worde Colligere alone. For so Tertullian speaketh in the ende of his booke, De fuga in persecutione. Sed quomodo colligemus, inquies? quomodo Dominica solennia celebrabimus? How shal we come to Churche together, thou wilt say? How shal we kepe our Lordes solemne feastes? So Synaxis is a companie and an assemblie of faithful folke together to serue God. Which by one woorde in Latine is called

Colligere.

Tertullian

Synaxis, & Collecta signifieth one thing verp often.

 Collecta.

Collecta. And this worde Collecta is found in the olde tran-
Leuit,23. slation of the Bible not seldome. Leuitici.cap.23. Dies octauus erit celeberrimus, atque sanctissimus, est enim dies cœtus atque collectæ. The eight day shal be the most solemne and holiest of al. for it is a day of comming together to serue God, as much to say, a holy day. The woorde is likewise vsed Deuter. 16. and 2. Paralipom. 7.

The place of Nicephorus tourned vpon M. Iewel.

Synaxis is a celebration of faithful peoples meeting at churche to serue God.

Concerning the place of Nicephorus, whereas at Alexandria vpon the Wenesdaies and Frydaies al thinges were donne that apperteine to an assemblie, or to a holy day (for so much the worde Synaxis soundeth) and the Masse specially and chiefly apperteined to such a solemnitie: thereof it appeareth, that they had the Masse done by the Priest, without the peoples receiuing of the Sacrament. For they had al thinges that apperteined vnto a Synaxis (which what it was, may be described with many wordes better, then signified with any one English woorde) and so it semeth to be an euident testimonie for Priuate Masse. For thus the Argument may be framed. what so euer belonged to Synaxis, that had they. The Masse chiefly belonged to Synaxis, ẏ is to say to the celebritie of a holy meeting at Church: Ergo they had the Masse. then further. But they had not the receiuing of the holy Mysteries: Ergo, the Priest celebrated Masse, that is to say, consecrated, offered, and receiued the body and bloud of Christe, without the people receiuing with him, which is that these men cal priuate Masse. Thus Nicephorus place is founde not onely impertinent to your purpose, but also such as may be retourned vpon your owne head.

Ievvel.

Touching these vvordes, Benedicere sancta, they do no more signifie the Consecration of the Sacrament, as M. Harding hath translated it,

then

then these vvordes, extollite manus vestras in sancta, *do signifie the lifting vp of handes to the Sacrament. Chrysostome in his Liturgie, vseth the same manner of speach to a farre other purpose. For after the Communion is ended, and the people ready to depart forth, he vvriteth thus*, Sacerdos benedicit Sancta, & exuit. *Here if M. Harding vvil take* Benedicere Sancta, *for Consecration, then must needes folovve a greate inconuenience, that there vvere tvvo Consecrations in one Communion, yea, and one Consecration, after al vvas ended. It may appeare, that Chrysostome by these vvoordes meant a solemne prayer to conclude the vvhole.*

Harding.

Were it so that S. Chrysostome by these wordes Benedicere Sancta, meant a solemne prayer to conclude the whole, as you ghesse, yet thereby in Leontius may be signified the Consecration of the holy Mysteries. For one worde may be taken in diuerse senses. Because this very worde Benedicere signifieth sometimes blessing on Gods behalfe towardes man, as where it is said, Benedixit Deus Noe, & filijs eius: God blessed Noe, and his children: shal we say therefore, that it is not an other where taken in an euil sense, as where it is said, Benedixit Naboth Deo & Regi, Naboth did blaspheme God and the King? Because this worde Calix, Cuppe, is taken for a Cuppe in one place, shal we therefore say, it is not taken for the passion in an other place? As where Christ said, O my Father if it be possible, let this cuppe passe from me. So what so euer Benedicere Sancta signifieth in S. Chrysostomes Liturgie, yet notwithstanding in this place of Leontius, it may be taken to signifie the Consecration of the Sacrament, as I haue before proued. And this your common manner of reasoning, which by the anouching of one truth, excludeth an other truth, is of al others the simplest, and weakest. Yet except an infinite

Gen. 9. 3. Reg. 21 1. Cor. 10 Mat. 26.

The chief furniture of M. Iewels whole booke is to exclude one truth by an other truth.

number of manifest vntruthes, it is the chiefe furniture of your whole booke.

Where you say further concerning this phrase, ẏ the meaning of it, semeth to be the same ẏ S. Chrysostomes is at the end of his Masse: your cōiecture had ben reasonable, if Leontius had attributed it vnto this holy Patriarke at the ende also of his Masse. But seing that his wordes be these, Cum ergo Sancta benedixisset Patriarcha, & orationem Dominicam inchoasset: who so euer hath skil of Ecclesiastical antiquities, can not but iudge these wordes to apperteine to that part of the Masse, that is about the Consecration of the Mysteries before the receiuing, and therfore much more before the end. For there be sundry aūcient recordes beside S. Hierome witnessing, that our Lordes prayer was said before the body and bloud of Christ were receiued. And some say that the Apostles them selues vsed so to doo, when so euer they celebrated the most holy Mysteries, according to the commaundement that Christ gaue them at his last Supper. This much being considered, my translation of benedicere sancta, is nothing disproued by the doubtful rubrice of S. Chrysostomes Masse. But let vs discusse your other good stuffe.

Vide Beatum Rhenanum in annotat. in Tertul. De Corona Militis

Ievvel.

Doubtlesse it vvas a very straite case, that a noble Man should be driuen to helpe the Priest to Masse.

Harding.

Doubtlesse it is a straite case, that M. Iewel for lacke of better mater, is driuen to stuffe his booke with such light ware, that better becommeth a mocking boy, then a Superintendent. And wherof gather you, ẏ the noble man holpe the Patriarke to Masse? Because he said our Lordes prayer with him? Remember you not, that in the Greeke Churche our Lordes prayer was said of the whole people at Masse, as it is said of the Priest only in the Latine Church? This much if you knewe not, you might haue learned of S. Gregory epist.63.ad Ioannem Episcop, Syracusan. This saying of the Pater noster with the Patriarke was donne after the manner of the Greke Churche, and not by way of seruing a Priest to Masse. Neither was he driuen so to do at al. That he did, was of common custome and of deuotion, not of compulsion, nor somuch as of request. Neither was he so noble, but that Patriarke both by dignitie of his rome, and by the high function of his Priesthod, specially whē in the person of Christe he consecrated his most pretious body and bloude at the aulter, was much nobler. If you had read the eloquent worke of S. Chrysostome, De dignitate Sacerdotali, and beleued it: you would not haue made so great a wōder, that any man, were he neuer so noble, should answere not onely the great Patriarke of Alexandria, the second Byshop of the worlde, but any Priest what so euer he were celebrating those honorable and dreadful mysteries.

Ievvel.

*It is a straite case for M. Harding, to renne to Alexandria * a thousand miles beyonde al Chrystendome to seeke his Masse, and that not in open Church neither, but onely in a priuate Oratorie.*

Harding.

It is a straite case that M. Iewel, who taketh vpon him to be a champion of the late deuised Gospel, is driuen to defende his vaine Chalenge with scorneful scoffes, and open lyes. When this holy Patriarke Iohn the merciful lyued, it is wel knowen, that Alexandria was one of the chiefe lightes of Christendome, howsoeuer it be of late yeres destroyd by warres, & now come into the Dominion of the Turkes, as Egypt and Syria is. Neither is it now in our time after so great mutations of thinges, a thousand miles from Christendome, as you say. For the

The.183. vntruth. Alexandria is yet neare to some parte of Christendome, and at that time was a chiefe light of al Christendom.

Landes of Cypres and Cādie, which are a parte of Christēdom, and at this day vnder the gouernement of the Venetians, are not farre from it, as Cosmographers can tel you.

M. Iew. taketh exception against places. *Alexandria.*

Verely it is a token that you mistrust your owne Chalenge, sith that you begynne now to take exception against places. For if you wil not alow vs Alexandria, where S. Marke first taught the faith, where many thousandes of Martyrs haue suffred death for Christe, where Papias, where Pantenus, where Clement, where Origen, where S. Athanasius, where Theophilus, where Dydimus, and many other excellent learned Fathers haue expounded ẏ scriptures, preached, written, & by al meanes set forth ẏ faith and defended it against tyrauntes and heretikes: I know not what is that place, against which you wil not take exceptiō. By as good right you may refuse the proufes of thinges in olde time donne, at Constantinople, at Carthage, at Chalcedon, at Ephesus, at Nice, in Græcia, Asia, Syria, Aegypte, Africa, at Antiochia, Yea at Hierusalem it selfe: because al these cities and Countries be now come into the handes of miscreantes, and be at this day no parte of Christendome. And so by this reason we may allege nothing out of the first Councels for proufe of any necessary doctrine, because it might be said, that we ranne many hundred miles beyonde al Christendome for our proufes.

M. Iew. altereth the state and purport of his Chalenge.

Neither be you now driuen to take exception against Cities and Countries only, that be taken from the possession of Christen men: but also against priuate Oratories, and against certaine Fathers. For now begynning to staggar, you alter the former purport of your Chalenge, and require vs to shewe you proufe of priuate Masse said, not in Oratories, but in open Churche, in the face and sight of al the people, and the same witnessed by S. Augustine, S. Hierome, S. Chrysostome,

sostome, or some other auncient Fathers, which your selfe can be content to allowe. These your tergiuersations and bare shiftes, do manifestly bewray both ye weakenes of your cause, and your great impudencie.

Ievvel.

*In the Tripartite Storie it is vvritten *thus: Gregorie Nazianzen at Constantinople in a litle Oratorie, σωναγωγὰς ἐποιεῖτο, made assemblies of the people. Here vve see the Actiō vvas common, and a ful Communion ministred, notvvithstanding the place vvere priuate.*

The. 184 vntruth. It is not written thus. Let the booke be trial.

Hist. tripart. li. 9. cap. 8.

Harding.

First the Greke of Sozomenus who is the author of the Storie here alleged, hath not those wordes σωναγωγὰς ἐποιεῖτο, as much to say, by your translation, *he made assemblies of the people.* Next neither hath the Latine booke, from whence you tooke the place, so as you haue falsified, but thus: in paruo oratorio sacra celebrabat, that is, S. Gregorie Nazianzene kept diuine Seruice in a litle Oratorie or chappel. This is a place by you of purpose falsified, neither can it by any way or colour be excused. If such manifest lyes and falsifyinges may stande for good proufes, you may be let slippe to make a new Chalenge to morow nexte, not only against the present Catholike Church, but also against the olde Fathers, yea against S. Paule and Christe him selfe. For this libertie being graunted you, wordes shal not lacke, at least to make a shewe.

Vide Sozomenum Græcum. li. 7. cap. 5.

The tripartite Storie falsified by M. Iewel.

The. 185. vntruth. It was not forbidden by Decrees, that the Sacramēt in some cases should be ministred in houses, it was cōmaunded.

Ievvel.

*Thus then gentle Reader, standeth my ansvvere to this tale. Firste, *that it vvas forbidden by many Decrees to minister the Sacrament in priuate houses: and therfore vnlikely that Iohn Almonar being a godly man vvould presume to doo the Contrarie.*

Harding.

Conc. Nicen. ca. 12.

To this I haue answered before. It was not forbidden, but rather commaunded by sundry Decrees in certaine cases to minister the Sacrament in priuate houses. As for example, if any had layen at pointe of death, and required to receiue his viage prouision, the blessed Sacrament was ministred vnto him in his priuate house, yea in his priuey bedchamber. If you meane, that the Masse was forbidden to be celebrated in priuate houses, I graunte: onlesse for some necessitie leaue of the Bishop therto had ben obteined. Whiles you be afraid to name the Masse, and to signifie the same, terme it to minister the Sacramēt: you shew your selfe to be lesse a shamed of making a lye, then of vsing that terme, which the Decrees that you allege for you, haue vsed. You be not a shamed to allege the Decrees, you be a shamed to recite their wordes.

De Cons. dist. 1. Missarum solennia. Item nullus presbyter. Item Clericos qui ministrant.

M. Iew. allegeth Decrees for him selfe, whose wordes being contrary to him, he is ashamed to vtter.

Here I might say, the Patriarkes house of Alexandria, was not priuate, and therfore those Decrees pertcine not vnto it. But Leontius nameth not his house, but his Oratorie. which Oratorie was consecrated, and therfore was it lawful in the same to celebrate Masse. The Decrees that forbid Masse to be donne in houses, are to be vnderstanded to speake of common and prophane dwilling houses, and not of consecrated places. So this godly man saying Masse in his Oratorie presumed nothing contrary to the Decrees made in that behalfe.

Ievvel.

Secondly, that this vvorde Missa vsed here by the rude and vtterly vnlearned Interpreter, doth not necessarily import the Masse.

Harding.

The interpreters smal skil of the Latine tongue, maketh no argument, that Missa doth not import the Masse. Though his Latine were meane, yet the Doctrine of the Catholike Churche is is not to be condemned. The circumstance of the place argueth it was the Masse. He had Latine ynough to signifie so much. If it like you not, that Missa shal signifie the Masse, then cause your frende M. Cooper of Oxford to set forth a new Dictionarie, and tell him that from hence forth Missa must not be Englished the Masse, but the new Communion, the ministration of the Sacramentes, the assemblie of the people, or some other preaty thing, wherby it may be put out of euery mans head, that the Church of Christe in olde time had Masse. If you could bring this to passe, and withal burne the bookes of so many auncient Fathers, and Councels, and olde Decrees: I promise you it were a notable feate, and a great furtherance to your Gospel. For as long as these continew, the Masse wil neuer out of memorie.

A shifting deuise, to abolish the name and memorie of the Masse.

Ievvel.

*Thirdly that M.Harding the better to furnish out the mater, hath violently, and *of purpose, falsified the Translation.*

The.186. Untruth. There is neither violence, nor any false purpose in my translation, as I haue proued.

Harding.

Had I so donne, I perceiue your courtesie would not haue sticked violently to charge me therwith. My translation is true and good, as the same I haue before iustified.

Ievvel.

Fourthly, that notvvithstanding here vvere graunted the Celebration of the Sacrament, yet it can not be forced thereof, that the priest receiued alone.

Harding.

What meane you by the celebration of the Sacrament? You vse termes of doubteful and manifold signification, to haue starting holes at nede. Wil you stil be afraid to name that you persecute, except you name it with spite? I can not force it of this holy Fathers Masse, you say, that the priest receiued alone.

M. Iew. purposeth to graunt nomore then he is enforced to graunt.

Wherby he sheweth what reuerence & obedience he beareth towardes the church

Why syr be you at that point with vs, that you wil graunt nothing more, then we can enforce you vnto? wel then, this much can we enforce vpon you touching this place. That any person receiued with the Patriarke, it is not reported. There were but two others present, when he said Masse. Of them the one, I meane the noble man, for good cause was not, (as in my booke

Fol. 27. a

I haue declared) to be admitted vnto the receiuing of the mysteries. Then if any receiued with the Patriarke, it was but one onely person. But to a Communion thre be necessarily required at least besides the priest, by your owne Doctrine, as we fynde in your Communion booke that is of the last and fynest making, and most Geneuian like: ergo, it was a Masse without a companie receiuing the Communion together with the priest, which your Gospel calleth a Priuate Masse. For plainesse sake, this is my argument. where so euer a priest saith Masse without a companie receiuing with him, there is (if I may vse your terme) a priuate Masse said. But this Patriarke at his Masse had not a companie receiuing with him: Ergo, he said Priuate Masse.

An argument prouing that S. Iohn the Patriarke of Alexandria said priuate masse.

Iewel.

Fifthly, that although this vvere proued a priuate Masse, yet hath M. Harding vtterly missereckened him selfe and so gotten nothing. For it vvas vvithout the compasse of sixe hundred yeres.

Harding.

M. Iew. sticketh at a yere or two, as though time made the Masse good or il.

It appeareth by the wordes of the second Nicen Councel aboue rehersed, by which it is reported, that Leontius the writer of this holy Fathers life, lyued in the time of Mauricius the Emperour: that he might haue said this Masse within the sixe hundred yeres. For certaine it is that Leontius wrote his life, after the time that he had goten renome and fame for his great vertue. which maketh an argument that he lyued within the six hundred yeres. For Mauricius was lyuing at the very terme

of

of those yeres, as it may wel be proued by the stories of that age. Now take you this withal, that the second Councel of Nice, is to be credited before Vincentius. But for this I wil not striue with M. Iewel. If he graunt it was a priuate Masse, I would faine learne of him, why it should be condemned being said nine or ten yeares after the date of the said six hundred yeares, and allowed for good, if it had ben said a day or two, or a yeare, before the terme of the six hundred yeares. If it had ben good & godly before, why was it not so after? If it were good & godly after, why might it not be so before? Verely the time maketh it neither better, nor worse. Graunt it once to haue ben a Masse, & afterwardes it shal be proued, that it was good and godly. If that be proued, as in dede you haue no reason to disproue any parte of the Masse: what cause haue you now to impugne it? And if it may be found good now, then had it not ben euil within the six hundred yeares. And that is ynough.

Ievvel.

Last of al herevnto I adde, that the place, vvhere these thinges are imagined to be done, vvas il chosen, and very vnlikely to serue this purpose. For M. Harding is not able to proue, that in the Citie of Alexandria, vvas euer any one priuate Masse said, either before that time, or sithens.

Harding.

What is this other, but vaine trifling, and Petitio principij, as they cal it in schooles? You seme to haue spent your stuffe, that you prouided for this Diuision. And to say the truth, fewer wordes would better haue serued. If I haue so wel proued Masse without a company of receiuers in Alexandria, which place you say is il chose, and very vnlikely to serue this purpose: then may the discrete Reader iudge therof, how much better able I maye be to proue it by the practise of the Church in other places. Petitio principij.

The.xxxiij. Diuision.

IN this place I report a storie thought to be written by Amphilochius the famous bishop of Iconium, declaring how S. Basile celebrated Masse in a vision. For alleging which storie M. Iewel thinketh himselfe to haue great aduantage against me. And because through my whole booke he findeth not the like aduantage, therefore he maketh the most of it. How be it if al be duly considered, it shal appeare to the indifferent reader, that he hath not gayned so much by shewing the storie to be of suspecte credite, as he hath lost, by his vaine and vntrue dealing in disprouing the same. If it be but a dreame, and a fable, as he saith it is, what nede was there to make so much adoo about nought? who geueth that Capitain the praise of noble courage, that bendeth his whole strength and power against a weake forte? Yet this fable, as light as he maketh of it, must be talked of at Paules Crosse, aduise must be taken how it might be blowen ouer al England, to the discredite of my Answere vnto his Chalenge. And now al the circumstances be rehersed againe in this place, and nothing lefte vntouched, that may helpe to deface it. So great stirre, as he maketh about it, were ynough to make a wise man beleue, it were no fable, but rather a true tale, specially being so vehemently, and with so many wordes impugned by one, that faine would haue it seme a fable.

As touching myne owne parte, whether it be a vaine fable, or a true storie, I define nothing, as neither whether Amphilochius be the author of it, or any other man. Certaine it is, I am not the first that haue said, that Amphilochius wrote S. Basiles life, nor that haue made mention of these very thinges in the same conteined. For this hath ben acknowleged & reported by sundry learned men both of this age, and oftimes past, by Aloysius Lipomanus in vitis Patrum, by Gropperus in his boke of the blessed Sacrament, by Raphael Volaterranus in Monodia Gregorij Nazianzeni, by Iacobus Philippus Bergomensis in supplemento, by Antoninus Archebishop of Florence, by Vincentius Bellouacensis in speculo historiali, by Sigebertus in Chronicis. And, which M. Iewel esteemeth more then al these, by Mathias Flacius Illyricus and his felowes hote Gospellers, that be the gatherers of the storie of Magdeburg. who very oftentimes speaking of S. Basile do allege this Amphilochius, although I confesse sometimes they seme to doubt of that is extant in Amphilochius name. So that I returne M. Iewel ouer vnto al these, and require him to bestowe his scoffes and mockes vpon them, who haue herein ben deceiued before me, if they were deceiued at al.

What learned wryters haue made mētion of the life of S. Basil, as written by Amphilochius, or of the thinges cōcerning S. Basil in the story of this Amphilochius conteined.

parte. 2. tit. 10. ca. 4

lib. 16. cap. 94

But whether this be Amphilochius or no, let vs consider partly the weaknesse of M. Iewels argumentes, and partly the vntrue reportes that he maketh to disproue him. Of the booke that he hath had in his owne librarie these. xx. yeres, he may say what him listeth. It maketh nothing against the authoritie of other bookes, that be founde els where conteining this storie. It appeareth that his booke and myne be not one. For certainely he allegeth many thinges, that my booke hath not. And he him selfe here saith, that his booke beareth not the name of Amphilochius. Perhaps it is some Collection out of that they cal Vitas patrum, wherein part of Amphilochius is conteined. Reason would, he should not ground himselfe, and affirme so much vpon the credite of an vncertaine booke.

XX iij. That

That the life of S. Thomas the Martyr and Archebishop of Cantorbury, was ioyned with his booke, it maketh no argumẽt against Amphilochius. For treatises of men of diuerse ages may be bounde together within one volume at the pleasure of the owner, and yet shal not the author of the former, be thought (as M. Jewel obiecteth) to write a prophecy, and to be a prophet in respect of the later. For els Cato the elder writing De re rustica, should seme to haue written a Prophecie of Palladius, that lyued long after him, whose bookes be printed and bound in one volume. Likewise Titus Liuius should be taken for a Prophete in respecte of Lucius Florus, that is printed with him. This was a very fonde reason, neither worthy to be tolde at Paules Crosse, as it was with great reioysing of mo then young prentises, nor to be set forth in Print to stuffe his Replie.

Iewel.

The.187. Untruth. The life of S. Basil hathe not ben set forthe fully by these Fathers, their bookes do control this Untruth.

*The life of S. Basil hath ben set forth *fully, and faithfully, by sundry olde vvorthy vvryters, as by his ovvne brother* Gregorius Nyssenus, *by his dere frende* Gregorie Nazianzene, *by* Gregorius *presbyter, by* Socrates, *by* Theodoretus, *by* Sozomenus, *by* Necephorus, *touched also in diuerse places by* Chrysostom. *And notvvithstanding of late yeres he that vvrote* Vitas patrum, *and* Iacobus de Voragine, *and* Vincentius in speculo, *vvho seme to intitle this booke by the name of* Amphilochius, *haue furnished the same vvith many vnsauery vaine tales, *yet vvas there none of them so impudent, once to make any mention of this peeuish tale of M. Hardinges Masse.*

The.188. Untruth. *Vincentius in Speculo* maketh mẽtion of the miraculous Masse of S. Basil, as here it is shewed.

Harding

Harding.

There is neuer a one of al these olde writers, that hath fully set forth the life of S. Basile. Gregorius Nyssenus his brother doth but praise his vertues, and for the same compareth him with the Saincetes of the Olde and newe Testament. S. Gregorie Nazianzene writeth much, yet not a ful storie of his life, but onely an Oration to be made in his praise at his burial, and so it is called in Greke Λόγοσ ἐπιτάφιος a funeral oration: though he came to Cesarea, where S. Basile was bishop, and there pronounced it a long time after he had ben buried, as Gregorius presbyter writeth. Gregorius presbyter, wrote the life of Gregorie Nazianzene, but that euer he wrote the life of S. Basile, I haue not yet learned. As for Socrates, Theodoritus, Sozomenus, and Nicephorus, they can not be said to haue written his life: In their Stories they haue only as it were by the way, and vpon an occasion geuen, touched somewhat concerning his life. But that is farre from writing a ful Storie of his life.

Gregorius Nyssenus wrote not S. Basils life. *Gregorie Nazianzene.* *Gregorius presbyter in vita Nazianzeni.*

Of al others S. Gregorie Nazianzene wrote thereof most amply, yet of his Miracles, which doubtelesse he had vertue to worke sundry and great, (for els how could he haue ben iustly compared with the chiefe Fathers of both testamentes?) he made no mention. The storie of whose Miracles semeth to be the profession of the booke, that beareth the name of Amphilochius, which notwithstanding I auouch not to be his. For here I shewe only the vntruthes of your sayinges, and the feeblenesse of your reasons.

Wheras you say of the rest, that none of thẽ was so impudẽt as once to make any mẽtion of this strange mãner of S. Basiles Masse, which wordes import an vncourteous & bitter surmise of me: it may please you to rebuke your selfe of an vntruth.

For Vincentius maketh mention of it in speculo. Where he saith this much alleged out of Sigebertus. Basilius Cæsariensis gemina philosophia, & sanctitate claruerat. Cui Deus apparens ad precem eius eum docuit, vt proprijs verbis sanctum Sacrificiū consecraret. Basile Bishop of Cesarea had goten him a fame through both his philosophies and holinesse. Whom God appearing vnto him at the prayer which he made, taught to Consecrate the holy Sacrifice, with prayers of his owne making. Furthermore if it wil plese you to read Antoninus before named Parte. 2. titulo. 10. cap. 4. you shal finde the same very thing, which you cal a peeuish fable of M. Hardings Masse, that here I haue alleged, fully and wholly rehersed worde for worde. Which when you shal haue read, I trust you wil discharge me of the foule crime of impudencie, sith the storie is mentioned by Antoninus, Vincentius, and Sigebertus.

Vincentius lib. 16. cap. 94.

Antoninus Archiepiscopus Florentinus.

Ievvel.

Socrates and Sozomenus say, that Basil in his youth vvas Libanius scholar: M. Hardings Amphilochius saith, Basil vvas Libanius schoolfellovve.

Harding.

Both Socrates and Sozomenus say, that S. Basile and S. Gregorie Naziāzen when they were yong men at Athens, went to the Schooles of Himerius and Proeresius the most famous Sophistes of that time: and that afterward they went to heare Libanius at Antiochia. Concerning both their going to schoole with Libanius, notwithstanding what so euer they wrote, it may be doubted of. For neither Gregorius presbyter, maketh any mention of it in S. Gregorie Nazianzens life, reporting to what places for learning he went vnto; first, to Cesarea, next in to Palestina, after that to Alexandria and to Pharos, and last of al to Athens, where he found S. Basile: And S. Gregorie Nazianzene in Epitaphio saith of S. Basile, that first he went to

Socrat. lib. 4. cap. 26. Sozom. li. 6. cap. 17.

The places that S. Gregorie Nazianzen and S. Basil went vnto for learning.

to schoole at Cesarea, next at Bizantium, after that at Athens, and that from Athens he retourned home to Cesarea. From thence after a while by occasion of troubles that rose through heretiques, he went into Pontus, and there remained in studie of Diuinitie conferring with the said Gregorie thirteen yeares, and then retourned home vnto his Countrie Cesarea, where at length he was made Bishop. That he was at any time Libanius scholar, it can not by these two Gregories appeare.

Coniectures y S. Basile was neuer Libanius scholar in his youth.

And very likely it is, that if he had ben Libanius scholar, some mention therof should haue ben made, either by S. Basile him selfe, or by Libanius, in one or other of those sundry familiar Epistles, which they wrote one to the other, specially whereas in the same they speake most of Eloquence, and of Scholars which S. Basile sent from Cappadocia to Libanius, and of the profession of Rethorique, for which at those daies Libanius at Antiochia was famous. Libanius in an Epistle to S. Basile, to persuade him that he had not forgoten him, saith that he knew him, when he was a yong man. But that he was his Schoolemaister he saith it not, where place was to say it, if he had euer so ben: and S. Basile would gently haue acknowleged the same, specially whereas he made sute vnto him to take Scholars to teach sent out of Capadocia, at his request.

But what if it be graunted that S. Basile was Libanius scholar? Might not he at an other time be his schoolefellow? Though S. Basile were his scholar in Rhetorique, yet they might be Schoolefellowes in Philosophie, and in the Mathematicals. Were not some your scholars M. Iewel in Corpus Christi Colledge when you taught Rhetorique there, who were your Schoolefellowes in Diuinitie, when Peter Martyr came to Oxford? What so euer this Amphilochius was, by this reason he is not disproued.

Ievvel.

Nazianzene and Gregorius Presbiter saye, that Basile continu-
The.189. untruth. My Amphilochius saith no such thing. *ing at Cæsarea, vvas vvel acquainted vvith Eusebius the Bishop there, before he vvent into Pontus:* * *M. Hardinges Amphilochius saith, that at his returne from Pontus, vvhich vvas sone after, Eusebius knevve him not, neither had euer spoken vvith him or sene him before.*

Harding.

Of any great acquaintance that was between S. Basile and Eusebius before S. Basiles going into Pontus, neyther Gregorie Nazianzene, nor Gregorius Presbyter speaketh. Of ennemitie between them they speake. And that you reporte of my Amphilochius, I assure you my booke hath no mention of it.

Ievvel.

The.190. untruth. Nazianzen saith not this much, as by ŷ boke it may be tried. *M. Hardinges Amphilochius saith, Basile vvas Bishop of Cæsarea, in the time of the Emperour Iulianus: vvherevpon also are founded a great many fonde fables, Nazianzene his nearest frende saith, he vvas chosen Bishop there a long vvhile after, in the time of the Emperour Valens,* * *and vvas not Bishop there at al during the vvhole time of Iulianus.*

Harding.

About the time when S. Basile was made Bishop, there may a varietie be espied in writers without their greate discredite. For in the accompt of times, seldome do writers eyther Prophane, or Ecclesiastical thoroughly agree. Which appeareth euidently in the conference of the Greeke historiographers with Titus Liuius in the reckening of the yeares, and specially in the booke of Councels. In Monodia Nazianzeni which Volaterranus wrote, touching this mater, we finde these woordes, Itaq; non vt quidam existimant, Basilius sub Iuliano principe, sed post Valentis mortem Episcopus fuit.

Basile

Basile was not Bishop in the time of Julian the Emperour as some thinke, but after the death of Valens. By which wordes it appeareth that mennes opinions herein haue ben diuerse. But for my selfe I beleue he was Bishop in the time of Valens. That he was not Bishop at al during the whole time of Julianus, though perhappes it be true, yet S. Gregorie Nazianzene expressely saith it not, as you reporte.

The 191. vntruth. Theodoritus saith not that Julius Sabba foretolde Julians death.

Ievvel.

*M. Hardings Amphilochius saith, Basile foretolde the death of Iulian: Theodoretus saith, it vvas one Iulianus Sabba, that * foretolde it, * and not S. Basile.*

The 192. vntruth. That is not in Theodoritus.

Harding.

It might haue ben tolde by both. Albeit, Julianus Sabba did not foretel his death, but tolde miraculously he was dead after that he was slaine. That S. Basile tolde it not, so much Theodoritus saith not. Didymus also of Alexandria told it, hauing learned the same by a marueilous vision, as Sozomenus declareth.

Theodorit. lib. 3. c. 23. Sozom. lib. 6. cap. 2.

Ievvel.

M. Hardinges Amphilochius saith the Emperour Valens yelded and gaue place vnto Basile. Sozomenus saith, the Emperour continued stil his purpose, and vvould not yelde.

Harding.

Theodor. lib. 4. c. 19. Nazian. in Monodia.

Both S. Gregorie Nazianzene, and Theodoritus, and others that write of S. Basiles persecution, confesse that at length Valens yelded in some parte, and proceded not so rigorously, as he had intended.

The 193. vntruth. Naziãzen saith not so in Monodia.

Ievvel.

*M. Hardinges Amphilochius saith, Nazianzene vvas present at S Basiles burial. Nazianzene him selfe, that ought to knovve it best, * saith he came aftervvard, and vvas not present.*

XX ij Harding.

Harding.

Whether he was at S. Basiles burial or no, I neither deny, nor affirme. That Nazianzene him selfe saith, he came afterward, and was not present: that I denye. For he saith no such thing at al, at least in Monodia, as you haue coted your Margent.

Ievvel.

The. 194 Vntruth. This is not said by this Amphilochius. It is M. Iewels false addition.

Gregorius presbyter saith, Nazianzene came a great vvhile after that Basile vvas buried. M. Hardinges Amphilochius is so impudent, that he saith, Nazianzenus came in al haste, and savv the blessed bodie, and fel vpon it, **vvhen it vvas buried. Vvherby it semeth, that this Amphilochius vvas not very vvise, nor circumspect in his talke. For if Nazianzene savv S. Basiles bodie, hovv vvas it buried? If it vvere buried, hovv could he see it?*

Harding.

Gregorius presbyter saith, Quum multum effluxisset temporis. &c. a long time after that S. Basile was departed from this life to God, Gregorie Nazianzene wrote Epitaphium, an Oration in praise of him, which is extant in Greke, and then came to Cæsarea, and there before the Citie pronounced it openly. This excludeth not, but that he might haue ben there before at his burial. But whether he were so or no, I say not. Only I note the feblenesse of M. Iewels reasons, and the vntruthes of his sayinges. Now saith he, *this Amphilochius is so impudent, as to say, that Nazianzene came in hast, savv, and fel vpon the blessed bodie, vvhen it vvas buried.* No syr he saith it not. These wordes, *vvhen it vvas buried,* be of your own false addition, they be not in this Amphilochius. Wherefore he was not impudent, that wrote thē not, but you were impudēt that put them in, & with the same so fowly bely him. For al this he may seme wise & circūspect ynough in his talke, mary you proue your self a false lyer in reprouing him.

M. Iew. by false addition corrupteth & falsifieth ẏ place which he impugneth.

If

If you deale so falsly with my Amphilochius, for so it liketh you to cal hi: you shal cause mē to geue more credite vnto his autoritie, then I claime to be geuen. Thus I haue shewed ẏ weaknesse of M. Iew. reasons which he bringeth to desproue this Amphilochius, & the falshed of his reportes. As for Amphilochius him selfe, be he as he is, I neither defend him, nor condemne him.

Ievvel.

VVe may novv the better beleue Homer, that Iuppiter vvith his Goddes vvente dovvne sometime for his pleasure to banket in Ethiopia. &cat.

Harding.

It hath euer ben the manner of heretikes to skoffe at miracles, visions, and apparitions, S. Ambrose sheweth, that the Arians, after ẏ one Seuerus in Millan, who had ben long blinde, miraculously recouered his sight at the touch of holy Martyrs reliques, would not beleue it, though it were most certainly knowen. As concerning visions, al seme ridiculous and foolish to some, saith S. Cyprian: sed vtique illis, qui malunt contra sacerdotes credere, quàm sacerdoti. But they be such, saith he, as had rather beleue against the Priestes, then beleue a Priest.

Heretikes haue euer mocked visions, and miracles. Ambro. in Sermo. 91. Cypr. li. 4. epist. 9.

But syr, you that compare the apparition of Christe with the poetical fiction of Iuppiters coming downe into the earth, thinke you it to be a mater al together vaine, and so to be laughed at? Trowe you that holy mē haue not sometimes for their comfort the benefite of such apparitions? wil you make Egesippus, who was so nigh the Apostles time, & S. Ambrose, false fablers, who constantly report how Christe appeared vnto S. Peter, as he was flying from Rome for feare of death? wil you scoffe at the whole Church, in which the sounde of these wordes is oftentimes hearde, Martinus Catechumenus hac me veste contexit.

Of visiōs and apparitions made to holy men.

Christe appered vnto S. Peter, as Egesippus, & S. Ambros do reporte.

Christe appeared to S. Martine.

Martine the Catechumen hath couered me with this garment? wil you scoffe at the learned Father Gregorius presbyter, whose autoritie you haue so much vsed in this article? If you discredite others, yet him I trowe you wil not refuse as a vaine fabler. Reade in him the life of S. Gregorie Nazianzene: and there you shal finde these very wordes. πολλάκις γοῦν καὶ χριστὸν ἑώρα ἐναργῶς ἐν ὕπνοις, καὶ ἐν μελέτῃ νυκτερινῇ ταύτην τῆς καθαρότητος λαμβάνων ἀντίδοσιν. that is to say. Many times he sawe Christe manifestly in his sleape, and in his night meditation, receiuing this rewarde for his pure life. If S. Gregorie Nazianzen sawe Christe many times in some recompense as it were of his purenesse. why may we not thinke the same of S. Basile, who in al vertue & holinesse of life by report of al was rather passing, then inferiour to Nazianzene?

The apparition of Christe to a good mā is a reward of purenesse.

Christe appeared to S. Gregorie Nazianzen.

Here could I say much for prouffe, that it is neither an incredible, nor strange, nor vnwonte thing, Christe, his Mother the blessed virgin Marie, Angels, Apostles, and other Saincttes, to appeare vnto men, and one liue man in a vision to appeare vnto an other liue man, as the holy mounke Johannes appeared vnto a godly woman, whereof S. Augustine speaketh, and disputeth how it might be, in his booke de cura pro mortuis agenda ad Paulinum: and this would I here doo, but that it would aske a larger treatise then this Article requireth, and that I stay not much vpon this vision of S. Basile set forth by this Amphilochius, what so euer he was. For in dede we haue no nede for prouffe of the Masse, to allege visions. It is and may be otherwise sufficiently proued.

Aug. de cura pro mort. agēda cap. 17.

The. xxxiiij Diuision.

This is the last Diuision of this Article, in which I allege for proufe of the Priestes sole receiuing at Masse, that M. Iewel and his companions cal priuate Masse, a place of S. Chrysostome out of the. 61. homilie ad populum Antiochenum. where complayning of the peoples slaknesse in receiuing their rightes, he saith, the Sacrifice is daily offred, the priestes stande at the aulter, but nullus est qui communicetur, there is not one (saith he) that wil be houseled. This place witnesseth with most cleare wordes, that Masse was daily celebrated (for therin the eternal Sacrifice of the Church, that is to say, the body and bloud of Christe is consecrated, offred, and receiued by the Priest) and that none came to receiue with the Priest. And so is it founde, that in S. Chrysostomes time long with in the terme of the first sixe hundred yeres, Masse was said and donne, though sometimes the Priest had no companie to receiue the Communion in the same place with him. This being proued, M. Iewel is duly required to yelde and subscribe. *Chrys. ho. 61. ad pop. Antioche.*

Against this, it stoode you vpon M. Iewel, to replie with reason, not to make your reader mery with scoffing. It is not vnknowen vnto you, that wynding vp of a mater, is by commō vse of speach made an English terme. wherefore your iesting at it toucheth not me so much as the language of your Countrie. Of Clew or twined thread, wherewith you make your selfe pleasant, there was no mention. If you would nedes shewe that you had a feat grace in iesting, you should haue taken iust occasion offred, and not breede the occasion of the whole sporte your selfe. As one said once in Rome of a mery Consul, *Winding vp of a mater.*

quàm ridiculum habemus consulem? I see it may as wel be said of you, quàm ridiculum habemus Ecclesiasten, what a sporting preacher haue we? But let vs heare, what you say.

Ievvel.

Here vvould I first knovve, vvhether M. Harding vvil rest vpon the bare vvordes of Chrysostome, or rather qualifie them somevvhat, and take his meaning. If he presse the vvordes precisely, as he semeth to doo, then did not Chrysostome him selfe communicate, for he vvas some body: and the plaine vvordes be, no body doth communicate. By vvhich vvordes doubtlesse Chrysostome him selfe is excluded, as vvel as others. And so there vvas no sole receiuing, nor any receiuing at al: and therfore no Priuate Masse.

Harding.

To satisfie your desire, I tel you for answere, that I wil rest vpon the wordes of S. Chrysostome, not bare, but taking also his meaning: which is to meane as he spake, and not contrary to his speach. Neither wil I the wordes so precisely to be pressed, that S. Chysostome him selfe by them should be made not to cōmunicate. Such precisenes is besides al reason. And your selfe pardy are not so simple, but you knowe, that in an vniuersal speach, the common rule taketh place, semper excipitur persona loquentis. Alwaies the party that speaketh is excepted: namely in such speaches as signifie an action not touching the speaker him selfe. As here, S. Chrysostom saing, that there was none to communicate, spake it of the cōmunicating of others with him, not of his owne receiuing of the Sacrifice which he had consecrated. Now you come to dispute vpon S. Chrysostomes meaning, and that by a gheasse of your owne vtterly vntrue, as here it shal appeare.

Ievvel.

It appeareth Chrysostomes purpose vvas, to rebuke the negligence of the people, for that of so populous a Citie they came to the holy communion in so smal companies. VVhich companies he in a vehemencie of speache by an exaggeration in respect of the vvhole, calleth no body. The like manner of speache is vsed also sometimes in the scriptures. S. Iohn saith of Christe, Testimonium eius nemo accipit. & c.

Harding.

You tel vs two thinges. The one, that S. Chrysostomes purpose was to rebuke the negligence of the people, for that they came to the Communion in smal companies. The other, that in a vehemencie of speache he calleth a smal companie by a cōparison to the whole, no body. The one you proue not, towardes the other you say somewhat, though to litle purpose. Touching the first, you say, it appeareth: And I say, it appeareth not. whether is more to be beleued, your yea, or my nay? If it appeare, as you say, then tel vs whereof it appeareth. which be the wordes, that shewe it? If you haue no such wordes in S. Chrysostome ỷ may seme to shew it, thē how doth it appeare? Or wil you say, it appeareth to you, when no man els can see it besides your self?

Verely it is cleare ỷ S. Chrysostomes purpose was, not to rebuke the negligence of the people for cōming to the Cōmunion in smal companies, as you beare vs in hande: but to withdrawe them from their euil custome of receiuing their rightes once in the yere, which was at Easter, and that though they were not duly and worthily prepared therefore, and to persuade them to receiue oftner. So to vnderstādhim, ỷ circumstance of the place, and his owne wordes do leade vs, whereof this saying, there is none that wil be houseled, doth immediatly depēde & folow. I see (saith he) great inequalitie of thinges among you. At other times when as for the most parte ye are in cleane life, ye come not (to receiue your rightes) But at Easter, though ye haue done somewhat amisse, yet ye come. O what a custome is this? O what a presumption is this? The daily Sacrfice is offered in vaine, we stand at the

What was S. Chrysostomes purpose.

Chryso. Hom. 61. ad pop. Antiochen.

aulter for nought, there is not one that wilbe houseled. What man of any iudgement is there, to whom these wordes of S. Chrysostome do not plainely report, what was his purpose in this sharpnes of speache? who seeth not how he rebuketh them for that they forbearing to receiue at other times, when they were in cleane life, they would receiue at Easter, yea though somewhat were amisse? wherein they folowed more the commō custome at that time vsed, thē considered vprightly, what the dutie of Christian people required. This he calleth inequalitie of thinges, this he calleth presumption. As in deede howe vneuen dealing is it, a man to forebeare the enioying of that great benefite, when he might worthely receiue it, and for customes sake to come vnto it, when he is vnworthy of it? to shunne it when it geueth life, and to take it, when it procureth damnation? And what a great presumption is it, a man to come to that holy table of the high kinge, not hauing on him his wedding garment? This inequalitie of thinges, this presumption, and peruersitie of custome, is that against which S. Chrysostomes special purpose was to speake.

Inequalitie of thinges.

If his mynde had ben to rebuke the negligence of the people, for that they came to the Communion in smal companies, that is to say, because the more parte of thē refrayned from comming vnto it: he would not haue called it a custome, nor a presumption. For custome hath his name of a thing oftentimes and vsually donne, and not of that a thing is omitted and not donne. Presumption likewise is of a thing donne rashly, vnreuerently, and vnworthily, which requireth great reuerence, feare, and honour, and is not so called, when a thing is lefte vndonne. Againe if his purpose had ben to rebuke them for their comming to the Communion in smal companies, then as he would haue commended some for that they

Custome.

Presumption

came

came, so he would haue blamed others, for that they came not.

And whereas you bring an example of a like phrase out of the Scripture, and also out of S. Chrysostome, in which a fewe are to be vnderstanded, though Nemo be expressed, it is to no purpose, onlesse you could proue, that S. Chrysostome founde fault with the fewnes of the Communicantes, and not with the euil custome of receiuing the Communion at Easter onely though they were not in worthy sorte disposed. For what if in S. John Nemo signifie a fewe, where it is said, Testimonium eius nemo accipit, wil it folow thereof that in this place also it must so signifie? Remember you not that examples serue to make cleare that is obscure, and not also to proue that is denied? Haue you forgoten the olde saying, Exempla rem ostendunt, non probant? First you should haue shewed, that in this very place Nemo is taken for smal companies, and then you might wel haue declared by other like examples of the Scriptures and Doctours, that the worde to importe that signification were not a thing vnwont and strange. Wherefore seing that (as it is now declared) S. Chrysostomes wordes conteine a rebuke not of the peoples comming to the Communion in smal companies, but of their vneuen dealing, and of their vngodly custome, in that they forebare to receiue the Communion at other times when their life was purer, and presumed to receiue at Easter, how impure soeuer they were: and seing there appeareth nothing whereby the daily receiuing of other Priestes and Deacons with the Prieste that daily celebrated the Sacrifice is clearely proued: I say stil, that this place of S. Chrysostome witnesseth the Priestes standing at the aulter, and the oblation of the Sacrifice, when none others communicated Sacramentally with him, which is that these men cal priuate Masse.

Iohn. 3.

Ievvel.

And albeit, this onely ansvvere compared vvith the manner of Chrysostomes eloquence, vvhich commonly is hoate and feruent, and vvith the common practise of the Churche then, may suffice a man more desyrous of truth, then of contention, yet I haue good hope, it may be proued, not vvithstanding M. Hardinges Nemo, *that Chrysostome neither vvas alone, nor could be alone at the holy Ministration, and therefore could say no priuate Masse.*

Harding.

You do wel and wisely to geue ouer your holde, and not to stand vnto your former Answere. Let it be graunted, that oftentimes S. Chrysostome speaketh in great heate against those, whose eares and hartes the custome of synne hath dulled, as becommeth a preacher to speake: wil you therfore charge him with an vntruth in this place, as making smal companies to be no body? But he vseth the like speach in an other homilie, and the Scripture speaketh likewise sometimes. Yet if you could allege a hundred such phrases, al they would not proue your conceiued meaning of this place. As concerning the practise of the Churche then, though very commonly some others wel disposed of the people or of the Clergie receiued with the Priest that sacrificed: Yet that proueth not but sometimes the Priest might receiue that he had offered alone, whereof S. Chrysostome here complaineth, not that they of Antioch came to the Communion in smal companies, but that many times they came not at al, for that is it he meaneth by his word οὐδείς, that is to say, nullus, none.

But what is the good hope you haue conceiued? Mary that it may be proued (say you) notwithstanding M. Hardinges Nemo, that S. Chrysostome neither was alone, nor

could

could be alone at *the holy Ministration,* and therfore could say no priuate Masse. what bring you the mater now from receiuing alone, to being alone? who spake of the Priestes being alone? Is not our question of the Priestes sole receiuing? why speake you of S. Chrysostomes not being alone?

Ievvel.

For if the vvhole companie of the laye people vvold haue forsaken him, yet had he companie sufficient of the Priestes and Deacons, and others of the Quiere. And if the vvhole Quiere vvoulde haue forsaken him, yet had he companie sufficient of the laye people: as it may be clearely proued.

Harding.

What nede is there to proue that no man denyeth? what if S. Chrysostome were not forsaken so of al companie, but that some or other were present, when so euer he said Masse? wil you thereof conclude, that he neuer said priuate Masse, as much to say, that at his Masse he neuer receiued the Communion alone? For that is it you vnderstand by a Priuate Masse, how so euer you iangle here. He saith not, I am destitute of companie, or that, no body is present at the celebration of the holy Misteries, but, οὐδ' εἰς ὁ μετέχων, nullus est qui participet, there is none to receiue with me. Your parte had ben substantially to proue, that S. Chrysostome & al other Priestes had euermore companies to receiue with them, when so euer they celebrated the daily Sacrifice, or that they forebare to do it for lacke of companies to be partakers of the Mysteries with them. Not being hable to proue this, you thought it best to proue an other mater, that no mā doubteth of and which is easy to be proued. Then thus you make your entrie into an vnnecessary, idle, & impertinent Common place.

Ievvel.

That there vvas then a greate number to serue in the Ministerie, it

Ignat. ad Trallian.

may diuersly vvel appeare. Ignatius calleth Presbyterium, *the sacred Colledge, the Councel and companie of the Bishop.*

Harding.

Who denieth, but that the Bishop had of olde time a companie about him in his Churche? So is it now in euery Bishops See, or Cathedral Churche. But this proueth not that alwaies they communicated sacramentally with him, when so euer he said Masse.

Ievvel.

Chrysostome him selfe in his Liturgie, saith thus. The Deacons bring the disshes vvith the holy bread vnto the holy Aulter, the rest carrie the holy Cuppes. By vvhich vvordes appeareth bothe a number of the Ministerie, and also prouision for them that vvould receiue.

Harding.

At certaine times the people receiued the Communion, it is not denyed. At such times the Deacons in semely wise brought breade, and wine vnto the Aulter to be consecrated. Neither is it denied, though this place proued it not, that Churches of olde time had Deacons and other Ministers in holy Orders, and that some prouision of bread and wine was made for them that receiued then the body and bloud of Christe vnder the formes of Bread & wine, as we see now prouision of Breade made at Easter and other feastes, when faithful and deuoute people be disposed to receiue their maker vnder the forme of bread. But that there was no Masse, or Sacrifice celebrated, in which such order was not taken for a companie of communicantes: that (say wee) by S. Chrysostomes Liturgie here alleged, nor by any other place that M. Jewel can bring, is yet proued.

Epist. Cornelij ad Fab. ex Euseb. lib. 6. cap. 23.

Ievvel.

Cornelius vvriteth, that in the Church of Rome, there vvere fourty and sixe Priestes, seuē Deacōs, seuē Subdeacons, fourty and tvvo Acolutes, Exorcistes,

stes, Readers and other officers of the Church, fiftie and tvvo: VVidovves, and other afflicted people that there vvere releued, a thousand fiue hūdred. Nazianzene complaineth of the nūber of the Clergie in his time, that they semed to be moe then the rest of the people. And therfore the Emperour Iustinian afteruvard thought it nedeful to abridg the number, and to make a lavve, that in the great Churche of Constantinople, vvhere Chrysostome vvas Bishop, there should not be aboue the number of three score Priestes, one hundred Deacons, forty vvemen, foure score and ten Subdeacons, one hundred and tenne Readers, and fiue and tvventy Singers.

Nazian. in Apologetico. In authēt. col. 1. tit. vt determinatus.

Harding.

Truth it is, there was a great companie of Clerkes, widowes, and other afflicted people in the time of S. Cornelius that blessed Pope and Martyr, belonging to the Church of Rome. What conclude you thereof? Because at those daies the Church had so many, wil it folow thereof, that they did alwaies receiue the Communion, when any Priest there offered the Sacrifice? We striue not with you for the presence of a companie, but we require you to proue, that the Mysteries were neuer celebrated, or to speake as now we speake, the Masse was neuer said, but when a companie receiued with the Priest. This place as it proueth not so much, so it sheweth manifestly how farre vnlike your new Congregation is to the Churche of that time, what difference there is betwen your Clergie & that Clergie, and how ẏ Churche then had the same degrees of holy Orders, that the Catholique Churche hath at this day.

In that Epistle of S. Cornelius to Fabianus Bishop of Antioche we finde the seuen Orders that in holy Church are genē, expressely named, which are these. Priestes, Deacons, Subdeacons, Acolutes, Exorcistes, Readers, Porters or waiters at the Churche dores, which worde you couered with your false

M. Iew. falsifieth S. Cornelius epistle.

translation of other Officers of the Churche, contrary to the Greke, where you found these two wordes, ἅμα πυλωροῖς, ỳ is, vnà cum hostiariis, least you should put the Reader in mynde of the iust number of the holy Orders of the Churche, which the Churche of your new Gospel vtterly contemneth, the Clergie whereof consisteth in manner al together of craftesmen whom after your owne deuise ye dubbe Ministers. That you allege of Nazianzene and Iustinian, proueth nothing, but that at that time the Clergy was great. It were good you would stand vpon the point, and leaue such nedelesse vagares. Now let vs vnderstand of al this what conclusion you inferre.

Ievvel.

Hereby vve may see, that Chrysostome being at Antioche in so populous a Citie, although he had none of the Lay people vvith him, yet coulde not be lefte alone.

Harding.

Is this the conclusion, whereunto you driue al that you haue alleged hitherto, that S. Chrysostome could not be alone? And how is that concluded? By witnesse of S. Cornelius the number of the Clergie in his time was great at Rome, so was it also in other places by reporte of S. Gregorie Natianzene. The Emperour also Iustinian abridged the number of the Clergie of Constantinople: what foloweth of al this, Ergo S. Chrysostome in the populous Citie of Antioche could not be lefte alone? what meane you M. Iewel, could he not be lefte alone at Antioch, because there were many Clerkes in the Church of Rome, and of Constantinople? what reason is this? where is your Logique? where is the sharpnesse of your witte? Although your argumẽt in this place be absurd & foolish, yet if we graunt it, what proue you thereby, but onely ỳ there was a companie present? But when will you shewe vs by any point of learning, that a

Prieste

priest might not Consecrate and offer the Sacrifice, except a companie receiued it with him? why doth he not allege S. Chrysostome, S. Augustine, S. Hierome, S. Ambrose, S. Basile, or some one of al the holy and learned Fathers, that wrote from the Apostles time vntil M. Luther blasted abroad this new Gospel, who affirmeth plainely, that Masse can not be said, or that the vnbloudy and external Sacrifice of the Churche can not be celebrated, onlesse a companie receiue with the priest in the same place? If the priest may not lawfully receiue alone, why doth he not allege one Father or one learned man olde or new, that is Catholike, who saith so? why doth he not shewe vs, where complaint was made by any Father, of the ceasing of the Daily Sacrifice for lacke of Communicantes? This were directly to the purpose. And men that take vpon them to defende any new Doctrine, and to impugne the olde so generally receiued, and so continually mainteined, as the Doctrine of the Churche concerning the Masse is, ought to shewe cleare and euident reasons, and such as could with no learning and contrary reason be disproued.

Ievvel.

Novv if vve say, that some of the priestes, Deacons, or other communicated vvith the Bishop, I tel them (saith M. Harding) boldely and vvith a solemne countenance, vvhich must nedes make good prouse, this is but a poore shifte, and vvil not serue their purpose.

Harding.

How so euer it becommeth a Superintendent to scorne and skoffe at my countenance, I tel you now againe no lesse boldely, then I tolde you before, that such answere is but a poore shift in dede, and wil not fully serue your purpose. Yet to say the truth, here you belye me. For I said not I tel them, which might be wel said: but we tel them, and that for modesties sake, foreseing

as it were, with what an Hickescorner I had to doo. But lying
Pag.31. I trow to this fellow, is accidens inseparabile. Neither yet
did I onely say so, but I added also a reason wherefore. which
reason you haue craftily dissembled, because you can not answer
it. Now let vs see what shifte you can make, that your answere pretending a sufficient companie of priestes and Deacons to receiue with euery priest that in any place saith Masse beside Cathedral Churches, seme not to be a poore shifte. Thus you say.

Ievvel.

But if it be true, it is rich ynough. If it agree vvith Chrysostomes ovvne meaning, it is no shifte, and therfore sufficiently serueth our purpose.

Harding.

Proue it to be true, then it shalbe rich ynough. Proue it to agree with S. Chrysostomes meaning, then it shalbe no shifte.

Ievvel.

And because he sitteth so fast vpon the bare vvordes, and reposeth al his hope in Nemo, if vve liste to cauil in like sorte, vve might soone finde vvarrant sufficient to ansvvere this mater, euen in the very plaine vvords of Chrysostome. For thus they lie. Frustra assistimus altari, *in vaine vve stande at the aulter. VVe stande saith he, and not I stande: and therfore includeth a number, and not one alone.*

Hardiug.

To presse the Doctours wordes with his meaning, that is not to cauil. To wrest the Doctour to that he neuer meant, as you do, making him say one thing, and meane an other, that in dede is to cauil. It is very vaine, that you claime aduantage of the plural number, because he saith, *vve stande*, and not I stande. As though he spake it not both of him selfe, and of many

Aduātage claimed of the plural number. *VVe stand.*

many other Priestes, that did the like, who in their seueral churches stoode oftentimes at the Aultare, and celebrated the Sacrifice, when they had no companie to receiue with them. S. Paule (you knowe) very oftentimes speaketh in the plural number, when he meaneth him selfe, and others, that attended the businesse of the Apostleship, though they were farre a sundre: as (for example) where he saith, Habemus thesaurum istum in vasis fictilibus. We haue this treasure in earthen vessels. 2. Cor. 4.

So S. Chrysostome, *VVe stande,* saith he, that is, I and others that be likewise priestes, stande at the Aultare, we offer the Daily Sacrifice, and yet, Nullus qui communicetur, there is not one that doth Communicate.

If you wil nedes haue, this worde of the plural number assistimus, we stande, to comprehend a number of others that stoode with S. Chrysostome at the aultare: yet that moueth not, that they receiued, onlesse you make vs beleue, that to stand at the Aultare is to receiue. Verely I maruel, how you dare stand so long vpon this place, in which you see so manifest a Testimonie for Aultares, which wickedlye ye haue throwen downe, and for the Daily Sacrifice of the body and bloud of Christe, which like Antichristes forerouners ye haue abolished.

A testimonie for aultares, and for the daily sacrifice

Iewel.

It is prouided by the Canons of the Apostles, that if any Bishop, or Priest, or Deacon, or any other of the Quiere, after the Oblation is made, do not receiue, onlesse he shevve some reasonable cause of his so doing, that he stand excommunicate. The like lavve in the Church of Rome vvas afteruvard renevved by Pope Anacletus.

Can. Apo. ca. 9. ἐκ τοῦ καταλόγου τοῦ ἱερατικοῦ.

Harding.

If by your false Translation, you make them to be of the Quiere, which by the Canons of the Apostles be

False translation.

Canon. Apost. ca. 17. οἰκέτιν ἐκ τοῦ καταλόγου τοῦ ἱερατικοῦ: thē who so euer hath maried a widow, a harlot, or a house maid, he can not be a Bishop, nor Priest, nor Deacon, no neither so much as of the Quiere, For so saith the. xvij. Canon of the Apostles Canons, ἢ ὅλως τοῦ καταλόγου τοῦ ἱερατικοῦ. If you stand to your translation, and to those Canons, where wil you place your false named Bishops, Priestes, and Deacons, which haue maried widowes, I wil not say which haue yoked them selues vnto harlottes?

But touching the Canons of the Apostles, they bound them onely that were of that first age. After that the number of Christian people was increased, the great rigour of them was remitted. Neither were al faithful persons that came to the common place of prayer, stil bound to receiue the Communion after the Oblation was made, vnder the paine of excommunication, as it is decred by those Canons. For at length it was decreed by. S. Fabian the Pope, that men should not be bound to Communicate oftener then thrise in the yeare, at Christmasse, Easter, and witsonday. The like Decree was made touching the Laie people, in the Councel of Agatha. Wherefore the Canons of the Apostles were no necessarie Lawe nor rule of the Church in S. Chrysostomes time. Yet by those Canons also as hard as they were, they of the Clergie vpon a reasonable cause, sometimes were excused for not receiuing the Communion, when the Oblation was made.

Canon. Apost. ca. 10. De cons. dist. 1. & si non. Concil. Agathen. ca. 18.

Anaclet. epist. 1. As for the Decree of Anacletus that you speake of, it is to be vnderstanded onely of those, that attended vpon the Bishop at the celebration of the Sacrifice, and that onely vpon solemne feastes, as I haue before declared.

Ievvel.

Cōcil. Nicen. ca. 14. *The Councel of Nice decreeth thus.* Accipiant Diaconi secundum ordinem post presbyteros ab Episcopis, vel a Presbytero Communio-

Communionem. *Let the Deacons in order after the priestes receiue of the Bishops, or of the priest the holy Communion.*

Harding.

This sheweth onely in what order the Deacons should receiue the Communion, it conteineth not a commaundement binding them at euery Oblation to receiue. How be it you haue parcially and vntruly alleged the wordes of this Decree, by taking parte for your purpose, and leauing out parte which maketh against you, and by which the whole may the better be vnderstanded. That Decree of the Nicene Councel truly alleged, hath thus. It is reported vnto the holy Councel, that in certain places, and cities, the Deacons do geue the Sacramentes vnto priestes. But this neither rule, neither custome hath delyuered vnto vs, that they who haue not power to offer the Sacrifice, should geue the Sacramentes vnto them that offer. (where this much is to be noted by the way, that by the most auncient and allowed Councel of Nice, the Oblation of the Sacrifice, and of such a Sacrifice as none haue power to offer but priestes, is anounched. It foloweth.) But this hath come vnto our knowledge, that certaine Deacons receiue the Sacramentes before the Bishops. Let al these thinges therfore be cut away, and let them receiue the holy Communion in order after rhe priestes, of the Bishop, or of a priest. In case there be no Bishop nor priest present, then let the Deacons bring it forth and eate it. By which wordes reseruation is proued, and that of one kinde, as reason geueth. For neither can wine be long kept, neither thereof would the Fathers of that Councel haue sayd, edant, let them eate: but edant & bibant, let them eate it, and drinke it, if they had meant both. As this Decree then proueth not that at euery Masse Deacons ought of necessitie to receiue the Sacrament, so it geueth vs a manifest witnesse of the Oblation of the Sacri-

M. Iew. corrupteth the Nicen Councel, by hewing and mangling.

Reseruation is proued bi this canon of the Nicen Councel, and that of one kinde, as it appeareth.

Witnesse of oblatiō.

fice, which is donne in the Masse, and of Reseruation, and that (as it appeareth) vnder one kinde. And so the Councel of Nice proueth the Catholike Doctrine, it proueth nothing for you. But let vs heare more of your proufes, that S. Chryso-stome could not say priuate Masse, and receiue alone, For that you haue taken in hande to proue.

Ievvel.

Concil. Carthag. 6. Ca.18. Concil. Laodicé. Ca.59. Concil. Toletan. 4. Ca.17.

Likevvise in the Councel of Carthage, Accipiant Diaconi, ex ordine Eucharistiam post Presbyteros, eis dante Episcopo, vel Presbytero. *Let the Deacons receiue the Comunion in order after the priestes, either the Bishop or the priest ministring it. So the Councel of Laodicea,* It is lawful onely for the priestes of the Church to enter into the place, where the aultare standeth, and there to Communicate. *So the Councel of Toledo,* Let the priestes and Deacons Communicate before the Aultare, the clerkes in the Quiere, and the people without the Quiere.

Harding.

To these Councels I answere as before. There is declared an order how the Deacons should receiue, there is no commandement geuen, when and how often they should receiue. Againe it is to be noted, that these Councels, specially the two former,

Concil. Laodicé. Ca.19.

speake of the manner and custome of the Churches, in which the bishops offered the Sacrifice, who in solemne feastes, when they celebrated, had certaine priestes and Deacons about them, who also Communicated with them, according to S. Anacletus Decree. It was not so in other places, where there was not such number of Priestes and Deacons. For to beleue that such lacke was in some places, we are perswaded by the Decree of S. So-

De Con. dist.1. vt illud.

ter: who ordeined that when a priest celebrateth Masse, he haue an other priest by him to supply his Office, if any suddaine infirmitie happen. But where? in euery place? No, but vbi cleri copia suffragatur, that is as much to say, where there is such a

num-

number of Priestes, that if one fal sicke, an other maye be present to performe that is to be done. Which had ben absurd so to haue said, onlesse in some certaine places, there had ben but one priest.

Againe the Decrees of these prouincial Councels binde not generally. For els no priest might go to Church before the bishop go. For so it is Decreed by the Councel of Laodicea here mentioned. And so where there is no bishop, there should no priest come to Churche. And so it was not to be alleged against priuate Masse. Concil. Laodicē. Ca 56.

Ievvel.

Nicolaus Cusanus vvriting vnto the Clergie and learned of Bohemia, hath these vvordes: Hoc est singulariter attendendum, quod Sacerdotes nunquam sine Diacono celebrabant: & in omni Missa Diaconus de manu sacerdotis accepit Eucharistiam sub specie Panis, & Sacerdos de manu Diaconi Calicem. *This thing is specially to be noted, that the priest did neuer celebrate vvithout a Deacon: and that in euery Masse the Deacon receiued the Sacrament in the kinde of bread, at the priestes hande: and the priest the cuppe at the Deacons hande.* Nic. Cusanus ad Cerum & literatos Bohomiæ.

Harding.

This place is of smal authoritie. First I finde it farre otherwise reported in the booke that was Printed at Basile euen among thē of your own sect. Vew the place who wil in the print of Henricus Petri, Anno. M.D.XLV. and he shal finde it altogether otherwise then you haue alleged. It is to be sene Pagina 854 in fine paginæ. Againe though it were as you reherse the wordes, yet is Nicolaus Cusanus a late writer. He lyued about a C. yeres past. If you would stād to his iudgemēt touching not only this Article of the Masse, but also al other your Articles, in which you and your felowes vary from the Catholike Church: we would sone say vnto you, ye are welcome home, In that Cusanus epist. 7. ad Bohemos.

Cusanus epist. 7. ad Bohemos.

very Epistle, yea in this very place he proueth Communion vnder one kinde against the Jacobellians. If you folowe his autoritie in that, you may be the bolder to require vs to heare him in this. If you contemne him in that, and in a number of other Articles: what reason is it, you should bynde vs to stand to his autoritie in this? And make the best you cā of this place, yet by it you can not proue a Communion lawful by your owne tradition: for you teach that it is not a sufficient Communion, except there be three that receiue with the priest at least. But what so euer he say, that is beside that the Church obserueth generally, concerning certaine olde customes: we wil so farre beleue him, as he proueth it. If he proue it not, we may reasonably suspende our assent, vntil you or some other proue it for him. Wheras you exclude vs from alleging al that wrote without the first sixe hundred yeres, it is not euen dealing you should be admitted to take your aduantage of euery thing that is without proufe reported by al that euer wrote sithens the Apostles time to this present age.

Answer to the place of Cusanus.

Yet least you should crake of the force of this place alleged out of Cusanus, I answer, that it is to be vnderstanded onely of the custome of Cathedral Churches, where priestes had alwaies Deacons attending vpon them at the holy Oblation, and of those Masses, which were celebrated with solemnitie in the high and principal Feastes. Which manner disproueth not but that in Oratories and other Churches, where such number of clergie was not stil resident, Masse might vpon necessitie be said, to recorde the memorie of our Lordes death, without any such seruice of a Deacon at al. Example whereof I alleged here before out of Leontius writing of the Masse, which the blessed man S. John surnamed the Merciful Patriarke of Alexandria celebrated in his Oratorie.

Ievvel.

Ieuvel.

Chrysostome him.selfe in the Liturgie,that commonly beareth his name, foloweth the same order. After that the Priestes haue receiued (saith he) *the Archedeacon commaundeth the deacons to come forth, and they so coming receiue, as the Priestes did before. This was the very order of Chrysostomes Masse, touching the Clergie, and that by Chrysostome him selfe.*

Harding.

This witnesseth, they did so in the Cathedral or metropolitan Churche in Constantinople at solemne feastes, when the Bishop him selfe did celebrate a solemne Masse, when the Archedeacon attended vpon him, & gaue order what the inferiour Deacons should doo. But that this was donne at al times, and in al places when soeuer and wheresoeuer the Masse was said, and that they were bounde thus to doo, (whereby S. Chrysostome could at no time possibly receiue the Communion alone no not when he was a priuate Priest at Antioche): this much by the wordes of the Liturgie can not be proued. Had euery Parrish Churche and Chappel within the large Diocesse of Constantinople an Archedeacon? If it had not, and if the Archedeacon were attending vpon the Bishop, or some other Priest, that did the Bishops stede: this place cā not be alleged, as to declare what was the order in euery Church, where Masse was said, but what was the order in the Cathedral Church.

How be it these wordes be not at al in S. Chrysostomes Greke Liturgie, nor in the translation of Erasmus, ẏ is nearest vnto the Greke. But they are the words only of the Rubrice of a Greke Masse booke, which one Leo Thuscus in the time of Emanuel Emperour of Constantinople turned into Latine. I maruel that M. Jewel would allege S. Chrysostomes Liturgie or Masse, seing that he refused it before, and would not stand to it. Thus he saith, and vnsaith, alloweth and condemneth, what

M. Iew. now seeketh helpe at S. Chrysostomes Massebooke, whose Masse before he refused for witnesse of the Sacrifice.

him list for better shifting of the mater, that is presently handled.

If I should folowe him herein, and take for myne aduantage what so euer semeth to sownde on our side, I could out of this very place, where he founde these wordes concerning ŷ receiuing of the deacons with the Priest, allege the wordes put immediatly before, that seme to make a cleare prouse of the priuate Masse. For there it is said thus. Deinde Sacerdos sumit corpus Dominicum, si solus fuerit. After that the Priest receiueth our lordes body, if he be alone. If he be alone at ŷ aulter, & receiue alone, thē hath he donne ŷ, which these men cal priuate Masse. And so far is priuate Masse proued by S. Chrysostome him selfe. But whether the deacons, or the people receiue afterward or no: ŷ Oblation is made, Sacrifice is perfitely done, & so the Masse is done, by what name so euer it be called, neither can ŷ which is afterward done, alter the nature & cōdition of that was before done. So whether any others receiue with the Priest or no, yet that which the Priest hath donne is the Masse. And as if others receiue, that maketh not the Sacrifice publike or common, so if they receiue not, that maketh it not priuate. For in dede, as I haue before said, there is no Masse priuate in respect of the Sacrifice that is offered, of which specially it is named. That M. Iewel calleth priuate Masse, is none other but the Priestes priuate receiuing.

An apparent testimonie for priuate Masse in S. Chrysostomes Liturgie.

Ievvel.

Novv let M. Harding iudge vprightly, vvhether these shiftes be so poore as he vvould make them.

Harding.

I iudged these to be but poore shiftes before. Now againe the more I weigh & consider thē, the poorer I iudge them. And al others ŷ be learned and can iudge, yea M. Iewel him selfe (if he cā iudge vprightly of ought that maketh against him) I dout not, wil iudge the same. Litle cause had he thus to bragge.

But

But here I must require the Reader to take ỹ paines to read, what I haue said in this place of my boke. which if he do, he may soone perceiue, what is that I cal a poore shifte, & for what cause I cal it so. And thus it is. whereas to auoide this place of s. Chrysostome, saying there was none ỹ would be houseled, when the daily Sacrifice was offered, if the Gospellers by way of ghesse would say, ỹ the Priestes & deacons cōmunicated daily with him ỹ offered, though none of the people did: then we tel them say I (& not I tel thē as M. Iewel falsly reporteth ỹ place) ỹ this poore shifte wil not serue their purpose. And there I shewe good cause why. For (say I) though they say ỹ in the great Church of Antioche some sufficiēt number alwaies cōmunicated with ỹ Priest that said Masse, where many Priests & deacons were, which neither being denied they shal euer be able to proue: what may be thought of many thousand other Churches abroad in the world, where ỹ Priest ỹ celebrated Masse, had not alwaies in readinesse a sufficient number of other Priests & deacons to receiue with him, and so to make vp a ful Communion? Of such Churches it must be said, that there either the Sacrifice ceassed, and that was not donne, which Christe commaunded to be donne in his remembrance, which is not to be graunted: or that the memorie of our lords death was oftentimes celebrated of ỹ Priestes without tarying for others to cōmunicate with thē, & so had these Churches priuate Masse, as the Churches now adaies haue. Thus there. pag. 31.

For this cause I cal that surmised answere a poore shifte, as I might right wel doo. For by it the force of the obiection is not taken away. This much could M. Iewel craftily dissēble, & passe ouer wͭ silence, & vttereth a long processe for proufe ỹ the clergie alwaies receiued with S. Chrysostome. Neither that can he proue sufficiently, and though he could, yet my reason remaineth vnanswered. For if he had cause to complaine of lacke of Cōmunicantes at Antioch, how much more cause had the Priestes of other lesser Churches to complaine thereof?

At length M. Iewel seeing him selfe not yet to haue proued sufficiently, that the Clergy of bounden duetie receiued the Communion alwaies, where so euer a Priest said Masse, he turneth his tale, and speaketh of the people, and would his Reader to beleue, that there was at euery Oblation of the Sacrifice a number of the people receiuing with the priest, whereby it might follow that S. Chrysostome could not receiue alone, when he said Masse.

Ievvel.

Chrysostome in diuerse places semeth to diuide the vvhole multitude into three sortes, vvhereof some vvere Penitent, *some* Negligent, *and some* Deuoute.

Harding.

If S. Chrysostome haue in diuerse places made such a diuisiō of ẏ whole people into these three sorts, as you say, you should haue done wel for your credites sake, to haue directed vs by your quotations (of which in maters of smal weight you are not spareful) to some of those places, that by conference we might see whether you dealt plainely or no. Now your other dealings be euery where found so vntrue, that for good cause you be suspected. Yet to saue your credite, for so much as this is but your vncertaine gheasse, you do wel to say, Chrysostome semeth to diuide. Such doubtful seeming maketh smal proufe. Whether he euer so diuided the people or no, I know not, certaine it is, ẏ of them som did their open penance, who were named Pœnitentes, some were Negligent, & some were Deuoute, as of men some be white, some be blacke, and some be browne. Many such diuisions may soone be made, But to what ende bring you this coniecture?

Ievvel.

Iewel.

The Penitent vvere commaunded avvay, and might not communicate. The Negligent sometime departed of them selues, and vvould not cōmunicate. The Deuoute remained, and receiued together.

Harding.

That such as were enioyned publique penaunce were not admitted to receiue the Cōmunion, it can not be denied. What you say of the Negligent, it is your owne, neither maketh it matter greatly, what you say of them. They that departed of them selues, and would not presume to receiue, because they fealt some secret grudge in conscience, for that, they are not to be reputed for negligent, but rather for reuerent, and such as feared God. And so might they be deuoute, though they departed, and receiued not. But the Deuoute say you remained, and receiued together, Thus you say, but you proue it not. And though you were able to proue, they did so sometimes, which is not to be denied: yet if they omitted to receiue at certaine times, then is priuate Masse confessed. So that now your part was to proue, that at euery Masse the Deuoute receiued, and that there was neuer any Masse for the first six hundred yeares, but a Deuoute companie receiued the Communion at it, which you shal neuer be able to proue.

Ievvel.

Novv that the Deuoute remained stil vvith Chrysostome the vvhole time of the holy Mysteries, it is plaine by the very same place, that M. Harding here allegeth for his purpose.

Harding.

Here you trauaile much to proue that the Deuoute remained at the holy Mysteries. I pray you Syr who denied it? If no man denied it, what meane you to dwel so long in it? Be it graunted you, they remained, how proue you that they receiued?

wander not abroad, come close to the point, bring vrgent reasons, bring not your vncertaine gheasses. Thus you would seme to proue it.

Ievvel.

Ad popul. Antiochen hom. 61.

For thus Chrysostome saith vnto the people, Thou art come into the Churche, and hast song praises vnto God with the rest, and hast confessed thee selfe to be one of the worthy in that thou departedst not forth with the vnworthy. *By these vvoordes he shevveth that some vvere vvorthy, and some vnvvorthy: that the vnvvorthy departed, and the vvorthy remained.*

Harding.

In the Apostles age and long after, during the time of persecution, the deuoute and holy people remained at the celebration of the Mysteries, and receiued. In processe of time, and after that peace was procured to the Churche through that the Emperours became Christians, which came to passe long before S. Chrysostomes time: the peoples deuotion slaked, and though they came to the Churche, and were present at the Sacrifice, yet for the more parte they receiued not: and in the East Churche it was growen vnto a custome, that commonly they receiued but at Easter onely, and that though they were not then best prepared, which is the thing that S. Chrysostome complaineth of. They that remained, shewed them selues outwardly as though they were worthy. But their remaining is no necessary Argument of their receiuing. For euen in that Homilie the contrary is auouched immediatly vpon the wordes by M. Jewel alleged. Quomodo mansisti, neq; participas de mensa? How hast thou taried (saith he) and doest not partake of the table? which M. Jewel craftily and falsly nipped away from the sentence, because he saw they made cleare against him. Such sinceritie is in these sincere Gospellers. Now then for al that he hath brought hitherto,

Homil. eadem.

M. Jew. nippeth S. Chrysostom.

therto, he concludeth no more but that the people remained at the holy Mysteries, that they receiued at euery celebration, he is not able to conclude. And so there was Masse, when ẏ people receiued not. Of al this directly he can gather nothing against the offering of ẏ daily Sacrifice without companie receiuing ẏ Communion with ẏ priest, which thei cal priuate Masse. And because ẏ Scripture hath no cōmaundement binding ẏ laie folke to receiue the blessed Sacrament oftentimes, therfore S. Chrysostom vseth not wordes of commaundement vnto them, but only of exhortation, which he would haue vttered otherwise, if it had been expressely commaunded by Scripture.

M. Iew. patcheth peeces of S. Chrysostomes sentences together, & thereby corrupteth and falsifieth his meaning.

Iewel.

And againe in the same Homilie he saith, The Deacon standing on high, calleth some to the Communion, and putteth of some: thrusteth out some, and bringeth in some. *Chrysostome saith,* some are called, *and* some are brought in * *to receiue with the Priest. Where then is now M. Hardinges Nemo?*

The. 195. vntruth. S. Chrysostome saith not so.

Harding.

You make your selfe mery like a pleasant Diuine with the terme Nemo, and cal it *M. Hardinges Nemo*: wherein you do S. Chrysostome wrong, for the worde wherupon I grownd is his, it is not mine. This ẏ you allege here, was not done at al times, when so euer any Priest offered the daily Sacrifice, nor in euery Church: but at certaine solemne feastes specially at Easter, and in Cathedral churches, & where els a nūber of Priestes & Deacons were alwaies remaining. S. Chrysostom in ẏ place out of which you pieced this allegation, declareth the manner that the Deacons vsed at Easter chiefly, and at other high feastes, when the people generally, or for a great parte, receiued the Communion. That this custome was ordinarie at euery celebration of the Sacrifice, of his woordes it can not necessarilie be gathered.

M. Iew. hath litle cause here so to triumph.

He mangleth & cutteth his Authors sentences.

And whereas you make S. Chrysostome to say, that *some are* (by the Deacon) *called*, and *some are brought in*, and thereupon triumph as though you had wonne the feelde, *Vvhere then is novv M. Hardinges nemo?* I must tel you, y͏ͤ smal occasion of such a vaine bragge had ben geuen you, if you had not fowly mangled the sentence, and cut away certaine wordes, that disclose the whole meaning of S. Chrysostome. A man that readeth but your bare wordes, would thinke the Deacon brought in some by the hande or otherwise, to receiue with the Priest, for so you frame your tale. But S. Chrysostome reporteth y͏ͤ mater thus. The Deacon standing vpright in the sight of al the people, and crying out alowde, in that dreadful silence, some he calleth, and some he putteth of, non manu hoc faciens, not doing this with his hand, but with his tongue more effectuously, then with his hand. For that worde (he meaneth this worde Sancti, holy) falling into their eares, euen as a hand driueth out some and bringeth in others. And to signifie what manner a driuing out and bringing in this was, he saith afterward more plainely. Stat apud nos & nunc Preco, nō capite quenque tenens & producens, sed omnes pariter interiori detinens capite. Among vs also now (at the great assemblies) standeth the Cryer, not holding euery one & bringing him forth by the head, but staying altogether by y͏ͤ inward head.

Chrysost. ad popul. Antiochē. Hom. 61.

what was ment by the Deacons crie, Sancta sanctis.

Deceiue your Reader no more M. Iewel, with hewing away of that which declareth the truth in any doubt. The crie of the Deacon sounding in their eares, Sancta sanctis, holy things for the holy, gaue warning that they came not vnworthily to that holy table: as it required them to be holy that came, which was a bringing in, so it fraid away and excluded them, who fouͤd them selues in conscience vnholy and vnworthy. So that this bringing in, and thrusting out, was altogether spiritual. Of al which S. Chrysostome made mention, onely to set before the

peoples

peoples eyes, how none but holy and worthy might be admitted to receiue those holy mysteries. He speaketh not in expresse wordes of the peoples communicating with him: but quite contrarywise he rebuketh their once coming in the yere, not so much for that they came but once, as for that they came euen then also vnworthily, or els soone after Easter fel vnto their olde disorder of life againe.

Ievvel.

Chrysostome saith, Some are called, *and* some are brought in *to receiue vvith the priest. VVhere then is novv M. Hardinges Nemo?*

Harding,

S. Chrysostom saith not, some are brought in *to receiue vvith the priest. To receiue vvith the priest,* is your owne addition. And although the Deacon made his solemne proclamation, by which he called the people to come forth and receiue, vpon high and solemne feastes, as at Easter, Witsonneday, Christmasse, Epiphanie. &c: yet at sundry other times might the priestes stand at the aultare, and offer the Daily Sacrifice, when none came to receiue, as here he maketh cōplaint. And so nowe S. Chrysostomes *Nemo,* whereat after your scoffing manner you ieast, calling it M. Hardinges *Nemo,* hath his place.

M. Iew. falsifieth S. Chrysostome by wordes of his owne addition.

S. Chrysostomes Nemo hath his place.

Ievvel.

*Verely if there vvere some people vvith the priest, then vvas there no place for no body: If no body receiued, then is it not true that Chrysostome * saith, that some receiued.*

The. 196. Untruth. S. Chrysostome saith not there that some receiued.

Harding.

Though there were some people present with the Priest, when he celebrated, yet might it be, that none receiued the Sacrament with him, as S. Chrysostome by his complaint signifieth. And so was there place for no body. And though no body received, yet S. Chrysostome said truth, for he said not, that some received, as you report him vntruly. It were better you were no body, then thus to teache false Doctrine, belying euery body.

Ievvel.

Here of a false principle, M. Harding, as his vvont is, gheasseth out the like conclusion: If there vvere so fevve Communicantes in that populous Citie of Antioche, vvhere the scriptures vvere daily expounded, then it is likely in Countrie Churches there vvere none at al. This argument hangeth onely by likelyhoode, as do the reast of his making: and being set in order it standeth thus. There vvas no Priuate Masse in the great Citie of Antioche: Ergo, there vvas priuate Masse in the Countrie. Surely (good reader) this is a very country argument, vvhat so euer it seme to M. Harding.

Harding.

If the principle be false, why haue you not by good reason disproued it? That you replie out of S. Chrysostome in Acta Apost. Hom. 45. concerning them of Constantinople, is beside the purpose, for I speake of Antioche. If my wonte be to gheasse out Conclusions, how is it, that you haue filled your boke with so litle certainty and assured mater, but altogether with light and vnsauery pelse? My Countrie argument shal seme probable to the wiser sorte of ỹ Citie, I doubt not, if it be thoroughly weighed and considered. Because you haue weighed it with false balance, and taken away parte of the weight, who liste to weigh it better, thus in my booke it is reported. See reader, and iudge.

Fol. 30. b Now if Chrysostome had cause to complaine of the peoples slaknesse in coming to the Communion, in that great and populous Citie of Antioche, where the scriptures were daily expounded and Preached, where Discipline and good order was more straightly exacted, where in so great number some of likelyhode were of more Deuotion then others: what is to be thought of many other litle townes and villages through the world, where little litle preaching was hearde, where discipline slaked, where the number of the faithful being smal, and they occupied altogether in worldly affaires, fewe gaue good ensample of Deuotion to others? Doubtlesse in such places was much lesse resorte of the people at the Masse time, to receiue the Sacrament with theyr Priestes. Thus there.

Now onlesse you wil say, there were moe wel disposed and deuout people in euery village & smal parrish, then in the great Citie of Antioche, of reason you must graunt, that if there wāted number of Communicantes at Antioche, much more it wanted in some parrish churches. If it were so, then it foloweth, that either they had the Sacrifice without a companie receiuing with the priest, which you make to be priuate Masse, or that commonly they had no Sacrifice at al, which is not to be graunted. For abroade out of the great Cities Christen people had then their ordinarie synaxes, that is, meetinges and assemblies, holydaies & Seruice, whereof the Masse was the chiefe, as it may wel be proued by sundry auncient Councels. And thus is the weight of my Countrie argument, (as M. Iewel iesteth) heuier, then that it may so easily be lifted away by his light scoffe.

Iewel.

And further vvhereas to aduance the Citie, *and to abase the Countrie *he saith, the people in* Cities *vvere Daily taught by open sermons, here in he must nedes be content, that his gheasse geue place vnto the truth. For Chrysostom him selfe saith farre othervvise. Thus he speaketh vnto the people of the* Citie: Dum per hebdomadem semel vocamus vos. &c. *(see the place Reader.) I note not this for that I misselike vvith daily preaching, but for that *vntruth so boldly presumed should not passe vntouched.*

The. 197. Untruth. I say not so, let my booke be sene.

Pag. 91.

The. 198. Untruth. It is no Untruth, I speake it only of Antioch.

Harding.

Nay here rather must M. Iewel be content to hear, that his dealing is first very false. For S. Chrysostō hath no such saying at al

M. Iew. vseth false allegatiō.

neither in Acta hom.45.neither in Matth.hom.5.as he hath caused his booke to be quoted: next, very vniust, and vncourteous, so bitterly to charge me with vntruth, where none is. For if S. Chrysostome haue any such place, very like it is, that it maketh more against him then with him, els by his false quotation he would not haue lead the reader from it. And yet for the vntruth as he calleth it, to be tryed out, reade my boke ouer againe and againe gentle Reader, and (trust me) thou shalt no where finde the wordes, with which M. Iewel burtheneth me. If he make me to say what pleaseth him, what maruel is it, if he blame me, where no fault is? If this then be an vntruth, it is M. Iewels vntruth, verely myne it is not.

Ievvel.

The.199. Vntruth. I say not so. This is altogether falsified.

*Yet *saieth M. Harding, in smal countrie Churches either the priest let cease the Daily Sacrifice, or els he receiued alone. But the Daily Sacrifice ceassed not: for then that had ben left vndone, that Christe commaunded to be donne: Ergo, there vvas Priuate Masse. O M. Harding, is it not poßible, your doctrine may stande vvithout lyes? So many vntruthes, in so litle roome, vvithout shame of the vvorlde, vvithout feare of God? VVhere did Christe euer commaunde you to make your Sacrifice? By vvhat commißion? By vvhat vvordes? VVhere did Christe vvil you to doo it euery day? VVhere did Christ euer cal it the Daily Sacrifice? Or vvhere euer learned you that the remembrance perteineth more to the priest, then to the people? &c.*

The.200. Vntruth. I say it not, it is falsly imputed vnto me.

Harding.

M. Iew. corrupteth and falsifieth my wordes & my reasōs.

You falsifie my wordes, and set forth my reasons to disaduantage, and then you make your outcrie, and say, *O M. Harding. &c.* But if the Reader wil be indifferent, and peruse what I say in dede, and not what you report of me, he shal fynde you a false Merchant I doubt not, and so be moued on the other syde to crye out, O M. Iewel, what false partes be these? Hath your aduersarie the truth so farre on his syde, that you can not replie,

but

but with falsifying his wordes, and misreporting his reasons? Neither is this spoken of this place onely, but in general of his whole booke.

And Syr demaunde you, where Christe euer commaunded vs to doo this Sacrifice? If you were a member of Christes Churche, I would say vnto you as Christe said to Nicodemus: Are you a Doctour in Israel, and knowe not this? If telling it would euer haue donne you good, you would not now so blasphemously haue asked it by way of contempt. For the auncient and holy Fathers, Martyrs, and Confessours, that from the Apostles time to our dais haue writtē, haue euery one most plainly tolde it you. And yet you beleue it not: at least whereas once you beleued it, now you are departed from it. Whereas once you confessed it, and witnessed it with your hand writing, before a multitude of learned men in the Uniuersitie of Oxford, now with hand and tongue you impugne it. So of a Iewel, you are become a Iulian. Ioan.3.

For the Christian Readers sake, I make this brief answer to your demaunde. Christe at his last supper commaunded his Apostles, and their successours to offer this Sacrifice of the Aultare (for so S. Augustine calleth it) saying, Doo ye, or make ye this in my remembrance. So hath the holy ghost euer taught the Church by the mouthes and pennes of the Fathers: of whom many haue confirmed the same Doctrine with their bloude. Because I haue spoken hereof before, and more is hereafter to be spoken in confutation of the Replie vpon the. 17. Article, where it is specially treated: fewe testimonies may suffice in this place. The making of the Sacrifice, was instituted and commaunded at Christes last Supper. Mat.26.

S. Dionysius that blessed bishop and Martyr, who learned the truth of S. Paule him selfe, wryteth thus. Wherefore the Bishop both reuerently and according vnto his bishoply office, after the holy praises of Gods workes, excuseth him self, for that he Testimonies for the Sacrifice. *Dionys.ec. hier.part. 1.ca 3.*

offereth vp the healthful Sacrifice which is aboue his degree, first crying out vnto him in seemely wise, Tu dixisti, hoc facite in meam commemorationem. Thou hast said the worde, Do ye this in my remembrance. The sense whereof is this, as though the Bishop should say vnto god. Verely I should not be so hardy as to offer the Sacrifice vnto thee my Lord God, except, that I should do it, with these wordes thou hadst commaunded me.

Christ said. Doo this. &c.

The holy Martyr and Bishop S. Ireneus, who was nigh the Apostles time, saith likewise speaking of this vnbloudy Sacrifice: Christe tooke that which is by creation bread, and gaue thankes, saying, this is my body. And the cuppe likewise which is of a creature that is with vs, and confessed it to be his bloud, and taught vs the newe Oblation of the newe Testament, which the Church receiuing it of the Apostles, offereth vp vnto God ouer the whole worlde.

Iren. cōtra hæreses. lib. 4. ca. 32

Christe taught the Sacrifice.

If in the Sacrifice, which is Christe, (saith S. Cyprian) none but Christ be to be folowed, Verely it behoueth vs to obey and doo that, which Christ hath done, and which he hath cōmaunded to be done. For if Iesus Christ our Lord and God be the highest priest of God the Father, and if he first haue offred Sacrifice vnto God the Father, and commaunded this to be made in remēbrāce of him: then that priest doth the stede of Christ truly, which foloweth that as Christe did, and then he offereth a true and ful Sacrifice vnto God the Father in the Churche, if he begyn so to offer, as he seeth Christe him selfe to haue offred.

Cyprian. *lib. 2. epi. 3.*

Christe hath commaunded the Satrifice to be donne.

A true and ful Sacrifice.

Here haue we, that Christ is the Sacrifice, ẏ he Sacrificed himself, that he is to be folowed of priestes, in that which he did, & cōmaunded to be done, that this is a true & ful Sacrifice offred vnto God in the Church. what can be said more plainely?

To these three blessed and learned Martyrs, let vs ioyne S. Chrysostome a blessed Confessour, who wrote the whole order & seruice

seruice of the Masse in which this Sacrifice is offred. Thou O Lord (saith he) hast ordeined the rite of Sacrifices, and hast deliuered vnto vs the celebration of this solemne and vnspotted Sacrifice, as being the Lorde of al. &c. I besech thee therfore looke vnto me a synner, and thy vnprofitable seruaunt, purge my soule and hart of euil conscience, and make me meete with the vertue of thy spirite, and grace of thy priesthod, that I may stande at this thy holy table, and consecrate thy holy and immaculate body, and pretious bloud. For to thee I come. &c. And suffer, that these giftes may be offred vnto thee of me a synner, and thy vnworthy seruaunt. For thou arte he that offerest, and arte offred, both that takest and geuest, Christ our God. Lo Christ is the Sacrifice that we offer as S. Cyprian said, he is the offrer, and the thing offred, he both taketh the Sacrifice of vs, and geueth the Sacrifice to vs. He hath instituted the rite and manner, and hath deliuered vnto vs the celebration of this Sacrifice. And this hath he done, as the Lord of al. For els no man could of his owne power and auctoritie haue ordeined this so high and so diuine a thing.

Christ hath ordeined the sacrifice. Chryso. in Liturgia.

Christ offereth, and is offred.

After this he acknowlegeth the making of this Sacrifice to be Christes commaundement, for immediatly after consecration he saith thus, Memoriam igitur agentes salutaris huius mandati. &c: therfore we calling to remembrance, or performing the memorie of this healthful commaundement, of al thinges donne for vs, of thy Crosse, sepulchre, resurrection, &c. At length also he commeth to make his prayer for the dead, and for the quicke, and saith: Remember (O Lorde) al them that be a sleape in the hope of resurrection and life euerlasting, and make them to be at rest, where the light of thy countenance is seene. Now cal no more vpon vs M. Iewel so malapertly to shew you, where and by what wordes Christ cōmaunded vs to celebrate this Sacrifice.

S. Chrysostom expressely calleth the sacrifice a Commaundement.

S. Chrysostome praieth for the dead at his Masse.

you see what worthy Fathers they be , that haue auouched it, and vpon what grounde they haue donne it.

M. Iew. demaundeth malapert and needelesse questions.

To your other captious questions, I answere negatiuely. What so euer Christe would vs to do touching the diuine Oblation, that it be made by ech particular priest euery day: it is not so expressed in Scripture. Neither that euer he called it the Daily Sacrifice. What nede had you, or what moued you to aske these questions? And who euer said, the remembrance of Christes death perteineth more to the Priest, then to the people? If no man euer said these thinges, what spite is there in you, so odiously to demaunde of vs these questions, as though they apperteined to our Doctrine? Touching this last, the people is bound to remember Christes death, as wel as the priestes: but to do this holy Ministerie, and to celebrate this high Sacrifice, to consecrate the body and bloud of Christe, and to offer the same in cōmemoration or remembrance of Christes death, it belongeth specially to priestes, and though with the vowe also of the faithful people, yet by the Ministerie of the priestes onely is this donne, to whom it is said, Doo ye this in my remembrance.

The people is boūd to remember Christes death, ỳ priestes are bound by celebration of the Sacrifice to bring the same to remēbrāce

After this, as though your Conscience gaue you, that you should be ouerthrowen in the other questiōs, you renue the feeld as it were, & come in with a new band of vaine questions cōcerning Daily Masse, as though if we could sufficiently proue the Masse, yet we should sticke at the daily Masse. Therfore you say.

A new band of vain questions.

Ievvel.

VVho euer commaunded your priest to say your daily Masse? VVhat lavve, vvhat Decree, vvhat Decretal, vvhat Legantine, vvhat prouincial? Or vvhat priest euer vvas there, that said it Daily?

Harding.

Here is much a doo, but answer is sone made. Though no one Priest euer said it Daily, yet is it, and long hath it ben euery day said by sundry priestes, verely within the first

six

six. C. yeres, was very often said and celebrated, and thereof it is called, not the daily Masse, but the daily Sacrifice in manner euerywhere in the Fathers, as they knowe, who be conuersant in their writinges.

Daily Sacrifice.

And that the Masse be celebrated, we haue lawes, Decrees, and auncient Councels, moe then I thinke it necessary to recite here. When any man professing defence of the Catholike religiō, wil be so far ouerseene as to mainteine opinion, that eche Priest ought of bounden dutie to say Masse euery day, then against such a one wil al that serue you which you haue raked here together, out of Peccham, Linwode, Innocentius the third, Thomas of Aquine, and out of Vitas Patrum, for stuffing of your booke. But when noman affirmeth any such absurditie, you may vnload such nedelesse wares in some other voyde roome. With this and such other trash you haue raised the price of your booke, and haue damnaged the common welth, causing so bad stuffe to be so derely solde.

Vnnecessary stuffing of M. Iewels boke

As for Cusanus the Cardinal whom here you repeate againe, it is a token you are neare dryuen, that you are faine to runne to him for helpe, specially out of that treatise, which he maketh purposely against the heretikes of Bohemia your predecessours. So souldiers in the chase to escape the hādes of their ennemies, oftentimes leap into the Sea, and the poore birde to escape the hawke sometime taketh succour of a house, whereof otherwise he would be afraide. What corners haue not you serched, what booke is there so litle worth, what rotten ragges be so vile, which you and your felowes for you haue not turned and tossed, to finde out somewhat (not so much for the defence of your Gospel, for litle can you defende, your profession is rather to impugne) that may haue some colour contrary to that the Churche now (I wil not say beleueth, but) obserueth?

Cusanus is drawē in to helpe, where of purpose he impugneth this new Gospel.

The mater is answered before. Though it witnesse that the deacon receiued the Sacrament vnder the forme of breade onely at the Priestes hande, whereby receiuing vnder one kinde is auouched, which maketh against you: yet your communion, wherto a companie of three at the least is requisite to receiue whith the priest, is not thereof inferred. So at Cardinal Cusanus handes, your cause fyndeth no succour at al, but contrarywise hinderance and control. And though a deacon receiued at euery solemne Masse the one kinde of the priest, yet that forbiddeth not, but that it was lauful for a Priest to say Masse, without a deacon in time and place, where a deacon was not alwaies ready and disposed. Cusanus there telleth what was of custome donne, and that in cathedral Churches, and at solemne feastes: he sheweth not what was euery where, and alwaies of necessitie to be donne.

One kinde receiued.

The obiection made out of Cusanus answered.

Now this was your parte and promise, to proue, that S. Chrysostome, or any other Priest could not possibly say Masse, onlesse there were a companie to receiue with him. But when you come to shew the proufes of your doctrine, thanked be God, they be as weake as ye aduersarie would wish. And therfore you haue dōne politikely in taking vpon you to disproue the Catholike doctrine, & not to proue your owne. For who knoweth not how much easier it is, rashly to deny, thē with reason to affirme, to disproue, then to proue, as easier it is to throwe downe, then to set vp, to destroy, then to buylde? As it is said in the gospel of that blessed womā Marie, S. Marthas sister, that she had chosen the best parte, wherby to serue God: so it may be said of you M. Jewel and of your felowes, you haue chosen the easiest parte, whereby to serue Antichriste.

M. Jew. chosing ye easier part impugneth the doctrine of the Church & proueth not his owne.

Luc. 10.

Ievvel.

But vvhat a vvonderful case is this? The Masse, that vve must nedes beleue.

*beleue is so auncient, so vniuersal, so Catholique, so holy, so glorious, * cannot be founde neither in Churches, nor in Chapels, nor in Secrete Oratories, nor in priuate houses in Tovvne or Citie, but must be sought out in some petie parish in the Countrie, and that by coniecture onely, and by gheasse, and by such recordes, as directly condemne the vvhole order of the Masse, and vvil suffer no man to be present there at, but onely such as vvil receiue.*

The.201. vntruth. The Sacrifice of y Masse is proued to haue ben made in Churches, & oratories, & that in Townes & Cities, as here it is proued.

Harding.

Al this wynde shaketh no corne. This tale sheweth more spice, than maketh prouse. And as it proueth nothing, so it disproueth nothing. As you take vpon you to denye the Masse impudently, so on the contrary side, I wil be bolde to affirme it truly. And to adde authoritie vnto boldenesse, forasmuch as here I meane by the name of Masse, specially the vnbloudy Oblation of Christe in the Daily Sacrifice of the Churche, which Cōsecration presupposed, is dōne in the holy seruice of the Masse: I haue proued it in the begynning of this treatise by witnesse of sundry fathers, and euen here in this very Diuision, by the witnesse of S. Dionysius. S. Ireneus, S. Cyprian, and S. Chrysostom. Neither were it hard, if I would in this place tarrye vpon it, and enlarge my booke, to proue it by a farre greater number of testimonies.

And because we are now in hande with a place of S. Chrysostome, it shal not be beside the purpose out of the same place to allege you his testimonie for the Masse. As when a lorde (saith he) commeth vnto the table, the seruauntes that haue offended him, must not be present, but be put out of his sight: so euen here also whiles the Sacrifice is brought forth, and Christe is Sacrificed, and the sheepe of our lorde, &cæter. the like he saith an other where τοῦ Χριςοῦ τιθυμένου, that is to say, when Christe is Sacrificed. So then you haue testimonies for the Masse celebrated not only in some petie parish

Chrysost. hom. 61. ad popul. Antiochen. Et Christus immolatur. *Ad Ephes. ca. hom. 3.*

as you terme it, but also in two of the greatest Cities of the worlde, Constantinople, and Antioche, for of them speaketh S. Chrysostome, in those two homilies: As S Cyprian is to be vnderstanded to meane of the Sacrifice celebrated in the Citie of Carthage, S. Ireneus of Lios, S. Dionysius of Athens. which famous Cities I trowe, you wil not accompt for petie Parishes in the Countrie.

Ad popul. Antioche. hom.61.& ad Ephes. hom.3.

If S. Chrysostome would suffer no man to be present at Masse, but onely such as would receiue, for so you say, although vntruly, (for he was faine to suffer them though to some grief of his mynde, as it appeareth by the two forementioned homilies): yet, were it true, the Masse of it selfe for al that is neuer the more vnlauful, or a thing the more vngodly. For whether many receiue with the priest, or the priest receiue alone, if the one Masse, where many receiue be good, the other can not be euil: because the vertue of the Sacrifice consisteth not in the receiuers, or communicantes, but in the Institution of Christe, and in the thing offred. The vertue of that which we cal the Masse, standeth in the Consecration, which Consecration is as good in a priuate Masse, that is, when a Priest receiueth alone, as in the publike, or whē he hath a multitude to receiue with him. For such multitude of receiuers geueth no vertue to the wordes, by power of which the body and bloud of Christe are consecrated.

The vertue of a priuate Masse is nolesse thē of a publike Masse.

Thus then is the Masse in it selfe of one substance, vertue, and force, whether many receiue the Sacrament with the Priest, or he receiue alone, and so farre is priuate Masse auouched. If ỹ people be so vndeuoute, as they can not be brought to receiue, that is their default, against whō you may speake your pleasure an other while, it is not the Priestes default, nor any diminishing of the vertue of the Sacrifice. That great benefite is enio-

enioyed of the fewer, the benefite it selfe by their vndeuotion is not diminished. As the benefite of Christes passion is neuer the lesse, though many men through infidelitie, heresie, and wicked life departe from Christe, and ioyne them selues vnto Antichriste.

Ievvel.

*For thus saith Chrysostome * If thou stand by, and do not communicate, thou arte malaprete, thou arte shamelesse, thou arte impudent. 2. Thine eies be vnvvorthy the sight hereof, vnvvorthy be thine eares. 3. O thou vvilt say: I am vnvvorthy to be partaker of the holy Mysteries, Then arte thou vnvvorthy to be partaker of the prayers: 4 Thou maist no more stande here, then a * Heathen, that neuer vvas Christened.*

Chrysost. ad Ephes. hom. 3.

The. 202. vntruth. These be M. Iewels forged wordes they be not S. Chrysostomes owne wordes.

Harding.

Good Reader this saying is altogether falsified. Though S. Chrysostom haue the like wordes in sundry places, yet speaketh he not in this sorte and order, as M. Iewel, would thee to beleue. Much lesse meaneth he, as this falsifier reporteth his sense, with wordes of his owne forging. This whole allegation is patched together out of foure diuerse places of his thirde Homilie vpon the Epistle to the Ephesians, between ech parte sundry sentences intermedled.

The. 203. vntruth. S. Chrysostome saith not thus.

M. Iew. corrupteth & falsifieth S. Chrysostome, & patcheth together diuers sentences, which in him be laid forth in sundry places.

The first parte conteineth not S. Chrysostomes wordes. That which he saith, is thus. Πᾶς ὁ μὴ μετέχων τῶν μυστηρίων, ἀναίσχυντος, καὶ ἵσταμαι ὡς ἑστηκώς. that is to say: Euery one that receiueth not the Mysteries, is impudent, and hath stād here rashly. For thou must vnderstand Reader these wordes, as spoken by S. Chrysostome, after that Masse is done, and after that the Priest hath receiued. For after al this, did the people Communicate, when so euer they Communicated. And thus he spake to the intent he might moue them to receiue oftener, specially at euery such solemne Masse. M. Iewel hath added vnto the sentence by his rhetorical exaggeration, more then the Doctour meant.

If such heate and vehemencie of speach would stirre the people at this day vnto worthy receiuing of the Communion with the Priest euery day, or at least euery Sonday: would God the like tale were now also tolde them. Euery good Catholique man doubtlesse would be glad of it, and praise God for it. But if they vpon reuerence, and of a deuout feare, refraine to receiue: I thinke it not good now to driue them out of the church at Masse time. For neither S. Chrysostom commaunded that to be done: Neither doth he order his talke otherwise, then as one that maketh an exhortation. You heare him allege no scripture that commaūdeth the people at euery time to receiue with the priest when he sacrificeth: he complaineth nowhere of breach of any precept.

The second parte of this saying is in an other place spoken of them, who not being cleane in conscience, but hauing the spot and wrinckle of deadly sinne in their soule, be vnworthy not only to receiue, but also to beholde and heare these Mysteries. Of such he saith, vnworthy be their eies, vnworthy be their eares. And to put the more terrour in their heartes, comparing them to beastes in consideration of their filthy sinnes, he allegeth the
Exod.19 Scripture saying, Si bestia tetigerit montem, lapidibus obruetur, If a beast touch the hil, it shalbe stoned to death. Now M. Iewel being loth the people should be present at Masse, referreth this indifferently to al them that stand by, and do not Communicate, of what merite so euer they be. And what in him lyeth, driueth them from the Church.

The third parte is found a sundre from the reste of this saying in an other place. And it is vnderstanded to be spoken of one ỳ putteth a barre against the grace of the holy Ghoste, so as it can not enter: As if a man beare malice to an other, wil not forgeue, or otherwise haue a minde and wil to sinne. To such a one saith S. Chrysostome: How tarriedst thou, and didst not participate of the holy table? I am vnworthy, thou saist. Then arte thou vnworthy to communicate in prayers. And he meaneth it of the prayers that be made at Masse, after the Penitentes and Catechumens were commaunded out of the Church.

The fourth parte of this allegation is placed an otherwhere, and is by M. Iewel falsified worst of al. Chrysostomes wordes be these. If a beast saith the Scripture, touch the hil, it shal be oppressed with stones. So the Iewes were not worthy so much as to go vp: albeit afterwarde they went, and saw where God had stand. Then foloweth that which he speaketh vnto the vnworthy looker on. ἔξεστι μετὰ ταῦτα προσελθεῖν, καὶ ἰδεῖν, ὅταν μὲν γὰρ παρῇ, ἄπιθι. οὐκ ἔξεστί σοι μᾶλλον, ἢ τῷ κατηχουμένῳ. As much to say, It is lauful for thee anonne to come and see. But when he is present, go thy way. It is no more lauful for thee, then for a Catechumen, as much to say, a learner of the faith, not yet baptized.

Here is to be noted by the way, that S. Chrysostome in this place acknowlegeth a special presence of Christe in the blessed Sacrament. For if Christe were not present in the Mysteries otherwise then he is by his diuine Maiestie euerywhere: he would not haue said, anonne (when the Communiō is al receiued) thou maist come (to the aulter) and see, but when he is present, gete thee hence. So by S. Chrysostome Christ is presente in the Mysteries: when they are ended, he is not so present, and therefore a sinner may come to the place where he was, and see.

A special presence of Christ acknowleged by S. Chrysostom to be in the Sacrament.

But that any person which receiueth not, may stand at the

A Catechumen is in better state then a heathen as we meane speaking of an heathen.

Masse and be presente, no more then a heathen that neuer was Christened, so much S. Chrysostome saith not. Although a Catechumen be not yet Christened, yet he is in farre better state then a heathen, by whom we vnderstand an Infidel. For the Catechumens many of them were perfite beleuers, though they differred to be baptized for a time. Thus hast thou good Reader the wordes of this holy Doctour truly laid before thee. which as they conteine an ernest and vehement exhortation to the people to receiue the Sacrament, & to roote out al such vices that made them vnworthy of it: so they be not spoken against the blessed Sacrifice of the Masse, to which purpose they are by M. Iewel vntruely applyed.

Ievvel.

The. 204 vntruth. This is a false reporte both of S. Chrisostomes wordes & of his meaning.

And touching him selfe he saith, In vaine vve come to offer the daily Sacrifice: In vaine vve stande at the Aulter. Meaning thereby, as may appeare, that if he said priuate Masse, for lacke of companie, it vvas in vaine.

Harding.

This man almost neuer allegeth his Doctour truely. He saith not, *In vaine vve come to offer the daily Sacrifice*. Neither that he saith there, toucheth him selfe, as M. Iewel would the Reader to vnderstand, but rather the people, who were present at the Sacrifice, and receiued not. But he woulde faine haue this pointe beleeued, that the Priest in saying Masse, doth al in vaine, if the people receiue not. And therefore he forgeth a false sense, saying. *And touching him selfe, he saith, &c.* And yet if the people receiued neuer so much (as in these Countries and in other places out of England they receiue very often) would not he so be content, and allowe the Masse: so great hatred by the inspiration of Satan hath he conceiued against the external Sacrifice of the Church.

But

But if the people forslow to do their dutie, and dispose not them selfe to come and receiue, yet doth not the Priest in vaine touching him self (as this great ennemie of this Sacrifice saith) come to offer the daily Sacrifice. For touching him self, he doth that which Christ commaunded his Disciples, and their sucessours to do. He consecrateth the body and bloud of Christe, he offereth and presenteth him vnto God, he prayeth for the people, and for him selfe, in presence of which Sacrifice teares craue not forgeuenesse in vaine, saith S. Cyprian: he celebrateth the memorie of Christes death, he geueth thankes to God for Christes sake. This and much more he doth, to the inestimable benifite of him selfe, and of the people, specially of such as be in state to receiue grace, whose publike Minister he is. Therefore false it is that M. Iewel fathereth vpon S. Chrysostom, that he should say touching him selfe, as in the behalfe of euery Priest, when the people receiued not, he came in vaine to offer the Daily Sacrifice.

The priest offereth not in vaine touching him selfe, though ŷ people do not receiue with him.
Mat. 26.
Luc. 22.
1. Cor. 11
Cyprian. de cœna Domini.

The worde of S. Chrysostome is this: The daily Sacrifice is in vaine. He saith not, we come in vaine to offer the daily Sacrifice. Our comming to the Aulter, and our offering is not in vaine. But the Sacrifice θυσία, (for that is the worde) the consecrated hoste, is in vaine, not touching him self, that is to say the priest, as M. Iew. would haue it vnderstanded, nor touching ŷ hoste it self, but touching ŷ people, and how, I shal here declare anon. Againe he saith, παρεστήκαμεν we haue stand at ŷ Aulter in vaine: wherby he meaneth a long stãding & waiting of ŷ priestes (after ŷ oblatiõ was done) to see who would come & receiue. But none came, and in that respect their standing was in vaine. So that al is to be referred to them that refused to receiue, not to the Priestes office, that said Masse, nor to the Sacrifice it self: which Masse M. Iewel gheasseth to be in vain, because it is said

Frustra quotitianum Sacrificium.
The masse is not in vaine in it selfe, but ŷ priestes standing & waiting for the people is in vaine whẽ they refuse to receiue the Communion.

Sacrifice & Aulter. without companie of receiuers. Among other thinges, this much is not to be dissembled. How so euer M. Iewel handls this place of S. Chrysostome, he can not with al his Rhetorike, nor with any other shifte auoide, but he must nedes graunt the Sacrifice, and that daily, and an Aulter, which he, as also the rest of those Gospellers deny vtterly.

Ievvel.

The. 105. vntruth. This much I see not here, neither is there any cause why I should see it. *Here M. Harding *seeing that his Masse, euen by his ovvne authoritie is shrevvdly crackte, and least for vaine, assayeth to salue it, as vvel as he may, *The Masse (saith he) is not in vaine in it selfe, but vnto the people that vvil not come. This is a glose beside the text: yet let vs take it as it vvere true. But if hearing of the Masse be a thing pleasant vnto God, and meritorious vnto the people: if Christ be there offered in dede for the sinnes of the vvorlde, if the Priest alone may receiue for al the reste, if it be sufficiēt for the people to cōmunicate spiritually, as M. Harding hath auouched, then is not the saying of the Masse in vaine, no not vnto the people, no although they neuer vvould cōmunicate. Chrysostom saith, It is in vaine, M. Harding saith, it is not in vaine. And yet to see a greater contradiction, M. Harding him selfe in this place saith, it is in vaine vnto the people: And yet the same M. Harding hath saide before, it is commaunded by Councels, it is sufficient for the people to communicate in spirit, it is not in vaine vnto the people.*

The. 106. vntruth. I say not so. Al this paragraph is a continual falsifiyng of my wordes & sense, as here I declare, and my booke witnesseth Diuisio. 9

Harding.

Fol. 13 b. If lyes were good proufes, I were confuted. But the Masse (say you) is shrewdly crackte. By whome I pray you? By you M. Iewel? Alas good Syr, though you be a greate craker, yet be you in these points but a weake cracker. No no Syr, falshed can not cracke the truth. Had your mattockes and pickeaxes ben of no more strength in hewing and tearing downe the aulters of God, that S. Chrysostome so many hundred yeares past, said to haue ben set vp in our countries of Britaine, then your lying Replie is of reasō or learning in cracking the

Chrysost. in Demonstratione aduersus Gentiles, quod Christus sit Deus.

the Masse: the aulters (wherof S. Chrysostome here speaketh) had stil remained whole, as yet for al your Replie the Masse remaineth vncrackte, and to the ende shal remaine in al places, but where Antichrist shal be folowed, and Christ forsaken. For confutation of al that you say here to proue me contrary to this holy Doctour, and contrary to my selfe, I require no more of the Reader, but to peruse my wordes, and consider, whether I say, as you reporte me to say, or whether the Repliemaker hath said vntruely, and made his apparent gaine of lying, or no.

Foreseeing this Replie would be made, in my boke I say thus. Whereas S. Chrysostome saith, the Daily Sacrifice was in vaine, and the Priestes stoode at the Aulter in vaine: it is not to be vnderstanded of the Sacrifice in it selfe (that is my terme there, the Masse I named not) as though it were in vaine and frustrate: but this is to be referred to the people, it was in vaine for their parte, that should haue receiued the Communion with the Priestes, who waited daily for them, and cryed out as the manner was, Sancta Sanctis, Holy thinges for the holy. And after that they had receiued the bread (that is, the Body of Christe vnder the forme of bread) them selues, shewing the chalice to the people, said, Come ye vp to receiue, with the feare of God, with faith and charitie. But al was in vaine. For none came, so colde was their deuotion in that behalfe. Thus there. Fol.30.b

Now iudge good Reader, how truly M. Iewel dealeth. He nameth the Masse, to make the mater more odious. I name not the Masse, but the Sacrifice, as S. Chrysostome doth. He maketh me to say, *the Masse is not in vaine in it selfe, but vnto the people that wil not come.* I say, whereas S. Chrysostom saith, the Daily Sacrifice was in vaine, it is not to be vnderstanded of the Sacrifice in it selfe, as though it were vaine and frustrate: but that this is to be referred to the people, it was in vaine for their part, that should haue receiued the Communion. I say not the Masse is in vaine vnto the people. That would you faine haue me say, I suppose. Forged dedes and counterfeite writes make no good proufe in Lawe, they be punished by Lawe.

Againe say you, *Chrysostome saith, It is in vaine, M. Harding saith, it is not in vaine.* Which it M. Iewel? Nameth S. Chrysostome the Masse? Name I the Masse? he nameth the daily Sacrifice, and so do I, which is done and made in the Masse. And say I determinatly, it is not in vaine? Do I not qualifie my wordes, and say, It is not in vaine and frustrate in it selfe, but for the the peoples parte?

As you would make S. Chrysostome and me to seme to be at variance, so you go about to make your Reader beleue, I am at variance with my selfe. And yet say you, *to see a greater contradiction* (you might better haue said to see me make a greater lye) *M. Harding him selfe in this place saith, It is in vaine vnto the people, and yet the same M. Harding hath said before, It is not in vaine vnto the people.* To this what shal shal I say, but that al is a Lye? I say not in al my booke, the Masse is in vaine vnto the people, Neither say I, the Masse is not in vaine vnto the people. Onely I expounde S. Chrysostostome, seeking how to iustifie his saying, and how to saue the truth from slaunderous wranglers, of which sorte you shewe your selfe to be.

M. Iew. maketh a false tale of his owne, and fathereth it vpon mee.

And whiles I do this, I confesse with S. Chrysostome the Sacrifice, whereby I meane as he doth, the hoste sacrificed, that is, the body of Christe, is in vaine, not in it selfe, not per se, as the Learned do speake, but on the peoples behalfe, for theyr parte that shoulde haue receiued it sacramentally.

καθημερινὴ θυσία

S. Chry-

S.Chrysostome saith it is in vaine, because it hath not the ful effect it should haue in the nature of a Sacrament receiued. This is no contradiction at al. Christes death is in vaine on their behalfe that beleue not, or diuide them selues from the Church his body mystical. Christes death is not in vaine for their parte that beleue, and perseuer in keping his preceptes vnto the ende. If I say thus, I say truly, who denieth? Yet shal a wrangler, as you are, replie and say: why then Christes death is in vaine, and it is not in vaine. It is no contradiction, nor inconuenience to say: a thing is in vaine, and not in vaine, in sundry respectes. Frustra percussi filios vestros, I haue striken your sonnes in vaine, saith God in ye prophete Ieremie cap. 2. On Gods behalfe, they were not striken in vaine, for God doth nothing in vaine. For their parte, it was in vaine. For they were not amended by it, as there it foloweth, disciplinam non receperunt. They receiued no correction therby. Thus a thing may be donne in vaine, and not in vaine: and so to say, it is no absurde contradiction, as M. Iewel maketh of this.

Touching this blessed Sacrifice, the body of Christe, it is cōsecrated specially and chiefly both for the representation of Christes death who is there present, & also that it be receiued sacramentally to our spiritual comfort. For those two endes is Consecration. Now if the Priest receiue it, and the people receiue it not: then for him it is not in vaine, and for their parte it is in vaine, quoad participationem sacramentalem, as concerning the sacramental participation and receiuing only. Yet is it not hereby denied, but that the Masse, in which the Sacrifice is consecrated, offred, and receiued of the Priest, may in other respectes be good and profitable to ye people otherwise deuoutly disposed, for that they may communicate with the Priest spiritually in the liuely remembrance of the passion of Christe with thankes geuing, be-

How the Sacrifice is in vain.

In vaine absolutely, and in vaine with respect. cause Christ who suffered passion and death, is there present.

And therfore whereas S. Chrysostome saith here in a vehemencie of speach, the daily Sacrifice is in vaine, yet is it not necessary to vnderstand him so precisely, as though he had meant, it were absolutely and simply in vaine. For his manner is to vse

Εἰκῆ this worde εἰκῆ, in vaine, sometimes so, as it may beare a reasonable qualification. Complaining in an homilie of the peoples negligence, that regarded litle the scriptures, the reader (saith he) goeth vp (twise or thrise euery weeke) and telleth you first, whose

Chrysost. ad heb. hom. 8 ex cap. 5. booke it is, that he readeth out of, as for exãple, the booke of such or such a prophete. and then he vttereth what he saith. Therefore the thinges ought to be cleere vnto you, and ye should knowe not

The 107 vntruth. M. Chrysostom neuer spake so. here is a burthen of lyes and blasphemies laid together. onely the texte it selfe, but also the very causes of the thinges that be written, and who spake them: sed omnia frustra, & sine fructu. But al is in vaine, and without fruite. He meant not in this place, that al was in vaine absolutely, both on the readers behalfe, and the peoples too. For euen there a litle before he excepteth a fewe, whom he thought not to be altogether ignorant of the thinges that were so commonly rehersed by the reader. Yet because they

The 108. vntruth. This is not S. Chrysostomes sense, as here I proue. It is the sẽse of Satan, & of Antichrist his Captaine, and of M. Iew. Antichristes forerõner. profited lesse then his desire was they should, he saith, al is in vaine, and no good is donne at al.

Ievvel.

*If M. Harding vvil stande vnto the authoritie of Chrysostome. let him not dissemble, but speake plainely vnto the people, * as Chrysostome spake. Let him say to them that come to heare his Masse, 1 If ye receiue not, ye are shamelesse, ye are impudent : 2 Ye are not vvorthy to be partakers of the cõmõ prayers: 3 Departe ye from the church: 4 ye haue nomore place here, then Turkes and heathens: 5 your eies be vnvvorthy to see these thinges, vnvvorthy be your eares: 6 Our Masses cã not profite you: 7 they are not meritorious for you: 8 they please not God: 9 they prouoke his anger: 10 they are al in vaine.* This is Chrysostomes sense, and plaine meaning: and this is a fayre vvinding vp of M. Hardinges Clevve.*

Harding

Harding.

No syr, not so, this is a fowle and a blasphemous winding vp of M. Iewels Clewe. Of any Clewe at al I made no mention: it is but a toye of his head to sporte withal. But beware he (I ernestly aduise him) least, if he recant not and repent by time, being at length pulled into hel with the twined thread of such blasphemous Clewes, he be bounde hande and foote with cordes of the deuils Clewe, and caste into the outward darkenesse, where shalbe weeping and grinding of teeth.

Beware good reader of this false and wicked doctrine, if thou loue thy soule health. M. Iewel beareth thee in hande, that S. Chrysostome hath spoken these wordes: and to cause thee the rather so to beleue, he hath printed them in that distinct letter, in which the Fathers saiinges in his booke are printed. Now ẏ truth is, S. Chrysostome is here altogether falsified. Touching the first and second sentence, he hath the like wordes, I graunt, and calleth him impudent and rash, that standeth at the Mysteries, and receiueth not. Likewise he that for his excuse saith, he is not worthy to participate, is by him admonished, to be vnworthy also of the Communion of prayers. That euery such a one is vnworthy to be partaker of the Common prayers, it is false, and S. Chrysostome him selfe hath the contrary in his Liturgie, where he maketh special mention of the Catechumens, and prayeth specially for them.

M. Iew: fowly corrupteth and falsifieth S. Chrysost.

In this place he speaketh not of the Common prayers, as M. Iewel reporteth, to exclude (as it semeth) Gods people from the hope of al benefite of prayers: but onely of the mystical prayers, or such as were said about the Consecration of the Mysteries.

Common prayers.

For this it is to be considered, that S. Chrysostome spake these wordes in respect of the custome and condition of that time. The Christen people and Infidels dwelled together. At the former parte of the Masse came the Catechumens, the possessed of sprites, the Penitents, and at the Sermons the Infidels were permitted to be present. After Sermon, when ẏ Mysteries were to be celebrated, al these were put out of the Churche, and none remained, but they who both were called, and also should be perfecti, perfite. These at the begynning, and long after, when the Sacrefice was celebrated, in many places commonly vsed to communicate.

Chrysost. hom. 61. ad popul. Antiochen.

In S. Chrysostomes time, the heate of this deuotion slaked among many. Most receiued not the communion but at certaine high feastes, as S. Chrysostome him selfe saith, some thrise, some twise, some but once in the yere, and some but once in two yeres. S. Ambros and S. Augustine said of the Grekes, and of them in the East, that they receiued our lordes body but once in the yere, as is before mentioned. To bring the people to this auncient deuotion againe, and to stirre them to receiue oftener, S. Chrysostome vsed this vehemencie of speache as out of the two forsaid homilies is by diuerse alleged. And because when the Deacon made his proclamation, come ye vp with faith and charitie and with the feare of God, they came, and yet receiued not: S. Chrysostome saith, that who so euer so came, and would not receiue, he was impudent and rash. And verely who so euer would at this day come to the place, where the blessed Sacrament is deliuered, and kneele downe, making resemblance to receiue, and yet would not receiue: worthily might he be rebuked, of impudencie and rashnes.

Who are they whō S. Chrysostom called impudent and rash.

But syr where did euer S. Chrysostome speake thus to the people, If ye receiue not, departe ye from the Churche? Do

M. Iew. would haue vs dryue al gods

Do ye driue your congregations out of the Churche, so often- times as they be not disposed to receiue your Communion? If S.Chrysostome did it, why do not ye folow him? If he did it not, why woulde you haue me so to speake vnto the people? Surely he neuer spake it, and therfore you belye him. Where said he, that *if the people receiue not at the Masse, they haue no more place there, then Turkes and Heathens?* Verely this is too Turkish and too Heathenish a saying, for S.Chrysostome to haue vttered. Who they are whose eyes be vnworthy to see these Mysteries, and eares to heare them, I haue declared before.

people out of the church, that do not receiue

M.Iew. Turkish and heathenish doctrine.

You would me to speake vnto the people, as S.Chrysostome spake, *Our Masses can not profite you*. Why then did S.Chrysostome speake of Masses? You haue oftentimes denied it pardy. If he dyd, we haue a witnesse more for the name of the Masse, then I was ware of. If he did not, then reporte you vntruly of him. Verely he neuer spake any such thing at al, as neither that which foloweth in your next sentence. As for the thre last sayinges, *The Masses please not God: they prouoke his anger: they are al in vaine*: These are not S.Chrysostomes sayinges, they are M. Iewels cankred blasphemies, geuing witnesse of his perfite hatred against the Churche of God. It had ben better he had neuer worne thread, then to haue winded vp such a wicked Clewe.

He maketh S.Chrysostome speake of Masses.

M.Iew. raileth out wicked blasphemy

Now good Reader I pray thee looke once backe againe, and reade what M.Iewel saith in the begynning of this Paragraph. There thou readest thus. *If M. Harding vvil stande vnto the authoritie of Chrysostome, let him not dissemble, but speake plainely vnto the people, as Chrysostome spake*. This condition I accept with a good wil. Vnto the authoritie of S.Chrysostom I wil stand, neither wil I dissemble, but speake plainely as he spake. If I alter his wordes, it shalbe litle, the sense I wil not alter at al. Now I require M.Iewel to stande hereunto also as reason is.

And let the worlde iudge, (though rather had I that learned men shoulde iudge) which is more agreable to the Doctrine of S. Chrysostome, either the new Communion of England, or the Masse of the Catholike Church, which it pleaseth M. Iewel to cal my Masse. For thereof is our controuersie.

Here is plain speaking, as S. Chrysostō speaketh which M. Iewel requireth. The real presence. Chryso. hom. 3. ad Ephe. Ibidem. Ad popul. Antiochen. hom. 61. cognatus vester factus sum. Ibidem. Ibidem.

First touching the truth and real presence of Christes body and bloud, which we consecrate in the Masse, if I shal speake plainely, as S. Chrysostome spake, then thus must I speake. This body is nothing different from that body, which was fastened vnto the Crosse, which was pearsed with nailes, which was Sacrificed. Againe. Who so euer of vs do participate of this body, who so euer do taste this bloud: consider ye, that we taste his bloud that sitteth aboue, that is adoured of the Angels, that is nigh vnto the immortal power. Item, if I wil speake plainely as S. Chrysostome spake, then must I thus speake vnto faithful people in the person of Christe. Volui frater vester esse, My wil hath ben to be your brother, for your sake haue I taken vnto me flesh and bloud. And to you now I deliuer the selfe same flesh and blood, by the which I became your cousin, or became to be of your nature. Item, If the figure of this bloud had so greate vertue both in the Temple of the Hebrewes, and in Egypt, when the postes of the dores were therwith anoincted: much more thē hath the truth. Weigh wel this worde, truth, reader, and thou shalt see, that the blood which we haue in the Sacrifice of the Churche, is not a Figure, as the Sacramentaries make it, but in comparison of the Figure of the olde lawe, the very truth. To conclude, here of I must say vnto the people with S. Chrysostome. Hic terrarum orbis est pretium, hoc Christus emit Ecclesiam. This is the price of the worlde, with this Christe hath bought his Churche.

This much is plainly spoken by S. Chrysostome touching the veritie of the body and bloud of Christe in this blessed Sacrament.

crament. The Doctrine of the English Communion is farre vnlike to this, for therby the people is taught the true body & bloud of Christe not to be here in dede, but the thinges that be layd vpon their table, to be the creatures of bread and wine, and them to be in dede but tokens, signes, and figures of the holy thinges. What differēce then is betwen the signe & figure of Christes flesh, & the flesh it self, betwen bread and wine, and that pretious body and bloud it selfe: so much oddes there is betwen this new Gospel, and the Doctrine of S. Chrysostom, betwen the new Communion, and his and our Masse.

The ods betwen our Masse or S. Chrisostomes masse, and the New Commu-nion of England.

Furthermore to compare table with table, *Isti mensæ administrant angeli, ipse rex adest*, at this table angels do serue, the king him selfe, (that is to say Christe) is present, saith S. Chrysostome. He saith more ouer, the holy ghost commeth downe in to vs Διὰ τῶν προκειμένων, through the holy thinges that be laid forth vpon the table. I trowe M. Iewel him selfe wil not tel the people, to thintent they should honour and worship Christe really present on the table of their Communion, that angels waite vpon the bread and wine: neither that the holy ghost commeth down vnto them through the creatures of bread and wine.

Ad Ephes. hom. 3.
Ibidem.

Now as S. Chrysostome, and we with him, do acknowledge Christes body and bloud verely present in the Mysteries, so he confesseth that Christ is there by way of Sacrifice, and that he is offred vp in Sacrifice. For so be his plaine wordes. *Profertur Sacrificium, & Christus immolatur.* The Sacrifice is brought forth, and Christe is Sacrificed.

Christe is sacrificed.
Chrysost. ad popul. Antiochē. hom. 61.

In the begynning of his Masse, (so Erasmus calleth his Liturgie) he maketh his prayer to our Lorde, that he may stande at the dreadful aulter without condemnation, and make the pure Sacrifice. These Gospellers as they haue euery where destroyed the aulters, so neither haue they any such Sacrifice at al.

Chrysost. in Liturg.

In Liturg. S. Chrysostome vseth at his Masse such Ceremonies, as if he were now lyuing, he were like to be wel scoffed at of M. Iewel, and accompted for a superstitious Papist of the rest. He kisseth the table foure times in forme of a Crosse, he taketh a lynnen vestiment with his right hande, he kisseth and blesseth it. Then he putteth on his Stole, his girdle, and his pal, at euery one making a seueral and special prayer.

The ceremonies of S. Chrysostomes Masse vsed by the Grekes at this daye.

At his Masse he commendeth himself and the people to god through the prayers of Saintes, saying thus. Haue mercie, and saue vs O Lorde for the prayers of her, that brought thee forth Gods Mother, euermore virgin Marie, of al the holy spiritual powers, of thy pretious Prophete, foreronner and Baptiste Iohn, of thy holy glorious Apostles, and of S. Nicolas, whose memorie we celebrate.

S. Chrysostom commendeth him selfe and the people to god through the praiers of our Lady and al other Saintes.

The like memorie he maketh there, desiring God to helpe for the prayers of his Saintes, and specially of the blessed virgin Mary, alwais calling her Deipará, seuen or eight times. Precibus sanctorum serua nos. Kepe vs (saith he) by, for, or through the prayers of Saintes. In one place he saith the Aue Maria, that our new Gospellers set so litle by. Haile Marie ful of grace, our Lord is with thee, blessed arte thou among wemen, and blessed is the fruite of thy wombe: because thou hast brought forth the Sauiour of our soules.

The Aue Maria.

He prayeth also vnto our Lady and praiseth her, saying. It is a worthy and a iust thing to glorifie thee the mother of God, euermore most blessed, and the vtterly vndefiled mother of our God, more honorable then Cherubin, and incomparably more glorious then Seraphin, who broughtest forth God without corruption.

Prayer vnto our Lady S. Marie.

He prayeth at sundry times for the Dead, beseching God to remember them, and for the same also he offereth. He putteth

Praier for the dead.

wine into the Chalice, saying thus, And one of the souldiers opened his side, and forthwith issued out bloud. And when he mingleth therto the water, he saith, And water, and he that saw it hath borne witnesse of it, and his witnesse is true.

Mingling of water and wyne.

Then he offereth incense. Light is borne before the priest bearing the Gospel. The priest turneth vnto the Image of Christe. The Deacon readeth the Epistle, geuing warning whose Epistle it is, saying, the Epistle of S. Paule. Then after a Psalme song, the Deacon stoupeth downe, and the priest prayeth ouer him, beseeching God to geue vtterance vnto tellers of the glad tidinges with much power, through the prayers of our Lady, Gods mother, and euer virgin Marie, and the holy and glorious Apostle, and Euangeliste, whose gospel is read.

Incense, light, the image of Christ.

Concerning the rest of S. Chrysostomes Masse, what prayers are made, much like (though moe in number) to the prayers of the Latine Masse, for al states, both quicke and dead, how the body and bloud of Christe are consecrated, how reuerently and with deuoute manner they are adoured, and incensed, how the blessed Sacramentes are lifted vp and shewed vnto the people, how the hoste is broken, and parte of it put into the Chalice, how lightes be hanged vp before the Sacramentes, how the Deacō calleth vp the people to come and receiue the Communion, and how in the end they are dimissed with the priestes blessing, to declare al this at large, it were ouer long. Verely most thinges are donne agreably to the Latine Masse, whereof the ministration of this new deuised Communion hath not so much as a shadow.

Adoratiō, lifting vp and shewing of the Sacramentes, lightes &c.

Thus this mater is to be tolde, if we stand to the authoritie of S. Chrysostome, and speake plainly as S. Chrysostom spake, which M. Iewel requireth, wherby the catholike Doctrine touching the Masse, is in euery point auouched and confirmed: and the new deuise of the English Communion is quite discredited. The thing is plaine, what nede many wordes?

Hereby it appeareth clearly what a Turkish and Heathenish harte M. Iewel hath, in that he would haue me speake vnto the people that resorte deuoutly vnto the Masse, & say, they haue no more place there, then the Turkes and Heathens. I trust good people, and al such as shal vnderstand, how falsely he hath fathered this wicked doctrine vpon S. Chrysostome, wil beleue him herein so farre as Turkes and Heathens the ennemies of God are to be beleued. Verely there is no Turke or Heathen so to be feared, as a Minister of such Turkish doctrine. For whereas the Turkes at the vttermost cã but destroy our bodies, these Turkish ministers destroy both bodies and soules euerlastigly. Good Reader it shal be holesome for thee to beleue S. Chrysostome him selfe, who teacheth the doctrine concerning the most blessed Sacrifice of the Masse, that the holy Ghoste hath taught the Catholike church, which also we teach: and not to beleue M. Iewel, or any of his companions scholers of Caluines wicked schole, whose study and endeuour is to withdraw thee from thy olde faith and religion that S. Chrysostom and al holy Fathers sith the Apostles time professed, and bring thee vnto their vncerteine nouelties by them selues not agreed vpon, which if thou yelde vnto, and remaine therein impenitent, at the end thy part shalbe with Turkes and Heathens. God geue the grace not to trust to lies.

Ievvel.

The.209. Untruth. I say otherwise. Looke in my booke.

*Novv let vs examine this inuincible Argument, vvherevvith euery childe, *as M. Harding vaunteth, is able to proue the Priuate Masse. The Maior is this: The Sacrifice in Chrysostomes time vvas daily offered. The Minor is this: But many times no man came to communicate vvith the Priest: The Conclusion, Ergo, there vvas priuate Masse.*

Harding.

Wil you neuer reporte my wordes truly? As to Midas, what so euer he touched it became golde: so what so euer M. Iewel taketh in hande, I see wel, it shalbe falsified. But of al other your infinite falsifyinges, this is one of the least. I vaunt not, as you say, that with this argument euery childe is able to proue priuate Masse. But say I in that place, Of this most euident place of S. Chrysostome, euery childe is hable to make an inuincible argument against M. Iewel for the priuate Masse, as they cal it, in this sorte. M. Iew. falsifieth al that he taketh in hande. Pag. 31. a.

By reporte of S. Chrysostome, the Sacrifice in his time was Daily offred, that is to say, the Masse was celebrated. But many times nobody came to Communicate Sacramentally with the Priestes, as it is before proued: Ergo there were Masses donne without others receiuing the Sacrament with the Priestes. Ergo, Priuate Masses (being taken for the Priest sole receiuing) in S. Chrysostoms daies were not straūge. Now what answer you to this argument? This is my argumēt there.

Ievvel.

* Here the Maior is apparent false.

* The Minor proued at aduentures onely by blinde gheasse, and so not proued at al. Therfore the Conclusion must needes folovve after as it may. Onlesse M. Harding looke better to it, I trovv it vvil proue but a childish argument.

The. 210. Untruth. The Maior is S. Chrysostoms, to whose verdite M. Iewel hath promised to stande.

The. 211. Untruth. The Minor likewise is S. Chrysostomes, as here it is shewed.

Harding.

Why syr know we you not being so olde a one as you are, that the argument may be good, though the antecedent be false?

This Argumẽt is not to be blamed, being such as may easily be brought into the forme of a perfite syllogismus. But the Maior (you say) is apparent false. You say so, but you proue it not. Saying so, you deny the Doctours, to whose iudgement you haue promised to stand, and by whose verdite you haue offered your Chalenge to be tried. For prouse of the Maior, S. Chrysostome saith, ἐικῆ καθημερινὴ θυσία, the daily Sacrifice is in vaine. If it were daily in vaine, then was it daily. If it were not daily, then neither was it daily in vaine. Omni die populis immolatur, Christe is sacrificed for the people euery day, saith S. Augustine. Epist. 23.

Chrysost. ad Ephes. hom. 3.

The Minor is proued by the plaine wordes of S. Chrysostome. οὐδεὶς ὁ μετέχων. There is none that receiueth, saith he. If there were none that receiued with the Priest, then the Priest, as of necessitie he was bounde, receiued the Oblation alone. And so was that done which you cal priuate Masse. That others receiued with the Priest, as Deacons and Priestes, when the people refused, or some of the people, when the Deacons and Priestes refused: that is your blinde gheasse M. Jewel, and seely coniecture, contrary to the plaine wordes of S. Chrysostome. The conclusion therfore foloweth wel ynough, and according to the rules of Logique.

Ievvel.

The. 212. vntruth. S. Augustine hath the contrarie.

Canon. 52. Aug. tract 26. Concil. Laodicen. Can. 49.

As for the Maior it is plaine by the sixth Councel of Constantinople. * *by S. Augustine vpon S. Iohn, by S. Basil Ad Cæsariam Patritiam, by the Epistle of the Councel of Alexandria in the defence of Macarius, and by the Councel holden at Laodicea, and by sundry other aucthorities to that purpose before alleged, that the Sacrifice vvas not daily offered, as M. Harding imagineth.*

Harding.

This is answered before in the. ix. Diuisiõ. Your three Councels

cels, the sixth of Constantinople, that of Alexādria, and the other of Laodicea, and S. Basiles epistle to Cesaria, shew the custome onely of particular Churches. And for the exception of a fewe certaine places, it is not reason, that you conclude the exception of al other places. A particularibus non sufficienter enumeratis ad vniuersalia you know, it is no good argument. As for S. Augustine, he is quite contrary to you in that very place which you allege, and more plainely in sundry other places. In his tenth booke de ciuitate Dei cap. 20. he calleth ẏ Sacrifice of our Masse, quotidianū Ecclesiæ Sacrificiū, ẏ daily Sacrifice of ẏ Church. To Ianuarius he saith, Alibi nullus dies intermittitur, quo nō offeratur. Alibi Sabbato tantū & Dominico. Alibi tantū Dominico. One where no day passeth, but the Sacrifice is offred. An other where it is offred onely vpon the Saterday and Sonneday. An other where vpon the Sonneday onely. But most plainely he auoucheth this in an epistle to Bonifacius. Hath not Christe (saith he) ben offred once in him selfe, and yet in the Sacrament he is sacrificed for the people, not onely through al the solemne feastes of Easter, but also euery day?

The daily Sacrifice proued.

Aug. epist. 118.

Aug. epist. 23.

And to what purpose is the sixth Councel of Constantinople, that was holden long after S. Chrysostomes time, alleged against the custome of the Churche in his time? That the Sacrifice was daily offred in the time that he lyued in, it is manifest by his owne testimonie. After that he hath expounded S. Paule affirming Christe to haue offred him selfe once to the destruction of synne, there vpon he addeth. Quid ergo nos? Nonne per singulos dies offerimus? offerimus quidem, sed ad recordationem mortis eius facientes. Then wat is that we do? Do we not offer euery day, day by day? Yeas we do so verely: but that as we do, we do it in remembrance of his death.

Heb. 10.

Chrys. ad heb. ho. 17.

But what nede is there to heape here together testimonies for the daily Sacrifice, sith that al the auncient Fathers writinges minister them to the diligent reader almost in euery place? Let vs therfore briefly conclude with the witnesse of S. Ciprian. who saith, Nos Sacerdotes Sacrificia Dei quotidiè celebramus. We that be Priestes de celebrate the Sacrifices of God daily. And so haue you good authoritie for that the Sacrifice was daily offred, which you denye.

Cypri. li. 1. epist. 2.

Ievvel.

Touching the Minor, it is not proued, but hangeth, as I haue said, onely by gheasse. * *M. Harding him selfe savve, that this is but a slender proufe, Chrysostome ministred euery day,* ergo, *he receiued alone. And therfore he sought further to finde his Single Communion in the Countrie. But Chrysostome saith, There is no body to communicate. By this it may appeare, as I haue already said, that Chrysostome him selfe did not communicate: onlesse vve vvil say, Chrysostome vvas No body: and so No body receiued alone: and No body him selfe said M. Hardinges priuate Masse. And therefore No body may come forth, and iustly require me to subscribe. Thus the Maior being false, the Minor not proued, the conclusion not folovving, thou seest good Christian reader, vvhat inuincible force M. Harding hath brought to proue his Masse.*

The. 213. vntruth. M. Harding could not see y in S. Chrysostome, which is not in him to be sene. M. Jew. deliteth in a vaine toy of his No body.

Harding.

What this man lacketh in truth and reason, he supplieth with wordes. And that wordes should not be tedious, he saweth them with scoffes. Such of the audience perhaps may he please, who haue more delight to heare Hickescorner vpō the stage, then to consider the profitable drifte of the mater. The Minor is proued by the credite of S. Chrysostome, whose worde is plaine, there is none to receiue. The disprouse of it hangeth al together by gheasse.

Neither

Neither sawe I this prouse to be sclender, Chrysostome ministred euery day, ergo, he receiued alone: for I neuer sawe it at al. It may be an argument of some Minister, verely myne it is not. Neither meaneth S. Chrysostome where he speaketh of that standing at the aulter in vaine, onely of him selfe, but also of other priestes in his time indifferently, and therfore he speketh in the plural number, we stand. But when I sawe S. Chrysostome, by his owne reporte, to offer the Sacrifice, and to stand at the aulter, loking for others to come and receiue, whē none came for so signifieth his worde οὐδ' εἷς: then sawe I the prouse good and sufficient, that he receiued alone.

οὐδ' εἷς nullus, none, or not one.

The whole commeth to this issue, whether we shal beleue S. Chrysostome him selfe, who saith, there was none to communicate, when the sacrifice was offred, or M. Iewel, that saith, there were others to communicate. Now if S. Chrysostome be a man rather to be beleued, then M. Iewel, who is so notoriously knowe to halte: then is not the Single Communion or sole receiuing founde only in the Countrie, whereof he iesteth, but also in the great Cities of Antioche, and Constantinople, as before we founde it in Carthage, and Alexandria, in Millan, and by great probabilitie in Rome. which are the greatest and ẏ most famous Cities of the worlde.

The single Communiō is founde in great Cities.

pag. 17. b. 18 b 21. b. 20. a.

Among other bad shiftes that M. Iewel is driuen vnto for auoiding this place, he vseth this for one, that, forasmuch as S. Chrysostome saith there is no body to communicate, he would it by this to appeare, that S. Chrysostome him selfe did not communicate. But this shifte is the worst of al others. For both in al such speaches, not to except the person of him that speaketh, it is beside reason: And in this case not to except the person of S. Chrysostome, or of whom so euer he meant, it is beside learning. For where as he confesseth a sacrifice offred, & to ẏ ende a priestes standing at the aulter: we must vnderstand there to be

The exception that M. Iew. maketh of S. Chrysostomes owne person is vaine, beside learning, and reasō.

Sacrifice alwaies requireth receiuing.

to be included the receiuing. The Fathers of the twelfth Toletane Councel excõmunicated al Priestes, that presumed to offer the holy Sacrifice of the aulter, and forbare to receiue the Communion. For what manner a sacrifice is that (say they) whereof neither he him selfe that sacrificeth is partaker? Thereof in that Councel we finde this expresse doctrine, which there they proue by the wordes of S. Paule to the Corinthians. Omnibus modis est tenendum, vt quotiescunque sacrificans corpus & sanguinem Iesu Christi Domini nostri in altario immolat, toties perceptionis corporis & sanguinis Christi se participem præbeat. By al meanes this is to be kepte, that how oftẽtimes so euer the priest doth sacrifice the body and bloud of Iesus Christe our lorde on the aulter, so oftentimes he receiue, and make him selfe partaker of the body and bloud of Christe. And further. It is ceataine (saith that Councel) that they, who doing sacrifice do not eate there of, be gylty of our lordes Sacrament. Wherfore if M. Iewel wil haue it appeare, because S. Chrysostome said, there is none to receiue, that neither S. Chrysostome him selfe receiued: then must he shewe vs, that he offered no Sacrifice. And that can not he doo, for expressely he witnesseth the Sacrifice. Otherwise the excepting of his person from receiuing the Communiõ, standeth not with the graunting of his Oblation, according to learning.

Conc. Toletan. 12. c. 7

1. Cor. 10

It may appeare, that Chrysostome him selfe did not Communicate, saith M. Iewel, *onlesse vve say, Chrysostome vvas No body: and so No body receiued alone: and No body him selfe said M. Hardinges priuate Masse. And therfore No body may come forth, and iustly require me to subscribe.* To dally thus vpon No body in so graue a mater, I doubte, whether it become any body. Though Vlysses, as homere ẏ poete faineth, vpõ good policie named hĩ selfe Vtis, as much to say, No body, vnto Polyphemus ẏ cruel Gyant: yet

Vtis.

it not semely for a Diuine, & a minister of the word, to bestow such a nickename vpon the holy Father S. Chrysostome. But let vs leaue to this Replier such toyes, least if we take them from him, we plucke from him his fairest feathers.

Now if for his sake, to maintaine his mery point, we wil not say, that S. Chrysostome was No body: then is he put to silence, and al the sporte is dasshed. Let then S. Chrysostome be as he was, Some body. If we say so, then Some body receiued alone, and Somebody him selfe said priuate Masse. And therfore Somebody may now come forth and iustly require this mery body to subscribe. Thus the Maior being true, the Minor proued by thaffirmation of S. Chrysostom, the Conclusion of the premisses by right Logique folowing, thou seest Christian Reader, how weakly this Argument is answered.

Ievvel.

But because he semeth to set somevvhat by the vvinding vp of his Clevv, it shal not be from the purpose, to vnvvinde it againe, and to lay it abroad, and to consider the stuffing of it, and to see hovv closely and handsomly it is vvound together.

Harding.

This Clew that you haue neuer done withal, is of thread of your owne spinning: as for me, I neither made any, nor spake at al of any. If you had good mater ynough for disprouse of the Catholique doctrine, you should not haue neded to spend so many idle wordes in pursuing such a light toye. Now let vs see your vnwinding, wherin I suppose you are prompter then in winding together: for the profession of your Gospel is, to loose and vnwinde, what Christe, and the Apostles, and their successours these. xv C. yeares haue bounde and wounde together.

Ievvel.

First there is not one thread of the holy Scriptures in al this Clevv.

but the plaine example of Christ and the Apostles quite refused.

Harding.

If you meane by this Clew my Answere to the first Article of your vaine Chalenge, as it semeth you do: for ẏ Cōsecration and the vnbloudy Oblation of the body and bloud of our Lorde, we haue the Institution of Christ, who taught the new Oblation of the new testament, which the Church tooke of the Apostles, aud offereth the same to God through the whole worlde, as S. Ireneus saith. This Oblation I haue proued by Scriptures, the Institution of Christ, who said Do ye this in my remēbrance, by the example of the Apostles, and the general doctrine of the Fathers. And more amply hereafter it shal be proued.

Irenæus. lib.4.c.32.

Ievvel.

Secondly the priuate Masse is founded vpon the negligence, and as M. Harding calleth it the vndeuotion of the people.

Harding.

The Consecration and Oblation, is founded vpon Christes Institution, practised by the Apostles, and continued by the Church. That the people many times receiueth not with the Priest, it is not a thing positiue, and therfore properly to speake, it is not founded. Priuate Masse being taken for the Sacrifice of the Church we acknowledge none. The Priest that offereth, is bound to receiue. The people be not alwaies bound to receiue with him. If lacking companie he receiue alone, thereby Christes Institution of his part is not broken. If the people be herein negligent and vndeuout, the more grieuous is their offence.

The.214. vntruth. It is not said that ij. priestes in sundry places do communicate together in breaking bread, this terme is here falsly conueyed in.

Ievvel.

*Thirdly, there is a vvay deuised, hovv tvvo Priestes saying their Masses in diuerse Countries, may communicate together *in breaking bread, be the distance betvveen them neuer so great, and that vvithout any manner vvarrant of Scripture or Doctour.*

Harding.

Harding.

Your terme of Breaking Breade is suspitious, what you meane thereby we know not. But for as much as many that do participate of one bread, that is to say, of the body of Christ, and of one cuppe, to witte, of the bloud of Christe worthily, be made one bread and one body, as S. Paul saith: not onely two Priestes, but al faithful persons that do the same worthily, do communicate together, be the distance betwene them neuer so great. They breake not bread together, neither do they receiue together in one place: but they cōmunicate together, & be made one body by the participation of Christes flesh both with Christ, and within them selues, as I haue at large before declared, out of S. Hilarie, Cyrillus, and other auncient Fathers. 1.Cor.10

Ievvel.

Fourthly, Laie people, vvemen, sicke folkes, and boyes, that receiued or ministred the Sacrament alone, * *are brought in for this purpose: as though it had ben lavvful for vvemen or boyes to say Masse.*

The. 215. vntruth. They are not brought in to this purpose, as is sufficiētly declared, but to proue sole Receiuing.

Harding.

This replie of boyes is very boyish, and yet very common in al your first Article. An example in my boke is alleged, where a lad is sent to the priest to come and minister the blessed Sacrament to Serapion lying at the point of death. The Priest him selfe being very sicke, and not able to come, sendeth the Sacrament by the lad. Which is wel allowed by S. Dionysius of Alexandria, and recorded by Eusebius, but this Replier scoffeth much at it. That lay people, wemen, and sicke folkes, haue receiued the Sacrament alone, examples haue been alleged: yet thereby it is not made lauful, that wemen and boyes should say Masse, as your boyish scoffing pretendeth. But if it were lawful for them to receiue alone, why shew you not some good reason, why a Priest may not receiue alone, whose sole receiuing, you cal Priuate Masse?

Euseb. Eccles. hist. lib. 6. c. 34.

Ievvel.

The.216. vntruth. That al be not of doubteful credite, I haue sufficiently proued, as now it is euident. *Basil & Chrysost. in Liturgijs.*

*Fifthly, because S. Ambrose, S. Augustine, S. Hierome, S. Chrysostome, S. Basil, and such others vvould not serue, there is brought in a great number of pety Doctours, *al of doubteful credite, and many of them long sithence misseliked, and condemned by the Churche.*

Harding.

For the Sacrifice I haue brought the Testimonies and authorities of S. Basil, and of S. Chrysostome. The rest that you name, I might haue brought, as you may iudge by this treatise. Many other good and auncient Fathers I brought in, whose authoritie and estimation you haue donne what you could to deface, but al in vaine. Therein you haue shewed your impudent malapertnesse, their fame and worthinesse you haue caused the more to be knowen. Neither were they condemned by the Churche, as you belye the Churche.

Ievvel.

The.217. vntruth, I auouch not this mater by visions & dreames Neither be visions & dreames one thing. Ioan.20.

*Sixthly, the mater is made good by Visions, *dreames and fables.*

Harding.

Dreames, and fables my booke hath none. One Vision of S. Basil it reporteth, auouched by that appeared to me good autoritie. If your incredulous harte can beleue no visions, I can not say vnto you, as Christe said vnto S. Thomas, Inter digitum tuum huc: Come and put in thy finger hither. Albeit if that Vision moue you not, there is other prouse ynough for the Masse, beside the infallible tradition of the Churche, which you ought to beleue.

Ievvel.

Seuenthly there are alleged Canons of Councels not extant in any Councel, gathered vvithout great iudgement by one Grattan, and yet none of them neither prouing, nor once naming the Priuate Masse.

Harding.

Harding.

This is meant of the. 47. Canon of the Councel of Agatha. Though the booke of Gemlak, which was Peter Crabbes copie to the Printe, had not this, as also certaine other Canons, yet an other booke that Gratian had, might haue had it. This is answered before. Here I must warne the Reader of your craft. When you be not hable to auoid a manifest place brought against you, the best shifte you haue is, to denye the author. No man allegeth Gratian more then your selfe, though to litle purpose: but when ought that is in Gratian maketh against you, and is contrary to any parte of your Gospel, then is Gratian a man of litle iudgement, and of light auctoritie. This vantage you vsurp ouer vs, to allow, and disallow, whom, and what you liste, to binde vs to the writers of the first six hundred yeres, and your selfe to make your market the best you can, of al that euer wrote from S. Mathew to Cassander, that at these dayes writeth partly on your side, and partly on our side, whom ye allege, and we reproue. M. Iewels craft and shift.

An other false caste that you vse much, is this. There is but one boy here mentioned, and to good purpose: and you to make the mater more odious, name boyes: but one Vision, you name Visions, Dreames, and fables: one Canon of one Coūcel, that Peter Crabbes Copie had not, and you speake of Canons of Councels. Wel may your Rhetorique teach you this, verely the holy Scriptures haue not so taught you. Whereas you say, the Canons I haue alleged, proue not, nor once name the Priuate Masse: they both proue and name the Masse, and that is ynough. If they name not Priuate Masse, no maruel, the terme, as you take it, is a newe founde deuise of your first Euangeliste Martin Luthers Schoole. If we finde it not in the olde Fathers, crake not of it, we seeke not for it, nor looke to finde it much in the new writers, that be Catholike. It is a fowle wrangling to require a new deuised terme in old writers. You haue the thing, what can you aske more? Shal I denye, and put any man to proue, that there was bread catē within the first six hundred yeres, because this English terme bread, can not in al the writers of that age be found? It is a tokē you are ouercome in the mater, when thus ye stande vpon the terme.

Ievvel.

The. 218. Vntruth, These cities be yet farre within halfe a M. miles of christendome, and at ẏ time were ẏ principal partes, and as it wer the harte of christēdō.

Eightly because M. Harding could not finde his Masse in the vvhole Churche of Rome, vvithin the space of six hundred yeres after Christe, he hath therfore made search at Alexandria in Egypte, at Antioche in Syria, at Cæsarea in Cappadocia, * *a thousand Myles beyonde the limites of al Christendome, vvhereas vvas neuer priuate Masse said, neither then, nor before that time, nor neuer sithence.*

Harding.

M. Iew. forgoeth his owne Chalēge, & semeth to make exception of certaine Cities & Coūtries.

Why syr, was not your Chalenge general? Did you excepte the landes of Egypte, Syria, and Cappadocia? Did you not make your Proclamation of any one example of the Primitiue Churche? And in the time of the primitiue Church, where florished the faith more, then at Alexandria, where S. Marke the Euangeliste, then at Antioche, where S. Peter him selfe preached the Gospel, and founded the Churches? Cesarea likewise at length, specially in the time of S. Basil, became it not to be a famous Church? Neither were these great Cities in the time of the first six hundred yeres a thousand Myles beyond the limites, but rather a thousand myles within the limites of Christendom. And at this day Alexandria is neare, and Antioche is as it were a neighbour vnto the lande of Cypres, which is a parte of Christendome: and Cesarea is not very farre of.

If you disallow the Masse, because it is founde to haue ben

vsed

vsed in places now farre distant from Christendome: by like argument you may disallow the actes of Christe, his baptisme, his Passion, Resurrection, and Ascension, and that ye ministers talk so much of, the Supper of the Lord it selfe: For al these be found to haue ben donne at the flond of Iordan, and Ierusalem, that are now farther from the boundes of Christendome, then Antioche is. At other times you like any Churche better then the Church of Rome: yet now because for witnesse of the Masse I seme not to referre the reader vnto it: you finde fault for not alleging thexample of the Church of Rome. So that your trauaile is not so much to fynde the truth, as to finde some occasion of cauil against me. Of al other your light deuises inuented by you against the Sacrifice of the Church, this was the fondest. So much the lesse, you should haue vttered it at Paules Crosse. For therby what did you els, but make al the worlde witnesse of your folishnesse? For wel it is knowen, though Alexandria, Antioche, and Cesarea, be not now partes of Christendome, yet within the first six hundred yeres, they were of the chiefe members of al Christendome.

A most fond deuise of M. Iewel.

Iewel.

*Nienthly, for that he stoode in despaire of Cathedral and other like great Churches, he hath sought out Chappels, Celles, Oratories, and priuate houses: and because he had no hope to spede *in Townes, or Cities, he hath sought out the litle Churches in the countrie.*

The. 119. vntruth. I haue proued that masse was celebrated both in Cathedral Churches & in great Cities, as here it is euident.

Harding.

If your mynde was to exclude these, why did you not expresse them in your Challenge? You shew your selfe now not to haue made your Chalenge wisely. And syr I pray you, shal not an olde Father of the first six hundred yeres, be accompted an olde Father, because vpon some good occasion he said Masse in a Chappel, or Oratorie? Is Sole receiuing of the blessed Sacrament no sole receiuing, because it was in Priuate houses? Is the Masse proued no Masse, because it was celebrated in Churches of lesse frequencie, then Cathedral Churches be? And yet for them also, what make you of the Churches of Antioche, and Constantinople? were they not Cathedral? were they not great Churches? Rome excepted, were there euer any greater? How out of two Homilies of S. Chrysostome, we haue proued that there was Masse said, and that without a companie receiuing with the Priest, you haue now sene. And touching the testimonie of Leontius reporting the Masse of S. Iohn the Patriarke without Communicantes, wil you say, the great Citie of Alexandria was no Towne, but a countrie village?

Antioche, Constantinople, Alexādria

Ievvel.

Tenthly, notvvithstanding al this inquirie, he hath not yet founde neither the name of priuate Masse, nor any priest that euer ministred, and receiued alone.

Harding.

If it be proued to haue ben de iure, what skilleth it, whether it be proued, that it was donne also de facto? Particular factes, specially particular circumstances of factes, be not commonly written. The Masse we haue founde, and single Communion we haue founde, and the Priest also that hath offred the Sacrifice without others receiuing the Sacrament with him, we haue founde. As for the name of Priuate Masse, how could it be foūd in any auncient wryter, sith it is a new inuention of Luther? I meane, for that the Sacrifice cannot be Priuate. The thing then being founde, ye haue no colour of reason, in that so busily ye cal for the name, Remember you not, what S. Augustine saith to Pascen-

Now M. Iewel bringeth his Chalenge to the bare name of Priuate Masse, there he were best to holde him, for ye thing he seeth proued.

Pascentius a professour of the Arians heresie? Quid est contentiosius, quàm vbi de re constat, certare de nomine? What is more contentious, then where as the thing is certaine, to striue about the name? *Augustin. Epi.174.*

Iewel.

To be shorte, the vvhole substauce of his proufes hangeth onely vpon his ovvne surmise, vvithout any certaintie, or appearance of truth.

Harding.

He saith so, that is disposed to say any thing, rather then to subscribe. He that duly considereth the proufes, thinketh otherwise.

Ievvel.

These be the contentes of M. Hardinges Clevv, and thus substantially hath he proued the antiquitie, and vniuersalitie of his Masse.

Harding.

The toye of your Clew I leaue to you, make of it what you list. The antiquitie of the Masse is proued, because I shewe that it was within the first six hundred yeres after Christe. The vniuersalitie of it, I was not moued to proue, by the purporte of your Challenge. Al be it sith that Christe taught the new Oblation of the new Testament, and the Churche receiued it of the Apostles, & offereth it vp vnto God in vniuerso mundo, through the whole worlde, as S. Ireneus saith: there is no cause, that being the Masse wherein that Oblation is made, why any man should doubte, whether it were vniuersal, or no. *Ireneus lib.4. cap.32.* The masse hath ben vniuersally vsed through al the worlde.

What so euer the Apostles receiued of Christe, the same did the Church receiue of them vniuersally. This new Oblation of the new Testament, (which is that we make in the Masse, and whereof the Masse chiefly consisteth) they receiued of Christe, as S. Ireneus saith: Ergo, the Churche receiued the new Oblation of the new Testament of the Apostles vniuersally.

By this terme vniuersally, I vnderstand not euery particular member of the Church, but euery age and place, when and where by the Apostles, and their successours Churches were planted. And thus is proued, not onely the antiquitie, but also the vniuersalitie of the new Oblation of the new Testament, and consequently the Masse. For that new Oblation which Christ made at his last Supper, and taught his Apostles, is that thing which chiefely we vnderstand by the name of the Masse.

M. Iewels Conclusion of this Article.

Iewel.

Now good Reader, to geue thee only a taste of some part, that may be said of our side, first it is apparent, that Christ our Sauiour at his last Supper Ministred the holy Communion, and no priuate Masse, and bad his Disciples to do the same in his remembrance.

Harding.

Thou knowest Reader, the manner of Pearemongers is, the rather to allure byers vnto them, to set their best peares for shew in the vpper part of their Paniers, and when any byer commeth to geue him for a taste of the better sorte. The like policie here vseth M. Iewel. He bringeth forth the proufes of his doctrine, as it were summer fruit to a market, that is soone ripe, soone roten. And here setting forth to the eye his chiefe store, he geueth thee a taste of his best dish that he is able to make. Other foisty and rotten fruite he semeth to haue, whereof he would make shew, were not for feare it should offende, and marre the whole sale.

What is M. Iewels parte to proue.

That thou be not deceiued, remember, his part is to proue, that within the first. vi. C. yeres after Christ, any priest might not offer the new Oblation of the newe Testament (as S. Ireneus speaketh)

speaketh) which Christ taught his Apostles, that is to say; might not celebrate Masse at any time: except he had a companie to receiue the blessed Sacrament with him. If he proue not this, he proueth nothing contrary to the Doctrine herein and tradition of the whole Catholike Church. And if he proue this substantially and clearly, then is he worthy to be heard. The mater being so weighty, reason would, nothing be attempted against so auncient, so vniuersal, and so long continued an obseruation: onlesse the proufes be very manifest and such as can not be refuted. Let vs then examine the taste, which he geueth vs for commendatiõ, as the best and chiefe of the whole heape.

A taste of M. Iewels chief reasons against the Masse.

First, Christ (saith he) at his last Supper *Ministred the holy Communion, and no priuate Masse, and bad his Disciples to do the same in his remembrance.* What meane you M. Iewel by these wordes, *Ministred the holy Communion?* Make you Christ our Sauiour one of your Ministers? who euer spake so before you? where found you this phrase in al the Scriptures of the New or olde Testament, or in al the writinges of the olde Fathers? Ech worde is found a part, I denie not, but where is this very speach to be found? Thought you thus to begile the vnlearned people, and to bring your new deuised Communion into estimation, by bearing them in hãd, that Christ Ministred the holy Cõmunion? And for that policie was it thought good to print the first letter of your worde Ministred with a great M, that so your lewd Ministers might seme to practise that, whiche Christe did? No, No, M. Iewel, you and your Geneuian Ministers be farre from folowing Christes example and commaundement. Albeit I graunt, in a right sense it may be conceiued, how Christe at his last Supper ministred the holy Communion, but in you the worde is suspitious.

M. Iew. vseth a new and suspitious phrase.

Because the deuise of your Ministring liketh you wel, you

Luthers wicked intent in deuising the terme of priuate Masse after his own sense.

say, that Christe ministred no priuate Masse: as though this terme priuate Masse (in the sense that you take it to be of) were not a monster of Luthers owne begeting. wherby he sought to abrogate the external Sacrifice of the Churche, and euery sole receiuing of the blessed Sacrament. The Masse, as I haue before said, touching the Oblation and Sacrifice, is not, ne can not be priuate, as neither Christes death is, or can be priuate. The Communion also, that is to say, Christes flesh whereby we be incorporate and united unto him, and within our selues, is not ne can not be made priuate: the receiuing of the Communion may be priuate, single, or sole of one faithful person in respect of place.

The substance of the Masse considered according to Christes example of the Supper.

But forasmuch as the Masse is impugned by the example of Christes Supper: let vs consider, what Christ did at his Supper, and what is that, he bad his disciples do in his remẽbrance. If that which we do in the Masse, be that which Christe did, and commaunded to be donne at his Supper: then is the Masse not onely not impugned, but confirmed and made good by Christes example at the Supper. Christ then at his Supper, as S. Ireneus gathering the whole storie therof into a brief sũme writeth, toke the creature of bread, (or yͤ which by creation is bread,) and gaue thankes saying: This is my body. And the cuppe likewise, that is of a creature, which is with vs, he confessed to be his bloud, and taught the newe Oblation of the new Testament, which the Church receiued of the Apostles, and offereth it to God through the whole worlde.

Irenæus. lib.4. cap 32.

Now as the Church by report of that holy Martyr, who liued in the Apostles Scholers time, receiued this new Oblation of the new testamẽt of the Apostles, & offred it vnto god through the whole world: so we yͤ are priestes now continue the same, as Christ taught yͤ Apostles, as the Apostles deliuered to yͤ Church,

as

as the Churche hath obserued, and alwaies practised to these times. That is to say, we take bread, we blesse, we geue thankes, we make the Eucharist (for so the woorde is taken of S. Iustine, and other the moste auncient Fathers) we Consecrate the body of Christe, with and by the power of our Lordes owne worde which is workeful, as S. Ambrose calleth it, saying in the person of Christe, This is my body. Likewise we take the cuppe of wine mingled with water, we geue thankes, and speaking the woorde of Christe, we make and Consecrate by vertue of the same woorde, his pretious Bloud, that bloud which issued out of his side, saith S. Chrysostome. And thus we the publike Ministers of the Churche in this behalfe, geue, rendre, and offer vnto God an Hoste or Sacrifice of his owne giftes which he gaue vnto vs, the most pretious of al that we can geue, and most acceptable vnto him. In Apologia. 2.

This heauenly bread in the forme of common bread, for signification of Mysterie we breake, and distribute also vnto others hauing examined and proued them selues. which we neuer denie vnto such, when so euer they require it, or shew them selues desirous of it. If none of the people at sundry times finde them selues disposed, or so as it behoueth, prepared, the same notwithstanding for any notorious crime not being excommunicate, we admitte vnto the Communion of prayer, of peace, of holy bread (for so many Communions be commended vnto vs, beside the Communion of the most high Mysteries) and suffer them to be present at the celebration of the Sacrifice, and the Priest in that case receiueth the holy Mysteries alone.

And al this is donne vpon warrant of Christes woorde, who said, Do ye or make ye this in my remembraunce. The Bishop (saith S. Dionysius S. Paules scholer) excuseth him Luc. 22. 1. Cor. 11.

 selfe

Dionysius Eccles. Hierarch. p. 1 cap. 3. selfe that he taketh vpō him to sacrifice this helthful Sacrifice, that is so farre aboue his worthinesse, in semely manner crying out vnto him: thou hast spoken the worde, Do ye this in my remembrance. As touching that a number should alwaies of necessitie receiue with the Priest, and that it is of the substance and necessitie of the Sacrifice, it can not be proued. And therefore the ordinance of the Church therin is to be folowed.

Christ (say you) *bad his Disciples to do the same in his remembrance.* We do the same that Christe did, touching al that is of the substance of his Institution. As for euery Ceremonie which Christ obserued at his Supper, we are not bound to obserue. That his body and bloud be consecrated by a Priest with his wordes, that it be offered and receiued, it is conteined in the precept of Christ, as the holy Fathers haue taught vs hauing learned the same of the Apostles, and of the holy Ghost: but that this be neuer done, onelesse there be a number prepared to receiue the mysteries with the Priest: that is not necessarily gathered of the Luc. 22. 1. Cor. 11. wordes of Christ. For he said not, Do ye thus, but Do ye this, in my remembrance. Otherwise we might seme bound vnto many absurd & impossible things. So then number of receiuers being one of the thinges, which are left to the disposition of the Apostles, and consequently of their successours the gouernours of the Church: we do not offend, ne breake the Institution of Christ, in celebrating the vnblondy Sacrifice, & receiuing it alone when others be not therto disposed. But hereof we said ynough before. Now geue vs an other tast, for this is not to be liked.

The. 220. vntruth. S. paules wordes be not to be vnderstāded of the ministration of the sacramēt, but of the holy feastes. In 1 Cor. 11

Ievvel.

*Likevvise S. Paule vvilled the Corinthians one to vvaite and tarie for an other * in the holy Ministration, and to conforme them selues to Christes example. Vvhervpon S. Hierome saith, as it is before alleged, The Lordes supper must be common vnto al: For the Lorde deliuered the Sa-*

cramentes equally vnto al the disciples that vvere present. **And S.** *Ambrose likevvise expounding these vvordes, Inuicem expectate, VVaite one for other, saith thus, that the Oblation of many may be celebrate together, and may be ministred vnto al.* 1. Cor. 11.

Harding.

This place of S. Paule, Inuicem expectate, wait ye one for an other, is vnderstanded of S. Chrysostome, Theodoritus, and others Fathers, to be spoken not of the administration or receiuing of the blessed Sacrament, but of the feastes, which at that time they made in the place of common prayer, or where els they might most conueniently. These feastes they called ἀγάπας, as I haue before declared, where I spake of this place. S. Chrysostom calleth them κοινὰς τραπέζας, common tables, and κοινὴν εὐωχίαν, Common feaste. He declareth they were kept after the Seruice was done, and after ẏ the Cōmunion had ben receiued. Theodoritus calleth them Communes cœnas, Common suppers. Because these feastes that were wel vsed at the beginning to a godly exercise of humilitie, and charitie, in processe of time were abused of ẏ Corinthians, ẏ rich making cheere by them selues, and contemning the poore, contrary to the example of Christes Supper: the Apostle to cal them backe vnto the imitation of Christes example, requireth them to tarie one for an other, and not to sit downe and eate their meat, before the poore came. So this place serueth not the turne.

See before Fol. 92. a. *Chrysost. In. 1 cor. 11 Hom. 27.* *Theodorit. In 1. Cor. 11*

The wordes that you father vpon S. Hierome, be not S. Hieromes. Yet vnder his name you haue alleged them diuerse times in this Article. You seme to repose greate trust in them. But I maruel you would vse the helpe of such pety Doctours, you I say, that take your pleasure so much at me for bringing in them, whom it liketh not your self to allowe, though of others not vnlearned they be neuer so well alowed.

M. Iew. vseth the helpe of an vnknowē Doctour, vnder the name of S. Hierome

That S. Paules woordes waite ye one for an other, are meant of the supper of Common meates, whichwas called our Lordes supper.

But who so euer wrote those briefe Commentaries vpon S. Paules Epistles, by the woordes that you allege, he meaneth not the blessed Sacrament, but the supper or feastes of common meates, which was called also Cœna Dominica, our Lordes Supper, because it was made immediatly after they had receiued the Mysteries according to the example of our Lordes last Supper.

Comunem cœnam.

He signifieth no lesse him selfe in that very place, for thus there it foloweth. The Apostle saith this because as they came together in the Churche, thei offered their offeringes seuerally, and there in the Church eating the common Supper, withal they consumed what so euer remained of the Sacrifices after the Communion. Loe Syr, heare you not the very worde Communem cœnam. The common Supper? This common supper, which was named also our Lordes Supper, and is so called τὸ κυριακὸν δεῖπνον of S. Chrysostom, Dominicum conuiuium, our Lordes feast of Tertullian, should not haue ben priuate to the richer sort that had abundance whereof they made their offeringes, and consumed al them selues disdaining to waite and tarie for the poore: but it should haue been common as wel to the poore, that were not of habilitie to bring so large and so liberal offeringes, as to the rich. Therefore said S. Paule, Itaq; fratres mei cum conuenitis ad manducandum, inuicem expectate. Brethren when ye come together to eate, tarie one for an other, ad manducandum, to eate he saith, whereby he meaneth the eating of common meates at their Church feastes, not the participation of the body and bloud of Christ: although ere they came to their common meates, they receiued the Cōmunion before. And that it may be thought, that so he meant, it foloweth, Si quis esurit, domi manducet, If any be a hungred, let him eate at home. The place of S. Ambrose is to be vnderstanded likewise of those holy Suppers. Now let vs assay more of your taste.

By what names the supper is called of the Fathers.

Chrysost. In 1 Cor. 11 Hom. 27.

Tertullian lib. 2. ad Vxorem.

1. Cor. 11.

Ievvel.

*In the Canons of the Apostles it is Decreed, that if any man resorte vnto the church, and heare the scriptures, and absteine from the Communion: he stande excommunicate, as one that troubleth the Congregation. The like decrees are found vnder the names, of Calixtus, *Anacletus, Martinus, Hilarius, and others: by vvhich it is certaine, that the vvhole church then receiued together.*

Can. Apo. can. 9.

The. 221. vntruth. It is not certaine by the Decrees of Anacletus & Calixtus, ye the whole church thē receiued together at euery Oblation, for ye Decree is to be vnderstanded of ye priestes & others of ye clergie only, as I haue proued.

Harding.

Here you geue vs a false taste M. Iewel. You haue falsified the. 9. Canon of the Apostolike Canons. parte you haue cut away, and parte you haue falsly translated. The Canon is thus. Quicunque fideles Ecclesiam ingrediuntur, & scripturas audiunt (μὴ παραμένοντας δὲ τῇ προσευχῇ, καὶ τῇ ἁγίᾳ μεταλήψει) neque apud preces & sanctam participationem permanent, eos, tanquam qui ordinis in Ecclesia perturbationē inducant, à communione arceri oportet. What faithful persons so euer enter into the Churche, and heare the scriptures, and do not abyde at the prayers, and at the holy participation (or receiuing of the mysteries): it behoueth them to be excōmunicate, as them which bring trouble vnto the Churche. The Canō speaketh of such as would heare the Scriptures, but would not tarye in the Churche whiles the prayers were said, and the Mysteries were receiued. For that they were to be excommunicate, and not for that they refused to receiue the Communion, as you meane.

M. Iew. falsifieth the Canons of the Apostles.

But though euery faithful person in the Apostles time vsed to receiue very often, when fewe were yet come vnto the faith, and they alwaies in feare of their life through the cruel persecutions of the Infidels, vnder whom they lyued: yet at length when the multitude of beleuers was increased, the rigour of ye order was remitted by Fabian & others, and they were vnder paine of excommunication bounde to receiue but thrise in ye yere,

De cons. dist. 2. Etsi non.

at Easter, witsonneday, and Christmasse. Now though in the Apostles time their deuotion were such, yet when the number was greatly multiplied, the Oblation was at sometimes celebrate, when a companie was not disposed to receiue with the Priest, as it is proued by S. Chrysostomes complaint made in that behalfe.

Chryso. ad pop. Antioche. ho. 61.

By the decrees, that be vnder the names of Calixtus, Anacletus, Martinus, Hilarius, and others (I know not what others you meane) which you haue here confusely shuffled together, it doth not certainely appeare, that the whole Churche then receiued together, as you say. And were it graunted, that at certaine solemne feastes great companies receiued, as certainely they did in many places: yet wil it not thereof folowe, that within the space of the first six hundred yeres, there was no where at any time, any Masse celebrated without a companie receiuing with the priest. That is the point you must proue, els you proue nothing against vs.

The very point, that M. Iew. ought to proue.

Al that you bring, is to proue there was a Communion, which we denie not. Neither now repine we against that some of the people be alwaies disposed and ready to receiue with the Priest at euery Masse, if it might be brought to passe. But if the people be not alwaies so disposed, and if, as commonly it happeneth, there come none at al to be houseled: in this case the Churche hath thought good, the Priest offer the Sacrifice at the Masse, and so celebrate the memorie of Christes death not with standing. This case is directly to be impugned of you M. Iew. if you wil seme to fight against vs. For els your prouing of a Communion is but a needelesse multiplying of wordes.

This is ye case of our cõtrouersie, against which M. Iew. great Replie directly briegeth nothing.

The true vnderstanding of Anacletus Decree.

Touching the Decrees by you here alleged, they are answered before. The Decree of Anacletus, whereof a parte is is set forth by Gratian vnder the name of Calixtus, speaketh not of the whole Churche, that is to say, of al, both Clergie, and Laitie: but onely of such of the Clergie, as attended vpon the Bishop celebrating the Sacrifice vpon solemne feastes. They were Priestes and Deacons. And when the Sacrifice was donne, the Decree required them to receiue the Communion, or to be put out of the Churche. And that the request of the Decree perteined onely vnto them, it is euident both by the circumstance of the place, and by the wordes of the original, which hath thus, as Nicolaus Cusanus reciteth out of Burchardus: Sic enim Apostoli statuerunt, & Sancta Romana tenet Ecclesia, & si hoc neglexerint, degradentur. Let al communicate that were present at the Consecration. For so the Apostles haue ordeined, and the holy Romaine Churche holdeth, and if they omit it by contempt, let them be deposed from their degree. Loe, it saith, degradentur, saith Cusanus. And therfore it is not meant but of those holy persons which were presene at the Consecration, and were admitted into the most holy place, as they be, who be constituted in holy Orders.

Ex epist. 1. Anacleti. De cons. dist. 1. Episcopus Deo.

Nic. Cusanus epist. 7 ad Clerū et literatos Bohemia.

The Decree which folowing Gratian you do attribute vnto Martinus the Pope, willeth him to be thrust out of the Churche, that commeth to Church, heareth the scriptures, & forbeareth to receiue the Communion to enioy his vncleane lustes, and breaketh the settled rule of discipline. What maketh this against the Masse, that none may be said without companie of receiuers?

De cons. dist. 2. Si quis Ecclesiam.

Martinus Decree.

The wordes of Pope Hilarie reporte, that a man separate not him selfe from the Communion, onlesse his synnes be so great, that for them he be excommunicate. They commaunde him not at euery Masse to communicate Sacramentally, neither, that no Priest celebrate the Sacrifice,

Pope Hilaries Decree.

except he haue a number to receiue whith him. Therfore as we holde with this counsel of his, so we finde it not contrary to that we defende. Seing that then this is not to your purpose, gene vs an other taste.

Ievvel.

Clemens stromat. lib.1.

Clemens Alexandrinus saith. After that certaine, as the manner is, haue deuided the Sacrament, they geue euery of the people leaue to take parte of it.

Harding.

Clemens Alexandrinus.

Be it so. the manner was so then in Alexandria before Origens time, where this holy and learned Priest Clement liued. This doth not witnesse what was donne in other times, and in other places of ye worlde within the first six hundred yeres. And although this were the manner there in solemne feastes, yet this Clement denieth not, but a Priest might consecrate and receiue alone, when at some other time his Deuotion therto moued him lacking others to be partakers of the Mysteries with him.

Ievvel.

Chry. in 1. Cor. hom. 27.

S. Chrysostome plainely describeth the very order of the Communion, that vvas vsed in his time, by these very vvordes: The spiritual and reuerende Sacramentes, are set forth equally to riche and poore: neither doth the rich man enioy them more, and the poore man lesse: they haue al like honour, and like coming vnto them. The Sacramentes being once laid forth (as then the manner vvas for the people to receiue) are not taken in againe, vntil al the people haue communicate, and taken parte of that spiritual meate: but the priestes stand stil and vvaite for al, euen for the poorest of them al.

Harding.

M. Iew. forgeth wordes of his owne.

These wordes be not in S. Chrysostomes. 27. homilie vpō the first epistle to the Corinthians, as you haue quoted the place, nor

nor nowhere els I beleue. And though he had the like wordes somewhere, yet proue they no more then we confesse, that the Cōmunion was ministred to ye people equally as wel to ye poore as to ye riche. So is it now also, at Easter euery where among ye Catholikes, and at other solemne feastes in many places. If you say S. Chrysostomes wordes are to be vnderstanded of the manner, that was vsed euery day, when the Sacrifice was offred, or euery Sonneday in the yere, and adde further, that no Priest did euer ne might not celebrate the Sacrifice, except he had present a companie to receiue with him: this if you say, we tel you, the wordes expresse not so much, though they were supposed to be his, and that this much can not be proued out of al that euer S. Chrysostome wrote. Nowe geue vs an other taste. For this tasteth nothing of S. Chrysostome.

and saith they be Chrysostomes.

Ievvel.

*Againe he saith there are thinges, vvherein the priest differeth nothing from the people as vvhen vve must vse the feareful Mysteries. For vve are al * of one vvorthinesse to receiue the same.*

Chrysost. 2. Cor. Hom. 18.

Harding.

In this place S. Chrysostome making a comparison betwen the state of the new Testament, and of the olde, saith, that when the dreadful mysteries are to be receiued, the Priest differeth nothing from the subiect, for so he calleth euery one of the people. For (saith he) we are accompted worthy of the same selfe thinges in like sorte. That we are al of one worthinesse, so much neither the Greke original, nor the common translation geueth to vnderstande. In the olde lawe saith he, it was not so. For the Priest might eate of certaine portions of the sacrifices, of which it was not lauful for the people to eate. But now it is not so. For now one Body is set before al, and one Cuppe.

The 222. Untruth. S. Chrysostō saith not so. neither is it vtterly true. του ἀρχομένου.

Here I might demaunde of M. Iewel, what Body is that

What is this one body and one cup, ẏ serueth al, but ẏ body & bloud of Christe?

one body, that is set before al to receiue? what cuppe is that one Cuppe, whereof al do drinke? Bread it can not be. For what one bread, or loaf of bread, or what body is ẏ of bread, whereof being but one al take their parte? what one Cup is that which geueth drinke to al? Soothly this one Body, & this one Cuppe cā not be understanded any other, thē the Body and Blood of our Lorde, which we receiue in the Sacrament. Which though it be receiued of al, yet is neuer consumed. And what if the subiect, or euery of the people receiue this body of Christe, no lesse then the Priest, for that is the thing which S. Chrysostome speaketh, maketh this any argument against the Masse, at which none receiueth with the Priest? Verely I can not see, to what purpose this is brought in, but onely to proue that the people sometime were admitted to receiue, which no wise man euer denied. But this is M. Iewels Rhetorike, to bring thicke proufes for confirmation of one truth, to discredite an other truth. How so euer this like your taste, it semeth to vs not to taste wel for your purpose. Set vs forth therfore an other dish.

Ievvel.

Dial. li. 2. cap. 23.

S. Gregorie saith, that euen in his time the order vvas, that in the time of the holy Communion, the Deacon should stand vp, and say alovvde vnto the people, Si quis non communicat, det locum. If there be any body that is not disposed to communicate, let him geue place.

Harding.

By that place of S. Gregorie it appeareth, that in solemne Masses the Deacon admonished the people to come & receiue the Communion: but whether the people alwaies came and receiued, and that if none were disposed to receiue, the Priest himselfe should not celebrate Masse, and receiue: that are you not able to proue, neither by S. Gregorie, nor by any other Father. And this is your parte to proue, which you haue taken in

hand

hand, and nowe you are dryuen to let it fal, and slincke away.

But Syr howe could you finde in your harte to allege that chapter of S. Gregorye, which as it maketh nothing for you, so very much against you? For there haue you a plaine mention of Masse, and that Masse was sayd in a Church, and the Sacrifice offered by the Prieste for the soules of two Nonnes there buried, and that their Spirites obtined reste, by the holy Oblation offered for them, at the Masse. If you haue no better dyshe to geue vs a taste of then this that you haue hytherto brought, you may keepe your taste to your selfe, for thys sheweth what smale store you haue. I thought you would haue deuised some fine delicates, that we neuer tasted of before.

M. Iew. allegeth a chapter of S. Gregorie, that maketh much against him.

Ievvel.

This Latine vvorde Missa, *in the time of Tertullian, and S. Cyprian, signified a dimissing, or a licence to departe. and vvas specially applied vnto * the Communion, vpon this occasion that I must here declare. They that vvere then named Catechumeni, that is to saye Nouices of the faith, and not yet Christened, * vvere suffred to be present at the Communion, vntil the Gospel vvas ended. Then the Deacon commaunded them forth, pronouncing these vvordes alovvde, Catechumeni exeunto: or thus* Ite Missa est. Goe ye forth ye haue licence to departe. *Of this dimissing or departing forth of the Catechumeni and others, the seruice it selfe vvas then called* Missa. *The reste remained stil in the Churche. and receiued the Comunion together vvith the Priest.*

This is but a geasse of M. Iewels fantasie.

The. 223. vntruth. It was not specially applied vnto the Communion, as you meane, but vnto the Sacrifice. And so saith B. Rhenanus, of whom you borow part of that you bring here, and parte you falsifie.

The. 224. vntruth. That whereat the Catechumens were suffred to be present, was not the Cōmunion, it was called the Masse of the Catechumens.

Harding

Harding.

If in the time of Tertullian and S. Cyprian this worde Missa signified a dimissing or licence to departe, and was specially applied vnto the Communion, as you say, though vntruly: then was the name by men of that age vsed. If you wil abyde by this, what answere can you make to your selfe in the. 13. Article, pagina. 492. where you say the contrary? There among other thinges you say touching this worde: Missa, ỷ it is very seldome vsed of the olde Latine writers: of S. Augustine, S. Hierome, Tertullian, S. Cyprian, Arnobius, Lactantius, and others of that age, neuer. How standeth this together, in that time it signified so, and was applied vnto that, and of men of that time it was neuer vsed? If it were neuer vsed, thẽ it signified not, as you say, if it signified & was applied, thẽ was it vsed. Fy what cõtradiction is this? Such fonde ouersightes men fal into ỷ fal frõ the Church, and from the Doctrine of ỷ auncient and holy Fathers. Although I wil not striue much with you about ỷ worde Missa, yet that in the time of Tertullian and S. Cyprian, it signified a dimissing, or a licẽce to departe, and that it was specially applied vnto ỷ Communion: it is but your gheasse & coniecture. Wherein neuerthelesse you folow Beatus Rhenanus, out of whose annotations vpon Tertullian you haue taken this not without a manifest falsifying. For whereas he saith, Sacrificio id vocabulum accommodatum, that this worde Missa was applied vnto the Sacrifice, and, that properly Masse was in the time of The Sacrifice, when the Catechumens were put forth (for so be his very wordes, proprie Missa erat tempore Sacrificij, quando Catechumeni foras mittebantur): you say, it was specially applied vnto the Communion. Which is a special vntruth, and a special deuise of yours to abolish the memorie of the Sacrifice of the Aulter.

M. Iew. contrarieth him selfe.

In scholijs Rhenani in lib. Tertul. de corona militis. Item. in. 4 librũ contra Marcionem.

And

And here to aduance and set vp the memorie of your English Cōmunion, you say the Catechumens were suffered to be present at the Communion, as though that seruice of the Church, which in olde time was called Missa, bare then the name of Communion. Where euer read you M. Iewel, the Catechumens were suffered to be present at the Communion? Were they not put forth of the Church before the cōsecration was begonne? And did not the prayers said about the Consecration occupy a time, before they went to the Communion? Can you not bring your Communion into thestimation of antiquitie, but by suche manifest vntruth?

Let it be graunted, that as in Tertullian, and S. Cyprian remissa is somtimes vsed for remissio, so Missa be takē for missio, and then let Missio signifie as much as Dimissio, a dimissing, as you would haue it, and licence to departe, in consideration of the Catechumens departing forth of the Churche, when the Priest beganne to consecrate the body and bloud of our Lorde: what can you inferre of this? Mary say you, a Cōmunion. Who denieth, but that in the Primitiue Churche, they receiued the Communion? Why speake you not of the body and bloud of Christe? Why speake you not of the Sacrifice, of Consecration, Oblation? Is there nothing but Communion with you? And why doe you neuer declare, what you meane by your Communion? Can the people iudge you meane any other thing, then eatinge of bread, and drinking of wine together in the Church after your new deuise? And was Missa (the Masse) such Communion during the time of the first six hundred yeres? O miserable and vnfortunate people, that is thus deceiued, and lead into damnable erroures by such false guides.

As for the true Communion of the body of Christe good Reader, we esteme it, as it becommeth vs, and with harty the people would dispose them selues to such cleannes of conscience, and earnest deuotion, as they might more oftentimes receiue that heauenly foode. But if they can not be brought vnto it, yet is it not onely lawful, but also due for Priestes to celebrate the Masse, wherein that is done, which Christ at his Supper commaunded to be done, saying, Do ye this in my remembrance. Against which al that M. Iewel here saith of the woorde Missa, maketh no Argument at al.

He semeth to finde fault with the Masse, because it is celebrated many times without a number receiuing with the priest. But if we could persuade the people to come and receiue at euery Masse, that would not content him and his fellowes. For then would they finde fault with the doctrine of the Consecration, as they who can not abide the blessed Sacrifice of the Aulter. Then would they further impugne the faith of the Churche, as they doe busily, touching the true presence of Christes body in the Sacrament.

The marke that our Gospelers shoote at.

The marke they shoote at semeth to be nothing els, but to abolish the external Sacrifice of the Church, wherby the death of Christ is represented vnto vs, and kept in thankeful memorie: to bereue Christen people of the benefite of Christes true body in the Sacrament, to put away quite the holy and auncient seruice of the church: to displace the true and real presence of Christ and serue the people with common bread and wine: finally to bring them from humilitie and the feare of God, to cōtempt and dissolutenesse, from holsom obedience to damnable disobedience, from godlinesse to wickednesse, from the Catholique Churche, to the confuse wandringes of the Sacramentaries, from Christ to Antichrist.

Iewel.

Further the breaking of the bread, vvhich euen novv is vsed in the Masse it selfe, signifieth a distribution of the Sacrament vnto the people. as

S. Au-

S. Augustine saith vnto Paulinus, Ad distribuendum comminuitur, *It is broken to the ende it may be diuided. Moreouer the Priest him selfe in his Masse saith thus: This holy mixture and Consecration, &c. be vnto me, & to al that shal receiue it vnto saluatiō. Thus the very name of the Masse, the very breaking of the bread, the very gestures and vvordes that the Priest vseth at his Masse, beare manifest vvitnesse against priuate Masse.*

Harding.

It appeareth that in S. Augustines time when the people were disposed oftentimes to receiue, the Sacrament of Christes body was diuided into sundry portions to be distributed. Now the Church for more reuerence of so great a Sacrament, vseth an other ceremonie, & distributeth the body of Christ, vnder ẏ forme of bread made in litle cakes. That place maketh an obscure shew of a Cōmunion of moe then one, or rather of a purpose in ẏ priest to distribute the Communion. But that he may not in no wise Consecrate the body and bloud of Christe, offer it vp in Sacrifice, and receiue him selfe in remembrance of his death, onlesse he be sure of a multitude to receiue with him: that neither out of S. Augustine, nor out of any other Father olde or new haue you yet proued. And that is the point, which you should proue, els you spende wordes in vaine.

M. Iewel neuer proueth the special point of this Article.

But as here you haue noted three woordes of S. Augustine to litle purpose, so woulde God you woulde note certaine other woordes in the same place by him vttered, which were for you to very good purpose. The wordes are these. Eligo in his verbis hoc intelligere, quod omnis, uel penè omnis frequentat ecclesia. I choose in these woordes to vnderstand that, which al, or in manner al the Churche doth commonly beleue. O that you M. Iewel would humbly submit your selfe and your learning vnto the Catholique Church, the pillour and sure stay of truth, and would with that most learned Bishop choose in al doubtes and controuersies to hold, vnderstand, and maintaine,

Aug. ad Paulinū. Epist. 59.

1. Tim. 3.

what soeuer al, or in maner al the Church frequenteth, and hath customably obserued. Verely then would you not vpon so light growndes, and persuasions of Caluine, Peter Martyr, Hooper, Bale, and others of that riffe raffe, with your most certaine damnation, suffer your selfe to be lead away from the Catholike Church into what opinion soeuer at this day is by Apostates and Rebelles stubbornly holden against and in despite of the Church.

Concerning the wordes that the Priest him self saith at his Masse, whatsoeuer by his booke he is admonished there to say, it is expressed in consideration of them, that oftentimes do receiue. As that place presupposeth a Communion of others besyde the Priest, so it forbiddeth not Masse to be said onlesse the Priest haue prouided him a companie to receiue with hym. As the Masse with a number of worthy Communicantes is a godly thing, so can you not thereof proue the Masse whereat none other companie receiueth with the Priest, to be a thing vngodly.

The blessed Sacrifice is nothing impaired by lacke of companie to receiue.

If the Sacrifice be a holy thing, and acceptable vnto God, as most certaine we are, it is: what reason haue you or all your felowes, who worke al the spite ye can against the Sacrifice: why the peoples forbearing to receiue with the Priest, should make that naught and vngodly, which otherwise were good and godly? Doth the vertue of the Sacrifice consiste in the receiuers, and not rather in the Institution of Christe, and in the thing it self that is offered? If the Consecration be done according to the ordinance and commaundement of Christe, whereat the Prieste pronounceth not his owne wordes, but the wordes of our Lord, saying in his person, this is my body, this is my bloud: is it not as good in a priuate Masse (so you cal it) as in a publike Masse? Can the multitude that commeth to receiue, geue vertue and force to the operations (as S. Ambrose termeth them) or workeful

Mat. 26
Luc. 22
1. Cor. 11

The number of receiuers with the priest doth not make good ye sacrifice.

ful wordes of the Sacramentes? Is not the power of Christes diuine and eternal worde sufficient to make this Sacrifice without the helpe of others that come to cōmunicate with the priest? Verely this is a thing very ridiculous and vaine to beleue, that the number of people standing by the Priest and receiuing with him, should make good the Sacrifice. For so should the vertue of it depende of the power of the companie, and not of the worde of God, by vertue whereof the hoste is consecrate and made, before it be eaten.

Thus thou maist easily see Christian Reader, if thou haue not vtterly forsaken the Churche, and departed away from the faith of al the auncient and holy Fathers into the infidelitie of these Geneuians: how litle good this taste shal do thee, which M. Iewel hath here geuen thee: if thou receiue it, and feede of it. Onely he impugneth the Sacrifice that is offered in the Masse with wordes, and which is easy to do, gainesaith: but God be thanked, thou seest, he proueth nothing, that is contrary to the Catholique doctrine, which we mainteine.

Ievvel.

Here I leaue out a great number of Councels, and Canons, and olde Fathers, as Iustinus Martyr, Dionysius, Tertullian, Epiphanius, and Eusebius, vvith other auncient vvriters, both Greekes and Latines: thinking it sufficient by these fevve to haue geuen a taste of the reste. Our proufes hang not vpon coniecture or vncertaine gheasses: vve praye not aide of sicke folke, Vvemen, Boyes, and Children for the proufe of the holy Communion, * *as M. Harding is driuen to do for proufe of his Masse: vve seeke not out secrete Oratories, or priuy Chappels: vve forge no nevve Doctours, such as the vvorlde neuer knevve before, as these men do for lacke of others: vve allege neither Dreames nor visions, nor phantastical fables: vve rest vpon the Scriptures of God, vpon the auctoritie of the auncient Doctours, and*

These be wordes of boast whē the victorie is lost.

The. 225. vntruth. This is a slaunderous vanitie. It is euident in it selfe ŷ I proue not the Masse by boyes wemen, and children.

Councels, and vpon the vniuersal practise of the most famous cities and Churches of the vvorlde. These thinges vvel compared and vveighed together, iudge thou novv (gentle Reader) vvhether M. Harding haue hitherto iust cause, either to blovv vp the triumph vvith such courage, or to require any man to subscribe.

A heape of Lyes boldly faced out.

Harding.

Now at the end, this doughty Chalenger like a Maister of Fence fetcheth certaine floorishes, and so dischargeth his weapon. But thanked be God, his blowes be void, they beate the ayer, they light not vpon vs. Yet like a worthy Captaine, he craketh of his olde souldiers, that he hath leaft at home, which doubtlesse he would haue brought forth into the feeld with him, if they could but with a bare worde haue holpen him. But Syr if you haue leaft out such a great number of Councels and Canons, and olde Fathers, both Grekes and Latines, as you say you haue: in case your harte shal serue you againe to encounter, and trie whether you may defend your first Chalenge any better then hitherto you haue done: bring them al forth in Gods name, leaue none at home: specially if they be such olde Fathers in dede as you speake of.

Albeit I trowe no wise man wil beleue, you haue any great number of such, sith you make your most aduantage of certaine pety Doctours of later age, of which some are of very smal estimation, some of no credite but among your owne side, and that not generally, but in a point or two, wherein they swarue from the vnitie and consent of the Churche. For if you had so great a number of the most aũcient and best learned Fathers, to what purpose was it to allege Gerardus Lorichius, and Georgius Cassander, being both in many points Lutherans, either of late, or yet liuing?

If you leaft out such a great number of auncient writers,

Grekes,

Grekes, and Latines, what an ouersight was it for you, to alledge such a company of late writers, Schoolemen, and others, who as they had no great sight in Greeke, so to your fine eares (I am sure) they seme not to speake Latine? If you could haue brought in S. Iustinus Martyr, S. Dionysius, Tertullian, Epiphanius, and Eusebius, as you say: why haue you been so busy euen in this Article, with Haimo, Anselmus, Rupertus, Innocentius. 3. Hugo, Alexander de Hales, S. Thomas of Aquine, Bonauentura, Scotus, Durandus, Gratian, Nicolaus de lyra, Gabriel Biel, Hugo Cardinalis, Speculum Vincentij, Nicolaus de Cusa, the Glose vpon the Canon lawe, Hermanus Contractus, Micrologus, Summa Angelica, Bessarion, Eckius, Albertus Pighius, Doctor Smith? These do not I despise, but honor them, and reuerence them both for learning and vertue, ech one in their degree. Yet whereas your selfe do not allow them in vs, and contemne them vtterly when so euer they be alleged against you: you shewe hereby, how litle those olde Fathers, of whom you speake, do helpe your cause.

M. Iewels chief Doctours

Your proufes (you say) hang not vpon coniecture, or vncertaine gheasses: I pray you Syr, whereupon hang they then? Or rather what is that you proue at al? Is not your profession onely to stande vpon the negatiue, to denie, and disproue? As for example, touching this Article, that it is not, ne neuer was lawful, a Priest to say Masse without a companie of Communicantes with him in the same place, and that any such thing was neuer seene or hearde of within the first six hundred yeares, which was your part to proue, and which you promised to doo: how clerkely haue you proued it? what one cleare sentence haue you brought for it? And stil we cal vpon you, what one sufficient place haue ye to shewe vs for it. If you haue not, why trouble ye vs, and with force of the swoorde, more then with reason or

The Replier proueth nothing, but denieth what is catholike.

learning, driue vs from that, which we haue had in quiet possession almost these thousande yeares, by your owne confession?

The communion is not denied, therfore the profe of it is nedelesse.

The communion of Geneua set vp in England.

O you say, you haue sufficiently proued the holy Communion. who euer denyed it? what nede was there to bestowe so much labour to obteine that, which is freely graunted, and agreed vpon? The holy Communion I say, is sone proued, and of vs al throughly confessed. But your Communion of England, and of Geneua, we denie, we disproue and reproue, we vtterly deteste, as schismatical, as heretical, as wholy vnknowen vnto the Primitiue Church.

The holy and right Communion which we meane, is of the real body of our Sauiour Christe, duly consecrated by a Priest, and offered in Sacrifice vnto God, before it be receiued. Your eating of bread, and sipping of wine, which by the doctrine and belefe of your congregation that holdeth of Caluin, remaine and continew the common creatures of bread and wine, after al that ye haue said and donne: is not the Communion, which by the Scriptures of God, auncient Fathers, Councels, and the vniuersal practise of the Church, is recommended vnto vs. wherefore when so euer you make proufe of the holy Communion, the same perteineth not to the proufe of that which you cal your Communion. Your Communion is a separation from the Catholique Churche the spouse of Christe, a diuision of vnitie, a cutting away from Christes Mystical body: and therefore it is not holy but wicked and damnable, and no Communion at al, but in respecte of your owne fugitiue troupes.

Your often mention of sicke folke, wemen, boyes and children here repeated againe, geueth a testimonie of your boyish & childish disposition. It is knowen, I pray no aide of them

for

for proufe of the Masse. For single Communion or sole receiuing sundry testimonies be alleged, for which onely you condemne the Masse.

Newe Doctours I forge not. Those whom you with great rashnesse haue condemned, I haue sufficiently proued. I put not the confidence of our cause in visions. If that one vision of S. Basils miraculous Masse, which I allege, serue not, there be other proufes ynough: and your Challenge required but one sentence pardye.

You say, that ye rest vpon the Scriptures, the auncient Doctours, Councels, and the vniuersal practise of the chiefe Churches of the worlde. But we say, and now haue proued, that ye are departed from the Scriptures, from the auncient Doctours, and Councels, and from the Uniuersal practise of al the Churches of the worlde. If it be not so, defende your selues, shewe vs but one Churche of the whole worlde accompted Catholike, that euer taught within the first six hundred yeres the body and bloud of Christe not to be in the Sacrament of the Aultare, that vtterly denied the singular & external Sacrifice of the Churche, that held opinion, that Priestes haue not auctoritie to offer vp Christe vnto his Father, that a Priest may not Consecrate and offer the Sacrifice without a companie of Communicantes, that vsed to Communicate in breade and wine onely no special Consecration going before, as ye doo, and not of the body of our Lorde.

If you can not shew vs this, as sure we are you cā not, (for if you could, you wold haue made no deinty of it in your Reply) crake no more of your resting vpō the Scriptures, Doctors, Councels, general practise of al Churches. As we graūt, ẏ for the true & catholike Cōmuniō you haue al these, as also for ẏ real presence, and

The Gospellers haue no olde Fathers, nor Councels nor practise of the Church to shew for their Sacramentarie heresie, and for their new Communion.

and for the Sacrifice: so verely for your new devised Communion you haue none of these, no not so much as any reasonable gheasse, but altogether shamefull lyes. This being so, consider thou now good Reader, how weake proufes this man hath brought for maintenance of his Challenge, and how iust cause I had to require him to subscribe, according to his owne promise.

Hieron. aduersus Iouinianum. lib. 2.

Quòd multi acquiescunt sententiæ tuæ, indicium voluptatis est: Non enim tàm te loquentem probant, quàm suis fauent vitiis.

That many be of thy opinion, it is a signe they folow pleasure: For they do not so much allow what thou saist, as they fauour their owne vices.

A TABLE OF THE CHIEFE MATTERS, CONTEINED IN this Booke.

M.

serue

Tametsi liber iste lectus & approbatus sit à viris Theologiæ & Idiomatis Anglici peritissimis, author tamen M. N. Thomas Hardingus eius apud nos est fidei & eruditionis, vt solum eius nomen nobis sufficiat, vt eius opera tutò euulgari possint.

Ita testor, Cunerus, Pastor S. Petri Louanij. 7. Maij. Anno. 1566.